Contributions to Finance and Accounting

The book series 'Contributions to Finance and Accounting' features the latest research from research areas like financial management, investment, capital markets, financial institutions, FinTech and financial innovation, accounting methods and standards, reporting, and corporate governance, among others. Books published in this series are primarily monographs and edited volumes that present new research results, both theoretical and empirical, on a clearly defined topic. All books are published in print and digital formats and disseminated globally. This book series is indexed in Scopus.

Narmin Nahidi • Alex Zarifis
Editors

AI, FinTech, and the Future of Robo-Advisory

Risk Management and Ethical Considerations

Springer

Editors

Narmin Nahidi
Business School
University of Exeter
Exeter, UK

Alex Zarifis
Southampton Business School
University of Southampton
Southampton, UK

Cambridge Centre for Alternative Finance
Cambridge, UK

ISSN 2730-6038 ISSN 2730-6046 (electronic)
Contributions to Finance and Accounting
ISBN 978-3-032-18108-4 ISBN 978-3-032-18109-1 (eBook)
https://doi.org/10.1007/978-3-032-18109-1

This work was supported by University of Exeter.

This Springer imprint is published by the registered company Springer Nature Switzerland AG
The registered company address is: Gewerbestrasse 11, 6330 Cham, Switzerland

Contents

Contributors

Abdollah Ah Mand holds a PhD in Economics, a Master's in Finance, and an undergraduate degree in Engineering, bringing a multidisciplinary perspective to his research and teaching. He is currently a Senior Lecturer at Bristol Business School, University of the West of England, where he also serves as Programme Director for Accounting and Finance degrees. Prior to his current role, Dr Abdollah was a faculty member at Sunway University Business School in Malaysia. His research expertise lies in Behavioural Finance, FinTech, Energy Finance, and Sustainable Finance, with a strong track record of publications in reputable peer-reviewed journals. His work primarily explores the integration and dynamics of financial markets and emerging financial technologies. Dr Abdollah teaches a range of modules in FinTech, Finance, Economics, and Statistics at both undergraduate and postgraduate levels.

Mohammed Al-Khalidi is a senior lecturer in cyber security at the Department of Computing and Mathematics, Manchester Metropolitan University, Manchester, UK. He has 20 years of academic and industrial experience in the fields of cyber security, networking, and AI. He has been awarded research funding by UKRI's Global Challenges Research Fund (GCRF), the Department for Science, Innovation and Technology (DSIT), and other government bodies focusing on AI security and network security. His past assignments include lecturer with the Department of Computer Science, Edge Hill University, UK, and research officer with the School of Computer Science and Electronic Engineering, University of Essex, UK, where he also received his PhD degree. Prior to that, he worked in industry as a senior core network engineer at several multinational telecommunication companies. His research interests include AI security, IoT security, Mobile Computing, Cloud Computing, Ad-Hoc Networks, and Information Centric Networks.

Christian Bozzetto is a Risk Analyst at Intesa Sanpaolo, overseeing risk appetite frameworks for the Group's international subsidiaries. He holds a Master of Science in Economics and Finance from Ca' Foscari University of Venice, where he graduated with honors. His research interests include market microstructure and the application of artificial intelligence and machine learning in financial services. Christian has gained professional experience in financial consulting, risk management, and investment advisory through previous roles at Oliver Wyman, OTB Group, and Fineco.

Xusen Cheng is a Professor of Information Systems and Department Chair at the Department of Economics Information Management in the School of Information, Renmin University of China. He obtained his Ph.D. from Manchester Business School in the University of Manchester. His research interests include e-commerce and digital economy, and behaviour and design issues in information management. His research has been published in MIS Quarterly, Production and Operations Management, Journal of Management Information Systems, and Nature, among others.

Fabio Dias is a senior lecturer at the University of Surrey and program director for the master's degree program in financial technology at the Surrey Business School. Prior to becoming an academic, he earned 20 years of experience in the financial services industry across several roles in multinational banks and investment consulting companies. Besides being a technology expert, he is also a fully qualified financial advisor.

Ahmad Hatamabadi Farahani is a lecturer and researcher in accounting and finance at the University of Salford. He teaches modules such as *Financing Your Business and Entrepreneurial Accounting and Finance*. With over 20 years of experience in academia and industry, Ahmad has held roles from financial manager to auditor, showcasing expertise in strategic financial management and sustainable business practices.

He earned his PhD in Methods and Models for Economic Decisions from Insubria University (Italy), focusing on sustainable accounting in the transport sector. His international career spans Iran, Italy, and the UK, including positions like Financial Controller at Kuehne + Nagel and audit supervisor at top CPA firms. A Fellow of the Higher Education Academy (FHEA), Ahmad is committed to practical, globally minded teaching. He actively mentors dissertation students and supervises research, emphasizing real-world applications and entrepreneurial skill development.

Yan Huang is a senior lecturer in finance and the programme director for the Financial Services Professional Apprenticeship programme. Yan obtained a Bachelor's degree in Accounting from Shanghai University of Finance and Economics, a Master's degree in Finance and Investment from the University of Durham, and a Master's degree in Economics from the University of Exeter. She gained her PhD in Finance from the University of Exeter. Her research interests are empirical finance (asset pricing), corporate finance (mergers and acquisitions), and financial markets (insider trading and market efficiency). Before her appointment at the University of Exeter, she was a senior lecturer in finance in Oxford Brookes university. She has several years of consultancy experience on equities with investment banks such as UniCredit Group, Canaccord Genuity and Barclays.

Indigo Jones is Head of Research at the Elinor Ostrom Research Unit. The EORU is an independent laboratory associated with the moOngy group, a network of French and European consulting firms, in which consultants who are between assignments contribute to scientific projects organized by Dr. Jones. In addition, Dr. Jones has published papers in academic journals such as Finance and Annals of Economics and Statistics and has taught courses at Sorbonne University and the University of Orléans.

Narmin Nahidi is a finance scholar whose research examines how cognitive processes, technological innovation, and environmental risks shape financial behavior and corporate decision-making. Her work spans corporate finance, fintech, behavioral and Neurofinance, and biodiversity-related financial risks. She investigates how AI-enabled advisory systems influence investor judgment and portfolio formation, how attention and affect shape managerial behavior, and how biodiversity loss and ecological uncertainty feed into firms' investment, disclosure, and governance choices. Her research portfolio is grounded in empirical corporate finance, behavioural analysis, experimental methods, and data-intensive approaches to financial technology. She has produced studies on information frictions in corporate transactions, including the effects of digital rights management on M&A due diligence and media-driven variations in valuation and bargaining. Her work increasingly focuses on biodiversity–finance linkages, analyzing how ecological shocks transmit into financial markets, how environmental data integrity affects risk assessment, and how policy frameworks can improve biodiversity-related disclosure and accountability. A parallel stream of her work contributes to Neurofinance, examining how cognitive load, emotional regulation, and neural reward mechanisms influence risk-taking, ethical judgment, and strategic decision-making under uncertainty. She collaborates across disciplines, including neuroscience, environmental economics, computer science, and behavioral science, bringing together theoretical insights and empirical methods to study financial behavior through a multi-layered cognitive and technological lens. Dr. Nahidi brings over two decades of combined academic and industry experience. Before joining academia full-time, she held roles in consultancy, financial management, and corporate training across sectors, where she worked on projects related to financial analysis, risk assessment, organizational governance, and digital transformation. She is a Senior Fellow of the Higher Education Academy (SFHEA) and a Certified Management & Business Educator (CMBE). At the University of Exeter Business School, she contributes to program leadership, curriculum development, and industry-engaged teaching. She is an active participant in international research networks and policy-facing discussions on fintech, AI governance, sustainable finance, and behavioral decision-making.

Joep Noot is currently pursuing a Master's degree in Quantitative Finance at Erasmus University Rotterdam, where he also received a Bachelor's degree in

Econometrics and Operations Research in 2024. His research interests include exploring the intersection between econometrics and machine learning, with a focus on their applications to financial forecasting, volatility modelling, and credit risk analysis.

Manuel Nunes is a Lecturer in Banking and Finance and the Deputy Director of the Centre for Digital Finance at Southampton Business School, University of Southampton. Manuel is a researcher in Finance and Financial Technologies (Fintech), specialising in the use of artificial intelligence (AI) and machine learning tools for asset pricing and portfolio management in financial markets. He is a Fellow of the Higher Education Academy (FHEA) by Advance HE, York, UK, and the Centre for Higher Education Practice, University of Southampton.

Nader Virk is a Reader in Finance at Manchester Metropolitan University Business School. He has been working in HEIs internationally since 2010. His research interests in financial economics focus on factor models in asset pricing, volatility & extreme risk, and corporate governance. His research agenda entails Fintech applications such as P2P lending platforms, AI integration, and ESG issues in entrepreneurial finance, investments, and corporate governance. His research work has been funded by the UK and international funding agencies, including the British Academy, UKRI's Global Challenges Research Fund, Sveriges Riksbank & Nasdaq Nordic Foundation, Sweden, and Hilda and Nissi Foundation, Finland, among others. He is passionate about developing future researchers focusing on dealing with critical challenges of time through a financial market perspective. He has initiated and is leading the AI@Biz industry engagement series with a focus on enhancing academic-industry collaboration, training doctoral students and ECRs, and engaging the public in the discussion around AI utility, disruption, and impact. Dr Virk collaborates with industry on sustainability and AI, and reviews for the British Academy, ESRC, and Horizon Europe funding instruments. He writes for public and industry outlets and has contributed to UK Treasury Committee inquiries on AI in financial services, energy transition, and NetZero targets.

Larisa Yarovaya is an Associate Professor of Finance and the Director of the Centre for Digital Finance at Southampton Business School, University of Southampton, UK. Larisa is also an Advisory Board member of the British Blockchain Association, which also serves as the secretariat of the All-Party Parliamentary Group on Blockchain Technologies. With a profound expertise in international finance and Fintech, Larisa has contributed significantly to the academic landscape, authoring over 80 papers and co-editing the book "Cryptocurrency and Blockchain Technology". Recognised for her outstanding contributions, Larisa has earned a spot in Stanford's top 2% Global Scientists list, and her research has garnered more than 10,000 citations. Larisa is also ranked among the top 5 in the Top 200 Young Economists by RePEc, selected from a pool of 14,784 economists who have published their first work within the last 10 years. Her impactful work has been widely disseminated through esteemed media outlets such as BBC, MarketWatch,

FT Live, CBC, Euronews, and Bloomberg, showcasing her influence in both academic and public spheres. She has also appeared as an expert in the CNBC series on "Ethereum" and "Stablecoins". Larisa is actively engaged in policy debates and consultancy to influence the regulatory landscape in the UK and abroad. Larisa is the Chair and founding organiser of the annual Cryptocurrency Research Conference, established in 2018 and growing to become the largest niche academic conference in cryptocurrency and DeFi (https://cryptorc.org).

Alex Zarifis' research is on the applications of technology in business. Before the University of Southampton, he worked at the University of Cambridge, the University of Manchester, and the University of Mannheim. He is currently a research affiliate of the Cambridge Centre for Alternative Finance (CCAF). Dr Alex has worked on large EU- and UK-funded research projects at the Karlsruhe Institute of Technology (KIT) and Loughborough University. He obtained his PhD from the University of Manchester. His research interests include trust, artificial intelligence, blockchain, cryptocurrencies, Fintech, and Insurtech. He has over forty publications, and his work has featured in journals such as Computers in Human Behaviour, Information Technology and People, Electronic Commerce Research, and International Journal of Electronic Business and Internet Research. He has explored cryptoassets such as cryptocurrencies since 2012. As part of this research, he published the first peer-reviewed research on trust in digital currencies in the world in 2014. He also participated in creating the first government-recognised university degree on blockchain technologies in the world.

Part I
Foundations and Market Evolution

The Rise of Robo-Advisory in FinTech

Alex Zarifis, Narmin Nahidi, and Larisa Yarovaya

Abstract This chapter explores the transformative rise of robo-advisory within the broader FinTech revolution, tracing its evolution from traditional human advisors to AI-driven platforms that democratise financial services. The chapter begins by situating robo-advisory within the rapidly evolving financial landscape shaped by digitalisation, disintermediation, and changing client expectations. It examines the drivers behind this shift, including advancements in AI and data analytics, evolving investor demands for personalisation and accessibility, as well as the cost and scalability pressures facing financial institutions. The chapter differentiates between rule-based and AI-powered systems, highlighting how modern robo-advisors increasingly leverage machine learning, behavioural insights, and alternative data to offer dynamic and adaptive services. Emerging trends, such as hybrid advisory models, behavioural nudges, ethical challenges surrounding algorithmic transparency, and inclusivity concerns, are also addressed. Moreover, the chapter maps out key players and market trends, emphasising regional variations, consolidation patterns, and niche market opportunities. A novel framework of six AI-driven business models is introduced to explain how robo-advisory is strategically deployed across incumbent and disruptive financial organisations. The chapter concludes by underscoring that success in robo-advisory is not solely a

The original version of the chapter has been revised. A correction to this chapter can be found at https://doi.org/10.1007/978-3-032-18109-1_17

A. Zarifis
Southampton Business School, University of Southampton, Southampton, UK

Cambridge Centre for Alternative Finance, Cambridge, UK
e-mail: A.Zarifis@soton.ac.uk

N. Nahidi
Business School, University of Exeter, Exeter, UK
e-mail: n.nahidi@exeter.ac.uk

L. Yarovaya
Southampton Business School, University of Southampton, Southampton, UK
e-mail: L.Yarovaya@soton.ac.uk

N. Nahidi, A. Zarifis (eds.), *AI, FinTech, and the Future of Robo-Advisory*,
Contributions to Finance and Accounting,
https://doi.org/10.1007/978-3-032-18109-1_1

technological feat but hinges on trust, transparency, user experience, and regulatory alignment. Ultimately, robo-advisors serve as a lens to understand the future trajectory of financial services where AI, automation, and behavioural design converge to reshape how individuals engage with money, risk, and long-term financial planning.

Keywords Robo-advisory · FinTech · Artificial intelligence · Financial innovation · Behavioural finance · Hybrid advisory models · Market evolution · Trust and transparency

JEL Classification: G23, G24, O33, D83

1 Introduction

1.1 The FinTech Landscape and the Rise of Robo-Advisory

The financial landscape is undergoing a fundamental transformation driven by technological innovation, societal shifts, and evolving stakeholder expectations. At the heart of this transformation lies financial technology (FinTech), which is challenging traditional models and reshaping how financial services are delivered, consumed, and regulated. Among the many FinTech innovations, robo-advisors offering algorithm-based financial planning and investment services are rapidly rising to prominence. Their emergence signals a shift not only in how financial advice is delivered but also in the broader relationship between finance, technology, and society.

The integration of AI into financial services is occurring alongside a societal movement towards personalisation, accessibility, and digital empowerment. Consumers now expect real-time, tailored services delivered with the speed and convenience characteristic of digital platforms. Financial services are no longer the exclusive domain of affluent clients or institutional investors; rather, a new generation of retail investors is gaining access to sophisticated tools once reserved for wealth management elites. This democratisation of finance is a key hallmark of the FinTech era. At the same time, this empowerment is not entirely organic; it reflects both a "push" by providers keen to scale and automate services, and a "pull" from users demanding more control, transparency, and value.

Stakeholders in this ecosystem include individual investors, financial institutions, FinTech startups, regulators, and AI developers. Each group plays a different role and experiences unique challenges. Financial institutions face the dual pressure of integrating new technologies while preserving trust and compliance. For them, robo-advisory offers both opportunity and threat: a means to scale operations and reach new markets, but also a potential disruption to traditional advisory models. Startups, on the other hand, often position themselves as agile disruptors, leveraging automation to enter markets with lower overheads and more streamlined offerings. Regulators must balance the need for innovation with the imperatives of investor protection, fairness, and systemic stability. AI developers are tasked with creating systems that are not only technically robust but also ethically sound, interpretable, and aligned with human financial goals.

Robo-advisors exemplify how digital innovation is blurring the boundaries between finance and technology. At a basic level, these platforms use algorithms to assess an investor's profile based on factors such as risk tolerance, financial goals, and investment horizon and then propose and manage portfolios accordingly. Many also provide supplementary services like retirement planning, ESG investing, and debt management. Although the sophistication of these platforms varies, some incorporate advanced AI techniques, including natural language processing and machine learning, to offer more dynamic, conversational, and predictive services.

This revolution goes beyond digitising traditional services; it introduces entirely new ways of interacting with, accessing, and delivering financial products. FinTech lowers barriers to entry, expands financial inclusion, and enables the rise of automation-driven platforms like robo-advisors. These platforms exemplify how financial services are evolving from static, manual systems into dynamic, data-intensive ecosystems. The robo-advisor may use generative AI in both the frontend and the backend, both in the interaction and the analysis. This is not, however, necessarily the case, and there are robo-advisors that do not use advanced AI in either the frontend or the backend and are as effective. The varying use of AI highlights a key insight: success in robo-advisory does not always require the latest technological sophistication. Some effective robo-advisors use simple rule-based systems, prioritising user trust and clarity over complexity. Others push the frontier with real-time natural language processing, predictive analytics, and adaptive learning. This divergence reflects the broader diversity of strategies in FinTech, where innovation can take the form of both cutting-edge tech and user-friendly minimalism.

Robo-advisors are digital platforms that offer investment advice and typically create customised portfolios for individuals based on their preferences. These automated investment advisors are guiding an increasing volume of people and resources. They are growing in their ability and influence. The AI used can draw on a huge breadth of data and identify patterns that a human would miss and that may even defy a rational explanation. In practice, however, customisation is often limited, and the investors are simply put in a number of categories based on their dispositions to risk and their goals. The state of the art of what generative AI can do in this context and what is offered can be quite different, with some simpler services riding the wave of popularity of AI.

While neither the service nor the technology underpinning it is completely new, the scale at which it is being used now is very different from even a few years ago. The recent explosive growth of this innovation has clearly moved forward to the next stage of its diffusion to far wider audiences.

Despite their limitations, from the consumer's perspective they are liberating finance, making financial services available to far more people. Retail and novice investors can act in a more informed way even if they have limited money and time. From the perspective of the financial organisations, this will be their decisive battle, which will either enable them to scale dramatically or fall victim to the consolidation that typically comes with disruptive technologies like this. In an age where little is certain, there is one certainty for financial robo-advisors: Competitions will be fierce. Robo-advisors are not only easier to adopt, but they are also easier to evaluate and compare with each other. Along with Fintech, comparison websites are disrupting finance making the competition fiercer, and this applies to automated advisors. People are willing to give their money to a machine to manage, but they want to know from other people which is the best machine to give it to.

Those that are left standing in the end may or may not closely resemble the financial institutions of today. This is therefore one of the key battles where the smallest edge may tip things in one's favour. The old barriers to entry that provided some certainty and stability in the past are no longer as high as they used to be. So, in a new world with minimal barriers and many options, which will be the decisive factors? These will range from the usability, which can involve some nuanced subjective feelings about the experience, to the far more objective performance in hard numbers. It is therefore crucial for organisations to understand every dimension of this innovation and make the right moves at the right time.

This book covers the key issues related to robo-advisors, covering both the financial and technological dimensions. Using robo-advisors effectively may involve using the latest versions of generative AI or applying completely commoditised solutions with an effective business model. There isn't one answer, but it is necessary to understand this service and more broadly the role of Fintech in disrupting finance. To be successful, those from finance must understand robo-advisors as a technology and as an innovation, while people from a technology background must understand the financial dimension. In addition to the typical service of portfolio management, other common services are retirement planning, financial planning tools, fractional share investing, thematic and ESG investing, dividend reinvestment, crypto investments, estate planning, insurance advice and debt management.

Yet the evolution from rule-based to AI-powered advisory is far from linear. Some platforms continue to rely on predefined rules and rigid categorisation, offering only superficial customisation. Others are beginning to exploit the capabilities of generative AI to provide more intuitive and responsive user interactions, including real-time adjustments based on behavioural data and market changes. The gap between what the most advanced technologies can theoretically offer and what is actually implemented at scale remains significant. Many robo-advisors trade on the aura of AI innovation without deploying cutting-edge methods under the hood. The adoption of robo-advisory systems reflects a mixture of push and pull dynamics. From the "push" perspective, financial institutions and FinTechs are driving adoption through business models that rely on automation for scalability, cost-efficiency, and regulatory compliance. These platforms reduce the need for human labour and standardise decision-making, appealing to firms under pressure to do more with less. On the "pull" side, consumers, particularly millennials and digital natives, are increasingly comfortable with technology-based solutions and attracted to platforms that promise lower fees, greater transparency, and always-on availability. This convergence of supply-side innovation and demand-side readiness has accelerated the spread of robo-advisors into mainstream financial services.

Despite their growing popularity, robo-advisors are not without controversy. Critics question their ability to handle nuanced financial situations, their transparency in risk modelling, and their capacity to adapt to clients' changing needs. Others warn about the risks of over-reliance on algorithms, particularly when users lack the financial literacy to critically assess the advice they receive. From a regulatory standpoint, challenges include ensuring algorithmic accountability, preventing discriminatory outcomes, and maintaining investor protection in the face of opaque decision-making processes. Nonetheless, the benefits are considerable. Robo-advisors make investing accessible to a broader population, including those previously excluded due to high fees or complexity. They offer a scalable way to provide financial advice that can adapt in real time, potentially reducing behavioural biases and enhancing outcomes. They also increase transparency, as platforms often include clear dashboards and performance metrics, allowing clients to monitor their investments with unprecedented ease.

The rise of robo-advisors is also emblematic of deeper structural changes in finance. Traditional barriers to entry such as regulatory capital, brand trust, or branch infrastructure are eroding. Digital platforms can launch quickly, iterate rapidly, and scale globally. At the same time, the ability to compare financial products and services online puts incumbent institutions under pressure to compete not just on performance, but also on usability, personalisation, and customer experience. In this increasingly competitive landscape, having even a small technological or operational edge can be decisive. This book situates robo-advisory within the broader evolution of FinTech and financial services. It explores the historical development of digital investment tools, the transition from static rule-based systems to dynamic AI-driven models, and the interplay between business strategy, user experience, and regulatory frameworks. We argue that robo-advisors are not merely a new type of financial product, but a lens through which we can understand the future of finance itself where automation, data, and design converge to reshape how people save, invest, and plan.

1.2 Drivers, Challenges, and the Road Ahead

Understanding robo-advisors requires more than just awareness of their growing market presence. It demands an appreciation of both their technological underpinnings and financial logic. For finance professionals, this means engaging with the mechanisms of algorithmic decision-making and user interface design. For technologists, it means understanding risk management, asset allocation, and client segmentation. This interdisciplinary perspective is vital to harnessing the potential of robo-advisory while mitigating its risks. With such a disruptive technology, operating on such a large scale, there are challenges for all the stakeholders, not just the customers and the financial organisations, but also the regulators. For consumers, a key challenge is trust (Zarifis and Cheng 2022), understanding how a platform works, whether its advice is suitable, and whether they are protected in case of errors or unexpected outcomes. Financial literacy varies widely, and many investors may not realise they are engaging with AI rather than a human advisor. For financial organisations, the stakes are high: integrating robo-advisory into existing operations requires balancing cost-efficiency with risk management and client experience. Firms that fail to adopt may fall behind, while those that rush may suffer reputational or regulatory consequences. Regulators, in turn, must navigate the twin pressures of encouraging innovation and ensuring consumer protection. Questions of explainability, algorithmic fairness, data use, and fiduciary responsibility are central to regulatory debates. These issues raise urgent research questions: How should we evaluate robo-advisory outcomes? What kinds of disclosures should platforms provide? Can regulatory frameworks evolve quickly enough to match the pace of innovation? Ultimately, robo-advisors are part of a broader trend towards digital transformation in finance. Their success depends not only on algorithmic accuracy but also on trust, transparency, and alignment with human goals. In the chapters that follow, we examine how these platforms are built, adopted, regulated, and evaluated, offering insights for academics, practitioners, policymakers, and users alike. As this field evolves, the balance between innovation and accountability will determine whether robo-advisors fulfil their promise or fall short of it.

2 Evolution from Traditional Advisors to AI-driven Models

The evolution of financial advisory services from traditional human advisors to AI-driven robo-advisors represents a paradigm shift in how financial guidance is conceptualised, delivered, and experienced. This transformation is underpinned by broader trends in digitalisation, disintermediation, and datafication that are reshaping financial markets and institutions. Historically, financial advice was a high-touch, relationship-based service delivered by trained professionals, often operating under commission-based models or fee-based structures. Clients sought human expertise, not only for investment allocation but also for reassurance, trust, and behavioural coaching. However, this model was inherently limited by its cost, scalability, and access, especially for retail or low-net-worth investors. The emergence of robo-advisors in the post-2008 financial crisis era marked a response to these limitations. Early platforms such as Betterment and Wealthfront in the USA began offering algorithm-driven investment portfolios with lower fees, minimal entry thresholds, and a high degree of automation. These platforms aimed to democratise financial advice by using technology to reduce overheads and pass on savings to clients. As the market matured, incumbents like Vanguard and Schwab introduced their own hybrid robo offerings, blending automated models with optional human support.

A key driver of this shift has been the rapid development of financial algorithms and the availability of structured data on investor behaviour, market trends, and macroeconomic conditions. Initially, the algorithms were grounded in Modern Portfolio Theory (MPT) and offered asset allocations based on risk questionnaires and time horizons. However, the growing sophistication of machine learning and natural language processing has enabled robo-advisors to evolve from passive allocators to proactive, adaptive financial agents. AI-powered systems can now interpret textual data from news and social media, recognise sentiment shifts, and factor real-time economic indicators into investment decisions (Gomber et al. 2018; Sironi 2016).

Unlike their human counterparts, robo-advisors can scale effortlessly across geographies and client segments. They operate with 24/7 availability, consistent logic, and a high degree of transparency. While traditional advisors may offer a more holistic, empathetic, and customised approach, their performance and advice quality can vary significantly depending on individual skill, incentives, and behavioural biases. Robo-advisors, in contrast, offer standardisation and predictability, albeit with some loss of nuance and human judgement. Nonetheless, recent empirical studies suggest that the portfolio outcomes from robo-advisors are often comparable to those produced by traditional advisors, especially for passive investment strategies (Belanche et al. 2020; Fein 2015).

One of the turning points in this evolution has been the integration of behavioural finance principles into robo-advisory interfaces. Traditional advisors have long played a behavioural coaching role, helping clients resist herd behaviour, panic selling, or overtrading. Modern robo-advisors increasingly incorporate nudges, visual dashboards, and predictive alerts to guide users towards better financial habits (Lo 2017). This incorporation reflects a convergence of psychological insights, data analytics, and interface design, placing robo-advisory at the nexus of finance, computer science, and behavioural economics. At an institutional level, the evolution towards AI-driven advisory also reflects changing cost structures and regulatory pressures. With tightening margins, banks and asset managers view robo-advisory as a tool for operational efficiency and client segmentation. For example, high-net-worth clients may continue to receive bespoke advisory services, while entry-level clients are channelled through automated platforms. This "barbell" strategy allows firms to optimise resources and expand their reach without compromising compliance. According to Deloitte (2018), nearly half of wealth managers globally were investing in robo capabilities by 2020, with most adopting a hybrid advisory model.

Importantly, the rise of AI in financial advisory does not imply the obsolescence of human advisors. Instead, a "human + machine" model is emerging in which algorithms handle routine tasks, such as rebalancing, tax-loss harvesting, and risk profiling, while human advisors focus on complex financial planning and emotional engagement. This shift parallels trends in other professional services where AI augments rather than replaces human expertise. As pointed out by Brynjolfsson and McAfee (2014), the highest value lies not in pure automation but in collaborative intelligence, where machines enhance human decision-making. The transition to AI-driven models has also sparked ethical and regulatory debates. Concerns have been raised about algorithmic transparency, data privacy, and fairness in portfolio recommendations. Regulators are increasingly scrutinising the use of personal data, algorithmic biases, and the fiduciary responsibilities of robo-advisors (Baker and Dellaert 2019). While some jurisdictions have embraced innovation with regulatory sandboxes, others have taken a more cautious stance, imposing stricter licensing and disclosure requirements. This variation reflects broader tensions in global financial governance between fostering innovation and ensuring investor protection. The evolution from traditional to AI-driven financial advisors is not a linear replacement but a multifaceted transformation. It reflects broader shifts in technology, economics, and client expectations. While traditional advisory models continue to hold relevance in certain segments, the future of financial advice will likely be hybrid, data-informed, and increasingly digital. The next frontier involves not only refining the algorithms that drive these platforms but also enhancing their capacity for trust, adaptability, and ethical alignment.

3 Differentiating Rule-based and AI-powered Systems

The field of robo-advisory encompasses a wide spectrum of technological sophistication, from static rule-based systems to dynamic learning-based AI models. Distinguishing between these two categories is essential to understanding not only how robo-advisors function, but also their capacity for personalisation, adaptability, and long-term value creation. Rule-based systems, while often labelled as "robo-advisors", differ substantially in capabilities and risks compared to AI-powered platforms. Rule-based robo-advisors are grounded in predefined decision trees, heuristics, and fixed allocation models. These systems typically use structured inputs such as client age, income, risk tolerance, and investment horizon to generate asset allocations based on Modern Portfolio Theory (MPT). The advice is deterministic: given the same input, the system will always produce the same output. This structure ensures consistency, transparency, and regulatory clarity. For example, platforms like Vanguard Personal Advisor Services or early versions of Betterment followed this approach to offer low-cost, diversified portfolios built around passive investment strategies (Fein 2015).

Despite their simplicity, rule-based systems offer several advantages. First, they are easier to audit, explain, and regulate an important consideration in a highly scrutinised industry. Second, they are cost-effective, making them suitable for entry-level investors. Third, they reflect a conservative approach to technology deployment, limiting potential risks arising from opaque algorithms or spurious correlations. However, this rigidity also means that rule-based advisors often fall short in handling complex financial situations, adjusting to market shifts, or learning from new data. As Belanche et al. (2020) note, users may become disengaged over time if the system does not evolve with their preferences or behaviour. In contrast, AI-powered robo-advisors leverage machine learning, natural language processing, and other forms of artificial intelligence to deliver more adaptive and personalised services. Rather than relying solely on static inputs, these systems can incorporate unstructured data (e.g. financial news, social media sentiment), behavioural cues (e.g. login frequency, withdrawal patterns), and even voice or chat interactions to refine recommendations. This dynamic capability allows AI-based platforms to recognise emerging trends, predict customer needs, and proactively suggest financial actions (Gomber et al. 2018).

One of the key features of AI-powered systems is continuous learning. Algorithms can update their models as new data becomes available, allowing the advisor to recalibrate portfolios based on market volatility, client behaviour, or updated macroeconomic forecasts. For example, systems using reinforcement learning can optimise asset allocations over time based on the outcomes of previous decisions, improving performance while adapting to evolving investor preferences. As Sironi (2016) suggests, the most advanced robo-advisors behave more like "financial assistants" than mere portfolio generators.

However, these advantages come with trade-offs. AI-based systems are often less transparent, raising concerns about explainability, algorithmic bias, and accountability. Users may not fully understand how recommendations are generated, especially if the underlying models are black-box neural networks. Regulatory bodies such as the European Securities and Markets Authority (ESMA) have called for greater algorithmic transparency in digital finance, highlighting the tension between innovation and investor protection. Baker and Dellaert (2019) argue that the fiduciary responsibilities of robo-advisors must be reinterpreted in light of AI's growing role in decision-making. There is also the question of data privacy and ethical use. AI systems require large volumes of personal and behavioural data to function effectively. The more data they have, the better they can personalise. But this raises risks related to data breaches, misuse, and surveillance issues that are increasingly salient in jurisdictions with strict data protection laws like GDPR. Furthermore, the performance of AI-powered advisors can be uneven across different client segments. While tech-savvy users may appreciate adaptive interfaces and real-time insights, other investors may find them confusing or intimidating. This raises an important strategic decision for platforms: should they prioritise automation and sophistication, or maintain simplicity and clarity?

In practice, many robo-advisors fall somewhere along a continuum. Hybrid models combining rule-based decision trees with machine-learning enhancements are becoming increasingly common. Some firms also offer "human-in-the-loop" designs where advisors oversee AI recommendations and intervene when necessary. This approach aims to balance scalability and precision with human judgement and empathy. Ultimately, the differentiation between rule-based and AI-powered systems is not just technical; it reflects deeper questions about trust, control, and the nature of financial decision-making. As the industry matures, the challenge will be to develop systems that are not only intelligent but also interpretable, secure, and aligned with investor values.

3.1 Emerging Themes in Robo-Advisory

Robo-advisory services have evolved from niche innovations into robust, multi-functional financial tools embedded within the wider digital finance ecosystem. As the field matures, several key themes have begun to shape its trajectory. These emerging patterns are not only technological but also behavioural, regulatory, and ethical, revealing the expanding responsibilities and possibilities associated with algorithmic financial advice.

One of the most notable developments is the hybridisation of services. Early robo-advisors positioned themselves as fully automated alternatives to traditional financial planners. However, as adoption broadened, it became clear that many users, especially those with complex financial needs, preferred having some level of human interaction. In response, leading platforms have adopted hybrid models that combine algorithm-driven portfolio management with optional access to human advisors. This blended approach enhances trust, supports client retention during market turbulence, and acknowledges the psychological dimensions of financial decision-making (Jung et al. 2018). Rather than replacing human advisors outright, robo-advisors now often complement them, streamlining routine tasks while preserving empathy and flexibility for nuanced cases.

Another defining theme is the integration of behavioural finance into platform design. Traditional risk tolerance questionnaires are increasingly being replaced or supplemented by goal-based planning interfaces that reflect users' evolving life contexts. Rather than focusing narrowly on asset allocation, these platforms now guide users through savings milestones, retirement planning, and behavioural nudges designed to reduce impulsive decisions. Features such as progress dashboards, auto-reminders, and scenario planning tools are increasingly common, aligning robo-advisory interfaces with behavioural design principles that support financial well-being (Lo 2017).

Closely related to this is the rise of personalisation through alternative data. AI-powered robo-advisors now have the capacity to move beyond traditional demographic inputs. By analysing behavioural data, lifestyle patterns, and even psychometric signals, platforms can offer more refined and responsive investment strategies. This allows advisors to tailor portfolios based not just on income and age, but on personality traits, spending habits, and digital engagement profiles. Di Maggio et al. (2020) note that such approaches can significantly enhance portfolio alignment with investor goals, but they also raise ethical questions around data privacy, user consent, and algorithmic profiling. The promise of personalisation must therefore be balanced with responsible data governance.

Robo-advisors are also broadening their scope beyond investment management. What began as a service focused on low-cost, passive portfolios has now evolved into a suite of financial planning tools. Many platforms offer tax optimisation, debt reduction strategies, ESG screening, insurance matching, and estate planning, all within a unified digital interface. This shift reflects a strategic move towards lifecycle financial coaching, where the robo-advisor becomes a long-term partner in financial decision-making (Sironi 2016). The bundling of services also supports platform stickiness, as users are more likely to stay engaged when their broader financial lives are integrated into a single system.

Trust and transparency have simultaneously emerged as central concerns. As algorithms become more complex and less interpretable, users may feel uncertain about how decisions are made on their behalf. To address this, many platforms are now incorporating explainability features such as visualisation of allocation logic, plain-language disclosures, or simulation tools that show how portfolios respond to different market scenarios. This development is not merely cosmetic. Research has shown that perceived fairness and trustworthiness of algorithmic decisions improve when users understand how those decisions are made (Kleinberg et al. 2020). Regulators are also pressuring platforms to meet higher standards of disclosure, particularly under rules like GDPR and MiFID II, which directly address automated decision-making.

Finally, there is a growing emphasis on inclusion and accessibility. Robo-advisors have the potential to democratise finance by reducing entry barriers, offering multilingual interfaces, and lowering minimum investment thresholds. In developing economies, mobile-first robo-advisors are bringing investment services to new populations, bypassing the need for traditional banking infrastructure (Arner et al. 2016). Yet, challenges remain. Digital illiteracy, algorithmic bias, and accessibility limitations may still prevent marginalised groups from fully benefiting. Therefore, platforms must not only offer inclusive access but also be designed with diversity in mind, ensuring that users of varying backgrounds, ages, and digital proficiencies can engage meaningfully with the service. Together, these themes mark the expansion of robo-advisory from a narrowly defined technological solution to a broader institutional and behavioural phenomenon. The platforms are no longer only defined by their algorithms, but by how they engage users, address regulation, incorporate data ethics, and adapt across cultures and markets. Understanding these shifts is essential to grasping the future of digital financial advice not only in terms of innovation, but also in terms of responsibility, reach, and resilience.

4 Key Players and Market Trends in Robo-Advisory

In the future, there may be a small number of global robo-advisors, but currently, due to regulation and cultural differences, different robo-advisors are popular in each country. If we just take Europe as an example, in the UK, robo-advisors include Nutmeg; in German-speaking countries, Scalable Capital and Whitebox are popular; in France, there is Yomoni; in Spain, there is InbestMe; and in Switzerland, there is Simple Wealth. Countries that are known as financial innovators and are strong in Fintech and crypto, such as Singapore, are also particularly strong in providing several successful robo-advisors, such as StashAway and Endowus.

In North America, the robo-advisory space is led by early pioneers like Betterment and Wealthfront, which remain dominant due to first-mover advantage and consistent innovation in user experience. These platforms focus heavily on passive investing and automated tax-loss harvesting, offering a clean, intuitive interface for millennials and tech-savvy investors. However, major incumbents such as Vanguard, Fidelity, and Charles Schwab have also entered the space with hybrid models that combine algorithmic allocation with optional human advice. The success of these incumbents underscores a broader market trend: robo-advisory is no longer the exclusive domain of startups, but a capability that is rapidly being absorbed into the core offerings of traditional financial institutions.

Market penetration and client acquisition strategies vary by region and provider. In developed economies, most robo-advisors target digitally native retail investors, especially those in younger age cohorts with long investment horizons but limited capital. Conversely, in emerging markets, platforms are experimenting with alternative business models, including subscription-based plans, micro-investing, and integration with mobile wallets to reach users outside the traditional banking system. For example, platforms in India and Indonesia are leveraging partnerships with telecom providers and mobile-first banks to offer robo-investing services via super apps. These strategies reflect the adaptability of the robo-advisory model to different regulatory environments, financial infrastructures, and consumer behaviours.

Consolidation is another emerging trend. As the market matures, smaller robo-advisors are being acquired by banks, asset managers, or private equity firms seeking to expand their digital capabilities. This wave of mergers and acquisitions suggests a convergence between FinTech innovation and institutional finance, driven by the need for scale, trust, and regulatory compliance. At the same time, new entrants continue to emerge, particularly niche robo-advisors focused on ESG investing, Sharia-compliant portfolios, or crypto-asset management. These specialised platforms cater to increasingly segmented investor preferences, illustrating the potential for robo-advisors to not only generalise but also differentiate within the digital advice space.

These developments suggest that the future of robo-advisory will be both global and fragmented. While a few dominant players may emerge at scale, the landscape is likely to retain a diverse mix of local champions, hybrid models, and niche providers. The dynamics of trust, regulation, cultural fit, and technological infrastructure will continue to shape how robo-advisory evolves in different markets. Rather than converging towards a single model, robo-advisory is likely to diversify, reflecting not just financial logic, but also social, legal, and behavioural contexts unique to each region.

4.1 Digital Transformation in Finance and Emerging Business Models

The effectiveness and popularity of financial robo-advisors do not just depend on the technology they utilise but also on the broader strategy they are part of.

Digital transformation in finance is an ongoing process, but there are six AI-focused business models that have been proven and should stand the test of time. The six business models proven to be ideal for a modern organisation with AI at its centre (Zarifis and Cheng 2023, 2024) are: (1) an incumbent focusing on one part of the value chain and disaggregating, (2) an incumbent absorbing AI into an existing model, (3) an incumbent expanding beyond the current model to fully utilise the opportunities of AI and access new data, (4) a startup disruptor focused on one sector, built from the start to be highly automated, (5) a disruptor focused on tech adding a new service like insurance, and (6) a disruptor that is not necessarily tech-focused, with an extensive user or fanbase.

Robo-advisors are central to all six business models, but they will be used very differently depending on the chosen strategy. The business model may influence the technology and the data used by the robo-advisor. For example, if the strategy is to keep the business model the same and adapt technology to it, there will typically be some in-house customisation of the robo-advisor. The priority is that the robo-advisor accurately represents the organisation as opposed to fully utilising its capabilities.

As shown in Fig. 1, the deployment of robo-advisory services varies significantly depending on the business model of the financial organisation. These six AI-focused models illustrate not only how firms structure their operations around automation but also how they leverage data, scale, and customer engagement. The distinction between incumbents and disruptors, each adopting AI in different ways, highlights that there is no one-size-fits-all approach. Some models prioritise legacy integration, while others are built from the ground up with digital-native strategies. Understanding where a robo-advisor fits within this typology provides crucial insight into its strategic potential, technological constraints, and long-term sustainability in an increasingly competitive financial ecosystem.

The influence of the business model on the data available to the robo-advisor is important. The AI-focused business models put more emphasis on data than the older, outdated models they are replacing. It is not simply a case of more or less data; the different data make the assessment different. For example, the first three business models involve incumbents that have data on their customers and their investment results in the past that can inform the analysis the AI does. The fourth model is a startup that does not have its own data. The fifth is a tech-savvy company with data from its existing customer base, and the sixth is a company that is not tech-focused and has data from its existing customer base. If the customer behaviour available is not financial, it can still be useful in understanding their perspective on things like risk, trust, the point they are at in their lives, and their goals.

4.2 Robo-Advisors in Cryptocurrency Investment

In the context of cryptocurrencies, the concept of robo-advisory extends beyond simple portfolio rebalancing. Given the 24/7 nature of crypto markets and their

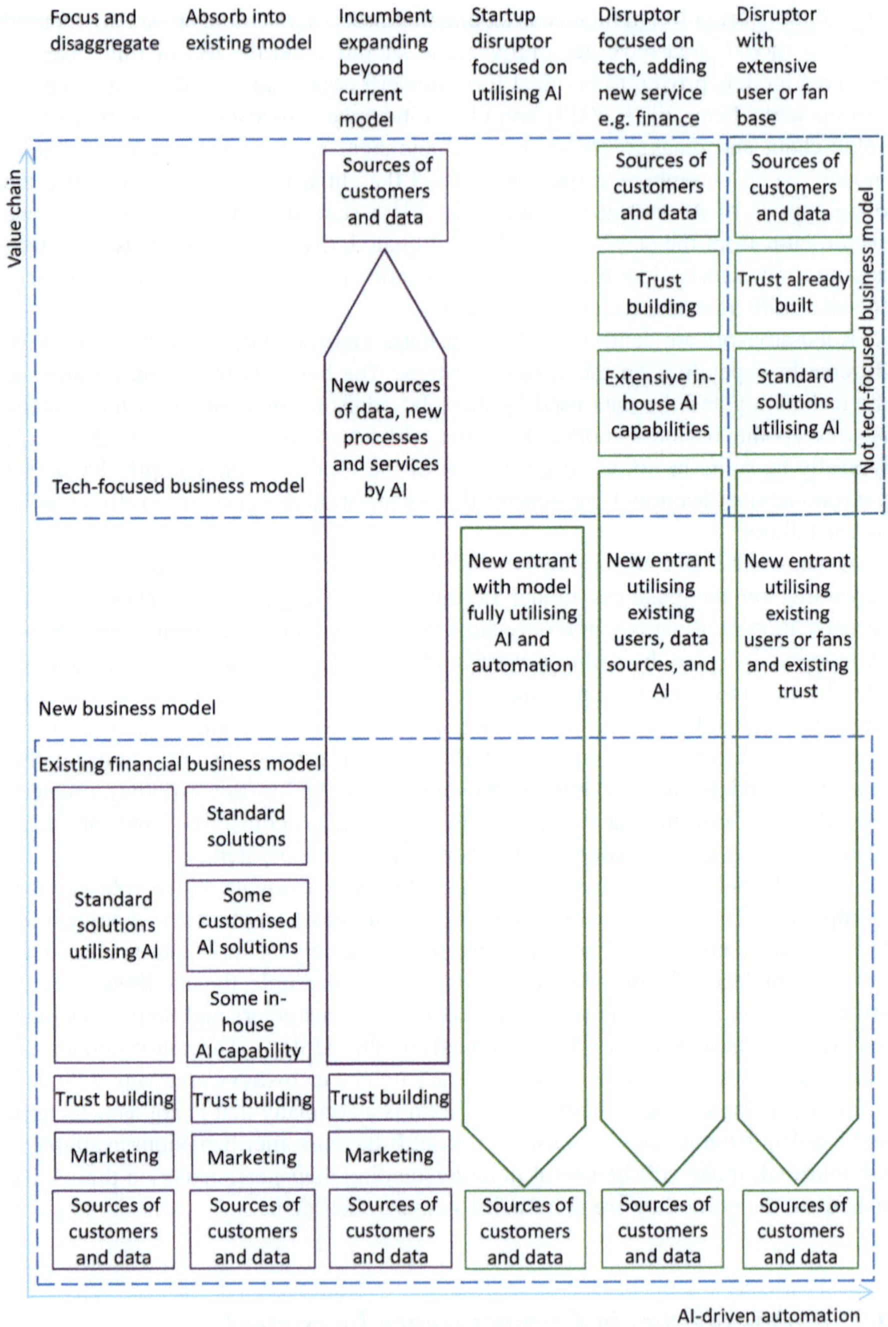

Fig. 1 Six financial services business models with AI at their centre

extreme volatility, algorithms must adapt to rapid price movements, liquidity shocks, and regime change challenges much more severe than in traditional markets (Luo et al. 2021). The integration of blockchain analytics, sentiment data, and real-time volatility metrics into advisory algorithms allows these tools to provide dynamic recommendations. For example, research has shown that ML-based trading strategies for cryptocurrencies significantly outperform simple buy-and-hold approaches, underscoring the importance of adaptive algorithmic design in this domain (Cohen 2023; Li et al. 2025). Thus, the evolution of robo-advisors for digital assets reflects not only the democratisation of investment management but also the technological sophistication required to operate effectively in decentralised markets, which exhibit distinct long-memory properties, trading environments, and arguably different investor behaviours.

While traditional robo-advisors (e.g., in equities or bonds) have been widely discussed (Judijanto 2025), the growing popularity of digital assets has prompted several fintech and wealth management platforms to expand their offerings into cryptocurrency investment. Several mainstream robo-advisory platforms, such as Betterment, have begun to offer diversified crypto-asset portfolios, while specialist firms like Bitwise Asset Management provide dedicated algorithmically managed crypto index funds. Other platforms, such as Wealthfront and SwissBorg, offer more limited or niche crypto exposure, indicating a spectrum of service depth in the robo-advisor crypto space. These systems utilise quantitative risk models to allocate investments between major cryptocurrencies, stablecoins, and occasionally DeFi assets, aiming to provide exposure while mitigating downside risks.

However, the operational logic of crypto robo-advisors differs significantly from that of traditional counterparts. Unlike equity or bond portfolios that rely on established valuation metrics and long-term fundamentals, crypto portfolios require real-time sentiment analysis, on-chain network data, and liquidity assessments (Li 2023). This complexity challenges the robustness of standard mean-variance optimisation frameworks and prompts developers to adopt hybrid models that combine algorithmic rebalancing with heuristic or rule-based triggers. Consequently, robo-advisors in the crypto domain embody a fusion of classical portfolio theory and behavioural-fintech adaptation to a novel asset class.

Robo-advisors offer a potential antidote to the behavioural biases that pervade cryptocurrency investing. Retail investors often fall victim to emotional trading, driven by fear of missing out (FOMO), loss aversion, and herding effects. By delegating portfolio decisions to an algorithm, investors may reduce impulsive behaviour and maintain more disciplined, long-term strategies. Automated systems also eliminate the cognitive overload caused by the high-frequency and often contradictory information flow within crypto markets.

Yet, reliance on algorithmic advice introduces its own psychological complexities. Some investors may develop an "illusion of control", assuming that the algorithm guarantees superior outcomes, while others may experience discomfort with the lack of human interaction or transparency in decision-making. Moreover, algorithmic biases embedded in model training data could reproduce systemic errors, particularly if models rely on historical patterns that are poorly suited to the rapidly evolving crypto environment. Thus, while robo-advisors can mitigate emotional biases, they simultaneously create new cognitive dependencies that warrant careful study (Filiz et al. 2022).

The regulatory landscape surrounding robo-advisors in traditional finance is still evolving, and the inclusion of cryptocurrencies further complicates the picture. In most jurisdictions, robo-advisors must comply with fiduciary and suitability requirements, ensuring that automated recommendations align with clients' profiles. However, when the underlying assets are decentralised and globally traded, the regulatory jurisdiction becomes ambiguous. Platforms offering crypto robo-advisory often face challenges in meeting disclosure standards, anti-money laundering (AML) compliance, and investor protection obligations.

The regulatory frameworks governing digital assets and artificial intelligence are rapidly evolving, shaping the environment in which robo-advisors operate. In the European Union, the Markets in Crypto-Assets Regulation (MiCA) (Regulation (EU) 2023/1114) represents a milestone in the legal recognition and supervision of crypto-asset activities. MiCA establishes harmonised rules for issuers of crypto-assets and for crypto-asset service providers (CASPs), introducing obligations related to investor protection, transparency, and operational governance. Robo-advisory platforms that offer automated investment strategies involving crypto-assets may fall within the MiCA definition of a CASP, particularly when providing portfolio management or investment advice. This means they must adhere to MiCA's authorisation, conduct-of-business, and disclosure requirements. The regulation also emphasises the need for algorithmic transparency and the management of technology-related risks, indirectly setting expectations for the explainability and accountability of AI-driven decision-making tools used in automated advisory services. In this sense, MiCA not only brings regulatory clarity to the crypto market but also indirectly establishes governance standards relevant to algorithmic and data-driven investment technologies.

Ethical concerns also arise from the opaque nature of algorithmic decision-making. Investors seldom understand how recommendation engines weigh different variables or respond to market stress, leading to a potential lack of accountability. Data privacy adds another dimension of risk, particularly when algorithms rely on personal financial data combined with blockchain analytics. Addressing these ethical and legal challenges is critical for building investor trust and ensuring the long-term sustainability of robo-advisory models in cryptocurrency markets.

The performance of robo-advised cryptocurrency portfolios remains a contested issue. Empirical evidence is still emerging, but early analyses suggest that algorithmic rebalancing can improve risk-adjusted returns by enforcing diversification and disciplined trading. In particular, automated systems can respond to volatility spikes more efficiently than human investors, reducing exposure during downturns and re-entering positions systematically. These advantages position robo-advisors as effective tools for smoothing returns in an otherwise turbulent market.

Nonetheless, algorithmic strategies are not immune to systemic risk. Model overfitting, delayed responses to black-swan events, and cascading sell-offs triggered by simultaneous algorithmic signals can amplify market instability (Paulin et al.

2019; Gort et al. 2022). The absence of standardised benchmarks also makes it difficult to assess performance objectively. In highly correlated markets such as cryptocurrencies, where diversification benefits might be limited within the crypto-assets ecosystem, robo-advisors may inadvertently provide a false sense of risk management. Therefore, continuous monitoring and adaptive-learning mechanisms are essential for maintaining robustness and investor confidence.

Looking ahead, the convergence of robo-advisory, decentralised finance, and artificial intelligence heralds a new phase of autonomous wealth management. Smart contracts could soon enable fully decentralised robo-advisors that operate without intermediaries, executing trades and rebalancing portfolios transparently on blockchain networks. Integration with decentralised oracles and predictive analytics could further enhance these systems' ability to anticipate market shifts, offering real-time, self-executing financial guidance.

However, the expansion of robo-advisory into crypto ecosystems also raises questions about inclusivity and systemic risk. While automation can democratise access to sophisticated investment tools, it might also lead to herding behaviour if thousands of investors follow identical algorithmic signals. Balancing efficiency with diversity, and automation with human oversight, will define the next stage in the evolution of robo-advisory technology. As digital assets mature, the key challenge will be ensuring that these innovations enhance financial stability and investor welfare rather than amplify speculative excesses.

5 Conclusion

Robo-advisory represents one of the most transformative developments within the broader FinTech revolution. As this chapter has shown, the shift from traditional human advisors to digital, and increasingly AI-driven, platforms is not simply a technological progression; it is a systemic change in how financial services are conceptualised, delivered, and consumed. This evolution reflects deeper shifts in client expectations, regulatory pressures, and institutional strategies, signalling a redefinition of the advisor–client relationship in the digital age. From their early days as low-cost, rule-based tools offering passive investment portfolios, robo-advisors have grown into complex, multifaceted platforms capable of delivering personalised and dynamic financial guidance. Today, many are embedded with machine-learning capabilities, natural language interfaces, and behavioural insights, enabling them to serve as adaptive financial companions rather than static allocation engines. The transition from deterministic models to predictive, data-driven systems illustrates how innovation in this space is driven not only by advances in technology but also by the growing demand for accessible, responsive, and transparent financial solutions.

At the same time, the chapter has highlighted that this transformation is not uniform or universal. Robo-advisors span a wide spectrum, from simple decision trees to sophisticated AI-driven assistants, and their capabilities, cost structures, and user experiences vary accordingly. This variation is shaped by a number of factors, chief among them the business model of the organisation deploying the technology. As Fig. 1 illustrates, six dominant models define how institutions integrate robo-advisory into their broader digital strategies. Whether these platforms are developed in-house by incumbents or launched by digital-native startups, the role of data, scalability, and trust is central to their success. Market structures and regulatory environments also play a critical role in shaping the landscape. Robo-advisory growth is uneven across geographies, with different players gaining traction depending on local consumer behaviour, cultural preferences, and compliance requirements. From Nutmeg in the UK to Betterment in the USA, to StashAway in Singapore, providers are adapting their models to meet regional needs while leveraging global technological trends. This duality, global convergence of digital finance with localised execution, will likely define the next decade of robo-advisory expansion.

Importantly, the rise of robo-advisory is not without risks and unresolved tensions. As outlined in this chapter, questions remain around transparency, algorithmic bias, user understanding, and regulatory oversight. The very features that make robo-advisors efficient and scalable—automation, opacity, and reliance on data—are also those that generate ethical and operational challenges. These tensions underscore the need for an interdisciplinary approach to evaluating robo-advisors, one that incorporates insights from finance, computer science, psychology, and law. What also emerges clearly is that success in robo-advisory cannot be reduced to technology alone. Platforms that thrive are those that blend usability with regulatory compliance, technical capability with behavioural insight, and scalability with personalisation. As we move further into the age of algorithmic finance, the key differentiator will likely be trust: platforms must not only deliver strong outcomes but also provide users with confidence in how those outcomes are achieved.

This chapter has laid the groundwork for understanding the rise of robo-advisory by tracing its origins, differentiating its technological forms, examining its business contexts, and highlighting its most pressing challenges and opportunities. In the chapters that follow, we delve deeper into the architecture, governance, and societal implications of robo-advisory platforms. We examine not just how they work, but how they are adopted, regulated, and evaluated across different stakeholder groups. Ultimately, robo-advisory is not merely a financial tool; it is a test case for how artificial intelligence, behavioural design, and digital infrastructure can be combined to reshape one of the most human of endeavours: making decisions about money, risk, and the future.

6 Overview of the Chapters

This book is organised into five interconnected parts that collectively examine how robo-advisory technologies are transforming the finance industry. It begins with the foundations of this transformation and then explores the behavioural and ethical dimensions of investor interaction, the regulatory and risk frameworks that underpin system integrity, the technological innovations driving new applications, and finally, the sustainability and future trajectory of AI-driven financial services.

Part I: Foundations and Market Evolution

The opening part establishes the conceptual and market foundations of robo-advisory. It charts the field's evolution within the broader FinTech movement and introduces the drivers that shaped its emergence. This chapter introduces the rise of robo-advisory, situating it within the broader context of the digital transformation of financial services. It examines how artificial intelligence, behavioural design, and data analytics have converged to democratise access to financial advice. The chapter concludes with a framework of six AI-driven business models that reveal the strategic diversity of robo-advisory across traditional and disruptive financial firms. Chapter "Current Trends for Robo-Advisors" continues by mapping current trends and developments in digital wealth management. It highlights the industry's shift from fully automated to hybrid advisory models that blend algorithmic precision with human insight. The discussion underscores how global adoption, client sophistication, and regulatory adaptation are collectively maturing the sector into a resilient and customer-centric ecosystem.

Part II: Behavioural and Ethical Dimensions

The second part turns to the human and ethical aspects of robo-advisory. It examines how cognitive biases shape investment decisions, how artificial intelligence can personalise advice, and how trust and transparency determine user adoption. Chapter "Behavioral Biases in Investment Decisions" analyses behavioural biases such as overconfidence, herding, and loss aversion that distort investor judgment and market efficiency. Drawing on insights from behavioural finance and neuroscience, it links these biases to financial instability and discusses AI-based techniques that can correct or reduce them responsibly. Chapter "AI in Personalized Financial Decision-Making" explores the growing role of artificial intelligence in tailoring financial advice to individual preferences and behavioural tendencies. By applying machine learning and reinforcement learning, robo-advisors can anticipate investor responses and adjust recommendations dynamically. The chapter also warns of ethical concerns around consent, fairness, and privacy, urging a balance between innovation and investor protection. Chapter "Building Trust in Financial Robo-Advisory and Overcoming Ethical Challenges"addresses the central challenge of building trust in financial automation. It outlines five key dimensions—human oversight, transparency, accuracy, usability, and human-like interaction—and proposes specific strategies to strengthen confidence and ethical reliability in AI-based financial systems. Chapter "A Theory of Investment Simplification and an Experiment with AI Large Language Models" moves the discussion towards the complexity of digital finance itself. Through an experimental comparison of human advisors and large language models, it demonstrates that advanced AI systems can simplify decision-making and even outperform humans in navigating the diversity of advisory platforms.

Part III: Regulation, Compliance, and Risk Management
Part III focuses on governance, risk, and accountability. It explores how AI introduces new risk categories, how regulators are adapting, and how auditing and cybersecurity frameworks evolve to maintain market integrity. Chapter "Identifying and Ranking the Eight Risks of AI for Each of the Six Main AI Focused Fintech Business Models" identifies eight key risks facing AI-focused FinTech business models, ranging from data privacy to strategic misalignment, and ranks their significance using a Delphi methodology. The analysis reveals that while established models reduce some forms of risk, they remain vulnerable to technological and ecosystem dependencies. Chapter "Regulatory and Compliance Issues in AI-Driven Financial Services" examines the regulatory and compliance issues that shape AI-enabled advisory services across major jurisdictions. It translates global regulatory expectations such as those of the SEC, FCA, ESMA, and MAS into actionable control frameworks, demonstrating how firms can integrate compliance into product design, testing, and deployment. Chapter "Robo-Advisory and Auditing: Internal and External Controls" explores how AI is reshaping both internal and external auditing. It introduces a dual-layer model that combines real-time technological oversight with ethical and governance assurance, positioning auditing as a continuous, predictive, and trust-building function in AI finance. Chapter "Cybersecurity risk and Robo-advisory" delves into the cybersecurity challenges of digital advisory systems. It explains how adversarial machine learning, data leaks, and model manipulation create new vulnerabilities and proposes a defensive architecture built on explainable AI, encryption, and zero-trust principles. Chapter "Progress in Contemporary Fraud Detection through the Fintech Application of Artificial Intelligence" extends the discussion to fraud detection and prevention. It highlights AI's potential to enhance financial transparency and reduce misconduct while stressing that lasting progress depends on ethical accountability, regulatory vigilance, and responsible innovation.

Part IV: Technological Innovations and Financial Integration
This part investigates the technological frontier of robo-advisory from data-driven forecasting and market microstructure to the transformative promise of quantum computing. Chapter "Enhanced Cryptocurrency Volatility Forecasting via Local Linear Forests" evaluates Local Linear Forests as a machine-learning approach for forecasting cryptocurrency volatility. The findings demonstrate that these models outperform traditional econometric frameworks, particularly in unstable market phases, offering practical insights for investors and regulators. Chapter "Fee Structure and Order Flow Informativeness in the Cryptocurrency Market" studies how trading fees influence the efficiency of digital markets. Using Binance's policy shift from zero to commission-based trading as a natural experiment, it shows that modest transaction costs enhance the informativeness of order flow and improve price discovery. Chapter "Quantum Computing and the Next Generation of Robo-

Advisory" explores quantum computing as a transformative force in financial modelling. It explains how quantum algorithms can advance portfolio optimisation, risk simulation, and data encryption while also acknowledging the current technical and adoption challenges that accompany this emerging paradigm.

Part V: Sustainability, Market Impact, and Future Directions
The final part looks towards the broader implications of robo-advisory for sustainable finance and market evolution. It considers how AI-enabled platforms contribute to ESG integration, investor alignment, and the long-term viability of the digital wealth sector. Chapter "Sustainable Investing and the Role of AI-Driven Robo-Advisors" discusses the intersection of sustainability and technology in asset management. It highlights how AI-driven robo-advisors enhance ESG investing by improving data consistency, transparency, and adaptability while helping mitigate greenwashing and aligning with evolving sustainability standards. Chapter "Robo-Advisory Under Review: The Market's Verdict" concludes the volume by examining how markets have responded to the emergence of robo-advisory services. By contrasting the withdrawal of several incumbent institutions with the success of specialised digital platforms and the rise of robo-advisory in emerging economies, it identifies the strategic and regulatory conditions under which digital advice will thrive.

References

Arner DW, Barberis J, Buckley RP, Nos Barberist J, Buckley RP (2016) The evolution of FinTech: a new post-crisis paradigm. Georgetown J Int Law 47(4):1271–1320

Baker T, Dellaert B (2019) Regulating Robo advice across the financial services industry. Iowa Law Rev. https://doi.org/10.2139/ssrn.2932189

Belanche D, Casaló LV, Flavián C (2020) Customer's acceptance of humanoid robots in services: the moderating role of risk aversion. Smart Innov Syst Technol 167:449–458. https://doi.org/10.1007/978-981-15-1564-4_42

Brynjolfsson E, McAfee A (2014) The second machine age: work, progress, and prosperity in a time of brilliant technologies. W.W. Norton & Company, 5(2014–1). https://doi.org/10.35562/alyoda.310

Cohen G (2023) Intraday algorithmic trading strategies for cryptocurrencies. Rev Quant Finance Account 61:395–409

Deloitte (2018) 2019 Investment Management Outlook - A mix of opportunity and challenge. https://www2.deloitte.com/content/dam/Deloitte/lu/Documents/financial-services/IM/lu-2019-investment-management-outlook.pdf

Di Maggio M, Liu J, Rizova S, Wiley R (2020) Exchange fees and overall trading costs. J Empir Finance, June. https://doi.org/10.2139/ssrn.3625801

Fein ML (2015) Robo-Advisors: a closer look by Melanie L. Fein. Fein Law Offices, 1–33. https://ssrn.com/abstract=2658701

Filiz I, Judek JR, Lorenz M, Spiwoks M (2022) Algorithm aversion as an obstacle in the establishment of Robo advisors. J Risk Financ Manage 15(8)

Gomber P, Kauffman RJ, Parker C, Weber BW (2018) On the fintech revolution: interpreting the forces of innovation, disruption, and transformation in financial services. J Manage Inform Syst 35(1):220–265. https://doi.org/10.1080/07421222.2018.1440766

Gort BJD, Liu X-Y, Sun X, Gao J, Chen S, & Wang CD (2022). Deep reinforcement learning for cryptocurrency trading: practical approach to address backtest overfitting

Jung D, Dorner V, Glaser F, Morana S (2018) Robo-Advisory: digitalization and automation of financial advisory. Bus Inform Syst Eng 60(1):81–86. https://doi.org/10.1007/s12599-018-0521-9

Judijanto L (2025) Robo-advisors in wealth management: a bibliometric study of research evolution. ES Account Finance 3(02):137–149. https://doi.org/10.58812/esaf.v3i02.501

Kleinberg J, Udwig J, Mullainathan S, Rambachan A (2020) Shrinking capitalism. AEA Papers and Proceedings, May, 2020. https://doi.org/10.1257/pandp.20201001

Lo AW (2017) Adaptive markets. Princeton University Press. https://doi.org/10.2307/j.ctvc77k3n

Luo D, Mishra T, Yarovaya L, Zhang Z (2021) Investing in times of Fintech revolution: ambiguity and return risk in cryptocurrencies. J Int Financ Mark Inst Money, 73

Li S, Yarovaya L, Mishra T (2025) Machine learning, memory and efficiency in cryptocurrency markets. Journal of International Financial Markets, Institutions and Money 105. https://doi.org/10.1016/j.intfin.2025.102210

Li Z (2023) The application of blockchain and robo-advisors in wealth management literature review. Adv Econ Management Polit Sci

Sironi (2016) FinTech innovation: From Robo-Advisors to goal based investing and Gamification

Paulin J, Calinescu A, Wooldridge M (2019) Understanding flash crash contagion and systemic risk: a micro–macro agent-based approach. J Econ Dyn Contr 100:200–229

Zarifis A, Cheng X (2022) A model of trust in Fintech and trust in Insurtech: how Artificial Intelligence and the context influence it. J Behav Exp Finance 36. https://doi.org/10.1016/j.jbef.2022.100739

Zarifis A, Cheng X (2023) The five emerging business models of fintech for AI adoption, growth and building trust. Business Digital Transformation: Selected Cases from Industry Leaders, 73–97. https://doi.org/10.1007/978-3-031-33665-2_4

Zarifis A, Cheng X (2024) How to build trust in answers given by Generative AI for specific and vague financial questions. J Electr Bus Dig Econ. https://doi.org/10.1108/jebde-11-2023-0028

Current Trends for Robo-Advisors

Fabio Silva Dias

Abstract FinTech innovation and changing customer demands for more affordable, always-available, and user-friendly services are driving a significant global transformation in the wealth management sector. Robo-advisors, which are automated investment platforms that use quantitative algorithms to manage portfolios, first appeared in the USA but have since quickly expanded throughout Europe and Asia. These platforms have solidified their position in digital wealth management by going beyond basic advice to provide full portfolio management, which now includes trade execution, monitoring, and automated rebalancing. In order to manage the growing complexity of clients and finances globally, the market is clearly maturing from fully automated services to more intricate hybrid models that combine technology and human expertise. This chapter explains the fundamental shift from purely automated services, which dominated the initial phase of the industry's development, towards more complex models that offer a careful balance of technology and human expertise.

Keywords Robo-advisory · Fintech · Wealthtech · Financial planning

FinTech innovation and changing customer demands for more affordable, always-available, and user-friendly services are driving a significant global transformation in the wealth management sector. Robo-advisors, which are automated investment platforms that use quantitative algorithms to manage portfolios, first appeared in the USA but have since quickly expanded throughout Europe and Asia. These platforms have solidified their position in digital wealth management by going beyond basic advice to provide full portfolio management, which now includes trade execution, monitoring, and automated rebalancing. In order to manage the growing complexity of clients and finances globally, the market is clearly maturing from fully

F. S. Dias (✉)
Surrey Business School, University of Surrey, Guildford, UK
e-mail: f.dias@surrey.ac.uk

N. Nahidi, A. Zarifis (eds.), *AI, FinTech, and the Future of Robo-Advisory*, Contributions to Finance and Accounting,
https://doi.org/10.1007/978-3-032-18109-1_2

automated services to more intricate hybrid models that combine technology and human expertise. This chapter explains the fundamental shift from purely automated services, which dominated the initial phase of the industry's development, towards more complex models that offer a careful balance of technology and human expertise.

1 Introduction and Overview

The emergence of robo-advisors can be attributed to their fundamental role in **democratising investment** through automated services. These online platforms, which were first envisioned as inexpensive substitutes for conventional human advisors, automatically create and manage client portfolios using algorithms. In the years after the global financial crisis of 2007–2008, this democratisation process was accelerated because of stricter regulations on established banks and the rapid advancements in computer science, which strongly encouraged technology-based financial firms to create non-bank solutions. Mass market investors can now open accounts, get financial advice, and automate their investment decisions more easily and affordably thanks to robo-advisors, which drastically reduce the financial barriers to entry.

The earliest and simplest iteration of these platforms was the **pure robo-advisor model**, characterised by a fully automated investment advisory process driven by algorithms with no direct human interaction for the user. This pure approach prioritised cost reduction and scalability, enabling providers to service a large number of retail investors with limited capital amounts. However, as the industry matured and competition intensified, providers began to recognise the inherent limitations of a model devoid of human touch, especially for handling complex or emotionally charged financial decisions. The industry began a discernible shift towards models that offered a balance of technology and human expertise, seeking to maintain efficiency while overcoming the challenges of complete automation.

This market evolution has resulted in the increasing prevalence of the **hybrid robo-advisor model**, which deliberately combines automated methods with additional human oversight in varying degrees. The hybrid structure allows for additional human interaction in the financial advisory process, a component that many investors, including wealthier and older clients, actively desire. A study of the US market by Metzler et al. (2022) clearly illustrates this split, showing that many of the largest players have adopted a hybrid approach to service their extensive client bases. This development highlights that the evolution of robo-advising is not a move towards a complete replacement of human professionals, but rather towards a partnership where technology augments and enhances the advisor's role.

Table 1, derived from an analysis of major US-based providers, demonstrates the early success and client acquisition of both pure and hybrid models, though hybrid systems often dominate the top tier of assets under management due to their appeal to high-net-worth individuals. The data shows that the largest firms

Table 1 Breakdown of major US-based robo-advisor providers

Type	Robo-Advisor Provider	Parent Company	AuM in bn USD	Number of Clients
Hybrid	Vanguard Advisors	Vanguard Group	>270.00	>1 million
Hybrid	Edelman Online	Edelman Financial Engines	>250.00	>1.3 million
Hybrid	Merril Edge Guided Investing	Merrill Lynch	>200.00	>2.5 million
Pure	Schwab Intelligent Portfolios	Charles Schwab and Co	>60.00	>400 thousand
Pure	Betterment	Independent	>25.00	>616 thousand
Hybrid	Personal Capital Advisors	Personal Capital Corp	>15.00	>27 thousand

are often traditional players or large subsidiaries that have successfully integrated a human-plus-machine offering. The crucial element here is the acknowledgment that while automation offers unparalleled efficiency, the element of human control remains an important factor for clients engaging in digital investment management. This evolving business model directly influences how firms structure their value proposition and manage client relationships, moving away from purely digital communication towards a blend of automated and personalised contact.

1.1 Defining the Hybrid Model

The **hybrid model** represents a strategic and practical combination of automated algorithms with human financial advisors, aiming to capture the best attributes of both service delivery methods. The core premise is that algorithms are deployed for their inherent **efficiency and scalability**, excelling at quantitative tasks that require speed and consistency. These automated systems perform key activities such as continuous portfolio monitoring, trade execution, and the systematic rebalancing of assets to maintain targeted risk levels. This machine-based approach dramatically lowers operational costs and ensures that standard investment processes are executed without human bias or error.

Conversely, the model purposefully integrates **human financial advisors** to provide a **personalised touch and nuanced understanding**, qualities that are fundamentally challenging for current technology to replicate. The human component is typically reserved for complex, non-standard situations, such as comprehensive financial planning, debt management, tax strategy, and, most importantly, providing emotional guidance during periods of market volatility. This additional human advice gives advisors the authorisation to discuss personal preferences and even override the algorithm's portfolio allocation, injecting a necessary element of flexibility and tailored judgement. Jung et al. (2018) underscore the reality that most investors still feel a need for an additional human advisor, reinforcing the viability of this blended approach.

This structural composition is designed to address a critical tension in the market: the investor desire for both **cost-effectiveness and human expertise**. Pure robo-advisors meet the cost-effectiveness need but often fall short when clients face complex life events or require empathetic counsel, prompting them to seek external validation or control. By offering various service tiers, often including premium subscriptions with permanent access to an advisory network via phone or chat, hybrid firms capture segments of the market that demand higher-touch service without paying the full price of traditional private wealth management. Furthermore, the customisation capabilities inherent in this model, explored in research such as Faloon and Scherer (2017), are greatly enhanced, moving beyond simple risk profile questionnaires to offer highly individualised portfolios developed through human consultations.

From an academic perspective, this hybridisation trend reflects a maturation of digital business models within the financial domain. The framework introduced by Osterwalder and Pigneur (2010), the Business Model Canvas, provides a structured lens through which Metzler et al. (2022) analyse the differing characteristics of pure versus hybrid RAs. Their analysis demonstrates that hybrid RAs strategically differentiate themselves through superior value propositions like 'additional human portfolio advice' and specific 'human advisory networks'. This requires them to manage a different infrastructure, including slightly higher staff payment costs compared to the 'very low staff payment' characteristic of their pure counterparts.

The differences extend directly into the customer interface, where hybrid RAs target customer segments that often require a 'mostly high capital minimum' and maintain 'additional personal communication' channels beyond purely automated ones. Ultimately, the hybrid model, as highlighted by Rühr et al. (2019), addresses the psychological trade-offs in automation by ensuring users feel they have a level of control and personal recourse, which is vital for building trust in the management of long-term wealth. The hybrid model thus serves as a contemporary benchmark for digital investment management, offering a comprehensive and psychologically reassuring service that technology alone cannot yet deliver.

2 The Rise and Mechanics of Hybrid Robo-Advisory Models

The evolution of digital wealth management has been marked by a critical strategic pivot: the shift from the purely algorithmic efficiency of the original robo-advisors to the balanced, client-centric design of the **hybrid model**. This model, which combines automated technology with human financial expertise, is rapidly becoming the industry standard, particularly for firms targeting the mass affluent and high-net-worth segments. The mechanics of the hybrid approach are built upon a complementary division of labour, where machines handle the routine, quantitative tasks, and human advisors focus on the complex, qualitative aspects of financial well-being. This symbiotic relationship not only enhances efficiency but also addresses the fundamental psychological needs of investors who often require the reassurance of a human expert during turbulent times or major life transitions.

2.1 Components of a Hybrid Robo-Advisor Model

The hybrid model in wealth management takes advantage of the best parts of both automated and human advisors. The automated system can do things like portfolio monitoring, rebalancing, and tax-loss harvesting that are quantitative and can be done repeatedly. This lowers the cost of providing services and makes it possible to reach the mass affluent market. On the other hand, the expensive human advisor focusses on qualitative, relationship-dependent tasks like complex financial planning, behavioural coaching, and custom problem-solving. These tasks build trust, give clients peace of mind, and provide emotional support that keeps clients through market fluctuations. This strategic integration helps businesses get around the problems with standalone models and build a complete, affordable, and strong service architecture that meets the needs of all types of wealth, providing clients with both affordable institutional-grade investment management and personal advice that is high-touch.

The **automated component** forms the technological backbone of the hybrid robo-advisor, primarily leveraging **Artificial Intelligence (AI)** and **machine learning (ML)** capabilities. These technologies are tasked with executing routine, high-volume tasks with speed, precision, and consistency that human advisors cannot match. Key functions include continuous **portfolio rebalancing**, where algorithms monitor deviations from the client's target asset allocation and automatically execute trades to restore balance, often using sophisticated techniques like dynamic rebalancing thresholds. The system is also responsible for extensive **data analysis**, processing vast amounts of market information, economic indicators, and client transaction data to generate predictive insights and suggest potential optimisations. This data-driven approach underpins all investment decisions, ensuring portfolios are managed according to quantitative models such as Modern Portfolio Theory (Markowitz 1952), thereby eliminating emotional bias from the investment process. Furthermore, the automated engine handles critical administrative functions, such as tax-loss harvesting in taxable accounts, seamlessly identifying opportunities to sell assets at a loss to offset capital gains, which is a key value proposition for clients.

In contrast, the **human advisor role** is strategically repositioned to focus exclusively on activities that require emotional intelligence, nuanced understanding, and bespoke solutions. Rather than spending time on trade execution or rebalancing, the human expert concentrates on **relationship building**, establishing the trust necessary to retain clients through market cycles. A primary focus is **complex financial planning**, covering areas far beyond simple investment returns, such as **estate planning**, where an advisor helps structure wills and trusts; **significant life events**, such as inheritance, divorce, or business sale; and long-term goal setting for intergenerational wealth transfer. Crucially, the advisor provides essential **emotional support and guidance**, acting as a behavioural coach to dissuade clients from making impulsive decisions driven by fear or greed during periods of market volatility. This human touch addresses the finding by Rühr et al. (2019) that many investors value a level of control and personal recourse, which the human advisor effectively provides by interpreting the algorithm's recommendations and communicating them in a personally relevant context. Metzler et al. (2022) confirm that this advisory network, often composed of Certified Financial Planners (CFPs), is a key value driver and cost centre differentiating hybrid models from their purely digital competitors.

The distinction between the roles can be summarised as a strategic separation of the **mechanical** and the **conceptual**. The automated system is the efficient engine of execution and monitoring, while the human advisor is the perceptive strategic planner and empathetic communicator. This is evident in the fact that while the algorithms manage the daily performance of the portfolio, the human advisor takes the lead in discussing non-standard products, complex debt strategies, and the integration of external accounts to form a truly holistic financial picture. The human advisor's ability to engage with client psychology and long-term motivations ensures the financial plan remains aligned with the individual's evolving personal and financial circumstances. The successful implementation of this duality is what defines the next generation of digital wealth management.

2.2 Integration of Insurance Products

A critical element of the hybrid model's advanced value proposition is the seamless **integration of insurance products** into the comprehensive financial planning service. Traditionally, investment management and insurance planning have been siloed, handled by separate professionals or institutions, which often results in fragmented and incomplete client financial health. The hybrid robo-advisor is uniquely positioned to **bridge this gap**, shifting the focus from a narrow concentration on investment growth to the broader **necessity of a holistic financial plan** that includes a thorough insurance needs review. This integration acknowledges that securing a client's current assets and future income against unexpected risks is just as vital as growing their capital.

The **hybrid advantage** in this area is powered by the synergistic relationship between the machine and the human advisor. The **automated system identifies potential insurance gaps** by analysing client data ingested during the onboarding process, which includes income stability, marital status, dependent children, mortgage debt, and existing policies. Using algorithms, the platform can quickly

Table 2 Differences in focus between pure and hybrid robo-advisors

Pure Robo-Advisor Focus	Hybrid Robo-Advisor Focus
Single goal: Investment Growth	Holistic Goals: Investment Growth and Risk Protection
Limited Human Interaction	Human Advisor for Complex Issues
Automated Tax-Loss Harvesting	Human Tax Strategy with Automated Tax-Loss Harvesting
Focus on Low-Cost ETFs	Focus on ETFs and Low-Cost Insurance Products

flag areas of underinsurance, such as insufficient life cover or a lack of long-term disability protection, based on quantitative financial modelling. Once the gap is identified, the **human advisor discusses specific policy options, terms, and helps navigate the insurance landscape**, providing the necessary qualitative advice on complex products like annuities, long-term care insurance, or variable life policies. This high-touch, tailored discussion overcomes the limitations of purely digital services, as the complexity of insurance terms and the profound personal implications of coverage often require human explanation and reassurance.

This combination creates a powerful **value proposition** for the client, explicitly **moving beyond investment growth to include crucial risk management**. The hybrid model provides a single, convenient point of access for managing both asset accumulation and asset protection, ensuring that the client's financial fortress is built on a solid foundation of security. For the firm, integrating insurance introduces a new stream of fee-based or commission-based revenue and significantly improves client retention by deepening the advisory relationship (Tereszkiewicz and Skalski 2025). The ability to offer advice on both sides of the balance sheet fundamentally distinguishes the hybrid service from pure robo-advisors, positioning it as a comprehensive financial partner rather than just a portfolio manager. Table 2 summarises the main differences in focus between pure and hybrid robo-advisors.

2.3 Catering to Individual Investor Needs

The flexible service delivery inherent in hybrid models allows them to effectively segment and cater to the diverse needs of the modern investor base, offering a broad **spectrum of engagement** based on **comfort, complexity, and budget**. This adaptability is a key commercial advantage, enabling firms to service a wider range of clients than either traditional advisors (who often require high minimum assets) or pure robo-advisors (who may struggle to retain clients as their wealth and financial complexity grow). The ability to scale the human touch up or down, based on a client's stage of life and financial magnitude, is the central mechanism of this customisation.

For **digitally native investors**, who are typically younger and highly comfortable with technology, the service leans heavily on the automated features for day-to-day management. These clients rely on the platform for portfolio monitoring and automated rebalancing, appreciating the convenience and low cost. They reserve **human advice for major milestones**, such as structuring investments for a new home purchase, planning complex educational savings, or consolidating various retirement accounts. The human advisor acts as an occasional consultant for validation and specialised guidance, a service that is often bundled into a low-cost subscription or offered for a nominal fee. This approach provides the digital generation with the professional assurance they need without compromising the seamless online experience they prefer.

Conversely, **higher-net-worth individuals** receive a significantly different service, with **regular consultations with a human advisor** becoming the norm, if not the expectation. For these clients, the digital platform functions primarily as a sophisticated **analytical and execution tool**; it provides detailed performance reporting, advanced scenario planning, and real-time access to their holdings, which can be critical for large, multi-faceted portfolios. The advisor uses the platform's analytical output to inform face-to-face or video-conference discussions on intricate topics like philanthropic giving, complex options trading, or trust administration. The advisor–client relationship here is central, allowing the firm to capture the higher advisory fees associated with customised, high-touch wealth management. This tiered approach, as discussed by Jung et al. (2018), allows the firm to generate significant and differentiated value from different customer segments.

The overall effect of the hybrid model is enhanced **accessibility**, making sophisticated financial advice available to a broader demographic, notably the **mass affluent**. By offering an affordable base service (the automated engine) with an accessible upgrade path (the human advisor), hybrid platforms democratise expertise that was previously only available to the ultra-wealthy. This fulfils the original promise of robo-advisors, as noted by Abraham et al. (2019), but in a more complete and sustainable manner. By retaining human accountability and offering tiered flexibility, hybrid models represent a crucial step forward in extending quality financial guidance to millions of investors worldwide.

2.4 Overcoming Non-Acceptance Challenges

The rapid digitalisation of the financial industry, propelled by FinTech innovation, presented a clear opportunity for pure robo-advisors to democratise investment through automated, low-cost services. These platforms offered a model of pure algorithmic efficiency, yet they encountered a significant barrier in the form of client **non-acceptance** (Sayeed and Kapoor 2025), particularly as they attempted to displace established, human-centric advisory models. While the millennial demographic is generally drawn to technological convenience and makes an attractive target, a substantial segment of potential users does not perceive purely automated platforms as a viable substitute for traditional personal advisory services or retail investing. This market resistance stems from both psychological factors and concerns about the complexity of advice provided.

The core issue underlying client resistance is the persistent **investor preference for human interaction and trust** in wealth management, a critical component that pure models intentionally bypassed. Surveys consistently indicate that a large majority of wealth management clients trust their human financial advisors and fundamentally value face-to-face communication. This preference for personal interaction is vital because financial planning often involves emotionally charged, non-standard life events, such as inheritance, retirement, or market crises, where investors seek empathetic guidance and validation rather than just cold, algorithmic data. Financial advisory clients expect technology to be only an enabler of custom experiences and differentiated services, but still expect to interact with a human advisor, a finding evidenced by research such as that of Reddel et al. (2021).

Because investors believed that basic, survey-based techniques were insufficient for thorough planning involving tax or estate issues, pure robo-advisors were initially unpopular. The hybrid model was created to solve this by deliberately reintroducing the human element. It combines the individualised knowledge of human financial professionals for intricate, emotionally charged conversations with the cost-effectiveness of automated platforms for repetitive tasks like rebalancing. Due to this integration, businesses are able to provide a tiered approach that appeals to a wider range of consumers, including those who are cost-conscious and those who are prepared to pay more for the emotional support of a human expert. This creates a win-win situation that is probably crucial to the general adoption of automated advice.

3 Leading Examples in the Hybrid Space

The proliferation of hybrid robo-advisory models is best understood by examining the strategies of market leaders who have successfully blended technology and human expertise. These firms, often major incumbent financial institutions, leverage their vast resources and existing client trust to offer a compelling value proposition that pure FinTech startups struggle to match. By offering varying degrees of human interaction, these examples demonstrate a mature understanding of investor psychology, where confidence and personal validation remain essential complements to algorithmic efficiency. The structures adopted by these industry heavyweights illustrate the practical mechanics of the hybrid model and its viability as the dominant approach in the future of wealth management.

3.1 Vanguard Personal Advisor Services

Particularly within the mass affluent and high-net-worth brackets, Vanguard Personal Advisor Services (VPAS) stands as a great example of the hybrid model's scalability and success. As a firm already celebrated for its low-cost investment

Table 3 Main features of Vanguard Personal Advisor Services

Feature	Explanation
Asset Minimum	Generally requires a significant minimum threshold
Fee Structure	Percentage of Assets Under Management (AUM), tiered and very low (e.g., 0.30%)
Perceived Advantages	Unlimited access to salaried CFPs for guidance; use of low-cost Vanguard funds; strong investment discipline and tax efficiency
Perceived Disadvantages	Higher initial asset minimum than most robo-advisors; limited investment choices (primarily Vanguard funds)

philosophy, VPAS successfully married its core strength with the provision of sophisticated, unlimited human advice. The service is predicated on the **integration of low-cost Exchange-Traded Funds (ETFs)** and mutual funds, primarily from its own fund family, with direct and unrestricted **access to Certified Financial Planners (CFPs)**. This combination delivers professional guidance without the high fees typically associated with full-service private wealth managers.

The service is generally tiered, requiring clients to maintain assets **above a certain asset threshold** (historically around $50,000 to $500,000, depending on the service level) to enrol. This threshold ensures the firm can profitably allocate its salaried CFP staff to clients who genuinely require comprehensive planning. The automated component of VPAS is robust, managing daily portfolio monitoring, strategic asset allocation, and rebalancing with Vanguard's signature disciplined approach. The human advisor, however, engages with clients on complex and highly personal matters, including retirement withdrawal strategies, estate planning considerations, and the integration of outside assets, which algorithms are incapable of handling with the required discretion.

This model, focusing on behavioural coaching and broad financial strategy over product sales, reinforces client loyalty and is a testament to the idea that advice, not just execution, is a key value differentiator. The blend of low-cost Vanguard products and high-quality CFP advice creates a highly compelling and transparent offering in the industry. Table 3 provides a summary.

3.2 *Schwab Intelligent Portfolios Premium*

Schwab Intelligent Portfolios Premium is another leading hybrid offering that demonstrates an alternative approach to pricing and service delivery compared to VPAS. The base offering, Schwab Intelligent Portfolios, is a **digital-only service** that charges no advisory fees but maintains a cash allocation component from which the firm earns revenue. The 'Premium' tier is an optional upgrade for clients who desire the human element, which they obtain for a flat, recurring **monthly fee** rather than a percentage of AUM. This fixed-fee structure makes the Premium service

Table 4 Main features of Schwab Intelligent Portfolios Premium

Feature	Explanation
Asset Minimum	Requires a moderate initial minimum threshold to enrol in the Premium service
Fee Structure	Initial planning fee plus a flat monthly advisory fee (e.g., $300 initial plus $30/month), regardless of AuM
Perceived Advantages	Unlimited, on-demand CFP access for a predictable flat fee; includes tax-loss harvesting and robust planning tools; zero advisory fee on the base automated service
Perceived Disadvantages	High minimum initial balance required for Premium; substantial cash allocation in portfolios may reduce potential returns

increasingly cost-effective for high-net-worth clients, demonstrating a strategic move to capture that affluent segment with transparent and predictable pricing.

This Premium upgrade grants the client **unlimited one-on-one guidance from human advisors**, typically Certified Financial Planners (CFPs), for a comprehensive financial planning experience. The service **includes advanced planning tools** that allow clients to model various financial scenarios, such as retirement projections or college savings paths, collaboratively with their advisor. Furthermore, the automated engine provides sophisticated services like **tax-loss harvesting** on eligible accounts, maintaining the cost and tax efficiency expected of a modern robo-advisor. The Schwab model is designed to be highly accessible and appealing to individuals who value the predictability of a subscription-like fee for unlimited advice, successfully merging the advanced capabilities of the digital platform with the personal reassurance of a dedicated advisor. Table 4 provides a summary.

3.3 Common Themes

Schwab Intelligent Portfolios Premium and Vanguard Personal Advisor Services' success is not a coincidence; rather, it stems from similar strategic choices that support the hybrid concept as a whole. Analysing these two prominent examples reveals important common themes that show how combining human expertise and technology results in a valuable and appealing offer for investors of all wealth levels. The main takeaway is that while efficiency is important in wealth management, personal involvement and trust are still crucial.

One central theme is the strategic use of **human advice as a retention mechanism** and a premium service differentiator, not merely a cost centre. Both firms employ human advisors, often CFPs, to handle the complex, non-routine scenarios that trigger an investor's emotional response, such as major life changes or significant market downturns. Research by Sayeed and Kapoor (2025) confirms that many clients, even in a digital world, still feel the need for an additional human advisor to validate investment decisions, especially during volatile periods. By providing unlimited or easy access to an advisor, these firms build the crucial **trust and accountability** that pure robo-advisors struggle to cultivate, thereby reducing client attrition and securing their long-term assets.

Secondly, both models meticulously structure their service tiers and fee schedules to offer **price predictability and perceived value** tailored to specific client segments. VPAS appeals to clients who prefer the low AUM-based fee and trust Vanguard's investment philosophy, while Schwab's fixed monthly fee highly favours high-net-worth clients who see the flat rate as a significant discount compared to the traditional 1% AUM fee. This targeted pricing strategy is a key component of their business models, as noted in the analysis of digital investment management by Metzler et al. (2022). The goal is to move beyond mere low-cost competition and create a value perception where the fee is justified by the tangible, high-quality, human-delivered advice provided.

A third common theme is the focus on **holistic financial planning over mere portfolio management**. Neither leading example limits the human advisor to just discussing the client's automated portfolio. Instead, they encourage discussions around estate planning, debt strategies, tax optimisation, and retirement income planning. The automated component handles the day-to-day investing, freeing the human expert to manage the client's entire financial picture. This focus aligns with the work of Abraham et al. (2019), who note that while robo-advisors expand access to *advice*, the ultimate goal is to enable comprehensive planning. The platforms serve as a convenient, data-rich hub that supports the advisor's ability to offer bespoke, integrated solutions, thereby moving the client relationship to a much deeper and more permanent footing.

Finally, the success of these models validates the power of **integrating technology with trusted brand legacy**. Both Vanguard and Charles Schwab were established financial powerhouses before the rise of FinTech, giving their robo-advisor offerings an immediate advantage in terms of regulatory confidence and investor recognition. The technology provides the operational efficiency needed to scale their business, but their existing decades of client trust and brand capital provide the crucial psychological comfort that encourages clients to commit large sums of money. This demonstrated blend of reliable, cutting-edge technology (efficiency) and a pre-existing commitment to client-first principles (trust) represents the most compelling and enduring value proposition in the modern wealth management arena.

4 Global Perspectives: Trends Beyond the US and Europe

The global trajectory of the robo-advisory market reveals a pattern of rapidly accelerating adoption (Zavialova, 2021), particularly as service models move from pure automation to the more palatable and comprehensive hybrid structure. While the initial focus of the FinTech revolution in wealth management was largely centred in North America and Western Europe, the most dynamic growth and compelling model adaptation are now manifesting across the Asian continent. This expansion is driven by unique demographic factors, high rates of technological absorption, and the strategic positioning of local financial institutions and agile technology startups. The embrace of hybrid platforms across Asia demonstrates a clear understanding that while efficiency is paramount, success in diverse and culturally sensitive markets requires bespoke solutions and the psychological reassurance of human expertise.

4.1 Leading Countries in Asia

Asia has cemented its position as a powerhouse for FinTech innovation and adoption, with a **strong and growing adoption of hybrid robo-advisory models** being a critical trend in its wealth management sector. The sheer scale and speed of digital transformation across the continent provide a fertile environment for technology-driven financial services, often bypassing the legacy systems that slow innovation in older markets. This growth is underpinned by rapid urbanisation, an expanding middle class seeking accessible investment avenues, and government policies actively encouraging FinTech sector development. Consequently, the region's hybrid platforms are not merely copies of Western models but are finely tuned to regional specificities, including unique regulatory frameworks and local investment preferences.

The leading countries in the robo-advisor market in Asia as of 2025 are shown in Table 5, obtained from Dharmadhikari (2025). China, Japan, and India retain the largest percentage of the market share, as measured by percentage of the total robo-advisory revenue on the continent.

Platforms in Asia are notable for offering solutions customised to the needs of the continent, such as in the case of Malaysia and the need for **Shariah-compliant portfolios**, which screen investments according to Islamic ethical and financial principles, as explained by Kasim (2023). Compliance with local regulations is also a must to thrive in the region.

4.2 Growth Trajectory: The Case of India

India presents an illuminating case study in the rapid ascent of the hybrid model, demonstrating that **despite evolving regulatory frameworks, growth remains robust**, indicating a **significant shift in wealth management delivery in the region**. The Indian market is characterised by millions of first-time investors entering the digital realm, driven by increased smartphone adoption and the rapid penetration of low-cost internet access. This demographic shift necessitates a financial advisory model that is both highly scalable and highly trustworthy, which the hybrid approach uniquely provides by blending technological efficiency

Table 5 Adoption of robo-advisory services in Asia

Country or Region	Market Share Percentage 2025	Primary Market Driver	Specific Hybrid Feature
China	32.60	Large FinTech Ecosystem and Volume	Integrated Wealth Management within Super Apps
Japan	14.05	High Internet Penetration and Traditional Finance Digitisation	Established Financial Institutions Leading Adoption
India	13.65	High Growth Potential and Digital Financial Inclusion	Focus on Mass Market and Smartphone Usage
South Korea	8.99	Advanced Technological Infrastructure	Technology-driven integration with Human Oversight
Singapore	3.76	Regulatory Clarity and Regional Wealth Hub Status	Gateway for International and Regional Expansion
Southeast Asia	7.83	Expanding Middle Class and Youthful Population	Shariah-Compliant Investment Options in Muslim Markets

with accessible human guidance. The sheer scale of the opportunity for financial inclusion is propelling both domestic FinTech unicorns and major international players to establish hybrid advisory operations in the country.

The adoption trajectory in India is, however, heavily influenced by investor psychology and the inherent anxieties associated with delegating financial control to an algorithm. The study by Singh and Kumar (2024) reveals the fundamental factors that shape the acceptability and adoption of robo-advisory services with AI integration: testing the Technology Acceptance Model (TAM) based on responses from Indian FinTech users, they found that **trust, perceived usefulness, and perceived risk all significantly impact users' attitudes** towards these automated platforms. This underscores the reality that technological performance alone is insufficient; client comfort is equally reliant on psychological assurance.

Crucially, the study by Biswas et al. (2022) **emphasises perceived risk and the preference for human oversight** as powerful determinants of adoption intention in the Indian market. This finding aligns with broader trends noted across Asia, where investors often have a lower tolerance for risk when entrusting capital to entirely digital platforms, and often require a visible layer of human accountability.

Specifically, the reluctance to adopt pure robo-advisors often stems from investors perceiving them as **riskier than traditional options**. The integration of human advisors in the hybrid model helps to mitigate this crucial barrier, as the human element serves as a trust anchor, assuring clients that a qualified professional is overseeing the automated decisions and is available for consultation during volatile times. The ability of hybrid platforms to offer personalised, human-led support transforms the perceived risk from a technical failure into a manageable relationship with a designated expert.

Users of new financial technologies are most concerned about factors pertaining to security and privacy risks. The hybrid model tackles this by utilising the perceived accountability of the human advisor or the brand trust of the underlying traditional financial institution in addition to putting strong digital security measures in place. In a world where investors frequently perceive FinTech services to have greater security and confidentiality concerns than traditional financial institutions, this dual-assurance system is essential. As a result, hybrid models are becoming the most popular and reliable service-delivery method for the rapidly growing wealth-management industry in India and throughout Asia by delivering the effectiveness of AI while controlling the perceived and psychological risks associated with digital delegation.

5 The Role of AI and Regulatory Constraints

The continuous expansion of artificial intelligence (AI) is reshaping the financial advisory landscape, with sophisticated tools like Large Language Models (LLMs) holding immense, yet problematic, potential. While algorithms are the engine of efficiency for hybrid robo-advisors, the limitations of these advanced AI systems, particularly concerning regulatory compliance, implicitly build the case for retaining high levels of human control. This tension between automated innovation and necessary regulatory stringency forms the current frontier of digital wealth management, driving the industry towards models that prioritise auditability and human-centred design over pure automation. The analysis of these constraints reveals why the hybrid approach, with its defined roles for human oversight, is becoming the only viable and responsible path for scaled financial advice.

5.1 Limitations of Large Language Models (LLMs) in Advice

The main problem with using Large Language Models (LLMs) for financial advice is that their algorithms are stochastic, which means that they use random processes instead of fixed logic. This makes their output inherently variable and unreliable. This inconsistency in output is a serious problem because financial regulation and the fiduciary duty say that all advice must be accurate, repeatable, and legal every time to protect consumers and hold firms accountable. Because an LLM is a 'black box' and is prone to statistical deviation, it can't give a consistent and auditable reason for its recommendations. This means that it doesn't yet meet the regulatory requirements for explainability and suitability. Therefore, a human advisor must filter and validate all machine-generated guidance.

Moreover, the **risk of 'hallucinations'** (the generation of plausible but factually incorrect information) inherent in LLMs presents a direct threat to the principle of correct advice. A human advisor must stay up-to-date on their field and give advice based on facts that can be checked and established financial law. An LLM, on the other hand, can confidently make up plausible but completely false information, like getting the rules for capital gains tax wrong or talking about investment products that don't exist. In a fiduciary context, giving out false information can lead to harsh regulatory penalties or professional censure. In a hybrid model, the human advisor is an important part of the compliance filter. They are in charge of turning the AI's complicated insights into advice that is legally sound, factually correct, and, most importantly, stable across multiple queries.

5.2 Regulatory Requirements for Financial Advice

The financial services industry is governed by stringent rules designed to protect consumers from misconduct and ensure fair practice, creating specific hurdles for AI implementation. A core requirement is the **need for reproducibility and auditability** of advice to ensure clear accountability. Regulators must be able to trace a specific recommendation back through the firm's processes to the data, logic, and policy that informed it, allowing them to verify compliance and assign responsibility if harm occurs. Purely automated systems must therefore possess clear, explainable decision-making pathways that can be reviewed externally.

However, the operating principles of advanced AI systems directly challenge this mandate. The **LLM 'black box' operation** and its potential for **'hallucinations'** fundamentally **conflict with stringent requirements** for transparency and explainability. The 'black box' refers to the difficulty, often impossibility, of fully understanding how a complex deep learning model arrived at a specific decision, while 'hallucinations' pose a direct and serious legal threat in a context where factual accuracy and legal correctness are paramount. As Zhu et al. (2024) observe, regulatory compliance is a significant challenge, especially since robo-advisor developers often operate internationally, yet their implementations must adhere to predominantly local legal frameworks.

Such a discrepancy necessitates a strategic approach to AI adoption that integrates regulatory compliance from the design phase onwards. The authors note that addressing these issues could involve various methods, such as employing comprehensible data visualisation or utilising advanced AI technologies like OpenAI's ChatGPT, developed with optimised language models and learning techniques. Nevertheless, these potential solutions currently lack sufficient investigation or practical design implementation. The research explicitly suggests that future research could focus on involving end customers in the design and implementation process to gather empirical evidence and refine these approaches. This proposed direction highlights a fundamental shift towards integrating the user experience with regulatory necessity, moving beyond mere technological capability.

This suggestion aligns closely with the **human-centred AI (HCAI) approach**, which emphasises that **high-level human control**, including usability testing, iterative refinement, and evaluation, should hold equal importance to high-level automation in AI-empowered systems (Shneiderman 2022). Applying HCAI principles to robo-advisory means that the system must be designed for both technological performance and human comprehensibility. This ensures that when the AI presents a recommendation, the human advisor can easily understand the underlying logic, identify potential errors or hallucinations, and take responsibility for the final advice, thus satisfying auditability requirements.

The conflict between the probabilistic nature of Large Language Models (LLMs) and the deterministic requirements of financial regulation and fiduciary duties is the primary obstacle to the deployment of fully automated robo-advisors. The challenge of adapting globally designed AI to various local legal frameworks must be overcome by developers. More importantly, they must solve the 'black box' problem, in which the complex reasoning of the AI lacks the transparency and explainability required to prove regulatory compliance. A qualified human advisor must serve as the accountable final sign-off, ensuring that the AI's output is suitable, preventing errors like hallucinations, and guaranteeing that the delivered service is legally sound and fully auditable. This inherent limitation further supports the strategic necessity of the hybrid model.

5.3 The Hybrid Solution and Human Accountability

Should a regulatory body investigate an LLM-generated recommendation that resulted in client harm (for example, an unsuitable portfolio allocation that led to excessive losses) **the firm would be fundamentally unable to provide a consistent explanation of the advice-generating process** due to the main flaws in an LLM:

1. **Non-Reproducibility:** If the regulator runs the exact same client data and prompt through the LLM again, the model, due to its probabilistic design, may produce a slightly different or even contradictory recommendation. This **non-reproducible** output fails the most basic test of auditability. The firm cannot demonstrate that the original, harmful advice was a stable, predictable outcome of the system's logic.
2. **The 'Black Box' Problem:** The complex, non-linear deep learning architecture of the LLM makes its decision-making process an **inscrutable 'black box'.** The firm cannot articulate *why* the LLM chose specific investment weights or applied a particular tax assumption. This failure to explain the rationale means the firm cannot satisfy the legal and ethical requirement to prove the advice was **objectively suitable** or in the client's **best interest**, as it cannot trace the recommendation back to a logical, auditable set of rules.
3. **Undermining Professional Diligence:** This failure to demonstrate systemic reliability **undermines the core legal requirement for professional diligence and**

integrity. Professional diligence mandates that a financial institution exercises the care and judgement expected of an expert. When the advice source is an inconsistent, unexplainable black box prone to factual errors (hallucinations), the firm cannot prove it exercised this required duty of care. The legal burden of proof lies with the firm to show that proper processes were followed; the LLM's architecture makes this proof impossible.

This regulatory and legal impasse confirms that full automation using current LLM technology is practically unworkable for client-facing financial advice. Consequently, the deployment of LLMs ends up being limited to back-office functions where human supervisors can transform the model's probabilistic insights into deterministic, legally verified client communications.

In this hybrid structure, **LLMs** are used as **sophisticated drafting tools** or **research engines** to quickly process market data, summarise documents, or draft initial client correspondence. Their output is treated as a **provisional, unverified input**. At the same time, **Human supervisors** (Certified Financial Planners, compliance officers) act as the **legal gatekeepers**. They review the LLM's suggested advice, verify its factual accuracy (checking for hallucinations), confirm its legal compliance with local regulations, and provide the final **deterministic sign-off**. This human intermediary assumes the **accountability** that the machine cannot, thereby satisfying the core legal requirement for an identifiable and responsible advice-giver.

Such a division of labour is arguably the only robust method for incorporating the speed of AI while maintaining regulatory adherence.

6 Conclusion and Future Outlook

The decade of development in the wealth management industry has solidified the hybrid model as the dominant and most comprehensive approach, confirming that both pure automation and pure human advice are ultimately insufficient due to issues of scalability, cost, and complexity management. Combining the low cost, efficiency, and consistency of automated platforms with the emotional intelligence, fiduciary accountability, and complexity management of human advisors solves the critical trade-off that constrained earlier digital solutions. Market leaders successfully use the human element as a premium retention mechanism, while the global growth of robo-advice requires a human layer for hyper localisation and cultural sensitivity. Most critically, the inherent stochastic nature and black box operation of advanced AI like LLMs directly conflict with stringent regulatory requirements for reproducibility and legal accountability, making the human advisor a non-negotiable compliance filter and accountable sign-off that solidifies the hybrid model as the only viable path for scaled, responsible financial advice.

6.1 Future Applications

The dominance of the hybrid model is further validated by its rapid adoption in emerging and complex financial domains, proving its adaptability beyond basic portfolio management. One significant area of growth is the management of **green investments through robo-advisors**, representing a crucial **future application** of the hybrid framework.

Research by Barile et al. (2025) offers evidence about the role of AI in empowering financial advisory services by investigating how leading robo-advisory platforms are integrating Environmental, Social, and Governance (ESG) and Socially Responsible Investments (SRIs). This trend reflects a growing client demand to align investment portfolios with personal values, a task that requires both sophisticated algorithmic screening and nuanced human consultation.

The automated component of the hybrid model excels at **ESG data integration**, using AI to screen vast amounts of non-financial data, company disclosures, and sustainability ratings to select appropriate green Exchange-Traded Funds (ETFs). However, the human advisor remains essential because **defining 'green' or 'ethical' is a qualitative, value-driven discussion** that algorithms cannot fully resolve. Clients may have specific exclusions (e.g., fossil fuels, tobacco) or preferences that require careful interpretation and detailed trade-offs: a task ideally suited for a human. This application demonstrates that as investment complexity increases, requiring the reconciliation of objective data (financial returns) with subjective values (ethics), the blend of machine-driven analysis and human-driven dialogue becomes even more crucial.

6.2 Concluding Thoughts

The increasing integration of AI and the shift towards hybrid models continues to redefine the wealth management landscape, moving it towards greater accessibility, lower cost, and enhanced complexity management. Looking forward, the true impact of this transformation remains a fertile ground for research, particularly as the distinction between human and robo-advice continues to blur. As Abraham et al. (2019) concluded, as robo-advisors expand and more information on them becomes available, more analyses could try to shed light on these issues, directing the path for future development.

For example, **future work could analyse in detail the profiles of robo-advisor users**, and thus to what extent these tools are contributing to better financial decisions by a wider array of investors. Understanding the demographic, wealth, and financial literacy profiles of users will determine if robo-advisors are truly fulfilling their promise of democratising wealth management, or if they are simply attracting clients already served by established providers.

Further analyses could also focus on whether human and robo-advisors are substitutes or complements: do they cater to entirely different population segments, or are sophisticated individuals increasingly using both simultaneously to manage different aspects of their wealth? This insight is essential for determining the ultimate steady-state market structure of the advisory industry and informing strategic business decisions.

Furthermore, a comparative financial analysis would prove highly insightful, focusing **on how the profit margins and cost structures compare between the two** model types, which would clarify the long-term economic viability of both pure and hybrid models at scale. The study should look into how advisory activities are distributed geographically from a global standpoint. It would be interesting to investigate whether robo-advising activity is concentrated in a few economies and accessible by investors worldwide, or if economies have their own robo-advisors tailored to their own domestic investors, given that robo-advisors are accessible to anyone, anywhere. This deals with the possibility of regulatory arbitrage or the concentration of systemic risk in major international financial centres.

Finally, the challenge of localisation remains paramount for international platforms. It would be useful to **analyse if the same robo-advisor gives consumers in different economies tailored recommendations based on local products and environments (such as tax codes), or instead provides standard international products**. The answer to this question speaks directly to the quality of the service provided by hybrid firms and their ability to ethically meet fiduciary standards in diverse regulatory environments. **Further insights on these topics would help to better understand the true potential and pitfalls of robo-advisors**, ultimately guiding policymakers and practitioners towards a future where technology responsibly serves the financial health of the global population.

Disclaimer on the Use of Large Language Models Large Language Models (LLMs) were used to proof edit this chapter and ensure optimal grammar and flow. LLMs were not used to autonomously generate any content or references in this chapter; any errors or omissions are the sole responsibility of the author.

Declaration:

Acknowledgements The author is thankful to Nahidi Narmin and Alex Zarifis for helpful comments while drafting this chapter.

Competing Interests The author is the CEO and majority shareholder of Stalwart Holdings, a provider of regulated financial advisory services.

References

Abraham F, Schmukler SL, Tessada J (2019) Robo-Advisors: Investing through Machines. Research & Policy Briefs, No. 21. World Bank Group. Washington DC, At https://documents1.worldbank.org/curated/en/275041551196836758/pdf/Robo-Advisors-Investing-through-Machines.pdf. Accessed 13 Oct 2025

Barile D, Secundo G, Mariani M, Brandonisio A (2025) 'A new era: managing green investments through Robo-Advisors', Management Decision. https://doi.org/10.1108/MD-06-2024-1268

Biswas A, Jaiswal D, Kant R (2022) Investigating service innovation, bank reputation and customer trust: evidence from Indian retail banking. Int J Qual Serv Sci 14(1):1–17. https://doi.org/10.1108/IJQSS-03-2021-0042

Dharmadhikari S (2025) Robo Advisor Market Report 2025 (Global Edition). 8th edn. Available at: https://www.cognitivemarketresearch.com/robo-advisor-market-report. Accessed 4 Oct 2025

Faloon M, Scherer B (2017) Individualization of Robo-Advice. J Wealth Manage 20(1):30–36. https://doi.org/10.3905/jwm.2017.20.1.030

Jung D, Dorner V, Weinhardt C, Pusmaz H (2018) Designing a Robo-advisor for risk-averse, low-budget consumers. Electr Mark 28(3):367–380. https://link.springer.com/article/10.1007/s12525-017-0279-9. Accessed 13 Oct 2025

Kasim RSR (2023) A smart Shariah-based decision-making in Islamic Fintech. in IIECONS 2023 STEM Conference Proceedings. https://doi.org/10.33102/iiecons.v10i1.77. Accessed 16 Sept 2025

Markowitz H (1952) Portfolio selection. J Finance 7(1):77–91. https://doi.org/10.2307/2975974

Metzler DR, Neuss N, Torno A (2022) The digitization of investment management – an analysis of Robo-advisor business models. Wirtschaftsinformatik 2022 Proceedings, 2. At https://aisel.aisnet.org/wi2022/finance_and_blockchain/finance_and_blockchain/2/. Accessed 5 Oct 2025

Osterwalder A, Pigneur Y (2010) Business model generation – a handbook for visionaries, game changers, and challengers. John Wiley and Sons, Hoboken, NJ. https://doi.org/10.1111/j.1540-5885.2012.00977_2.x

Reddel S, Silver R, Haggerty M (2021) Wealth management: The new state of advice, Accenture Consulting. At https://www.accenture.com/us-en/insights/capital-markets/wealth-management-financial-advice. Accessed 13 Oct 2025

Rühr A, Berger B, Hess T (2019) Can I control my Robo-Advisor? Trade-offs in automation and user control in (digital) investment management. In: AMCIS 2019 Proceedings. At https://aisel.aisnet.org/amcis2019/cognitive_in_is/cognitive_in_is/2/. Accessed 13 Oct 2025

Sayeed A, Kapoor GT (2025) Behavioural biases and Robo-Advisors: analysing the role of automated financial guidance in shaping investor choices. Int J Res Rev 12(4):124–132. https://doi.org/10.52403/ijrr.20250416

Shneiderman B (2022) Human-Centered AI, 1st edn. Oxford University Press, Oxford. https://doi.org/10.1093/oso/9780192845290.001.0001

Singh S, Kumar A (2024) Investing in the future: an integrated model for analysing user attitudes towards Robo-advisory services with AI integration. Vilakshan-XIMB J Manage 22(1):158–175. https://doi.org/10.1108/XJM-03-2024-0046

Tereszkiewicz P, Skalski S (2025) Robo-advisory services in the insurance sector under the EU regulatory framework. Geneva Pap Risk Insur Iss Pract 50:545–564. https://doi.org/10.1057/s41288-025-00358-z

Zavialova S (2021) FinTech Report 2021 – personal finance. Hamburg: Statista. At https://www.statista.com/study/44525/fintech-report/. Accessed 13 Oct 2025

Zhu H, Vigren O, Söderberg I-L (2024) Implementing artificial intelligence empowered financial advisory services: a literature review and critical research agenda. J Bus Res 174:114494. https://doi.org/10.1016/j.jbusres.2023.114494

Part II
Behavioral and Ethical Dimensions

Behavioral Biases in Investment Decisions

Narmin Nahidi

Abstract This chapter investigates behavioral biases influencing investment decisions, specifically loss aversion, herding, overconfidence, and recency bias. Integrating insights from behavioral finance and neuroscience, it reveals that these biases originate in brain regions linked to emotional processing, social cognition, and reward anticipation, resulting in systematic deviations from rational investment behavior. Historical case studies, including the Dotcom bubble, 2008 financial crisis, and Black Monday, illustrate how aggregated biases can trigger market-wide instability. The chapter further explores cognitive load as a critical factor exacerbating biases, demonstrating that decision fatigue significantly impairs investors' rational decision-making capabilities. It evaluates bias-mitigation strategies, emphasizing the effectiveness of financial education, behavioral nudging, and adaptive AI-driven interventions. Finally, the chapter addresses ethical considerations associated with using AI to correct biases, stressing the importance of transparency, informed consent, privacy, and autonomy in deploying these technologies to safeguard investor welfare and maintain market integrity.

Keywords Behavioral finance · Investor psychology · Loss aversion · Overconfidence · Herding · Cognitive load · AI bias mitigation · Ethical investing

JEL Classification: G41, D91, D87, C91

N. Nahidi (✉)
Business School, University of Exeter, Exeter, UK
e-mail: n.nahidi@exeter.ac.uk

N. Nahidi, A. Zarifis (eds.), *AI, FinTech, and the Future of Robo-Advisory*, Contributions to Finance and Accounting,
https://doi.org/10.1007/978-3-032-18109-1_3

1 Introduction

Investment decision-making was traditionally explained through rational economic theories, which assume investors act logically to maximize their financial returns. According to classical financial models, investors are expected to evaluate risks objectively, gather comprehensive information, and make consistently rational choices. However, extensive empirical evidence suggests that actual investor behavior frequently deviates from this rational ideal, influenced instead by cognitive and emotional biases. The recognition of these biases has been crucial in shaping the field of behavioral finance, which integrates insights from psychology and neuroscience to explain and predict financial behaviors that traditional models fail to capture (Barberis 2018; Hirshleifer 2015). Behavioral finance highlights the systematic and predictable nature of investor biases, such as loss aversion, herding, overconfidence, and recency bias, demonstrating how these psychological factors can significantly affect financial outcomes. Unlike random errors or anomalies, these biases reflect deeply ingrained cognitive tendencies that consistently skew investment decisions across various contexts. Acknowledging these psychological distortions is not merely an academic exercise but a necessary step toward developing practical strategies to mitigate their negative impact on investor welfare and market efficiency (Kuhnen and Knutson 2005).

Recent advances in neuroscience have profoundly enriched our understanding of the cognitive processes underlying investor biases. Neuroeconomic research, employing sophisticated brain-imaging techniques such as functional magnetic resonance imaging (fMRI), has provided compelling evidence of specific neurological mechanisms associated with biased decision-making. These neuroscientific insights clarify how emotional and psychological biases originate from brain regions responsible for emotional processing, social influence, and reward anticipation, demonstrating that investor biases are biologically grounded rather than merely cognitive misjudgments (Moore and Healy 2008; Tom et al. 2007). The identification of these neurological underpinnings has significant implications. It explains why biases such as loss aversion or herding are not easily eliminated simply by informing investors about them. Understanding that these biases are rooted in automatic and subconscious neural processes emphasizes the importance of adopting strategic interventions ranging from behavioral nudging to artificial intelligence solutions designed to counteract biases at a deeper cognitive level rather than relying solely on rational appeals or informational disclosures (Burke et al. 2010).

Historical financial crises serve as critical real-world demonstrations of how collective investor biases significantly affect market stability. Episodes such as the Dotcom bubble, the 2008 global financial crisis, and Black Monday in 1987 reveal that biases do not merely impact isolated investment decisions but can propagate widely, causing severe disruptions at the market level. During such crises, investor behaviors fueled by biases intensify market volatility, lead to asset mispricing, and significantly disrupt financial stability, resulting in prolonged economic consequences (Scheinkman and Xiong 2005; Shiller 2005). Analyzing these historical market events emphasizes the practical relevance of studying investor biases. It highlights that managing biases is not only beneficial at the individual investor level but also crucial for regulatory bodies, financial institutions, and market stakeholders aiming to promote market resilience. Systematically addressing these biases through regulatory frameworks, improved investor education, and targeted technological interventions could enhance market efficiency and investor protection during future financial crises (Barberis 2013).

Investor decision-making quality further deteriorates under conditions of cognitive load, a common yet underappreciated factor in financial behavior. Cognitive load refers to mental resource depletion caused by complex, continuous, or high-stakes decision-making scenarios. As cognitive fatigue sets in, investors increasingly rely on heuristic-driven judgments and emotional reactions, amplifying biases and reducing the quality of their financial choices. Empirical studies consistently demonstrate that cognitive overload correlates with increased trading frequency, impulsivity, and suboptimal portfolio diversification, leading to diminished financial performance (Barber and Odean 2000). Moreover, neurological studies confirm that cognitive load significantly impairs the functioning of the prefrontal cortex, a region essential for rational decision-making and executive functioning. Under sustained cognitive stress, investors find it difficult to regulate impulsive emotional responses effectively, exacerbating their vulnerability to cognitive biases and leading to poorer investment outcomes. Addressing cognitive load through structured interventions and cognitive management strategies thus becomes a crucial element in promoting rational investment decision-making and improved financial outcomes (Baumeister et al. 2008).

Given the systematic nature of cognitive biases, developing effective mitigation strategies is vital. Financial education has emerged as a foundational intervention, empowering investors with awareness and cognitive frameworks to recognize and manage biases proactively. Such structured educational initiatives significantly reduce susceptibility to biases, improving long-term decision-making quality and fostering greater financial resilience among investors. Empirical research consistently shows that informed investors are better equipped to avoid common pitfalls associated with biased decision-making (Fernandes 2014b). In addition to education, behavioral nudging techniques and AI-driven interventions have shown considerable promise in addressing cognitive biases practically and effectively. Nudging methods subtly influence decision environments to encourage rational behavior without limiting investor autonomy. Simultaneously, advanced AI technologies, particularly adaptive machine learning systems used in robo-advisory platforms, provide personalized, real-time bias correction interventions. These innovative approaches significantly enhance the quality and effectiveness of investor decisions, demonstrating practical success in improving financial outcomes and reducing biases (Thaler and Sunstein 2008).

However, the growing reliance on artificial intelligence for behavioral correction also introduces substantial ethical and regulatory considerations. While AI interventions offer significant benefits in reducing biases, they raise concerns regarding transparency, informed consent, data privacy, and the potential for manipulation.

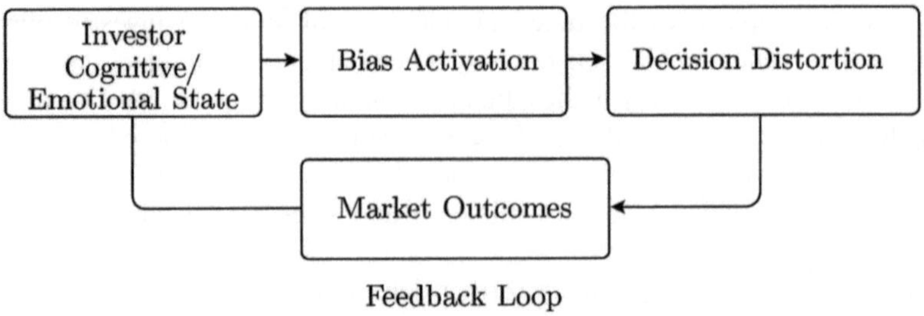

Fig. 1 Conceptual framework of investor biases and market dynamics (This framework illustrates how investors' cognitive and emotional states lead to bias activation, which distorts decision-making and generates market outcomes. A feedback loop reinforces these states, sustaining cycles of irrationality and instability.)

Notably, controversies around AI-driven gamification in investment platforms illustrate risks of ethical misconduct, reinforcing the necessity for rigorous oversight and clear ethical standards in deploying AI technologies within financial contexts (Cowls et al. 2021; Floridi et al. 2018). To sustainably harness AI's potential benefits while mitigating ethical risks, continuous evaluation and refinement of bias-correction strategies are essential. Financial institutions and regulatory bodies must implement transparent processes, rigorous consent procedures, and stringent privacy measures. Regular empirical assessment of intervention efficacy, investor feedback, and adaptation to evolving market conditions and technological advancements will ensure ethical compliance and effectiveness. This chapter, therefore, aims not only to highlight the critical influence of behavioral biases on financial decision-making but also to explore how ethical, strategically managed AI interventions can contribute to investor welfare and market stability (Fernandes 2014b; Jobin et al. 2019).

The conceptual framework presented in Fig. 1 captures the cyclical and reinforcing nature of investor decision-making under the influence of behavioral biases. At its foundation, the model begins with the cognitive and emotional states of investors, which form the substrate of all subsequent financial choices. Decades of research in behavioral finance have shown that decision-making is not purely rational but is instead deeply shaped by affective responses and cognitive load (Barberis 2018; Hirshleifer 2015). Neuroscientific evidence corroborates this view, indicating that regions such as the amygdala, prefrontal cortex, and striatum activate under conditions of fear, excitement, and reward anticipation, thereby priming investors to deviate from rational expectations (Kuhnen and Knutson 2005; Tom et al. 2007). These underlying states serve as the entry point in the framework, highlighting that biases are not anomalies but structural features of human cognition.

Once these states are triggered, they activate biases that systematically distort how information is perceived, processed, and integrated. Bias activation is not random but follows predictable psychological patterns, as established in behavioral finance literature (Barberis and Thaler 2003). For example, cognitive strain under information overload predisposes investors to heuristic shortcuts, while heightened emotional arousal increases susceptibility to impulsive behaviors (Baumeister et al. 2008). This stage of the framework underscores that biases function as mediating mechanisms between internal states and external decision outcomes. In line with advances in neurofinance, this perspective demonstrates that biases operate at the intersection of psychology and biology, which explains their persistence despite investor awareness and education (Moore and Healy 2008).

The third component of the framework, decision distortion, reflects the observable manifestations of these biases in the investment process. Distortions typically appear as misjudgments of risk, reliance on heuristics, and short-term orientation (Shiller 2005). Such distortions aggregate across market participants to influence pricing, liquidity, and volatility. Historical evidence demonstrates that when biases converge at scale, they amplify systemic instability: the herd dynamics of the Dotcom bubble, the loss-averse panic selling of 2008, and the recency bias underlying Black Monday all exemplify this pathway (Barberis 2013; Scheinkman and Xiong 2005). Thus, decision distortion operates as the critical link between individual psychology and macro-financial dynamics.

This framework situates these distortions within market outcomes that complete a feedback loop. Market volatility, asset mispricing, and crisis episodes feed back into investor emotions and cognitions, reinforcing the very biases that initiated the cycle (Shiller 2005). This recursive relationship highlights the systemic dimension of behavioral finance: biases are not merely micro-level deviations but drivers of collective market phenomena. Importantly, the feedback loop aligns with theories of reflexivity and adaptive markets, which posit that financial systems evolve in response to participants' biased perceptions and actions (Loewenstein and O'Donoghue 2011). By emphasizing this loop, the framework underscores the necessity of interventions that address not only individual investor behavior but also market structures and regulatory safeguards to break cycles of irrationality.

2 Common Investor Biases (Loss Aversion, Herding, Overconfidence, Recency Bias)

2.1 Neuroscientific Insights Into Biases

Cognitive biases such as loss aversion, herding, overconfidence, and recency bias are deeply rooted in the neurological processes that govern human decision-making. Loss aversion, one of the most extensively studied biases, demonstrates that investors tend to experience the pain associated with financial losses more intensely than the joy derived from equivalent gains. Neuroscientific research, particularly involving functional magnetic resonance imaging (fMRI), has revealed that the anticipation or experience of loss is strongly correlated with heightened activation of the amygdala, a brain region primarily associated with processing fear and negative emotional responses (Tom et al. 2007). This increased amygdala activity triggers neural pathways that prompt defensive and conservative decision-making patterns, often causing investors to forgo potentially profitable opportunities in an overly cautious attempt to avoid losses. Additionally, these neural responses explain not only the prevalent cautiousness in investor behavior but also why individuals persistently struggle to manage risks rationally, even when presented with clear statistical evidence favoring gains (Kuhnen and Knutson 2005).

Similarly, herding behavior, which describes investors' tendency to follow the actions or investment choices of others rather than relying on independent analyses, originates from intricate neurological processes involving social cognition. Key brain regions, such as the medial prefrontal cortex (mPFC) and the anterior cingulate cortex (ACC), are significantly activated when individuals engage in social decision-making processes (Burke et al. 2010). The mPFC is particularly crucial in evaluating and integrating social information, helping individuals understand others' actions and intentions, whereas the ACC plays an essential role in managing internal conflict and making decisions under uncertainty. When investors observe peers or a majority of market participants engaging in specific financial behaviors, these brain regions facilitate conformity by amplifying the perceived importance and validity of the group's actions. Consequently, individual investors are neurologically driven to align with collective decisions, even when these choices contradict their private evaluations. This herding impulse often contributes to the formation of financial bubbles and subsequent crashes, as collective overreactions lead to severe market imbalances (Hirshleifer 2015).

Overconfidence bias, another prominent cognitive distortion influencing investor behavior, involves excessive confidence in one's judgments and decision-making abilities, disproportionately underestimating the risks involved in financial decisions. Neuroeconomically, overconfidence bias is closely associated with the brain's reward system, particularly dopamine release within the ventral striatum (Moore and Healy 2008). Dopamine, a neurotransmitter integral to reward anticipation and motivation, intensifies feelings of optimism, pleasure, and confidence. When investors experience success, even minor victories, dopamine surges reinforce their perceived skills and analytical capabilities, increasing confidence levels and consequently reducing their sensitivity to risk signals and negative outcomes. Neuroimaging studies consistently find that individuals exhibiting overconfidence display distinctive neural activity, marked by diminished neural responses to uncertainty and enhanced activation during reward anticipation. These physiological patterns lead to consistently risky and speculative investment behaviors, often disconnected from rational assessments of financial realities, subsequently amplifying market volatility and investor vulnerability during downturns (Scheinkman and Xiong 2005).

Recency bias, another fundamental behavioral distortion, is characterized by the tendency to disproportionately prioritize recent experiences, news, or data while discounting historical trends and long-term evidence. Neurologically, recency bias is linked to the function of short-term memory regions, particularly involving the hippocampus and prefrontal cortex (Glaser and Weber 2007). The hippocampus plays a crucial role in the formation and retrieval of recent memories, making investors more inclined to rely heavily on information that is readily accessible or recently experienced. Additionally, the prefrontal cortex, responsible for executive functions such as decision-making and integrating various pieces of information, further exacerbates this bias by prioritizing recent data over historical evidence. Investors influenced by recency bias often demonstrate reactionary behaviors, making swift investment decisions based solely on the latest market movements or news headlines. This neurological propensity not only reduces investors' ability to engage in balanced, historically informed analysis but also leads to shortsighted decision-making strategies that can result in suboptimal financial outcomes, increased market volatility, and substantial portfolio losses (Shiller 2005).

The neuroscientific mapping of investor biases emphasizes that financial decision-making is not solely a cognitive or rational exercise but is deeply embedded in the brain's emotional and memory systems. Loss aversion, one of the most prominent behavioral biases, is strongly associated with the amygdala, a brain region central to processing fear and negative emotions. Functional magnetic resonance imaging (fMRI) studies demonstrate that amygdala activation increases when individuals anticipate or experience financial losses, leading to heightened risk aversion and defensive decision-making (De Martino et al. 2010; Tom et al. 2007). This explains why losses are often perceived as more painful than equivalent gains are pleasurable. Importantly, neuroscientific evidence suggests that this neural response operates at an automatic and subconscious level, reinforcing why loss aversion is so resistant to traditional educational interventions (Sokol-Hessner et al. 2013).

Herding behavior is mapped to the medial prefrontal cortex (mPFC) and the anterior cingulate cortex (ACC), both of which are central to social cognition and conformity. Neuroimaging research shows that the mPFC plays a crucial role in encoding social norms, interpreting others' intentions, and guiding behavior in line with group consensus (Behrens et al. 2009). The ACC, on the other hand, is strongly implicated in conflict monitoring and decision-making under uncertainty, particularly when individual preferences diverge from social expectations (Apps et al. 2013). Together, these regions drive conformity pressures that explain why investors often mimic the actions of peers or the market majority, even when such behavior contradicts their own private information. This neurological basis underlines why herding is such a persistent and destabilizing force in financial markets, as collective behavior magnifies volatility and contributes to bubble formation (Hirshleifer 2015).

The bias of overconfidence is primarily linked to the ventral striatum, a central node in the brain's reward circuitry. The ventral striatum is strongly modulated by dopamine, a neurotransmitter involved in reward anticipation and reinforcement learning (Knutson and Greer 2008). When investors experience gains or successful predictions, the resulting dopamine release reinforces feelings of skill and predictive ability, fostering an inflated sense of confidence in their judgment. Neuroeconomic research demonstrates that overconfident individuals exhibit heightened striatal activation even under conditions of uncertainty, which leads them to underestimate risk and overestimate their control over outcomes (De La Vega et al. 2016; Moore and Healy 2008). In financial contexts, this neural reinforcement loop explains why investors often persist in speculative strategies or excessive trading despite accumulating evidence of deteriorating conditions, thereby amplifying systemic risk.

Recency bias, characterized by the overweighting of recent information relative to historical context, is associated with the hippocampus and the dorsolateral prefrontal cortex (dlPFC). The hippocampus is central to the formation and retrieval of episodic memories, which makes recently encoded information more accessible and salient during decision-making (Eichenbaum 2017). The dlPFC, by contrast, is responsible for executive control functions, including integrating information across time horizons and regulating impulsive responses (Miller & Cummings, 2017). Under cognitive stress or uncertainty, the dlPFC's capacity for long-term integration weakens, leaving investors more reliant on the hippocampus and short-term cues. This neural imbalance explains why market participants often extrapolate from the latest news or price movements while neglecting broader historical patterns, thereby making financial systems more vulnerable to short-term overreactions and abrupt corrections.

Taken together, the mapping in Fig. 2 shows that investor biases are deeply rooted in neurobiological substrates. Far from being random errors, these behaviors emerge from the functional specialization of different brain regions for processing fear, social norms, rewards, and memory. This neuroscientific perspective aligns with the broader field of neurofinance, which integrates insights from psychology, economics, and neuroscience to explain systematic deviations from rationality

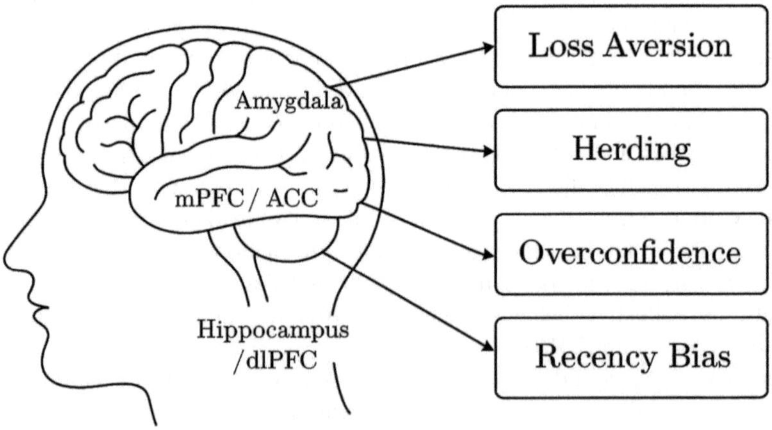

Fig. 2 Neuroscientific mapping of investor biases. Illustrates the neural basis of common investor biases. Loss aversion is linked to the amygdala, herding to the medial prefrontal cortex (mPFC) and anterior cingulate cortex (ACC), overconfidence to the ventral striatum, and recency bias to the hippocampus and dorsolateral prefrontal cortex (dlPFC). These associations show how investor decision-making is shaped by brain mechanisms governing emotion, social cognition, reward anticipation, and memory

(Camerer et al. 2005; Kuhnen and Knutson 2005). The framework suggests that attempts to mitigate biases must consider not only cognitive education but also interventions that account for these automatic neural processes, such as decision aids, adaptive algorithms, or structured choice environments. By situating investor behavior within its biological foundations, the figure underscores both the explanatory power of neuroscience and the limits of purely rational models in capturing the complexity of financial decision-making.

2.2 *Historical Market Events and Bias-Driven Crashes*

Historical financial crises vividly illustrate how investor biases significantly impact market dynamics and stability. The 2008 global financial crisis exemplifies loss aversion, where investors irrationally withdrew funds in panic selling, exacerbating market instability and deepening financial losses. Investors, influenced by exaggerated fear responses triggered by potential losses, rapidly liquidated positions, leading to cascading market declines. Behavioral finance studies reveal that loss aversion can create self-perpetuating cycles of panic, fueling systemic risk as investors' neurological reactions escalate into collective market disruptions. This contagion effect, amplified by loss aversion, illustrates how individual neurological responses aggregate into large-scale economic downturns, magnifying financial distress across global markets (Barberis 2013).

The Dotcom bubble of the late 1990s and early 2000s offers a clear example of herding behavior. During this period, investors systematically ignored fundamental financial analysis, instead following collective enthusiasm and the imitation of popular investment trends. Herd behavior was primarily driven by social conformity pressures, where investors' decisions became increasingly aligned with perceived market consensus rather than rational assessment of intrinsic asset value. This conformity significantly inflated asset valuations, especially within technology-related sectors. Neuroeconomic research highlights how the medial prefrontal cortex and anterior cingulate cortex actively contribute to herding, as these brain regions intensify the perceived legitimacy of collective actions. Consequently, when investor sentiment reversed due to unmet expectations or market fatigue, the rapid collective reversal precipitated severe market corrections and substantial financial losses, clearly demonstrating the detrimental impact of herding behavior on market stability (Hirshleifer 2015).

Similarly, overconfidence bias contributed notably to the stock market crash of 1929. In the years leading up to the crash, an extended period of rising stock prices significantly bolstered investor confidence, leading many to discount risks and speculative warnings. Investors engaged in aggressive and risky financial strategies such as margin buying, strongly believing in their abilities to predict and control market outcomes accurately. Neuroeconomic insights into overconfidence suggest that dopamine-driven optimism significantly exacerbates risk-taking behavior, reducing investor sensitivity to potential adverse outcomes. The inflated valuations and speculative frenzy ultimately collided with economic reality when signs of market weakening became apparent. Investors' hubris quickly gave way to panic selling once they recognized their miscalculations, triggering a catastrophic market collapse that underscored the devastating consequences of unchecked investor confidence (Scheinkman and Xiong 2005).

Recency bias notably influenced market behavior during the 1987 stock market crash, commonly referred to as Black Monday. Investors heavily relied on recent bullish market conditions, largely neglecting historical volatility patterns and long-term market performance indicators. This bias fostered widespread complacency among market participants, making them vulnerable to unexpected market shocks. The sudden emergence of instability quickly disrupted investors' overly optimistic expectations, prompting a swift and largely uncoordinated sell-off. Neuropsychological studies indicate that recency bias stems from cognitive mechanisms involving the hippocampus and prefrontal cortex, which disproportionately favor recent experiences in decision-making processes. This neurological predisposition toward recent information exacerbated the crisis, highlighting how short-term memory biases can drastically undermine market resilience and lead to severe financial disruptions (Shiller 2005).

The historical record of financial crises demonstrates that investor biases are not isolated psychological quirks but systemic forces that repeatedly shape market outcomes. The 1929 U.S. stock market crash, for instance, exemplifies the destructive role of overconfidence. As asset prices rose during the late 1920s, investors increasingly engaged in speculative margin trading, assuming their predictive abilities were superior to underlying risks. Neuroeconomic research connects such overconfidence to the ventral striatum, which reinforces reward-seeking behavior under conditions of optimism (Moore and Healy 2008). When overconfidence is shared across a broad investor base, it inflates valuations and amplifies leverage, leaving markets vulnerable to sudden reversals. The ensuing collapse in 1929 triggered the Great Depression, highlighting how unchecked confidence can transform into systemic fragility (Aliber and Kindleberger 2015; Scheinkman and Xiong 2005).

The 1987 Black Monday crash illustrates the destabilizing effects of recency bias. Investors extrapolated recent bullish market conditions into expectations of continued growth, neglecting longer-term volatility patterns. When instability emerged, this shortsighted reliance on recent information fostered panic selling, leading to a 22% decline in the Dow Jones Industrial Average in a single day. Behavioral finance research shows that recency bias stems from overreliance on short-term memory processes, which privilege accessible information over historical context (Shiller 2005). This episode demonstrates that biases rooted in cognitive heuristics can have macro-level consequences, undermining market resilience when investor expectations are systematically distorted.

The Dotcom bubble of 1999–2000 and the Japanese asset price bubble of the late 1980s and early 1990s both reflect the power of herding behavior. In both cases, investors disregarded fundamental valuation metrics in favor of collective enthusiasm for technology firms or real estate assets. Neuroimaging evidence links herding to the medial prefrontal cortex (mPFC) and anterior cingulate cortex

(ACC), which drive conformity under social pressure (Behrens et al. 2009). Herding produces positive feedback loops: rising asset prices attract more investors, which further inflates valuations. When expectations are disappointed, mass exits from these markets precipitate sharp corrections, as seen in the collapse of internet stocks and the prolonged stagnation of Japan's "Lost Decade." These episodes underscore how socially driven biases intensify asset bubbles, reinforcing the necessity for regulatory vigilance in periods of speculative euphoria (Hirshleifer 2015).

Finally, the 2008 global financial crisis highlights the pervasive role of loss aversion. Faced with collapsing housing markets and deteriorating financial assets, investors rushed to liquidate positions in a desperate attempt to avoid further losses. Neuroscientific studies show that loss aversion is rooted in the amygdala, which processes fear and negative emotional responses (Tom et al. 2007). This collective retreat not only deepened the liquidity crisis but also amplified systemic contagion, demonstrating how an individually rational desire to minimize losses can become collectively destabilizing. Barberis (2013) emphasizes that such panic-driven behaviors perpetuate cycles of volatility, as investor withdrawals accelerate market declines and reinforce systemic fragility. Taken together, the crises outlined in Table 2 highlight the enduring relevance of behavioral biases across contexts, demonstrating that financial instability is often a product of predictable cognitive distortions rather than random shocks.

Another compelling example of bias-driven financial disruption is the Japanese asset price bubble in the late 1980s and early 1990s. Driven by overconfidence and herding behaviors, Japanese investors and institutions aggressively invested in real estate and equities, buoyed by sustained economic growth and increasing asset prices. The prolonged optimism and collective belief in perpetual economic expansion resulted in significantly inflated asset valuations. When economic conditions eventually shifted and speculative excess became apparent, the market experienced a prolonged and severe correction. Neuroeconomic research suggests that the combination of overconfidence and herding amplified investors' unrealistic expectations, setting the stage for one of the most prolonged and economically damaging recessions in history, known as Japan's "Lost Decade" (Aliber and Kindleberger 2015).

2.3 Case Studies for Common Investor Biases

Case Study: The Housing Market Crash (2008 Financial Crisis)

The 2008 financial crisis offers a profound example of loss aversion. During this period, investors were faced with rapidly declining housing prices, triggering extreme emotional responses. Investors, driven by fear of losses, aggressively withdrew investments from various financial instruments, intensifying liquidity shortages. Neuroeconomic research supports that heightened amygdala activation from potential losses can explain the panic-driven market sell-offs witnessed during the crisis (Tom et al. 2007). Consequently, banks, hedge funds, and retail investors all engaged in irrational sell-offs, exacerbating economic instability. Loss aversion further fueled a severe liquidity crisis as banks stopped lending to each other due to uncertainty and fear of incurring additional losses. The breakdown of financial trust networks illustrates how behavioral biases, deeply embedded in neurological responses to risk, can result in widespread systemic disruptions, magnifying market declines and amplifying global economic distress (Barberis 2013).

Case Study: The Dotcom Bubble Burst (1999–2000)

The Dotcom bubble clearly demonstrates investor herding behavior. Investors collectively disregarded fundamental valuation principles, instead driven by widespread enthusiasm and imitative behavior. During the late 1990s, the Internet sector attracted enormous speculative investment primarily due to collective investor euphoria, rather than solid financial fundamentals. Herd behavior escalated rapidly as investors observed others generating impressive returns, prompting further speculative investments irrespective of actual profitability (Hirshleifer 2015). When reality failed to match inflated expectations, investor sentiment quickly reversed. The collective panic selling that ensued was equally herding-driven, resulting in dramatic market corrections and significant financial losses, clearly demonstrating how herding behavior can inflate market bubbles and magnify downturns.

Case Study: Stock Market Crash of 1929 (Overconfidence Bias)

The 1929 stock market crash is a prime historical example of overconfidence bias in action. Investors in the preceding decade experienced significant market growth, leading them to believe in their exceptional forecasting capabilities. This confidence fostered risky investment strategies, notably margin trading, which allowed investors to borrow money to invest, multiplying potential gains and losses (Scheinkman and Xiong 2005). When the stock prices began to falter, many overconfident investors maintained their positions, mistakenly convinced they could accurately anticipate market trends and promptly recover losses. This misjudgment and subsequent panic led to massive sell-offs, triggering one of history's most severe financial collapses and demonstrating the devastating market impact of overconfidence (Scheinkman and Xiong 2005).

Case Study: Black Monday 1987 (Recency Bias)

The 1987 stock market crash (Black Monday) illustrates recency bias vividly. Prior to the crash, investors had experienced prolonged bullish market conditions, leading them to underestimate the likelihood of volatility based on recent optimistic market trends. Consequently, when market corrections began, investors were unprepared and overly reliant on recent positive trends, prompting rapid panic selling when the market began to decline unexpectedly. The sharp market drop on Black Monday underscores how recency bias can result in significant, unanticipated losses due to excessive optimism and insufficient historical perspective (Shiller 2005).

3 How Biases Lead to Suboptimal Financial Decisions

3.1 Cognitive Load and Investment Choices

Decision fatigue, a direct consequence of cognitive overload, significantly exacerbates investor biases, negatively affecting investment quality and outcomes. Cognitive load refers to the inherent limitations in human cognitive capacity to process complex and extensive information, especially under continuous or demanding decision-making scenarios. As investors repeatedly face critical financial decisions, their mental resources become depleted, causing a shift toward reliance on simplified decision-making heuristics or mental shortcuts. These heuristics, although useful in conserving cognitive resources, often lead investors to neglect comprehensive analytical methods and rational evaluation of financial data. Consequently, biases such as loss aversion, overconfidence, and recency bias are amplified, as cognitively fatigued investors become increasingly vulnerable to making impulsive and emotionally driven investment choices rather than carefully reasoned decisions (Baumeister et al. 2008).

Extensive research consistently demonstrates the negative impact of high cognitive load on investors' abilities to critically analyze financial information and manage risk effectively. Investors experiencing cognitive strain frequently revert to intuitive decision-making processes characterized by emotional reactions and simplified heuristic reasoning. Experimental studies in behavioral finance and cognitive psychology illustrate a robust correlation between cognitive fatigue and decreased accuracy in risk assessment, prediction of market outcomes, and effective portfolio diversification. Under high cognitive load, investors tend to overlook crucial financial indicators, misjudge risks, and make rapid, unreflective investment decisions. This compromised cognitive state directly contributes to poorer financial performance, reduced profitability, and diminished overall investment returns, underscoring the critical importance of cognitive resource management in investment decision-making contexts (Hirshleifer and Teoh 2003).

Neuroeconomic research provides further insight into the neural basis of how cognitive load adversely impacts decision-making capabilities. The prefrontal cortex, responsible for executive functions including planning, risk assessment, and decision-making, becomes significantly less efficient when subjected to sustained cognitive stress. Reduced prefrontal cortical activity directly impairs the brain's ability to regulate emotional impulses and manage conflicting information effectively, making it difficult for investors to maintain rational oversight of their decisions. Under cognitive overload conditions, investors' neural pathways are more likely to default to emotionally influenced, impulsive responses, increasing susceptibility to cognitive biases. The resulting investment decisions, therefore, often reflect diminished rationality, greater emotional reactivity, and suboptimal risk management, directly contributing to lower overall investment performance (Loewenstein and O'Donoghue 2011).

Empirical analyses of market behavior reinforce the theoretical and experimental findings regarding the detrimental impacts of decision fatigue. Observational studies show that investors under significant cognitive strain tend to trade more frequently but with substantially less strategic intent and effectiveness. These investors often react hastily to market fluctuations, making frequent and inadequately informed adjustments to their portfolios. Such impulsive behavior not only increases transaction costs but also leads to reduced portfolio optimization and consistently lower investment returns. Additionally, frequent trading driven by cognitive fatigue can magnify emotional and reactive behaviors, exacerbating volatility and market instability. These empirical observations conclusively confirm that cognitive load significantly intensifies cognitive biases, adversely impacting investor performance and highlighting the need for strategic interventions aimed at reducing decision fatigue in financial decision-making processes (Barber and Odean 2000).

Moreover, recent evidence from behavioral finance indicates that professional investors are not immune to the adverse effects of cognitive load. Even seasoned financial experts display significantly impaired judgment and heightened susceptibility to cognitive biases under conditions of cognitive overload, such as during extended trading hours, market volatility periods, or stressful market events. These findings emphasize that cognitive load-induced decision fatigue is not merely a challenge for inexperienced or retail investors but constitutes a pervasive and critical issue affecting the entire investment community. Consequently, institutions and financial advisory services increasingly recognize the necessity of implementing structured interventions, such as periodic breaks, decision support tools, and cognitive load management strategies, to maintain optimal decision-making effectiveness and reduce the prevalence and impact of investor biases (Kuhnen and Knutson 2005).

3.2 *Bias Mitigation Strategies for Investors*

Financial education constitutes a foundational approach in addressing cognitive biases among investors. Structured educational programs are carefully designed to equip investors with the necessary skills and knowledge to recognize, understand, and mitigate biases such as loss aversion, herding, overconfidence, and recency bias. Empirical evidence consistently demonstrates that investors who participate in targeted financial education programs display notably reduced susceptibility to cognitive distortions. These programs often incorporate theoretical explanations, real-world case studies, interactive simulations, and self-assessment exercises, which collectively enhance an investor's ability to critically evaluate their decision-making patterns. Moreover, Fernandes (2014b) suggests that education instills a framework that promotes deliberate, rational consideration of financial data and market conditions, significantly improving investment effectiveness and decision-making outcomes.

Behavioral nudging techniques serve as powerful supplementary strategies for mitigating investor biases. Nudging involves the subtle manipulation of decision-making environments to encourage more rational and informed choices without restricting investor autonomy or freedom of choice. These methods include decision prompts, strategically timed reminders, explicit warnings about potential biases, and simplified information presentation, all designed to counteract impulsive trading behaviors driven by cognitive biases. Experimental studies and real-world applications in financial platforms provide compelling evidence of nudging's effectiveness in significantly reducing impulsive and emotionally driven financial decisions. Thaler and Sunstein (2008) show that nudging effectively encourages investors to pause, reflect, and consider broader analytical insights, ultimately promoting more thoughtful and informed decision-making processes and resulting in enhanced investor performance and greater portfolio resilience.

Recent advances in artificial intelligence (AI) and machine learning technologies offer increasingly innovative and sophisticated strategies for directly addressing investor biases. AI-driven systems can monitor, identify, and predict biased behaviors in real time, proactively offering corrective recommendations tailored precisely to individual investor profiles and behaviors. These AI systems utilize extensive historical financial data, behavioral analytics, and predictive modeling to adapt dynamically to investors' evolving behaviors, effectively targeting specific biases such as loss aversion, herding, overconfidence, and recency bias. By providing real-time, personalized interventions, AI-driven platforms such as robo-advisors have significantly enhanced investment outcomes by reducing the negative impact of cognitive biases. Furthermore, continuous AI learning allows these platforms to refine their intervention strategies over time, progressively enhancing their effectiveness in bias correction and overall investment decision optimization (Philps et al. 2018).

The framework in Table 1 underscores the layered nature of bias mitigation in financial decision-making, beginning with foundational education. Investor education builds awareness by equipping individuals with the cognitive tools to identify and manage their own biases. Programs that incorporate interactive simulations, feedback mechanisms, and case-based learning have consistently shown improvements in investor knowledge and self-monitoring (Fernandes 2014a). By fostering bias literacy, education provides the groundwork for more deliberate decision-making and helps reduce reliance on emotional heuristics. Yet, education alone has limitations: empirical evidence suggests that knowledge does not always translate into behavior, particularly when decisions are made under stress or cognitive load (Willis 2008). This highlights why education should be viewed as the first but not the final layer of effective bias mitigation.

Table 1 Education, nudging, and AI interventions in investor decision-making

Layer	Goal	Mechanisms	Expected Outcomes	Ethical Safeguards
Education (Awareness)	Build bias literacy and self-monitoring	Curricula, workshops, simulations, performance feedback	Improved financial knowledge; reduced impulsivity	Transparency in training content and methods
Nudging (Choice Architecture)	Structure decision environments to reduce frictions	Defaults, reminders, warnings, cooling-off periods	Increased adherence to rational choices; reduced reactive trading	Respect for autonomy; informed consent in nudges
AI (Real-Time Correction)	Provide personalized, timely decision support	Bias detection, adaptive alerts, counterfactual scenarios, explainable AI (XAI)	Reduced expression of biases; stronger portfolio discipline	Data privacy; non-manipulation; accountability

Table 1 outlines a three-layer bias mitigation framework. Education develops investor awareness, nudging improves choice architecture, and AI provides real-time bias correction. Each layer is supported by ethical safeguards, transparency, consent, privacy, and autonomy to ensure interventions enhance decision-making while protecting investor rights

The second layer, nudging, intervenes by shaping the decision environment in ways that reduce frictions and encourage rational outcomes. Drawing on insights from behavioral economics, nudges alter the architecture of financial choices without constraining autonomy (Thaler and Sunstein 2008). Practical mechanisms include default options in retirement savings plans, reminders that reduce procrastination, or cooling-off periods to prevent impulsive trading. These interventions have proven effective at curbing reactive decision-making while preserving investor freedom (Madrian and Shea 2001). Importantly, nudges act as a bridge between education and AI by making rational choices easier and more intuitive, thereby compensating for the persistent gap between awareness and behavior. However, critics caution that nudges can become manipulative if not transparently designed and disclosed, making ethical safeguards a necessary companion to this layer (Bovens 2018).

The third layer of the framework, AI-driven real-time correction, represents the most technologically advanced form of intervention. Unlike education or nudging, which are typically static, adaptive AI systems provide continuous and personalized monitoring of investor behavior. By analyzing large datasets of transactions and behavioral patterns, AI can detect when an investor is about to act under the influence of biases such as loss aversion or recency bias and intervene with timely corrective suggestions (Li et al. 2024). Empirical evidence from robo-advisory platforms shows that such systems improve portfolio discipline, reduce impulsivity, and enhance returns over time (Feinstein et al. 2023). The dynamic, feedback-based nature of AI makes it particularly suited to environments where biases are recurrent and context-dependent. Yet, its very power underscores the importance of robust ethical safeguards to prevent misuse.

Across all three layers, ethical safeguards are not an optional add-on but an integral element of bias mitigation. Transparency, informed consent, privacy protections, and respect for investor autonomy are essential to ensure that interventions enhance decision-making without veering into manipulation (Floridi et al. 2018). For example, while nudges can be effective, undisclosed default settings risk undermining investor trust if perceived as covert. Similarly, AI systems that use behavioral data must balance predictive accuracy with privacy rights, ensuring that investors retain control over both their data and their financial autonomy. Ethical frameworks such as "AI4People" have already proposed guiding principles to align technological innovation with social good, highlighting that trust and legitimacy are prerequisites for sustainable adoption (Cowls et al. 2021).

The framework emphasizes the need for monitoring and continuous evaluation. Interventions cannot be assumed effective or ethical without ongoing assessment of outcomes, investor feedback, and unintended consequences. For instance, educational programs should be tested for their long-term retention of bias literacy, nudging mechanisms should be evaluated for both effectiveness and perceptions of autonomy, and AI-driven platforms must be audited for fairness, transparency, and systemic impact. Continuous improvement not only ensures that interventions remain relevant to changing market conditions but also reinforces accountability among financial institutions deploying them. By embedding monitoring within the framework, bias mitigation evolves from a static toolkit into a dynamic system of governance capable of adapting to investor behavior and technological change.

However, the integration of educational, behavioral nudging, and AI-driven strategies into investor decision-making processes necessitates careful consideration of ethical and regulatory implications. Central ethical principles, including transparency, informed consent, and investor autonomy, must remain paramount when implementing these bias mitigation strategies. Transparency entails clearly disclosing how, why, and when interventions occur, ensuring investors understand the rationale behind suggested actions. Informed consent involves obtaining explicit investor agreement before deploying interventions that significantly alter decision-making behaviors. Additionally, preserving investor autonomy is critical to avoid perceptions of undue manipulation or coercion, which could undermine trust and willingness to engage with these technologies. Regulatory oversight also plays a crucial role in maintaining ethical standards, ensuring bias correction methodologies are employed responsibly, safeguarding investor privacy, and reinforcing trust and acceptance among users of financial advisory services (Cowls et al. 2021).

An additional important consideration involves the necessity for ongoing assessment and improvement of these strategies. Institutions and platforms must regularly evaluate the effectiveness of educational programs, behavioral nudging techniques, and AI-driven interventions to ensure continued alignment with evolving investor behaviors and market conditions. Continuous improvement processes, driven by robust feedback mechanisms and rigorous empirical analysis, are essential to maintaining the effectiveness and ethical integrity of these bias mitigation tools.

Table 2 Historical market events and bias-driven crashes

Year / Period	Market Event	Dominant Bias	Manifestation in Investor Behavior	Market Consequence
1929	U.S. Stock Market Crash	Overconfidence	Excessive speculation, margin trading, underestimation of risks	Severe market collapse; onset of Great Depression
1987 (Black Monday)	Global Stock Market Crash	Recency Bias	Extrapolating from recent bullish trends; neglect of volatility	Rapid sell-off; largest one-day percentage drop
1999–2000	Dotcom Bubble and Burst	Herding	Collective enthusiasm for internet stocks; imitation of peers	Asset bubble; dramatic correction in tech sector
2008	Global Financial Crisis	Loss Aversion	Panic-driven withdrawals; fire sales to avoid further losses	Liquidity crisis; prolonged global recession
Late 1980s–1990s	Japanese Asset Price Bubble & Lost Decade	Overconfidence & Herding	Aggressive equity and real estate speculation; conformity pressures	Prolonged stagnation; collapse of asset prices

Table 2 summarizes major financial crises of the twentieth and twenty-first centuries, highlighting the dominant behavioral biases underlying each episode. Overconfidence, herding, recency bias, and loss aversion manifested in distinct ways across crises, yet all contributed to systemic instability and large-scale market disruptions

By systematically monitoring and refining interventions based on investor feedback and empirical performance data, Jobin et al. (2019) suggest that financial services can sustainably enhance investor decision-making, reduce biases, and promote long-term financial well-being (Table 2).

3.3 *Case Studies on How Biases Lead to Suboptimal Financial Decisions*

Case Study: Excessive Trading Due to Decision Fatigue

A well-documented phenomenon demonstrating the impact of cognitive load on investor decisions is observed in the day-trading activities of retail investors. Studies have shown that investors who trade excessively due to cognitive fatigue often perform worse than less active investors. Barber and Odean (2000) observed that high-frequency traders, experiencing decision fatigue from constant engagement with market fluctuations, exhibited reduced portfolio performance due to impulsive trading behaviors and inadequate analysis of market signals. This case demonstrates clearly that investors suffering from cognitive overload make impulsive decisions, frequently ignoring rational analyses and thereby reducing investment returns significantly. Continuous exposure to complex market decisions intensifies cognitive strain, reinforcing suboptimal trading strategies and exacerbating financial losses (Barber and Odean 2000).

3.4 *Case Study: Educational Intervention in Retirement Savings*

A comprehensive educational program implemented by a major U.S. financial services provider aimed to reduce cognitive biases such as overconfidence and herding. The program included workshops, online modules, and interactive simulations, helping investors identify their personal biases and develop strategies for rational decision-making. Studies evaluating the program found participants significantly improved their investment decisions, exhibiting reduced susceptibility to biases and enhanced portfolio diversification and long-term performance (Fernandes 2014b). This practical example highlights education as a powerful tool for mitigating biases, ultimately enhancing investor decision-making quality and promoting financial resilience and stability.

4 Can AI Learn to Correct Human Biases?

4.1 *Adaptive AI Models for Behavioral Correction*

Artificial intelligence (AI), particularly adaptive machine learning models, has emerged as a powerful tool for correcting human biases in investment decision-making. Adaptive AI systems utilize algorithms capable of continuously learning from historical investor behaviors, dynamically adjusting their intervention strategies based on evolving investor profiles and changing market conditions. By analyzing large datasets of investor transactions and behaviors, AI models identify patterns indicative of cognitive biases such as loss aversion, herding, overconfidence, and recency bias. These sophisticated systems then provide real-time feedback and tailored recommendations to counteract these biases, encouraging investors to adopt more rational, balanced decision-making processes (Li et al. 2024). The effectiveness of adaptive AI models stems from their ability to process vast and complex datasets swiftly and efficiently, enabling them to detect subtle behavioral cues and bias tendencies that human advisors might overlook. Reinforcement learning, a subset of adaptive AI, exemplifies this capability by iteratively learning optimal intervention strategies through continuous interaction with investor decisions and feedback. These reinforcement learning models continuously update their predictive accuracy and intervention techniques based on the observed effectiveness of previous recommendations. Consequently, these AI-driven adaptive models progressively refine their interventions, making them increasingly precise and effective at mitigating investor biases over time (Oehler and Schneider 2022).

Moreover, adaptive AI models integrate insights from behavioral finance with predictive analytics to deliver proactive interventions. For instance, predictive neural network algorithms can forecast when an investor is likely to exhibit biased behavior, such as panic selling or impulsive buying, based on historical behavioral patterns and real-time market conditions. Upon identifying these scenarios, AI-driven systems provide targeted and timely nudges or reminders, prompting investors to reconsider potentially biased decisions. This approach significantly enhances the efficacy of interventions, offering support precisely when investors are most vulnerable to cognitive biases (Barberis and Thaler 2003).

Hybrid AI models, which blend machine intelligence with human advisory capabilities, represent another promising avenue for behavioral correction. These hybrid systems utilize AI's predictive power to flag potential bias-driven decisions, then incorporate human insights to provide nuanced, empathetic advice. This collaborative approach not only preserves investor autonomy but also leverages human judgment and emotional intelligence, fostering greater acceptance and effectiveness of AI recommendations. Such hybrid approaches can effectively address biases by combining the analytical strength of AI with the intuitive judgment and empathy inherent to human advisors, creating a balanced and powerful tool for enhancing investor decisions (Gomber et al. 2018). Moreover, recent advancements in explainable AI (XAI) enhance transparency and trust in adaptive AI models. Explainable AI technologies provide clear, understandable justifications for AI-generated recommendations, allowing investors to comprehend the rationale behind corrective interventions. Transparent explanations reduce resistance to AI-driven interventions, fostering greater investor acceptance and engagement. Enhanced investor understanding of AI-driven recommendations promotes informed consent, reduces skepticism, and significantly increases the likelihood that investors will integrate AI suggestions into their decision-making processes effectively, thus improving investment outcomes (Jobin et al. 2019).

4.2 Ethical Concerns in Bias Correction

While AI-driven bias correction techniques offer significant advantages for investor decision-making, they also raise critical ethical considerations related to autonomy, consent, and potential manipulation. A primary ethical concern involves the potential for AI interventions to infringe upon investor autonomy by excessively steering or influencing decisions. If AI interventions become overly directive or aggressive, they risk being perceived as manipulative, undermining the principle of investor self-determination. Consequently, maintaining clear boundaries between supportive nudging and intrusive manipulation is paramount in ethically deploying AI-driven interventions (Floridi et al. 2018). Transparency represents a core ethical requirement in deploying AI for behavioral bias correction. Investors must fully understand why specific recommendations or interventions are suggested to avoid the perception of covert manipulation or coercion. Explainable AI methodologies, which clearly articulate the rationale and underlying logic of interventions, play a crucial role in addressing ethical transparency. By ensuring investors can readily comprehend AI decision-making processes, financial institutions reinforce investor trust, enhance compliance with AI recommendations, and reduce resistance stemming from perceived opaque or manipulative practices (Cowls et al. 2021).

Informed consent is another pivotal ethical factor. Investors must explicitly agree to AI-driven interventions, especially those significantly influencing their decision-making behaviors. Without clear and informed consent, AI-based interventions risk crossing ethical boundaries into manipulation. Ensuring robust consent processes involves clearly communicating the nature, purpose, and potential impacts of interventions, allowing investors to retain control over their financial decision-making processes. Such transparent and consent-driven frameworks maintain investor autonomy, enhancing trust and ethical compliance while ensuring investors remain comfortable engaging with AI-enhanced decision-support tools (Mittelstadt et al. 2016). Privacy concerns constitute another significant ethical dimension in deploying AI systems that monitor investor behavior. AI-driven bias correction inherently involves collecting and analyzing detailed behavioral data, raising privacy concerns. Strict data governance protocols and privacy safeguards are essential to ensure ethical handling of sensitive investor data. Regulatory oversight must reinforce stringent privacy standards and ethical practices, preventing potential misuse of investor information and ensuring responsible AI deployment (Cowls et al. 2021).

Finally, addressing the broader societal implications of AI-driven bias correction requires ongoing ethical and regulatory vigilance. Policymakers, financial institutions, and technology providers must collaborate to establish clear ethical guidelines and oversight mechanisms for deploying these technologies. Establishing comprehensive ethical standards and accountability mechanisms helps balance the benefits of AI interventions against potential risks, fostering investor trust and societal acceptance. Continuous ethical scrutiny and adaptive regulatory frameworks will be crucial as AI systems become increasingly integrated into financial decision-making, ensuring balanced, ethical, and beneficial outcomes for investors and society at large (Mittelstadt et al. 2016).

4.3 *Case Studies on How AI Can Learn to Correct Human Biases?*

Case Study: Robo-Advisors and Behavioral Correction

Robo-advisory platforms provide clear evidence of adaptive AI models effectively addressing behavioral biases. Companies like Betterment and Wealthfront use AI-driven algorithms to identify and correct biased investment decisions in real time. These robo-advisors analyze past investor behavior and proactively intervene with targeted nudges and recommendations designed to counteract biases such as loss aversion, recency bias, and herding behavior (Feinstein et al. 2023). Empirical research supports these systems' efficacy, demonstrating that investors using robo-advisors show improved investment discipline, reduced impulsivity, and enhanced portfolio returns. This example effectively illustrates the practical applicability and effectiveness of AI-driven behavioral interventions in correcting investor biases and optimizing financial outcomes.

Case Study: Ethical Challenges in Robinhood's Gamification Controversy

The ethical implications of AI-driven interventions are illustrated by controversies such as Robinhood's gamification of investing, which illustrate the ethical implications of AI-driven interventions. Robinhood's platform utilized behavioral nudges, rewards, and simplified visuals designed by AI algorithms to encourage more frequent trading. However, regulators and critics argued these interventions crossed ethical boundaries by exploiting behavioral biases, such as overconfidence and impulsivity, to drive transaction volumes rather than encourage prudent investment strategies (Floridi et al. 2018).

5 Conclusion

Behavioral biases significantly influence investor decision-making, causing systematic deviations from rational economic models. The recognition that biases such as loss aversion, herding, overconfidence, and recency are embedded in human cognition and neural processes is vital for understanding the complexities of financial decisions (Kuhnen and Knutson 2005; Tom et al. 2007). Addressing these biases requires moving beyond simplistic educational measures toward integrating nuanced psychological and neuroscientific insights into investor advisory practices. An acknowledgment of these biases not only helps explain past financial anomalies but also lays a critical foundation for developing targeted interventions to promote more rational investor behaviors. Historical financial events offer powerful illustrations of how cognitive biases aggregate, leading to market-wide instability and economic disruptions. Crises such as the Dotcom bubble burst, the 2008 global financial crisis, and the 1987 stock market crash clearly show that biases are more than individual errors; they can profoundly influence broader market dynamics. Understanding the role biases play in these market phenomena emphasizes the necessity for policymakers, financial advisors, and regulators to incorporate behavioral insights into their frameworks. By doing so, stakeholders can better anticipate investor behaviors, prepare for potential market shocks, and take preventive measures that stabilize markets during turbulent periods (Scheinkman and Xiong 2005; Shiller 2005).

Cognitive overload and decision fatigue compound investor susceptibility to biases, intensifying emotional and impulsive behaviors that result in suboptimal financial outcomes. Investors facing continuous and complex decisions often experience cognitive depletion, impairing their ability to critically assess risks and leading to frequent, poorly informed trading. Empirical studies consistently demonstrate that cognitively strained investors exhibit decreased portfolio performance, increased transaction costs, and poor diversification strategies (Mittelstadt et al. 2016). Hence, effectively managing cognitive resources through structured interventions becomes essential for financial institutions and individual investors seeking sustainable financial performance and portfolio stability. Several effective mitigation strategies, including structured financial education, behavioral nudging, and AI-driven interventions, have emerged as practical solutions to investor biases. Financial education significantly reduces susceptibility to cognitive biases by equipping investors with robust frameworks for rational decision-making. Behavioral nudging techniques further complement education, guiding investors subtly yet effectively toward rational investment choices, enhancing outcomes without infringing on autonomy. Adaptive AI technologies, particularly those utilized in robo-advisory platforms, have proven highly effective by offering personalized, real-time feedback to investors, directly addressing and correcting biased decision-making in practice (Feinstein et al. 2023; Fernandes 2014b).

Despite these technological advancements, the ethical considerations surrounding the use of AI to correct human biases cannot be overstated. Issues such as autonomy infringement, manipulation risk, and privacy concerns present real challenges to widespread adoption. Recent examples like Robinhood's gamification controversies highlight how AI-driven bias corrections could cross ethical boundaries, reinforcing the necessity of transparent operations, explicit informed consent processes, and robust privacy protections (Cowls et al. 2021; Floridi et al. 2018). Ensuring ethical usage is critical not only to protecting investor rights but also to maintaining the integrity and public trust essential to the successful integration of these technologies. Looking forward, continued research and practical innovation in behavioral finance and AI-driven bias mitigation remain essential. Future studies must focus on refining these interventions' effectiveness, exploring emerging biases in evolving market contexts, and addressing increasingly complex ethical and regulatory challenges. Institutions must commit to ongoing evaluation and adaptation of educational programs, nudging techniques, and AI models, continuously aligning them with investor behaviors and market dynamics. Ultimately, these concerted efforts in understanding and mitigating investor biases promise not only enhanced individual investor welfare but also more resilient and efficient financial markets, benefiting society at large (Fernandes 2014b; Jobin et al. 2019).

References

Aliber RZ, Kindleberger CP (2015) In: Aliber RZ, Kindleberger CP (eds) Financial crises: a Hardy Perennial BT - Manias, Panics, and Crashes: a history of financial crises. Palgrave Macmillan, UK, pp 5–37. https://doi.org/10.1007/978-1-137-52574-1_2

Apps MAJ, Lockwood PL, Balsters JH (2013) The role of the midcingulate cortex in monitoring others' decisions. Front Neurosci 7(7 DEC):1–7. https://doi.org/10.3389/fnins.2013.00251

Barber BM, Odean T (2000) Trading is hazardous to your wealth: the common stock investment performance of individual investors. J Finance. https://doi.org/10.2139/ssrn.94140

Barberis NC (2013) Thirty years of prospect theory in economics: a review and assessment. J Econ Persp 27(1):173–196. https://doi.org/10.1257/jep.27.1.173

Barberis NC (2018) Psychology-based models of asset prices and trading volume. National Bureau of Economic Research. http://www.nber.org/papers/w24723

Barberis, Thaler R (2003) Chapter 18 A survey of behavioral finance. In: Handbook of the Economics of Finance, 1(SUPPL. PART B), 1053–1128. https://doi.org/10.1016/S1574-0102(03)01027-6

Baumeister RF, Sparks EA, Stillman TF, Vohs KD (2008) Free will in consumer behavior: self-control, ego depletion, and choice. Journal of Consumer Psychology 18(1):4–13. https://doi.org/10.1016/j.jcps.2007.10.002

Behrens TEJ, Hunt LT, Rushworth MFS (2009) The computation of social behavior. Science 324(5931):1160–1164. https://doi.org/10.1126/science.1169694

Bovens L (2018) The ethics of nudge. How Far to Nudge?, 2008, 108–121. https://doi.org/10.4337/9781786430557.00012

Burke M, Marlow C, Lento T (2010) Social network activity and social well-being. In: Conference on Human Factors in Computing Systems - Proceedings, 3, 1909–1912. https://doi.org/10.1145/1753326.1753613

Camerer C, Loewenstein G, Prelec D (2005) Neuroeconomics: how neuroscience can inform economics. J Econ Liter 43(1):9–64. https://doi.org/10.1257/0022051053737843

Cowls J, Tsamados A, Taddeo M, Floridi L (2021) A definition, benchmark and database of AI for social good initiatives. Nat Mach Intell 3(2):111–115. https://doi.org/10.1038/s42256-021-00296-0

De La Vega A, Chang LJ, Banich MT, Wager TD, Yarkoni T (2016) Large-scale meta-analysis of human medial frontal cortex reveals tripartite functional organization. J Neurosci 36(24):6553–6562. https://doi.org/10.1523/JNEUROSCI.4402-15.2016

De Martino B, Camerer CF, Adolphs R (2010) Amygdala damage eliminates monetary loss aversion. Proc Natl Acad Sci USA 107(8):3788–3792. https://doi.org/10.1073/pnas.0910230107

Eichenbaum H (2017) Memory: organization and control. Ann Rev Psychol 68:19–45. https://doi.org/10.1146/annurev-psych-010416-044131

Feinstein AD, Radica M, Welbanks L, Murray CA, Ohno K, Coulombe LP, Espinoza N, Bean JL, Teske JK, Benneke B, Line MR, Rustamkulov Z, Saba A, Tsiaras A, Barstow JK, Fortney JJ, Gao P, Knutson HA, MacDonald RJ et al (2023) Early release science of the exoplanet WASP-39b with JWST NIRISS. Nature 614(7949):670–675. https://doi.org/10.1038/s41586-022-05674-1

Fernandes D (2014b) Financial literacy, financial education and downstream financial behaviors. Manage Sci:1–23. https://doi.org/10.1287/mnsc.2013.1849

Fernandes N (2014a) The impact of sovereign wealth funds on corporate value and performance. J Appl Corporate Finance 26(1):76–84. https://doi.org/10.1111/jacf.12056
Floridi L, Cowls J, Beltrametti M, Chatila R, Chazerand P, Dignum V, Luetge C, Madelin R, Pagallo U, Rossi F, Schafer B, Valcke P, Vayena E (2018) AI4People—an ethical framework for a good AI society: opportunities, risks, principles, and recommendations. Minds Mach 28(4):689–707. https://doi.org/10.1007/s11023-018-9482-5
Glaser M, Weber M (2007) Overconfidence and trading volume. GENEVA Risk Insur Rev 32(1):1–36. https://doi.org/10.1007/s10713-007-0003-3
Gomber P, Kauffman RJ, Parker C, Weber BW (2018) On the Fintech revolution: interpreting the forces of innovation, disruption, and transformation in financial services. J Manage Inform Syst 35(1):220–265. https://doi.org/10.1080/07421222.2018.1440766
Hirshleifer D (2015) Behavioral finance. Ann Rev Financ Econ 7:133–159. https://doi.org/10.1146/annurev-financial-092214-043752
Hirshleifer, Teoh SH (2003) Limited attention, information disclosure, and financial reporting. J Account Econ. https://doi.org/10.2139/ssrn.334940
Jobin A, Ienca M, Vayena E (2019) Artificial intelligence: the global landscape of ethics guidelines. Nat Mach Intell. http://arxiv.org/abs/1906.11668
Knutson B, Greer SM (2008) Review. Anticipatory affect: neural correlates and consequences for choice. Philos Transact Royal Soc B Biol Sci 363(1511):3771–3786. https://doi.org/10.1098/rstb.2008.0155
Kuhnen CM, Knutson B (2005) The neural basis of financial risk taking. Neuron 47(5):763–770. https://doi.org/10.1016/j.neuron.2005.08.008
Li Z, Lu Z, Yin M (2024) Decoding AI's nudge: a unified framework to predict human behavior in AI-assisted decision making. Arxiv 38(9):10083–10091. https://doi.org/10.1609/aaai.v38i9.28872
Loewenstein GF, O'Donoghue T (2011) Animal spirits: affective and deliberative processes in economic behavior. Cornell University, Center for Analytic Economics https://doi.org/10.2139/ssrn.539843
Madrian BC, Shea DF (2001) The power of suggestion: Inertia in 401(k) participation and Savings behavior*. Quart J Econ 116(4):1149–1187. https://doi.org/10.1162/003355301753265543
Mittelstadt BD, Allo P, Taddeo M, Wachter S, Floridi L (2016) The ethics of algorithms: mapping the debate. Big Data Soc 3(2):1–21. https://doi.org/10.1177/2053951716679679
Moore DA, Healy PJ (2008) The trouble with overconfidence. Psychol Rev 115(2):502–517. https://doi.org/10.1037/0033-295X.115.2.502
Oehler A, Schneider J (2022) Gambling with lottery stocks? J Asset Manage 23(6):477–503. https://doi.org/10.1057/s41260-022-00268-y
Philps D, Weyde T, Garcez Ad'Avila, Batchelor R (2018) Continual learning augmented investment decisions. Arxiv, NeurIPS. http://arxiv.org/abs/1812.02340
Scheinkman JA, Xiong W (2005) Overconfidence and speculative bubbles. J Polit Econ 609:258–282. https://doi.org/10.2139/ssrn.298865
Shiller RJ (2005) Irrational Exuberance: second edition. Princeton University Press. ISBN 9780691123356
Sokol-Hessner P, Camerer CF, Phelps EA (2013) Emotion regulation reduces loss aversion and decreases amygdala responses to losses. Soc Cogn Affect Neurosci 8(3):341–350. https://doi.org/10.1093/scan/nss002
Thaler RH, Sunstein CR (2008) Nudge: improving decisions about health, wealth, and happiness. Yale University Press, 19(4), 356–360. https://doi.org/10.1007/s10602-008-9056-2
Tom SM, Fox CR, Trepel C, Poldrack RA (2007) The neural basis of loss aversion in decision-making under risk. Science 315(5811):515–518. https://doi.org/10.1126/science.1134239
Willis, L. E. (Iowa). (2008). Against financial literacy. Iowa Law Rev, 94(January), 197–285.

AI in Personalized Financial Decision-Making

Narmin Nahidi

Abstract This chapter explores the transformative role of artificial intelligence (AI) in personalized financial decision-making, highlighting how robo-advisors utilize advanced machine learning to detect and respond dynamically to investor behavioral biases such as loss aversion, overconfidence, anchoring, and recency effects. By employing predictive analytics and reinforcement learning models, robo-advisory platforms can anticipate investor behavior and proactively tailor interventions, significantly improving both financial outcomes and user satisfaction. Real-world case studies from wealth management and retirement planning illustrate the successful deployment of hyper-personalized strategies, demonstrating AI's capacity for nuanced portfolio adjustments and behavioral nudges. Despite promising advancements, the chapter addresses critical ethical challenges, including transparency, informed consent, data privacy, and the risks of reinforcing demographic biases or manipulative practices. The chapter concludes by advocating continuous refinement of AI strategies to balance technological sophistication with ethical responsibility, ensuring personalized finance genuinely serves investor welfare and market integrity.

Keywords Artificial intelligence · Personalization · Machine learning · Behavioral nudges · Predictive analytics · Ethical AI · Data privacy · Investor welfare

JEL Classification: G11, G41, O33, D83

N. Nahidi (✉)
Business School, University of Exeter, Exeter, UK
e-mail: n.nahidi@exeter.ac.uk

N. Nahidi, A. Zarifis (eds.), *AI, FinTech, and the Future of Robo-Advisory*, Contributions to Finance and Accounting,
https://doi.org/10.1007/978-3-032-18109-1_4

1 Introduction

Artificial Intelligence (AI) has profoundly reshaped the landscape of personal finance, shifting the emphasis from generic financial advice to finely tuned, user-specific strategies. As the democratization of investment services accelerates, robo-advisors AI-powered digital platforms have emerged as pivotal agents of this transformation. Initially designed to provide low-cost, algorithm-driven portfolio management, these platforms have evolved into sophisticated systems capable of complex behavioral modeling. No longer limited to static portfolio recommendations, today's robo-advisors actively learn from individual user behavior, integrating behavioral finance principles into their algorithms to offer increasingly personalized experiences (Jung et al. 2018). This evolution reflects a broader trend in financial services: leveraging AI to address the cognitive and emotional biases that traditionally impair financial decision-making. Importantly, this technological shift is not simply about automation; it is about fundamentally redesigning the advisory process to align better with how individuals think, feel, and act when managing their finances. Consequently, AI's role in personal finance is not merely operational but also deeply cognitive, aiming to improve both outcomes and experiences.

Central to this shift is the ability of AI systems to detect and respond to behavioral anomalies that manifest in financial decision-making. Cognitive biases such as loss aversion, overconfidence, anchoring, and recency effects often lead investors to make suboptimal choices, particularly under conditions of uncertainty or market volatility (Baker and Ricciardi 2010). Traditional advisory models struggled to consistently identify these biases, relying heavily on self-reported data and periodic advisor–client interactions. In contrast, advanced machine learning models now enable robo-advisors to monitor user behaviors in real time, using digital footprints such as changes in asset allocation preferences, trading frequency, or reactions to market news to infer the presence of biases. Sophisticated behavioral profiling techniques allow these systems to build dynamic models of each investor's psychological tendencies, updating continuously with new data inputs. Recent studies suggest that AI-driven detection mechanisms not only improve individual financial outcomes by mitigating bias-driven errors but also increase client satisfaction and retention by providing a sense of being genuinely understood (Jung et al. 2018).

Beyond the detection of biases, AI's capacity for targeted behavioral intervention has opened new frontiers in personalized finance. Robo-advisors are now increasingly designed to adapt their communication strategies, portfolio recommendations, and even timing of advice delivery based on inferred user biases. For example, investors displaying loss aversion might receive notifications framed to highlight potential long-term gains rather than short-term losses. Similarly, clients prone to overtrading due to overconfidence could be gently nudged toward more passive investment strategies. These adaptive responses are rooted in behavioral economics theories but are significantly amplified by AI's ability to scale these interventions across millions of users simultaneously (D'Acunto et al. 2019). Unlike traditional human advisors who must manually adjust their strategies for each client, AI systems automate this personalization at unprecedented levels of precision and responsiveness. Importantly, these nudges are often subtle, designed to preserve user autonomy while encouraging more rational decision-making, a balance that continues to be a subject of ethical debate within the field.

At the heart of these developments lies the application of machine learning models specifically designed for behavioral finance. Predictive analytics models, for instance, analyze historical behavioral data to forecast the likelihood of specific future actions, such as panic selling during a downturn. Natural language processing (NLP) algorithms assess sentiment in client communications or social media activity to gauge emotional states that may influence financial choices. Reinforcement learning models, in particular, stand out for their ability to optimize advisory strategies by learning from repeated interactions and feedback loops (Sironi 2016). Unlike static predictive models, reinforcement learning allows robo-advisors to dynamically adjust their approaches in real time, rewarding strategies that yield better client outcomes while penalizing those that do not. The fusion of these technologies signals a major paradigm shift in the advisory model, moving beyond retrospective performance analysis toward anticipatory guidance. As a result, machine learning not only helps predict individual behavior but also enables proactive shaping of that behavior toward improved financial wellness.

Real-world implementations provide compelling evidence of the efficacy of AI-driven personalized financial strategies. Leading robo-advisory firms such as Betterment and Wealthfront now offer hyper-personalized portfolio management services, adjusting asset allocations dynamically in response to both macroeconomic shifts and subtle user behavior changes (Belanche et al. 2020). These platforms integrate user-specific data, such as cash flow patterns, employment status, and spending habits, into their investment algorithms, creating a holistic picture of each client's financial life. Similarly, in the domain of retirement planning, AI-based tools are increasingly being used to customize saving trajectories based on personal longevity risk, expected healthcare costs, and even individual lifestyle preferences. Importantly, these innovations are not restricted to high-net-worth individuals; they are increasingly being made accessible to a broader retail clientele, democratizing access to sophisticated financial planning. Such developments highlight that personalization, once a premium service available only through private wealth managers, is becoming an expected standard feature in digital financial services.

Despite these promising advances, significant challenges remain in the deployment of AI in personalized financial decision-making. Algorithmic transparency remains a pressing concern: clients often lack clear insight into how and why specific recommendations are made, raising issues of trust and accountability (Jagtiani and Lemieux 2019). Furthermore, the ethical use of behavioral data is under increasing scrutiny, particularly regarding the fine line between helpful nudging and manipulative steering. Differential performance across demographic groups also poses challenges, as machine learning models trained on biased or incomplete data may inadvertently reinforce existing inequalities in financial outcomes. Cultural factors further complicate personalization efforts: strategies that work effectively in one country or demographic group may fail or even backfire in another. As such, there is a growing recognition that effective personalization must go beyond technical sophistication to incorporate considerations of fairness, inclusivity, and contextual sensitivity. This chapter addresses these complex issues by systematically exploring how robo-advisors detect and respond to user biases, the development and application of machine learning models for behavioral finance, and real-world case studies illustrating both the promises and limitations of AI-driven personalized financial strategies.

2 How Robo-Advisors Detect and Respond to User Biases

2.1 Detection of Behavioral Biases Through AI

The detection of behavioral biases in financial decision-making marks a critical advancement in robo-advisory services. Traditionally, financial advisors relied on questionnaires, interviews, and periodic reviews to infer client behavior. However, these approaches were often limited by self-reporting biases, infrequent interactions, and subjective interpretations. Robo-advisors, powered by artificial intelligence (AI) and machine learning, now analyze vast and diverse datasets, including user activity logs, transaction histories, device usage patterns, and even cursor movement on websites to infer user behavior in ways not possible before (Jung et al. 2018). This allows them to detect subtle manifestations of biases such as overconfidence, anchoring, or loss aversion without direct self-disclosure by users. Early detection, often unnoticed by clients themselves, becomes critical because even minor biases can compound over time to significantly harm long-term financial outcomes.

Modern AI systems use supervised and unsupervised learning techniques to uncover patterns that indicate the presence of biases. Deep learning techniques, particularly recurrent neural networks (RNNs) and long short-term memory (LSTM) models, have enhanced the detection of temporal patterns in investor behavior (Baker and Ricciardi 2010). These models capture dependencies across time allowing the system to recognize that an investor's trading behavior after a series of market losses may be driven more by emotions than by rational strategy. In addition, clustering algorithms enable robo-advisors to create investor archetypes, such as "risk-averse optimizers" or "momentum-driven traders," without pre-labeling users, offering a more nuanced understanding of how behavioral biases manifest across different segments. This transition from static client segmentation to dynamic behavioral profiling significantly improves the system's ability to preempt problematic decision patterns before they escalate.

Recent studies also highlight that real-time behavioral monitoring offers major advantages over periodic behavioral assessments. Real-time detection enables systems to track emotional volatility, sudden deviations from established investment preferences, or impulsive reactions to news events, allowing for immediate and context-specific interventions (Belanche et al. 2020). Techniques such as sentiment analysis through Natural Language Processing (NLP) have enabled some robo-advisors to gauge user emotions from support chat interactions or feedback responses, further enriching the behavioral data pool. Importantly, such approaches reduce reliance on self-reported risk tolerance questionnaires, which have long been criticized for their lack of predictive validity. Behavioral data, continuously updated and passively collected, provides a more authentic and adaptive measure of the investor's true risk attitudes and emotional resilience.

However, while AI-based bias detection offers significant promise, it also presents technical and ethical challenges that merit careful consideration. Detection models are only as good as the data and assumptions they are built on. If training data lacks demographic diversity, the model's predictions may systematically misinterpret or overlook important cultural or socioeconomic variations in financial behavior. Furthermore, the risk of "labeling" clients prematurely based on early behavior patterns can create self-fulfilling prophecies, whereby users are nudged into behavioral categories they might have otherwise grown out of. Addressing these limitations requires careful model validation, periodic retraining with updated datasets, and a commitment to maintaining a flexible rather than deterministic view of client behavior (Jagtiani and Lemieux 2019). Thus, while detection is a critical first step, its efficacy depends on both technical rigor and ethical safeguards (Fig. 1).

In the framework for behavioral bias detection by robo-advisors, the financial journey begins with the continuous acquisition of client behavioral data. This data, encompassing transaction histories, trade frequencies, emotional reactions inferred through digital interactions, and evolving risk appetite, is more granular and dynamic than what traditional risk-profiling questionnaires could ever capture (Baker and Ricciardi 2010). AI-driven systems process this vast and noisy data landscape using a combination of advanced machine learning methods: recurrent neural networks (RNNs) to identify temporal behavioral patterns, clustering algorithms (such as k-means and hierarchical clustering) to categorize investors based on shared behavioral traits, and sentiment analysis via natural language processing (NLP) to detect emotional volatility from user interactions (Jagtiani and Lemieux 2019; Jung et al. 2018). These techniques allow the system to construct dynamic investor profiles that continuously update in response to real-time actions rather than relying on static, outdated assumptions.

Once user behaviors are modeled, the system identifies specific behavioral biases such as loss aversion, overconfidence, anchoring effects, and recency bias, all of which have been empirically shown to distort financial decision-making (D'Acunto et al. 2019). By mapping behavioral triggers and recognizing bias-prone patterns, robo-advisors can develop tailored intervention strategies. Adaptive interventions include subtle nudges framed to counteract specific biases, such as emphasizing long-term gains to mitigate short-term loss aversion or designing "cooling-off" mechanisms to temper overconfident trading behaviors. These interventions are grounded in behavioral economics and choice architecture theories but are dynamically applied at scale through AI personalization engines (Belanche et al. 2024). Importantly, the system does not merely provide one-off advice but continuously

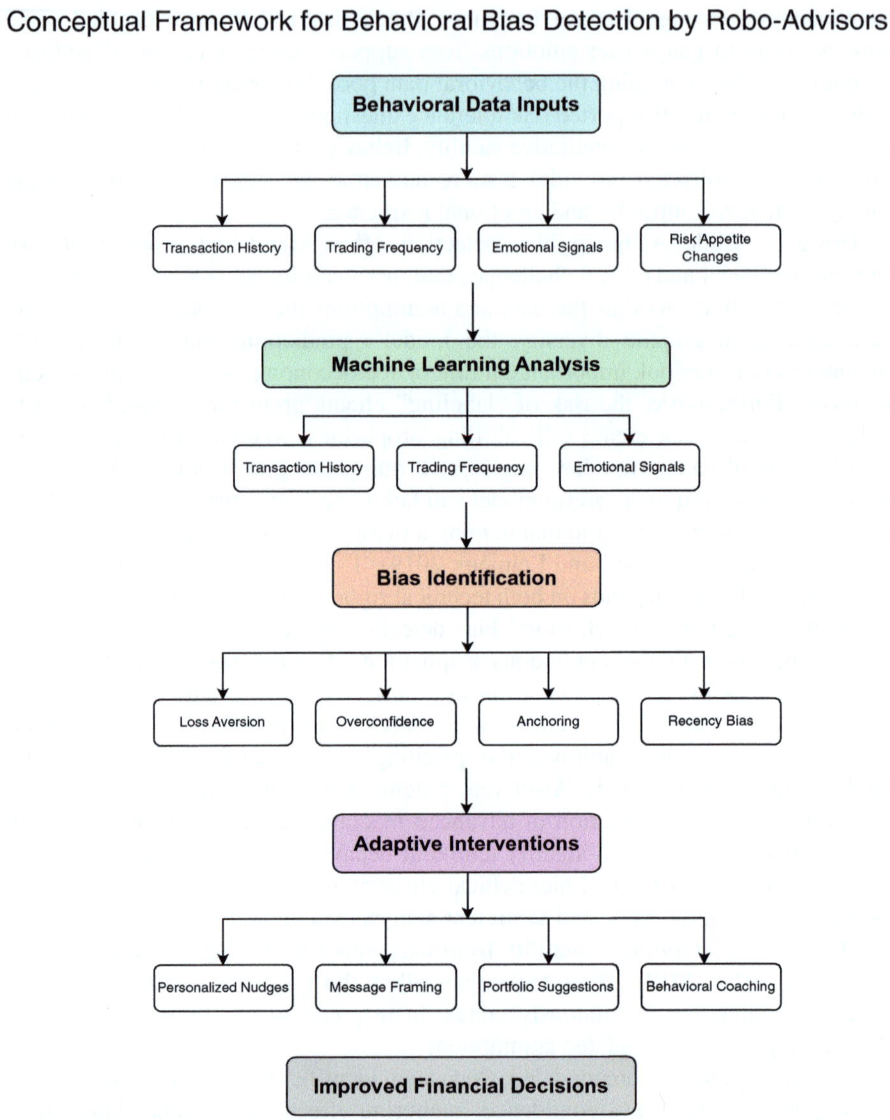

Fig. 1 Conceptual framework illustrating behavioral bias detection by robo-advisors. Behavioral data inputs are analyzed through machine learning models to identify client-specific cognitive biases. Adaptive interventions are then applied to correct these biases dynamically, promoting improved financial decision-making. The process is cyclical, reinforcing continuous behavioral learning and personalization

monitors behavioral feedback, closing the learning loop and recalibrating interventions over time.

The ethical dimension of such AI-driven behavioral correction systems deserves careful attention. As Martin (2019) discusses, algorithmic decision systems in finance raise critical issues around transparency, informed consent, and the potential for manipulation. While personalized nudging can empower investors to make better decisions, it also introduces the risk that poorly designed or opaque systems might steer clients in ways that benefit the platform rather than the user. Therefore, the framework implicitly requires robust governance structures, ongoing fairness audits, and clear user disclosures to ensure that bias correction remains aligned with the client's best interests.

The conceptualization outlined here not only synthesizes behavioral finance insights with modern AI capabilities but also opens new avenues for future development. Particularly, reinforcement learning models could be layered on top of bias detection to dynamically adjust nudging strategies based on real-world outcomes (Sironi 2016). Similarly, more sophisticated emotional modeling, drawing on advances in affective computing, could enhance the system's ability to detect early signs of behavioral instability before they translate into harmful financial actions. Such innovations could further improve the long-term financial well-being of investors by evolving beyond reactive interventions toward predictive behavioral support ecosystems.

2.2 *Adaptive Responses and Nudges by Robo-Advisors*

After detecting behavioral biases, robo-advisors deploy a range of adaptive responses designed to improve client decision-making without restricting their autonomy. Drawing on choice architecture and behavioral economics, these platforms implement "nudges" subtle modifications in how choices are presented to influence behavior without altering the actual options available (D'Acunto et al. 2019). For instance, investors prone to panic selling during downturns may receive encouraging notifications that reframe volatility as a normal, temporary phenomenon, helping to reduce anxiety-driven reactions. Similarly, investors exhibiting confirmation bias—favoring information that supports their existing beliefs—may be exposed to balanced market analysis reports that gently introduce alternative viewpoints. These interventions aim to recalibrate decision frames at critical junctures without appearing intrusive or paternalistic.

Personalization of nudges is a critical differentiator enabled by AI. Rather than applying uniform nudging techniques across all clients, advanced robo-advisors tailor interventions based on a user's detected behavioral profile, historical responses to past interventions, and evolving financial goals (Jung et al. 2018). Natural Language Processing (NLP) techniques fine-tune the language, emotional tone, and timing of messages to fit individual preferences, making advisory interactions feel more organic and less scripted. For instance, users identified as highly loss-averse may receive reassurance-focused updates after market dips, while overconfident investors may be nudged toward educational modules emphasizing the value of diversification. Reinforcement learning models continuously optimize these nudges, testing variations and learning from which ones result in improved user engagement and better financial decisions over time.

Several practical examples illustrate the effectiveness of AI-driven adaptive responses in financial advisory contexts. Platforms like Betterment, Wealthfront, and Nutmeg use algorithmic nudging techniques to automate tax-loss harvesting reminders, encourage automatic rebalancing, and reinforce goal-based investing behaviors. When users attempt to deviate from pre-set investment plans during periods of high market volatility, gentle reminders emphasizing long-term investment horizons are automatically triggered (Belanche et al. 2020, 2024). Other platforms have begun experimenting with gamification strategies, awarding virtual badges or progress milestones when users adhere to disciplined saving or investment behaviors. These subtle reinforcement mechanisms serve to internalize positive habits, transforming initially externally prompted actions into intrinsic behavioral patterns over time.

While the potential of AI-driven nudges is considerable, their design and deployment raise complex ethical issues. In particular, the line between helpful nudging and manipulation can become blurry when systems are optimized purely for engagement or profitability rather than client welfare (Jagtiani and Lemieux 2019). Transparency becomes essential: users must be informed when their behaviors are being influenced by design choices, and they should retain meaningful opt-out options if desired. Additionally, the risk of reinforcing harmful stereotypes, such as assuming lower risk tolerance based solely on age or gender, without continuous validation, must be actively managed through fair model practices and ongoing bias audits. Therefore, while adaptive responses represent a powerful tool for improving financial behaviors, their success depends as much on ethical system design and responsible governance as on technical sophistication.

3 Machine Learning Models for Behavioral Finance

3.1 Predictive Modeling of Investor Behavior

The application of machine learning (ML) to predict investor behavior represents a pivotal development in behavioral finance. Traditional financial theories assumed rational agents operating with perfect information, but decades of empirical research have demonstrated the pervasive influence of cognitive and emotional biases on decision-making (Baker and Ricciardi 2010). Predictive modeling techniques aim to bridge this gap by analyzing patterns in historical and real-time data to forecast future behavior more accurately. Supervised learning algorithms, such as logistic regression, decision trees, and gradient boosting machines, are commonly employed to predict outcomes like trade frequency, asset class preferences, risk tolerance shifts, or likelihood of panic selling during market downturns (Jagtiani and Lemieux 2019). These models incorporate diverse inputs, ranging from macroeconomic indicators to granular user-level data, offering a multidimensional view of investor psychology that static questionnaires could never capture (Fig. 2).

The conceptual framework for predictive modeling of investor behavior captures the intricate process by which personal and market-level data are systematically transformed into behavioral insights and financial recommendations. At the foundational level, the system collects granular personal data such as income patterns, age, past trading behaviors, and portfolio diversification history alongside broader market data including volatility indices, interest rate trends, and macroeconomic news sentiment. Unlike traditional econometric models that assume stable relationships between economic variables, predictive modeling in modern finance leverages machine learning algorithms like Random Forests, XGBoost, and deep neural networks to uncover complex, nonlinear patterns across vast multidimensional datasets (Belanche et al. 2020; Gomber et al. 2018). These models can flexibly accommodate non-stationary relationships and behavioral drift, providing a richer and more dynamic understanding of how external shocks and internal predispositions interact to shape investor decision-making. By structuring inputs at both the personal and market levels, the framework emphasizes that investor behavior cannot be predicted accurately without considering both micro-level psychological tendencies and macro-level financial environments.

The predictive modeling process culminates in the generation of anticipated investor behaviors, such as tendencies toward panic selling during downturns, herding behavior in bubbles, overtrading driven by overconfidence, or inertia characterized by the reluctance to rebalance portfolios even when optimal. These predicted behaviors, informed by complex interactions between user-specific and market-specific factors, allow robo-advisors and digital financial platforms to tailor interventions proactively. Rather than waiting for biases to manifest in destructive investment decisions, the system uses predictive signals to preemptively adjust portfolio recommendations, risk profiles, or communication strategies (D'Acunto et al. 2019). As discussed in Sect. 3.1 of the chapter, this shift from retrospective to anticipatory advisory models marks a profound departure from traditional financial advising, positioning predictive analytics as a behavioral shield rather than a mere diagnostic tool. The hierarchical structure of the framework flowing from data inputs through predictive modeling to behavioral outputs and personalized advice maps logically onto the chapter's theoretical emphasis on machine learning as a behavioral finance accelerator.

A deeper reflection on this framework reveals important ethical and technical challenges that warrant attention. Predictive modeling raises concerns about algorithmic bias, especially if training datasets underrepresent certain demographic or behavioral groups, potentially leading to mispredictions or unfair treatment (Martin 2019). Furthermore, the opacity of complex models like deep neural networks can obscure the logic behind specific behavioral forecasts, undermining client trust unless explainability mechanisms are integrated (Jagtiani and Lemieux 2019).

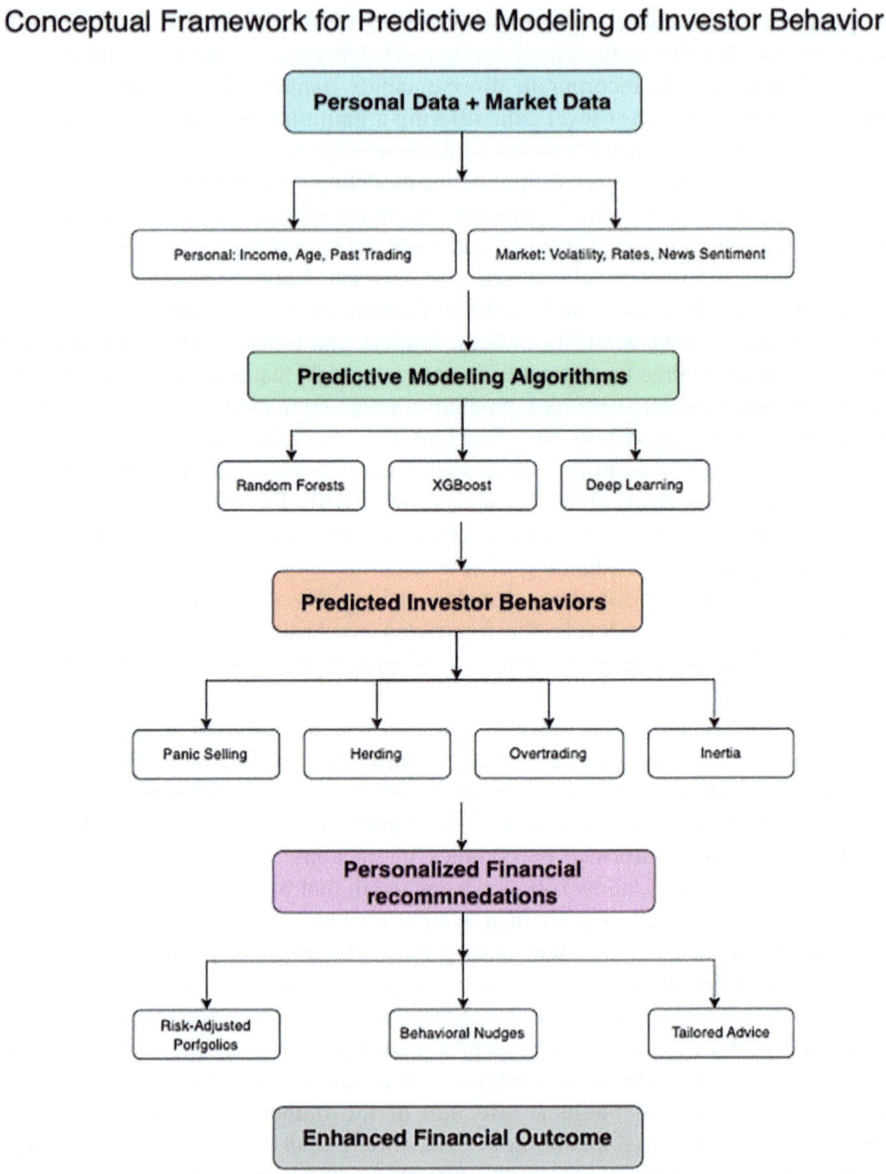

Fig. 2 Conceptual framework outlining predictive modeling of investor behavior. Personal and market-level data inputs are processed through machine learning algorithms to forecast behavioral outcomes such as panic selling, herding, and overtrading. Predicted behaviors inform proactive financial recommendations, aiming to enhance long-term investor outcomes through personalized, anticipatory strategies

One of the notable strengths of predictive modeling in finance is its ability to uncover nonlinear relationships between variables that traditional econometric models often miss. For example, neural networks can model complex interactions between investor age, income volatility, past investment experiences, and current market sentiment to predict susceptibility to herding behavior during bubbles (Belanche et al. 2020). Moreover, ensemble methods like random forests and XGBoost improve prediction accuracy by combining multiple weak learners, mitigating overfitting risks commonly encountered with individual models. Researchers have demonstrated that these techniques significantly outperform classical risk-profiling methods in predicting investment decisions under stress scenarios, particularly when behavioral variables such as sentiment scores and trading inertia are included as features (D'Acunto et al. 2019). Thus, machine learning offers a more realistic and nuanced lens for anticipating behavioral deviations from rational benchmarks.

However, the success of predictive models in behavioral finance hinges critically on the quality and richness of the underlying data (Gomber et al. 2018). Behavioral signals are often noisy, context-dependent, and influenced by latent factors that are difficult to observe directly. To address these challenges, financial technology firms increasingly integrate alternative data sources such as mobile device usage patterns, social media sentiment, geolocation data, and wearable device metrics into their models (Jung et al. 2018). While the incorporation of such data improves predictive accuracy, it also raises important questions about user privacy, data governance, and regulatory compliance. In response, some firms have adopted privacy-preserving machine learning techniques, such as federated learning, which allow model training across decentralized devices without transmitting raw data. These innovations represent an important step toward balancing personalization benefits with ethical data stewardship in behavioral prediction.

Another critical limitation of predictive modeling lies in its temporal stability. Investor behavior is not static; it evolves in response to changing personal circumstances, learning effects, and shifting macroeconomic conditions (Schoar and Sun 2024). Models trained on past behavior may quickly become obsolete if they fail to account for behavioral drift. Addressing this requires continuous model retraining, adaptive learning architectures, and the incorporation of online learning algorithms that can update predictions based on the latest behavioral inputs (Sironi 2016). Additionally, explainability remains a major concern. Black-box models, while often more accurate, risk losing client trust if their decision logic cannot be adequately communicated. Recent research emphasizes the importance of adopting explainable AI (XAI) frameworks that provide interpretable outputs, allowing users and advisors alike to understand the behavioral factors driving model predictions. Thus, while predictive modeling holds immense promise, its success ultimately depends on dynamic updating, ethical data usage, and transparent user engagement.

3.2 Reinforcement Learning for Dynamic Financial Advice

Reinforcement learning (RL) introduces a powerful paradigm for enhancing robo-advisory services by enabling systems to dynamically adapt their financial advice based on user interactions and outcomes. Unlike traditional supervised learning, which predicts a static outcome based on labeled data, RL algorithms learn optimal strategies by exploring different actions and receiving feedback through reward signals (D'Acunto et al. 2019). In the context of financial decision-making, these rewards can be defined in terms of user satisfaction, portfolio performance, or behavioral improvements such as reduced trading frequency or increased savings rates. Over time, the system refines its advisory strategies to maximize cumulative rewards, offering personalized, context-sensitive financial guidance that evolves alongside the client.

One of the key strengths of reinforcement learning in personalized finance is its capacity for continuous learning and adaptation. In environments characterized by uncertainty and dynamic user preferences, static models quickly become outdated. RL frameworks, particularly those based on Q-learning and deep reinforcement learning (DRL), allow robo-advisors to update their policy functions in real time as new information becomes available (Belanche et al. 2020). For instance, if a user's risk tolerance decreases following a personal life event such as job loss or family expansion, the RL agent can detect deviations from expected behavior and adjust portfolio recommendations accordingly. Importantly, this adaptability enables the system to remain aligned with the user's evolving financial goals and emotional states, providing a level of personalization that static advisory models cannot match.

Recent applications of RL in finance illustrate its potential for revolutionizing client engagement strategies. For example, some robo-advisors use multi-armed bandit algorithms to dynamically select the most effective nudging interventions based on real-time user responses (Jung et al. 2018). Others employ policy gradient methods to optimize asset reallocation strategies that balance expected returns with behavioral considerations such as loss aversion. Furthermore, hierarchical reinforcement learning models have been proposed to structure complex financial advice tasks into subgoals, improving learning efficiency and user interpretability. These developments suggest that reinforcement learning is not merely an academic curiosity but a practical tool capable of substantially enhancing advisory effectiveness, particularly in volatile or highly personalized client environments.

Nevertheless, deploying reinforcement learning systems in financial services entails substantial challenges. One major concern is the definition of appropriate reward functions. If rewards are too narrowly tied to short-term portfolio performance, the system may inadvertently encourage excessive risk-taking or short-termism, undermining broader financial wellness objectives (Jagtiani and Lemieux 2019). Additionally, exploration strategies necessary for the RL agent to discover better advisory actions carry inherent risks; poorly timed or inappropriate interventions can erode client trust and satisfaction. There are also regulatory and ethical considerations: how much autonomy should be delegated to an AI system in managing user finances? How should conflicts between user preferences and long-term welfare be resolved? Addressing these challenges requires a careful blend of technical safeguards, human oversight, and transparent client communication, ensuring that reinforcement learning is harnessed responsibly and effectively in personalized financial decision-making (Martin 2019).

4 Case Studies on AI-Driven Personalized Financial Strategies

4.1 Robo-Advisory Personalization in Wealth Management

The deployment of AI-powered personalization in wealth management has radically altered the traditional client–advisor relationship, turning what was once an elite, high-cost service into a widely accessible financial planning solution (Puschmann 2017). A particularly illustrative example is Betterment, one of the first and most successful robo-advisory platforms, which applies machine learning algorithms to tailor portfolios based on individual client profiles. Betterment collects detailed client information through onboarding questionnaires that assess risk tolerance, investment horizon, and financial goals. However, what sets it apart is the platform's ability to integrate behavioral data post-onboarding, such as deposit habits, withdrawal frequencies, and emotional responses to market fluctuations, into its continuous recommendation engine (Belanche et al. 2020). This results in a dynamic investment strategy that evolves alongside the client's financial journey, adjusting asset allocations proactively rather than reactively. For instance, if a user begins saving more aggressively than initially projected, Betterment's algorithms will recommend more aggressive equity exposure if risk tolerance allows, or alternatively may suggest moving surplus funds into new financial goals like a travel fund or early retirement account (Anagnostopoulos 2018). Similarly, if a user hesitates to rebalance a portfolio despite significant drift from the target asset allocation, behavioral markers of risk aversion are flagged, and the system subtly adapts its communication strategy using reassuring language or milestone framing to encourage corrective action without creating client anxiety (Gomber et al. 2017). Betterment's Tax Loss Harvesting+ product further customizes after-tax returns by monitoring portfolios daily for tax-optimization opportunities, a service that would have required bespoke wealth managers in the past. Importantly, the success of such personalization is not only technical but psychological: client surveys reveal that users who perceive their financial advisor (human or digital) as understanding their unique needs are significantly more likely to adhere to investment plans during volatile markets (Jagtiani and Lemieux 2019). Therefore, platforms like Betterment illustrate how AI personalization is not confined to portfolio construction alone but extends into continuous behavioral adaptation and emotional support mechanisms that were once the sole preserve of highly trained wealth managers.

Wealthfront offers another compelling case study in advanced personalization, particularly through the integration of real-world financial data into comprehensive wealth-building advice. Wealthfront's Path tool leverages machine learning models to create detailed, customized life-planning simulations by ingesting granular user data from bank accounts, investment portfolios, mortgages, and even credit card spending (D'Acunto et al. 2019). Unlike traditional financial plans that offer static projections based on generalized assumptions, Path adjusts in real time as user behavior evolves, offering continuous feedback loops that refine the retirement, housing, and family planning forecasts (Stolper and Walter 2017). For instance, if a user begins spending more heavily on travel or luxury goods, Path recalculates the probability of meeting retirement goals and suggests either increased savings rates or adjusted retirement dates to maintain financial sustainability. Furthermore, Wealthfront has incorporated sophisticated direct indexing options, replacing broad ETFs with customized baskets of securities tailored to client preferences, tax situations, and ESG considerations (Brandl and Hornuf 2020). By enabling tax-loss harvesting on individual securities rather than at the fund level, clients can significantly improve after-tax returns, achieving a form of hyper-personalized portfolio management once accessible only through private banking services (Sironi 2016). Wealthfront's behavioral nudging, such as automatic reminders to set financial goals or to capitalize on employer 401(k) matching programs, further ensures that users are continuously engaged in beneficial financial habits. These features demonstrate that the future of wealth management lies not merely in reducing advisory costs through automation but in delivering highly nuanced, individualized financial ecosystems capable of adapting fluidly to the evolving contours of each client's financial and emotional life.

4.2 *AI-Based Customization in Retirement Planning*

The integration of AI into retirement planning marks a fundamental shift away from static, one-size-fits-all strategies toward dynamic, personalized retirement ecosystems (Boreiko and Massarotti 2020). Personal Capital's Retirement Planner offers a clear case study in this transformation. Unlike traditional retirement calculators, which require manual input and assume linear progression of financial variables, Personal Capital aggregates real-time financial data across all linked accounts—bank savings, investment portfolios, real estate equity, debts, and pension plans—and continuously feeds this information into a machine learning model to simulate thousands of possible retirement outcomes under different market and life event scenarios (Belanche et al. 2020) (Fig. 3).

The conceptual framework for AI personalization in retirement planning captures the shift from static, one-size-fits-all models to dynamic, individualized financial life management. The starting point of the process is the continuous collection of real-time financial inputs, such as fluctuations in income, spending habits, savings contributions, and unexpected expenses, combined with the detection of life event

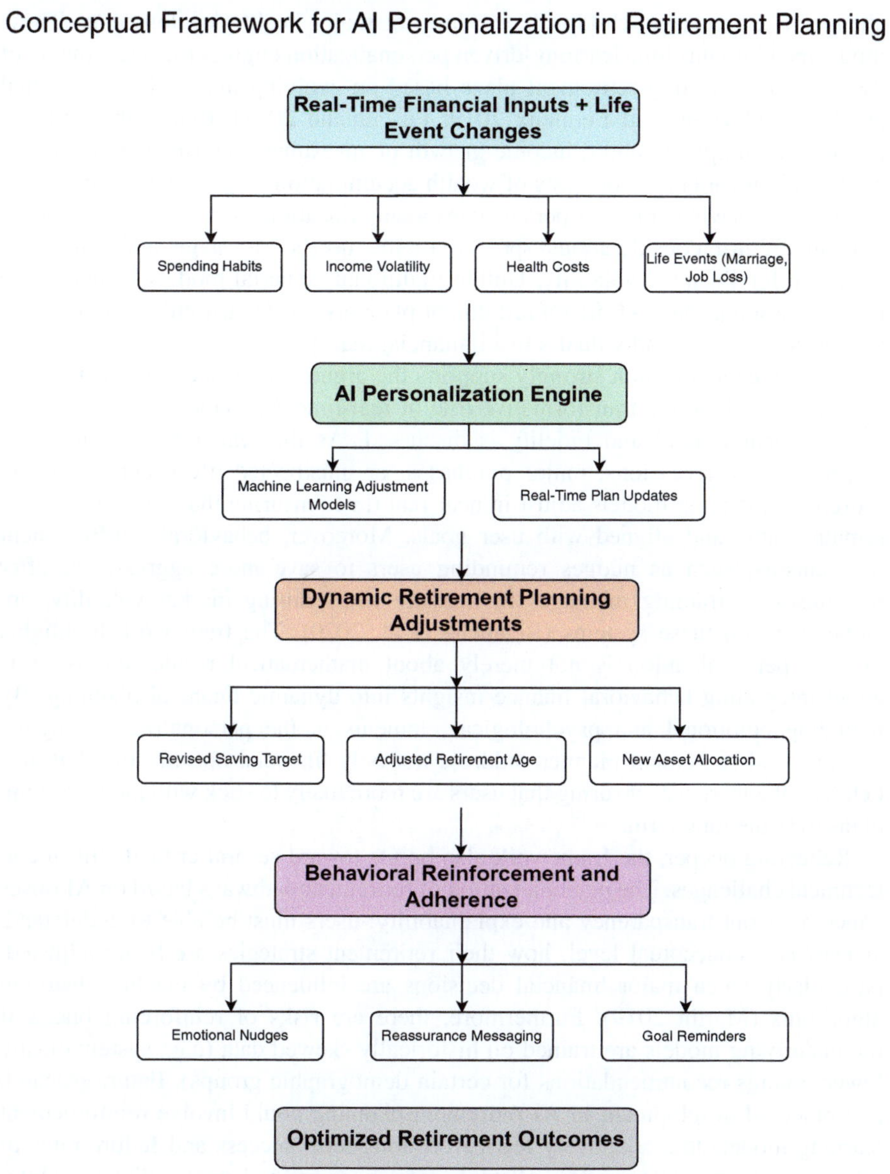

Fig. 3 Conceptual framework for AI personalization in retirement planning. Real-time financial inputs and life event changes are processed through machine-learning-driven engines to dynamically adjust retirement strategies. Behavioral reinforcement mechanisms are integrated to support emotional engagement and adherence, promoting optimized long-term retirement outcomes

changes like marriage, childbirth, job loss, or major health developments. These inputs feed into machine learning-driven personalization engines that are capable of dynamically adjusting retirement plans based on evolving financial and personal conditions (Jagtiani and Lemieux 2019; Puschmann 2017). Rather than relying on static assumptions about income growth or investment returns, the AI engine continually recalibrates forecasts of wealth accumulation, expected retirement age, and required savings rates. It personalizes asset allocations dynamically, balancing risk and return considerations specific to the user's life stage and emotional tolerance for financial volatility. Unlike traditional actuarial models, which make uniform assumptions, AI-driven retirement planners create customized trajectories that respond to each individual's lived financial reality.

This conceptualization strongly supports the argument advanced in Sect. 4.2 of the chapter, where the transformative role of real-time AI adaptation in platforms like Personal Capital and Fidelity is discussed. As financial inputs change due to promotions, recessions, major purchases, or unexpected life events, dynamic retirement planning models adjust in near real time, ensuring that retirement paths remain viable and aligned with user goals. Moreover, behavioral reinforcement mechanisms, such as nudges reminding users to save more aggressively after pay raises or framing messages to reassure users during market volatility, are embedded into these systems (Belanche et al. 2020). The framework highlights that AI personalization is not merely about mathematical recalculations; it is about integrating behavioral finance insights into dynamic financial planning. By including emotional and psychological elements in the personalization engine, AI-enhanced retirement planners address not only financial optimization but also behavioral adherence, ensuring that users are more likely to stick with their evolving plans over the long term.

Reflecting deeper, the framework also points toward several critical ethical and technical challenges. The personalization of retirement pathways based on AI raises concerns about transparency and explainability: users must be able to understand, at least at a conceptual level, how their retirement strategies are being adjusted, particularly when major financial decisions are influenced by machine learning algorithms (Martin 2019). Furthermore, there are risks of reinforcing biases if the underlying models are trained on historically skewed data (e.g., systematically lower savings recommendations for certain demographic groups). Future research and practical development in AI retirement planning could involve reinforcement learning models that adaptively learn from long-term success and failure rates of different retirement strategies, offering even finer-grained personalization. Integrating physiological data (such as stress indicators) or cognitive assessments could eventually enhance retirement planning further, creating systems that are not only financially adaptive but also emotionally intelligent. By offering this layered, adaptive, and ethically mindful perspective, the framework ensures that AI-driven retirement personalization remains not only technically sophisticated but also aligned with client welfare and broader societal goals.

This allows for a highly personalized stress-testing of retirement plans, dynamically adjusting for changes such as unexpected health costs, early retirement desires, or bear market scenarios. For example, if a user increases discretionary spending after a major lifestyle change (such as marriage or moving to a more expensive city), the Retirement Planner recalibrates forecasted retirement dates, suggests adjusted savings targets, or recommends more conservative investment allocations to safeguard retirement readiness. The system also flags shortfalls proactively rather than reactively, alerting users when spending behaviors threaten long-term goals and offering actionable strategies to get back on track. Beyond numeric adjustments, Personal Capital's interface uses visualizations like probability bands and worst-case projections to make complex uncertainty intuitively understandable to clients, thereby empowering more informed, emotionally resilient financial decision-making (Baker and Ricciardi 2010). The platform's ability to synthesize real-time financial behavior, market uncertainty, and individualized psychological patterns into a cohesive retirement strategy exemplifies how AI elevates retirement planning from a static, spreadsheet-driven process into a dynamic, adaptive life management system.

Other platforms, like Fidelity's Personalized Planning and Advice service, extend the AI-driven retirement customization model even further by incorporating behavioral segmentation into their retirement advice frameworks. Fidelity's system analyzes user behaviors such as login frequency, risk rebalancing hesitation, cash flow volatility, and savings consistency to create psychographic profiles that inform retirement advice (Jagtiani and Lemieux 2019). Rather than assuming a uniform decline in risk tolerance with age, the standard "glide path," Fidelity's AI adapts de-risking strategies based on how individuals actually behave when confronted with volatility. For instance, if a 60-year-old user displays the same emotional resilience and savings aggressiveness as a typical 45-year-old investor, the model adjusts the glide path to maintain higher equity exposure for longer, maximizing growth potential without unnecessarily increasing perceived risk. Conversely, users who exhibit flight-to-safety behaviors during minor market corrections are steered toward more conservative allocations well before traditional age-based models would suggest. Importantly, this dynamic personalization also extends to communication strategies: users prone to financial anxiety receive calming, reassurance-based updates framed around long-term goals, while financially confident users receive performance-driven analytics designed to maintain engagement without introducing unwarranted risk appetite. Such levels of behavioral sensitivity ensure that retirement advice remains not only financially sound but also emotionally attuned to the client, increasing the likelihood of adherence to long-term plans. By integrating these behavioral and financial dimensions, Fidelity exemplifies how AI-based retirement customization moves beyond portfolio optimization to support holistic financial well-being throughout an individual's retirement journey.

5 Conclusion

Artificial intelligence continues to redefine the boundaries of personalized financial decision-making, particularly by enabling systems that not only react to user behaviors but also anticipate and adapt to emotional and cognitive fluctuations. A key advance lies in the integration of psychographic data information—about user lifestyles, values, and motivations—into AI advisory models (Bendig et al. 2018). Unlike traditional demographic segmentation, psychographic profiling allows platforms to predict how different users will respond to market turbulence, interest rate shifts, or life events, thereby fine-tuning advice beyond purely financial variables. Studies in behavioral economics have long emphasized that financial choices are often driven more by identity and life goals than by objective optimization (Thaler and Sunstein 2008), and AI systems are increasingly capable of capturing these dimensions. This shift aligns closely with the rise of goal-based investing, where financial strategies are constructed around personalized milestones such as homeownership, education, or early retirement, rather than abstract benchmarks like portfolio alpha.

Beyond technical advancements, the deeper integration of behavioral finance principles into AI systems marks a paradigm shift. Traditional financial advice models operated under the assumption of stable risk preferences and rational actor models, but empirical research reveals that investor preferences are fluid, context-dependent, and heavily influenced by emotional states (Kahneman and Tversky 2021) Modern robo-advisors increasingly utilize dynamic risk profiling, wherein client risk tolerance is continuously assessed and updated based on behavior rather than static surveys (Imas 2016). For instance, observed trading hesitation during volatile periods or increased liquidity hoarding can trigger an automatic reassessment of a user's risk profile, prompting adaptive portfolio rebalancing. Such systems represent a fusion of machine learning capabilities with foundational theories from behavioral economics, operationalizing concepts like prospect theory into real-time financial advising.

However, the deployment of AI in personalized finance also introduces significant ethical complexities. Concerns about transparency, fairness, and informed consent are magnified in environments where user data is not only passively collected but actively used to steer behavior (Martin 2019). For example, if an AI advisor detects increased financial anxiety, it might nudge the client toward more conservative investment choices. While this appears benevolent, it also raises the risk of systematically disadvantaging certain groups if not carefully audited. Disparities in data availability and model performance across demographic cohorts can inadvertently reinforce financial inequalities, a phenomenon well-documented in the broader AI fairness literature (Cowgill et al. 2020). Addressing these issues demands robust bias detection frameworks, transparency in advisory logic, and the development of standards for explainable AI in finance, ensuring that personalization enhances client agency rather than undermining it.

Another underexplored challenge in personalized financial AI is the risk of "overpersonalization." While dynamic adjustment is valuable, excessive sensitivity to short-term behavioral signals can cause frequent, destabilizing changes to financial advice (Wang et al. 2018). For instance, a temporary spike in market anxiety could trigger a series of increasingly conservative portfolio adjustments, locking users into suboptimal strategies. Balancing personalization with strategic consistency requires careful calibration of model responsiveness thresholds and the integration of countercyclical behavioral nudges. Moreover, firms must recognize that not all deviations from optimal financial behavior are inherently irrational; users may have private information or life circumstances unknown to the model. Thus, AI systems must be designed to accommodate a degree of user autonomy and dissent without categorizing it immediately as an error to be corrected.

Looking forward, future research in AI-driven personalized finance could benefit from integrating emotional AI and affective computing techniques (Lemke et al. 2011). These technologies aim to detect and respond to user emotions in real time, offering an even deeper layer of behavioral understanding. For instance, physiological indicators such as heart rate variability or galvanic skin response, captured through wearable devices, could provide additional inputs into financial advice algorithms, allowing them to detect stress or excitement before these emotions manifest behaviorally. Combined with advancements in reinforcement learning, such systems could optimize not just financial metrics but emotional resilience and well-being as part of their advisory goals. However, such capabilities would necessitate even stricter ethical guidelines around consent, data usage, and emotional manipulation risks. By embedding emotional intelligence into financial advisory systems, the next generation of personalized finance could offer not only smarter but more humane and empathetic financial guidance.

References

Anagnostopoulos I (2018) FinTech and RegTech: impact on regulators and banks. J Econ Bus

Baker BHK, Ricciardi V (2010) Professionals and their clients. Econ Voice 7(October):3–5. https://doi.org/10.1016/j.jeconbus.2018.07.003

Belanche D, Casaló LV, Flavián C (2020) Customer's acceptance of humanoid Robots in services: the moderating role of risk aversion. Smart Innov Syst Technol 167:449–458. https://doi.org/10.1007/978-981-15-1564-4_42

Belanche D, Casaló LV, Flavián M (2024) Human versus virtual influences, a comparative study. J Bus Res 173(January). https://doi.org/10.1016/j.jbusres.2023.114493

Bendig D, Strese S, Flatten TC, da Costa MES, Brettel M (2018) On micro-foundations of dynamic capabilities: a multi-level perspective based on CEO personality and knowledge-based capital. Long Range Plan 51(6):797–814. https://doi.org/10.1016/j.lrp.2017.08.002

Boreiko D, Massarotti F (2020) How risk profiles of investors Affect Robo-advised portfolios. Front Artif Intell 3(September):1–9. https://doi.org/10.3389/frai.2020.00060

Brandl B, Hornuf L (2020) Where Did FinTechs come from, and where do they go? The transformation of the financial industry in Germany after digitalization. Front Artif Intell 3(March):1–12. https://doi.org/10.3389/frai.2020.00008

Cowgill, B., Dell'acqua, F., Deng, S., Hsu, D., Verma, N., & Chaintreau, A. (2020). Biased programmers? or biased data? A field experiment in operationalizing AI ethics. In EC 2020 - Proceedings of the 21st ACM Conference on Economics and Computation, Neur IPS, 679–681. https://doi.org/10.1145/3391403.3399545

D'Acunto F, Prabhala N, Rossi AG (2019) The promises and pitfalls of Robo-advising. Rev Financ Stud 32(5):1983–2020. https://doi.org/10.1093/rfs/hhz014

Gomber P, Koch J-A, Siering M (2017) Digital finance and FinTech: current research and future research directions. J Bus Econ 87(5):537–580. https://doi.org/10.1007/s11573-017-0852-x

Gomber P, Robert JK, Chris P, Weber BW (2018) On the Fintech revolution: interpreting the forces of innovation, disruption, and transformation in financial services. J Manag Inf Syst 35(1):220–265. https://doi.org/10.1080/07421222.2018.1440766

Imas A (2016) The realization effect: risk-taking after realized versus paper losses. Am Econ Rev:1–28. https://doi.org/10.2139/ssrn.2403865

Jagtiani J, Lemieux C (2019) The roles of alternative data and machine learning in fintech lending: evidence from the LendingClub consumer platform. Financ Manage 48(4). https://doi.org/10.1111/fima.12295

Jung D, Dorner V, Glaser F, Morana S (2018) Robo-advisory: digitalization and automation of financial advisory. Bus Inf Syst Eng 60(1):81–86. https://doi.org/10.1007/s12599-018-0521-9

Kahneman D, Tversky A (2021) Prospect theory: an analysis of decision under risk Daniel. Passion Perpetua Felicitas Late Antiq 47(2):293–298. https://doi.org/10.2307/j.ctv1kr4n03.21

Lemke F, Clark M, Wilson H (2011) Customer experience quality: an exploration in business and consumer contexts using repertory grid technique. J Acad Mark Sci 39:846–869

Martin K (2019) Ethical implications and accountability of algorithms. J Bus Ethics 160(4):835–850. https://doi.org/10.1007/s10551-018-3921-3

Puschmann T (2017) Fintech. Bus Inf Syst Eng 59(1):69–76. https://doi.org/10.1007/s12599-017-0464-6

Schoar A, Sun Y (2024) Financial advice and investor beliefs: experimental evidence on active vs. passive strategies. American Economic Association

Sironi (2016) FinTech Innovation: From Robo-Advisors to Goal Based Investing and Gamification

Stolper OA, Walter A (2017) Financial literacy, financial advice, and financial behavior. J Bus Econ 87(5):581–643. https://doi.org/10.1007/s11573-017-0853-9

Thaler RH, Sunstein CR (2008) Nudge: improving decisions about health, wealth, and happiness. Yale University Press 19(4):356–360. https://doi.org/10.1007/s10602-008-9056-2

Wang Y, Kung LA, Byrd TA (2018) Big data analytics: Understanding its capabilities and potential benefits for healthcare organizations. Technol Forecast Soc Chang 126:3–13. https://doi.org/10.1016/j.techfore.2015.12.019

Building Trust in Financial Robo-Advisory and Overcoming Ethical Challenges

Alex Zarifis and Manuel Nunes

Abstract Previous research identified five areas where trust could be built for financial robo-advisors. This research identifies the specific methods for building trust for each of these five areas. Building trust with human oversight can be done in three specific ways: (1) oversight of AI model and service it provides, (2) human explanations for advice and processes, and (3) regular human communication outside specific processes. Building trust with transparency and control can be done by: (1) recognise that there are beliefs that do not immediately lead to action, (2) explain actions and demonstrating ability and integrity, and (3) balance automation with control to avoid disempowering users. Building trust with accuracy and usefulness can be done by: (1) accurate and relevant information conveying competence and integrity, (2) usefulness supported by back testing and multiple methods, and (3) enhanced usefulness through personalisation. Building trust with ease of use and support can be done by: (1) achieve ease of use while keeping all the necessary functionality, (2) support time management with nudges, and (3) useful and reliable service with high performance. Building trust with a humanlike interaction can be done by: (1) utilise the latest sentiment analysis and longest contextual memory, (2) the robo-advisor should have a clear persona, and (3) build a relationship and a feeling of friendship and partnership.

Keywords Robo-advisors · Fintech · Insurtech · Trust · Chatbot · Agentic AI

A. Zarifis (✉)
Southampton Business School, University of Southampton, Southampton, UK

Cambridge Centre for Alternative Finance, Cambridge, UK
e-mail: a.zarifis@soton.ac.uk

M. Nunes
University of Southampton, Southampton, UK
e-mail: manuel.nunes@soton.ac.uk

N. Nahidi, A. Zarifis (eds.), *AI, FinTech, and the Future of Robo-Advisory*, Contributions to Finance and Accounting,
https://doi.org/10.1007/978-3-032-18109-1_5

1 Introduction

Most financial institutions can meet their short-term targets by offering competitive services that are attractive. The best financial institutions go beyond simply meeting short-term targets and build strong relationships. Even in the age of AI and data-driven decisions, evidence of the value of building strong relationships is all around us. Both retail customers and organisations show trust and loyalty to financial institutions they have a deeper emotional connection with. Until now, this usually happened naturally with the face-to-face interaction. Even when we interacted with systems on the internet, until recently these systems did not use AI but human logic coded into them. Now with the prevalence of AI and financial robo-advisory, new ways are needed to build trust (Cheng et al. 2021; Dietzmann et al. 2023). A typical AI implementation is naturally good at many aspects of financial services, but it is not naturally effective at building trust. Typically, some human intervention, such as supervised learning and specific instructions given before every answer the AI gives, are necessary to create an interaction that builds trust. Unfortunately, trying to get the AI to build trust in the way humans build trust doesn't usually work. There is extensive evidence that AI behaving as a human can often backfire or even be creepy, so new methods to build trust are necessary (Mori 2012). This research identifies specific methods to build trust in financial robo-advisors.

If we look for a similar case to the disruption AI is causing, the closest case that has this scale is the internet. The internet is not just a technology, but a series of standards created by Tim Burners-Lee and others over many years to structure the technology so that it delivers a service people trust.

The capabilities of AI increase on a weekly basis but implementing AI in a way that builds trust is still the responsibility of the humans in the organisation. There is a technical and business dimension to this. We often refer to the AI stack, as an AI implementation is not typically one application but a series of systems. We can also consider the other aspects of the financial institution as additional layers. All these technical and business layers to the 'financial robo-advisor stack' must be aligned to a trust-building strategy. AI can offer us many things such as near-infinite scaling but for effective relationships with humans, whether they are employees, customers, regulators, or other stakeholders, there needs to be a human behind the robo-advisor, a puppet master, a ghost in the machine (Fügener et al. 2021).

Previous research has identified four issues that affect trust in robo-advisors for specific financial questions, and five that affect trust in robo-advisors for vague financial questions (Zarifis and Cheng 2024). The four issues are the same for both specific and vague questions, but vague questions have one additional issue. The four issues that affect trust in all financial questions are human oversight, transparency and control, accuracy and usefulness, ease of use, and support. The additional, fifth issue that builds trust in vague questions is humanlike interaction.

While identifying these five areas is helpful, they are not specific methods to build trust but broad issues to focus on to build trust. It is difficult to have specific methods to build trust in financial robo-advisors, as each organisation and their context are different. Nevertheless, this research attempts to identify some more specific methods to build trust for each of these five issues. Therefore, the research question is:

What are the specific, practical methods to build trust in financial robo-advisors?

The previous research that identified the five trust-building areas had surveyed users of financial robo-advisors. As the user's perspective on these issues has already been recorded, this research implemented focus groups with finance experts to discuss with them the specific ways they would build trust for these five areas.

This research finds that building trust with human oversight can be done in three specific ways: (1) oversight of AI model and service it provides, (2) human explanations for advice and processes, and (3) regular human communication outside specific processes. Building trust with transparency and control can be done by: (1) recognise that there are beliefs that do not immediately lead to action, (2) explain actions and demonstrating ability and integrity, and (3) balance automation with control to avoid disempowering users. Building trust with accuracy and usefulness can be done by: (1) accurate and relevant information conveying competence and integrity, (2) usefulness supported by back testing and multiple methods, and (3) enhanced usefulness through personalisation. Building trust with ease of use and support can be done by: (1) achieve ease of use while keeping all the necessary functionality, (2) support time management with nudges, and (3) useful and reliable service with high performance. Building trust with a humanlike interaction can be done by: (1) utilise the latest sentiment analysis and longest contextual memory, (2) the robo-advisor should have a clear persona, and (3) build a relationship and a feeling of friendship and partnership.

The following section is the theoretical foundation, followed by the methodology section, where the data collection using focus groups and thematic analysis are discussed. The fourth section on the analysis and findings presents the specific methods to implement for each of the five trust-building areas. Finally, the conclusion summarises the main findings.

2 Theoretical Foundation

This section first looks at the challenges to trust in financial robo-advisors before identifying the five issues that build trust in robo-advisory that form the basis for the data collection.

2.1 The Challenges to Trust in Financial Robo-Advisors

Despite the impressive performance of generative AI transforming finance (Chui et al. 2023), receiving financial advice from a robo-advisor still raises several challenges to trust. From the user's perspective, there are several risks, each of which requires that they have trust in a positive outcome. Where there is risk, trust is needed (Lankton et al. 2015; McKnight and Chervany 2002). The risks from using a financial robo-advisor include that the AI does not understand their real motivation and intentions, technology supporting the robo-advisor does not work correctly, receiving damaging financial advice (Dietzmann et al. 2023), their sensitive personal information leaking, and having a cybersecurity breach (Jain et al. 2023). All these risks are exacerbated by the feeling a user can have that a human on the side of the financial institution is not responsible and anything that happens can be explained away as a technical issue.

There is also the additional potential risk of the robo-advisor making the consumer feel uneasy or even creepy. When we interact with traditional information systems, the interaction is similar to using a tool that has no thought process. When the user interacts with a robo-advisor, it may communicate in an inappropriate way, and this can create an additional feeling of insecurity or even creepiness (Mori 2012; Rajaobelina et al. 2021).

2.2 *The Five Issues That Build Trust in Robo-Advisory*

Research has found that when interacting with generative AI the nature of the task or questions can influence the perception of risk and trust (Cheng et al. 2021). Previous systems that used static code and not AI were limited to specific processes, such as reporting the price of a share. Because robo-advisors are more versatile and do not operate in a rigid way, they handle a breadth of questions and interact in a quasi-social way (Cheng et al. 2024). While there are many different questions asked, in terms of trust building, an important distinction must be made between specific and vague questions. There is a proven difference in how to build trust in these two different scenarios (Fig. 1).

Recent research has identified four issues that affect trust in robo-advisors for specific financial questions, and five that affect trust in robo-advisors for vague financial questions (Zarifis and Cheng 2024). The four issues are the same for both specific and vague questions, but vague questions have one additional issue. The four issues that affect trust in all financial questions are human oversight, transparency and control, accuracy and usefulness, ease of use, and support. The additional, fifth issue that builds trust in vague questions is humanlike interaction. These five trust-building areas are the starting point for this research, which will explore each of them further. These five areas should be further investigated to identify the specific practical ways to build trust (Fig. 2).

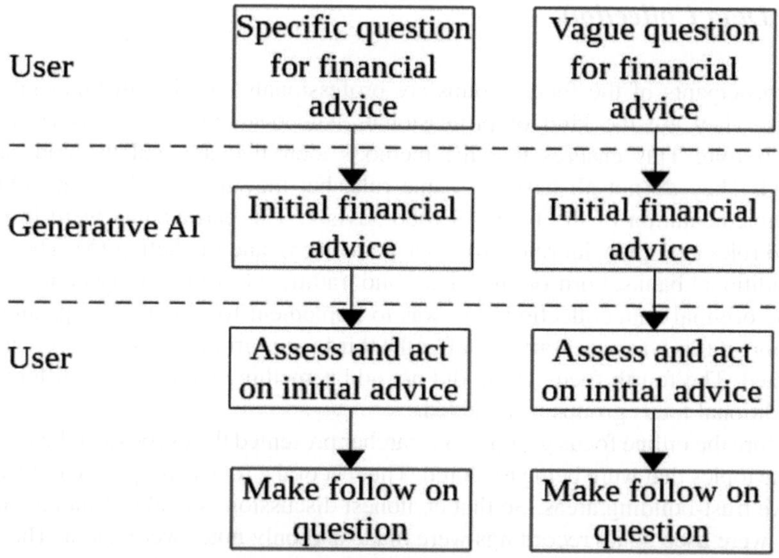

Fig. 1 The process of asking specific and vague financial questions

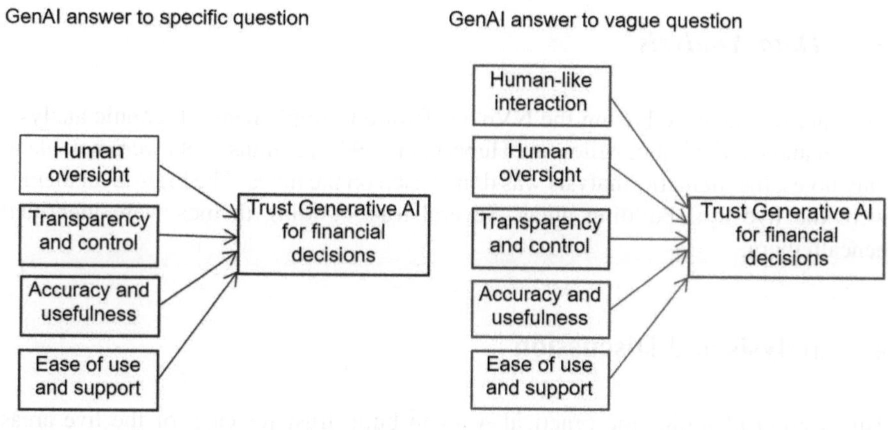

Fig. 2 The trust-building areas for specific and vague financial questions (Based on Zarifis and Cheng 2024)

3 Method

This research attempts to identify specific practical steps to build trust. Previous research identified five areas where trust can be built (Zarifis and Cheng 2024), so this research attempts to find realistic ways practitioners can implement them. For this reason, a qualitative approach with four focus groups was implemented.

3.1 Data Collection

The participants of the focus groups are professionals working in financial institutions. They are the kind of professionals who deal with these issues as part of their role. This ensures that the methods identified are realistic and can be applied. They do not all have the same role, but they are in roles that influence the implementation of the financial robo-advisor. The participants were from IT-related roles (9), financial roles (8), management (5), and marketing (5). They work for traditional banks, born-online banks, and traditional insurers in EU countries.

The original data collection plan was to implement four focus groups and then add more if this was necessary, but after the third focus group, the topics were indeed saturated. The fourth focus group did not add something significantly different, so no additional focus groups were added.

Before the online focus groups, a researcher presented the purpose of the research and the topics that were being explored. The rest of the focus group was divided into the five trust-building areas. So that an honest discussion is made, 'Chatham house rules' were used so no recordings were made and only notes were taken. The notes did not record the identities of the participants, just the main points that were made.

3.2 Data Analysis

The data was analysed using the NVivo software to implement a thematic analysis (Braun and Clarke 2006; Miles and Huberman 1994). As transcripts were not taken, only notes, the thematic analysis was done based on the notes. The high-level themes were the five trust-building areas. Several trust-building themes were identified beneath them.

4 Analysis and Discussion

This section identifies the practical ways to build trust for each of the five areas identified in previous research (Zarifis and Cheng 2024). There are four areas to build trust in both vague and specific questions, and one additional area that only helps for vague questions. There are some common themes such as transparency and having extensive safeguards and checks in place, but each area also has its idiosyncrasies and attempting to oversimplify these issues will not bring the best results. Each of these five areas needs to be handled individually for the best results.

4.1 Human Oversight

Despite the many challenges in keeping a human in the loop, including the problems humans can make, this is still the best way forward. Keeping humans in the loop ensures a more human character to the process. Despite the capabilities of AI, a real person's judgement and empathy are beneficial. Equally importantly, someone always needs to be responsible. Those using robo-advisors to make financial decisions need to know who is behind the tool they are using. They should also know where the responsibility of those creating and maintaining the chatbot starts and ends, and where their responsibility starts and ends. Human oversight needs to be implemented effectively and then communicated effectively.

Having a team of humans in the loop, in itself, does not guarantee any benefit; it needs to be implemented in a targeted way. Those involved in the human oversight will almost inevitably also be involved in troubleshooting unexpected day-to-day problems, which often take many professionals more time than they plan to spend.

4.1.1 Oversight of AI Model and Service It Provides

The first way to build trust is the oversight of the AI models. The model needs to be regularly checked by humans in quantitative and qualitative ways. Tests can be made for AI model drift, but humans can also regularly go through the process themselves. The 'mystery shopper' has been an effective method to check quality and fix issues that could damage trust before AI emerged, and it is still entirely relevant. AI cannot empathise with the problems the people that use it have. AI can give the appearance that it empathises, but it benefits from supervised learning and human instructions before each response it makes to do this effectively. Additionally, a robo-advisor may be well suited for the regular events it deals with, but less common events such as cyberattacks may need some human intervention.

If these proactive oversight processes are in place this will reduce problems, but reactive oversight will still be needed. It is inevitable that those that use robo-advisors will have both valid and less valid complaints. There will be complaints that are not valid, but the users believe them to be valid. The processing of these complaints should not be done with the priority to achieve efficiency. AI offers scale; these processes should focus on empathy and human interaction. Users must feel there is an organisation full of experts behind the machine they are interacting with, not just a server room and an organisation left on autopilot. The problem escalation path should be clear and as painless as possible. It should be seen as an opportunity to touch bases, not a process that should be stripped down to its most basic and automated.

This layer of human oversight managing the AI model and the service should be overseen by a team of middle managers with a range of expertise, including an understanding of the technical, business, psychological, and sociological dimensions.

4.1.2 Human Explanations for Advice and Processes

In marketing literature, they emphasise the importance of the specific 'touchpoints' a user has with an organisation. The main value of focusing on the interactions the user has with the organisation is that those resonate more than advertising or back-office operations not visible to the user.

There are opportunities during the process of using financial robo-advisors to get the best of both worlds, the performance of AI and the human touch. As already happens in some implementations, an explanation written by a human can accompany some advice. It does not have to be made for a specific question but for a type of situation, such as an unexpected event. Processes implemented with AI and automation are often effective in providing a good service when the user has their regular needs but often underperform when the user wants to make a big change to what they are doing such a changing their role in an organisation, or when they have a major change in their life. The effectiveness of generative AI is partly down to remembering previous conversations with a user but when there is a sharp change, these previous patterns are a hindrance, not a help.

Clear accountability that is regularly communicated is also important. There are no tricks to building trust; the humans in the financial institution cannot hide behind the robo-advisor. There should be regular updates that include the name of the human who wrote them. Any checks made by a human can also be logged with the person's name. The accountability does not always need to be communicated to the user, in some cases it just needs to be there in case they need it.

4.1.3 Regular Human Communication Outside Specific Processes

It is human nature to not only build an impression of a financial institution, but even give it human attributes such as traditional, aggressive, innovative, caring, friendly, kind, or unreliable. These human attributes we associate with an organisation influence trust. The performance of the organisation inevitably affects these issues, but it is not just about the performance. The communication should convey a coherent message and character both when reacting to requests and outside of specific processes. This is what the best organisations with strong values achieved before AI dominated the interaction with the user, and this is what should still happen today.

The communication must outline how experienced professionals with a successful track record are developing and validating the portfolios and handling exceptions. The more specific this is, the better. Including names, pictures, and where their office is emphasises that these are real people (Table 1).

4.2 Transparency and Control

Transparency and control are two different things, but we cannot have one without the other, so they are discussed together. If there is transparency but no control, what is the benefit of transparency? Similarly, if there is control but no transparency, how can the user utilise the control they have effectively? Financial professionals and

Table 1 How human oversight can build trust in robo-advisors

Trust-building area: Human oversight	
Trust-building method	Specific tips
Oversight of AI model and service it provides	The 'mystery shopper' is still an effective method to check quality and fix issues that could damage trust. The instructions given to AI before each answer it gives must be reviewed and updated regularly. Humans should intervene and tweak the instructions the robo-advisor receives before it replies when there are special events outside the regular routine. Empathetically process complaints. Complaints should be seen as an opportunity to build the relationship, not as a drain on efficiency.
Human explanations for advice and processes	Regularly offer an explanation written by a human to accompany some advice. When there are big changes in the user's life, past performance may not be the best guide so AI must be prepared to adapt. Regularly explain the accountability of humans involved including their names and what measures they take.
Regular human communication outside specific processes	Decide what character the financial institution should have and communicate this consistently. The character of the organisation should be conveyed in terms of human characteristics such as traditional, innovative, or friendly. Regularly communicate how human financial professionals shape the service. Mention their names.

consumers that use robo-advisors are willing to trust robo-advisors under some conditions. They know AI is playing a central role, but they want the process to be transparent. Interacting with a machine for important issues is inherently disempowering, so we start the relationship with a deficit of trust that needs to be dealt with. It needs to be clear what exactly the process is, what data is being used, and what data is being collected. These things need to be done effectively in a way that benefits the user, not a superficial way.

4.2.1 Recognise That There Are Beliefs That Do Not Immediately Lead to Action

The fashion of being 'data-driven' based on users' actions often misses people's feelings as they don't always act on them immediately. However, bad feelings building up can lead to negative actions further down the line. Feelings of a lack of transparency and control may not immediately be apparent in the data that come from measuring behaviour. Consumers can often be trapped in a situation where they do not have better options, so they do not change their behaviour for some time. However, as soon as an alternative appears they will change their behaviour. It is common for people to expect linear change in behaviour, but this is not always the case. There is often a sudden inflection point in behaviour that came from longer-held beliefs. Feelings are not always easy to understand when the interaction is online; we cannot read the persons face for example, but they are powerful and decisive.

It is important to appreciate that AI effectiveness is not enough on its own, as even with an excellent financial robo-advisor there will be both valid and less valid concerns and fears. All these things are dealt with instinctively when humans interact with each other. A professional in insurance or finance would do these without thinking. When we moved to online services these relationships were weakened but people knew that, ultimately, humans were making the decisions as they made the code and the algorithms. This applies to all five areas of trust building, but it is particularly important for transparency and control.

4.2.2 Explaining Actions and Demonstrating Ability and Integrity

The robo-advisor can make an excellent recommendation, but the user may still feel some anxiety and uncertainty. For example, if AI makes a change to a user's investment portfolio, a short explanation of why this was done is necessary. This is an opportunity for the robo-advisor to explain what methods it uses and how capable it is. If the robo-advisor makes a significant change, then it needs to inform the user. The user must not be left in uncertainty. As far as possible, the explanation must be in plain English avoiding specialised terminology and acronyms.

A separate section on the website can be dedicated to more information on the methodologies behind the actions and recommendations. If the user wants more information beyond the messages they receive, they will be able to find it at this methodology hub. These forms of communication not only reduce uncertainty and the perceived risk involved, but they build more realistic expectations.

4.2.3 Balancing Automation with Control to Avoid Disempowering Users

The robo-advisor must make it easy for the user to be in control by providing a range of tools. These are usually simple but give the user a quick way to take action to implement their will. A slider can enable them to adjust the risk level. Switches can be used to make typical investment exclusions such as weapons manufacturers, or organisations that are considered unethical such as cannabis and alcohol producers. There should also be a button that can be pushed that stops each process such as a new investment until it is checked by the user and confirmed. Additional buttons should enable the user to pause or undo a decision. The line between work and leisure time has been blurred and both professionals and retail investors may be making decisions when they are not entirely in their work mindset. This is the current reality so the financial robo-advisor must make it as easy as possible to understand the implications of decisions and correct mistakes where possible. These features create a psychological safety net for users.

Table 2 How transparency and control can build trust in financial robo-advisors

Trust-building area: Transparency and control	
Trust-building method	Specific tips
Recognise that there are beliefs that do not immediately lead to action	Current user behaviour does not tell the whole story. Bad feelings about the lack of transparency and control can build up and can lead to negative actions further down the line. AI's effectiveness is not enough on its own, as even with an excellent financial robo-advisor there will be both valid, and less valid, concerns and fears. The concerns should be understood, and empathy should be shown.
Explaining actions and demonstrating ability and integrity	An explanation in plain English of all the implications of an action should be made. The methods used to reach the decision and all the implications, such as changes to fees, must be explained. A section on the website can be dedicated to more information on the methodologies behind the recommendations. This not only reduces uncertainty, but it builds more realistic expectations.
Balance automation with control to avoid disempowering users	It must be made easy for the user to be in control by providing a range of tools. The tools give the user a quick way to implement their will. These features create a psychological safety net for users. The user can be encouraged to develop their knowledge where necessary. If they are doing something they have not done before, the robo-advisor can check if they are familiar with the implications.

The robo-advisor can also guide the user to develop their knowledge where necessary. If they are doing something they have not done before, such as buying precious metals, the robo-advisor can check if they are familiar with the implications (Table 2).

4.3 *Accuracy and Usefulness*

It is not a surprise that the accuracy and usefulness of the information build trust in the robo-advisor. The role accuracy and usefulness play in this context, however, is worth exploring further. Understanding their role in this specific context will make it easier to develop a comprehensive approach to building trust.

4.3.1 Accurate and Relevant Information Conveys Competence and Integrity

The robo-advisor must provide precise, reliable, and relevant information. There are many things an organisation can do to convey their competence, but if the accuracy is not there, all the other measures will be in vain. If there is accuracy, then other measures, such as communicating the value of the advice, can reinforce the feeling of competence. This is an obvious point but it needs to be made as AI often struggles with accuracy, especially if it is bringing a lot of information together such as the user's risk tolerance, fees, and so on. If there is a lack of accuracy, it may be perceived as a lack of competence, or a lack of integrity, or both. A lack of accuracy in any aspect may be perceived as dishonesty and may damage trust. With the risk involved in financial decisions people are particularly sensitive to the possibility of being misled.

4.3.2 Usefulness Supported by Back Testing and Multiple Methods

Generative AI has impressive capabilities, but the accuracy of the most popular generative AI most people use is achieved by implementing unsupervised and supervised training, along with several special commands. For financial questions, additional layers must be added on top of these typical layers. For example, AI can identify patterns in a wide range of data that influence risk. An example is that some insurers track alternative behavioural data such as a user typing speed, as slow typing has been linked to higher risk. These strengths of AI must be combined with traditional methods and back testing to previous scenarios. Finance and insurance are particularly challenging for generative AI, whose characteristics bring both strengths and weaknesses in this area. There are many unexpected sudden twists in these areas that are hard to predict by AI if it just plays to its natural strengths. The multiple AI models and methods will enhance the usefulness. The saying 'two minds are better than one' could be adapted here to 'multiple AI models and methodologies are better than one'.

4.3.3 Enhanced Usefulness Through Personalisation

While AI has both strengths and weaknesses in making financial predictions, personalising a service is something AI is naturally very strong at. The obvious strength of AI here is bringing data on the user's behaviour together to understand their specific needs. Less obvious is that AI can encourage more interaction from the user, so they keep sharing their needs as they evolve. In addition to measuring behaviour, surveys, and other opportunities to encourage feedback can be used. This dialogue can be elicited when there is unexpected performance or unexpected events. This should not come across as nudges but as opportunities for the user to have their say (Table 3).

4.4 Ease of Use and Support

When there is a big disruption with new technologies and new capabilities emerging, it is tempting to assume that getting the basics right, such as ease of use, is

Table 3 How accuracy and usefulness can build trust in financial robo-advisors

Trust-building area: Accuracy and usefulness	
Trust-building method	Specific tips
Accurate and relevant information conveys competence and integrity	AI often struggles with accuracy. The robo-advisor must provide precise, reliable, and relevant information. If there is a lack of accuracy, it may be perceived as a lack of competence, or a lack of integrity, or both.
Usefulness supported by back testing and multiple methods	Finance and insurance are a particularly challenging for generative AI, whose characteristics bring both strengths and weaknesses in this area. Multiple AI models and methods will enhance the usefulness.
Enhanced usefulness through personalisation	AI brings data on the user's behaviour together to understand their specific needs. AI can encourage more interaction from the user, so they keep sharing their needs as they evolve.

guaranteed. Unfortunately, this is not always the case. There are some issues that have an effect in one context of using a technology but do not have a decisive effect in others. For example, the role of institutions in building trust is a significant factor in some contexts but not others. Ease of use, however, almost always has a significant influence on users' trust and intention to use a technology.

4.4.1 Achieve Ease of Use While Keeping All the Necessary Functionality

As with other trust-building areas discussed here, in principle they are straightforward but when it comes to the implementation things can get tricky. For example, to build trust in the other areas discussed here additional functionality is needed to provide more information to the user and elicit more feedback from them. All this functionality adds complexity which could reduce the ease of use. That is why many financial organisations, especially the born-online banks prioritise simplicity. However, the best way to build trust is to have all the functionality necessary and still manage to keep it simple to use.

By managing to keep everything intuitive, anxiety is reduced and the robo-advisor appears more competent. Users are not always in a critical mood, but when dealing with a lot of information and important financial decisions, it creates anxiety. If the robo-advisor is hard to use, this creates negative emotions and makes the user question whether the aspects of the service they cannot see, the back-office functions, are working correctly. The friction must be reduced as far as possible, and the confidence should be increased. Processes such as onboarding and security checks used to take a lot of time and effort, but the best financial organisations are finding ways to reduce the time and effort needed.

4.4.2 Support Time Management with Nudges

The robo-advisor can give updates and remind the user when they need to check something or if there is something they might be interested in. Effective proactive communication from the robo-advisor benefits trust in several ways but here the purpose is to reduce the cognitive load. The nudges can be based on what usually works for most users but over time it can be personalised to the individual. Milestones can also be celebrated, as this is an additional way to enhance the user's contextual awareness.

4.4.3 Useful and Reliable Service with High Performance

The more useful the robo-advisor is, the more trust it will build and sustain. This does not mean that an extremely useful robo-advisor does not need to build trust in other ways. Trust must be built in all the areas identified, as being weak in some of them will undo the benefit from the others. The usefulness can be enhanced by showing a deeper understanding of the implications of the financial actions on a person's life. Each action can be annotated with a simple explanation. Ideally, the user will feel that the robo-advisor has been sent on a clear mission and will continue to pursue the agreed goals without the need for oversight or micromanaging (Table 4).

Table 4 How ease of use and support can build trust in financial robo-advisors

Trust-building area: Ease of use and support	
Trust-building method	Specific tips
Achieve ease of use while keeping all the necessary functionality	Achieving ease of use by providing a stripped-down basic service is easier to achieve but this means missing other opportunities to build trust. All the trust-building areas must be implemented while still achieving ease of use. By keeping everything intuitive anxiety is reduced and the robo-advisor seems more competent. The friction must be reduced as far as possible, and the confidence should be increased.
Support time management with nudges	The robo-advisor can give updates and remind the user when they need to check something or if there is something they might be interested in.
Useful and reliable service with high performance	The usefulness can be enhanced by showing a deeper understanding of the implications of the financial actions on a person's life. The user should feel that the robo-advisor has been sent on a clear mission and will continue to pursue the agreed goals without the need for oversight or micromanaging.

4.5 Humanlike Interaction

An attempt at humanness that is out of place, or in any other way ineffective, can backfire and even feel creepy. However, with the capabilities of robo-advisors today and the effort that is put into training them and fine-tuning their behaviour, it is feasible to reliably achieve a positive result from humanlike behaviour. Previous research has found that humanlike behaviour should be limited to the interactions where the user asks broader vague questions. A more human, quasi-social interaction does not build trust when a specific question is asked and might seem out of place.

4.5.1 Utilise the Latest Sentiment Analysis and Longest Contextual Memory

The advisor must be updated constantly so it is at the cutting edge of understanding context, sentiment, and intent. This is the 'arms race' between the AI different financial institutions use. The previous conversations must be remembered and linked to current discussions, so the context is clear. Whether voice or text is used to communicate, the sentiment analysis must be able to identify feelings such as frustration and anxiety. The intent should be understood as quickly as possible so the user can use shorter simpler commands and not need extensive prompt engineering, or inputting a whole specification, to get the result they need. This technical prowess is necessary to implement the other trust-building methods in this area.

4.5.2 The Robo-Advisor Should Have a Clear Persona

The robo-advisor must convey an identity and personality. As with many things, the AI is presenting this without it being real, so it is a persona and not a real personality. Each financial institution has a certain image, but its employees still have room to show their different personalities. In a similar way, the robo-advisor must have a persona that fits the institutions image but there is still room for customisation to each user. For example, it is well documented that younger traders often make more regular trades than older traders. The robo-advisor can use data on demographics to customise their persona up to a certain point, and then do the final customisation based on the individual's behaviour. Another option is for humans to prepare several personas for the robo-advisor to choose from based on what the specific user would probably appreciate more.

4.5.3 Build a Relationship and a Feeling of Friendship and Partnership

Inclusive language can be used to give the user the sense that the robo-advisor is on its side. An example is 'Let's review this week's performance'. This inclusive

Table 5 How humanlike interaction can build trust in financial robo-advisors

Trust-building area: Humanlike interaction	
Trust-building method	Specific tips
Utilise the latest sentiment analysis and longest contextual memory	The previous conversations must be remembered and linked to current discussions, so the context is clear. Whether voice or text is used to communicate, the sentiment analysis must be able to identify feelings such as frustration and anxiety. The intent should be understood as quickly as possible so the user can use shorter simpler commands and not need prompt engineering.
The robo-advisor should have a clear persona	The robo-advisor can use data on demographics to customise up to a certain point, and then do the final customisation based on the individual's behaviour. Humans can prepare several personas that the robo-advisor chooses from, based on what the specific user would probably appreciate more.
Build a relationship and a feeling of friendship and partnership	Inclusive language can be used to give the user the sense that the robo-advisor is on its side. An example is 'Let's review this week's performance'.

language makes the user feel like they are partners with the robo-advisor and it is not just a tool. The user will not perceive this as fake but as empathetic. As long as this is not taken too far this is effective (Table 5).

5 Conclusion

Previous research has identified four issues that affect trust in robo-advisors for specific financial questions, and five that affect trust in robo-advisors for vague financial questions (Zarifis and Cheng 2024). The four issues that affect trust in all financial questions are human oversight, transparency and control, accuracy and usefulness, ease of use, and support. The additional, fifth issue that builds trust in vague questions is humanlike interaction. Knowing these five areas is helpful, but in order to take action, specific methods to build trust for each of them are necessary. Therefore, this research identified the specific methods to build trust in robo-advisors for each of the five areas.

This research finds that building trust with human oversight can be done in three specific ways: (1) oversight of AI model and service it provides, (2) human explanations for advice and processes, and (3) regular human communication outside specific processes. Building trust with transparency and control can be done by: (1) recognise that there are beliefs that do not immediately lead to action, (2) explain actions and demonstrating ability and integrity, and (3) balance automation with control to avoid disempowering users. Building trust with accuracy and usefulness can be done by: (1) accurate and relevant information conveying competence and integrity, (2) usefulness supported by back testing and multiple methods, and (3) enhanced usefulness through personalisation. Building trust with ease of use and support can be done by: (1) achieve ease of use while keeping all the necessary functionality, (2) support time management with nudges, and (3) useful and reliable service with high performance. Building trust with a humanlike interaction can be done by: (1) utilise the latest sentiment analysis and longest contextual memory, (2) the robo-advisor should have a clear persona, and (3) build a relationship and a feeling of friendship and partnership.

Yet these trust-building methods do not operate in isolation. Algorithmic bias and ethical trade-offs represent systemic risks that can undermine client confidence if left unaddressed. Bias can enter robo-advisory systems through data, features, model design, and deployment choices, producing suitability failures, excess trading costs, and inappropriate drawdown exposure. Practitioners must also navigate genuine tensions between personalisation and fairness, transparency and proprietary interest, automation and human oversight, and predictive accuracy and interpretability. The governance architecture of model risk management, suitability assurance, fairness monitoring, and documentation provides the institutional foundation without which the practitioner strategies identified in Sect. 4 cannot be sustained at scale.

This analysis carries implications for investors, firms, and regulators alike. Investors benefit from understanding that robo-advisory trust is multidimensional and that the presence of sophisticated technology does not guarantee aligned interests. Questions about oversight, transparency, and fairness monitoring are reasonable to ask and material to the advisory relationship. Firms benefit from recognising that trust-building is not merely a marketing exercise but requires genuine investment in governance infrastructure, bias testing, and explainability. The competitive advantage of robo-advisory, scalable personalised advice at low cost, can only be sustained if clients believe the system operates in their interest. Regulators benefit from the framework's emphasis on outcomes rather than prescriptive rules. Suitability, fairness, and transparency can be assessed through the lens of client experience and distributional analysis, without requiring detailed algorithmic audits that may be impractical at scale.

The chapter began by observing that trust, built naturally through face-to-face interaction in traditional advisory relationships, must be deliberately constructed in the age of AI-driven financial services. The trust-building areas identified in Sect. 2 and operationalised in Sect. 4 provide the conceptual and practical architecture for this construction. They offer a comprehensive approach to building financial robo-advisory systems that are not merely efficient and scalable, but genuinely worthy of client confidence.

We thank Dr Peng Xu for proofreading the paper.

References

Braun V, Clarke V (2006) Using thematic analysis in psychology. Qual Res Psychol 3(2):77–101. https://doi.org/10.1191/1478088706qp063oa

Cheng X, Bao Y, Zarifis A, Gong W, Mou J (2021) Exploring consumers' response to text-based chatbots in e-commerce: the moderating role of task complexity and chatbot disclosure. Inter Res 21. https://doi.org/10.1108/INTR-08-2020-0460

Cheng X, Yan Y, Zarifis A (2024) Understanding users' response to Chatbots from the perspective of interactive ritual Chain. In: Americas Conference on Information Systems (AMCIS), 1–5

Chui M, Hazan E, Roberts R, Singla A, Smaje K, Sukharevsky A, Yee L, Zemmel R (2023) The economic potential of generative AI (Issue June)

Dietzmann C, Jaeggi T, Alt R (2023) Implications of AI-based robo-advisory for private banking investment advisory. J Electr Bus Dig Econ 2(1):3–23. https://doi.org/10.1108/jebde-09-2022-0037

Fügener A, Grahl J, Gupta A, Ketter W (2021) Will humans-in-the-loop become Borgs? Merits and pitfalls of working with AI. MIS Quart 45(3):1527–1556. https://doi.org/10.25300/MISQ/2021/16553

Jain R, Kumar S, Sood K, Grima S, Rupeika-Apoga R (2023) A systematic literature review of the risk landscape in Fintech. Risks 11(2). https://doi.org/10.3390/risks11020036

Lankton N, McKnight H, Tripp J (2015) Technology, humanness, and trust: rethinking trust in technology. J Assoc Inf Technol 16(10):880–918

McKnight H, Chervany NL (2002) What trust means in E-Commerce customer relationships: an interdisciplinary conceptual typology. Int J Electr Commer 6(2):35–59

Miles MB, Huberman AM (1994) Qualitative data analysis. Sage Publications

Mori M (2012) The Uncanny Valley: the original Essay by Masahiro Mori. IEEE Robot Automat Magaz 12(Figure 1):1–6. https://spectrum.ieee.org/automaton/robotics/humanoids/the-uncanny-valley

Rajaobelina L, Prom Tep S, Arcand M, Ricard L (2021) Creepiness: its antecedents and impact on loyalty when interacting with a Chatbot. Psychol Mark 38(12):2339–2356. https://doi.org/10.1002/mar.21548

Zarifis A, Cheng X (2024) How to build trust in answers given by Generative AI for specific and vague financial questions. J Electr Bus Dig Econ 3(3):236–250. https://doi.org/10.1108/JEBDE-11-2023-0028

A Theory of Investment Simplification and an Experiment with AI Large Language Models

J. Indigo Jones

Abstract The complexity of investing in financial markets creates demand to simplify it; but competition to meet this demand creates a new layer of complexity, restarting the cycle. Robo-advisors are but one link in a long chain of financial technology seeking to scale and simplify access to financial markets, and there are now too many to know them all. The next link in the chain of creative destruction is the robo-"robo-advisor"-advisor: A technology which helps retail investor chooses the right robo-advisor for them. One non-AI advisor and five AI large language models (LLMs) are tested to see whether at least one can provide complete advice that can navigate complicated jurisdictional problems and robo-advisor service heterogeneity without producing hallucinations. Since there are no switching costs, only one is necessary. Four out of five LLMs outperform the human team, and with a sophisticated prompt, Anthropic's Claude can solve this problem without error. The prompt is provided such that readers can benefit directly from this research.

Keywords Household finance · FinTech · Large language models · Generative AI · Wealth management

JEL Classification G11, G15, G24, G28, G51

Parts of this paper draws on the author's PhD thesis, "Behavioral Household Finance and Robo-Advising" (University of Orléans, 2024). The author thanks the participants of the AFSE 2025 Annual Congress and the AFREN Digital Economics Conference E3N#11 for their comments on earlier drafts of this work and acknowledges Paolo Georges Cirne for his help in validating the final draft.

J. I. Jones (✉)
Elinor Ostrom Research Unit, Paris, France
e-mail: indigo.jones@gmx.com

N. Nahidi, A. Zarifis (eds.), *AI, FinTech, and the Future of Robo-Advisory*, Contributions to Finance and Accounting,
https://doi.org/10.1007/978-3-032-18109-1_6

1 Introduction

In 1924, there was only one mutual fund. For the layman, investing in financial markets suddenly became simpler: Just invest in MITTX. Then competitors started offering different kinds of mutual funds. This broadened the choice set for investors, which is always good, but as a byproduct of having to understand the differences among the mutual funds in order to make an informed choice, investing in financial markets became complicated again. Then in 1975, there was only one index fund. For the layman, investing in financial markets suddenly became simpler: Just invest in VFIAX. Then the cycle repeated—bond indexes, the Wilshire 4500, maturity dates. Then in 1993, there was only one Exchange Traded Fund (ETF): Just invest in SPY. And the cycle repeats: inverse, leverage, tilt. Then in 2008, there was only one robo-advisor: Just invest with Betterment. Rinse and repeat: REITs, crypto, tax-loss harvesting. This is creative destruction (Aghion and Howitt 1990), where a financial innovation's proliferation sows the seeds of its own eventual replacement.

Two stylized facts emerge from this brief history: Investors demand both simplification and diversification. But these two demands are in conflict. The demand for simplification is met by a supplier with a financial innovation: mutual fund, index fund, ETF, robo-advisor, whereas the demand for diversification is met by multiple suppliers with specialized services catering to a specific portfolio need, investor demographic, or wealth bracket. This is the situation in which the latest evolution in this history, robo-advisors, finds themselves in.

Could generative AI, and specifically large language models (LLMs), help build this hypothetical robo-"robo-advisor"-advisor? Capable of referencing the breadth of the published content on the Internet and eminently scalable (List 2022), but also prone to hallucinations, LLMs may or may not be capable of performing this role.

The outline of this chapter is as follows. Section 2 reviews the literature on simplifying financial technology and describes the complex current state of robo-advisors. Section 3 considers a theory of conflict between demand for simplicity and diversity in investment options. Section 4 describes the methods used to construct the task for the experiment with the AI LLMs and their comparison with human financial advisors. Section 5 states the results of the experiment with a discussion in Sect. 6. Section 7 concludes by placing this study within a wider economic context of automatization of financial advice.

In this chapter, five of the most popular LLMs are given a complex intellectual task of recommending a robo-advisor to an investor, and their answers are compared against a baseline of human financial advisors. Because these LLMs are all free and giving them this task is as simple as copying and pasting it from this study, there are no upfront or switching costs among the LLMs. As such, if there is at least one LLM that is capable of solving the task, then the robo-"robo-advisor"-advisor exists. The human financial advisors failed the task. As did four of the five LLMs. But one LLM, Anthropic's Claude, produced advice without error.

This study contributes to the literatures of financial technology (FinTech), human financial advisors compared to robo-advisors, and the extent to which AI can replace professional services. Furthermore, this study provides an economic theory explaining the cyclical evolution of simplifying financial services, a framework for thinking through stumbling blocks and edge cases when choosing a robo-advisor, and a specifically engineered prompt which readers can use to recover their lost utility predicted from the theory.

2 Literature Review

2.1 The Steady March Toward Simplification

Owning and maintaining a diversified portfolio is more complicated than holding a single stock, but investors accept this additional complication because the lowered risk is worth the trade-off in expectation. Nobel prize-winning economist Harry Markowitz (1952) outlined that an investor could construct a portfolio which maximizes an expected return for a given level of risk through diversification of nonperfectly correlated assets, inventing modern portfolio theory (MPT). MPT largely replaced the naive diversification strategy that investors used prior to its invention. Extensions of MPT, such as the capital asset pricing model (CAPM) by Nobel prize-winning economist William Sharpe (1964) or the three- or five-factor model by Nobel prize-winning economist Eugene (Fama and French 1992, 2015), are industry standards. If only this was easier.

Saving is common, and the benefits of diversification are well-known, but building and especially maintaining a scientifically diversified portfolio that suits an investor's unique financial situation is difficult. Therefore, financial technologies have been invented to make diversification easier. Since at least 1924, investors have pooled their resources and delegated the task of managing a diversified investment portfolio, called a mutual fund (Farina et al. 1969). However, the fees associated with paying the manager and reimbursing their trades meant most mutual funds had below-average returns (Sharpe 1966). Furthermore, mutual funds that outperformed in 1 year rarely maintained this streak in subsequent years (Carhart 1997). This is predictable. In any given trade, the average return of the buyer and seller is slightly negative: One makes a profit and the other makes a loss, but they both pay transaction fees. If financial markets are efficient (Fama 1970), an imperfect but plausible and widely held view, the fact that few managers can reliably earn above-average returns after deducting transaction fees logically follows. To address this shortcoming with the typical mutual fund, Jack Bogle launched Vanguard in 1975 with a mutual fund called an "index fund," which gives up the chance of outperformance to guarantee average returns by tracking a broad stock market index such as the S&P 500 (Bogle 1999). Further financial technologies improved on this model. Buying and selling shares of a mutual fund can be tricky, so exchange traded funds (ETFs) were invented in 1989 to make trading index funds easier. Eventually, there were so many ETFs on the market that investors needed help choosing among them, so robo-advisors were invented in 2008 to give advice on and manage portfolios composed purely of ETFs (Fisch et al. 2019).

With each new simplifying technology, portfolio diversification becomes more accessible to and inclusive of diverse audiences (see Chatterjee 2020). Whereas once only the wealthiest institutions and individuals could access sophisticated diversification, with ETFs and especially robo-advisors, the financial and informational barriers to entry have been greatly reduced. Just as other technologies which have reduced the barriers to stock market participation have raised participation rates (Bogan 2008), robo-advisors are bringing new entrants into financial markets as well (Reher and Sokolinski 2019). Choi (2022) summarized that across eight dimensions, consensus popular and academic household finance agreed on just one: to invest in passive index funds, e.g., with robo-advisors.

2.2 *The Benefits of Robo-Advisors*

The actions taken by these untrained, middle-class individuals are of great interest to governments, regulators, asset managers, financial markets, and academics exactly because they are so typical of the median person, a person who has either very little experience in finance or has not yet even entered financial markets. As more people enter the global middle class (Kochhar 2015), as stock market participation rises across many countries (Campbell 2006), and as more individuals' pensions are covered by defined contribution instead of defined benefit plans (Broadbent et al. 2006; Gomes et al. 2021), the number of household investors participating in the stock market will only grow.

The question then is how to properly advise this growing stream of new investors, those without experience and uncertain financial literacy, cost-effectively at scale (List 2022). Here, there is a large cleavage between popular and academic household finance. If popular household finance is pessimistic about the ordinary person's capabilities, academic household finance is optimistic. To avoid taking on debt, Dave Ramsey (2013) encourages his readers to rent until they have the money to buy their primary residence in cash because they cannot be trusted with debt. Meanwhile, Ando and Modigliani (1963) assume that people can solve lifetime consumption optimization problems or at least behave as if they have done so. These two perspectives have little in common.

Robo-advisors can improve upon human performance (including well-trained financial managers) in many ways. In reality, investors underdiversify (Benartzi and Thaler 2001). Investors hold too much company stock (Benartzi 2001) and home-country stock (French and Poterba 1991), and trade excessively (Barber and Odean 2000, 2001). Perhaps this is the bounded rationality mentioned by Simon (1955), regular humans' limited omniscience. But investors do not always do much better with human financial managers. Certain flaws among human financial advisors have been well documented. To start, human financial advisors can advise their clients to hold portfolios that reflect their own portfolios (Foerster et al. 2017; Linnainmaa et al. 2021). This is not necessarily good advice. Not only is each client in need of different advice that fits their unique financial situation, in the words of Linnainmaa et al. (2021), human advisors can "trade frequently, chase returns, prefer expensive, actively managed funds, and underdiversify." Chalmers and Reuter (2020) found that the portfolios of clients who sought financial advice from brokers underperformed target date funds, in part because advisors steered clients toward higher fee products. Human advisors can steer their clients to high fee, often self-serving financial instruments (Mullainathan et al. 2012). Mullainathan et al. (2012) also documented evidence of age and gender discrimination toward clients. Sharpe (1966) observed that the average mutual fund performed below the market average; half a century later, it is still the case that the average human financial advisor underperforms the market and sometimes even naive retail investors without advice (Hackethal et al. 2012; Chalmers and Reuter 2020).

Robo-advisors do not have these problems. It is not surprising then that even when retail investors like and trust their financial advisor, they may seek a second opinion with robo-advisors (Zhang et al. 2021). Some users prefer robo-advisors because they are more accountable (Philippon 2019), objective Jung et al. (2019), precise (Wexler and Oberlander 2021), or convenient (Mesbah et al. 2019) than human financial advisors. Robo-advisors can also act as infinitely patient AI teachers, demonstrating to investors how to better diversify their portfolio without necessarily taking up the time of or replacing a human financial advisor (Loos et al. 2020).

2.3 *The Limits of Having Hundreds of Robo-Advisors*

Up to this point, robo-advisors have been presented as a natural evolution in the journey to make modern portfolio diversification a la Markowitz (1952) or Fama and French (2015) simple enough for retail investors to perform en masse. But that is speaking of robo-advisors as a general concept: How does it look in the field?

Because of the Foreign Account Tax Compliance Act (FATCA), an American living in France cannot open an account with Betterment. Nor can a Frenchman living in the United States open an account with Yomoni. Automatic rebalancing is standard practice with most robo-advisors, but not Amundi's. Furthermore, Amundi's robo-advisor is business to business (B2B), as are Advize, FundShop, Fundvisory, and many others. By default, Nalo's portfolios operate like target date funds, decreasing stock market exposure over time, though this option can be deactivated. As a promotional offer at time of writing, SoFi automated investing matches individual retirement account (IRA) contributions at 1%. Ramify allows investment in art. Every portfolio with Fidelity Go includes cryptocurrency. Acorns, Ellevest, SoFi, and Stash have no minimum investment threshold. Some robo-advisors have ESG options, some do not; Goodvest has *exclusively* ESG portfolios. There are no fees at either Schwab Intelligent Portfolios or at SoFi; 6% of a Schwab portfolio is kept in cash that is then loaned out, while SoFi directs its investors to its proprietary ETFs that have relatively high expense ratios. Speaking of Schwab, tax-loss harvesting is available above $50,000 in assets under management. Can the average robo-advisor client handle this complexity? If they can, then it is questionable such a financially literate investor would even need a robo-advisor. If they cannot, then there is a latent demand, an unmet need, for the next simplifying financial technology.

Retail investors employ financial advisors because they want help understanding and managing an investment portfolio. Robo-advisors automate this transaction, making it more transparent and accessible. But now there are hundreds of robo-advisors, each with their own services, entry barriers, and jurisdictions. Robo-advisors aim to simplify ETFs, a technology aimed to simplify mutual funds, which itself is a technology aimed to simplify trading individual stocks. The next stage in this evolution of simplification, indeed the next step for robo-advice itself, is to advise retail investors which robo-advisor to choose.

There is room for improvement in robo-advisors. Mutual funds were simple until there were hundreds of them. ETFs were simple until there were hundreds of them. The same has happened to robo-advisors. How can a retail investor with barely a concept of compound interest possibly choose among the hundreds of robo-advisors today, which compete with each other on services like tax-loss harvesting and exposure to real estate investment trusts (REIT)? Each incremental innovation in the robo-advisory market increases the risk of choice overload (Chernev et al. 2015) and thus reduces the scalability of the underlying technology (Al-Ubaydli et al. 2019). The logical next step is for retail investors to seek an advisor to help them choose a robo-advisor: a "robo-advisor"-advisor. Reasonably, this advice could itself be automated: a robo-"robo-advisor"-advisor.

3 Theory

3.1 A Theory of Investment Simplification

A few key financial concepts such as adding and subtracting currency are taught in elementary school and are essential for life. The classic three-question financial literacy survey by Lusardi and Mitchell (2011) measures a population's rate of understanding of just slightly more advanced financial concepts, with around half of the population answering correctly depending on the country. Meanwhile, tests

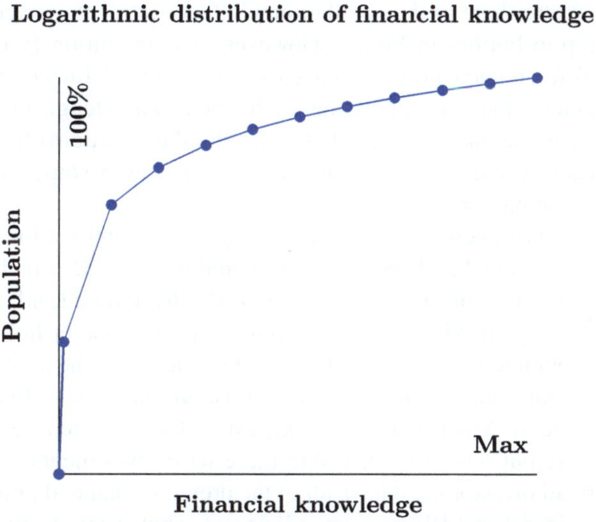

Fig. 1 Logarithmic distribution of financial knowledge

used to qualify professionals to give investment advice such as the certified financial analyst (CFA) or certified financial planner (CFP) exams are much longer and much more difficult, with very few people earning these credentials (Terry and Vibhakar 2006). A stylized fact can be extrapolated from this information: Financial knowledge has a logarithmic distribution, as described in Fig. 1, which plots the equation $log_{10}(x) + 2$ as an example.

If stock returns are inexplicably high and Treasury bill returns are inexplicably low, then one would expect that all households in an economy of rational agents would hold some equity. Indeed, this is an implication of MPT (Markowitz 1952). But this is far from the case, and this incongruity is known as the stock market participation puzzle (Mankiw and Zeldes 1991). No plausible rational explanation exists for the stock market participation puzzle (Haliassos and Bertaut 1995). Stock market participation rates in the United States have doubled since the puzzle was first identified, but the current rate of around 50% participation is still far below 100%, and many other wealthy countries have participation rates near 0% (Campbell 2006).

Because of dramatic episodes like the Great Depression and the Great Financial Crisis, it has become common knowledge that people can lose money in financial markets. A risk-averse and particularly a loss-averse individual, with an understanding of financial markets that they themselves judge to be insufficient, might then rationally choose not to participate (Kahneman and Tversky 1979). Innovations which reduce information costs have been shown both theoretically and empirically to increase stock market participation rates (Bogan 2008).

If a simplifying financial technology reduces the financial knowledge threshold for participating in financial markets (moves from right to left in Fig. 1), then a greater share of the population will feel confident enough to participate (moves from top to bottom in Fig. 1). However, as competition enters the market with slightly differentiated products based on the original financial innovation, distinguishing among these products makes financial knowledge more, not less, important. As such, the financial knowledge threshold for participating in financial markets moves back to the right and once again discourages some of the population away from participating.

One concrete example of this cycle of simplification and diversification is ETFs. The original ETF, SPY, is based on the S&P 500, which is a broad market index of U.S. large cap stocks. SPY is a highly diversified fund, and a portfolio that contains nothing but SPY is exposed to little specific risk or liquidity risk. Feeling confident enough to invest in SPY requires knowledge of the aforementioned concepts, which is more than what is tested by Lusardi and Mitchell (2011) but not exceptionally difficult. Much later, 2x-, 3x-, even 10x-leveraged version of the S&P 500 index were put on the market. Are these wise investments? To answer this question, the retail investor must have all of the previous financial knowledge necessary to choose to invest in SPY *plus* knowledge of what it means to be leveraged. A choice set of ETFs that contains nothing but variations on the S&P 500 can wind up being intimidating (Chernev et al. 2015). Such may be the case for robo-advisors today.

4 Methods

4.1 Human Financial Advisors' Attempt

The robo-"robo-advisor"-advisor already exists: *Investing in the Web* gives retail investors a questionnaire to determine which robo-advisors would be right for them. Investing in the Web also has a companion website aptly named *Robo-Advisor Finder*.[1] This tool can be used as a baseline of professional, educated, experienced human performance against which to compare LLM performance. As a form of qualitative research, I explored this tool until I exhausted it of all the advice it could give, testing different situations and noting any mistakes that it made. At the time of writing, Investing in the Web's service has at least three flaws that prevent it from working effectively: jurisdictional blindness, heterogeneity insensitivity, and incompleteness.

First, jurisdictional blindness. After filling out the survey, I was suggested four robo-advisors, none of which would accept me as an American client. Investing in the Web does not know about FATCA. Nor does it know about the regulations about Passive Foreign Investment Companies (PFIC)—investing with any of the companies suggested would likely trigger this tax penalty. I tried once again, wondering whether Investing in the Web knew about the sanctions imposed on

[1] The website for Robo-Advisor Finder can be found in here.

investment by Russian citizens and residents. Investing in the Web suggested Sarwa; Sarwa lists on its website that it does not accept Russian resident clients. Investing in the Web has a very limited understanding of jurisdiction, steering clients toward robo-advisors that do not take them as clients.

Second, heterogeneity insensitivity. Investing in the Web groups unlike robo-advisors together, and the minimum investment threshold is a clear example of this. The lowest minimum investment threshold an investor can specify with Investing in the Web is "less than 500 [of a currency, e.g. $ or]," which obscures the distinctions among robo-advisors with no minimum (e.g., Acorns, SoFi), those with a $100 minimum (e.g., Vanguard Digital Advisor, Ally Invest Robo Portfolios), or a 300 minimum (e.g., Goodvest, Mon Petit Placement). It is a mistake to paper over these thresholds. New retail investors may find it intimidating to deposit anything at all into an online investment account, especially with a FinTech that is not a household name like Bank of America or BNP Paribas.

Third, incompleteness. Investing in the Web does not show France's largest, second largest, *or* third largest robo-advisors (Yomoni, Ramify, and Nalo), and it is not clear why these would be omitted.

Investing in the Web represents humanity's attempt at responding to investors' demand to simplify robo-advisors, and it missed the mark in three ways: jurisdictional blindness, heterogeneity insensitivity, and incompleteness.

Creating a complete robo-"robo-advisor"-advisor would clearly help retail investors navigate the growing complexities of choosing a robo-advisor, but it will not be easy. Very few financial professionals master the diversity of services and the jurisdictional headaches that come with the territory of advising financial services to all the world at once. Nor is any one person, even a team of skilled professionals, likely to have the encyclopedic knowledge that keeping up-to-date records on hundreds of worldwide robo-advisors entails.

In the next section, these shortcomings will be used to create a sophisticated prompt to give to the AI LLMs. In this way, the responses of the LLMs can be compared with those of Investing in the Web's human financial advisors.

4.2 AI LLMs' Attempt

To answer whether current-gen LLMs can respond to investors' demand for the simplification of robo-advisors and competently act as a robo-"robo-advisor"-advisor, five of the most popular current-gen LLMs will be asked two prompts: one naive and one sophisticated. The naive prompt will ask the LLM to recommend a robo-advisor in the way a naive, would-be new retail investor would ask for advice. That is to say, without clearly sign-posting the pitfalls surrounding jurisdiction and heterogeneity, and completeness identified in the previous section as shortcomings to the human financial advisors' advice. Meanwhile, the sophisticated prompt will highlight these three problems, phrasing the question in a way that guides the LLM to give a fuller answer. The quality of each LLM's response will be judged by whether it gives information on or asks follow-up questions about jurisdiction, heterogeneity, and completeness. This will result in a grade of zero to three for each LLM's response, with one point awarded for each category. To be clear, an LLM getting even one point on this metric would mean that it outperformed a team of educated professionals with work experience, time, and a budget.

The five LLMs used in this experiment are the following: OpenAI's ChatGPT-4o mini, Microsoft's Copilot, Mistral's Large 2, Anthropic's Claude 3.5 Sonnet, and Google's Gemini.[2] The naive prompt is "Which robo-advisor should I use?" The sophisticated prompt is "I am an American living in France with $500 to invest. What are all the robo-advisors that I could use?" The sophisticated prompt is posed in a new chat, not as a follow-up question. Each chat was launched with a clear cache such that no personal information about the researcher could be accessed by the LLM (e.g., location, language preferences). Some LLMs have implemented memory of previous conversations; this option has been disabled for this test.

5 Results

The responses each LLM gave to the naive prompt, "Which robo-advisor should I use?", are available in Tables 1, 2, 3, 4, and 5. The responses each LLM gave to the sophisticated prompt, "I am an American living in France with $500 to invest. What are all the robo-advisors that I could use?", are available in Tables 6, 7, 8, 9, and 10. In each table, the "Response" column is the unedited, AI-generated text from each LLM, while the score and notes in the other column are my own analysis.

Accompanying each table are four summary statistics in which the LLMs' responses are judged as to whether they are complete (C), take into account the investor's legal jurisdiction (J) and minimum account balance heterogeneity (H), and contain hallucinations (errors). If the LLM provides misinformation, what about the response was incorrect is clarified.

In response to the naive prompt, no LLM gave a complete response which took into account the investor's legal jurisdiction. However, four out of five LLMs took into account the minimum account balance of different robo-advisors, and all five LLMs made no hallucinations. That said, the responses were often surface level, a depth at which LLMs tend to perform with the fewest hallucinations (Zhang et al. 2025).

[2] The test was performed on October 30th, 2024 using the most recent models available at that time.

Table 1 ChatGPT-4o mini's AI-generated response to the naive prompt

Human evaluation	Response created with ChatGPT-4o mini
of the response created with ChatGPT-4o mini J: 0 H: 1 C: 0 Total: 1/3 Errors: No	Choosing the right robo-advisor depends on your specific needs, financial goals, and preferences. Here's a breakdown of popular options, along with what each is best for: 1. Betterment Best For: Beginners, goal-based investing, tax optimization Features: Betterment offers a range of goal-based investment options, retirement planning tools, and socially responsible investing (SRI) portfolios. It includes a unique feature called Tax Loss Harvesting, which can help reduce your tax bill. Fees: 0.25% for digital, 0.4% for premium with access to financial advisors Minimum Investment: $0 for digital, $100,000 for premium 2. Wealthfront Best For: Comprehensive financial planning, tax-optimized investing, crypto exposure Features: Wealthfront offers strong tax-loss harvesting, college savings planning, and customizable portfolios. Its Path tool lets you simulate different life goals (like buying a home or early retirement). Recently, they've also added crypto exposure. Fees: 0.25% Minimum Investment: $500 3. Schwab Intelligent Portfolios Best For: No-fee options, broad investment choices Features: Schwab's robo-advisor doesn't charge a management fee, which is rare. You'll get access to a wide array of Schwab's ETFs and automatic rebalancing. They also offer a premium plan for access to CFPs and human advisors. Fees: $0, but Premium plan has a $300 one-time fee plus $30 per month Minimum Investment: $5,000 4. Fidelity Go Best For: Low fees for smaller accounts, brand reliability Features: Fidelity Go is a great option if you already have a Fidelity account. It offers solid portfolio management and tools, and has lower fees for smaller accounts. Fees: No fees under $25,000, 0.35% for $25,000 and above Minimum Investment: $0, with a $10/month minimum for funded accounts 5. Ellevest Best For: Women, socially responsible investing (SRI) Features: Designed with women in mind, Ellevest focuses on creating financial plans that consider unique life factors such as gender pay gap and career breaks. It offers SRI portfolios and personalized financial planning. Fees: $1, $5, or $9 monthly subscription depending on the tier Minimum Investment: $0 for managed accounts 6. Vanguard Digital Advisor Best For: Vanguard loyalists, long-term retirement savers Features: Vanguard's robo-advisor primarily uses its own low-cost funds and focuses on long-term retirement planning. If you're already familiar with Vanguard's funds, this is an affordable option. Fees: 0.15% in addition to fund expenses Minimum Investment: $3,000 7. SoFi Automated Investing Best For: Free management, SoFi ecosystem users Features: SoFi's robo-advisor is free, and offers perks like financial planning sessions with advisors. It's best if you also use SoFi for other financial products, as the ecosystem integration can simplify your finances. Fees: $0 management fee Minimum Investment: $1 Tips to Choose: Low Fees: Schwab Intelligent Portfolios and SoFi Automated Investing are great options for low or no fees. Human Advisors Access: Betterment, Schwab, and Fidelity Go's higher tiers offer human advisors. Tax Efficiency: Betterment and Wealthfront have robust tax strategies, like Tax-Loss Harvesting. Socially Responsible Investing (SRI): Ellevest and Betterment are popular for socially conscious investing. If your main goal is a hands-off investment approach with low fees, SoFi or Wealthfront could be ideal, while Betterment and Ellevest might be more attractive if you're seeking goal-specific, socially responsible options.

Table 2 Copilot's AI-generated response to the naive prompt

Human evaluation	Response created with Copilot
of the response created with Copilot J: 0 H: 0 C: 0 Total: 0/3 Errors: No	Depends on what you're looking for. Betterment and Wealthfront are popular choices for their low fees and user-friendly platforms. Ellevest is great if you're into investing with a focus on women. Do you have any particular investment goals in mind?

Table 3 Mistral Large 2's AI-generated response to the naive prompt

Human evaluation	Response created with Mistral Large 2
of the response created with Mistral Large 2 J: 0 H: 1 C: 0 Total: 1/3 Errors: No	Choosing a robo-advisor depends on your personal financial goals, investment style, and specific needs. Here are some popular robo-advisors and their key features to help you make an informed decision: Wealthfront: Ideal for: Investors looking for a comprehensive, hands-off approach. Key features: Tax-loss harvesting, automatic rebalancing, high-yield savings account, and portfolio line of credit. Minimum investment: $500 Fees: 0.25% annual advisory fee Betterment: Ideal for: Investors seeking goal-based investing and access to human advisors. Key features: Tax-loss harvesting, automatic rebalancing, goal-based investing, and access to human advisors with premium plans. Minimum investment: No minimum for digital plan, $100,000 for premium plan Fees: 0.25% annual fee for digital plan, 0.40% for premium plan Vanguard Digital Advisor: Ideal for: Investors who prefer low-cost, diversified portfolios from a well-established company. Key features: Low expense ratios, diverse investment options, and human advisor support for higher account balances. Minimum investment: $3,000 Fees: Approximately 0.15% annual fee (including both advisory fee and average fund expense ratio) Schwab Intelligent Portfolios: Ideal for: Investors looking for a low-cost, diversified portfolio with a cash buffer. Key features: Automatic rebalancing, tax-loss harvesting, and a cash allocation feature. Minimum investment: $5,000 Fees: No advisory fee, but there are underlying fund fees (average around 0.08%) M1 Finance: Ideal for: Investors seeking a customizable, automated investing experience. Key features: Customizable portfolios, automatic rebalancing, and fractional shares. Minimum investment: $100 for taxable accounts, $500 for retirement accounts Fees: No management fees, but there are underlying fund fees Before making a decision, consider factors such as fees, minimum investment requirements, account types, and additional features that align with your financial goals. It's also a good idea to research and compare other robo-advisors not mentioned here, as new platforms and features continuously emerge.

Table 4 Claude 3.5 Sonnet's AI-generated response to the naive prompt

Human evaluation	Response created with Claude 3.5 Sonnet
of the response created with Claude 3.5 Sonnet J: 0 H: 1 C: 0 Total: 1/3 Errors: No	I aim to help you think through this decision while noting that financial choices are personal and should account for your specific situation. Here are some key factors to consider when choosing a robo-advisor: Major considerations: Minimum investment requirements Management fees (typically 0.25-0.50% annually) Investment options and strategies offered Tax-loss harvesting availability Access to human advisors if needed User interface and ease of use Account types supported (IRA, taxable, etc.) Some popular options to research: Vanguard Digital Advisor: Known for very low fees (0.20%) and access to Vanguard's low-cost funds Betterment: Pioneer in the space with solid tax optimization and multiple portfolio options Wealthfront: Strong tax-loss harvesting and planning tools Schwab Intelligent Portfolios: No management fees but requires higher cash allocation Fidelity Go: Competitive fees and backed by major institution I'd encourage you to: Check minimum investments/fees for each Compare their investment approaches Read recent reviews and user experiences Consider whether you want access to human advisors Would you like me to elaborate on any specific aspect of these robo-advisors?

Table 5 Gemini's AI-generated response to the naive prompt

Human evaluation	Response created with Gemini
of the response created with Gemini J: 0 H: 1 C: 0 Total: 1/3 Errors: No	The best robo-advisor for you will depend on your individual needs and preferences. Some factors to consider include: * **Fees:** Robo-advisors typically charge a small percentage of your assets under management (AUM) as a fee. Some robo-advisors have lower fees than others, so it's important to compare fees before choosing a provider. * **Investment options:** Some robo-advisors offer a wider range of investment options than others. If you have specific investment goals or preferences, you may want to choose a robo-advisor that offers a wider range of investment options. * **Account minimums:** Some robo-advisors have higher account minimums than others. If you don't have a lot of money to invest, you may want to choose a robo-advisor with a lower account minimum. * **Human advisor access:** Some robo-advisors offer the option to speak with a human advisor for an additional fee. This can be helpful if you have complex financial needs or want personalized advice. * **Features:** Some robo-advisors offer additional features, such as tax-loss harvesting, goal-based investing, and financial planning tools. These features can be helpful if you want to get the most out of your investment experience. Here are some of the top-rated robo-advisors: * **Betterment:** Betterment is a popular robo-advisor with low fees, a wide range of investment options, and access to human advisors. [Image of Betterment robo-advisor] * **Wealthfront:** Wealthfront is another popular robo-advisor with low fees, a wide range of investment options, and a focus on tax-loss harvesting. [Image of Wealthfront robo-advisor] * **Vanguard Digital Advisor:** Vanguard Digital Advisor is a robo-advisor offered by Vanguard, a well-known investment firm. Vanguard Digital Advisor has low fees and a wide range of investment options. [Image of Vanguard Digital Advisor robo-advisor] * **Charles Schwab Intelligent Portfolios:** Charles Schwab Intelligent Portfolios is a robo-advisor offered by Charles Schwab, another well-known investment firm. Charles Schwab Intelligent Portfolios has low fees and a wide range of investment options. [Image of Charles Schwab Intelligent Portfolios robo-advisor] Ultimately, the best way to choose a robo-advisor is to do your research and compare different providers. You should also consider your own financial goals and risk tolerance when making your decision.

Table 6 ChatGPT-4o mini's AI-generated response to the sophisticated prompt

Human evaluation	Response created with ChatGPT-4o mini
of the response created with ChatGPT-4o mini J: 1 H: 1 C: 0 Total: 2/3 Errors: Yes. Fidelity Go, Betterment, and XTB do not accept US expat clients. N26 does not have a robo-advisor.	As an American living in France with $500 to invest, you have several robo-advisor options that cater to international clients, including expatriates. Some of the most accessible robo-advisors in your range include: Fidelity Go – Fidelity Go is accessible to Americans abroad and has no minimum balance, though it requires $10 to begin investing. With a management fee of 0.35% on larger balances (free for accounts under $25,000), it's a cost-effective choice if you're starting with a smaller amount. It is well-regarded for integration with Fidelity accounts, but it doesn't provide tax-loss harvesting. Betterment – Betterment offers a global reach and is particularly useful for U.S. expatriates, requiring no minimum balance for its basic digital account. It charges a 0.25% management fee, provides automatic rebalancing, and optimizes for tax efficiency, which can be beneficial depending on your tax situation. XTB Investment Plans – For those based in Europe, XTB offers a cost-effective way to invest in ETFs, with no management fees. However, you will manage the portfolio selection yourself, making it a good low-cost, customizable option, especially for ETF investors. Schwab Intelligent Portfolios – Schwab's robo-advisor is accessible to U.S. expats, requires no advisory fees, and offers automatic rebalancing and tax-loss harvesting. A minimum of $5,000 is generally needed, which may be a higher hurdle, but its low-cost model is an advantage if you can invest more in the future. N26 Invest – Tailored to European residents, N26 Invest offers investment plans with automatic management through the N26 mobile bank platform. The minimum investment is around €50, making it accessible if you're primarily operating in euros. While many U.S.-based robo-advisors have low minimums, not all are available internationally, so it's worth checking residency restrictions before opening an account. Platforms like Betterment, Fidelity, and Schwab are especially reliable for expats given their broad acceptance of U.S. citizens abroad.

Table 7 Copilot's AI-generated response to the sophisticated prompt

Human evaluation	Response created with Copilot
of the response created with Copilot J: 0 H: 0 C: 0 Total: 0/3 Errors: Yes. No suggestion accepts US expats. Indexa Capital's account minimum is €2,000. Yomoni does not offer real estate investments.	There are several robo-advisors available in France that you can consider for investing your $500. Here are some of the top options: Yomoni: Known for its user-friendly interface and personalized portfolios. It offers various investment strategies, including ETFs and real estate investments. Nalo: Focuses on creating personalized portfolios tailored to your specific investment goals. eToro: Offers smart portfolios and is popular for its social trading features. XTB Investment Plans: Ideal for DIY investors looking for low fees and long-term investment options. Indexa Capital: Known for its low fees and straightforward investment approach. Birdee: Focuses on responsible investing, aligning portfolios with ESG (Environmental, Social, and Governance) criteria. Each of these robo-advisors has its own unique features and benefits, so it's a good idea to explore them further to see which one aligns best with your investment goals and preferences. Do you have any specific investment goals or preferences that you'd like to share? That might help narrow down the options even more!

Table 8 Mistral Large 2's AI-generated response to the sophisticated prompt

Human evaluation	Response created with Mistral Large 2
of the response created with Mistral Large 2 J: 1 H: 1 C: 0 Total: 2/3 Yes. Betterment, Wealthfront, and Yomoni do not accept US expats. Vanguard's account minimum is $100.	As an American living in France, you have several robo-advisor options to consider for investing your $500. However, it's essential to ensure that the platforms you choose are available to U.S. citizens living abroad and comply with both U.S. and French regulations. Here are some robo-advisors you might consider: Vanguard Digital Advisor: Vanguard is a well-established investment company that offers a robo-advisor service. They require a minimum investment of $3,000, which is higher than your current investment amount, but it's an option to keep in mind for the future. Wealthfront: Wealthfront is a popular U.S.-based robo-advisor with a minimum investment of $500. They offer diversified portfolios and various account types. However, you should confirm that they accept U.S. citizens living in France. Betterment: Betterment is another well-known U.S. robo-advisor with no minimum investment requirement. They offer diversified portfolios, tax-loss harvesting, and other features. Like Wealthfront, you should verify that they accept clients in your situation. Schwab Intelligent Portfolios: Charles Schwab offers a robo-advisor service with a minimum investment of $5,000. They provide diversified portfolios and automatic rebalancing. Schwab is known for being expat-friendly, but you should still confirm that their robo-advisor service is available to you. Interactive Advisors: This service is offered by Interactive Brokers, which is known for being expat-friendly. They have a minimum investment of $100 and offer diversified portfolios, automatic rebalancing, and tax-loss harvesting. Yomoni: Yomoni is a French robo-advisor that offers diversified portfolios and is tailored to the French market. As a U.S. citizen living in France, you should confirm that you can open an account with them. Before choosing a robo-advisor, make sure to consider factors such as fees, investment strategies, and account types. Additionally, it's crucial to verify that the platform you choose is available to U.S. citizens living in France and complies with relevant regulations. Consulting with a financial advisor or tax professional familiar with both U.S. and French regulations can help ensure you make an informed decision.

Table 9 Claude 3.5 Sonnet's AI-generated response to the sophisticated prompt

Human evaluation	Response created with Claude 3.5 Sonnet
of the response created with Claude 3.5 Sonnet J: 1 H: 1 C: 1 Total: 3/3 Errors: No	Since you're an American living in France, your investment options are more limited due to regulations around serving US persons abroad. Let me suggest some available options while noting that my knowledge cutoff means you should verify current availability: Schwab Intelligent Portfolios Available to US citizens abroad No management fees Minimum investment: $5,000 (unfortunately above your current amount) Interactive Advisors Accepts US citizens living abroad Management fees: 0.08-1.5% Lower minimum investments available SoFi Automated Investing May work for US citizens abroad No management fees Minimum investment: $1 However, I recommend you: Double-check current availability to US citizens in France with each provider Consider traditional brokerages like Schwab or Interactive Brokers that definitely serve Americans abroad Consult with a tax professional about implications of investing while living in France Your $500 budget would work with some of these options, though having additional savings for emergencies before investing would be ideal. Would you like me to explain more about any particular option?

Table 10 Gemini's AI-generated response to the sophisticated prompt

Human evaluation	Response created with Gemini
of the response created with Gemini J: 1 H: 1 C: 0 Total: 2/3 Errors: Yes. Betterment and Wealthfront do not accept US expats; Indexa Capital, Yomoni, and Nalo do not accept US citizens or residents.	As a US citizen living in France, you'll likely have more options for robo-advisors than those explicitly marketed in France. Here are some to consider: Robo-advisors with global reach: Betterment: Known for its low fees and tax-loss harvesting. Wealthfront: Offers tax-loss harvesting and financial planning tools. Charles Schwab: Provides a robo-advisor service with access to a broader range of investment options. Robo-advisors with French presence: Indexa Capital: Specifically caters to French investors, offering low fees and a focus on index funds. Yomoni: Another French robo-advisor with a good reputation and competitive fees. Nalo: Offers personalized portfolios and a user-friendly platform. Important Considerations: Tax Implications: Be aware of the tax implications of investing as a US citizen living abroad. Consult with a tax advisor to understand your specific situation. Currency Exchange: Consider the costs associated with currency exchange when investing in foreign markets. Regulatory Differences: Ensure that the robo-advisor you choose is compliant with both US and French regulations. Customer Support: Check if the robo-advisor offers customer support in English or French. Additional Tips: Research: Before investing, do thorough research on each robo-advisor, considering factors like fees, investment options, and customer service. Diversification: Diversify your investments across different asset classes and geographies to manage risk. Long-term Perspective: Adopt a long-term investment horizon and avoid making impulsive decisions based on short-term market fluctuations. Remember, this is not financial advice. It's always recommended to consult with a qualified financial advisor to make informed investment decisions tailored to your specific needs and circumstances.

In response to the sophisticated prompt, the response of Anthropic's Claude satisfied all three conditions and without hallucinations, the only LLM to do so. At this more challenging depth, all four other LLMs failed to meet all three conditions and produced misinformation with respect to the legal jurisdiction of the client. Microsoft's Copilot failed to meet any condition with either prompt *and* produced misinformation in the sophisticated prompt. Though, to be fair, this is to say that Copilot performed at the same level as the human financial advisors.

6 Discussion

The human financial advisors' shortcomings were used as a basis to create a task against which five of the most popular free LLMs could compete. Because there are no upfront or switching costs among the LLMs, all that matters is that at least one of the LLMs is able to solve the task. Only one LLM failed in all of the same ways that the human financial advisors failed: Microsoft's Copilot. Three of the five LLMs beat the human financial advisors in at least one dimension: OpenAI's ChatGPT-4o mini, Mistral's Large 2, and Google's Gemini. And one LLM, Anthropic's Claude 3.5 Sonnet, solved the task without mistakes when given a sophisticated prompt. This is surprising. Until recently, this was thought to have been impossible. One LLM performed as well as humans, and four performed better, with one performing perfectly.

The naive prompt did not provoke the LLMs to spontaneously give a complete list of robo-advisor options or advice concerning an investor's legal jurisdiction, though four out of five mentioned that robo-advisors have heterogeneous minimum account balances. Though the advice varied in length and complexity, only Microsoft's Copilot responded to the naive prompt with a request for more information. And the specific request Copilot made, about the investor's goal, is important to giving good advice but hardly narrows down the list of options.

When given the sophisticated prompt, Anthropic's Claude provided a complete list of robo-advisors that cater to a client in a complicated jurisdictional situation (US citizen non-resident), with appropriate caveats about minimum account balance heterogeneity, and without any hallucinations. Compared to the other LLMs, which all delivered hallucinations and which all failed in at least one of the three categories, Claude's performance is surprising. However, Claude's response to the naive prompt only tackles minimum account balance heterogeneity; it does not lead a new retail investor to consider questions about jurisdiction or to ask for a complete list of options. Therefore, while Claude performed the best in the hands of a sophisticated user, a new retail investor may still struggle to use Claude to find the right robo-advisor for them.

To give good advice, a robo-"robo-advisor"-advisor must ask more questions. To reduce the hundreds of robo-advisors to a manageable list, the best questions to ask would be those that eliminate many robo-advisors from consideration in as few questions as possible. Two important questions include the client's legal jurisdiction and minimum account balance. The only human-led robo-"robo-advisor"-advisor effort, Investing in the Web's Robo-Advisor Finder, poses these two questions, though the advice the client receives is often inaccurate. Meanwhile, AI LLMs do not systematically ask these two questions or give advice such that these questions need not be asked. Furthermore, even if a sophisticated user brings up these two questions independently, most LLMs responded with hallucinations.

Anthropic's Claude stands out as an exception, giving decent advice without error when given a sophisticated prompt, resulting in a complete list of robo-advisor options for the user. Claude's acceptable performance as a robo-"robo-advisor"-advisor shows that simplifying robo-advisors further still is not the future, it is the now. AI can do it.

Though the abject failure of Microsoft's Copilot, which did not meet any objective in either test and still produced misinformation on top of that, offers a sober warning to anyone trusting the output of an LLM out of hand. To an inexperienced judge, the outputs of Claude and of Copilot are indistinguishable. AI can do it—but how can one know?

In addition, new retail investors must also be informed of the availability of financial instruments such as ETFs or REITs or financial technologies such as automatic rebalancing and tax-loss harvesting, and they must be given explanations as to what all of these concepts mean for them. In this respect, neither the non-AI nor AI options to date fully fill the void of a human financial advisor or a robo-advisor's website and sign-up questionnaire. AI LLMs are not currently prepared to spontaneously teach new retail investors what they really need to know before opening an investment account.

7 Conclusion

For over 100 years, investors have demanded financial services be both simple and diverse. The result of these two conflicting demands is a cycle of simplifying financial innovation followed by complexifying competition. As the global middle class continues to grow (Chatterjee 2020) and stock market participation continues to rise (Bogan 2008), new investors with less capital and financial literacy enter the arena of investment. Inheriting the lineage from mutual funds to index funds to ETFs, robo-advisors are the most recent link in the chain of financial technology simplifying scientific diversification—but surely not the last. Now that there are hundreds of robo-advisors competing in different legal jurisdictions and with many complicated services, a new need has arisen to simplify the search for robo-advisors. For the moment, this is a rather specific niche. If this advice is to exist at scale, a machine would have to give it. While a traditional database of robo-advisors may suffice, this need for another layer of simplification happens to coincide with the popularization of AI. Can AI LLMs be the robo-"robo-advisor" advisor? Can AI meet the need? This paper shows that at least one LLM can. And since there are no upfront or switching costs for using this LLM, "at least one" is enough.

All this indicates that the new role of robo-"robo-advisor"-advisor might be best filled by a "boutique" AI LLM trained specifically to give financial advice. Current-gen AI LLMs that new retail investors are likely to use are all general purpose. But from the consumer's perspective, all that may be necessary to solve the question of AI trustworthiness is a strong signal of its domain-specific competence (Lo and Ross 2024). Examples of these such "boutique" AIs have been popping up all over industry, from traditional finance behemoths such as Moody's Research Assistant to small FinTech startups such as Odonatech's LiLa. One or another may one day become the reference.

Acemoglu and Restrepo (2018) indicate three broad effects of technology: reinstatement (creating jobs), productivity, and displacement (removing jobs). In this chapter, the effect of AI was to displace the team behind Investing in the Web's Robo-Advisor Finder. Though it may make robo-advisors more productive as LLMs funnel investors into more appropriate wealth managers. And as a positive externality, financial markets would become incrementally more productive due to increased liquidity. To say nothing of the marginal investor who uses an LLM to start investing.

In living memory, robo-advisors shook up the financial advice industry, stoking fears among financial advisors that algorithms would put them all out of work. Somewhere in cyberspace, AI has given a robo-advisor a chill down its spine.

Funding Statement The Elinor Ostrom Research Unit is a multidisciplinary research laboratory associated with the moOngy group. All views expressed are my own and not necessarily reflections of the moOngy group or of its clientele. The moOngy group and its clientele exercise no editorial control over the research process, including but not limited to the conceptualization, design, data collection, analysis, decision to publish, or preparation of the manuscript. This research received no specific grant from any public, private, or non-profit funding agency.

References

Acemoglu D, Restrepo P (2018) The race between man and machine: implications of technology for growth, factor shares, and employment. Am Econ Rev 108(6):1488–1542

Aghion P, Howitt P (1990) A model of growth through creative destruction. Econometrica 60(2):323–351

Al-Ubaydli O, List JA, Suskind D (2019). The science of using science: towards an understanding of the threats to scaling experiments. Technical report, National Bureau of Economic Research, Cambridge

Ando A, Modigliani F (1963) The "life cycle" hypothesis of saving: aggregate implications and tests. Am Econ Rev 53(1):55–84

Barber BM, Odean T (2000) Trading is hazardous to your wealth: the common stock investment performance of individual investors. J Financ 55(2):773–806

Barber BM, Odean T (2001) Boys will be boys: gender, overconfidence, and common stock investment. Q J Econ 116(1):261–292

Benartzi S (2001) Excessive extrapolation and the allocation of 401 (k) accounts to company stock. J Financ 56(5):1747–1764

Benartzi S, Thaler RH (2001) Naive diversification strategies in defined contribution saving plans. Am Econ Rev 91(1):79–98

Bogan V (2008) Stock market participation and the internet. J Financ Quant Anal 43(1):191–211

Bogle JC (1999) Common sense on mutual funds: new imperatives for the intelligent investor. Wiley, New York

Broadbent J, Palumbo M, Woodman E (2006) The shift from defined benefit to defined contribution pension plans–implications for asset allocation and risk management. In: Reserve Bank of Australia, Board of Governors of the Federal Reserve System and Bank of Canada, vol 1, p 54

Campbell JY (2006) Household finance. J Financ 61(4):1553–1604

Carhart MM (1997) On persistence in mutual fund performance. J Financ 52(1):57–82

Chalmers J, Reuter J (2020) Is conflicted investment advice better than no advice? J Financ Econ 138(2):366–387

Chatterjee A (2020) Financial inclusion, information and communication technology diffusion, and economic growth: a panel data analysis. Inf Technol Dev 26(3):607–635

Chernev A, Böckenholt U, Goodman J (2015) Choice overload: a conceptual review and meta-analysis. J Consum Psychol 25(2):333–358

Choi JJ (2022) Popular personal financial advice versus the professors. J Econ Perspect 36(4):167–192

Fama EF (1970) Efficient capital markets. J Financ 25(2):383–417

Fama EF, French KR (1992) The cross-section of expected stock returns. J Financ 47(2):427–465

Fama EF, French KR (2015) A five-factor asset pricing model. J Financ Econ 116(1):1–22

Farina RH, Freeman JP, Webster J (1969) Mutual fund industry: a legal survey. Notre Dame Law Review 44(5):732

Fisch JE, Laboure M, Turner JA (2019) The emergence of the robo-advisor. The Disruptive Impact of FinTech on Retire Syst 13:13–37

Foerster S, Linnainmaa JT, Melzer BT, Previtero A (2017). Retail financial advice: does one size fit all? J Financ 72(4):1441–1482

French KR, Poterba J (1991) Investor diversification and international equity markets. Natl Bur Econ Res 81(2):222–226

Gomes F, Haliassos M, Ramadorai T (2021) Household finance. J Econ Lit 59(3):919–1000

Hackethal A, Haliassos M, Jappelli T (2012) Financial advisors: a case of babysitters? J Bank Financ 36(2):509–524

Haliassos M, Bertaut CC (1995) Why do so few hold stocks? Econ J 105(432):1110–1129

Jung D, Glaser F, Köpplin W (2019) Robo-advisory: opportunities and risks for the future of financial advisory. In: Advances in Consulting Research: Recent Findings and Practical Cases, pp 405–427

Kahneman D, Tversky A (1979) Prospect theory: an analysis of decision under risk. Econometrica, 47(2):263–291

Kochhar R (2015) A global middle class is more promise than reality: from 2001 to 2011, nearly 700 million step out of poverty, but most only barely. In: The Middle Class in World Society. Pew Research Center, Washington DC

Linnainmaa JT, Melzer BT, Previtero A (2021) The misguided beliefs of financial advisors. J Financ 76(2):587–621

List JA (2022) The Voltage Effect: How to Make Good Ideas Great and Great Ideas Scale. Crown Currency, New York

Lo AW, Ross J (2024) Can chatgpt plan your retirement? Generative AI and financial advice. Harvard Data Sci Rev (Special Issue 5). https://doi.org/10.1162/99608f92.ec74a002

Loos B, Previtero A, Scheurle S, Hackethal A (2020) Robo-advisers and investor behavior. Technical report

Lusardi A, Mitchell OS (2011) Financial literacy around the world: an overview. J Pension Econ Financ 10(4):497–508

Mankiw NG, Zeldes SP (1991) The consumption of stockholders and nonstockholders. J Financ Econ 29(1):97–112

Markowitz H (1952) The utility of wealth. J Polit Econ 60(2):151–158

Mesbah N, Tauchert C, Olt CM, Buxmann P (2019) Promoting trust in AI-based expert systems

Mullainathan S, Noeth M, Schoar A (2012) The market for financial advice: An audit study. Technical report, National Bureau of Economic Research, Cambridge

Philippon T (2019) On fintech and financial inclusion. Technical report, National Bureau of Economic Research, Cambridge

Ramsey D (2013) The total money makeover: a proven plan for financial fitness. Nelson Books, Nashville

Reher M, Sokolinski S (2019). Democratizing financial advice

Sharpe WF (1964) Capital asset prices: a theory of market equilibrium under conditions of risk. J Financ 19(3):425–442

Sharpe WF (1966) Mutual fund performance. J Bus 39(1):119–138

Simon HA (1955) A behavioral model of rational choice. Q J Econ, 69(1):99–118

Terry A, Vibhakar A (2006) A comparative analysis of the CFA and CFP designations. Adv Financ Edu 4(Fall):66–81

Wexler MN, Oberlander J (2021) Robo-advisors (RAs): the programmed self-service market for professional advice. J Serv Theory Pract 31(3):351–365

Zhang L, Pentina I, Fan Y (2021) Who do you choose? comparing perceptions of human vs robo-advisor in the context of financial services. J Serv Mark 35(5):634–646

Zhang Y, Li Y, Cui L, Cai D, Liu L, Fu T, Huang X, Zhao E, Zhang Y, Chen Y, et al. (2025) Siren's song in the AI ocean: A survey on hallucination in large language models. Comput Linguist, 51(4):1373–1418

Part III
Regulation, Compliance, and Risk Management

Identifying and Ranking the Eight Risks of AI for Each of the Six Main AI-Focused Fintech Business Models

Alex Zarifis and Xusen Cheng

Abstract This research explores the implications for risk of six AI-focused Fintech business models identified in the previous research. While each of the six business models has been validated in previous research, their typical influence on risk has not been sufficiently explored.

A Delphi method with two stages is used. In the first stage, the semi-structured interviews with experts identify the main risks each of the six models faces. For the second stage the participants are presented with a summary of all the risks identified by all the participants, and they are asked to rank them for their specific model.

Eight risks related to the application of an AI-focused business model are identified: (1) direct AI risks, (2) technology integration risk, (3) third-party vendor risk, (4) technology infrastructure risk, (5) data protection and privacy risk, (6) cybersecurity risk, (7) fraud and identity theft risk, and (8) strategic misalignment risk. The eight risks apply to all six models; however, they are not equally significant in all models.

The six business models reduce risk in two main ways: Firstly, because they are proven models and secondly because they have a proven place in the typical ecosystems that emerge.

Keywords Fintech · Business model · Risk · Finance · Insurance · AI · Digital transformation

---

A. Zarifis (✉)
Southampton Business School, University of Southampton, Southampton, UK

Cambridge Centre for Alternative Finance, Cambridge, UK
e-mail: a.zarifis@soton.ac.uk

X. Cheng
Renmin University of China, Beijing, China
e-mail: xusen.cheng@ruc.edu.cn

N. Nahidi, A. Zarifis (eds.), *AI, FinTech, and the Future of Robo-Advisory*, Contributions to Finance and Accounting,
https://doi.org/10.1007/978-3-032-18109-1_7

1 Introduction

AI in robo-advisors and elsewhere in financial institutions bring risks that must be addressed at the business model level. Fintech has reduced risks and crime in the physical world, but increased technology-related risks such as cybercrime (Jain et al. 2023). Financial institutions are not only faced with technology that is changing rapidly but rapid change across the environment they operate in. The rate of change and the fact that it often has far-reaching implications means that financial institutions need to adapt their business model far more regularly than in the recent past (Jorzik et al. 2024). Business model innovation needs an understanding of the process of changing a business model, and what business models typically work (Tucci 2022). Failure to innovate in the best way can cause long-term damage and make future attempts harder (Välikangas et al. 2009). With these fundamental changes to technology and the broader environment financial institutions need to identify a new business model that addresses the many challenges while not increasing risk. The risk still comes from all the usual sources but the lack of a shared vision at many levels is increasing risk. This lack of a shared vision is partly due to competing visions, but it is also due to a lack of clarity on what an organization's business model should be in five years' time and what the sectors of the economy they are engaged in will look like in five years' time. Therefore, having clarity on the business model not only helps internally in implementing the operations but also externally in creating a shared vision. The implications for risk of the Fintech business model chosen must be merged into the vision. If a shared vision is not possible at least it helps the stakeholders understand the organization's future model and adapt.

When the pace of change was slower most financial institutions gradually evolved, with more dramatic changes to the business model such as pivots to something new much rarer. The primary consideration was to continue to utilize the skills and capabilities within the organization. With the technologies today, especially AI with its near-infinite scalability, the main driver behind the choice of business model is no longer what the existing skills and capabilities are. The key driver behind a business model now is to identify the best business model for the current environment irrespective of what the current capabilities are. The most obvious example is from outside finance, but it illustrates this point clearly: Elon Musk bought Twitter and changed its business model from the first week. He was not motivated by what the current strengths of Twitter were, such as moderating discussions, but he was primarily motivated by what the best business model would be for today. Whether Elon Must is right or wrong time will tell but the decisive redesign of the business model is necessary in the fast-changing world. Organizations must be prepared for a purposeful leap to a new model, not just a gradual evolution.

The slower and less far-reaching change in the past meant there was more time to understand the risks directly and indirectly affecting an organization. The role of technology was smaller and more predictable than AI. Now, due to the need for more regular strategic adjustments, there is a need to have a broader understanding of risk and understand how changes to the business model can affect it. Both AI and the broader environment can be very unpredictable. While the capabilities of AI are irrefutable, there is a trade-off between more predictable and transparent AI and unleashing AI's full capabilities but losing some control, predictability, and transparency. In terms of the broader environment, after a period where countries had a degree of buy-in to some kind of shared vision of globalization there seems to be far less agreement on a shared vision. The importance of risk is multifaceted as understanding it better can support other key decisions relating to sustainability of the organization and building trust.

This research explores the implications for risk of six AI-focused financial business models identified in previous research (Zarifis and Cheng 2024). These business models reduce risk firstly because they have been repeatedly proven to be effective and secondly because they have a proven place in the typical ecosystems that emerge. Therefore, the research questions are:

How do the six prominent AI-focused financial business models influence risk?

What are the most important risks for each of the six prominent AI-focused financial business models?

The six AI-focused finance business models as identified by previous research are (1) disaggregate, concentrate on a reduced number of financial services and a smaller part of the value chain, (2) keep business model unchanged and absorb AI into existing processes, (3) incumbent in finance expanding beyond their current model, (4) dedicated finance disruptor, typically a startup, (5) tech company offering financial services, and (6) disruptor not focused on technology with large user-base offering new financial services (Zarifis 2025). The first three models involve organizations that have been offering financial services for many years. The last three involve organizations that did not offer financial services in the past but are utilizing the capabilities of AI to start offering them.

Eight risks related to the application of an AI-focused business model are identified. These are (1) direct AI risks, (2) technology integration risk, (3) third-party vendor risk, (4) technology infrastructure risk, (5) data protection and privacy risk, (6) cybersecurity risk, (7) fraud and identity theft risk, and (8) strategic misalignment risk. The second stage of the data collection asked participants to rank the eight risks for their specific business model. The eight risks apply to all six models; however, their significance is different for each model.

This research finds that the six business models do indeed offer clarity and reduce several risks. Clarity on the business model reduces risk. While the Fintech business models do not necessarily increase risk and may indeed reduce it, because of the change in the nature of the risk involved, trust needs to be built with all the stakeholders.

The next section is the theoretical foundation that covers three main areas. This is followed by the methodology section that explains how the qualitative Delphi method with two stages is implemented. This is followed by the findings, the discussion and conclusion and finally the limitations and suggestions for future research.

2 Theoretical Framework

This research is guided by two broad areas of literature, digital transformation and business model innovation, and the traditional and emerging risks in Finance and Fintech. Based on this literature, an existing framework with the six AI focused Fintech business models is adopted and further developed.

2.1 Digital Transformation and Business Model Innovation

Digital transformation does not always necessitate business model innovation but as the scale of disruption in finance is very high, transformation and business model innovation are increasingly coming together (Liu et al. 2025). The organization offering financial services must understand the implications of the transformation and model innovation so that they can implement the changes to their organization but also, so they fully understand what their existing, and emerging competitors are doing.

Digital transformation in finance is indeed driven by AI (Jorzik et al. 2024), but more fundamentally it is driven by the sharing and processing of information which is happening at a larger scale than before (Wu and Pambudi 2025).

While some argue that if one element of a business model is changing this can be considered as business model innovation, this term is usually reserved for significant changes that go beyond a gradual evolution (Tucci 2022). Companies offering financial services for the first time, and existing insurers automating services and calculating risk in a different way, certainly qualify as business model innovation. Many of the typical building blocks of a model are being transformed. The typical examples of business model building blocks are (1) value propositions, (2) customer relationships, (3) customer segments, (4) channels, (5) cost structure, (6) revenue streams, (7) key partnerships, (8) key activities, (9) key resources (Osterwalder and Pigneur 2010).

2.2 The Traditional and Emerging Risks in Finance and Fintech

There is a broad variety of risks that can impact a Fintech from those very closely monitored such as the various financial risks to the less closely monitored risks such as pandemics, often referred to as black swan events. While the wide variety of risks should not be ignored, when looking at the effect of Fintech business models on risk, the risks more closely related to the choice of business model and the process of implementing that business model should be prioritized. These are risks that have been either reduced or increased by the choice of business model. Framing the most closely related risks in this way means focusing on the Fintech business model risks. This is covered mostly in literature on Fintech, risk and business model risk (Brillinger et al. 2020; Dellermann et al. 2017).

There is evidence that not going through the digital transformation causes risks related to operating in an outdated inefficient way. While business model innovation traditionally benefitted from a high tolerance to risk in this disruptive period, the risks of not acting may even be larger. At the same time, the increased use of Fintech has been found to increase risk taking by an organization (Tang et al. 2024).

Literature on Fintech risk identifies five types of closely related risks (Tyagi 2024). These are technology, operational, compliance, strategic, and reputational risks. These five topics capture the key risks for a Fintech that is heavily reliant on AI. Beyond research publications these are hot topics practitioners, and the industry press often cover them.

The business model innovation in finance is primarily driven by trying to fully utilize AI. Therefore, the new business model also brings with it a new relationship with AI with all the benefits and new risks this involves. Given the increasing volume of personal data processed, the increased ability to draw insight and the increased ability to act on that insight there are increased privacy concerns and risks for trust (Canhoto et al. 2023).

2.3 The Six AI-Focused Fintech Business Models and Nine Building Blocks

In finance, it could be argued that all organizations in this area will meet the criteria of a Fintech soon as the dependence on AI is constantly increasing and financial technology is changing business models (Elia et al. 2023). While this may be true, there is still a useful distinction to be made between a more traditional financial organization with many offices, branches and many staff, and a leaner Fintech with less offices and staff and a higher dependence on technology. Fintechs are also typically created from the start with a business model designed to make the most out of a recent technology.

Business models are defined in a variety of ways (Tucci 2022). This lack of consensus is not necessarily a bad thing as some definitions of business models are more useful in some situations and others in other situations. Even within an organization there might be disagreement on what the business model is. While the many different approaches should be welcomed, it must be made clear which approach is being taken and why.

So that this research can evaluate the influence of a business model on risk in Fintech the prevailing business models need to be identified first. This research adopts six business models of Fintechs identified in previous research so that the implications of the business model to risk can be explored. This list has been updated recently so it should be representative of most organizations in this area.

The six Fintech business models are (1) disaggregate, concentrate on a reduced number of financial services and a smaller part of the value chain, (2) keep business model unchanged and absorb AI into existing processes, (3) incumbent in finance expanding beyond their current model, (4) dedicated finance disruptor, typically a startup, (5) tech company offering financial services, (6) disruptor not focused on technology with large user-base offering new financial services (Zarifis 2025; Zarifis and Cheng 2024).

The first three models include organizations that are already active in the financial sector. The last three models are organizations that were not involved in finance in the past but have used AI and other new technologies to offer services they couldn't in the past. Figure 1 illustrates the similarities and differences of these six models.

3 Methodology

This research attempts to capture the perspective of the experts working in Fintech organizations and not other stakeholders, such as the consumers or shareholders. The qualitative Delphi method is helpful in reaching a consensus among experts. The Delphi method has been used extensively to gain consensus on the use of technology (Gallego and Bueno 2014; Joia and Sily de Assis 2019), financial innovation (Peng et al. 2014), and business models (Effendi et al. 2024).

This research uses the Delphi method with two stages. In the first stage, the semi-structured interviews with experts identify the main risks each of the six models faces. For the second stage the researchers present the same participants with a summary of all the risks identified by all the participants, and they are asked if they want to revise their list of risks and if they can rank them from most serious, to least serious. The Nvivo software was used to analyse the transcribed interviews and identify the main themes.

With this method this research can extend the research on the six AI-focused Fintech business models. While each of the six business models has been validated and explained extensively in previous research their typical influence on risk has not been sufficiently explored (Fig. 2).

The data collection had to ensure that the semi-structured interview participants were professionals who had experience with one of the six AI-focused business models. For this reason, participants who worked for Fintech companies that matched one of the six models were approached.

Fintechs are heavily influenced by the geographic region they are active in, due to several reasons such as the local regulation and culture. For this reason, companies from one country, China, were targeted. While innovation in technology and finance can come from many different places in the modern world, China is one of the leaders in innovation in this area. Chinese Fintechs can be considered among the most advanced in terms of technology and business models.

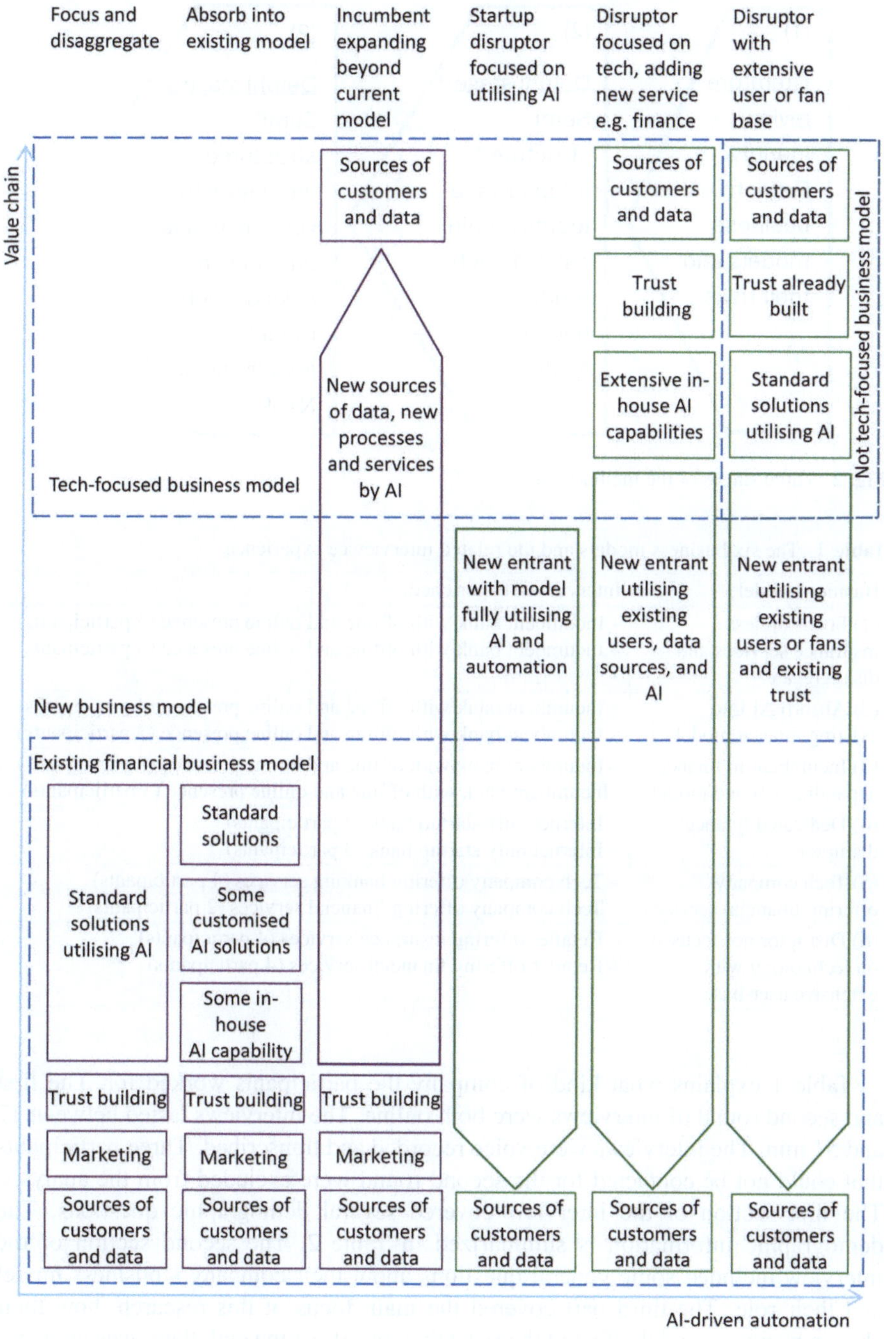

Fig. 1 The six AI-focused Fintech business models (based on Zarifis 2025)

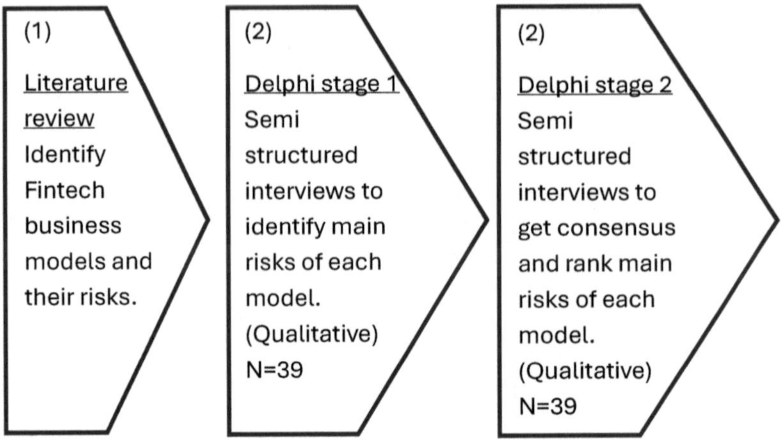

Fig. 2 Three stages of the methodology

Table 1 The six business models and the related interviewee experience

Business model	Interviewee experience
(1) Focus on less insurance services and disaggregate	– Incumbent bank with offline and online presence (3 participants) – Incumbent bank with offline and online presence (3 participants)
(2) Absorb AI into existing finance model	– Incumbent bank with offline and online presence (4 participants) – Incumbent bank with offline and online presence (3 participants)
(3) Incumbent in finance expanding beyond model	– Incumbent bank with offline and online presence (3 participants) –Incumbent bank with offline and online presence (3 participants)
(4) Dedicated finance disruptor	– Internet only startup bank (3 participants) – Internet only startup bank (3 participants)
(5) Tech company offering financial services	– Tech company offering banking services (4 participants) – Tech company offering financial services (2 participants)
(6) Disruptor not focused on technology with extensive user-base	– Retailer offering insurance services (4 participants) – Retailer offering financial services (4 participants)

Table 1 explains what kind of company the participants worked for. The first and second round of interviews were both online. The interviews lasted between 17 and 51 min. The interviews were voice recorded and transcribed. Three participants that could not be contacted for the second round were excluded from the analysis. The first section of the interview covered several demographic questions. The demographic information is summarized in Table 2. The second section of the interview included some general questions about their company's business model and their role. The third part covered the main focus of this research, how their chosen business model affected the risks they faced. At the end, there was an open-ended question asking them if they wanted to add something on the issues discussed that was not already covered (Table 2).

Table 2 Demographic information of interview participants

Measure	Variable	Participants
Gender	Male	7
	Female	5
Age	18–24	0
	25–39	4
	40–59	7
	60 or older	1
Highest education qualification	University bachelor's degree	10
	University postgraduate degree	2
Experience working for a Fintech	Under 1 year	7
	Between 1 and 3 years	26
	Over 3 years	6
Monthly income in pounds (EUR)	3001–5000	6
	5001–7000	2
	Over 7001	2
Chinese nationality and Chinese resident		38
Without Chinese nationality, but a Chinese resident		1

4 Findings

The purpose of the analysis is to identify and rank the main risks for each business model. For each model the participants were asked about risks across technology, operational, compliance, strategic, and reputational risks. These five categories of risk are considered the most suitable for Fintech (Tyagi 2024). Eight risks related to the application of an AI-focused business model are identified. These are (1) direct AI risks, (2) technology integration risk, (3) third-party vendor risk, (4) technology infrastructure risk, (5) data protection and privacy risk, (6) cybersecurity risk, (7) fraud and identity theft risk, and (8) strategic misalignment risk. The eight risks apply to all six models; however, they are not equally significant in all models.

The second stage of the data collection asked participants to rank the eight risks for their specific business model. Managers and their organizations have finite resources so knowing which risks to prioritize is beneficial. The risks identified for each of the six business models are discussed here.

4.1 The First Fintech Business Model and Its Risks: Focus on Less Financial Services and Disaggregate

The first business model relies heavily on an external value chain while only doing a small part of the value chain internally. This characteristic of the first business model influences many of the risks.

4.1.1 Direct AI Risks

There is a danger of basing financial and other decisions on inaccurate data. The increased automation and the lack of face-to-face interaction can have a detrimental effect on the quality of the data. One participant gave the example of the many problems with people entering false information during the onboarding process. While this usually stops short of becoming a security threat or a threat of fraud, the false information is still processed leading to a skewed understanding. Given the many partners involved, they may all allow some inaccurate information into the ecosystem. Given the complexity of the ecosystem, it is hard to identify and fix the problems with the data. One participant stated:

> The onboarding needs speed, no security vulnerability, and OK for regulation, the range of the data we get for analysis is not important... the wrong data from the onboarding makes worse analysis.

Data sovereignty is one of the most important issues when trying to achieve accurate and reliable results with AI. AI trained on a data set with very different characteristics to the one it is analysing now may not make the best decisions. For example, AI trained in one region, may not come to the best decisions with data that is very different to what it was trained on. Using blockchain as a shared infrastructure can provide clear provenance for the data across the ecosystem. One participant stated:

> who owns the data for the AI, who is allowed to change it, partners should agree on the this

Artificial intelligence-driven risk assessment: AI is being used to personalized financial products and calculate clients credit scoring. These processes have all the typical risks of using AI, but some are more profound. Typical issues around data quality are compounded by the lack of transparency and can lead to breaches of regulations and laws. The risks can be mitigated with more use of human oversight, explainable AI, governance frameworks, guardrails, and quality checks. These remedies can be harder to implement in a broadly distributed ecosystem. One participant said:

> Some processes are not very sensitive, we can reject a client, we are allowed to do that, we have no obligation, other processes are more sensitive, very regulated or financially high risk. AI automating risk assessment and AI using different criteria are different, if client facing then must be more careful.

4.1.2 Technology Integration Risk

The Fintech ecosystem of many organizations is also a technology ecosystem with many nodes that depend on each other to function properly. A problem in one of the ecosystem's nodes can cause the whole ecosystem to stop functioning properly. There needs to be alignment across the whole technology stack if possible. Using blockchain as a shared infrastructure can reduce several risks when integrating technology.

4.1.3 Third-Party Vendor Risk

This model creates a company narrowly focused on one part of the value chain such as validating the identity of the clients. By specializing in one narrow part of the value chain they can become very good at it and become a very appealing partner to many organizations in the financial ecosystem. This strategy has a similar logic to the very widely adopted strategy from IT of having the 'best of breed' for each system. However, with the large number of partners, and the limited control over them, the third-party risk increases. Security vulnerabilities or outages often come from third-party vendors. These vulnerabilities often cause problems and are not limited to the high profile cases such as the outage caused by Crowdstrike in 2024.

There is often extensive jurisdictional fragmentation. This fragmentation can mean that some members of the ecosystem are not fully aware of the risks that come from the third-party vendors their partners use.

Fintechs should take the security record of potential partners into account and have contracts that require any issue to be reported across the ecosystem.

4.1.4 Technology Infrastructure Risk

Organizations trying to increase security and reduce the risks in their infrastructure often find themselves in the situation where they have achieved strong internal controls, but have less control over their external value chain. Keeping the shared infrastructure secure can be more challenging than keeping the internal systems secure. On the other hand, modern technologies can also offer solutions for this model. For example, new partners can easily be added to the ecosystem by utilizing the blockchain infrastructure to share information.

4.1.5 Data Protection and Privacy Risk

Given that most people nowadays interact with Fintech on their phone and prove their identity with the fingerprint, protecting this biometric data is very important. There are different privacy requirements across different countries. EU countries are far stricter than most other countries. For a distributed ecosystem this presents challenges. The most common solution is to follow the strictest standards in the ecosystem. Data and privacy governance frameworks, traceability and privacy enhancing technologies can help.

4.1.6 Cybersecurity Risk

Fintechs are very attractive targets for cybercriminals because of the money and data they have. Unfortunately, with financial services there is a trade-off between security and accessibility, so some vulnerability is probably inevitable. Cybercriminals are skilled at identifying and targeting the weakness in a complex process, implemented by a complex ecosystem of organizations.

In many countries it is a regulatory requirement to report breaches. In addition to this, the nature of the attacks, with many ransomware attacks, makes them public. These breaches have become almost inevitable, and the effort is on limiting the damage caused. Breaches can come from applications used, file transfer systems, and cloud hosting.

4.1.7 Fraud and Identity Theft Risk

Financial institutions collect a lot of sensitive information. There is not only sensitive information collected on customers such as their passport number, but many insights can be deduced by how the customers spend their money. For example, if someone looks at how a person spends their money over a month, they can often draw insight about their current health based on medicines they buy, and future health based on their eating habits. As this information is spread across the ecosystem, the risk of it leaking out and enabling fraud and identity theft increases. Keeping data secure is more challenging across an extensively distributed ecosystem.

4.1.8 Strategic Misalignment Risk

The period when Fintechs started emerging and rapidly gained market share with the competitive advantage of the technology they used is gradually coming to an end. Incumbents have responded and are using AI effectively themselves. The rewards may be less certain now, so the acceptable risk to take on to pursue those reduced rewards is also often less. The clear path to growth is not as clear anymore. Strategic decisions have more risk of causing a misalignment between nodes of the ecosystem (Table 3a).

Strategic misalignment is not usually one of the main concerns for organizations that have a lower dependency on their partners. However, for many modern Fintechs that are a small part of a larger ecosystem, this becomes an ongoing concern. This is a risk that is increased by the Fintech business model of focusing on less financial services and disaggregating. The rate of change, across technology, regulation, international trade agreements and many other areas is increasing at a faster rate than before. What is an ideal financial ecosystem structure today may not be ideal tomorrow. One participant said:

> We have fabulous partners, they help us. We are good with our position. Five years from now will we be in the same agreement with the same people? We have to adapt, you see how fast things move now . . .

Table 3a The first Fintech business model and its risks ranked (focus on less financial services and disaggregate)

Rank	Risk
1	Data protection and privacy risk Distributed ecosystem presents challenges for data protection.
2	Strategic misalignment risk Strategic decisions have more risk of causing a misalignment between nodes of the ecosystem. Rate of change challenging.
3	Technology integration risk One of the ecosystems nodes can cause the whole ecosystem to stop functioning properly.
4	Technology infrastructure risk Can have strong internal controls, but have less control over their external value chain.
5	Third-party vendor risk With the large number of partners, and the limited control over them the third-party risk increases.
6	Direct AI risks AI and static models basing decisions on inaccurate data. The data may have been maliciously created or simply inaccurate. Some new technologies and services based on technologies not fully regulated yet.
7	Fraud and identity theft risk Information is spread across an ecosystem so risk of it leaking out and enabling fraud and identity theft increases.
8	Cybersecurity risk Security breaches are almost inevitable, and the effort is on limiting the damage caused. In most countries they must be reported.

4.2 The Second Fintech Business Model and Its Risks: Keep Business Model Unchanged and Absorb AI Into Existing Processes

The second business model does not change to fully utilize AI, but instead utilizes AI to make current processes and services more efficient and effective. Broadly speaking, AI is adapted to the model, the model is not adapted to AI. Organizations that see their business model as a strength and do not find alternative models appealing may choose this approach. Given the stability offered by a proven model, some risks are significantly reduced in comparison with the first model that adapt to fit into a new ecosystem. Nevertheless, some risks are higher. Equally importantly, the nature of the risk in each category can be very different. For example, the risk of strategic misalignment is now more about gradually drifting away from the ideal model for the constantly evolving technology.

4.2.1 Direct AI Risks

If AI is adapted to existing processes, it may not be fully utilized. The existing workflows were created in that way to fit the technology available at the time. This raises the key question of whether the existing processes are worth retaining. If the existing processes are retained, then the current roles and people may also be retained. This can create a situation where the organization is partly operating with an old model and partly with a new model.

The positive side of retaining some staff and existing processes is that they can shape the new AI implementations with their experience and knowledge. For example, an organization's staff usually know their customers better than anybody. This can reduce the risk of an AI implementation.

4.2.2 Technology Integration Risk

The technical challenges may seem less, as it is more a case of evolution than revolution, but the connections between the old and new infrastructure can be fragile and cause problems. Maintenance may be more complicated and scaling the operations in the future may be harder. The way legacy processes typically use data and the way AI uses data are different. Legacy processes can involve several complicated steps including manual decisions that prevent AI from functioning to its full potential. One participant said:

> . . . we have AI in the front end, risk analysis and some other things now we are connecting-putting AI in more places linking things the risk of unintended consequences with data and failures is more . . .

4.2.3 Third-Party Vendor Risk

Given that the process of integrating AI to the current model is more extensive with this approach, the technical skills to do this must be available to such an organization. Having access to such skills can reduce the risk caused by third-party integration. On the other hand, if third-party software is not used in the most typical way, unexpected risks may emerge.

4.2.4 Technology Infrastructure Risk

Despite the model staying the same, the infrastructure needs to be updated fully so that it can provide the processing and cooling needed by AI. While it is an honourable view that humans should be in the loop, this needs to be limited so that bottlenecks do not appear. Increasingly, AI solutions must be 'end-to-end', covering the whole process. If the infrastructure is customized extensively to the current model this may make innovating and scaling harder in the future. Additionally, there may be difficulties following the constantly changing regulation. At the same time, large organizations that have the capability to customize their infrastructure can gain an advantage from this and have their fate in their own hands, being less dependent on tech providers who regularly want another slice of the pie. One participant said:

> ... we want to our data, our ability to implement strategic decisions, we won't depend on others.

4.2.5 Data Protection and Privacy Risk

Extensively customizing AI solution to match the existing model can offer several benefits but it increases the responsibility of the Fintech implementing the changes. Data protection risks increase. If new customized AI is used it may need more training data in comparison with using existing models. If the right guardrails are not used, data from around the world may be used to train the AI causing risks of not complying with the regulation of some countries. Consent may not be taken correctly. While AI, like many innovations, can stretch some laws close to breaking point, at least if an organization does this in the same way as most of the others in the industry, there is strength in numbers. If most in the industry do something, the regulation may adapt to them. One participant said:

> ... these decisions are bigger than one of us they need to be decided together and we do it together to have clarity ...

4.2.6 Cybersecurity Risk

Extensively customizing a solution can increase the risk of cybersecurity threats. More responsibility for cybersecurity goes onto the Fintech in the same way more responsibility for all other aspects of the solution moves onto the Fintech. A more customized solution will rely on a variety of software libraries, APIs, and data. This creates a larger attack surface. With all the processing needed for the development and operation of more customized AI the organization becomes more vulnerable to denial-of-service attacks. With the increased burden of responsibility key actions may be missed, or slower than necessary. Updates may be slow leaving vulnerabilities. A more complex customized AI solution may make monitoring and auditing harder.

In addition to the traditional purposes of cyberattacks which are to stop an organization operating, request a ransom or steal data, there is now the additional risk of an adversary stealing a customized AI model by using repeated queries to essentially reverse engineering the boundaries of the decisions it takes. In finance the boundaries of the decisions are very important and can be a competitive advantage a Fintech would rather others did not know.

4.2.7 Fraud and Identity Theft Risk

With the AI adapted to the model and not vice versa, the risk of fraud can move from broad frauds targeting several Fintechs, to more customized frauds that can try to understand the parameters of the AI decision. When the parameters of a decision are known, it may be possible to trick the system. The customized AI requires extensive adversarial training to be able to identify these attempted frauds. Additionally, a model that is very focused on one dataset may not identify frauds that do not exist in that dataset. Furthermore, if unlawful access to the dataset is gained, fraudulent cases can be added as legitimate cases to mislead the AI.

4.2.8 Strategic Misalignment Risk

In this scenario, the risk of strategic misalignment is more about gradually drifting away from the ideal model for the constantly evolving technology. Keeping the model the same has many benefits, including that existing staff and customers are familiar with it. However, as competitors move forward transforming their business models, new staff and customers will become more familiar with the new AI-focused models. One participant said (Table 3b):

> Is the question what I want or what the new generation want? The question is what the new generation wants . . .

Table 3b The second Fintech business model and its risks ranked (keep business model unchanged and absorb AI into existing processes)

Rank	Risk
1	Direct AI risks AI and static models basing decisions on inaccurate data. The data may have been maliciously created or simply inaccurate.
2	Technology integration risk Speed of innovation and technology becoming obsolete.
3	Technology infrastructure risk Customizing infrastructure extensively to the current model makes innovating and scaling harder in the future.
4	Third-party vendor risk If third-party software is not used in the most typical way, unexpected risks may emerge.
5	Data protection and privacy risk New customized AI may need more training data in comparison with using existing models. If the right guardrails are not in place data from around the world may be used to train the AI breaching regulation.
6	Cybersecurity risk Extensively customizing of a solution can increase the risk of cybersecurity threats.
7	Fraud and identity theft risk The customized AI requires extensive adversarial training to be able to identify these attempted frauds.
8	Strategic misalignment risk By keeping the model the same, the organization may be gradually drifting away from the ideal model for the constantly evolving technology.

4.3 *The Third Fintech Business Model and Its Risks: Incumbent in Finance Expanding Beyond Their Current Model*

The third AI-focused business model attempts to get the most out of AI by keeping its existing services but also adding new ones to fully utilize the opportunities offered by AI. By adding new services often more bundled offers are made to consumers. This means that while changing existing services is not the starting point of the digital transformation the existing services usually evolve to fit in better with the new services added.

4.3.1 Direct AI Risks

The motivation behind this strategy is to keep the existing services and add new ones. In some ways this reduces risk as the disruption is limited mostly to the new services. However, if the AI solution fails publicly, this will cause reputational damage to the pre-existing services also. Therefore, despite limiting the risks, by not disrupting all the processes, the new AI-driven processes can still cause reputational damage to the whole organization.

When new AI is used on existing services, it benefits from the knowledge built up in the organization. When new AI is used on a new financial service it might be unreliable or fail, even if it appeared to work correctly during testing. Some AI models work well in testing but do not work so well in real scenarios with unexpected information.

Beyond the potential AI failures, the dehumanization of the new financial services may also affect reputation. While most people today typically use financial services without interacting with a human, they are still interacting with processes created by humans with decision making created by humans. A more extensive use of AI will be more dehumanizing.

The new AI powered financial services will also bring new liabilities when there is financial loss. Which part of the ecosystem those liabilities fall on is not always straightforward. One participant said:

> ... it is easier to add new teams to work on new products with new technology get the lessons and use them in the old teams. Going to the old teams and restructuring makes conflict the new technologies aren't liked by everyone.

4.3.2 Technology Integration Risk

Some organizations implementing this strategy choose to keep their current processes and systems operating in a similar fashion as before but add new processes that rely more heavily on AI and automation. Others overhaul all the systems despite keeping the existing services the same. The new services added inevitably need the latest technology as they have been created to take advantage of the new technologies' new capabilities.

4.3.3 Third-Party Vendor Risk

The new AI-focused services may create heavy dependencies on vendors the organization finds itself locked in with. With the fast pace of AI's progress, the companies providing AI change their models, pricing, and terms, quite regularly. One participant said:

> the promise of AI does not always materialize there are difficulties implementing the AI in the right way and costs not going out of control.

4.3.4 Technology Infrastructure Risk

The infrastructure risks of expanding the use of AI go beyond the usual IT risks. As AI stops being used as several tools in several different processes, and covers most of the operations in a coherent way, it becomes a single point of failure. Any failure in the AI stack can cause an immediate failure. The data pipeline can be vulnerable to false data that can degrade the AI model.

The challenges to system integration can also increase as the new AI *need*s to be integrated with existing systems, databases, and APIs. Most financial services need to be as close to instant as possible, and delays can harm the customers.

4.3.5 Data Protection and Privacy Risk

As a financial institution expands, using AI and deep learning more than before, more data is collected from the users. Additional data, not directly related to the service is collected so the privacy risks increase. This additional personal information may be used incorrectly by the organization. Additionally, a data breach would be more harmful as this information unnecessarily collected will also leak out. As several AI vendors are used in the AI pipeline this also makes it harder to protect customers privacy. The contracts with those vendors and others accessing data through APIs may not be sufficiently strict.

4.3.6 Cybersecurity Risk

An existing company that has built up a reputation over the years has more to lose from cybersecurity breaches either made possible by AI, or made worse by AI. The intention to move forward quickly must be balanced by ensuring the AI used is secure. There are vulnerabilities specific to AI such as data poisoning. One participant said:

> . . . the more AI we use the risks of degrading the quality of our data or criminals accessing it increases. Sometimes it is harder to identify irregular behaviour.

4.3.7 Fraud and Identity Theft Risk

The most obvious threat is the use of AI to create a digital doppelganger by creating deepfakes and synthetic identities that can apply for loans and other services. AI can also be used to adjust patterns of behaviour sufficiently to avoid detection. Security measures in place that are scanning for certain patterns of behaviour to identify as suspicious can be fooled. The various techniques for fraud and identity theft can be combined on a large scale across emails, voice, and even video to create a very convincing picture.

4.3.8 Strategic Misalignment Risk

This approach attempts to reduce the risk of strategic misalignment by keeping the current model and 'bolting on' the new services. There can, however, be tension and inconsistency among the old and the new. One participant said (Table 3c):

> Success depends on the new teams not just the technology. They need to make it work. If they fail we might not use AI in that way

Table 3c The third Fintech business model and its risks ranked (incumbent in finance expanding beyond their current model)

Rank	Risk
1	Direct AI risks When AI is used in a new financial service it might be unreliable or fail, even if it appeared to work correctly during testing.
2	Data protection and privacy risk Data, not directly related to the service is collected so the privacy risks increase. This additional personal information may be used incorrectly by the organization. Additionally, a data breach would be more harmful as this information unnecessarily collected will also leak out.
3	Cybersecurity risk Some cybersecurity breaches are made possible, or made worse, by AI. The reputation of the whole organization can be damaged, not just the new parts of the organization trying to innovate.
4	Fraud and identity theft risk AI can create a digital doppelganger by creating deepfakes and synthetic identities. AI can also adjust patterns of behaviour to avoid detection.
5	Technology infrastructure risk When AI is not just being used as several tools in several different processes, and covers most of the operations in a coherent way, it becomes a single point of failure.
6	Technology integration risk The new services added inevitably need the latest technology as they have been created to take advantage of technologies' new capabilities.
7	Strategic misalignment risk There can be tension and inconsistency between the old and the new models.
8	Third-party vendor risk The new AI-focused services may create heavy dependencies on vendors the organization finds itself locked in with them.

4.4 The Fourth Fintech Business Model and Its Risks: Dedicated Finance Disruptor, Typically a Startup

The dedicated finance disruptor, typically a startup, is an organization that was created to fully utilize the latest technologies with a new business model. They usually offer faster and cheaper services but can struggle with the quality of the service.

4.4.1 Direct AI Risks

A startup being created to fully utilize AI may be more optimized to benefit from this technology but there are also additional risks. There is no long track record that has built up trust, so one large-scale public failure can be fatal. A new organization using new models will not be well prepared for the variety of real-life scenarios. A lack of historical data increases the risk of wrong decisions. Additionally, with humans being mostly out of the loop in the decision-making process, and less experienced staff in the company because some were replaced by AI, experience, good judgement, and instincts are lost. One participant said:

> ...we have the best plan how to use AI and gain customers. We are cheaper with more automation. Others wait to see how many clients we get before they try to copy it. Comparison websites encourage more people to focus on price not extra services they are not interested in.

4.4.2 Technology Integration Risk

As the model is created to fully utilize the latest AI models the technology integration risks should be limited. However, due to the fast setup and high automation, cascading failures can be more dramatic and harder to resolve. While traditional businesses may face the challenge of reducing the number of employees they have, born digital companies may not have enough experts to resolve problems that arise as they go thorough automated processes.

4.4.3 Third-Party Vendor Risk

These born digital organizations are typically set up as fast as possible and at the lowest cost possible to take advantage of technology and undercut the existing financial organizations. This scenario typically means that there is a heavier reliance on third-party vendors in comparison with other models. These vendors may be used by other competitors also, so having a competitive advantage with better AI models is difficult. Furthermore, these vendors are being entrusted with the organization's most valuable asset, its data.

4.4.4 Technology Infrastructure Risk

For born online financial institutions AI is a layer of the infrastructure and not a series of AI applications on the infrastructure. This high dependence on AI has implications for operational stability and compliance. The driving motivation is for efficiency, but this must be balanced with resilience and transparency.

4.4.5 Data Protection and Privacy Risk

The more aggressive application of AI amplifies data protection and privacy concerns. If more data is collected, and more processing is done with it, there are higher risks to customers' privacy. As more data is collected and used the data lineage becomes more unclear. Additionally, sensitive private information about individuals such as their political views or health can be inferred from non-sensitive data such as their purchase history. There may also be various forms of function creep where insights gained for one purpose are used for other purposes. For example, insight gained from AI analysing fraud risks could be used for marketing. The initial insight may be ethical and legal, but the way it is subsequently used may be unethical and illegal.

4.4.6 Cybersecurity Risk

This model offers agility but the complete dependence on AI and other technologies also makes it vulnerable. This model typically uses a highly integrated AI stack. Attackers know that the company does not have physical branches to fall back on. There is a single point of failure and denial-of-service attacks can be effective. Customers may feel more feel more cut-off and lose trust faster when they lose access to the service. One participant said:

> Our simple structure makes it easier to operate but downtime from technical failures, ransomware attack would be a big problem. Some would leave. They can come to us easily and leave easily.

4.4.7 Fraud and Identity Theft Risk

The AI of the organization is in an ongoing 'war' with the AI of the fraudsters. The organization's AI must constantly improve to stay ahead. Adversarial AI can attack at much larger scale creating thousands of fake accounts or stealing the credentials of thousands of accounts. Attacks can mislabel fraudulent transactions as legitimate making the AI consider all future fraudulent transactions of that type as legitimate. Additionally, the more automation and less staff can create a blindness to what is happening, allowing more frauds to get past undetected.

4.4.8 Strategic Misalignment Risk

There is often a trade-off between optimizing a model to a specific situation and creating a flexible organization. This model is designed to make the most of the current situation, but it is not necessarily designed for an organization that will learn and adapt. Therefore, the strategic decisions need to be correct and taken at the right time. If the strategic advantage is using AI more effectively and the organization does not differentiate itself in any other way, then it is in a constant battle to stay ahead in how it uses AI.

Furthermore, overreliance on AI for strategic data-driven decisions may prevent the organization from thinking outside the box and innovating. The reduced human capital due to automation can make this worse (Table 3d).

Table 3d The fourth Fintech business model and its risks ranked (dedicated finance disruptor, typically a startup)

Rank	Risk
1	Direct AI risks A new organization using new models will not be ready for all real-life scenarios. A lack of historical data increases the risk of wrong decisions.
2	Cybersecurity risk When using a highly integrated AI stack there is a single point of failure and denial-of-service attacks can be effective.
3	Third-party vendor risk There is a heavy reliance on third-party vendors, and they are entrusted with the organization's data.
4	Technology infrastructure risk For born online financial institutions AI is a layer of the infrastructure and not a series of applications on the infrastructure, causing compliance problems.
5	Data protection and privacy risk As more data is collected and used the data lineage becomes more unclear. Sensitive private information about individuals can be inferred.
6	Fraud and identity theft risk The more automation and less staff can create a blindness to what is happening, allowing more frauds to get past undetected.
7	Technology integration risk Due to the fast setup and high automation cascading failures can be more dramatic and harder to resolve.
8	Strategic misalignment risk This model is designed to make the most of the current situation, but it is not necessarily designed for an organization that will learn and adapt.

4.5 *The Fifth Fintech Business Model and Its Risks: Tech Company Offering Financial Services*

This model typically involves a tech company or tech-savvy company that utilizes its existing infrastructure and customer base to offer new financial services. They were not involved in finance in the past, but are using AI and other new technologies to offer services they couldn't before.

4.5.1 Direct AI Risks

These tech savvy companies typically utilize AI in far less regulated services, and they need to adapt when using AI in the far more regulated financial sector. They may have technology capabilities the traditional financial institutions do not have, but the traditional financial institutions know how to shape and navigate regulation. A fundamentally different philosophy is needed where innovation should be done in a way that avoids mistakes and additional risks. The mindset of a financial institution needs to be created. A practical illustration of this is that more explainable AI may be needed, even if this sacrifices some performance. The level of automation achieved in other services may not be possible due to the regulation and broad variety of different situations in real life. One participant said:

> The team have the skills. Many were hired now, lawyers, financial professionals. We avoid the riskier products. We identify the ones that are profitable and we know we can do better than those doing them now. Our data and our models give us some advantages.

4.5.2 Technology Integration Risk

While the tech savvy company has already adopted the latest forms of AI their challenge is to ensure the way it is used meets regulatory requirements. Meeting the regulatory requirements at the point when the financial services are offered is only the start and an ongoing effort is needed to do this for all cases, into the future.

4.5.3 Third-Party Vendor Risk

While large tech savvy companies create and control more of the technology they use in comparison with the typical financial institution, they still use third parties for many technology solutions. However, these collaborations are done from a position of strength, and the tech savvy companies avoid the risk of being tied in or having their business cannibalized.

4.5.4 Technology Infrastructure Risk

The integration challenge is combining the highly regulated technology offering the financial services with the rest of the technology already used. This integration creates infrastructure risks. An infrastructure that was created for scalability and speed must now have very high integrity and resilience. Financial services are not always required at a uniform level and there are often sudden spikes in demand caused by an event or some news. This is a challenge for all systems but the heavier the use of AI the more challenging these spikes become due to the high processing requirements it has. One participant said:

> We can scale but not lowering performance and consistently delivering the low latency people expect needs investment.

4.5.5 Data Protection and Privacy Risk

Cross border flows of financial data are an example of the challenges that must be resolved. Additionally in many countries there are regulations on using non-financial data for financial decisions. The technology savvy company can still utilize their existing technology and data but this is not as straightforward as it may seem.

4.5.6 Cybersecurity Risk

While a tech savvy company is well positioned to deal with cybersecurity threats, the new threats caused by offering financial services need extra care. Some new vulnerabilities are created, and some existing vulnerabilities are amplified. The AI models are at the centre of the operations and if they, or their data, can be interfered with, there will be many problems. For example, chatbots have been hijacked and used to reveal sensitive information they were not supposed to.

4.5.7 Fraud and Identity Theft Risk

As is often the case with cybercrime, criminals find a way to turn an organization's strengths against them. The tech savvy company has a large existing customer base. This creates an additional liability as large-scale fraud can use those identities to extract money. Real identities can be stolen, or synthetic identities can be created with some real information to make them more convincing.

4.5.8 Strategic Misalignment Risk

With this model the key characteristic is to lead on technology and especially AI. This has benefits but attempting to constantly lead on AI implementing one

Table 3e The fifth Fintech business model and its risks ranked (tech company offering financial services)

Rank	Risk
1	Data protection and privacy risk Using existing technology and data for financial services may breach data protection and privacy laws of multiple countries.
2	Cybersecurity risk The AI models are at the centre of the operations and if they, or their data, can be interfered with, there will be many problems.
3	Direct AI risks Lack of experience navigating the regulatory implications of using AI in finance.
4	Technology infrastructure risk An infrastructure that was created for scalability and speed when used for non-financial services must now have very high integrity and resilience.
5	Technology integration risk AI capabilities evolve on a weekly basis, fully utilizing new forms of AI and adapting to changing regulation is challenging.
6	Fraud and identity theft risk The large existing customer base creates an additional liability as large-scale fraud can use those identities to extract money.
7	Strategic misalignment risk Attempting to constantly lead on AI, implementing one new model after another can cause problems. New models may not achieve strategic goals.
8	Third-party vendor risk These collaborations are done from a position of strength, and the tech savvy companies avoid the risk of being tied in or cannibalized.

new model after another can cause problems. Every innovation has its risks and constantly innovating on AI models increases the risk of pushing a model out that is flawed. A new AI model may not be technically flawed but may not achieve the organization's strategic goals (Table 3e).

4.6 The Sixth Fintech Business Model and Its Risks: Disruptor not Focused on Technology with Large User-Base Offering New Financial Services

This model involves a disruptor not focused on technology with large user-base offering new financial services. An example of this strategy is the EasyBitcoin platform Easyjet founder Stelios Hadjioannou created.

4.6.1 Direct AI Risks

The main reason these organizations want to embed financial services is that they already have a large customer base and they want to add a new revenue stream.

This is a benefit, but unlike the startups that have less to lose, these companies can lose the customers they have for other services if things go wrong. Relying heavily on AI for the customer interaction and decision making can create an unhelpful and opaque process and even mistakes. Highly automated processes make it hard to access a human and this becomes a serious problem with special cases, or when there is a problem.

When there is an existing customer base and existing data on them there is the obvious temptation to use that data to personalize the service. If the personalization is done inappropriately, this can backfire. Non-financial behaviours such as buying habits are not always the best predictors of financial behaviour.

The AI models using non-financial data may draw conclusions that were valid in the past but due to changing circumstances are no longer valid. The risk of model drift is amplified in this scenario.

An explanation for a financial decision, such as not to give a loan, is necessary. This can be difficult when AI is used but it becomes far harder when that AI is using non-financial data to make financial decisions. One participant said:

> You can either push your customers to buy more of the same, which works until they are completely saturated, then you need to offer them something different. AI can do this. The customer journey with AI should be smooth but the regulation and risks involved complicate this. We take it one step at a time.

4.6.2 Technology Integration Risk

Relying heavily on off-the-shelf solutions can save money. As these organizations are not trying to differentiate themselves with financial services, just further monetize existing customers, this may seem like the best approach. Adding off-the-shelf financial solutions to their existing solutions may create incompatibilities across the AI stack.

4.6.3 Third-Party Vendor Risk

Relying heavily on off-the-shelf solutions for an increasing number of services can cause problems. The organization may be limited in the strategic decisions it can make and become entirely dependent on the vendors and what their strategy is. There may also be limited control over the quality of the service. A faulty model update may stop the services being available.

4.6.4 Technology Infrastructure Risk

On the surface, adding one additional revenue stream to several other ones does not appear too challenging for the technology infrastructure. There are, however, serious computational and scalability risks. The temptation may be to utilize the existing infrastructure but the demands of AI for financial services are much higher. Far more calculations are made, utilizing more data. These processing requirements are even higher when there are unexpected spikes in demand. Additionally, given that the non-financial data will be used for real-time solutions there may be challenges here also.

4.6.5 Data Protection and Privacy Risk

The regulation around data protection and privacy is far stricter for financial services, so if the data from the non-financial services will be used there may be problems. Off-the-shelf solutions may not be preconfigured to each country's regulations. Additionally, repurposing data collected for one service to another service without consent is a violation of regulations in many places.

4.6.6 Cybersecurity Risk

A company that does not have a heritage in finance, entering the financial sector with mostly off-the-shelf solutions brings some cybersecurity risks with it. In addition to the typical cybersecurity risks, the company's existing customer base may be a more attractive target for phishing attacks now that financial services have also been added. The existing customers may have their guard down as they have an existing relationship with the organization and may not consider interactions with it as risky as interactions with a traditional bank. One participant said:

> We approach security differently here. We follow the financial sectors industry standards. We have risk-based security planning, use industry standard security assessment tools. There is layered defence. We prioritize critical assets.

4.6.7 Fraud and Identity Theft Risk

Possible flaws in the company's AI can create openings for fraud. In addition to the vulnerabilities created by the AI this organization uses, the data this organization has can also become a vulnerability if fraudsters gain access to it. As this organization has both financial and non-financial information on its customers, this can make hyper-personalized fraud easier.

4.6.8 Strategic Misalignment Risk

This company can have a misalignment between its previous and current strategies, and how these strategies use technology. The previous strategy would use AI for marketing, engagement, and convenience, while the new strategy offering financial services needs the technology to focus more on security, compliance, and accuracy.

Table 3f The sixth Fintech business model and its risks (disruptor not focused on technology with large user-base offering new financial services)

Rank	Risk
1	Direct AI risks The AI models using non-financial data may draw conclusions that were valid in the past but due to changing circumstances are no longer valid.
2	Data protection and privacy risk Off-the-shelf solutions may not be preconfigured to each country's regulations.
3	Third-party vendor risk These organizations may be limited in the strategic decisions they can make and become entirely dependent on the vendors and what their strategy is.
4	Cybersecurity risk Such an organization's existing customer base may be a more attractive target for phishing attacks now that financial services have also been added.
5	Technology integration risk Adding off-the-shelf financial solutions to their existing solutions may create incompatibilities across the AI stack.
6	Technology infrastructure risk The temptation may be to utilize the existing infrastructure but the demands of AI for financial services are much higher. Far more calculations are made.
7	Fraud and identity theft risk As these organizations have both financial and non-financial information on their customers, this can make hyper-personalized fraud easier.
8	Strategic misalignment risk These organizations can have a misalignment between their previous and current strategies, and how these strategies use technology.

If AI fails and hallucinates on financial services this is very serious, while if the AI failed when recommending a product such as clothes this would not be a big problem.

More broadly the character of the company when interacting with the customer will have to change and some customers may not like this. Whether this is intentionally crafted or left to chance, each organization projects a character in their interactions with their customers. Typically, organizations offering financial services must be more formal, precise while other organizations can be more informal and friendly. The more formal tone is necessary to put the customer in the mindset of making a serious financial decision. Whether the organization chooses to be more formal all the time, or to skip between the two, there are challenges in coming across as coherent and friendly as before.

The obvious solution for the misalignment between parts of the organization offering different services is to make them different companies, but this goes against the strategy of offering as many services in one place. Getting the right balance between how close and how separate the different parts of the organization should be can be tricky. While AI enables a breadth of services to be offered at scale, these issues illustrate how there are still challenges in doing this (Table 3f).

5 Discussion and Conclusion

The six business models discussed here are on a high level of abstraction and easy to understand. However, when we look at the implications for risk of these business models, things quickly become very complicated. In most cases, the risks are not necessarily problems to be solved but delicate balances. While cybersecurity can indeed be seen as a problem to solve, in most of the cases, the risk and the reward come together.

The six AI-focused finance business models as identified by previous research are (1) disaggregate, concentrate on a reduced number of financial services and a smaller part of the value chain, (2) keep business model unchanged and absorb AI into existing processes, (3) incumbent in finance expanding beyond their current model, (4) dedicated finance disruptor, typically a startup, (5) tech company offering financial services, (6) disruptor not focused on technology with large user-base offering new financial services (Zarifis 2025). The first three models involve organizations that have been offering financial services for many years. The last three involve organizations that did not offer financial services in the past but are utilizing the capabilities of AI to start offering them.

Eight risks related to the application of an AI-focused business model are identified. These are (1) direct AI risks, (2) technology integration risk, (3) third-party vendor risk, (4) technology infrastructure risk, (5) data protection and privacy risk, (6) cybersecurity risk, (7) fraud and identity theft risk, and (8) strategic misalignment risk. The second stage of the data collection asked participants to rank the eight risks for their specific business model. The eight risks apply to all six models; however, their significance is different for each model.

5.1 Contribution to Theory

This research focuses on the impact of the choice of AI-focused business model on risks. Initially the role of a broad range of risks across financial, legal, security, and operational (Ryu 2018) are explored. This research finds support for eight prominent types of risk across all six Fintech business models. This suggests that these eight types of risk are usually present when a Fintech adapts to use AI more extensively.

Additionally, the experts interviewed came to an agreement ranking the significance of the eight risks for their specific business model. This extends the literature on the six AI-focused Fintech business models to also cover the typical risks that come directly from how they apply AI. The areas of research on Fintech business models and risk are linked.

5.2 Contribution to Practice

These findings are useful for companies that would identify themselves as Fintechs and other financial organizations that rely heavily on AI. For financial institutions the risks they were preoccupied with in the past were financial, and the solutions to these risks were also financial, such as limiting credit. However, now one of the main sources of risk is the AI used, and the solutions are not simply financial. The solutions are not just about credit models but need to start at the business model level. The Fintech leadership must integrate risk management into the goals, so they are not seen as competing priorities. This integrated approach will align values, improve awareness and engagement. A risk culture that fits the specific AI-focused business model can be created and this can lead to a resilient culture. A narrow approach to risk management, not proactively shaping the AI focused business model is not the way forward.

While the Fintech business models do not necessarily increase risk and may indeed reduce it, because of the change in the nature of the risk involved, trust needs to be built with all the stakeholders. A Fintech can identify one of the six business models that fits them, or a combination of two or more business models that captures what they do. Based on their model, they can use the eight most important risks to adapt their plans and constantly audit their implementation of AI. This research enables Fintechs to target their finite resources more effectively to reduce risk. Having the link between risk management and the business model, and constantly developing both together means there is less chance of unpleasant surprises.

6 Limitations and Future Research

This research utilizes qualitative data collection from experts working in Fintech to evaluate the typical risks when applying AI. This research extended research on six AI-focused Fintech models. Future research can further extend these six business models by focusing on each one individually or testing them in other areas.

References

Brillinger AS, Els C, Schäfer B, Bender B (2020) Business model risk and uncertainty factors: toward building and maintaining profitable and sustainable business models. Bus Horiz 63(1):121–130. https://doi.org/10.1016/j.bushor.2019.09.009

Canhoto AI, Keegan BJ, Ryzhikh M (2023) Snakes and Ladders: unpacking the personalisation-privacy paradox in the context of AI-enabled personalisation in the physical retail environment. Inf Syst Front. https://doi.org/10.1007/s10796-023-10369-7

Dellermann D, Fliaster A, Kolloch M (2017) Innovation risk in digital business models: the German energy sector. J Bus Strat *38*(5):35–43. https://doi.org/10.1108/JBS-07-2016-0078

Effendi PL, Wirjodirdjo B, Rosdaniah SI (2024) Influence factors on sustainable business models for renewable energy supply: Indonesian electricity industry. Cogent Bus Manage 11(1). https://doi.org/10.1080/23311975.2023.2293303

Elia G, Stefanelli V, Ferilli GB (2023) Investigating the role of Fintech in the banking industry: what do we know? Eur J Innov Manage 26(5):1365–1393. https://doi.org/10.1108/EJIM-12-2021-0608

Gallego D, Bueno S (2014) Exploring the application of the Delphi method as a forecasting tool in information systems and technologies research. Technol Anal Strat Manage 26(9):987–999. https://doi.org/10.1080/09537325.2014.941348

Jain R, Kumar S, Sood K, Grima S, Rupeika-Apoga R (2023) A systematic literature review of the risk landscape in Fintech. Risks 11(2). https://doi.org/10.3390/risks11020036

Joia LA, Sily de Assis MF (2019) Motivations for the IT professional Turnaway intention: a Delphi approach. Inf Syst Manage 36(3):228–242. https://doi.org/10.1080/10580530.2019.1625239

Jorzik P, Klein SP, Kanbach DK, Kraus S (2024) AI-driven business model innovation: a systematic review and research agenda. J Bus Res 182(June):114764. https://doi.org/10.1016/j.jbusres.2024.114764

Liu J, Lv X, Zhang G, Zhang M (2025) Can fintech drive innovation in enterprise digital business models? Finance Res Lett 78(March). https://doi.org/10.1016/j.frl.2025.107237

Osterwalder A, Pigneur Y (2010) Business model generation: a handbook for visionaries, game changers, and challengers. Wiley

Peng J, Groenewold N, Fan X, Li G (2014) Financial system reform and economic growth in a transition economy: the case of China, 1978-2004. Emerg Mark Finance Trade 50(Suppl. 2):5–22. https://doi.org/10.2753/REE1540-496X5002S201

Ryu HS (2018) What makes users willing or hesitant to use Fintech?: the moderating effect of user type. Ind Manage Data Syst 118(3):541–569. https://doi.org/10.1108/IMDS-07-2017-0325

Tang M, Hou Y(G), Goodell JW, Hu Y (2024) Fintech and corporate risk-taking: evidence from China. Finance Res Lett 64(March):105411. https://doi.org/10.1016/j.frl.2024.105411

Tucci CL (2022) The many sides of business model innovation. Manage Org Rev 18(1):209–211. https://doi.org/10.1017/mor.2021.82

Tyagi A (2024) Risk management in Fintech. In: The Emerald handbook of Fintech. Emerald Publishing Limited, pp 157–175. https://doi.org/10.1108/978-1-83753-608-520241015

Välikangas L, Hoegl M, Gibbert M (2009) Why learning from failure isn't easy (and what to do about it): innovation trauma at Sun Microsystems. Eur Manage J *27*(4):225–233. https://doi.org/10.1016/j.emj.2008.12.001

Wu CH, Pambudi PDL (2025) Digital transformation in fintech: choosing between application and Software as a Service (SaaS). Asia Pac Manage Rev 30(2):100342. https://doi.org/10.1016/j.apmrv.2024.12.006

Zarifis, A. (2025). Leadership with AI and trust. De Gruyter. https://doi.org/10.1515/9783111630137

Zarifis A, Cheng X (2024) The five emerging business models of Fintech for AI adoption, growth and building trust. In: Zarifis A, Ktoridou D, Efthymiou L, Cheng X (eds) Business digital transformation. Palgrave Macmillan, pp 73–97. https://doi.org/10.1007/978-3-031-33665-2_4

Regulatory and Compliance Issues in AI-Driven Financial Services

Narmin Nahidi

Abstract This section examines how regulation shapes the design, operation, and oversight of AI-enabled and automated investment services ("robo-advice") across leading jurisdictions and distills the practical implications for firms building or scaling these models. We map convergence among functional regulators the U.S. Securities and Exchange Commission (SEC), the UK Financial Conduct Authority (FCA), the European Securities and Markets Authority (ESMA), and the Monetary Authority of Singapore (MAS)—showing that automation does not create a "lite" regime: fiduciary/suitability duties, fair marketing rules, technology and outsourcing controls, and record-keeping apply with equal or greater intensity when advice is delivered by algorithms. Horizontally, the EU's Digital Operational Resilience Act (DORA) and AI Act tighten governance, transparency, and resilience expectations that directly touch model development, deployment, monitoring, and rollback. We translate these frameworks into operational control sets data capture and suitability mapping (including sustainability preferences in Europe), model governance and change control, performance and "AI" claim substantiation, digital engagement practice (DEP) inventories, third-party/cloud oversight, and audit-grade books and records illustrating each with real enforcement and supervisory findings. The section also explores how to balance innovation and investor protection using sandboxes, "targeted support"/simplified advice initiatives in the UK, outcomes testing under the Consumer Duty, and DORA-style resilience drills, so product teams can iterate safely. Case studies (Schwab cash floors; Wealthfront/Hedgeable feature and marketing claims; Titan's hypothetical performance controls; Betterment's TLH disclosures; SoFi conflicts; SEC "AI-washing") show recurring failure modes and durable fixes: promise carefully, evidence continuously, explain plainly, and remediate fast. The overarching message is practical: build to the strictest common denominator across markets, wire compliance into the release pipeline, and treat

N. Nahidi (✉)
Business School, University of Exeter, Exeter, UK
e-mail: n.nahidi@exeter.ac.uk

N. Nahidi, A. Zarifis (eds.), *AI, FinTech, and the Future of Robo-Advisory*,
Contributions to Finance and Accounting,
https://doi.org/10.1007/978-3-032-18109-1_8

every client-facing statement, especially numbers and AI claims, as a regulated representation supported by contemporaneous evidence.

Keywords Financial regulation · Compliance · Artificial intelligence governance · Algorithmic accountability · Consumer protection · Digital operational resilience · Fiduciary duty · RegTech

JEL Classification: G28, G21, K23, O33

1 Introduction

AI is now embedded across retail investing and wealth management, with robo-advisers delivering onboarding, suitability assessment, portfolio construction, rebalancing, and client updates through fully digital journeys. Regulators have largely mapped these journeys onto existing investor-protection regimes rather than creating bespoke robo rules from scratch. In practice, that means U.S. advisers (including robo-platforms) operate under the Advisers Act's fiduciary and anti-fraud standards; UK firms face outcome-focused duties culminating in the FCA's Consumer Duty; EU firms must meet MiFID II suitability requirements updated by ESMA; and Singapore's MAS applies a technology-agnostic licensing and conduct framework tailored by pragmatic guidance for digital advisers. Across these regimes, the themes are strikingly consistent: robust client profiling and evidencable suitability; accurate, balanced marketing (including tight controls for hypothetical performance and honest "AI" claims); documented algorithm governance; and operational resilience with vendor/Cloud oversight. This chapter builds on those pillars and frames what "good" looks like in day-to-day product, model, legal, and compliance work.

In the United States, robo-advisers are simply investment advisers, so the same fiduciary duty and anti-fraud provisions apply to automated services and human advisers alike. Recent SEC actions show where digital models and marketing most often slip. The Schwab Intelligent Portfolios settlement in 2022 turned on disclosures that did not plainly convey how mandated cash allocations could depress expected returns; the three subsidiaries paid $187 million in disgorgement and penalties, and the case became a touchstone for aligning algorithm economics with client-facing language. The SEC's ongoing Marketing Rule sweeps (since 2023) and the Titan case underscore that hypothetical performance shown to broad audiences without strict controls is a violation; record-keeping, audience gating, and net-of-fees presentation are now non-negotiable mechanics for any growth team. And in 2024, the Commission fined Delphia and Global Predictions for "AI-washing," making clear that claims about AI capabilities are marketing statements subject to the anti-fraud rule, like any other. If you say a model "does X," you must be able to prove it. Together, these actions set the U.S. perimeter for robocompliance: don't oversell the model, don't misuse performance metrics, and ensure disclosures match how the algorithm really behaves.

The United Kingdom has taken an outcomes-based approach that treats automation as part of normal business rather than a special case. The FCA's 2018 multi-firm review of automated investment services flagged weaknesses in profiling, suitability evidence, and support for vulnerable customers; those gaps are amplified in click-through experiences where firms may collect too little information or lean too hard on defaults. Since July 2023, the Consumer Duty has raised the bar again: firms must design and distribute products and communications that deliver "good outcomes," which squarely covers risk-profiling journeys, portfolio templates, nudges, and post-sale support. Parallel policy work on the Advice–Guidance Boundary is creating a pathway for "targeted support" and simplified advice so firms can serve mass-market consumers without compromising protections; robo teams should monitor these consultations to scope constrained-advice flows with clear eligibility rules, human fallback, and audit trails. The direction of travel is clear: automation is welcome, provided firms can demonstrate suitability, fair value, and accessible communications in the round.

Across the European Union, MiFID II suitability remains the anchor for advice, including algorithmic advice, while horizontal digital rules now bite operationally. ESMA's 2022–2023 suitability guidelines clarify how firms must gather and use client information on knowledge/experience, risk tolerance, capacity for loss, objectives, and (since 2022) sustainability preferences, and how those inputs should flow through tools and recommendations. Two EU-wide frameworks now sit alongside: the AI Act, which entered into force on 1 August 2024 with phased application through 2025–2027 (including obligations for general-purpose AI from August 2025 and full application in August 2026); and DORA, applicable from 17 January 2025, which hardens ICT risk management, incident reporting, testing, and third-party oversight for financial entities. For robo-advisers, that translates into day-to-day obligations around model documentation and change control, resilience and failover testing, cloud/vendor governance, and clear, accessible disclosures, especially when sustainability preferences drive portfolio construction.

Singapore provides a concise, principle-based template that many Asia-Pacific (APAC) markets reference. MAS's Guidelines on the Provision of Digital Advisory Services clarify licensing under the Securities and Futures Act/Financial Advisers Act, set expectations for algorithm governance and back-testing, require ongoing monitoring, and mandate human escalation paths for edge cases while keeping the framework technology-agnostic so innovation isn't chilled. MAS couples this with a pragmatic stance on outsourcing and technology-risk controls, reflecting the reality that robo-platforms depend on APIs and cloud providers; firms must evidence vendor due diligence, performance monitoring, data protection, and exit plans. The net effect is a rules-light but expectations-clear environment: if a digital adviser claims it can profile, recommend, and rebalance appropriately, it must be able to show its working license in place, models documented, controls live, and customers supported.

A fast-emerging cross-cutting issue is digital conduct the way app design, prompts, and behavioral nudges embedded in digital financial platforms shape investor behavior. Internationally, IOSCO has examined Digital Engagement Practices (DEPs) such as default settings, push notifications, confetti, and prize draws, highlighting how they can increase trading, leverage, or risk-taking if not governed. The FCA has run controlled experiments showing that DEPs can materially affect trading frequency and risk appetite, reinforcing Consumer Duty expectations on customer understanding and foreseeable harm. For robo-advisers, this means inventorying every engagement element across onboarding, portfolio selection, and rebalancing; classifying which elements may constitute a recommendation or create bias; and building policies, sign-offs, and monitoring akin to financial promotions. Treat DEPs as part of the advice process, not just product design, and evidence how you mitigate harm while preserving beneficial nudges (e.g., reminders to review objectives or rebalance thresholds).

Enforcement history provides practical design lessons that teams can apply immediately. The SEC's first robo actions (Wealthfront and Hedgeable, 2018) targeted false statements about tax-loss-harvesting controls and misleading performance advertising, reminding firms that automation does not dilute the requirement to be fair, clear, and not misleading. The 2023 Titan case and the 2023–2024 Marketing Rule sweeps cemented operational expectations for hypothetical performance (audience gating, records, net-of-fees), which many growth teams had historically under-engineered. And the 2024 "AI-washing" cases against Delphia and Global Predictions translate cleanly to today's environment: inventory your AI uses, ensure claims match reality, and pre-clear every phrase that implies capability or advantage. A robust archive of marketing materials, model-change logs, and compliance approvals is no longer "nice to have"; it's table stakes.

An effective way to reconcile innovation with investor protection is to treat compliance as product design. Embed legal, compliance, and model-risk specialists into sprints; maintain end-to-end documentation (data lineage, features, training/validation, performance bounds, challenger models); define human-in-the-loop triggers, particularly for vulnerable customers or edge-case recommendations; and test resilience under DORA-style scenarios, including cloud outages and API breaks. Align all client-facing statements with reality, especially "AI" claims, and run pre-clearance for performance illustrations under the SEC Marketing Rule or local equivalents. As the EU AI Act phases in and DORA applies, and as the FCA tightens expectations under the Consumer Duty, firms that institutionalize this "compliance-by-design" approach will scale faster and safer across jurisdictions because they can show, not just tell, how their systems deliver suitable advice, robust operations, and fair outcomes.

2 Global Regulations on Robo-Advisory (SEC, FCA, ESMA, MAS)

Across major markets, there is no "lite" regime for robo-advisors, the same investor-protection rules that govern traditional advisers apply to automated services, with extra scrutiny on how algorithms are designed, monitored, and explained. In the United States, robo-platforms are investment advisers under the Investment Advisers Act, owing fiduciary and anti-fraud duties alongside compliance and recordkeeping obligations (SEC, 2022b). The UK's Financial Conduct Authority (FCA) supervises automated advice and online discretionary investment management under outcomes-based principles, now elevated by the Consumer Duty (FCA, 2022). In the European Union, MiFID II suitability rules refreshed by ESMA govern profiling and recommendations whether human- or algorithm-delivered (ESMA, 2022). Singapore's MAS sets a technology-agnostic framework that pairs licensing with specific expectations for digital advisory controls (MAS, 2018b). Conceptually, this alignment reflects the academic view that robo-advice should be regulated by function, not form (Baker & Dellaert, 2019).

In the U.S., the practical regulatory perimeter is defined as much by enforcement as by statutes and formal rules. Robo-advisers must make accurate Form ADV disclosures, operate under the Compliance Rule, and comply with the Marketing Rule when using testimonials, endorsements, or any hypothetical or back-tested performance (SEC, 2022b). Early enforcement actions against robo-advisory platforms highlighted recurring compliance weaknesses. In 2018, the SEC brought actions against Wealthfront and Hedgeable for misleading statements and insufficient controls, including issues related to tax-loss harvesting claims, client testimonials, and performance comparisons (SEC, 2018). Subsequent enforcement actions continued to emphasize similar risks, including cases involving SoFi Wealth, Schwab Intelligent Portfolios, and Titan Global Capital Management concerning conflicts of interest, undisclosed portfolio allocation effects, and misleading hypothetical performance claims (SEC, 2018, 2022b, 2023, 2024). More recently, the SEC pursued "AI-washing" actions against Delphia and Global Predictions for misleading statements regarding the use of artificial intelligence in investment processes (SEC, 2024). The operational lesson for U.S. robo-advisory firms is consistent: disclosures must align with actual model behavior, performance claims must be substantiated, and any AI-related representation should be treated as a regulated statement requiring verifiable evidence.

The UK approach treats automation as business as usual but demands robust evidence that retail clients receive suitable recommendations and fair value across the full digital journey. The FCA's multi-firm review of automated investment services highlighted gaps in data capture, suitability evidence, and support for vulnerable customers, weaknesses that can widen in click-through experiences if firms rely on defaults or shallow questionnaires (FCA, 2018). Since 2023, the Consumer Duty has made "good outcomes" the standard for product design, communications, and support, which squarely covers risk-profiling tools, portfolio templates, nudges, and post-sale prompts (FCA, 2022). Parallel policy work on the advice–guidance boundary seeks to enable "targeted support" and simplified advice journeys without diluting protections, a live track that robo teams should monitor when scoping constrained-scope use cases (FCA & (Dasgupta, 2021; FCA, 2024).

Within the EU, MiFID II suitability remains the anchor while horizontal digital rules now shape day-to-day model operations. ESMA's 2022 guidance clarifies how firms should capture and use knowledge/experience, objectives, risk tolerance, capacity for loss, and clients' sustainability preferences and how those inputs must flow into tools and recommendations, including algorithmic ones. Two EU-wide frameworks overlay the advice rules: the AI Act (entered into force in 2024 with phased obligations through 2025–2026) introduces governance and transparency duties, including for general-purpose AI used inside advice stacks; and DORA (applicable from January 2025) hardens ICT risk management, incident reporting, testing, and oversight of critical third-party providers (European Commission, 2024; European Union, 2022). For robo-advisers, that translates into model documentation and change control, resilience testing, cloud/vendor oversight, and accessible disclosures alongside classic suitability files (Table 1).

2.1 U.S. Enforcement Trajectory

The U.S. Securities and Exchange Commission (SEC) has taken the clearest stance that robo-advisors are subject to the same fiduciary and anti-fraud duties as traditional advisers, with enforcement actions setting the boundaries of permissible conduct. In In the Matter of Wealthfront Advisers, LLC (SEC, 2018), the Commission charged the platform for misleading tax-loss-harvesting claims, particularly the assurance that wash sales would be automatically avoided when, in practice, controls were incomplete. In a parallel case, In the Matter of Hedgeable, Inc. (SEC, 2018), false performance representations led to sanctions, reinforcing that automated services cannot dilute the "fair, clear, and not misleading" principle. Together, these early actions established that algorithmic advice is not exempt from core fiduciary duties and that every claim about automation must be verifiable across all edge cases.

2.2 Conflicts and Cash Floors

The 2022 Schwab case epitomizes how subtle algorithmic design choices can embed conflicts of interest. According to the SEC (2022a), Schwab's robo-portfolios included mandated cash allocations that depressed expected returns relative to alternatives, without prominently disclosing the impact or the affiliated benefits to Schwab's bank. The $187 million settlement demonstrated that regulators will treat cash "corridors" as material allocations that require plain-English disclosure and robust governance. As Baker and Dellaert (2018) argue, conflicts of interest in robo-advice are structurally harder for clients to perceive, making transparent disclosures not merely desirable but necessary to preserve trust. This case remains the most significant robo-advisory enforcement to date and sets a precedent for quantifying and communicating the economic implications of embedded rules.

Table 1 Enforcement actions and supervisory frameworks in robo-advisory services across jurisdictions

Jurisdiction /Regulator	Year	Firm/Entity	Business Model	Alleged Misconduct	Regulatory Basis	Outcome/ Sanction	Sanction Amount	Admission / Settlement	Remedies Ordered	Notes / Key Lessons
USA/SEC	2018	Wealthfront	Fully automated robo	Misleading TLH claims, wash-sale monitoring failures	Advisers Act (anti-fraud, compliance)	Settlement	N/A	Settled, no admission	Enhanced disclosure, compliance review	Automation ≠ diluted duty; every claim must match execution
USA/SEC	2018	Hedgeable	Robo discretionary	Misleading marketing, performance exaggeration	Advisers Act	Settlement	N/A	Settled	Disclosure fixes	Early case confirming "no carve-out" for robo
USA/SEC	2021	SoFi Wealth	Hybrid robo + proprietary ETFs	Conflicts of interest (proprietary ETF bias)	Advisers Act	Settlement	Not public	Settled	Conflict disclosure	Conflicts must be quantified and disclosed
USA/SEC	2022	Charles Schwab (3 subs.)	Robo discretionary	Undisclosed cash floors, misleading disclosures	Advisers Act	Fine + disgorgement	$187 m	Settled	Restitution + disclosure changes	Cash allocations = material economic decision, must disclose
USA/SEC	2023	Titan Global Capital	Robo / fintech app	Improper hypothetical performance marketing	SEC Marketing Rule	Fine	$1 m+	Settled	Marketing controls, record-keeping	Hypothetical results = "hazardous content"
USA/SEC	2023	Betterment	Large robo	Misstatements re: tax-loss harvesting	Advisers Act	Fine	$9 m	Settled	Monitoring + remediation	Release management = investor protection

(continued)

Table 1 (continued)

Jurisdiction/ Regulator	Year	Firm/Entity	Business Model	Alleged Misconduct	Regulatory Basis	Outcome/ Sanction	Sanction Amount	Admission / Settlement	Remedies Ordered	Notes / Key Lessons
USA/SEC	2024	Delphia (AI) & Global Predictions	AI-driven robo	Misleading "AI" claims ("AI-washing")	Advisers Act anti-fraud	Fine	~$400 k combined	Settled	AI claims substantiation	AI language is a regulated statement
UK / FCA	2018	Multi-firm robo review (10+ firms)	Online discretionary + automated advice	Weak profiling, suitability evidence gaps, poor support for vulnerable clients	FCA Conduct Rules	Supervisory notice, no monetary fine	N/A	N/A	Required remediation	FCA treats automation as BAU but demands outcomes
UK/FCA	2023	Consumer Duty roll-out	Sector-wide	Digital advice journeys must deliver "good outcomes"	Consumer Duty rules	Supervisory monitoring	N/A	N/A	Ongoing reporting + monitoring	Elevated bar for digital suitability and communications
EU/ESMA	2022–23	All EU firms under MiFID II	Robo and human advice	Suitability & sustainability preference integration	MiFID II + ESMA Guidelines	Supervisory	N/A	N/A	Periodic review/reporting	Sustainability preferences must be fully integrated
EU/ESMA	2024	Sector-wide guidance on AI in investment services	Robo firms using AI	Risks of bias, opacity, overreliance	MiFID II + AI Act	Guidance (non-binding yet)	N/A	N/A	Sandbox creation, transparency obligations	AI Act = governance + documentation expectations
Singapore/ MAS	2018	Robo advisory sector	Licensing & oversight	Guidance on algorithm governance, back-testing, outsourcing	Securities and Futures Act	Supervisory	N/A	N/A	Licensing conditions	Pragmatic template no carve-outs, must prove controls

This table summarizes major regulatory interventions affecting robo-advisory platforms. U.S. entries reflect formal SEC enforcement actions with monetary sanctions, while UK, EU, and Singapore entries represent supervisory reviews, policy frameworks, and guidance documents that shape compliance expectations

2.3 Performance Claims and Hypotheticals

Marketing remains a persistent pressure point where growth imperatives collide with regulatory boundaries. The Titan order in 2023 exemplifies this dynamic: the SEC found that hypothetical performance was disseminated to retail audiences without the gating, disclaimers, and reproducibility required under the amended Marketing Rule (SEC, 2023). Scholars note that retail investors often overweigh hypothetical returns, leading to distorted expectations (Lusardi & Mitchell, 2014). Titan's $1 million penalty shows that performance illustrations are treated as high-risk content, requiring not only accurate assumptions but also robust distribution controls. From a compliance-by-design perspective, this means embedding marketing review processes into content pipelines so that no chart, tweet, or landing page can circumvent regulatory filters.

2.4 AI-Washing as an Emerging Frontier

Most recently, the SEC's 2024 cases against Delphia and Global Predictions introduced the notion of "AI-washing" misleading statements about the use of artificial intelligence in investment processes (SEC, 2024). This aligns with broader concerns about "greenwashing" and other forms of exaggerated claims in finance. By sanctioning firms for overstating AI capabilities, the Commission clarified that language such as "predicts" or "optimizes" is a regulated representation requiring evidence. As Cruz et al. (2024) noted, this was the SEC's first explicit action targeting AI misrepresentation, and it signals that AI-related marketing will be policed with the same rigor as performance advertising. For robo-advisers, this introduces a new compliance perimeter: every AI-related phrase must be backed by model documentation, validation results, and contemporaneous evidence.

2.5 UK Supervisory Approach

In contrast to U.S. headline fines, the UK's Financial Conduct Authority (FCA) has pursued supervisory reviews and thematic interventions. Its 2018 multi-firm review of automated investment services flagged deficiencies in client profiling, suitability evidence, and treatment of vulnerable customers (FCA, 2018). Although no fines were imposed, firms were required to remediate weaknesses and demonstrate compliance improvements. Since July 2023, the Consumer Duty has raised the bar by obliging firms to evidence "good outcomes" across product design, communication, and post-sale support (FCA, 2022). As Black (2008) emphasizes, the UK tradition of "outcomes-based" regulation often relies on supervision and monitoring rather than punitive fines, aiming to shape firm behavior systemically. For robo-advisers, this translates into deeper evidence-gathering and user-testing of digital flows, even absent enforcement penalties.

2.6 European Convergence and Horizontal Rules

At the EU level, MiFID II remains the anchor for suitability obligations, but ESMA's 2022 guidelines clarified how sustainability preferences must be integrated into suitability assessments, including algorithmic advice (ESMA, 2022). This requirement adds a new layer of complexity, as robo-engines must now align portfolio construction with clients' environmental, social, and governance (ESG) preferences. The horizontal frameworks of the Digital Operational Resilience Act (DORA) and the AI Act go further: DORA hardens ICT risk management, testing, and vendor oversight (EU, 2022), while the AI Act mandates governance and transparency obligations for "high-risk" AI, including general-purpose AI used in financial services (EU, 2024). Scholars such as Gunningham et al. (2003) argue that layered regulatory approaches combining sectoral rules with horizontal resilience requirements create more robust guardrails but also increase compliance costs. For robo-platforms, the implication is that operational resilience and AI explainability are no longer optional extras but regulatory necessities.

2.7 Singapore's Pragmatic Template

Singapore's Monetary Authority of Singapore (MAS) has taken a technology-agnostic but principle-heavy approach. Its Guidelines on the Provision of Digital Advisory Services require algorithm governance, back-testing, ongoing monitoring, and escalation paths for edge cases (MAS, 2018a, 2018b). This is complemented by the Technology Risk Management Guidelines (MAS, 2021), which stress scenario testing, adversarial simulations, and vendor due diligence. As Tan (2020) notes, MAS's stance balances innovation encouragement with strict expectations that firms prove controls in practice. Unlike the U.S., penalties have been rare, but licensing conditions and supervisory scrutiny act as de facto enforcement tools. The lesson is clear: robo-platforms in Singapore operate under a rules-light but expectations-heavy regime where credibility depends on demonstrable governance.

2.8 Cross-Jurisdictional Lessons

Taken together, the global picture shows divergence in style but convergence in substance. The SEC leads with visible penalties, making enforcement a signaling device; the FCA and MAS rely more on supervisory engagement and guidance;

and ESMA leverages horizontal frameworks that embed digital resilience and AI accountability into sectoral rules. As Baldwin et al. (2012) argue, regulatory strategies oscillate between "command-and-control," "incentive-based," and "responsive" approaches. For robo-advisers operating cross-border, the safest path is to build to the strictest denominator: SEC-style claim substantiation, FCA-style outcome monitoring, ESMA-level sustainability and resilience documentation, and MAS-grade vendor oversight. This approach not only reduces retrofit costs but also positions firms as trustworthy players in a market where investor confidence hinges on transparency and evidence.

Singapore provides a concise, principle-based template that many APAC firms follow. The Guidelines on Provision of Digital Advisory Services confirm that licensing is technology-agnostic and set expectations for algorithm governance, back-testing, ongoing monitoring, and human escalation for edge cases (MAS, 2018a, 2018b). MAS complements this with Technology Risk Management guidance on scenario testing, adversarial simulations, and incident response, and with outsourcing expectations for cloud and critical vendors (MAS 2021). The message is clear: there is no robo carve-out, automate only what you can supervise and explain, and prove that controls work in production.

Convergence is strongest around digital conduct and communications. International work on Digital Engagement Practices (DEPs) shows that prompts, default settings, notifications, and gamified design can materially influence risk-taking and trading frequency in retail channels (IOSCO, 2024; IOSCO, 2025). UK experiments echo these findings and link them directly to Consumer Duty expectations on customer understanding and foreseeable harm (FCA, 2024). For robo-advisers, that means cataloguing every engagement element across onboarding, portfolio selection, and rebalancing; defining when a prompt might constitute a recommendation; and governing DEPs with the same controls and approvals used for financial promotions (FCA, 2022; ESMA, 2022).

Supervisors in all four jurisdictions increasingly expect compliance by design. Product squads should embed legal/compliance and model-risk specialists into sprints; maintain model cards, data-lineage documentation, challenger models, and performance bounds; and operate change-control processes that tie code releases to approvals and client-facing disclosures (ESMA, 2022; SEC, 2023). Operational resilience is now table stakes: define RTO/RPO for rebalancing engines, drill failover runbooks, secure audit and exit rights with cloud/data vendors, and monitor key risk indicators that link client outcomes to model and platform health (European Union, 2022; MAS, 2021). When platforms operate across borders, building to the strictest regulatory standard by default such as DORA-grade resilience, ESMA-level suitability evidence, FCA-style outcomes monitoring, and MAS-aligned technology risk management reduces retrofit risk.

Innovation remains encouraged within guardrails. The FCA's Innovation Pathways (and earlier Advice Unit), MAS's sandboxes, and the AI Act's requirement for national AI sandboxes provide structured ways to test novel features under supervisory visibility (FCA, 2022; MAS, 2018a, 2018b; European Commission, 2024). The practical win is not a lower bar but earlier alignment on controls, disclosures, and metrics that evidence client benefit. Teams that use these channels while treating marketing language (especially "AI" claims and hypothetical results) as regulated, and that hardwire suitability, resilience, and explainability into their CI/CD pipelines, will move faster with fewer regulatory surprises (SEC, 2023; FCA, 2022).

3 The Challenge of Ensuring Compliance with Financial Laws

Ensuring suitability remains the core challenge because automated journeys magnify both the benefits and the risks of scale. Firms must collect sufficiently granular data on knowledge/experience, objectives, risk tolerance, capacity for loss, and, since 2022 in the EU, sustainability preferences, then map those inputs to portfolios in a way that is explainable and evidenced (ESMA, 2022). UK supervision has repeatedly found that digital flows can under-collect or over-rely on defaults, which undermines suitability and the fair-value outcome now required by the Consumer Duty (FCA, 2018; FCA, 2022). A robust control environment therefore includes hard stops when inputs are incomplete, documented logic that links client attributes to portfolio selection, periodic re-profiling triggers tied to life events or market stress, and a clear human-in-the-loop path for edge cases and vulnerable customers (FCA, 2018; ESMA, 2022).

Marketing and performance communications are the next pressure point because they sit where growth targets meet regulatory obligations. Under the SEC's Marketing Rule, hypothetical and back-tested results require audience controls, relevance filters, prominent limitations, and durable recordkeeping; failures in any of these mechanics have led to enforcement against digital advisers who showcased eye-catching numbers to mass audiences (SEC, 2023). The broader lesson is operational: performance content must be treated as a high-risk asset with pre-clearance workflows, standardized disclaimers, net-of-fees presentation when applicable, and monitoring to ensure sales channels don't circumvent gating rules (SEC, 2023). UK and EU regimes reach similar conclusions through different legal routes: communications must be fair, clear, and not misleading, and firms must be able to evidence that customers genuinely understood key features and risks (FCA, 2022; ESMA, 2022). "AI" language is itself a regulated claim. In 2024, the SEC sanctioned firms for making false or misleading statements about their use of AI/ML, signaling that claims about models, data, and predictive capabilities must be substantiated like any other performance-adjacent statement (SEC, 2024). Practical compliance means maintaining an AI claims register that maps every public assertion to internal evidence (data lineage, training/testing summaries, validation metrics, and limits), enforcing pre-clearance of AI-related phrasing in all channels, and aligning investor presentations with what the production system actually does. When phrasing implies advantage "predicts," "detects," "optimizes," "learns" firms should expect to produce contemporaneous evidence on request (SEC, 2024).

Model governance ties the above together and determines whether the advice engine is controllable at scale. Supervisors expect firms to define model purpose, features, data sources and rights, training/validation methods, challenger approaches, performance bounds, and change-approval thresholds; they also expect drift, stability, and fairness monitoring, with documented interventions when thresholds are breached (ESMA, 2022; European Commission, 2024). The EU AI Act reinforces governance and transparency expectations, while DORA pushes financial entities toward disciplined ICT controls and resilience testing that directly affect model deployment and rollback procedures (European Union, 2022; European Commission, 2024). In APAC, MAS guidance makes the same point pragmatically: keep algorithms explainable, back-test them, monitor them continuously, and be ready to escalate to a human when the logic hits its limits (MAS, 2018a, 2018b).

Operational resilience and third-party risk have shifted from "sound practice" to mandatory in several jurisdictions, with particular implications for cloud-first robo stacks. DORA requires formal ICT risk frameworks, incident reporting, threat-led testing, and oversight of critical third-party providers expectations that map onto architectural choices like multi-region deployment, controlled failover, immutable config, and tested run-books for advice and rebalancing engines (European Union, 2022). MAS's Technology Risk Management and Outsourcing frameworks land similarly, requiring scenario exercises, adversarial simulations, vendor due diligence, audit/exit rights, and data portability practical guardrails for platforms built on external APIs and cloud services (MAS, 2021; MAS, 2018a, 2018b). Day-to-day, this means defined RTO/RPO targets for advice functions, telemetry to detect partial failures, and drill-proven incident communications to clients and regulators. Digital engagement practices (DEPs) prompts, defaults, leaderboards, prize draws, push notifications can tilt investor behavior and therefore attract conduct scrutiny. IOSCO's recent work finds that DEPs can raise trading frequency and risk-taking, while UK experiments show measurable shifts from small design changes in trading apps (IOSCO, 2024; IOSCO, 2025; FCA, 2024). Under the Consumer Duty, design choices that predictably cause harm breach expectations on customer understanding and foreseeable harm (FCA, 2022). Compliance therefore extends beyond words to interaction design: inventory DEPs, classify which elements might constitute a recommendation, apply financial-promotion style approvals, and monitor behavioral outcomes (e.g., migration into riskier portfolios after a specific prompt), with thresholds for remediation and product changes (FCA, 2022; ESMA, 2022).

Books and records complete the compliance perimeter and are often where otherwise good programs stumble. The SEC's sweeps routinely pair marketing findings with recordkeeping lapses; the same risk exists in UK/EU regimes that expect durable evidence of what clients saw, understood, and agreed to (SEC, 2023; FCA, 2022). For automated platforms, "records" must include versioned screenshots of every in-app screen and disclosure, all variants used in A/B tests, push-notification texts, social content, and app-store descriptions, plus model-change logs tied to release identifiers. When combined with suitability files and service-level telemetry, these artifacts let firms reconstruct the client experience and the state of the model at any point—often the difference between explaining a blip and defending a breach (ESMA, 2022; SEC, 2023).

Table 2 builds on the enforcement history and supervisory case studies summarized earlier by mapping four cross-cutting regulatory themes: suitability, truthfulness of AI and performance claims, digital conduct nudges, and operational resilience across the SEC, FCA, ESMA, and MAS.

The intensity ratings in Table 2 were derived from observable regulatory posture rather than subjective judgment. A "High" intensity designation reflects either direct enforcement actions with monetary sanctions (e.g., SEC penalties for misleading tax-loss harvesting claims, hypothetical performance disclosures, or AI-washing) or binding obligations with detailed guidance (e.g., ESMA's MiFID II suitability rules and the EU's Digital Operational Resilience Act). "Medium" intensity indicates areas where regulators have published thematic reviews or supervisory expectations but have not yet imposed widespread penalties, such as the FCA's Consumer Duty monitoring of suitability and digital nudges, or MAS's requirements for algorithm governance under its 2018 Guidelines. Finally, "Emerging" denotes themes where regulatory attention is visible through principle-based guidance or exploratory reports but without targeted enforcement to date, as with DEPs in Singapore or operational resilience in the United States. These classifications capture the present regulatory stance as of 2024–2025 and are designed to highlight both the variation in current supervisory approaches and the likely trajectory of future enforcement.

Empirical evidence from U.S. enforcement actions confirms that marketing and disclosure remain the dominant vulnerabilities in robo-advisory oversight. Since 2018, the SEC has repeatedly sanctioned firms for misleading statements, from Wealthfront's false claims about tax-loss harvesting to Titan's improper presentation of hypothetical returns (SEC, 2018; SEC, 2023). The case against Betterment in 2023 further reinforced that even partial misstatements about the frequency and scope of tax-loss harvesting monitoring constitute breaches of fiduciary duty (SEC, 2023). As Fig. 1 shows, these cases comprise the overwhelming majority of enforcement activity, illustrating the SEC's prioritization of transparency in automated advice. Conflicts of interest form a second, though less frequent, category. The SEC's 2022 action against Charles Schwab subsidiaries highlighted how platforms' use of cash "floors" in automated portfolios—directed into affiliated funds—created hidden conflicts that disadvantaged clients (SEC, 2022a). Similarly, SoFi Wealth was sanctioned for misstatements in its disclosures around investment strategies (SEC, 2021). These cases demonstrate that even where robo-advisory algorithms are technically functional, underlying commercial incentives can distort outcomes. The smaller number of conflicts cases in Fig. 2 suggests that regulators treat these as significant but episodic breaches, requiring targeted penalties rather than systemic reforms. A newer and growing frontier is the misrepresentation of artificial intelligence capabilities, or "AI-washing." In 2024, the SEC charged Delphia and Global Predictions with making false and misleading claims about their use of artificial intelligence in investment processes (SEC, 2024). These actions were the first of their kind and signaled a regulatory shift toward scrutinizing not

Table 2 Regulatory themes in robo-advisory oversight: Current intensity and future hotspots

Theme	SEC (U.S.)	FCA (UK)	ESMA / EU	MAS (Singapore)	Current Intensity	Future Hotspots
Suitability in digital contexts	Fiduciary duty; actions against Wealthfront, Betterment for suitability gaps (SEC, 2018, 2023).	Multi-firm review (2018) found weak profiling; Consumer Duty (2022) requires "good outcomes."	MiFID II guidelines (2022) mandate integration of ESG preferences.	Digital Advisory Guidelines (2018) require profiling + human fallback.	High (SEC, FCA, ESMA)/medium (MAS)	ESG-driven suitability (EU), vulnerable customer focus (UK).
Truthfulness in AI & performance claims	Titan (2023) on hypotheticals; Delphia/Global Predictions (2024) on AI-washing.	Consumer Duty + promotions oversight; no robo-specific fines yet.	MiFID II fairness rules; AI Act (2024) extends transparency to AI tools.	Back-testing and validation expected (TRM, 2021).	High (SEC)/medium (FCA, ESMA)/emerging (MAS)	AI Act enforcement (EU); AI marketing scrutiny (SEC).
Digital conduct nudges (DEPs)	Not yet direct but overlaps with anti-fraud standards.	DEP experiments (2024) show nudges drive risk-taking; subject to Consumer Duty.	Acknowledged in suitability/disclosure context; IOSCO 2024–25 reports highlight risks.	No explicit DEP enforcement, but MAS expects firms to mitigate harmful nudges.	Medium (FCA, ESMA)/emerging (SEC, MAS)	DEP enforcement (FCA); cross-border standards (IOSCO).
Resilience /outsourcing	Record-keeping and operational resilience under Compliance Rule.	Supervisory focus on resilience frameworks; tied to Consumer Duty.	DORA (2022, effective 2025) mandates ICT risk and vendor oversight.	TRM (2021) + Outsourcing Guidelines (2018) require vendor diligence, stress testing.	High (ESMA)/medium (MAS, FCA)/emerging (SEC)	Cloud/vendor failures; cross-border stress testing.

This table compares how major regulators address suitability, AI/performance claims, digital conduct nudges, and operational resilience in robo-advisory platforms. The "Current Intensity" column reflects whether enforcement is high (visible penalties or strict rules), medium (supervisory focus), or emerging (principle-based expectations without direct enforcement). The "Future Hotspots" column highlights likely areas of upcoming regulatory focus

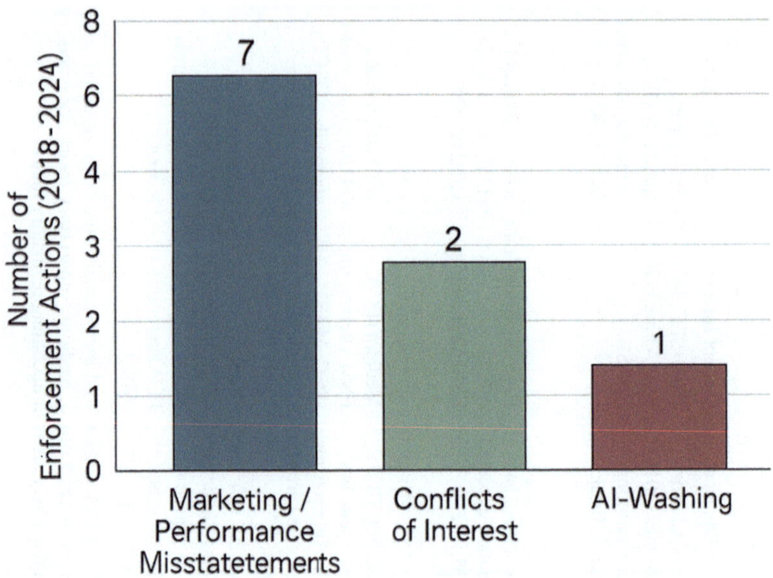

Fig. 1 Distribution of SEC robo-advisory enforcement actions by issue type (2018–2024). This figure aggregates all SEC robo-advisory enforcement actions between 2018 and 2024 into three categories. Seven of the cases, such as Wealthfront (2018), Hedgeable (2018), Titan (2023), and Betterment (2023), concerned misleading marketing or performance disclosures, making this the dominant enforcement focus. Two cases, including the 2022 action against Schwab and the 2021 sanction of SoFi Wealth, involved conflicts of interest or misaligned incentives within automated portfolios. Only one case to date, the 2024 charges against Delphia and Global Predictions, explicitly addressed misrepresentation of artificial intelligence capabilities, marking the beginning of an "AI-washing" enforcement trend. These proportions (7, 2, 1) reflect the SEC's emphasis on information accuracy and transparency in robo-advisory, while signaling that AI-related misstatements are emerging as a future priority

only performance disclosures but also the credibility of AI-based marketing claims. The emergence of AI-washing cases—though still a minority in Fig. 2—aligns with concerns raised by Mayer Brown (2024) and others that firms are increasingly tempted to exaggerate AI capabilities as a competitive differentiator.

Taken together, the distribution in Fig. 1 underscores two broader points. First, robo-advisory enforcement has been disproportionately concentrated on information asymmetries—misstatements, omissions, and claims that impair client decision-making—rather than on the technical functioning of algorithms. Second, the trajectory suggests a gradual expansion from traditional fiduciary issues (suitability, conflicts) toward digital-age risks such as AI marketing and engagement design. This pattern mirrors the regulatory dynamics described by Black (2008) and Baldwin, Cave, and Lodge (2012): regulators initially focus on visible misstatements, but over time extend oversight to systemic design features. As the FCA's (2024) experiments on digital engagement practices and ESMA's (2022)

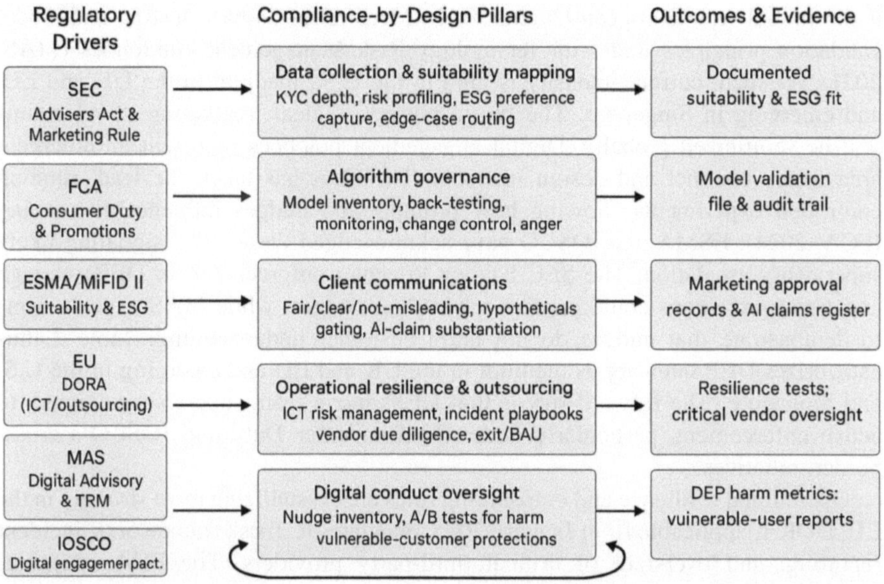

Fig. 2 Compliance-by-design model for robo-advisory regulation. This figure illustrates how regulatory drivers (SEC, FCA, ESMA/MiFID II, EU DORA and AI Act, MAS, IOSCO) feed into five compliance-by-design pillars: suitability, algorithm governance, client communications, operational resilience, and digital conduct oversight, producing auditable outcomes. Arrows indicate regulatory influence flowing into firm processes, and feedback loops represent continuous monitoring and governance

ESG suitability guidelines show, global regulators are converging on similar themes even if their enforcement modalities differ.

Instead of analyzing regulators in isolation, this comparative structure highlights both the areas of convergence and the dimensions where supervisory emphasis diverges. Suitability emerges as the universal anchor. U.S. enforcement has repeatedly sanctioned robo-advisers where claims about automated tax-loss harvesting or profiling overstated actual performance (SEC, 2018, 2023). In the UK, the FCA's 2018 review and the 2022 Consumer Duty require firms to evidence suitability across digital journeys, including protections for vulnerable customers. ESMA's 2022 guidelines add a further obligation: sustainability preferences must flow directly into recommendations, a change that materially increases the evidentiary burden on robo platforms. MAS (2018a, 2018b) likewise expects profiling and escalation paths, though its posture is supervisory rather than punitive. Accordingly, Table 2 ranks SEC, FCA, and ESMA as "high" intensity, and MAS as "medium."

The SEC has made marketing and AI claims a top priority, penalizing Titan for hypothetical performance disclosures (SEC, 2023) and Delphia/Global Predictions for AI-washing (SEC, 2024). The FCA applies Consumer Duty and promotions rules but has not yet fined robo-advisers specifically on this dimension. ESMA embeds truthfulness under MiFID II and will soon enforce transparency obligations under the AI Act (European Union, 2024). MAS relies on back-testing and model validation principles under its Technology Risk Management Guidelines (MAS, 2021). As such, current intensity is high in the U.S., medium in the UK and EU, and emerging in Singapore. The future hotspot is clear: marketing of AI claims will be scrutinized globally. Digital engagement practices represent an emergent area where conduct and design intersect. The FCA has taken the lead, running controlled experiments showing how prompts and nudges influence risk-taking (FCA, 2024). ESMA and IOSCO have acknowledged these risks, signaling likely supervisory escalation. The SEC has yet to center enforcement on DEPs, though anti-fraud provisions could capture misleading nudges, while MAS expects firms to demonstrate that nudges do not harm customer understanding. Table 2 thus categorizes DEP intensity as medium in the UK and EU and emerging in the U.S. and Singapore. The forward risk is that DEPs move from supervisory concern to active enforcement, particularly under the Consumer Duty and IOSCO's cross-border initiatives.

Operational resilience and outsourcing rules are crystallizing most strongly in the EU. DORA, applicable from January 2025, mandates ICT risk frameworks, incident reporting, and oversight of critical third-party providers. The FCA integrates resilience into its Consumer Duty monitoring, while MAS sets detailed expectations for vendor oversight in its TRM (2021) and Outsourcing Guidelines (2018). The SEC, by contrast, treats resilience largely through record-keeping and general compliance obligations. Hence Table 2 records high intensity for ESMA, medium for FCA and MAS, and emerging for the SEC. The clear future hotspot is cloud and vendor failures, which regulators increasingly treat as systemic risk triggers. Table 2 reframes robo-advisory oversight from a jurisdictional comparison to a thematic diagnosis. Suitability and truthfulness are already highly policed, while DEPs and resilience are the next enforcement frontiers. By incorporating a future-hotspot lens, the table highlights where platforms should pre-emptively invest in controls: AI claim substantiation, DEP inventories, ESG suitability mapping, and DORA-grade vendor governance. The message is clear: firms that build to the strictest denominator across jurisdictions are best positioned to scale safely while avoiding retrofit costs.

The compliance-by-design model in Fig. 1 shows how diverse regulatory mandates are absorbed into the operational structures of robo-advisers. In the United States, enforcement actions such as Wealthfront and Hedgeable (2018) and Betterment (2023) [Betterment (2023) refers to the SEC's enforcement action against Betterment LLC, announced on April 18, 2023. The SEC alleged that Betterment made misleading statements concerning its tax-loss harvesting service, including failures in disclosure about the frequency of monitoring for wash sales. The case was resolved through a settlement and a $9 million penalty (SEC, 2023).] show how fiduciary and disclosure duties under the Advisers Act are applied to automated tax-loss harvesting and profiling claims (SEC, 2018, 2023). In the United Kingdom, the FCA's multi-firm review of automated investment services and its subsequent Consumer Duty reforms have emphasized suitability and fairness across digital journeys, particularly for vulnerable customers (SEC, 2018, 2022b). At the EU level,

ESMA's suitability guidelines under MiFID II explicitly require ESG preference integration (ESMA, 2022), while the Digital Operational Resilience Act (DORA) introduces binding ICT and vendor governance (EU, 2022). Singapore's MAS has developed a more principles-based regime, through its Guidelines on Digital Advisory (2018) and TRM framework (2021), while IOSCO (2021, 2024) has signaled that digital engagement practices will soon be subject to cross-border scrutiny.

These drivers are translated into five operational pillars that together form the backbone of compliance by design. Suitability processes ensure that KYC data, risk profiles, and ESG preferences are captured with sufficient granularity to satisfy fiduciary and MiFID obligations. Algorithm governance requires inventorying, back-testing, and continuous monitoring of models, consistent with both SEC enforcement actions against Titan for hypothetical returns (SEC, 2023) and MAS requirements for lifecycle testing. Client communications obligations extend from prohibitions on misleading marketing in the SEC's Marketing Rule to the FCA's outcomes-based fairness test under the Consumer Duty, making substantiation of AI-related claims a critical control (Cruz et al., 2024). Resilience and outsourcing controls draw on systemic frameworks such as DORA and MAS outsourcing guidelines, embedding vendor diligence, continuity testing, and incident reporting into advisory platforms. Oversight of digital nudges responds to emerging supervisory concerns raised by the FCA's experiments on trading apps (FCA, 2024) and IOSCO's consultation on digital engagement practices (IOSCO, 2024).

Each of these pillars generates tangible artifacts that regulators increasingly demand as evidence. Suitability processes produce documented assessments of investor preferences and ESG fit; algorithm governance yields validation files and audit trails; client communication controls create marketing approval records and AI claims registers; resilience frameworks produce stress test results and vendor oversight reports; and nudge oversight generates DEP harm metrics and records of interventions for vulnerable clients. These outputs reflect a broader move toward evidence-based regulation, in which supervisory scrutiny hinges not on principles alone but on the demonstrability of compliance (Baldwin et al., 2012). The arrows in Fig. 1 represent this linear logic: regulatory expectations flow into firm-level processes, which in turn generate verifiable outputs.

The feedback loops illustrate that compliance is not static but iterative. Suitability records inform the refinement of profiling tools, validation outcomes feed back into model-risk management, claims registers shape future marketing practices, resilience test results drive vendor governance adjustments, and DEP metrics inform interface redesigns. This circularity resonates with Gunningham et al.'s (2003) concept of "smart regulation," in which compliance systems are designed to evolve in response to regulatory signals and market behavior. By showing how outputs become inputs for the next cycle of governance, the model highlights compliance-by-design as a dynamic system rather than a one-off obligation. This interpretation positions regulatory oversight as both constraint and enabler: a mechanism that, if well-embedded, supports investor protection while fostering trust in the scalability of AI-driven advisory services.

4 Balancing Innovation and Investor Protection

Regulatory on-ramps exist to help teams test new ideas transparently rather than quietly shipping and hoping for the best. The FCA's Innovation Pathways gives firms early engagement and structured feedback on novel advice/guidance journeys, building on the Advisory Unit's experience with automated models (FCA, 2022). MAS offers Sandbox, Sandbox Express, and enhanced support that allow time-boxed, parameterized testing with clear exit criteria (MAS, 2018a). The EU AI Act goes further by requiring each Member State to operate at least one AI regulatory sandbox by the mid-2020s, creating a supervised space to trial AI-enabled features that affect suitability, monitoring, or communications (EU, 2024). None of these lowers the bar on client protection; they reduce legal uncertainty and align controls before full launch (FCA, 2022; MAS, 2018a).

A practical way to widen access without diluting safeguards is to design constrained-scope advice with crisp eligibility rules and overt boundaries. UK policy work on the advice–guidance boundary is explicitly aimed at closing the "advice gap" by enabling "targeted support" and simplified advice for well-defined needs, supported by Consumer Duty outcomes on customer understanding and price/value (FCA, 2022). For robo teams, this translates into flows that clearly signpost when a client is outside the scope, default to guidance rather than advice when inputs are incomplete, and offer human fallback when the algorithm's confidence or coverage is low. Documenting those design decisions and measuring whether they drive better outcomes are as important as the code (FCA, 2022).

Explainability is both a technical and a communications discipline. Internally, model cards, data lineage, performance bounds, and challenger results anchor governance; externally, firms must explain, in plain language, why a recommendation fits a specific customer, including any sustainability-preference trade-offs required by MiFID II. Under the Consumer Duty, "customer understanding" requires testing whether disclosures actually land, not just presenting them (FCA, 2022). Effective robo-platforms, therefore, pair algorithmic explainers with UX that lets clients interrogate key drivers, risk capacity, horizon, sustainability preferences, and access an escalation route to a human when something does not look right (FCA, 2022).

Test-first engineering helps teams innovate quickly without outsourcing risk to end users. DORA expects EU firms to implement threat-led penetration testing and incident playbooks; MAS TRM encourages scenario-based and adversarial exercises (EU, 2022). For robo-advice, that means treating portfolio engines and profile-to-portfolio mapping as mission-critical services with defined RTO/RPO, running chaos tests on market data/API dependencies, and gating deployments on model-risk approvals. Canary releases and shadow-mode comparisons between challenger and champion models can catch regressions before they affect clients, with rollback procedures drilled like fire drills (EU, 2022).

Vendor and cloud strategies should be framed as investor-protection controls, not only cost or speed choices. DORA requires oversight of critical third parties, while MAS Outsourcing guidance expects due diligence, performance SLAs, audit rights, exit plans, and data-portability arrangements that survive stress (EU, 2022). Practically, robo platforms need dual data feeds where feasible, circuit-breakers for stale or anomalous inputs, and read-only fallbacks that pause rebalancing rather than propagate bad data. Contracts should encode supervisory access and exit timelines, and architecture should minimize single points of failure—decisions that materially improve client outcomes during disruptions (EU, 2022).

Measurement closes the loop and turns "we think this helps" into evidence. The Consumer Duty asks boards to monitor whether products deliver good outcomes; that invites metrics such as suitability exceptions, vulnerable-customer escalations, rebalancing error rates, and behavioral outcomes linked to DEPs (FCA, 2022). For firms that use sustainability preferences in Europe, tracking whether portfolio construction honors stated preferences without unintended concentration risk is similarly important. Publishing periodic outcome dashboards to governance committees and acting on signals demonstrates the culture that supervisors increasingly expect.

Roadmaps should be aligned to regulatory timelines, so innovation does not force late retrofits. The AI Act entered into force in 2024 with phased obligations through 2025–2026, including transparency and governance expectations for general-purpose AI that many firms will rely on. DORA has been applied since January 2025, and its testing, incident, and third-party oversight obligations are now live for EU financial entities (EU, 2022). A "strictest-standard-first" philosophy—DORA-grade resilience, ESMA-level suitability evidence, FCA-style outcomes monitoring, MAS-aligned TRM—lets cross-border robo-platforms scale without fragmenting their control stack, while still leaving room for product teams to iterate quickly within clear guardrails (FCA, 2022).

5 Case Studies

5.1 Charles Schwab Intelligent Portfolios Cash Floors & Conflicts

Schwab's automated portfolios brought the industry's attention to how apparently "neutral" portfolio rules can encode meaningful economic choices that must be explained with the same care as security selection. A mandated cash floor that is systematically higher than peers or than a purely mean–variance specification will tend to depress expected returns in many market states, yet clients can easily miss that trade-off if disclosures emphasize the elegance of the algorithmic process while relegating sweep mechanics or opportunity cost to footnotes. Properly engineered robo-advice treats cash like any other allocation: it has a thesis (liquidity, volatility dampening, rebalancing fuel), a measurable cost in forgone expected return, and observable dynamics when interest rates or spreads move. Compliance becomes the forcing function that aligns elegant math with plain-English truth-telling: if the engine's rules predictably change the client's long-run risk/return, what, why, how much, and for whom must appear prominently in onboarding screens, portfolio summaries, and ongoing communications (SEC, 2022a).

The U.S. fiduciary lens, the UK's Consumer Duty, and ESMA's MiFID II suitability all converge on the same outcome question: would a reasonable retail client understand the economic implications of this design, and is the recommendation still suitable and fair value for that client segment (ESMA, 2022)? That pushes teams to move beyond boilerplate risk factors toward concrete, decision-useful figures such as "in a 60/40 model, a 6–8% cash corridor would have reduced annualized returns by 0.5–1% bps over the past three rate cycles" alongside an explanation of why the platform nonetheless believes the corridor improves client outcomes (liquidity, smoother drawdowns, behavioral benefits). It also reframes "conflicts" as a quantitative discipline: if affiliated sweep revenue exists, quantify it, disclose it in context, and evidence governance that prevents revenue from silently overriding suitability. The objective is not to eliminate cash or affiliation per se, but to ensure clients and supervisors can see cause, effect, and control plainly (ESMA, 2022; SEC, 2024).

Turning that policy intent into daily practice starts with a conflict inventory wired directly into model governance. Each rule that can be advantageous to the firm (cash, affiliate ETFs, order routing) needs an owner, a metric, and board-level visibility. For cash, firms should backtest expected drag across rate regimes, track realized drag versus a benchmark model, and surface exceptions when the engine drifts beyond corridor bounds. Under the Consumer Duty, those data feed the product's price and value assessment; under MiFID II, they sit in the suitability file and periodic reviews; under the Advisers Act, they support "full and fair disclosure" and supervision evidence (ESMA, 2022). Importantly, this is not a one-time paper exercise: corridor changes, fee changes, or market conditions that materially alter the economics must trigger synchronized updates to disclosures, help-center content, adviser scripts, and client notifications.

Model governance must document who can change the cash logic, what evidence is required, how changes are rolled out, and how clients are told. Release trains should block any code/config change that affects cash unless the disclosure package has been refreshed and archived, with exact client-facing wording versioned alongside the code commit. Where sustainability preferences are collected (EU), the file should show how higher cash interacts with those preferences if it indirectly crowds out exposures necessary to honor them because suitability under MiFID II now includes sustainability-preference fit, not just risk/return fit (ESMA, 2022). In UK contexts, product and distribution assessments under the Consumer Duty should make explicit whether higher cash aligns with the target market and whether any segment is likely to experience foreseeable harm from persistent cash drag (FCA, 2022).

A final layer is client comprehension and ongoing outcome testing. Disclosing that "cash may reduce returns" is not the same as demonstrating that retail clients grasp the magnitude and conditions. Short, tested explanations ("Holding 8% cash in this model would have reduced average returns by about 0.8% per year in the last decade, but helped cushion 12% of drawdowns and reduced trading costs by

15 bps per trade") make the trade-off tangible. Periodic outcome reviews tracking realized performance deltas, complaint themes, opt-outs, and the incidence of "cash exceptions" give boards evidence that the design is delivering what it promises. The regulatory message across jurisdictions is consistent: automation is welcome, but if the algorithm bakes in a non-obvious economic effect that also touches a potential conflict, transparency, governance, and measurable outcomes must be the safeguards.

5.2 *Wealthfront and Hedgeable Automation Claims and TLH Reality*

The early robo cases established a durable principle: when a platform claims an automated feature will monitor, prevent, or optimize something on a client's behalf, that claim is an objective statement of fact, not brand rhetoric, and it must be consistently true across the messy edges of real accounts (SEC, 2018). Tax-loss harvesting (TLH) is a perfect stress test for this principle because it sits at the intersection of market timing, brokerage operations, lot selection, wash-sale rules, and client heterogeneity. A promise like "we monitor for wash sales" collapses into many fragile sub-promises once fractional shares, multiple custodians, external accounts, and settlement timing are in play. The lesson from enforcement is simple: if any of those sub-promises routinely fail for a material subset of users, the disclosure must reflect that reality before, not after, clients rely on it (SEC, 2018).

Re-engineering TLH for compliance means defining feature service-level objectives: what harvesting frequency and loss thresholds the system targets; when harvesting pauses (e.g., after buys that risk a wash sale); which account linkages are required for cross-account visibility; and how the system behaves when data are stale or incomplete. Each constraint must be surfaced in the UI the moment it applies ("We detected activity in your external IRA that could trigger a wash sale; harvesting is paused for 30 days"), paired with accessible help text and a human escalation path (ESMA, 2022). From a U.S. perspective, that is both anti-fraud (truthful statements) and supervision under the Compliance Rule; from a UK/EU perspective, it supports "fair, clear, not misleading" communications and suitability because tax outcomes depend on client circumstances (ESMA, 2022).

Suitability extends deeper than many product teams assume. Aggressive TLH can be unsuitable for thinly funded accounts with high transaction costs, for clients with limited current or future tax liability, or for those whose behavioral preferences favor simplicity over frequent trades. Under MiFID II, suitability documentation should explain why TLH is on, off, or constrained for a given profile, and under the Consumer Duty, firms should test whether clients understand the feature's caveats and potential side effects (ESMA, 2022). That nudges platforms to build a decision explainer that goes beyond marketing ("we add after-tax returns") to show the client their likely benefit distribution and the conditions under which benefit drops to near zero.

Marketing governance is the other half of the equation. Every sentence in a landing page, blog, email, or app-store listing that implies detection, prevention, or optimization must trace back to an internal evidence file: test cases, failure-mode analyses, incidence rates, and change-control history. Growth teams should adopt a content circuit-breaker that blocks campaigns if telemetry shows the feature is under-delivering for a segment ("<60% of eligible accounts harvested in the past 90 days" triggers a pause and a disclosure review). For U.S. advisers, this discipline aligns with the spirit of the Marketing Rule even if the content is not hypothetical performance; for UK/EU firms, it aligns with financial promotions rules and the Consumer Duty's customer understanding outcome (ESMA, 2022).

Books and records turn good intentions into demonstrable compliance. Keep exact versions of client-facing copy, in-app prompts, A/B variants, and help-center articles; tie them to code releases and feature flags so the firm can reconstruct what any client saw on any date. Archive internal validations and model/feature change logs and maintain a "known limitations" register that product, compliance, and support teams can reference. When regulators ask "How did you know this was working as claimed?" the answer should be produced, not reconstructed (SEC, 2023).

The thorniest operational risks arise at the edges: fractional-share rounding that trips wash-sale windows, delayed brokerage data that hides purchase activity, external accounts that break visibility, and seasonal crowding of harvest requests that push trades into less favorable liquidity. None of these absolves the firm of accurate claims; they simply demand robust fallbacks (graceful pausing, client alerts, human review) and transparent messaging about when the feature is constrained. Across jurisdictions, the regulatory expectation is that platforms either deliver what they promise or change the promise before clients are harmed (ESMA, 2022).

5.3 Titan Hypothetical Performance and the Marketing Rule

The Titan order crystallized how the amended U.S. Marketing Rule treats hypothetical and back-tested numbers in retail-facing materials: they are hazardous content that demands tight eligibility, careful presentation, and durable records (SEC, 2023). Hypothetical results are not inherently misleading, but they become so when broadcast to mass audiences that cannot reasonably contextualize assumptions, when the numbers are cherry-picked, or when a firm cannot reproduce the charts months later. For digital-first advisers whose growth relies on performance storytelling, the operational stakes are high: either build a publication factory that meets the rule's engineering standard, or minimize the use of hypotheticals in public channels. Eligibility is step one. The rule expects firms to limit the distribution of hypothetical performance to investors for whom it is relevant and likely to be understood, typically in controlled portals, after profiling, with acknowledgment flows, not on social feeds or open landing pages (SEC, 2023). That expectation must be implemented in code, not just policy: SSO-gated pages, role-limited CMS publishing, disable-by-default settings for affiliates and influencers, and automated checks that block upload of images containing performance figures to public channels. The more distributed your marketing operation, the more you need technical controls that make the compliant path the only path.

Presentation discipline is step two. Where applicable, show net-of-fees outcomes; disclose the central assumptions succinctly (rebalancing cadence, cash handling, trading costs, tax treatment, data vintage, benchmark construction); articulate limitations (model risk, survivorship bias); and avoid time-window cherry-picking (SEC, 2023). The communication should be written at a reading level appropriate for retail an explicit link to the UK Consumer Duty's "customer understanding" outcome and tested periodically with real users. In EU settings, similar expectations flow from MiFID II's requirements on fair, clear, and not misleading communications and from ESMA's stance on suitability and appropriateness (ESMA, 2022). Multi-channel governance is step three. It is not enough to police the corporate blog while ignoring app-store screenshots, PDFs, investor decks, or partner posts. Firms need a single source of truth for performance assets, route all variants through compliance, and hash/version each artifact so the archive proves exactly what was published, where, and when. Influencer or affiliate programs require specific rules: pre-approved scripts, no ad-libbing performance, and platform-level monitoring that flags uploads containing numbers that look like returns. If any channel cannot meet those standards reliably, it should not be used for performance content (SEC, 2023). Data lineage and reproducibility are step four. Hypothetical charts must be recreatable: the firm should retain the data inputs, back-test code, parameter files, and rendering scripts needed to generate the exact figure clients saw. That package sits alongside the approval memo and the campaign brief in the archive. Six months later, a reviewer should be able to press a button and regenerate the chart, including footnotes and disclaimers. This is where marketing operations intersects with model risk: if you cannot reproduce it, you probably should not publish it (SEC, 2023).

Cross-border platforms should design to the strictest common denominator. Even where the U.S. rule does not directly apply, UK financial promotions rules and the Consumer Duty's emphasis on comprehension, as well as EU MiFID II's fairness and suitability expectations, point in the same direction. It is cheaper to treat all hypothetical numbers as hazardous everywhere than to vary controls by region and hope distribution teams never mix assets (ESMA, 2022). Firms that sell into professional channels can build a parallel pipeline with different entitlements, but they must be confident that those materials never leak into retail spaces. Commercial pressures are the persistent friction. Performance sells, speed matters, and creators move fast. The operational antidote is to slow down the riskiest content by design: fewer users with publishing rights, longer SLAs for reviews, automatic expiry of approvals when numbers change, and telemetry that records views and audiences so you can show, not just assert, that distribution stayed within the intended perimeter. Regular retrospectives—how many assets were blocked by the gate, how many were corrected, how many comprehension tests failed—turn governance into a learning loop that growth leaders can respect (SEC, 2023).

Finally, remember that hypothetical performance often travels with AI claims in modern marketing. A chart that implies predictive power plus a caption that says "our AI finds the winners" is a two-fer: Marketing Rule exposure and potential "AI-washing" risk if the claim outpaces the evidence. The safest pattern is to build an AI claims register and subject any AI-plus-performance package to both review tracks before publication. The regulator's perspective is straightforward: if you are going to persuade retail investors with numbers and algorithms, build the controls that retail investors deserve (SEC, 2023).

5.4 Betterment Code, Disclosures, and Trust Loops in TLH

The Betterment matter highlights a deceptively simple truth: in automated advice, software release management is investor protection (SEC, 2023). When a change in code, configuration, or vendor behavior alters how a touted feature like TLH (Tax-Loss Harvesting) performs, the disclosure ecosystem must update in lockstep, or clients will continue making decisions on outdated assumptions. That means product teams need to treat compliance artifacts, client-facing explanations, eligibility criteria, risk factors, and limitations as dependencies of the release, not optional post-hoc edits. If the release toggles a constraint or changes expected benefits for a segment, the pipeline should fail safe until the wording, FAQs, and support scripts are refreshed and archived.

A robust telemetry layer is the practical heart of this posture. Measure realized harvests against model-expected opportunity; flag accounts or cohorts whose realized benefit persistently trails expectations; and monitor leading indicators (e.g., increased pause rates, spikes in wash-sale blocks, vendor latency). Tie those signals to content circuit-breakers that pause new campaigns or trigger in-app banners when the feature is under-delivering for meaningful segments. From a regulatory standpoint, this is simply good supervision and "books and records," but in the UK and EU settings, it also serves the Consumer Duty's good outcomes requirement and MiFID II's suitability reviews by showing that the firm is watching client benefit, not just code metrics (FCA, 2022).

Change control must also extend to explainability. If TLH is constrained for a client, the UI should say why in terms a layperson understands, and the suitability file should reflect the decision. Some clients may prefer to switch the feature off temporarily when constraints dominate; others may accept reduced benefit for continuity. Either way, a plain-language explainer coupled with a human escalation route preserves customer understanding and trust—the core currency under the Consumer Duty—and a practical defense in any supervisory dialogue (FCA, 2022).

Client remediation planning deserves the same engineering rigor as detection. Where constraints or bugs reduced expected benefits, quantify the tax impact by cohort, consider fee credits or other remediation, and communicate proactively with personalized letters that translate the technical issue into investor reality ("Because of Wash sales, your account harvested fewer losses than expected; here is what we did and what changes going forward"). The tone and timing of this communication are compliance choices: fast, transparent remediation aligns with fiduciary duties and fair-value expectations and prevents a technical problem from becoming a conduct problem (SEC, 2023).

The enduring constraint set is non-trivial: cross-custodian wash-sale interactions that the platform cannot see directly; brokerage API timing that hides same-day activity; tax-lot fragmentation that complicates lot selection; and jurisdictional differences in tax treatment. None of these absolves firms of accurate claims; they simply necessitate graceful fallbacks (pausing, alerts, human checks), humble copy that acknowledges limits up front, and governance that ties product ambition to evidence. Across the SEC, FCA, and ESMA regimes, the through-line is the same: promise carefully, instrument deeply, explain clearly, and fix quickly when reality diverges from the brochure (SEC, 2023).

References

Baker T, Dellaert BGC (2018) Regulating robo advice across the financial services industry. Iowa Law Rev 103(2):713–750. https://doi.org/10.2139/ssrn.2932189

Baker T, Dellaert B (2019) Regulating robo advice across the financial services industry. Iowa Law Rev. https://doi.org/10.2139/ssrn.2932189

Baldwin R, Cave M, Lodge M (2012) Understanding regulation: theory, strategy, and practice. Oxford University Press

Black J (2008) Forms and paradoxes of principles-based regulation. Cap Mark Law J 3(4):425–457. https://doi.org/10.1093/cmlj/kmn026

Cruz LS, Kanter AD, Smith CD (2024) Securities and exchange commission brings first enforcement actions over "AI-washing". Mayer Brown LLP

Dasgupta P (2021) The economics of biodiversity: the Dasgupta review. https://assets.publishing.service.gov.uk/media/602e92b2e90e07660f807b47/The_Economics_of_Biodiversity_The_Dasgupta_Review_Full_Report.pdf

ESMA (2022) Guidelines on certain aspects of the MiFID II suitability requirements (ESMA35-43-3172). https://www.esma.europa.eu/document/final-report-guidelines-certain-aspects-mifid-ii-suitability-requirements

EU (2022) Regulation (EU) 2022/2554 of the European Parliament and of the Council on digital operational resilience for the financial sector (DORA). https://eur-lex.europa.eu/eli/reg/2022/2554/oj/eng

EU (2024) Regulation (EU) 2024/1689 of the European Parliament and of the Council laying down harmonised rules on artificial intelligence (AI Act). https://eur-lex.europa.eu/eli/reg/2024/1689/oj/eng

FCA (2018) Automated investment services—our expectations (Multi-firm review). https://www.fca.org.uk/publications/multi-firm-reviews/automated-investment-services-our-expectations

FCA (2022) PS22/9: A new Consumer Duty (Policy statement and final guidance). https://www.fca.org.uk/publications/policy-statements/ps22-9-new-consumer-duty

FCA (2024) CP24/27: Advice Guidance Boundary Review—proposed targeted support reforms (pensions). https://www.fca.org.uk/publications/consultation-papers/cp24-27-advice-guidance-boundary-review-targeted-support-reforms-pensions

Gunningham N, Grabosky P, Sinclair D (2003) Smart regulation: designing environmental policy. Oxford University Press

IOSCO (2021) Report on sustainability-related issuer disclosures. The Board of the International Organization of Securities Commissions. https://www.iosco.org/library/pubdocs/pdf/IOSCOPD678.pdf

IOSCO (2024) Digital Engagement Practices (DEPs): Consultation report (CR/09/2024). https://www.iosco.org/library/pubdocs/pdf/IOSCOPD777.pdf

Lusardi A, Mitchell OS (2014) The economic importance of financial literacy: theory and evidence. J Econ Lit 52(1):5–44. https://doi.org/10.1257/jel.52.1.5

MAS (2018a) Guidelines on Outsourcing (Issued July 27, 2016; revised October 5, 2018). https://www.mas.gov.sg/-/media/mas/regulations-and-financial-stability/regulatory-and-supervisory-framework/risk-management/outsourcing-guidelines_jul-2016-revised-on-5-oct-2018.pdf

MAS (2018b) Guidelines on Provision of Digital Advisory Services (CMG-G02). https://www.mas.gov.sg/-/media/mas/regulations-and-financial-stability/regulations-guidance-and-licensing/securities-futures-and-fund-management/guidelines-on-provision-of-digital-advisory-services%2D%2Dcmgg02.pdf

MAS (2021) Technology risk management guidelines. https://www.mas.gov.sg/-/media/MAS/Regulations-and-Financial-Stability/Regulatory-and-Supervisory-Framework/Risk-Management/TRM-Guidelines-18-January-2021.pdf

SEC (2018) SEC charges two robo-advisers with false disclosures (Press Release No. 2018-300). https://www.sec.gov/newsroom/press-releases/2018-300

SEC (2022a) Schwab subsidiaries misled robo-adviser clients about absence of hidden fees (Press Release No. 2022-104). https://www.sec.gov/newsroom/press-releases/2022-104

SEC. (2022b). SEC charges investment adviser Betterment for misstatements concerning tax loss harvesting service (Press Release No. 2023-80). https://www.sec.gov/newsroom/press-releases/2023-80

SEC (2023) SEC charges FinTech investment adviser Titan for misrepresenting hypothetical performance (Press Release No. 2023-153). https://www.sec.gov/newsroom/press-releases/2023-153

SEC (2024) SEC charges two investment advisers with making false and misleading AI claims (Press Release No. 2024-36). https://www.sec.gov/newsroom/press-releases/2024-36

Robo-Advisory and Auditing: Internal and External Controls

Ahmad Hatamabadi Farahani and Narmin Nahidi

Abstract This study examines how artificial intelligence (AI) reshapes auditing practices in robo-advisory systems through the integration of internal and external control frameworks. It explains how internal audits ensure algorithmic reliability, data integrity, cybersecurity, and regulatory compliance, while external audits provide independent verification of financial reporting under IFRS, GAAP, Basel III, and MiFID II. The chapter highlights how AI technologies—machine learning, natural language processing, robotic process automation, and explainable AI—transform auditing into a continuous, data-driven, and predictive function. Ethical dimensions such as bias, transparency, accountability, and data privacy are also analyzed, emphasizing the importance of governance frameworks and regulatory oversight. Drawing on real-world examples from leading financial institutions and audit firms, the chapter proposes a dual-layer audit model combining technological and ethical assurance to enhance trust, transparency, and resilience in AI-driven financial ecosystems.

Keywords Auditing · FinTech governance · Internal control · External assurance · Explainable AI · Ethical accountability · Continuous auditing · Financial transparency

JEL Classification: M42, G21, G28, O33

A. H. Farahani
Salford Business School, University of Salford, Salford, UK
e-mail: a.hatamabadifarahani@salford.ac.uk

N. Nahidi (✉)
Business School, University of Exeter, Exeter, UK
e-mail: n.nahidi@exeter.ac.uk

N. Nahidi, A. Zarifis (eds.), *AI, FinTech, and the Future of Robo-Advisory*, Contributions to Finance and Accounting,
https://doi.org/10.1007/978-3-032-18109-1_9

1 Introduction

The integration of artificial intelligence (AI) into financial advisory systems, known as robo-advisors, has profoundly transformed investment management and financial planning. Robo-advisors automate portfolio management, risk assessment, and client interaction, providing scalable, cost-efficient services previously accessible only to high-net-worth individuals (Baker and Dellaert 2018; Hossnofsky and Junge 2019). These platforms leverage complex algorithms and vast datasets to deliver tailored investment solutions rapidly and efficiently (Phoon and Koh 2018). Despite their widespread adoption, the increased reliance on automated systems introduces new risks, necessitating sophisticated auditing practices to maintain accuracy, regulatory compliance, and consumer trust (Hossnofsky and Junge 2019).

Internal auditing serves as a critical safeguard in AI-driven financial systems by providing independent assurance over the efficiency and reliability of operations, particularly as robo-advisors automate complex financial decisions (Alles et al. 2008). Effective internal audits scrutinize the underlying algorithms for performance accuracy, data integrity, and security, ensuring continuous compliance with internal policies and external regulatory standards (Mittelstadt et al. 2016). Historically, internal audits focused primarily on financial statement accuracy and compliance; however, modern approaches have evolved significantly to address emerging risks associated with AI, such as algorithmic bias, data privacy concerns, and cybersecurity threats (Appelbaum et al. 2017). Contemporary internal auditing frameworks emphasize algorithm transparency, rigorous model governance, and proactive risk management to address the dynamic complexities of AI systems (Raji et al. 2020).

Concurrently, external auditing frameworks tailored for robo-advisory platforms have emerged as essential components for validating financial disclosures and regulatory compliance. External audits are mandated to attest to the accuracy and reliability of financial statements, compliance with accounting standards such as the International Financial Reporting Standards (IFRS) and Generally Accepted Accounting Principles (GAAP), and adherence to regulatory frameworks like Basel III and the Markets in Financial Instruments Directive II (MiFID II) (Zetzsche et al. 2016). Traditional auditing methods have primarily been manual, time-consuming, and prone to human error; however, modern external auditing practices increasingly incorporate digital technologies, blockchain, and advanced data analytics to enhance efficiency, accuracy, and transparency (Dai and Vasarhelyi 2017). This integration of advanced technology supports auditors in effectively navigating complex regulatory landscapes and ensuring robust compliance in rapidly evolving financial markets (Issa et al. 2016).

AI technologies themselves increasingly contribute to the auditing process by automating routine audit tasks and detecting anomalies with heightened accuracy and efficiency. Advanced data analytics, machine learning, and natural language processing allow auditors to swiftly identify irregularities and potential fraud, significantly reducing the likelihood of undetected errors in financial reporting (Appelbaum et al. 2017). Classical audit methods relied heavily on sampling and manual verification, which were often limited in scope and accuracy; however, contemporary practices harness sophisticated algorithms capable of analyzing vast datasets in real time, dramatically improving audit coverage and precision (Issa et al. 2016). This evolution in audit practices enhances overall audit quality, reduces operational costs, and enables auditors to proactively identify and mitigate emerging financial risks, fundamentally reshaping the landscape of traditional auditing methodologies (ACCA 2022).

Finally, ethical considerations remain paramount at the intersection of AI and auditing, particularly regarding automated financial reports. Concerns about fairness, accountability, and transparency in AI-generated financial outputs necessitate comprehensive ethical frameworks and guidelines (Floridi et al. 2018). Historically, ethical frameworks in financial auditing focused primarily on professional standards and compliance obligations; today, auditors must navigate complex ethical issues surrounding automated decision-making processes, algorithmic transparency, accountability, and data privacy (Mittelstadt et al. 2016). Contemporary ethical standards increasingly emphasize transparency in algorithmic decision-making, accountability in algorithmic governance, and safeguarding the privacy of sensitive financial data, underscoring the importance of maintaining both technical and ethical rigor in auditing practices (European Commission 2021). Addressing these ethical challenges is crucial not only for maintaining public trust but also for fostering sustainable and ethically responsible growth within AI-driven financial ecosystems (OECD 2020b).

2 The Role of Internal Auditing in AI-Driven Financial Systems

Internal auditing is essential in the governance of AI-driven financial systems, offering critical independent assurance over operational efficiency, algorithm reliability, and compliance with evolving regulatory frameworks (Institute of Internal Auditors (IIA) 2017). Internal auditors systematically evaluate the robustness of algorithms, data management practices, and cybersecurity measures, ensuring that financial institutions effectively mitigate the inherent risks associated with automated advisory processes (Appelbaum et al. 2017). A critical function of internal auditing involves assessing the transparency and fairness of algorithms employed by robo-advisors. Auditors verify that AI models produce consistent, unbiased outcomes across diverse client portfolios, thus protecting against discriminatory financial practices and ensuring fairness in automated decision-making processes (I. Lee and Shin 2018). Internal auditors also confirm the integrity and completeness of input data, recognizing that flawed or biased data can significantly impair algorithmic accuracy and financial reliability (IBM Research 2020).

Internal auditors play a crucial role in safeguarding sensitive client data by evaluating cybersecurity frameworks within AI-driven platforms. Given the heightened cybersecurity risks associated with digital financial services, auditors assess security protocols, encryption methods, and response strategies to potential breaches, ensuring robust protection against cyber threats (Chui et al. 2020). This responsibility extends to verifying adherence to data privacy regulations such as the General Data Protection Regulation (GDPR), further emphasizing the auditor's role in compliance oversight (Altman et al. 2018). Additionally, internal auditors contribute to regulatory compliance assurance by regularly evaluating adherence to standards such as Basel III, IFRS, and MiFID II. Continuous monitoring of compliance practices ensures that robo-advisors maintain necessary regulatory alignment, thus mitigating potential financial penalties and reputational risks associated with non-compliance (Financial Stability Board 2017).

For instance, JP Morgan's use of internal auditing for its AI-driven platform "Chase Digital Assistant" provides a clear demonstration of the critical role internal auditing plays in practical contexts. Internal auditors at JP Morgan regularly perform comprehensive assessments of the digital assistant's decision-making algorithms, ensuring their fairness and impartiality across diverse customer segments. They meticulously audit cybersecurity protocols, examining layers of security from data encryption to intrusion detection systems. Additionally, compliance with rigorous financial regulations such as Basel III, IFRS, and MiFID II is continuously validated through scheduled audits. The rigorous auditing practices at JP Morgan have notably enhanced the platform's operational reliability, significantly reducing both the frequency and severity of potential security breaches and ensuring regulatory adherence, thereby increasing client satisfaction and trust (IOSCO 2021).

Similarly, Wealthfront, a leading robo-advisory service provider, employs extensive internal auditing practices to ensure platform robustness and reliability. Internal audit teams at Wealthfront systematically review the accuracy of algorithms responsible for investment decisions, stress-testing these algorithms under diverse market scenarios to verify their stability and adaptability. Additionally, comprehensive data integrity audits are regularly conducted to ensure the accuracy and completeness of client data inputs, thus maintaining the reliability of automated advice provided to clients. Auditors at Wealthfront also emphasize verifying adherence to evolving regulatory frameworks, thereby proactively mitigating legal and compliance risks. These rigorous internal auditing measures have substantially improved Wealthfront's ability to detect and correct potential system weaknesses, maintain stringent regulatory compliance, and enhance consumer trust through demonstrated transparency and accountability (Jung et al. 2018).

Assignment: Evaluating Internal Auditing Practices in Robo-Advisory Platforms

Objective:

To critically analyze and assess the internal auditing practices and their effectiveness in a real-world robo-advisory platform, providing practical insights and recommendations for improvements.

Task:

1. **Select a Robo-Advisory Platform:**
   Choose an existing robo-advisor (e.g., Betterment, Wealthfront, JPMorgan Chase Digital Assistant, Vanguard Digital Advisor, or similar).
2. **Research the Platform's Internal Auditing Practices:**
   Investigate and document:
   - Algorithm transparency practices.
   - Measures for maintaining algorithmic fairness and avoiding bias.
   - Cybersecurity measures and compliance with data protection laws.
   - Procedures ensuring compliance with regulatory standards (IFRS, GAAP, Basel III, MiFID II).
3. **Interview or Communication (Optional but Recommended):**
   Attempt to reach out directly to professionals involved in internal auditing or compliance at the chosen firm to gather firsthand insights. Alternatively, you may rely on public reports, white papers, or case studies available from reputable sources.
4. **Critical Evaluation:**
   - Critically evaluate the strengths and weaknesses of the internal auditing approaches employed by your selected robo-advisor.
   - Identify areas of potential vulnerability or risk that may have been inadequately addressed.
5. **Recommendations:**
   Based on your findings, propose practical improvements to the internal auditing practices, addressing any gaps or limitations identified.

Deliverables:

- A detailed report (approximately 2500–3000 words) including:
  - Introduction and rationale for selecting the robo-advisor.
  - Methodology of research conducted.
  - Comprehensive evaluation of auditing practices.
  - Specific, actionable recommendations for improvement.
  - Conclusion summarizing your insights and their implications.

Evaluation Criteria:

- Depth and accuracy of research and analysis.
- Critical insight into the effectiveness and comprehensiveness of existing auditing practices.
- Practicality and feasibility of recommendations.
- Clarity, organization, and professionalism in written presentation.

Bridging Internal and External Oversight

Internal auditing practices in robo-advisory platforms are not merely about compliance but represent the foundation of operational trust in automated financial services. These audits go beyond verifying financial statements; they examine the heart of robo-advisory operations—the algorithms themselves. Internal auditors scrutinize whether investment models are transparent, reliable, and free from systemic bias. For example, Betterment, one of the earliest U.S. robo-advisors, integrates internal auditing into its product development cycle by continuously testing its asset allocation algorithms under different market scenarios. Such practices demonstrate how auditing safeguards both institutional integrity and client welfare, ensuring that digital platforms remain accountable to the same standards of fairness and prudence expected of traditional human advisors.

Yet, internal auditing on its own is insufficient in a financial environment defined by rapid innovation and global regulation. External auditing provides an additional, independent layer of oversight that ensures credibility for both regulators and investors. Independent auditors assess the completeness of financial disclosures, compliance with international standards such as IFRS and GAAP, and adherence to regulatory frameworks like Basel III and MiFID II. Consider the case of Nutmeg, the UK-based digital wealth manager, which has routinely subjected itself to external evaluations to validate its compliance with EU investor protection rules. Such independent verification strengthens market trust by assuring clients that algorithm-driven advice has been tested not only internally but also by third parties with no vested interest in the platform's success.

The interaction between internal and external auditing is particularly critical given the complexity of algorithmic finance. Robo-advisors execute thousands of client transactions daily, each influenced by real-time data and automated rebalancing. Traditional audit techniques, which relied on periodic sampling, cannot capture the full picture of such systems. As a result, firms like Vanguard Digital Advisor have adopted hybrid approaches, embedded internal continuous monitoring while cooperating with external auditors for annual and quarterly reviews. This dual model allows risks such as algorithmic drift, cybersecurity breaches, or compliance lapses to be addressed swiftly while maintaining external credibility. Together, these practices form a layered defense system, ensuring resilience in environments where financial advice is automated at scale.

Technology itself is reshaping how both internal and external audits are performed. Internal audit teams are increasingly using explainable AI to evaluate algorithm decisions and employing stress-testing to simulate extreme scenarios. Externally, audit firms have begun to rely on blockchain for transparent record-keeping and AI-driven anomaly detection for efficiency. A notable example is StashAway, a Singapore-based robo-advisor that uses advanced analytics to continuously audit its risk management models internally, while engaging independent auditors to verify cross-jurisdictional compliance. This dual adoption of cutting-edge technology demonstrates how the auditing profession is evolving into a real-time, proactive governance function rather than a backward-looking check on past performance.

These developments underscore why internal and external control frameworks are indispensable in AI-driven finance. Without clear frameworks, audits risk becoming fragmented and reactive, failing to keep up with the speed of technological change. Effective frameworks provide structure: they embed accountability at every organizational level, clarify responsibilities between internal auditors and external examiners, and ensure that compliance, transparency, and ethical conduct are integral to daily operations. As platforms such as Schwab Intelligent Portfolios and others demonstrate, when robust frameworks are in place, robo-advisors can balance innovation with accountability, reassuring both clients and regulators. The next section examines how these internal and external control frameworks are formally structured and applied, highlighting their role in strengthening reliability, transparency, and ethical responsibility in AI-driven financial ecosystems.

This conceptual framework illustrates how internal and external controls jointly safeguard robo-advisory platforms. Internal controls focus on operational reliability, including algorithm validation, data integrity, and cybersecurity. External controls provide independent oversight, reinforcing compliance with IFRS/GAAP, Basel III, and MiFID II. Together, these layers create a comprehensive assurance framework that integrates technological oversight with regulatory accountability.

The framework in Fig. 1 is designed around two concentric circles, which visually separate the scope of internal and external audit controls. The inner circle represents those processes that are embedded within the robo-advisory platform itself. These controls are the responsibility of the organization's management and audit teams, forming the platform's first line of defense. By placing them inside the

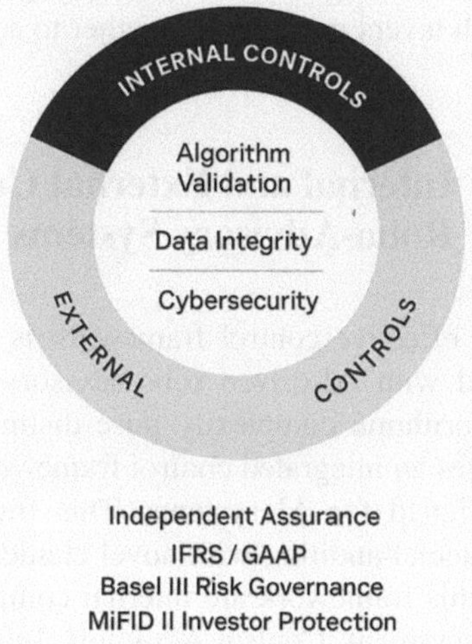

Fig. 1 Dual structureof audit oversight in AI-driven robo-advisory systems

circle, the framework highlights their proximity to day-to-day operations and their role in maintaining the reliability of the system from within.

Three main internal controls are emphasized: algorithm validation, data integrity, and cybersecurity. Algorithm validation ensures that decision models perform as expected under different conditions, reducing the risk of biased or flawed investment recommendations. Data integrity refers to the accuracy, consistency, and completeness of the information feeding into the algorithms; without trustworthy data, even the most advanced model will produce unreliable results. Cybersecurity represents protection against breaches, hacking, or data theft, which is particularly important in digital finance. Together, these internal elements focus on the technical and operational soundness of robo-advisory systems.

Surrounding the inner circle is the outer layer, which represents external controls. These are not managed by the organization itself but are imposed by independent auditors, regulators, or global standard-setting bodies. Their separation into the outer circle underlines their independence and their broader perspective, which extends beyond the boundaries of the firm. External controls are concerned not only with whether the robo-advisor is functioning internally but also with whether it aligns with the expectations of the wider financial system and global regulation.

Four external controls are highlighted. Independent assurance involves third-party auditors verifying financial reporting and governance. IFRS/GAAP compliance ensures that financial statements follow recognized accounting standards, promoting comparability and transparency. Basel III risk governance addresses capital adequacy and systemic resilience, a critical safeguard when AI models could amplify risks. Finally, MiFID II investor protection ensures that clients' interests are safeguarded, particularly in European markets. By surrounding the inner circle, these external controls provide a protective outer shell that validates and strengthens the work of internal controls. The separation between the circles symbolizes the different responsibilities and perspectives, while their concentric design shows that both layers must work together to achieve comprehensive oversight.

3 Internal and External Control Frameworks for AI-Driven Robo-Advisory Systems

An effective control framework is pivotal for managing the unique risks associated with AI-driven robo-advisory platforms, where rapid decision-making and algorithmic complexity pose distinctive auditing challenges. IOSCO (2021) proposes an integrated control framework, emphasizing essential activities specifically designed for AI systems. This framework combines principles from traditional financial auditing with novel elements required by emerging technologies. Central to this framework are internal components such as the Control Environment, Risk Assessment, Control Activities, Information and Communication, and Continuous Monitoring, alongside external auditing practices, each explicitly tailored to address the intricacies of robo-advisors and AI-driven financial services. The Control Environment component within the framework provides the foundational ethos and operational context, emphasizing management oversight, integrity, and ethical standards crucial for AI applications in finance. The European Commission (2021) emphasizes the importance of fostering an organizational culture that prioritizes transparency and accountability in automated decision-making processes, especially within high-risk AI systems. Establishing clear governance structures, defining explicit roles and responsibilities, and reinforcing ethical guidelines form the basis for robust AI governance, creating an environment where AI risks are systematically identified and managed.

The workflow in Fig. 2 outlines the sequence of steps involved in auditing AI-driven robo-advisory platforms. It begins with data input, where information from markets, clients, and risk assessments flows into the system. This stage is critical because the quality of outputs depends entirely on the reliability of inputs; inaccurate or biased data will compromise every subsequent step of the process. Once the data is processed, the system moves to internal audit checkpoints. At this stage, automated and human auditors verify three elements: bias detection, model

Fig. 2 Workflow of internal and external audit processes in AI-driven robo-advisory systems

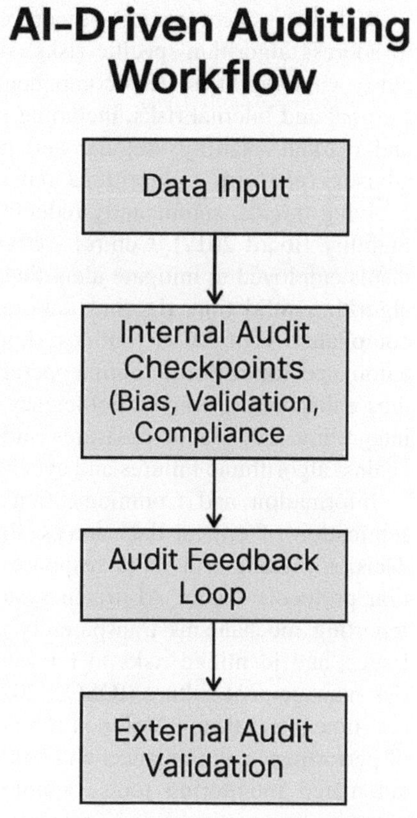

validation, and compliance monitoring. Bias detection ensures that algorithmic recommendations are not systematically unfair to certain groups of investors. Model validation checks whether algorithms perform as intended under various market conditions. Compliance monitoring confirms that the system aligns with internal policies and relevant financial regulations. The third component is the audit feedback loop, which differentiates AI-driven auditing from traditional, static methods. Instead of waiting for periodic reviews, the system provides continuous oversight by feeding audit findings back into the platform. This allows for ongoing corrections, real-time learning, and the early identification of risks or anomalies. It makes the audit function proactive, not just reactive, and ensures that errors are addressed before they escalate.

This process culminates in external audit validation. Here, independent auditors and regulators provide a third-party check on the system's performance and reporting. This stage verifies that financial statements comply with standards such as IFRS and GAAP, that risk management aligns with Basel III, and that client protections under MiFID II are being met. By placing this step at the end of the workflow, the framework highlights the complementary role of external oversight in confirming the robustness of internal audit processes and enhancing overall trust in robo-advisory platforms.

Risk Assessment forms the second critical internal component, explicitly tailored to address algorithm-specific risks, such as data bias, model drift, and cybersecurity vulnerabilities. This component necessitates continuous evaluation of both external and internal risks, including regulatory compliance, technological threats, and market volatility. Regular and proactive risk assessments ensure the robo-advisory platform's algorithms remain reliable, unbiased, and resilient against evolving threats, significantly reducing financial and reputational risks (Financial Stability Board 2017). Control Activities represent the practical internal mechanisms employed to mitigate identified risks. These include detailed procedures for algorithm validation, rigorous data quality checks, cybersecurity safeguards, and compliance verification routines. Appelbaum et al. (2017) highlight embedding automated controls into routine operations to swiftly detect and address anomalies, thus enhancing operational efficiency and accuracy. This component also stresses integrating redundancy measures and fallback mechanisms, enhancing resilience against algorithmic failures and cyber incidents.

Information and Communication practices ensure the timely, accurate dissemination of critical data across all organizational levels, facilitating informed decision-making and rapid response capabilities. Effective internal communication protocols within AI-driven systems involve continuous documentation and reporting mechanisms transparently conveying algorithmic changes, compliance issues, and identified risks to relevant stakeholders, thereby fostering a cohesive risk management culture (IOSCO 2021). Continuous Monitoring is pivotal for the real-time internal supervision of robo-advisory systems, enabling ongoing oversight of performance, compliance, and risk management. IOSCO (2021) advocate using automated monitoring tools capable of real-time data analysis and predictive analytics to swiftly identify emerging risks and operational irregularities. These advanced monitoring practices significantly enhance the capacity to pre-emptively identify and rectify issues, reinforcing platform reliability and regulatory adherence. Externally, auditing frameworks play a critical role in verifying the effectiveness and compliance of robo-advisory platforms with established financial and regulatory standards. External auditors perform independent evaluations of algorithm accuracy, data integrity, and adherence to financial reporting standards such as IFRS and GAAP, alongside regulatory compliance with frameworks like Basel III and MiFID II. These external audits provide third-party assurance, enhancing the credibility and transparency of robo-advisors in financial markets (Deloitte 2018).

As a practical illustration, BlackRock's Aladdin platform exemplifies the successful integration of both internal and external control frameworks. Internally, Aladdin employs rigorous continuous monitoring mechanisms, leveraging advanced analytics to assess algorithm performance, cybersecurity integrity, and compliance adherence constantly. Externally, independent audits validate Aladdin's adherence to regulatory standards, algorithm reliability, and data integrity, significantly improving risk management capabilities and enhancing market trust (BlackRock Sustainability Disclosure 2024). Similarly, Charles Schwab Intelligent Portfolios demonstrates effective implementation of comprehensive internal and external control practices. Internally, Schwab rigorously focuses on algorithm validation, data integrity checks, and proactive compliance monitoring. Externally, Schwab undergoes regular independent audits assessing compliance with regulatory frameworks and financial reporting standards. This dual internal and external approach ensures algorithmic reliability, regulatory compliance, and operational transparency, significantly enhancing client confidence and operational resilience (IOSCO 2021).

To further enrich understanding of auditing AI-driven systems, the UK's Digital Regulation Cooperation Forum (DRCF) emphasizes the necessity of a robust framework for algorithmic auditing. According to the DRCF (2023)'s findings, auditing algorithms involves systematically examining algorithmic systems to assess compliance with legal standards, ethical guidelines, and performance expectations. The report highlights current regulatory challenges, including transparency issues, data accessibility, and the need for clearly defined standards and competencies among auditors. Furthermore, it underscores the importance of collaboration among regulators, industry stakeholders, and auditors to establish comprehensive standards for auditing algorithms effectively. These insights from the DRCF underline the need for continuous evolution in auditing practices, reinforcing the critical role of regulation and oversight in maintaining trust and reliability in AI-driven financial advisory services (DRCF 2023).

Assignment: Designing an External Audit Plan for a Robo-Advisory Platform
Objective:
To critically design a real-world external auditing plan for a robo-advisory platform, applying theoretical concepts, regulatory frameworks, and best industry practices.

Task:

1. **Select a robo-advisor:** Choose an existing robo-advisor (Betterment, Wealthfront, Vanguard Digital Advisor, Nutmeg, etc.).
2. **Research its regulatory obligations:** Focus on IFRS, GAAP, Basel III, MiFID II, and applicable local standards.
3. **Design an audit plan:**
   - Define audit scope
   - Identify key risk areas
   - Propose techniques for validating algorithmic accuracy
   - Propose data integrity verification steps
   - Detail compliance checks
   - Define audit frequency and reporting structure
4. **Justify your plan:** Support choices using academic references and industry reports.

Deliverables:

- Detailed external audit plan (approx. 2500–3000 words).

Evaluation Criteria:

- Depth of regulatory understanding
- Creativity and practicality of audit design
- Use of academic and industry references
- Critical insight into challenges and limitations
- Professional structure and clarity

4 Ensuring Compliance with IFRS, GAAP, Basel III, and MiFID II

Ensuring compliance with global financial standards such as the International Financial Reporting Standards (IFRS), Generally Accepted Accounting Principles (GAAP), Basel III, and the Markets in Financial Instruments Directive II (MiFID II) is a cornerstone of sound governance for AI-driven robo-advisory platforms. As these platforms operate within complex, highly regulated financial ecosystems, maintaining compliance is essential for safeguarding market integrity, protecting investors, and fostering public trust (Rozario and Vasarhelyi 2018). However, the inherent opacity and complexity of AI-driven systems present significant challenges to traditional compliance methodologies, necessitating advanced auditing frameworks and adaptive regulatory approaches (Arrieta et al. 2019). Robo-advisors must implement sophisticated internal controls, robust data management practices, and advanced compliance monitoring tools to navigate this regulatory landscape effectively.

The International Financial Reporting Standards (IFRS), issued by the International Accounting Standards Board (IASB), provide a globally recognized framework for preparing and presenting financial statements (IASB 2019). For AI-driven robo-advisors, IFRS compliance involves ensuring the accuracy and transparency of financial reporting, particularly in areas such as fair value measurement, revenue recognition, and financial instrument disclosures (The IFRS Accounting Standards Navigator 2021). Given the reliance of robo-advisors on dynamic algorithmic models and real-time data, it is crucial to establish clear methodologies for valuing complex financial instruments and disclosing algorithm-driven financial outcomes. Furthermore, IFRS requires transparent documentation of model assumptions, risk exposures, and data sources, underscoring the importance of comprehensive algorithmic audit trails and model governance practices (PWC 2020).

Similarly, compliance with the Generally Accepted Accounting Principles (GAAP), particularly as applied in the United States, entails adhering to rigorous accounting standards concerning financial reporting, revenue recognition, and disclosure requirements (FASB 2021). Robo-advisory firms operating in or serving U.S. markets must align their financial reporting processes with GAAP principles, ensuring that automated systems accurately capture and report financial transactions. This includes establishing robust controls to verify the accuracy of automated bookkeeping processes, ensuring completeness and accuracy of financial data, and maintaining auditability of AI-driven financial operations (Kokina and Davenport 2017). The complexity of integrating AI-driven financial decisions with traditional accounting frameworks necessitates ongoing collaboration between auditors, data scientists, and compliance officers (Appelbaum et al. 2017).

Basel III, developed by the Basel Committee on Banking Supervision, introduces comprehensive risk management standards aimed at enhancing the resilience of financial institutions (Committee on Banking Supervision 2017). For robo-advisory platforms affiliated with or integrated into banking structures, Basel III compliance entails robust capital adequacy, liquidity risk management, and operational risk controls (Committee on Banking Supervision 2017). Given that AI-driven systems can amplify systemic risks through interconnected algorithms and data dependencies, ensuring compliance with Basel III requires continuous stress testing, scenario analysis, and dynamic risk modeling. Furthermore, the integration of AI into risk management processes demands enhanced model risk governance frameworks to mitigate potential unintended consequences of automated decision-making (EY 2020).

The Markets in Financial Instruments Directive II (MiFID II), a cornerstone of EU financial regulation, seeks to enhance investor protection, market transparency, and financial stability (ESMA 2018). For robo-advisors operating within the European market, MiFID II compliance is multifaceted, encompassing requirements for suitability assessments, product governance, best execution practices, and transparency in client communications (Ringe and Ruof 2018). AI-driven platforms must ensure that their recommendation algorithms adhere to suitability standards, taking into account individual client profiles, risk tolerances, and investment objectives. Additionally, MiFID II mandates rigorous disclosure requirements and transaction reporting, necessitating comprehensive data management and auditability of AI-driven advice (Buczynski et al. 2025).

A comparative analysis of these regulatory frameworks highlights both commonalities and distinctive challenges for robo-advisory compliance. While IFRS and GAAP primarily focus on financial reporting accuracy and transparency, Basel III emphasizes risk management and capital adequacy, and MiFID II prioritizes investor protection and market conduct. Together, these frameworks demand a holistic compliance strategy that integrates financial, operational, and conduct risk controls. Robo-advisors must adopt a unified compliance architecture, leveraging advanced data analytics, automated monitoring, and cross-functional collaboration to ensure seamless alignment with these diverse regulatory mandates (Gurrea-Martinez and Wan 2021).

A practical example of comprehensive regulatory compliance in action is seen in the operations of UBS Wealth Management's AI-driven advisory services. UBS employs a sophisticated compliance framework integrating IFRS-based financial reporting, GAAP alignment for U.S. operations, Basel III-compliant risk management practices, and full adherence to MiFID II standards for European clients (UBS 2022). Through advanced AI auditing tools, automated compliance monitoring, and proactive regulatory engagement, UBS successfully navigates the complex global regulatory landscape, demonstrating best practices for the industry. Another notable example is Revolut, which, as a fast-growing fintech, has developed agile compliance mechanisms that align its AI-driven offerings with the aforementioned regulatory frameworks, leveraging continuous auditing and real-time compliance dashboards to maintain regulatory alignment across jurisdictions.

Assignment: Comparative Compliance Analysis of Robo-Advisors
Objective:
To critically analyze and compare how AI-driven financial platforms comply with global financial regulations, identifying risks and improvement opportunities.
Task:

1. **Select two robo-advisors:** One EU-based and one US-based.
2. **Research their compliance practices:**
   - IFRS
   - GAAP
   - Basel III
   - MiFID II
3. **Compare and contrast:**
   - Highlight similarities, differences, and gaps
   - Discuss jurisdictional challenges
   - Identify areas of regulatory uncertainty for AI-driven systems
4. **Propose improvements:** Suggest harmonization strategies or enhanced compliance mechanisms.

Deliverables:

- Comparative analysis report (approx. 3000–3500 words).

Evaluation Criteria:

- Depth of regulatory analysis
- Quality of comparison
- Critical understanding of AI compliance challenges
- Practicality of recommendations
- Academic and professional rigor

5 AI's Role in Automating Audit Processes and Detecting Anomalies

The integration of AI technologies into auditing processes is transforming the landscape of financial oversight, particularly within AI-driven robo-advisory platforms. Traditional audit methodologies, which relied on manual sampling and retrospective reviews, are being replaced by continuous auditing frameworks powered by advanced AI tools (Lee et al. 2020). AI-driven audits enable real-time monitoring of financial transactions, detection of anomalies, and verification of compliance with regulatory requirements. This transformation not only enhances audit efficiency but also improves the accuracy and timeliness of financial oversight, thereby reducing operational and compliance risks (ICAEW 2019).

Machine learning (ML) plays a pivotal role in automating audit processes. By training models on historical financial data and audit outcomes, ML algorithms can learn to identify patterns associated with normal operations and flag deviations indicative of potential errors or fraud (Gallego Sánchez et al. 2021). For robo-advisors, this capability is particularly valuable given the volume and complexity of transactions processed by algorithmic systems. ML-driven audit tools can continuously analyze large datasets, detecting subtle anomalies that might elude traditional audit techniques (W S R 2025). Additionally, unsupervised learning techniques, such as clustering and anomaly detection algorithms, allow auditors to identify outliers without predefined rules, further enhancing audit coverage and precision (Thiprungsri and Vasarhelyi 2011).

Natural Language Processing (NLP) extends AI's auditing capabilities to unstructured data sources, such as contracts, client communications, and regulatory filings. NLP tools can automatically extract and analyze relevant information from these documents, facilitating compliance verification and risk assessment. For example, NLP algorithms can assess whether client communications adhere to MiFID II disclosure requirements or whether contract terms align with IFRS revenue recognition principles. By automating the analysis of unstructured data, NLP significantly broadens the scope of audit processes and enhances auditors' ability to identify compliance gaps (Fotoh and Mugwira 2025; Onyenahazi 2025).

AI-powered Robotic Process Automation (RPA) further streamlines audit workflows by automating routine, rule-based audit tasks. RPA tools can automatically perform data extraction, reconciliation, and reporting tasks, freeing auditors to focus on higher-value activities such as risk analysis and judgment-based evaluations. Within robo-advisory platforms, RPA can automate the reconciliation of transaction data with accounting records, the generation of audit reports, and the monitoring of key risk indicators, thereby enhancing audit efficiency and reducing operational costs (Charlotte and Jacob 2024; Lacurezeanu et al. 2020).

A key innovation in AI-driven auditing is the development of Continuous Auditing and Continuous Monitoring (CA/CM) frameworks. CA/CM leverages AI and real-time data analytics to provide ongoing assurance over financial processes, rather than periodic retrospective assessments. For robo-advisors, CA/CM enables real-time monitoring of algorithmic decisions, client transactions, and compliance metrics, allowing auditors to detect and address issues as they arise. This proactive approach enhances the resilience of financial systems and supports a culture of continuous improvement and regulatory compliance.

Explainable AI (XAI) is increasingly critical for ensuring the transparency and auditability of AI-driven financial processes (Barredo Arrieta et al. 2020). As robo-advisors rely on complex machine learning models, it is essential that auditors can understand and explain the rationale behind algorithmic decisions. XAI tools provide interpretable insights into model behavior, enabling auditors to verify compliance with fairness, accountability, and transparency standards. By enhancing the explainability of AI systems, XAI supports more effective audits and strengthens stakeholder trust in AI-driven financial services (Cheong 2024; Kuiper et al. 2021).

A practical example of advanced AI-driven auditing can be seen in the practices of KPMG's Clara platform. Clara integrates AI, ML, and NLP tools to automate audit processes, perform advanced data analytics, and provide continuous monitoring of client operations. By leveraging Clara, KPMG auditors can efficiently analyze large volumes of financial data, detect anomalies in real time, and generate insightful audit reports. This advanced auditing approach has been successfully applied to several fintech and robo-advisory clients, demonstrating its effectiveness in enhancing audit quality and regulatory compliance (KPMG 2024, 2025).

Another leading example is Deloitte's Cortex AI platform, which offers advanced anomaly detection and risk assessment capabilities. Cortex AI employs ML algorithms to continuously monitor transactional data, identify emerging risks, and provide real-time insights to auditors. In the context of robo-advisory platforms, Cortex AI enables proactive detection of compliance breaches, operational anomalies, and financial irregularities, thereby strengthening the platform's control environment and supporting robust regulatory compliance. These case studies illustrate the transformative potential of AI in automating audit processes and detecting anomalies, setting new benchmarks for audit quality and effectiveness in the era of AI-driven finance (Deloitte 2025).

Assignment: Conceptual Model for AI-Driven Continuous Auditing
Objective:
To design an advanced conceptual framework for integrating AI into continuous auditing and anomaly detection processes in financial services.
Task:

1. **Research AI technologies:**
   - ML
   - NLP
   - XAI
   - RPA
   - CA/CM best practices
2. **Develop a conceptual model:**
   - Define components of your framework
   - Describe AI tool integration at each stage
   - Explain anomaly detection mechanisms
   - Address explainability and ethical considerations
3. **Justify your model:** Link it to academic theory and industry trends.

Deliverables:

- Conceptual model and explanation (approx. 3000 words + model/diagram).

Evaluation Criteria:

- Innovation and originality of the model
- Technical soundness
- Theoretical grounding and use of references
- Practicality for auditing robo-advisors

6 Ethical Considerations in AI-Audited Financial Reports

The adoption of AI in auditing processes introduces a range of ethical challenges that demand critical attention from regulators, auditors, and financial institutions. As robo-advisory platforms increasingly rely on AI-driven audits for compliance and risk management, concerns arise regarding algorithmic bias, fairness, accountability, transparency, and data privacy (Deloitte 2025). The complexity and opacity of AI models, especially black-box machine learning systems, can obscure audit outcomes, leading to questions about the trustworthiness and ethical integrity of AI-audited financial reports. Addressing these concerns requires a multi-dimensional ethical framework that integrates technical, legal, and social perspectives (Barham et al. 2024).

One of the most pressing ethical risks in AI auditing is algorithmic bias. AI models used in financial audits are often trained on historical data that may reflect existing biases or structural inequalities. If unchecked, these biases can propagate through audit outcomes, leading to unfair or discriminatory financial reporting. For example, biased anomaly detection algorithms may disproportionately flag certain types of transactions or clients, thereby undermining the fairness and objectivity of the audit process. Ethical AI auditing requires rigorous bias detection and mitigation strategies, including diverse training datasets, fairness-aware machine learning techniques, and continuous monitoring for bias (Kamalaruban et al. 2024).

Transparency is another foundational ethical principle in AI auditing. Stakeholders including investors, regulators, and clients must be able to understand how AI-generated audit findings are produced (Mökander 2023). Yet, many modern AI models, especially deep learning algorithms, lack interpretability, posing a significant barrier to transparency (Doshi-Velez and Kim 2017). Explainable AI (XAI) is emerging as a crucial tool for addressing this challenge, offering interpretable insights into model behavior and decision-making processes (Regulation and Forum 2022). Integrating XAI into AI-audited financial reporting enables auditors to justify their conclusions and fosters trust among stakeholders (Guidotti et al. 2019).

Accountability is closely linked to transparency but extends to the assignment of responsibility for AI-driven audit outcomes. In traditional auditing, human auditors are held accountable for errors or misconduct. However, with AI-driven processes, responsibility can become diffused across multiple actors, including data scientists, software developers, and auditors (Cobbe et al. 2023). Ethical AI auditing requires clear accountability structures that define who is responsible for AI system design, deployment, oversight, and outcomes (Raji et al. 2020). Auditors must remain ultimately accountable for ensuring the integrity of financial reports, even when AI tools are used to automate audit tasks (OECD 2023).

Data privacy is another key ethical concern in AI-audited financial reports. Robo-advisory platforms process vast amounts of sensitive personal and financial data, which are used to train and operate AI audit models (Goodman and Flaxman 2017). Ethical auditing demands strict compliance with data protection regulations such as the General Data Protection Regulation (GDPR), as well as best practices for data anonymization, encryption, and secure storage (OECD 2023). Moreover, auditors must ensure that AI systems do not inadvertently expose or misuse personal data during audit processes (OECD 2024).

The UK's Digital Regulation Cooperation Forum (DRCF) highlights the evolving role of regulators in shaping ethical standards for algorithmic auditing. Their 2022 report emphasizes the need for collaboration between regulators, industry, and academia to develop ethical frameworks for auditing AI systems. The DRCF also underscores the importance of algorithmic transparency, regulator access to AI systems, and the creation of sector-specific ethical guidelines. Their findings offer a valuable roadmap for enhancing the ethical oversight of AI-audited financial reports, aligning with broader calls for responsible AI governance (DRCF 2022; PWC 2024).

A compelling real-world example of ethical AI auditing can be found in PwC's Halo for Blockchain platform. Halo is designed with embedded XAI tools and strict data privacy safeguards, enabling transparent, accountable, and privacy-preserving audits of blockchain-based financial systems. PwC's approach demonstrates how ethical considerations can be operationalized in AI auditing, balancing the benefits of automation with the imperatives of fairness, accountability, transparency, and privacy (PWC 2024).

Similarly, EY's use of XAI in AI-driven audits for financial services clients highlights best practices in ethical auditing. EY integrates XAI methods to provide interpretable audit outputs, while also employing comprehensive bias detection, accountability frameworks, and GDPR-compliant data practices. This ethical-by-design approach ensures that AI-audited financial reports uphold the highest standards of integrity and trustworthiness. As AI auditing continues to evolve, such examples set an important precedent for the industry (EY 2025).

Assignment: Ethical Risk Assessment and Mitigation Plan for AI Auditing
Objective:
To identify and evaluate ethical risks in AI-driven financial audits and propose a mitigation framework aligned with current regulatory and industry guidance.
Task:

1. **Select a robo-advisory platform or fintech:** Real-world or hypothetical.
2. **Conduct an ethical risk assessment:**
    - Algorithmic bias
    - Transparency and explainability
    - Accountability structures
    - Data privacy and security
    - Alignment with regulatory guidance (e.g., GDPR, DRCF 2022)
3. **Develop an ethical mitigation plan:**
    - Practical strategies for each risk area
    - Embedding ethical considerations into audit processes
    - Define monitoring and accountability mechanisms
4. **Justify the plan:** Support with ethical frameworks and academic sources.

Deliverables:

- Ethical risk assessment and mitigation plan (approx. 3000 words).

Evaluation Criteria:

- Depth of ethical analysis
- Practicality of the mitigation strategies
- Use of real-world regulatory guidance
- Academic and professional integration
- Clarity, structure, and critical thinking

7 Conclusion and Practical Implications

The integration of AI into auditing processes within robo-advisory platforms offers transformative potential, enabling continuous monitoring, enhanced anomaly detection, and more efficient, accurate financial oversight. However, this evolution also introduces complex regulatory, technical, and ethical challenges that must be carefully navigated. As demonstrated throughout this chapter, ensuring compliance with key global standards such as IFRS, GAAP, Basel III, and MiFID II requires robust internal and external control frameworks, supported by advanced AI-driven tools and transparent governance practices (Chang et al. 2018). AI's role in automating audit processes extends beyond efficiency gains; it enhances audit quality by enabling real-time insights and proactive risk management (Chang et al. 2018). Yet, the increasing reliance on complex algorithms necessitates the adoption of Explainable AI, bias mitigation strategies, and rigorous accountability mechanisms to ensure ethical integrity and stakeholder trust (Barredo Arrieta et al. 2020). These insights underscore the need for collaborative regulatory frameworks and sector-specific ethical standards to address emerging challenges in AI auditing.

For practitioners, this evolving landscape demands a shift in audit methodologies and skillsets. Auditors must increasingly collaborate with data scientists, AI engineers, and compliance officers to design, monitor, and interpret AI-driven audit systems (Chang et al. 2018). Furthermore, organizations should prioritize the development of ethical AI governance frameworks, embedding transparency, fairness, and accountability into the core of their audit practices (OECD 2020a).

For regulators, the rapid advancement of AI auditing technologies calls for adaptive and forward-looking policy development. This includes promoting transparency in algorithmic systems, fostering cross-sector collaboration, and enhancing regulators' technical capacity to audit AI systems effectively (DRCF 2022). Collaborative efforts between regulators, industry leaders, and academia will be essential to ensure that AI auditing serves the broader public interest, upholds market integrity, and protects consumer rights.

For students and future professionals, the key takeaway is that AI-driven auditing is not simply a technical enhancement; it is a paradigm shift that requires rethinking traditional audit roles, ethical responsibilities, and regulatory approaches. Developing interdisciplinary expertise in AI, finance, law, and ethics will be critical for succeeding in this dynamic and increasingly complex field. As AI continues to reshape the financial auditing landscape, a commitment to ethical, transparent, and accountable practices will remain the foundation of trust and resilience in AI-powered financial ecosystems.

References

ACCA (2022) The future of audit. www.GrantThornton.global

Alles MG, Kogan A, Vasarhelyi MA (2008) Putting continuous auditing theory into practice: lessons from two pilot implementations. J Inf Syst 22(2):195–214. https://doi.org/10.2308/jis.2008.22.2.195

Altman M, Wood A, O'Brien DR, Gasser U (2018) Practical approaches to big data privacy over time. Int Data Priv Law 8(1):29–51. https://doi.org/10.1093/idpl/ipx027

Appelbaum D, Kogan A, Vasarhelyi MA (2017) Big data and analytics in the modern audit engagement: research needs. Audit J Pract Theory 36(4):1–27. https://doi.org/10.2308/ajpt-51684

Arrieta, A. B., Díaz-Rodríguez, N., Del Ser, J., Bennetot, A., Tabik, S., Barbado, A., García, S., Gil-López, S., Molina, D., Benjamins, R., Chatila, R., & Herrera, F. (2019). Explainable artificial intelligence (XAI): concepts, taxonomies, opportunities and challenges toward responsible AI. http://arxiv.org/abs/1910.10045

Baker T, Dellaert B (2018) Regulating robo advice across the financial services industry. Iowa Law Rev 103(3) http://www.finra.org/

Barham G, Banzon A, Mercer A (2024) Artificial intelligence auditing framework. The Institute of Internal Auditors, pp 11–18

Barredo Arrieta A, Díaz-Rodríguez N, Del Ser J, Bennetot A, Tabik S, Barbado A, Garcia S, Gil-Lopez S, Molina D, Benjamins R, Chatila R, Herrera F (2020) Explainable artificial intelligence (XAI): concepts, taxonomies, opportunities and challenges toward responsible AI. Inf Fusion 58:82–115. https://doi.org/10.1016/j.inffus.2019.12.012

BlackRock Sustainability Disclosure (2024). www.blackrock.com

Buczynski W, Steffek F, Jamnik M, Cuzzaolin F, Sahakian B (2025) Future Themes in regulating artificial intelligence in investment management. Comput Law Secur Rev Int J Technol Law Practice. https://doi.org/10.1016/j.clsr.2025.106111

Chang M, Jackson AB, Wee M, Chen G, Keung EC, Geertsema PG, Lont DH, Lu H, Schultz E, Swieringa J (2018) Accounting & finance. Accounting & Finance 58(3):633–634. https://doi.org/10.1111/acfi.12291

Charlotte LJ, Jacob MW (2024) Automation and robotic process automation (RPA) in financial auditing: efficiency vs. job displacement. https://www.researchgate.net/publication/390662177

Cheong BC (2024) Transparency and accountability in AI systems: safeguarding wellbeing in the age of algorithmic decision-making. Front Hum Dyn 6. https://doi.org/10.3389/fhumd.2024.1421273

Chui, M., Manyika, J., Miremadi, M., Henke, N., Chung, R., Nel, P., & Malhotra, S. (2020). Notes from the AI frontier: applications and value of deep learning

Cobbe J, Veale M, Singh J (2023) Understanding accountability in algorithmic supply chains, ACM international conference proceeding series, pp 1186–1197. https://doi.org/10.1145/3593013.3594073

Committee on Banking Supervision B (2017) Basel Committee on Banking Supervision Basel III: finalising post-crisis reforms. https://www.bis.org/basel_framework/

Dai J, Vasarhelyi MA (2017) Toward blockchain-based accounting and assurance. J Inf Syst 31(3):5–21. https://doi.org/10.2308/isys-51804

Deloitte (2018) 2019 investment management outlook - a mix of opportunity and challenge. https://www2.deloitte.com/content/dam/Deloitte/lu/Documents/financial-services/IM/lu-2019-investment-management-outlook.pdf

Deloitte (2025) Finding irregularities fast. https://www.deloitte.com/de/de/products/aistudio/anomaly-detector-consistency.html?utm_source=chatgpt.com

Doshi-Velez F, Kim B (2017) Towards a rigorous science of interpretable machine learning. Ml:1–13. http://arxiv.org/abs/1702.08608

DRCF (2022) DRCF algorithmic processing workstream: response to call for input submissions

DRCF (2023, September 23) Auditing algorithms: the existing landscape, role of regulators and future outlook

ESMA (2018) ESMA publishes annual report. https://www.esma.europa.eu/press-news/esma-news/esma-publishes-2018-annual-report

European Commission (2021) Proposal for a Regulation laying down harmonised rules on artificial intelligence (Artificial Intelligence Act)

EY (2020) Supervisory expectations and sound model risk management practices for artificial intelligence and machine learning

EY (2025) Responsible AI in financial services. Responsible AI in financial services

FASB (2021) Accounting standards updates issued. https://www.fasb.org/standards/accounting-standard-updates

Financial Stability Board (2017) Artificial intelligence and machine learning in financial services - market developments and financial stability implications. Financial Stability Board, p 45. http://www.fsb.org/2017/11/artificial-intelligence-and-machine-learning-in-financial-service/

Floridi L, Cowls J, Beltrametti M, Chatila R, Chazerand P, Dignum V, Luetge C, Madelin R, Pagallo U, Rossi F, Schafer B, Valcke P, Vayena E (2018) AI4People—an ethical framework for a good AI society: opportunities, risks, principles, and recommendations. Mind Mach 28(4):689–707. https://doi.org/10.1007/s11023-018-9482-5

Fotoh LE, Mugwira T (2025) Exploring large language models in external audits: implications and ethical considerations. Int J Account Inf Syst 56. https://doi.org/10.1016/j.accinf.2025.100748

Gallego Sánchez MDC, De-Pablos-Heredero C, Medina-Merodio J-A, Robina-Ramírez R, Fernandez-Sanz L (2021) Relationships among relational coordination dimensions: impact on the quality of education online with a structural equations model. Technol Forecast Soc Chang 166. https://doi.org/10.1016/j.techfore.2021.120608

Goodman B, Flaxman S (2017) Counterfactual explanations without opening the black box. AI Mag 38(3):50–57

Guidotti R, Monreale A, Ruggieri S, Turini F, Giannotti F, Pedreschi D (2019) A survey of methods for explaining black box models. ACM Comput Surv 51(5). https://doi.org/10.1145/3236009

Gurrea-Martinez A, Wan WY (2021) The promises and perils of robo-advisers: challenges and regulatory responses. https://doi.org/10.2139/ssrn.3931448

Hossnofsky V, Junge S (2019) Does the market reward digitalization efforts? Evidence from securities analysts' investment recommendations. J Bus Econ 89(8–9):965–994. https://doi.org/10.1007/s11573-019-00949-y

IASB (2019) IFRS update December 2019. https://www.ifrs.org/news-and-events/updates/iasb/2019/iasb-update-december-2019/

IBM Research (2020) AI fairness 360: an open source toolkit for detecting and mitigating bias in machine learning models

ICAEW (2019) Fiscal risks report 2019. ICAEW. https://www.icaew.com/about-icaew/regulation-and-the-public-interest/policy/better-government-series/obr-fiscal-risks-report-2019

Institute of Internal Auditors (IIA) (2017) International professional practices framework (IPPF), 2017 edition

IOSCO (2021) Report on sustainability-related issuer disclosures. The Board of the International Organization of Securities Commissions. https://www.iosco.org/library/pubdocs/pdf/IOSCOPD678.pdf

Issa H, Sun T, Vasarhelyi MA (2016) Research ideas for artificial intelligence in auditing: the formalization of audit and workforce supplementation. J Emerging Technol Account 13(2):1–20. https://doi.org/10.2308/jeta-10511

Jung D, Dorner V, Glaser F, Morana S (2018) Robo-advisory: digitalization and automation of financial advisory. Bus Inf Syst Eng 60(1):81–86. https://doi.org/10.1007/s12599-018-0521-9

Kamalaruban P, Pi Y, Burrell S, Drage E, Skalski P, Wong J, Sutton D (2024) Evaluating fairness in transaction fraud models: fairness metrics, bias audits, and challenges. In: ICAIF 2024 - 5th ACM international conference on AI in finance, pp 555–563. https://doi.org/10.1145/3677052.3698666

Kokina J, Davenport TH (2017) The emergence of artificial intelligence: how automation is changing auditing. J Emerging Technol Account 14(1):115–122. https://doi.org/10.2308/jeta-51730

KPMG (2024) KPMG advances AI integration in KPMG Clara smart audit platform. https://kpmg.com/xx/en/media/press-releases/2025/04/kpmg-advances-ai-integration-in-kpmg-clara-smart-audit-platform.html

KPMG (2025) Transforming audit with AI and KPMG Clara. https://kpmg.com/dk/en/ai/transforming-audit-with-ai-and-kpmg-clara.html

Kuiper, O., Van Der Burgt, J., & Leijnen, S. (2021). Exploring explainable AI in the financial sector: perspectives of banks and supervisory authorities

Lacurezeanu R, Tiron-Tudor A, Bresfelean VP (2020) Robotic process automation in audit and accounting. Audit Financiar 18(160):752–770. https://doi.org/10.20869/AUDITF/2020/160/024

Lee I, Shin YJ (2018) Fintech: ecosystem, business models, investment decisions, and challenges. Bus Horiz 61(1):35–46. https://doi.org/10.1016/j.bushor.2017.09.003

Lee J, Feung C, Thiruchelvam IV (2020) A framework model for continuous auditing in financial statement audits using big data analytics. Int J Sci Technol Res. www.ijstr.org

Mittelstadt BD, Allo P, Taddeo M, Wachter S, Floridi L (2016) The ethics of algorithms: mapping the debate. Big Data Soc 3(2):2053951716679679. https://doi.org/10.1177/2053951716679679

Mökander J (2023) Auditing of AI: legal, ethical and technical approaches. In: Digital society, vol 2, Issue 3. Springer International Publishing. https://doi.org/10.1007/s44206-023-00074-y

OECD (2020a) Digital

OECD (2020b) OECD principles on artificial intelligence

OECD (2023) Advancing accountability in AI governing and managing risks throughout the lifecycle for trustworthy AI. www.oecd.ai/wips

OECD (2024) AI, data governance, and privacy: synergies and areas of international co-operation. OECD Artif Intell Pap 22:1–55. http://www.oecd.org/termsandconditions

Onyenahazi OB (2025) Integrating artificial intelligence in financial auditing to enhance accuracy, efficiency, and regulatory compliance outcomes. Int J Res Publ Rev 6(7):23–44. https://doi.org/10.55248/gengpi.6.0725.2402

Phoon KF, Koh CC (2018) Robo-advisors and wealth. J Altern Invest 20(3):79–94. https://doi.org/10.3905/jati.201

PWC (2020) Transparency report 2020. https://www.pwc.co.uk/who-we-are/transparency-report/2020.html

PWC (2024) Audit of general ledger with Halo. https://pwc.to/3Sj4u5J

Raji ID, Smart A, White RN, Mitchell M, Gebru T, Hutchinson B, Smith-Loud J, Theron D, Barnes P (2020) Closing the AI accountability gap: defining an end-to-end framework for internal algorithmic auditing, Proceedings of the 2020 Conference on Fairness, Accountability, and Transparency, pp 33–44. https://doi.org/10.1145/3351095.3372873

Regulation D, Forum C (2022) DRCF algorithmic processing workstream: response to call for input submissions

Ringe W-G, Ruof C (2018) A regulatory sandbox for robo advice (May 31, 2018). European Banking Institute Working Paper Series 2018-no. 26, Available at SSRN: https://ssrn.com/abstract=3188828 or https://doi.org/10.2139/ssrn.3188828

Rozario AM, Vasarhelyi MA (2018) Auditing with smart contracts. Int J Digit Account Res

The European Commission (2021) Regulation of the European Parliament and of the Council, vol 0106. The European Commission, p 108

The IFRS Accounting Standards Navigator (2021) IFRS accounting standards navigator. https://www.ifrs.org/issued-standards/list-of-standards/

Thiprungsri S, Vasarhelyi MA (2011) Cluster analysis for anomaly detection in accounting data: an audit approach. Int J Digit Account Res 11:69–84. https://doi.org/10.4192/1577-8517-v11_4

UBS (2022) UBS first quarter 2022 report. https://www.ubs.com/global/en/investor-relations/financial-information/quarterly-reporting.html

W S R JE (2025) The impact of artificial intelligence on financial auditing practices. https://doi.org/10.2139/ssrn.5246758

Zetzsche, D. A., Buckley, R. P., Arner, D. W., & Barberis, J. N. (2016). EBI working paper series from FinTech to TechFin: the regulatory challenges of data-driven finance. https://ssrn.com/abstract=2959925

Cybersecurity Risk and Robo-Advisory

Nader Virk and Mohammed Al-Khalidi

Abstract This chapter outlines the increasing cybersecurity risks in digital and AI-driven finance while focusing on robo-advisors. This chapter contextualises robo-advisory architecture, threat taxonomy and entry points, and how AI presence adds to cybersecurity attack surface area. Then it moves into a deeper analysis of key attack vectors like insecure APIs, misconfigured cloud infrastructure, and exposed data pipelines as common entry points. Building on this, the chapter examines advanced attack techniques, including adversarial machine learning methods such as data poisoning, model evasion, and backdoor insertion, targeting AI decision-making reliability. These techniques exploit AI model complexity, highlighting the need for explainable AI (xAI). Advanced Persistent Threats increasingly deploy these for long-term unauthorised access. Furthermore, the chapter investigates systemic vulnerabilities from interconnected digital ecosystems, including cloud services and distributed computing. Decentralised finance (DeFi) asset risks like smart contract exploits, flash loan attacks, and oracle manipulation are given special attention as novel threats.

The chapter also addresses the growing importance of data privacy in AI-powered financial services, especially for robo-advisors handling sensitive client data. It examines increasing regulatory scrutiny and emphasises the need for compliance, transparency, and robust ethical standards. Ethical considerations like algorithmic bias and trust are integrated throughout. Towards the end, this chapter also explores the role played by AI and xAI applications in forensic accounting and auditing for fraud detection and investigations. It concludes with strategic recommendations for securing digital wealth management platforms, encompassing advanced encryption,

N. Virk (✉)
Manchester Metropolitan University Business School, Manchester Metropolitan University, Manchester, UK
e-mail: n.virk@mmu.ac.uk

M. Al-Khalidi
Department of Computing and Mathematics, Manchester Metropolitan University, Manchester, UK
e-mail: m.al-khalidi@mmu.ac.uk

N. Nahidi, A. Zarifis (eds.), *AI, FinTech, and the Future of Robo-Advisory*, Contributions to Finance and Accounting,
https://doi.org/10.1007/978-3-032-18109-1_10

multi-factor authentication, zero-trust architecture, AI-driven anomaly detection, and secure software development and robust data governance.

Keywords Cybersecurity risk · Robo-advisory · Attack vectors · Algorithmic bias · AI and explainable AI · Forensic accounting

1 Introduction

Cybersecurity risk is scaling in financial services as they are mapped increasingly into digital space. Global loss projections are expected to be approximately 10.5 trillion USD by the end of 2025. This underscores the macro relevance of cyber resilience for investors and policymakers (Morgan 2024). International Monetary Fund (2024) report highlights that for financial firms direct losses might appear relatively small; however, the risk of extreme losses—at least 2.5 billion USD—is on the rise and poses a threat to macro-financial stability. The emerging robo-advisory financial landscape is no exception. The widespread use of AI in robo-advisory platforms introduces significant systemic and cybersecurity risks. These challenges stem from the inherent characteristics of AI systems and their growing reliance on interconnected digital infrastructure. These may include the amplification of market instability and correlated trades for the reliance on a small number of data vendors, and increased adoption of similar AI models. Consequently, herding in financial markets—algorithmic synchronised trading—will amplify market volatility and increases systemic risk (Kirilenko et al. 2017; Budish et al. 2015). Automation and Autonomy features in robo-advisory architecture further inflate these risks and have been flagged by supervisors (FSB 2017, 2024; ESMA 2025).

This chapter outlines a typical robo-advisory architecture, attack surface area—taxonomy and entry points, and convergence and systemic nature of the cybersecurity threats. A deeper analysis of several attack vectors, data contamination in robo-advisory systems, and the convergence of attack vectors follows. Then dimensions of deepfake concerns, identity theft, and vulnerabilities linked to human inter-looping in robo-advisory are considered. This chapter allocates considerable space to the impact of AI and xAI in forensic accounting and auditing to handle typical reporting and corporate misconduct and evidential scope in compliance and legal settings.

2 Cybersecurity Threat Landscape in Robo-Advisory

Robo-advisory platforms aggregate private client information and operate over application programming interface (API)-driven and cloud and AI-enabled infrastructures. They also connect, assimilate, and transform data from external newsfeeds, data supply lines, and market rails. This architecture creates multiple

Fig. 1 Architecture of an AI-driven robo-advisor

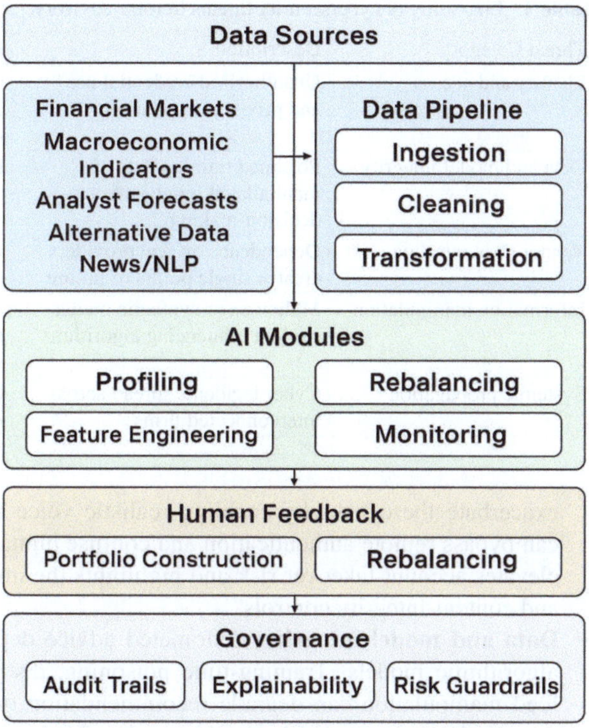

exposure points where cyber risk can materialise. Figure 1 showcases a typical robo-advisory architecture and each element of it for its digital interconnectedness. The increased use of AI approaches—from Gen-AI transformers to ML models—opens several cybersecurity threats at each point of data entry, processing, modelling, decision execution, and identity authentication.

Table 1 outlines and exemplifies cybersecurity threats. As shown, the threat taxonomy for robo-advisory can be divided into six areas:

- **Identity and access**: Credential abuse and privilege escalation are primary breach vectors for cloud-hosted portfolios and client portals. This risk is magnified where API-first architectures[1] expose control surfaces, leading to weak authorisation, excessive data exposure, or insufficient rate-limiting (Florackis et al. 2023). Misconfigured cloud resources and leaked credentials increase lateral-movement risk into data lakes and feature stores, concentrating the damage from a single key compromise (Aldasoro et al. 2022). In addition, phishing and social engineering remain persistent entry points for cyber attackers targeting human interaction in the robo-advisory decision loop. For robo-advisors, deepfakes

[1] Appendix Table 8 provides definitions and explanations for key terms in the robo-advisory, financial services, and cybersecurity risk domains of work.

Table 1 Taxonomy of cybersecurity threats in robo-advisory

Threat Category	Description	Example scenario
Identity and access	Unauthorised credential use and privilege escalation	Compromised API key allows attacker to access client portfolios
Data and model integrity	Poisoned training data or manipulated inputs affect decision-making	Fake market data feed biases asset allocation
Vendor concentration	Dependence on few providers creates single points of failure	Cloud outage disrupts all portfolio rebalancing
Information manipulation	Malicious or synthetic media content influencing algorithms	Fake news triggers robo-advisors to sell assets simultaneously
Systemic propagation	Cyber incidents spread across interconnected firms	Custodian breach leads to multi-platform disruption

exacerbate these risks by enabling realistic voice or video impersonation that can bypass remote authentication and confuse human-in-the-loop checks, which elevates account-takeover risk and highlights the importance of live verification and content-integrity controls.

- **Data and model integrity**: Automated advice depends on data pipelines and algorithmic models. Training-time poisoning, distribution shift, and real-time feed manipulation can degrade recommendation quality, triggering misallocations and erroneous and loss-prone trades. These risks grow with data volume, third-party sourcing, and model complexity (Aldasoro et al. 2022; Florackis et al. 2023). In Decentralised finance (DeFi), oracle design governs data accuracy and integrity when bridging off-chain information into on-chain venues. Poor choices like weak cryptography or single-source data vendors elevate manipulation risk (Eskandari et al. 2021). Market-microstructure vulnerabilities further widen the attack surface: transaction reordering and maximal extractable value (MEV) can distort prices (Daian et al. 2019), while flash loans allow capital-free, single-block exploit chains (Qin et al. 2021), with recent work even synthesising profitable transactions automatically (Chen et al. 2024). These dynamics imply a need for independent pricing, circuit breakers, and strict segregation between core advisory logic and any DeFi connectors.
- **Vendor concentration**: Dependence on a narrow set of providers for compute, analytics, and market data can synchronise failures and increase single-point-of-failure risk (Crosignani et al. 2023).
- **Information manipulation**: Automated channels ingest news and signals. Adversarial content, including synthetic media like deepfakes, increases the odds of reactive rebalancing and correlated errors (Jiang et al. 2024; Mirsky and Lee 2021; Tolosana et al. 2020).
- **Systemic propagation**: Empirical evidence shows that cyber incidents travel along supply chains. Robo-advisory systems that are linked to wider DeFi

configurations interlinked via custodians, market data vendors, and payment rails can magnify the blast radius (Crosignani et al. 2023).

3 Attack Vectors and Data Contamination in Robo-Advisory

DeFi platforms, particularly those powered by AI, and distributed ledger technologies (DLT), rely on a complex interplay of APIs, data flows, and chain securitised and smart contract infrastructures. While these interconnections drive efficiency and innovation, they simultaneously expand the scope of exposure to cybersecurity risks, offering adversaries multiple entry points into robo-advisory systems, Fig. 2 highlights different attack points in a typical robo-advisory platform. Table 2 outlines common attack vectors for robo-advisory systems and users. Three categories of attack vectors stand out as both prevalent and uniquely damaging: insecure APIs, data contamination, and robo-advisory-specific exploits targeting smart contracts, and oracle mechanisms—no cryptographic security, poor data latency, among others.

3.1 Insecure APIs

APIs form the connective tissue of robo-advisors, trading platforms, and digital banking systems. They enable seamless integration across services, including authentication, account management, transaction execution, and third-party analytics. However, poorly secured or misconfigured APIs are among the most exploited vulnerabilities for robo-advisory systems similar to other fintech ecosystems.

- **Authentication bypass:** Weak token management or missing authorisation checks allow attackers to impersonate users or escalate privileges. In 2019, a vulnerability in the Venmo payment API allowed attackers to scrape millions of transaction records because the API lacked proper access restrictions (Basak

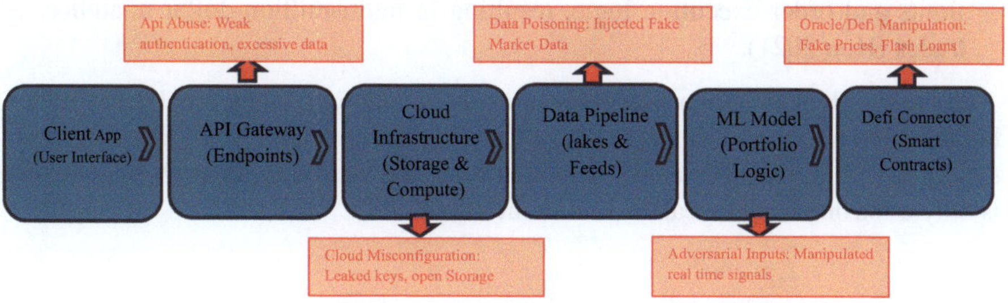

Fig. 2 Attack surface map of a robo-advisory platform

Table 2 Common attack vectors in robo-advisory

Vector	Technical mechanism	Exploit example	Consequences
Insecure APIs	Weak auth, overexposed endpoints	Attacker extracts client portfolio data	Privacy loss, fraud
Cloud misconfigurations	Exposed storage buckets, leaked credentials	Misconfigured Amazon S3 (Simple Storage Service) bucket with transaction history	Data breach, insider trading
Data poisoning	Insertion of malicious samples into training data	Fake trading volumes bias allocation model	Misallocation, losses
Adversarial inputs	Real-time manipulation of inputs	Adversarial signal fools rebalancing algorithm	Erroneous trades
Oracle manipulation	Exploiting off-chain → on-chain bridges	False price feed changes valuation of tokenised assets	Financial loss
Flash loans	Exploiting capital-free loans to manipulate protocols	Borrow → manipulate → profit → repay cycle	DeFi-linked loss

and Tiwari 2025). Table 3 outlines major cybersecurity breaches since 2016. Similarly, misconfigured API authentication in banking apps has been shown to allow attackers to bypass login processes entirely, accessing account details without user consent (Tandon et al. 2022).

- **Data leakage:** Excessive data exposure through verbose error messages or unprotected endpoints can reveal sensitive client information (Genfer and Zdun 2022). In 2020, the Robinhood trading app's API exposed personal details of around 2000 customers due to excessive response data in its backend (CNN, 2020). Attackers could use such leaks to craft spear-phishing campaigns targeting high-value investors.
- **Portfolio strategy abuse:** Exploiting API workflows, adversaries can automate fraudulent transactions or extract sensitive portfolio insights. In 2018, attackers exploited APIs of several cryptocurrency exchanges by manipulating withdrawal limits and order execution logic, resulting in multi-million-dollar unauthorised trades (Hou 2021).

As robo-advisors increasingly rely on APIs to interact with external data sources, brokers, and custodians, a single insecure endpoint can compromise the integrity of the entire digital wealth management chain—living well with the proverb that "one is only as strong as the weakest link in the chain".

Table 3 Major cybersecurity episodes in financial services

Year	Platform	Attack vector	Details from document	Impact/scale
2016	The DAO	Smart Contract Re-entrancy Bug	Attackers exploited a re-entrancy bug in the DAO's Ethereum smart contract	$60 million in Ether siphoned
2018	Several Cryptocurrency Exchanges	API Business Logic Abuse	Attackers exploited APIs by manipulating withdrawal limits and order execution logic	Multi-million-dollar unauthorised trades
2019	Venmo Payment API	API Vulnerability	Vulnerability allowed attackers to scrape transaction records because API lacked proper access restrictions	Millions of transaction records scraped
2020	Robinhood Trading App	API Data Exposure	API exposed personal details due to excessive response data in backend	Around 2000 customers affected
2020	bZx Protocol	Oracle Manipulation + Flash Loans	Flash loans used to distort price feeds; attackers borrowed and sold assets at artificially inflated valuations	Around $8 million extracted
2022	Wormhole Bridge	Smart Contract Bug	Bug in cross-chain bridge smart contract allowed hackers to mint tokens without proper collateralisation	120,000 ETH (then worth over $320 million)
2022	Mango Markets (Solana)	Oracle Manipulation	Attacker manipulated oracle-based collateral valuations to borrow far beyond actual holdings	$114 million drained

3.2 *Data Contamination and Model Integrity Attacks*

Robo-advisors and AI-driven financial platforms rely heavily on large, diverse datasets to train and update models for portfolio allocation, risk assessment, and fraud detection. This dependence makes them vulnerable to data contamination, a form of adversarial manipulation where malicious actors inject misleading or poisoned data into training or operational pipelines.

- **Data poisoning:** Corrupting datasets with biased or fraudulent entries can skew model outputs, leading to misallocation of funds or faulty risk assessments. In 2021, researchers demonstrated how adversarial data contamination could trick a robo-advisor prototype into systematically underweighting blue-chip equities, producing systematically unbalanced portfolios (Yussuf 2025). Similar risks have been highlighted in credit scoring where manipulated datasets can cause biased or fraudulent lending decisions.

- **Model evasion:** Carefully crafted adversarial inputs exploit model blind spots, bypassing fraud detection systems or misclassifying risk profiles. A notable case occurred when fraudsters exploited machine learning-driven anti-money-laundering (AML) systems by structuring transactions just below reporting thresholds, evading detection algorithms. These "structuring" attacks resemble adversarial examples in vision models, but in interconnected systems, they allow criminals to launder money without raising alarms (Borrajo et al. 2020). Conceptually, this threat is also applicable to robo-advisory systems: users might exploit these thresholds with the service providers.
- **Backdoor insertion:** Attackers embed triggers within training data that allow them to manipulate outputs later without raising suspicion. Academic studies have shown how backdoored financial prediction models can be induced to make specific trades when encountering hidden triggers such as acoustic data positioning (Mengara 2024). While not yet publicly tied to a real-world heist, the threat is emerging as financial institutions increasingly outsource AI model development.

These threats highlight the dual role of data: as a driver of financial intelligence and a potential attack vector. Contaminated data undermine not only technical reliability but also regulatory compliance and client trust.

3.3 DeFi-Specific Exploits Applicable to Robo-Advisory Systems

DeFi introduces unique systemic risks due to its reliance on immutable code and external data feeds. Unlike traditional financial systems, robo-advisors within the DeFi family of systems often lack intermediaries capable of halting malicious activities once they are in motion. Two exploit classes are particularly critical:

- **Smart contract vulnerabilities:** Errors in contract logic, such as re-entrancy flaws or unchecked arithmetic operations, can allow attackers to drain liquidity pools, mint unauthorised tokens, or trigger cascading failures across interconnected protocols. The DAO hack of 2016 remains the most famous example: attackers exploited a re-entrancy bug in the DAO's Ethereum smart contract to siphon $60 million in Ether (Li 2024). In 2022, a bug in the Wormhole bridge smart contract allowed hackers to mint 120,000 ETH (then worth over $320 million) without proper collateralisation, highlighting how contract logic flaws can be catastrophic (Azad et al. 2025).
- **Oracle manipulation:** Oracles bridge on-chain and off-chain environments, supplying asset prices and market data. Attackers can manipulate oracle inputs through flash loan-driven market swings or by compromising the oracle infras-

tructure itself. Distorted price feeds can lead to under-collateralised loans, forced liquidations, or arbitrage exploitation at systemic scale. In 2020, the bZx protocol suffered a series of oracle manipulation attacks, where flash loans were used to distort price feeds. Attackers extracted around $8 million by borrowing and selling assets at artificially inflated valuations (Deng 2024). More recently, in 2022, Mango Markets on Solana was drained of $114 million when an attacker manipulated oracle-based collateral valuations to borrow far beyond their actual holdings (Scharfman 2024).

These exploits illustrate how digital systems introduce not only technological vulnerabilities but also economic attack surfaces, where adversaries weaponise market dynamics in addition to code.

3.4 The Convergence of Attack Vectors Into Sophisticated Pathways

Attack vectors can be integrated into modular cyberattacks. A sophisticated adversary may chain them together—for example, by leveraging an insecure API to access training pipelines, contaminating models to influence trading strategies, and finally exploiting system protocols through manipulated oracles to maximise financial gain. This convergence of technical, economic, and data-driven attack vectors underscores the necessity for multi-layered defence strategies.

Robo-advisory platforms, which are API-first and cloud-hosted, have multiple exposure points. Authorisation flaws, excessive data exposure, and weak rate-limiting in API-first architectures can enable the enumeration of client data or tampering with configurations that influence model inputs (Florackis et al. 2023). Similarly, misconfigured cloud resources and leaked credentials increase lateral-movement risk into data lakes and feature stores, concentrating the damage from a single key compromise (Aldasoro et al. 2022). The model supply chain introduces additional attack surfaces: poisoning of historical market or behavioural data can bias training, while adversarial perturbations or manipulated feeds can cause real-time misallocation.

The use of blockchains: oracles bridging off-chain data to on-chain environments are a critical point of failure. Experimental systemisations show that design choices can affect truthfulness, latency, and manipulation resistance (Eskandari et al. 2021). DeFi exposures complicate matters when robo-advisors integrate tokenised products or yield strategies. Foundational analyses of decentralised exchanges show that transaction reordering and miner/maximal extractable value (MEV) can distort prices and create consensus instability, enabling adversaries to profit from frontrunning and sandwiching (Daian et al. 2019). Flash loans lower capital barriers for complex exploit chains; empirical and constructive work demonstrates how attackers can compose protocol vulnerabilities to manipulate prices within a single block (Qin et al. 2021). Recent program analysis advances can even synthesise profitable flash loan exploit transactions automatically, raising the baseline capability of adversaries (Chen et al. 2024).

For robo-advisory connectors, this implies a need for independent pricing, circuit breakers, and strict segregation between core advisory logic and experimental DeFi interfaces. Data governance should include source authentication, lineage tracking, canary datasets, and continuous monitoring to detect distribution shifts and anomalous correlations consistent with poisoning or feed tampering (Eskandari et al. 2021; Florackis et al. 2023).

4 Deepfake Concerns in Robo-Advisory

The rise of deepfakes has introduced a critical new dimension of cyber risk to the DeFi ecosystem. Within robo-advisory systems, deepfakes compromise identity verification, client authentication, data integrity, and the overall trust upon which automated financial advice depends (Chesney and Citron 2019; Maras and Alexandrou 2019).

4.1 Deepfakes and the Erosion of Digital Trust

Deepfakes exploit neural networks to produce highly realistic yet fabricated images, voices, and videos that convincingly impersonate real individuals. This technological capability poses a direct threat to digital trust, the foundation of online financial engagement. As robo-advisors rely on AI-mediated interactions, often without human oversight, synthetic identities can manipulate clients or staff to execute fraudulent transactions (Aithal and Aithal 2021).

Remote onboarding processes, particularly video-based Know Your Customer (KYC) protocols, are vulnerable to deepfake spoofing. A falsified video identity can subvert biometric verification and lead to unauthorised account creation or fund access (Europol 2022). Such attacks not only compromise individual clients but can also erode public confidence in the reliability of automated financial systems.

4.2 Threat Vectors and Attack Scenarios

Deepfakes intersect with and amplify existing attack vectors in AI-driven finance, transforming theoretical vulnerabilities into practical, high-impact risks. Several real-world incidents and credible demonstrations have illustrated how synthetic media can be weaponised to undermine financial integrity and client trust.

4.2.1 Synthetic Identity Fraud

Fraudsters increasingly use deepfake-generated images and videos to bypass biometric verification systems. A prominent example emerged in 2023, when the Hong Kong police reported a case in which criminals used AI-generated deepfake video calls to impersonate company executives and defraud a multinational firm of approximately HK$200 million (around USD 25 million) (South China Morning Post 2023). Attackers convincingly mimicked the facial and vocal features of legitimate employees during an online meeting, successfully authorising large-scale fund transfers. This incident demonstrates how deepfakes can be combined with synthetic identity creation and social engineering to exploit remote onboarding and transaction authorisation processes in fintech and robo-advisory platforms. Given the reliance of these systems on automated KYC and digital identity verification, the potential for similar exploitation is substantial.

4.2.2 Voice Phishing and AI-Driven Social Engineering

Deepfake voice technologies have already been deployed in financial fraud with significant success. In 2019, criminals used an AI-generated replica of a CEO's voice to convince an employee at a UK energy firm's German subsidiary to transfer €220,000 to a fraudulent account (The Wall Street Journal 2019). The attackers replicated the executive's accent and speech patterns so accurately that the employee believed the instructions were authentic. Such incidents exemplify the evolution of "vishing" (voice phishing) into AI-driven deception. As robo-advisors increasingly integrate voice-based user interfaces and hybrid human AI advisory models, the potential for adversaries to impersonate trusted individuals, including clients, advisors, or compliance officers, poses a major operational and reputational risk (Europol 2022).

4.2.3 Market Manipulation Via Fabricated Media

Deepfakes can also be leveraged for strategic disinformation and market manipulation. In 2020, a falsified video purporting to show a US CEO making a controversial statement briefly circulated online, leading to a measurable dip in the company's stock before the video was debunked (Nguyen et al. 2022). Similarly, in 2023, analysts at Reuters identified an emerging trend of AI-generated fake news anchors used in state-linked disinformation campaigns promoting false economic data and stock commentary (Reuters 2023). Such incidents demonstrate how deepfakes can indirectly influence robo-advisory algorithms that rely on sentiment analysis or news feeds for portfolio recommendations. A targeted synthetic video or voice clip could distort data inputs used for automated investment decisions, amplifying volatility and creating systemic information risks in digital wealth management systems.

Table 4 Real-world manifestations of deepfake risks in AI-driven financial services

Threat type	Mechanism	Real-world example	Implications for robo-advisory
Synthetic identity fraud	Deepfake-generated identities bypassing KYC	Hong Kong executive impersonation scam (2023)	Compromised client onboarding, fraudulent transactions
Voice phishing	Deepfake voice imitating executives or clients	UK CEO voice fraud (2019)	Social engineering of advisors, fraudulent fund transfers
Market manipulation	Deepfake media distorting financial news	Fake CEO videos and synthetic anchors (2020–2023)	Algorithmic misinference, market volatility, client misinformation

As shown above and summarised in Table 4, these examples underscore that deepfakes are not a hypothetical threat but a present and escalating risk vector in financial ecosystems. For robo-advisory platforms that depend on digital identity, automated communication, and data-driven decision-making, the convergence of deepfake media and cyber deception significantly raises both operational and systemic risk profiles.

4.3 *Model and Data Vulnerabilities*

Deepfakes also present indirect systemic risks by contaminating datasets or AI models used in robo-advisory. Synthetic data introduced into client communication logs or sentiment analysis systems can degrade model accuracy, bias financial recommendations, or trigger compliance violations (Goodfellow et al. 2020). As robo-advisors increasingly integrate natural language processing (NLP) and video interfaces, deepfake-generated inputs could be misclassified as legitimate. This contamination introduces feedback risks, whereby AI models inadvertently learn from manipulated data, reinforcing misinformation or unethical decision patterns (Brundage et al. 2018). In 2024, the UK's National Cyber Security Centre (NCSC) warned of model extraction attacks targeting financial sector chatbots, where attackers attempted to reconstruct proprietary algorithms through iterative querying (NCSC 2024). Accordingly, an attacker could probe a robo-advisor's Large Language Model (LLM) to infer risk models, investment strategies, or compliance thresholds, compromising intellectual property and enabling adversarial market behaviour.

4.4 Detection and Mitigation Strategies

Mitigating deepfake and AI-driven threats in robo-advisory systems requires a multi-layered approach that combines technological, operational, and regulatory measures. In addition to AI-based detection algorithms, several complementary strategies are critical for safeguarding digital wealth management platforms.

4.4.1 Liveness Detection

Liveness detection during video authentication ensures that clients are physically present and not represented by synthetic media such as deepfake videos or recorded clips. Modern systems confirm real-time interaction through motion and gesture verification, depth analysis, and behavioural cues, providing a robust defence against impersonation and identity fraud. Banks including HSBC and Standard Chartered have successfully deployed such systems to mitigate fraudulent remote account openings (Europol 2022).

4.4.2 Blockchain-Enabled Digital Identity Verification

This provides immutable and tamper-proof records of client identity. Decentralised identity frameworks and smart contracts allow institutions to verify credentials cryptographically while maintaining transparent, auditable trails. Pilot initiatives by the Sovrin Foundation and fintech projects in Singapore and Switzerland demonstrate improved security and regulatory compliance for KYC and AML processes (Mungai 2024).

4.4.3 Inter-institutional Intelligence Sharing

Intelligence sharing enhances early detection of synthetic identity threats, deepfake campaigns, and adversarial AI attacks. Financial institutions can contribute anonymised indicators of compromise to centralised repositories, enabling pattern recognition across organisations. Regulatory technology tools facilitate secure, compliant data exchange, while initiatives such as Financial Services Information Sharing and Analysis Center (FS-ISAC) provide global alerts on AI-driven scams affecting robo-advisory platforms.

Together, these measures form a layered defence that strengthens security, supports regulatory compliance, and protects client trust in AI-powered financial services.

4.5 Regulatory and Ethical Considerations

Regulatory frameworks are evolving to address synthetic media threats. The EU Artificial Intelligence Act (2024) mandates transparency and disclosure for AI-generated content, while GDPR provisions on data accuracy and consent apply directly to deepfake identity misuse. In the United States, the Federal Trade Commission (FTC) and Financial Crimes Enforcement Network (FinCEN) have both issued warnings regarding synthetic identity fraud in digital finance (FTC 2023).

Ethically, deepfake manipulation challenges principles of fairness, authenticity, and accountability in AI deployment (Floridi and Cowls 2019). For robo-advisory, maintaining transparency in client interactions and ensuring data authenticity are essential to sustaining consumer trust and upholding fiduciary duties.

4.6 Strategic Implications for Robo-Advisory Security

A holistic security approach must integrate deepfake detection and prevention within broader cybersecurity architectures. Recommended practices include:

- Continuous AI-based monitoring for synthetic media anomalies
- Behavioural analytics to identify inconsistencies with client interaction baselines
- Staff awareness training to recognise deepfake-enabled fraud tactics
- Collaborative partnerships with regulators, cybersecurity firms, and fintech associations to develop standardised response frameworks

Ultimately, shielding robo-advisory platforms from deepfake threats transcends a purely technical challenge; it becomes a fundamental test of infrastructural integrity, ethical resilience, and institutional trustworthiness within the age of synthetic reality.

5 Identity Theft and Human Elements in Robo-Advisory

While much of the cybersecurity discourse in digital finance focuses on technological vulnerabilities, human factors remain a decisive source of risk in robo-advisory systems. Identity theft, social engineering, insider threats, and jurisdictional inconsistencies in data protection laws all expose the human interface of digital wealth management to exploitation. Table 5 lists human-centred vulnerabilities in robo-advisory with examples and potential mitigation strategies. As clients, employees, and intermediaries interact with increasingly autonomous advisory platforms, cognitive biases, behavioural lapses, and weak security practices can undermine even the most advanced technical safeguards.

Table 5 Human-centred vulnerabilities in robo-advisory

Vulnerability	Example attack	Key study/source	Mitigation strategy
Phishing and social engineering	AI-generated emails and voice deepfakes impersonating robo-advisor support to obtain credentials	FS-ISAC (2024a, 2024b); Europol (2022)	AI-based phishing detection, client education, secure multi-channel transaction verification
Credential theft	Compromise of client login data via password reuse or API breach	Verizon (2024) *Data Breach Report*	Hardware-bound MFA, behavioural biometrics, zero-trust access control
Insider threat	Privileged employee extracts client data from analytics environment	European Union Agency for Cybersecurity (ENISA 2025)	Least-privilege principle, privileged-account monitoring, ethics training
Jurisdictional gaps	Cross-border identity theft exploiting inconsistent data protection regimes	OECD (2023) *Digital Identity Governance*	Unified global identity standards, regulatory sandboxes, international cooperation

5.1 Phishing and Social Engineering

Phishing remains one of the most prevalent enablers of identity theft in financial technology (Zhou et al. 2023). Attackers exploit clients' trust in branded communication to harvest login credentials, personal data, or multi-factor authentication tokens. In 2024, the FS-ISAC reported a marked increase in AI-generated phishing emails targeting investment clients. These campaigns often combine traditional phishing with "vishing" and "smishing" techniques, as well as deepfake voice or video impersonations of support staff (FS-ISAC 2024c).

Robo-advisory clients are particularly vulnerable because of limited direct human interaction—an environment that encourages implicit trust in automated digital communication. Mitigation strategies include adaptive phishing detection filters driven by natural language processing, client awareness campaigns, and transaction-level verification processes that require secondary confirmation through secure channels (e.g., in-app biometrics or time-locked approvals).

5.2 Credential Theft and Weak Authentication Practices

Credential theft is frequently facilitated by password reuse, inadequate multi-factor authentication, or insecure data storage. Compromised credentials can grant attackers full access to client portfolios, enabling unauthorised trades or fund withdrawals. According to Verizon's Data Breach Investigations Report (2024), over 60 per cent of financial sector breaches still originate from stolen or weak credentials.

In robo-advisory contexts, credential theft can occur through both client-side and back-office vulnerabilities. Cloud-based authentication services and third-party API integrations magnify the exposure. Advanced mitigation approaches include hardware-bound multi-factor authentication, behavioural biometrics that analyse keystroke or device usage patterns, and zero-trust identity frameworks that continuously verify both user and device integrity.

5.3 Insider Threats and Behavioural Risks

Even in highly automated systems, human operators—developers, analysts, and compliance officers—retain privileged access that can be exploited deliberately or inadvertently. Insider threats range from data exfiltration and model tampering to negligence leading to unauthorised exposure of client information. A notable example occurred in 2022 when a European wealth-management firm discovered that a contractor had exported anonymised but reconstructable client data from its robo-advisory analytics environment, breaching GDPR confidentiality requirements (ENISA 2025).

Mitigation requires a combination of least-privilege access control, continuous monitoring of privileged accounts, and organisational culture interventions.

Behavioural analytics can detect anomalous employee activity, while periodic ethics and cybersecurity training reinforce accountability. From a governance perspective, integrating insider-risk management into the firm's overall AI assurance framework aligns security with fiduciary responsibility.

5.4 Jurisdictional and Regulatory Human Factors

Identity management in global robo-advisory platforms often crosses multiple legal jurisdictions, each with distinct standards for privacy, authentication, and liability. Discrepancies between GDPR (EU), GLBA (US), and PDPA (Asia-Pacific) can result in regulatory blind spots that criminals exploit by routing identity theft operations through less stringent regions. Moreover, differences in reporting obligations may delay cross-border coordination and incident response.

To mitigate such jurisdictional vulnerabilities, firms are increasingly adopting unified identity governance frameworks anchored in international standards such as ISO 27701 and NIST 800-63. Participation in cross-jurisdictional regulatory sandboxes also promotes harmonisation of best practices for digital identity assurance and breach notification.

5.5 *Strategic Implications*

Human-centred vulnerabilities illustrate that even the most sophisticated AI infrastructures remain only as secure as the individuals who design, operate, and use them. For robo-advisory firms, embedding human-factor resilience into cybersecurity architectures—through continuous education, behavioural analytics, ethical governance, and cross-border policy alignment—is essential to preserving both operational integrity and public trust.

6 AI and xAI in Forensic Accounting and Auditing

Another area in financial services and DeFI solutions where AI and ML are increasingly reshaping is forensic accounting and auditing. Traditional methods in financial reporting and auditing work rely heavily on manual inspection, sampling, and rule-based analytics. Whereas AI systems enable detection of subtle and large-scale patterns that humans would miss. However, the adoption of black-box models introduces risks of opacity, due-diligence and legal liability, regulatory uncertainty, and ethical concerns. This is where xAI becomes indispensable. Explainable AI bridges the gap between predictive accuracy and interpretability, ensuring accountability and transparency in financial forensics (Zhang et al. 2022), which becomes essential evidence to track cybersecurity vulnerabilities that exploit the use of AI approaches—from data normalisation to portfolio choice/construction models—in the post-attack scenarios. That is xAI provides evidence (digital)—just not explanations—in adverse scenarios in responding to compliance, fiduciary, and legal challenges.

6.1 *The Role of AI in Forensic Accounting*

AI-enabled tools can process structured and unstructured financial data at scale, including general ledgers, invoices, contracts, and communications. ML models detect anomalies in transaction flows, classify potentially fraudulent entries, and flag irregularities that merit investigation. For instance, ensemble learning techniques have demonstrated significant effectiveness in identifying accounting fraud across large datasets, outperforming traditional regression and ratio analysis (Bao et al. 2020). Neural networks, decision trees, and support vector machines allow forensic auditors to capture nonlinear dependencies, and complex fraud schemes that conventional methods fail to identify.

Beyond fraud detection, AI is increasingly applied to compliance monitoring, AML surveillance, and detection of financial misstatements. By embedding AI in auditing workflows, firms can improve efficiency while reducing human error, thereby reallocating auditors' attention to higher-judgement tasks. Yet, these efficiency gains are tempered by the challenge of defending algorithmic conclusions in regulatory or courtroom settings.

6.2 *Why Explainability Matters*

The black-box nature of advanced ML models conflicts with the evidentiary requirements of forensic accounting. Courts, regulators, and professional standards require that decisions be justifiable, auditable, and replicable. xAI tools such as SHAP (Shapley Additive Explanations) and LIME (Local Interpretable Model-agnostic Explanations) clarify how input features contribute to model outputs, thereby providing an audit trail of algorithmic reasoning (Zhang et al. 2022). Zhou et al. (2023) emphasise that user-centred xAI can align investigative needs with model design, producing explanations that regulators and auditors can understand without diluting predictive accuracy. Table 6 lists the application of different xAI approaches in forensic accounting and auditing.

Virk (2025) stresses that trustworthy AI adoption in financial services depends on embedding explainability, ethical safeguards, and governance frameworks. Without these, AI risks amplifying systemic vulnerabilities, bias, and public mistrust. For forensic accounting, explainability thus transforms from a technical add-on to a legal and ethical necessity.

6.3 *Applications of xAI in Forensic Practice*

In forensic auditing, xAI contributes across three key areas:

Table 6 Explainable AI techniques in forensic accounting and auditing

xAI Technique—Reference	Application	Benefit
SHAP—Zhang et al. (2022)	Fraud detection and misstatement analysis	Quantifies variable contributions; builds audit trail
LIME—Zhou et al. (2023)	Transaction anomaly detection	Generates local explanations for flagged cases
Feature importance (tree-based)—Bao et al. (2020)	Prioritisation of risk factors	Highlights drivers of anomalies for case triage
Rule extraction (from neural networks)—Bertomeu et al. (2021)	Auditability of black-box models	Translates complex outputs into human-readable rules
Counterfactual explanations—Virk (2025)	Forensic investigations and litigation	Demonstrates how small data changes affect outcomes

- **Fraud detection and prioritisation**: xAI highlights which variable(s) drove anomaly scores, enabling investigators to triage cases and focus on high-risk areas.
- **Audit trail generation**: Transparent feature importance and decision pathways support professional scepticism and strengthen audit documentation.
- **Regulatory and courtroom defensibility**: xAI provides interpretable explanations admissible as evidence. Regulators may find it useful to develop early warning systems as ML models accurately identify firms with accounting misstatements. (Bertomeu et al. 2021).

Empirical studies confirm that when auditors are equipped with explanations, they exhibit greater trust in ML-generated fraud flags and make more consistent decisions (Bao et al. 2020; Zhou et al. 2023). This reinforces the dual role of xAI in enhancing both technical reliability and human accountability.

6.4 AI/ML Forensic Solution Development

AI systems are not standalone replacements for auditors; rather, they augment professional expertise and in an inexpensive fashion. In fraud analytics, supervised ML models trained on historical fraud cases classify transactions as normal or suspicious, while unsupervised anomaly detection uncovers novel fraud schemes. Semi-supervised and ensemble methods combine labelled and unlabelled data to enhance robustness. These approaches are particularly valuable where fraud patterns evolve rapidly, and labelled datasets are scarce. Table 7 lists AI/ML approaches, their use cases, and gains they bring in the forensic and auditing work streams.

Forensic auditing is also integrating NLP to analyse unstructured data such as emails, contracts, and whistleblower reports. Sentiment analysis, topic modelling, and entity recognition help identify collusion, insider trading, or concealment

Table 7 AI/ML approaches in forensic audit solutions

Approach	Use Case	Strength
Supervised learning (logistic regression, SVMs, neural nets)	Fraud classification in financial statements	High accuracy with labelled data
Unsupervised anomaly detection (clustering, autoencoders)	Discovery of unknown fraud patterns	Detects novel schemes without labels
Ensemble methods (random forests, boosting)	Fraud risk prediction	Reduces overfitting; improves generalisation
NLP (topic modelling, sentiment analysis)	Forensic text analysis (emails, contracts)	Detects collusion and concealment
Graph analytics	Network analysis of related parties	Reveals hidden connections and laundering pathways

behaviours. Additionally, graph analytics map networks of related parties, revealing hidden ownership structures or illicit payment flows.

6.5 Challenges and Policy Implications

While AI and xAI provide powerful capabilities, several challenges remain. First, forensic datasets are often imbalanced, with relatively few fraud cases compared to legitimate transactions. This complicates training and may yield biased models. Second, data privacy regulations constrain access to sensitive records, creating tension between investigative scope and compliance. Third, adversarial manipulation of inputs such as falsified invoices or doctored communications can mislead both humans and machines, requiring robust data validation. Addressing these limitations, the training datasets should therefore capitalise on audit logs, model interpretability, and mechanisms to correct for bias. These elements should be integrated into design processes from the outset.

Policy recommendations from the UK Parliament inquiry highlight the need for governance frameworks, auditability requirements, and professional training to ensure responsible AI deployment (Virk 2025). Crucially, achieving auditability requires that these deployed systems must develop tools that offer justifications for their actions; this need for fundamental AI/xAI utilisation is especially pronounced in forensic accounting and auditing where results have to be utilised in legal proceedings or compliance documentation. To support this shift, regulators may need to establish minimum standards for explainability in audit tools, alongside ethical guidelines to mitigate algorithmic bias. Firms adopting AI forensic solutions must, therefore, balance innovation with compliance, transparency, and societal trust.

7 Summary

Robo-advisors move beyond simple rule-based allocation to perform dynamic, multi-factor analysis, aligning a client's specific risk tolerance and financial goals with a diversified portfolio. This algorithmic approach ensures consistency and mitigates potential human biases in security or fund selection, providing a more transparent and auditable investment process. The convergence of automated technology and core financial services is set to accelerate, fundamentally reshaping capital allocation towards optimised efficiency, accessibility, and robust risk management. The emergence of agentic AI integration will further enable autonomous trading and hyper-personalisation.

Beyond robo-advisory, AI and xAI are also reshaping another critical area of financial services—forensic accounting and auditing. Traditional auditing and compliance functions, once reliant on manual sampling and rules-based checks, are being transformed through AI-driven anomaly detection and explainable modelling. xAI bridges predictive accuracy and interpretability, ensuring accountability and transparency in financial forensics. These tools allow auditors to trace how algorithms flag irregularities, detect information content in misstatements, or detect potential fraud, which becomes vital evidence in post-incident investigations involving cybersecurity breaches or data manipulation. In this way, AI and xAI not only enhance operational efficiency but also strengthen the evidentiary and compliance foundations of digital finance—complementing the automation and personalisation advances seen in robo-advisory systems.

Unfortunately, at the same time, this technological sophistication will heighten systemic exposures and risks. As highly interconnected, data-driven, and cloud-hosted systems, robo-advisory platforms face concentrated exposure to cybersecurity threats. Their inherent interconnectedness makes them susceptible to various cyber dangers, while their reliance on external data sources, NLP, Gen-AI textual analysis, and cloud infrastructure significantly expands the attack surface area. Moreover, the dependency on similar AI models and concentrated data vendors raises concerns of herding, procyclicality, and amplified volatility in stressed markets (FSB 2024; ESMA 2025).

The financial impact of cybersecurity threats is tangible and is expected to intensify as robo-advisory platforms become increasingly interconnected within digital financial ecosystems. The highly networked nature of these systems means that cyber incidents are rarely isolated; rather, they can propagate rapidly through supply chains, third-party vendors, data pipelines, correlated model errors, and opaque technological dependencies. Empirical evidence shows that cyber risk is already priced in equity markets, predicts stock performance, and spreads swiftly across financial networks, thereby elevating the likelihood of extreme event risk (Aldasoro et al. 2022; Florackis et al. 2023; Jiang et al. 2024; Crosignani et al. 2023).

To ensure robust protection, mitigation strategies should include the adoption of zero-trust architectures, which operate on the principle of "never trust, always verify", alongside the deployment of adversarial robustness techniques to defend against data poisoning (Biggio et al. 2012; Rose et al. 2020; Zhao et al. 2024). Adversarial attacks—where malicious data are intentionally introduced to corrupt an AI model—pose a direct threat to the integrity and reliability of automated investment advice.

Beyond cybersecurity, algorithmic bias represents an equally critical and interconnected risk. Adversarial attacks can intentionally exploit or amplify existing model biases by injecting data that reinforce discriminatory patterns, thereby undermining both the fairness and accuracy of automated investment decisions. Such biased algorithms can generate unfair or exclusionary outcomes, manifesting as disparate impact, where ostensibly neutral models disproportionately disadvantage protected groups of investors. To mitigate these vulnerabilities, robo-advisory platforms should adopt structured AI risk management frameworks, such as the NIST AI Risk Management Framework (RMF) and guidance from regulatory bodies like ENISA. Regular bias testing, adversarial stress testing, model auditing, and robust governance are essential to ensure algorithmic fairness, transparency, and accountability.

In parallel, the integration of AI and xAI into forensic accounting and auditing introduces a complementary governance dimension. While AI-driven analytics enhance fraud detection, compliance monitoring, and anomaly identification, xAI ensures transparency and accountability in these processes (Zhang et al. 2022; Bao et al. 2020; Zhou et al. 2023). By generating interpretable audit trails and clarifying model reasoning, xAI supports the evidentiary and regulatory defensibility of AI-based financial systems—particularly vital when addressing cybersecurity incidents or disputed algorithmic decisions. Embedding explainability within robo-advisory and auditing frameworks therefore strengthens both technical assurance and legal resilience, bridging compliance, forensic oversight, and trust in digital financial ecosystems.

The measurable market consequences of cybersecurity vulnerabilities and threats reinforce cyber risk management as a first-order concern for DeFi (Florackis et al. 2023; Jiang et al. 2024). Consequently, effective mitigations must move beyond perimeter defence, incorporating authenticated data sources, lineage tracking, hardened APIs, rigorous cloud security, and continuous monitoring to detect data anomalies (Eskandari et al. 2021; Aldasoro et al. 2022). Furthermore, strengthening user-oriented security controls—such as multi-factor authentication and targeted employee training—can complement these systemic measures by reducing human-related vulnerabilities and overall susceptibility to cyber threats (Franz et al. 2021; Zhuo et al. 2023).

Cybersecurity threats, data poisoning, and algorithmic bias collectively demand proactive and adaptive governance frameworks to maintain both resilience and fairness. These intertwined risks underscore the urgent need for responsive regulation and robust supervisory engagement, ensuring that technological innovation strengthens—rather than undermines—financial stability. These threats have significant governance implications. Markets increasingly penalise firms with high cyber exposure, creating incentives for measurable risk reduction and transparent controls (Jiang et al. 2024). Within firms, broad oversight should cover secure software development, dependency risk, and model lifecycle management. Across firms, heterogeneity in digitalisation and supervisory regimes—regulatory maturity—implies uneven baseline resilience, so cross-vendor testing and data lineage validation are critical for globally operating platforms (Aldasoro et al. 2022).

For robo-advisory platforms, these considerations apply not only to safeguarding their own operations but also to evaluating and pricing the cybersecurity vulnerabilities of investee firms during portfolio construction at both micro and macro levels. Ultimately, effective defence for robo-advisors blends identity-centric security, zero-trust architecture, and end-to-end ML operations (MLOps) assurance for data provenance and monitoring, aligning technical controls with the empirically observed pricing and propagation of cyber risk (Crosignani et al. 2023; Florackis et al. 2023; Jiang et al. 2024). Embedding MLOps into robo-advisory and forensic accounting frameworks will enhance documentation of model development and deployment, traceability, verifiability, and consequently, audit readiness and regulatory compliance. This will ensure not only transparency and model auditability but also the integrity of the underlying data and model logic. Integration of MLOps could pave the way for Regtech, transforming operational oversight into technical governance, bridging automated decision-making with accountability, and fortifying trust in digital financial infrastructures. This chapter concludes that tailored controls and governance for automated, autonomous, and personalised wealth management services are urgently needed: cybersecurity risks can propagate through financial markets, disrupt investment processes, and exacerbate systemic instability (Table 8).

Appendix

Table 8 Key terms in financial services, robo-advisory, and cybersecurity threat domains

Term	Technical description	Explanation
API-first architectures	A design approach where all functionality is built around application programming interfaces (APIs), enabling modular integration	Robo-advisors rely on APIs for connecting to brokers, data providers, and payment systems
Circuit breakers	Automated mechanisms that halt trading or system operations when thresholds (e.g., price or risk) are breached	Used in robo-advisory trading algorithms to prevent cascading losses or flash crashes
Data flows	The movement of data between sources, systems, and storage	Power the continuous learning and decision-making of robo-advisory models
Data lakes	Centralised repositories storing structured and unstructured data at scale	Used for aggregating client data, market signals, and behavioural analytics
Data leakage	The unintended exposure of confidential data to unauthorised entities	May occur when client data or proprietary algorithms are shared across integrated fintech ecosystems
Data poisoning	The deliberate corruption of training data to manipulate model behaviour	Adversaries can bias robo-advisory algorithms to misclassify risk or recommend suboptimal portfolios
Deepfakes	AI-generated synthetic media that impersonates real individuals or institutions	Could be used to mimic financial advisors, CEOs, or regulators in communication with clients

(continued)

Table 8 (continued)

Term	Technical description	Explanation
DeFi connectors	Interfaces that link robo-advisors with DeFi protocols for yield or liquidity management	Extend portfolio diversification and returns through on-chain instruments
Feature stores	Systems for storing and managing machine learning features used in model training and inference	Ensure consistent and high-quality data inputs for robo-advisory AI models
Flash loans	Uncollateralised loans executed within a single blockchain transaction	May be used indirectly in DeFi-integrated robo-advisory strategies
Lateral-movement risk	The ability of attackers to move within connected systems once initial access is gained	In integrated fintech ecosystems, attackers could move from CRM to portfolio management systems
Market-microstructure vulnerabilities	Weaknesses in the trading mechanics of markets (latency, order routing, liquidity)	Robo-advisors execute trades rapidly across fragmented venues
Miner/maximal extractable value (MEV)	Profit miners gain by reordering, inserting, or censoring blockchain transactions	Impacts robo-advisors interacting with DeFi or tokenised assets
MLOps	The practice of automating and managing machine learning lifecycle (development, deployment, monitoring)	Core to maintaining AI-driven advisory systems
Oracle design/-manipulation	Oracles provide off-chain data to blockchain smart contracts; manipulation occurs when inputs are corrupted	Used by DeFi-connected robo-advisors for pricing and market feeds
Phishing	Fraudulent attempts to obtain sensitive information by impersonating trusted entities	Commonly targets robo-advisory users via fake platforms or login portals
Social engineering	Psychological manipulation to trick individuals into divulging information or performing actions	Targets clients or employees of robo-advisory firms

References

Aithal A, Aithal PS (2021) Applications of artificial intelligence in FinTech: opportunities and cybersecurity challenges. Int J Appl Eng Manage Lett 5(2):30–46

Aldasoro I, Gambacorta L, Giudici P, Leach T (2022) The drivers of cyber risk. J Financ Stabil 60:100989

Azad P, Xu J, Feng Y, Strowbridge P, Akcora C (2025) Hedge funds on a swamp: analyzing patterns, vulnerabilities, and defense measures in Blockchain bridges. arXiv preprint arXiv:2507.06156

Bao Y, Ke B, Li B, Yu YJ, Zhang J (2020) Detecting accounting fraud in publicly traded U.S. firms using a machine learning approach. J Account Res 58(1):199–235

Basak A, Tiwari D (2025) API security risk and resilience in financial institutions. MBA Thesis. Laurea University of Applied Sciences

Bertomeu J, Cheynel E, Floyd E, Pan W (2021) Using machine learning to detect misstatements. Rev Account Stud 26(2):468–519

Biggio B, Nelson B, Laskov P (2012) Poisoning attacks against support vector machines. In: Proceedings of the 29th International Conference on Machine Learning (ICML). Edinburgh, UK, pp 1807–1814. Available at: https://arxiv.org/abs/1206.6389

Borrajo D, Veloso M, Shah S (2020) Simulating and classifying behavior in adversarial environments based on action-state traces: an application to money laundering. In Proceedings of the First ACM International Conference on AI in Finance (pp 1–8)

Brundage M et al (2018) The malicious use of artificial intelligence: forecasting, prevention, and mitigation. Future of Humanity Institute, University of Oxford

Budish E, Cramton P, Shim J (2015) The high-frequency trading arms race: frequent batch auctions as a market design response. Q J Econ 130(4):1547–1621

Chen Z, Beillahi SM, Long F (2024) Flashsyn: flash loan attack synthesis via counter example driven approximation. In Proceedings of the IEEE/ACM 46th International Conference on Software Engineering (pp 1–13)

Chesney R, Citron D (2019) Deep fakes: a looming challenge for privacy, democracy, and national security. Calif Law Rev 107(6):1753–1819

Crosignani M, Macchiavelli M, Silva AF (2023) Pirates without borders: the propagation of cyberattacks through firms' supply chains. J Financ Econ 147(2):432–448

Daian P, Goldfeder S, Kell T, Li Y, Zhao X, Bentov I, et al (2019) Flash boys 2.0: Frontrunning, transaction reordering, and consensus instability in decentralized exchanges. arXiv preprint arXiv:1904.05234

Deng X (2024) Enhancing smart contract security: front-running flash loan DeFi attacks and safeguarding smart contracts against oracle deviations, Master's thesis. University of Toronto (Canada)

Eskandari S, Salehi M, Gu WC, Clark J (2021) Sok: Oracles from the ground truth to market manipulation. In Proceedings of the 3rd ACM Conference on Advances in Financial Technologies (pp 127–141)

European Securities and Markets Authority (ESMA) (2025) Advice / report related to the retail investor journey and digital investment services. ESMA, Paris

European Union Agency for Cybersecurity (ENISA) (2025) ENISA threat landscape: finance sector. Athens: ENISA. Available at: ENISA Threat Landscape: Finance Sector. Accessed: 16 March 2026

Europol (2022) Facing reality? Law enforcement and the challenge of deepfakes. Europol Innovation Lab

Florackis C, Louca C, Michaely R, Weber M (2023) Cybersecurity risk. Rev Financ Stud 36(1):351–407

Floridi L, Cowls J (2019) A unified framework of five principles for AI in society. Harv Data Sci Rev 1(1)

Franz A, Zimmermann V, Albrecht G, Hartwig K, Reuter C, Benlian A, Vogt J (2021) {Sok}: Still plenty of phish in the sea—a taxonomy of {user-oriented} phishing interventions and avenues for future research. In Seventeenth Symposium on Usable Privacy and Security (SOUPS 2021) (pp. 339–358)

Financial Stability Board (FSB) (2017) Artificial intelligence and machine learning in financial services: Market developments and financial stability implications. Financial Stability Board, Basel

Financial Stability Board (FSB) (2024) The financial stability implications of artificial intelligence. Financial Stability Board, Basel

Financial Services Information Sharing and Analysis Center (FS-ISAC) (2024a) Combating threats and reducing risks posed by AI. https://www.fsisac.com/hubfs/Knowledge/AI/FSISAC_CombatingThreatsAndReducingRisksPosedByAI.pdf

FS-ISAC (2024b) Adversarial AI — framework, taxonomy, threat landscape and control frameworks. https://www.fsisac.com/hubfs/Knowledge/AI/FSISAC_Adversarial-AI-Framework-TaxonomyThreatLandscapeAndControlFrameworks.pdf

FS-ISAC (2024c) Stop the Scams: FS-ISAC's new Phishing Prevention framework helps financial sector counter surge in scams. https://www.fsisac.com/newsroom/stop-the-scams-fsisac-new-phishing-prevention-framework-to-counter-surge-in-financial-scams-targeting-financial-services-firms

Genfer P, Zdun U (2022) Avoiding excessive data exposure through microservice APIs. In: European conference on software architecture. Springer International Publishing, Cham, pp 3–18

Goodfellow I, Bengio Y, Courville A (2020) Deep learning. MIT Press

Hou G (2021). Cryptocurrency money laundering and exit scams: cases, regulatory responses and issues. In: Understanding cryptocurrency fraud: the challenges and headwinds to regulate digital currencies edited by Shean Corbet (Vol. 2). Walter de Gruyter GmbH & Co KG

International Monetary Fund (2024) Cyber risk and the financial sector: an assessment of costs and policy approaches. IMF. https://www.elibrary.imf.org/display/book/9798400257704/CH003.xml

Jiang H, Khanna N, Yang Q, Zhou J (2024) The cyber risk premium. Manage Sci 70(12):8791–8817

Kirilenko AA, Kyle AS, Samadi M, Tuzun T (2017) The flash crash: high-frequency trading in an electronic market. J Finance 72(3):967–998

Li Z (2024) On the automatic repair of smart contracts in Blockchain [Doctoral dissertation, Purdue University Graduate School]

Maras MH, Alexandrou A (2019) Determining authenticity of video evidence in the age of artificial intelligence and in the wake of deepfake videos. Int J Evid Proof 23(3):255–262

Mengara O (2024) Trading devil final: backdoor attack via stock market and Bayesian optimization. arXiv preprint arXiv:2407.14573

Mirsky Y, Lee W (2021) The creation and detection of deepfakes: a survey. ACM Comput Surv 54(1):1–41

Morgan S (2024) Boardroom Cybersecurity Report 2024. Secureworks. https://www.secureworks.com/centers/boardroom-cybersecurity-report-2024

Mungai R (2024) Synthetic identity fraud a critical primary national security priority. Authorea Preprints

National Cyber Security Centre (NCSC) (2024) The near-term impact of AI on the cyber threat. UK Government. https://www.ncsc.gov.uk/pdfs/report/impact-of-ai-on-cyber-threat.pdf

Nguyen TT et al (2022) Deepfakes and financial markets: emerging threats and policy responses. J Financ Regul Compl 30(4):512–529

OECD (2023) Digital identity governance: cross-border challenges and regulatory responses. OECD Publishing

Qin K, Zhou L, Livshits B, Gervais A (2021) Attacking the defi ecosystem with flash loans for fun and profit. In: International conference on financial cryptography and data security. Springer, Berlin Heidelberg, pp 3–32

Reuters (2023, June 28) AI-generated "news anchors" emerge in misinformation campaigns

Rose S, Borchert O, Mitchell S, Connelly S (2020) Zero trust architecture. NIST Special Publication 800–207. National Institute of Standards and Technology (NIST), Gaithersburg. Available at: https://doi.org/10.6028/NIST.SP.800-207

Scharfman J (2024). Decentralized finance (DeFi) fraud and hacks: Part 3. **In The cryptocurrency and digital asset fraud casebook, Volume II: DeFi, NFTs, DAOs, meme coins, and other digital asset hacks. Springer Nature Switzerland, pp 159–191

South China Morning Post (2023, February 23). Hong Kong firm loses HK$200 million in Deepfake video conference scam.

Tandon R, Charnsethikul P, Arora I, Murthy D, Mirkovic J (2022) I know what you did on Venmo: discovering privacy leaks in mobile social payments. Proc Priv Enhanc Technol 2022(3):633–654. [Assumed volume/issue based on typical format]

The Wall Street Journal (2019, August 30) Fraudsters Used AI to Mimic CEO's Voice in Unusual Cybercrime Case

Tolosana R, Vera-Rodriguez R, Fierrez J, Morales A, Ortega-Garcia J (2020) Deepfakes and beyond: a survey of face manipulation and fake detection. Inf Fusion *64*:131–148

U.S. Federal Trade Commission (2023) Consumer alert: synthetic identity fraud in financial transactions. FTC, Washington, DC

Verizon (2024) Data Breach Investigations Report 2024

Virk N (2025) UK financial services leadership in the AI age: opportunities and challenges [Written evidence submitted to the UK Parliament Treasury Committee, AIFS0033]. UK Parliament. https://committees.parliament.uk/writtenevidence/139822/html/

Yussuf M (2025) Advanced cyber risk containment in algorithmic trading: securing automated investment strategies from malicious data manipulation. Int Res J Mod Eng Technol Sci 7(3):883

Zhao M, Zhang L, Ye J, Lu H, Yin B, Wang X (2024) Adversarial training: a survey. Available at: https://arxiv.org/abs/2410.15042

Zhang CA, Cho S, Vasarhelyi M (2022) Explainable artificial intelligence (XAI) in auditing. Int J Account Inf Syst 46:100572

Zhou Y, Li H, Xiao Z, Qiu J (2023) A user-centered explainable artificial intelligence approach for financial fraud detection. Finance Res Lett 58:104309

Zhuo S, Biddle R, Koh YS, Lottridge D, Russello G (2023) SoK: Human-centered phishing susceptibility. ACM Transact Priv Secur 26(3):1–27

Progress in Contemporary Fraud Detection Through the Fintech Application of Artificial Intelligence

Aymen Turki

Abstract The Global Financial Crisis (GFC) served as a catalyst for the emergence of financial technology (Fintech), driven by a decline in trust towards traditional financial and a rise in financial irregularities. The COVID-19 pandemic later accelerated its adoption, leading to a notable surge in digital fraud threats and an arms race with fraudsters. This chapter concentrates on the application of Fintech innovations following the recent global crises, particularly those associated with the automation of fraud detection driven by artificial intelligence (AI). Fraud incidents and their associated losses are still troubling, creating a dual challenge that involves the effective deployment of innovative AI-based Fintech solutions together with the vital necessity for ethical transparency. The objective of this chapter is to identify advanced AI technologies that can offer a contemporary outlook on fraud detection within the modern finance sphere. AI-driven Fintech solutions tailored for various categories of fraud detection will enhance ethical transparency and aids in the prompt detection of fraudulent practices before they cause substantial damage. The chapter reaches the conclusion that the future of fraud detection depends not solely on advancements in AI technology but also on human accountability and a collective commitment to preserving ethical integrity and promoting responsible innovation.

Keywords Fraud detection · Fintech · Artificial intelligence

1 Introduction

In recent decades, Fintech, defined as the integration of digital technologies such as artificial intelligence (AI), blockchain, data and graph analytics, and cloud computing, has emerged as a potentially transformative game changer within the global financial markets (Schueffel 2016; Philippon 2016; Puschmann 2017;

A. Turki (✉)
Clermont School of Business, and CleRMa Research Lab, Clermont-Ferrand, France
e-mail: aymen.turki@clermont-sb.fr

N. Nahidi, A. Zarifis (eds.), *AI, FinTech, and the Future of Robo-Advisory*, Contributions to Finance and Accounting,
https://doi.org/10.1007/978-3-032-18109-1_11

Goldstein et al. 2019; Thakor 2020). As a leading technology, AI and Machine Learning (ML) facilitated fraud detection (Bao et al. 2020; Zhong and Goel 2024) and helped to automate risk management (Gu et al. 2020). Additionally, Regulatory Technology (RegTech), which automates compliance procedures such as KYC (Know Your Customer) and AML (Anti-Money Laundering), employed AI to help effectively adhere to regulatory requirements (Charoenwong et al. 2024). Also, Insurance Technology (InsurTech) integrates AI and data analytics to provide tailored insurance solutions, automated claims, and adaptive pricing (Debener et al. 2023). Other financial technologies used AI to automate, predict, and personalize customer consulting services through robo-advisory and chatbots (Tiberius et al. 2022). In our current economic landscape facing a dual challenge of the proper application of this emerging AI-based Fintech along with the imperative of ensuring ethical transparency, the role of AI technology in identifying financial irregularities to achieve transparency goals remains ambiguous and still unclear to implement.

To address this question, it is essential to explore in greater detail two concepts that are significantly involved in this debate, namely AI and fraud detection, and also to define the various forms that AI technology takes in the finance industry, particularly around fraud detection. From a technical standpoint, AI in finance integrates several components which are mainly based on data-driven learning algorithms with intelligent automation to enhance efficiency, decision-making quality, compliance, and customer experience (Ahmed et al. 2022). Given its widespread use, the key aspect of AI in the financial sector is ML, which translates to algorithms that learn from historical financial data to make predictions or decisions. Their applications involve credit scoring, fraud detection, and stock price forecasting, among others (Berdiyeva et al. 2021). Another principal component is the Natural Language Processing (NLP) which allows systems to understand and process human language. Their functionalities are generally associated with chatbots, customer support, and sentiment analysis of market news (Chen et al. 2023a). Predictive analytics is another segment of AI applied to finance which uses statistical and ML models to forecast future events or trends and is practically involved in predicting loan defaults, market movements, and customer behavior (Chhikara et al. 2025). Another technique of AI applied to finance involves Deep Learning which simulates complex patterns and connections within large datasets, and it effectively renders in algorithmic trading image recognition for financial document verification (Ng 2020). Lastly, AI that allows computers to process and interpret visual data translates into another component of AI in finance which is computer vision. It is used for KYC verification based on facial recognition, reading and validating documents (e.g., invoices), and biometric authentication of financial institutions' customers (Gupta et al. 2023; Entrust 2025).

Despite the algorithmic bias and explainability issues, these main technologies of AI applied in the different financial domains (i.e., banking, wealth management, risk management, fraud detection and security, RegTech, InsurTech) improved accuracy by reducing human error in analysis and decision-making and detected abnormal patterns faster than manual systems (AFME 2023). Undoubtedly, irregularities in finance constitute the cornerstone of regulatory compliance and ethical transparency's challenges (Puplampu 2024). In this regard, fraud detection, being among key aspects, refers to the process of detecting and preventing fraudulent or illegal financial activities before they inflict damage on individuals or organizations (Wells 2017). Within finance and Fintech, it predominantly involves the utilization of AI, ML, and data analytics to detect irregular or suspicious patterns in transactions, accounts, or customer behavior (EY 2024b; PwC 2023). More specifically, fraud categories can be sorted into payments and card-not-present (CNP)[1] fraud (Bodker et al. 2022), detecting account takeover (ATO), fraud in the process of onboarding and verifying identity (McKinsey 2019; Vanini et al. 2023), document forgery (Sukhija et al. 2025), AML transaction monitoring (Singh and Best 2019), procurement fraud problem (Rendon and Rendon 2016), and financial statement manipulation (Albrecht et al. 2015). In this chapter and based on these dimensions of fraud detection in conjunction with the assigned AI technologies, we will first explore the occurrences of fraud detection in the wake of the recent global crises. In the second section, we will outline the dimensions and categories of contemporary fraud detection within modern finance and accounting. The third section of the chapter presents examples of innovative and emerging solutions to address the different types of fraud, and finally, the last part concludes and discusses the challenges and ethical imperatives.

2 Occurrences of Fraud Detection in the Aftermath of the Last Global Crises

The Global Financial Crisis (GFC) of 2008 and the COVID-19 pandemic crisis were two major shocks that accelerated the emergence of Fintech and AI by revealing vulnerabilities in conventional finance and transforming regulatory and technological frameworks (Bartlett et al. 2022). More precisely, the GFC highlighted the breakdown of trust due to a lack of transparency, risky lending practices, and a deficiency in accountability. Consumers and businesses lost trust in incumbent banks and became more open to alternative and AI-driven financial services (Babina et al. 2025). Moreover, post-crisis reforms, such as Basel III and Dodd-Frank, have enhanced the safety of banking; however, they have also led to a higher need of developed compliance techniques, which have compelled incumbents to reduce their small-scale compliance activities (Gozman and Currie 2014). Fintech startups filled this gap by offering faster, cheaper, and more transparent financial services, and also by implementing innovative compliance mechanisms that facilitate fraud detection and credit scoring through the utilization of advanced technologies such as AI (Vives and Ye 2025).

[1] Card-not-present fraud refers to the unauthorized utilization of credit or debit card information to acquire goods and services in a non-face-to-face environment such as through e-commerce platforms.

On the other hand, the COVID-19 pandemic accelerated digital adoption through spurring AI innovation in RegTech such as compliance automation, and InsurTech, as seen in pandemic coverage (Ceron and Monge 2023; Erel and Liebersohn 2020). Traditional banks accelerated partnerships with Fintech ventures to digitize operations quickly and bridge resilience gaps amid the pandemic (Fu and Mishra 2022). Consequently, in conjunction with GFC, the pandemic created a disruptive legitimacy making financial technology not just an alternative, but a mainstream part of the global financial ecosystem (Kwan et al. 2024). In this regard, corporate surveys indicate an increased incidence of fraud throughout the 2010s. PwC's worldwide surveys conducted around 2011 revealed that approximately one-third of companies had encountered fraud in the preceding year; by 2018, the reported prevalence had risen to about 49% (based on a global sample). This represents a significant increase from the baseline observed in the early 2010s (PwC 2011).

The convergence of disruption and digitization has led to an increase in external, cyber-enabled fraud, with numerous organizations documenting new incidents associated with the disruptions caused by COVID-19. AI, in the hand of fraudsters, can create significant vulnerabilities. The increase in AI adoption has been made possible by the reduction of technical barriers to AI utilization, as demonstrated by accessible platforms such as ChatGPT and Copilot, which democratize access to advanced AI functionalities. Fraudsters are exploiting these same technologies to create more intricate schemes, thereby presenting challenges to current fraud detection systems (Deloitte 2024). According to PwC's 2022 Global Economic Crime and Fraud Survey (GECS), almost 70% of organizations that encountered fraud indicated that their most significant disruptive incident originated from an external attack or a combination of external and internal collusion; the report clearly associates the emergence of new fraud incidents with the disruptions related to the pandemic (PwC 2022). Levels of fraud incidents continue to be high during the last seventeen years, and the mix (according to fraud category and third-party exposure) is constantly changing. EY reports a rise in integrity incidents and observes that approximately 68% of significant incidents involve third parties (EY 2024a). KPMG's fraud barometer (2025b) reveals high volumes and values of fraud. Conversely, the report indicates a decrease in the total amount of losses due to payment transfer fraud from £83.7 million in 2023 to £11.2 million in 2024. The observed ongoing evolution of payment fraud has seen remote purchase fraud emerge as a key concern in addition to other fraud threats including phishing attacks and the utilization of automated bots for credential stuffing and the creation of fraudulent accounts. This same report attributes the downturn trend in payment fraud losses to the combined effect of regulatory enforcement and technological innovation, especially the advancements in AI and ML technologies such as generative AI and deepfakes. From another perspective, the most reliable global estimate by Nasdaq Verafin (2024) indicates that fraud losses for 2023 are projected to be around US$486 billion, highlighting a substantial and ongoing issue, even as certain categories show signs of stabilization. In the UK, the value of alleged fraud cases in the courts has bounced back to pre-pandemic levels by 2022 and has continued to exhibit significant case-driven volatility throughout 2023–2024

(KPMG 2021). Ultimately, there is no universally accepted global total in dollars from the major consulting firms such as PwC, EY, Deloitte, and KPMG, and even current empirical literature about the progression of the trend throughout time generates mixed inferences (Karpoff 2021), but one thing is certain: fraud incidents and their resulting losses are still alarming, and taking action to adequately address this issue has become a pressing necessity.

3 Dimensions of Contemporary Fraud Detection Across Modern Finance and Accounting

Contemporary fraud detection in modern finance and accounting has evolved into a multidimensional field where traditional scrutiny and control have to deal with new fraudulent practices' emergence, digitalization, advancement of AI technology, and the transition to proactive fraud management (Moody's 2023). In this regard, it can be comprehended through various complementary dimensions that together define the scope of contemporary fraud detection (Okur et al. 2021; Van Belle et al. 2023; Papadakis et al. 2020).

The first dimension is functional. It differentiates between fraudulent practices in finance and those in accounting. In the accounting field, when a manager commits fraud, they deliberately alter accounting records to present the company's financial situation as more favorable than it truly is (Punch 1996; Zimmer 1998; Clikeman 2010; Cooper et al. 2013). This includes financial reporting, which generally manifests as manipulated statements, earnings distortion, fictitious revenues, or understated liabilities (Adelberg 1979; LoPucki 1996; Beneish 1999). It also concerns procurement and payables through false invoicing, duplicate payments, or supplier collusion (Piper 2017). Payroll and expenses (e.g., ghost employees, inflated reimbursements) (Kelly 2023) and receivables and treasury (e.g., lapping, unauthorized transfers, diverted collections) illustrate additional forms of fraud within accounting practices (KPMG 2025a). In the finance area, fraud management extends to payments, lending, trading, and asset management, where fraud can take the form of payment scams (Toh 2024), insider trading (Esen et al. 2019; Liu et al. 2020; James et al. 2023), or misappropriation of client funds, among others. AI-enabled systems are becoming an integral part of these workflows, continuously auditing transactions, and identifying anomalies in real time.

Alongside this functional distinction (finance vs. accounting) in fraud detection, a second dimension classifies fraud by the type or nature of misconduct with the emergence of new types due to the advent of digitalization. The conventional practices such as asset misappropriation, along with financial statement fraud, still constitute the core of fraudulent activities. However, digitalization has introduced new typologies such as cyber-assisted payment fraud, illegal appropriation of personal information and the creation of artificial identities, account takeovers, and AML violations. Each type requires different data and different analytical techniques. For instance, AI applications in payment fraud depend on recognizing behavioral patterns and detecting anomalies, whereas AML analytics prioritize graph analysis and transaction network modeling to uncover hidden connections among entities. PwC's Global economic crime and Fraud survey (2022) shows that 44% of fraud experienced by the financial services industry are customer fraud, 38% refer to cybercrime, and 29% relate to know-your-customer failure. According to Visa Acceptance (2025)'s report, fraud in payment continues to be a global issue, with 98% of merchants encountering one or more forms of payment fraud over the last 12 months. The surveyed data indicate a steady decrease in the occurrence of fraud in digital payment to merchants, alongside notable reductions in fraud types like first-party misuse, phishing, and card testing, and a significant rise in real-time payment fraud affecting 45% of merchants worldwide in 2024.

A third and increasingly crucial dimension is the advancement of AI technology. AI-driven systems may greatly enhance accuracy in fraud detection and diminish the number of false positives that have overwhelmed fraud reports (Moody's 2025c). Traditional rule-based and statistical techniques, which are previously employed by auditors and controllers, are being replaced by ML-driven systems which utilize supervised models to categorize transactions as either fraudulent or legitimate based on historical data (Bao et al. 2020; Hunt et al. 2022; Bertomeu et al. 2021; Zhang Parker et al. 2025) and unsupervised models to identify new patterns without prior labels (Gomes et al. 2021; Debener et al. 2023). Additionally, techniques such as natural language processing (NLP) facilitate the automated examination of text-based evidence, including emails and invoices (Qatawneh 2025), whereas graph analytics uncover collusive networks among suppliers, customers, and bank accounts (Motie and Raahemi 2024). Within Fintech ecosystems, companies like Feedzai, Featurespace, and Forter have developed real-time AI engines that apply adaptive behavioral analytics to millions of transactions per second, consistently learning as new fraud typologies emerge (Omdia 2025).

Ultimately, a maturity dimension defines the transition from reactive fraud management to proactive strategies (Moody's July 2025a). Earlier systems were retrospective, focusing on the post-occurrence detection of fraud. In contrast, contemporary organizations leverage AI and a continuous flow of data to establish preventive strategies and implement predictive and prescriptive systems (Brown et al. 2020). Predictive models anticipate potential fraud scenarios, while prescriptive analytics trigger autonomous responses, such as blocking transactions, amplifying alerts, or dynamically adjusting thresholds (Zhang Parker et al. 2025). In the Fintech sector, this evolution occurs in the framework of the emergence of autonomous and self-learning risk management platforms that prioritize real-time prevention over retrospective detection (Moody's 2025b).

In summary, these dimensions form a comprehensive framework for understanding fraud detection in finance, accounting, auditing, and Fintech. Contemporary AI-driven solutions for fraud detection increasingly eliminate the boundaries between these domains (Vasarhelyi et al. 2018), which illustrates that the future of fraud detection is not merely dependent on improved controls, but rather on dynamic data-driven ecosystems where AI-based Fintech solutions continuously enhance compliance and ethical transparency (Financial Crime Academy 2025; ThreatMark 2025).

4 AI-Driven Fintech Solutions Tailored for Various Categories of Fraud Detection

The current landscape of AI-driven Fintech for fraud detection features several complementary solutions that have emerged to address each specific category of fraud. Indeed, and considering the different categories of fraud, there are specialized Fintech companies that utilize AI and ML along with associated data science techniques to identify, prevent, and address each fraud type. The key advantage of these solutions is their combination of ML, behavioral and device signals, graph networks, document forensics, and cloud-based real-time deployment, which is designed for the business process of each fraud vector (Moody's July 2025a).

In digital payments, especially in relation to CNP transactions and authorized push payment (APP) scams,[2] numerous prominent Fintech solutions utilize AI and ML to identify fraudulent patterns in real time (e.g., Freedzai, Seon, MevaL, Group-IB). For instance, Feedzai, a Portuguese Fintech founded in 2009, provides a platform that oversees payment flows and utilizes advanced AI to highlight suspicious transactions in real time (Zalcewicz 2018). Seon, a Hungarian Risktech[3] founded in 2017 by Tamas Kadar and Bence Jendruszak, provides AI-powered direct actions for fraud prevention and AML compliance. Likewise, ARIC RiskHub by Feature space utilizes the latest ML technology alongside cutting-edge behavioral models to monitor real-time customer data and spot suspicious activity in transaction behavior, while Fraud Management by SAS uses industry-leading data analytics and ML to implement enterprise real-time scoring to monitor payments, non-monetary transactions, and events. Many renowned banks are currently using SAS's Fraud Management like the Bank of America, HSBC, Citygroup, and the Commonwealth Bank of Australia (HGInsights 2025). On the merchant side, e-commerce-centric solutions like Forter and Riskified leverage identity-driven AI decision engines to determine the authenticity of users, integrating networked signals alongside behavioral models. Leveraging ML that benefits from a global merchant network, Riskified developed an advanced platform that enables online merchants to establish reliable connections with their customers. Companies adopting Riskifield include

[2] The occurrence of APP fraud is characterized by a scammer convincing a victim to willingly send money based on fraudulent pretenses.

[3] Risktech, which is more narrowly defined than Fintech, merges risk management practices with technological advancements to optimize decision-making processes and outcomes associated with risk. This field employs a range of technological tools, including AI, ML, and data analytics.

Farfetch Ltd, and Mastercard, while Stripe and Shopify are among their partners (HGInsights 2025).

Regarding the account takeover (ATO) category of fraud, Risktech companies have created more specialized behavioral and device-intelligence platforms related to digital identity exploitation. For example, BioCatch, founded in 2011, integrates ML, advanced visualization, and behavioral biometrics, such as mouse movements, typing patterns, and device context, to identify physical and cognitive digital behavior anomalies that induce fraudulent activity (Crunchbase[4] 2025). LexisNexis Risk Solutions, which is part of RELX, a global provider of information and analytics, integrates device fingerprinting, behavioral data, and consortium intelligence to assess risk during login and transaction activities (Pitchbook[5] 2025). TransUnion's TruValidate (previously known as iovation) uses device-risk scores and behavioral analytics to monitor transactions in real time and identify high-risk fraudulent behaviors (Digital Marketplace 2025). Arkose Labs, founded in 2013 and recognized by G2[6] as the 2023 leader in Bot detection and mitigation, incorporates intent analysis along with interactive challenges to mitigate fraud-farm traffic, which assist banks and Fintech companies in differentiating authentic users from bots or manipulated victims without introducing additional friction (Thales Imperva 2025).

In the context of onboarding new clients, whether for identity verification (KYC), business verification (KYB), or protection against synthetic identities and deepfake resistance, the use of AI has become a fundamental requirement. AI-driven Risktech solutions are becoming increasingly essential. For example, Socure, a cybersecurity Risktech founded in 2012 in Nevada (USA), integrates supervised ML with online/offline signals to defeat synthetic IDs and deepfakes. This solution is trusted by four of the five largest US banks, and the largest credit card issuers and e-commerce marketplaces according to Provenir.com (2025). Onfido, an AI-powered identity verification solution founded in 2012 and acquired by Entrust Corporation in 2024, incorporates live biometric and document verification processes to mitigate onboarding identity fraud for digital platforms. Onfido even runs a fraud laboratory to produce deepfake attack data aimed at strengthening models. Through Onfido's solution, Entrust conducts millions of identity verifications annually, contributing to an estimated savings of $5.5 billion in fraud losses (Entrust 2025). SentiLink, a venture capital-backed Fintech founded in 2017, concentrates on assessing

[4] Crunchbase is an American data platform that provides information about startups and tech businesses. Their content includes investment and funding information, individuals in leadership positions, and corporate news.

[5] PitchBook is a leading data resource providing comprehensive data on tech startups, companies, and industries, tracking every element of the public and private equity markets, including venture capital, private equity, and M&A. PitchBook gathers data regarding over 2 million global private firms, investors, transactions, M&A, limited partners, funds, financial information, advisors, personnel, news, and analytical assessments.

[6] G2 stands as the largest and most reputable software marketplace globally. Annually, over 100 million professionals, including those from every Fortune 500 company, rely on G2 to enhance their software selection process through authentic peer reviews (g2.com).

application fraud within Fintech and digital lending environments (Pitchbook 2025). SentiLink's ML algorithms are designed to prevent synthetic identity fraud, which occurs when fraudsters merge fictitious names with stolen Social Security numbers. In 2024, a solution was also developed by SentiLink to identify a new form of identity theft known as assumed identity abuse, which occurs when criminals take advantage of the genuine identities of individuals who entered the USA on temporary visas and are no longer present in the country (SentiLink 2025). In the meantime, Trulioo, an electronic identity verification platform founded in Vancouver and owning 7 granted patents, enables businesses to execute AI-driven assessments across different jurisdictions (Pitchbook 2025; Wakeham 2016; Ali et al. 2020).

As fraudsters submit forged documents (i.e., altered bank statements, manipulated paystubs,[7] fake invoices, falsified IDs) during onboarding or underwriting processes, the role of AI-based solutions specialized in counter-document forensics is becoming increasingly vital. Founded in 2019, Resistant AI, an AI-driven solution for fraud and financial crime prevention across document pipelines, focuses on identifying tampering and AI-generated documents through structural and forensic evaluations (TechCrunch[8] 2025). Established by Ronan and Conor Burke following their university graduation in 2017, Inscribe automates the document review process through the application of generative AI detection and verification mechanisms. Prominent firms such as BlueVine, Petal, Fair, and Ramp have placed their confidence in Inscribe. Supported by investors including Y Combinator, Uncork Capital, Crosslink Capital, and Foundry Group, Inscribe has created a worldwide footprint in North America and Europe (Crunchbase 2025)

In a wider context, particularly in the domain of AML and transaction monitoring where illicit activities might involve networks of individuals, layering[9] of funds, or organizational collusion, AI- and graph analytics-powered fraud detection platforms play a vital role. Established in 2014, ComplyAdvantage recently secured a late-stage venture capital investment from Prosper. This prominent and reliable SaaS platform utilizes AI to address financial crime, incorporating ML-driven transaction monitoring and screening systems designed to reduce false positives while detecting complex illicit financial flows (Pitchbook 2025). The mission of ComplyAdvantage is to counteract the risks associated with money laundering and terrorist financing (Lessambo 2023). Founded in 2016 and recently securing \$175 million in a Series F funding by Teachers' Venture Growth (TVG) at \$2.6B valuation (TechCrunch 2025), Quantexa leverages decision intelligence and graph analytics to reveal concealed relationships among entities, thus facilitating the identification of fraud

[7] Paystubs represent a record of salary details and wage information pertinent to employees and self-employed individuals, including independent contractors and freelancers.

[8] TechCrunch is an American news outlet dedicated to covering the latest developments related to high-tech companies and startups.

[9] Layering represents the second phase in the money laundering process, during which illegal funds are transferred through intricate transactions and accounts to obscure their origin. The objective is to dissociate the money from its illegal source, making it difficult to trace (LSEG glossary, 2025).

rings or collusive networks (Aziz and Dowling 2019; Harmon and Psaltis 2021). Quantexa is broadening its Microsoft partnership and plans to launch an AI-powered workload for the Microsoft Fabric data analytics platform. Quantexa is also developing its Databricks partnership to handle billions of data records, allowing companies to create generative AI applications with structured and unstructured data (Tech Times 2025).

Inside the enterprise, the fields of procurement, account payables (AP), and management expenses are increasingly handled by AI spend monitoring. Spend management is frequently associated with budgeting, procurement, AP, and payment, along with another critical department that plays a role in spend management: travel and expense (T&E). In this context, procure-to-pay (P2P),[10] T&E, and AP fraud where internal fraud frequently manifests as fraudulent invoices, duplicate payments, or collusion with suppliers, AI-driven Fintech solutions are gaining traction. In the absence of a system designed to ensure compliance with the company's spending policies (i.e., booking travel, making purchases, submitting expense reports), even minor discrepancies can rapidly increase, resulting in substantial financial losses for the organization. A notable example of practical solutions is AppZen which employs AI to audit 100% of expense reports in real time. AppZen enables the analysis of employee expenses to identify cases where an employee may be violating company policy or committing expense fraud, including the detection of duplicate claims, forgeries, suspicious merchants, and receipts generated by AI (NY Times 2025). Anant Kale, the CEO of AppZen and co-founder with Kunal Verma, stated that prior to engaging with AppZen, organizations were arbitrarily reviewing between five and twenty percent of their total expenses to ensure adherence to company policy, and now, every single expense is examined (TechCrunch 2018; Butcher 2021). Likewise, Concur Detect by Oversight uses AI and ML to automatically analyze expense reports, speed up the auditing process, and resolve issues before and after reimbursement. Concur Detect and Oversight Systems enforce regulations concerning various types of expenses, including travel, meal allowances, accommodation limits, and vendor purchases, thereby minimizing the likelihood of unintentional or deliberate policy violations (Discovery Consulting 2024).

In the area of financial statement fraud and journal entry manipulation, Fintech solutions leverage AI-driven audit analytics to evaluate entire sets of journal entries instead of depending on limited sample testing (Bao et al. 2020; Bertomeu et al. 2021). The first aspect of financial statement fraud concerns revenue and earnings management, which includes accrual-based manipulation (Dechow et al. 1995), revenues recognition tactics (Altamuro et al. 2005), and real activities manipulation (Roychowdhury 2006), among others. AI-based platforms such as MindBridge examine all entries rather than just samples, integrating statistical analyses to identify anomalies that may indicate potential management overrides or

[10] The Procure-to-Pay process serves to integrate procurement and supplier accounting systems to improve operational efficiency.

fraudulent entries (Leocádio et al. 2024). Founded in 2015, MindBridge platform detects unintentional errors and intentional financial misstatements through the application of ML technologies. In 2023, MindBridge and KPMG declared strategic partnership aiming at integrating advanced AI into the KPMG's intelligent audit platform, KPMG Clara, thereby facilitating the detection of high-risk transactions and contributing to improved audit quality of KPMG (KPMG 2023). The second aspect of financial statement fraud involves estimates and reserves fraud through cookie-jar strategy[11] via the allowance for doubtful accounts (McNichols and Wilson 1988), loan-loss provisions (Beaver and Engel 1996), restructuring reserves and reversals (Burgstahler et al. 2002), and deferred tax valuation allowance as hidden reserves (Schrand and Wong 2003). Other aspects include classification and presentation manipulations (McVay 2006; Kaplan et al. 2020), consolidation entries manipulations (Chen et al. 2023b), and narrative disclosure which won't change the trial balance but will change investor perception (Loughran and McDonald 2011; Mayew and Venkatachalam 2012). Other AI-driven solutions are effectively aligned with these aspects. Caseware IDEA is a comprehensive AI-powered data analysis tool that analyzes 100 percent of accounting data to detect reporting inconsistencies, unusual reversals, or manual credits that form the basis of premature revenue (Gee 2014). Founded in 2017 by Maarten Alblas in Amsterdam, DataSnipper is another AI-based accounting tool that transforms Excel into a powerful and intelligent platform for auditing and financial procedures. On the side of auditing firms, leading groups have integrated AI into their services such as KPMG Clara, which promotes real-time data analysis and risk identification throughout financial statements (Gultom et al. 2021), and PwC Halo, which highlights comprehensive population testing and journal entry analytics to uncover atypical relationships (Dlamini 2025); these AI functionalities are specifically designed to transform audit firms and steering them toward innovation in fraud detection.

AI-driven solutions, including those mentioned above, clearly address the needs of contemporary fraud detection in modern finance. They are also fundamentally transforming the landscape of auditing, compliance, and risk management globally, leading to questions about the future of the related professions and the evolving role of humans in light of the potentially dominant position that AI may assume in fraud detection objectives within the financial sector (Lucinity 2025).

[11] Cookie jar accounting, also known as cookie jar reserves, refers to an accounting method whereby a company allocates a portion of substantial reserves accumulated during a prosperous year to offset losses incurred in less profitable years. This practice can create a misleading impression for investors, leading them to perceive that the company's losses are smaller than they truly are.

5 Conclusions and Discussions of Challenges and Ethical Imperatives

The future of fraud detection is shaped by a complex interplay of AI-driven Fintech innovation, regulatory compliance, and ethical responsibility. The ongoing rise of AI solutions, driven by generative AI, deep learning, and NLP, heralds a significant transformation in fraud investigations. The reverse side of the coin is that in the possession of fraudsters, AI has the potential to create substantial vulnerabilities. Indeed, the progress in large language models (LLM) has enabled the creation of AI-generated text that closely resembles human-written material, thereby enhancing the effectiveness of scams. The rising use of deepfake technology and the creation of synthetic identities introduce new risks, as scammers can now mimic reputable figures, such as CEOs, using convincingly crafted audio and video. The central question is whether the two contradictory phenomena continue to evolve in the same manner and at the same pace; if they do, we will be trapped in a vicious cycle of being unable to outpace fraudsters, thereby compromising our goal of achieving enhanced ethical transparency. In this scenario, the impact of AI technology is trivial, and we inevitably revert to the solution that should serve as the engine, which is the ethical responsibility of financial actors.

Another primary challenge lies in maintaining data privacy while adopting new AI technologies and complying with changing regulatory frameworks, such as the General Data Protection Regulation (GDPR) and the upcoming EU AI Act. Financial institutions must navigate the tension between effective fraud prevention and the preservation of individual privacy, ensuring that AI-driven models do not violate user rights (Naim et al. 2023; Zhou et al. 2024).

Equally significant to note is the challenge regarding algorithmic bias and fairness. When AI systems are trained on historical data, they can accidentally reproduce systemic biases, which may lead to inequitable outcomes such as biased fraud classifications or misleading investment recommendations (Bao et al. 2022). To alleviate this issue, organizations need to carry out regular algorithmic audits, engage in bias testing, and implement explainable AI interfaces that enhance transparency and trust. This will lead to additional sources of costs and time-consuming tasks that are similar in volume to those existing without AI, thus creating a vicious cycle of a lengthy and expensive fraud detection process. Consequently, the role of human involvement is undeniable, and human accountability remains a vital ethical requirement.

As emphasized by Bianchi and Briére (2023) and PwC (2023), the frameworks that incorporate human oversight are crucial to ensure that the ultimate responsibility for decision-making lies with professionals instead of autonomous algorithms. PwC (2023) stresses the importance of integrating AI risk management into the overall enterprise strategy, which includes compliance, cybersecurity, and ethical governance across all AI-related activities. Overall, these challenges together indicate that the future of fraud detection relies not only on technological progress but also on the collective commitment to maintaining ethical integrity and responsible innovation.

References

Adelberg AH (1979) Narrative disclosures contained in financial reports: means of communication or manipulation? Account Bus Res 9(35):179–190

AFME (2023) Artificial Intelligence: Challenges and Opportunities for Compliance, September 2023. https://www.afme.eu/media/d5gm0fsu/finalafmeaicompliance202305.pdf

Ahmed S, Alshater MM, El Ammari A, Hammami H (2022) Artificial intelligence and machine learning in finance: a bibliometric review. Res Int Bus Finance 61:101646

Albrecht C, Holland D, Malagueño R, Dolan S, Tzafrir S (2015) The role of power in financial statement fraud schemes. J Bus Ethics 131(4):803–813

Ali G, Ally Dida M, Elikana Sam A (2020) Two-factor authentication scheme for mobile money: a review of threat models and countermeasures. Fut Inter 12(10):160

Altamuro J, Beatty AL, Weber J (2005) The effects of accelerated revenue recognition on earnings management and earnings informativeness: evidence from SEC Staff Accounting Bulletin No. 101. Account Rev 80(2):373–401

Aziz S, Dowling M (2019) Machine learning and AI for risk management. Disrupt Finance:33–50

Babina T, Bahaj S, Buchak G, De Marco F, Foulis A, Gornall W et al (2025) Customer data access and fintech entry: early evidence from open banking. J Financ Econ 169:103950

Bao Y, Ke B, Li B, Yu YJ, Zhang J (2020) Detecting accounting fraud in publicly traded US firms using a machine learning approach. J Account Res 58(1):199–235

Bao Y, Hilary G, Ke B (2022) Artificial intelligence and fraud detection. In: Innovative technology at the interface of finance and operations, vol I. Springer International Publishing, Cham, pp 223–247

Bartlett R, Morse A, Stanton R, Wallace N (2022) Consumer-lending discrimination in the FinTech Era. J Financ Econ 143(1):30–56

Beaver WH, Engel EE (1996) Discretionary behavior with respect to allowances for loan losses and the behavior of security prices. J Account Econ 22(1-3):177–206

Beneish MD (1999) The detection of earnings manipulation. Financ Anal J 55(5):24–36

Berdiyeva O, Islam MU, Saeedi M (2021) Artificial intelligence in accounting and finance: meta-analysis. Int Bus Rev 3(1):56–79

Bertomeu J, Cheynel E, Floyd E, Pan W (2021) Using machine learning to detect misstatements. Rev Account Stud 26(2):468–519

Bianchi M, Brière M (2023) Robo-advising: Less AI and more XAI? Augmenting algorithms with humans-in-the-loop. Mach Learn Data Sci Financ Mark:33–59

Bodker A, Connolly P, Sing O, Hutchins B, Townsley M, Drew J (2022) Card-not-present fraud: Using crime scripts to inform crime prevention initiatives. Secur J 1

Brown NC, Crowley RM, Elliott WB (2020) What are you saying? Using topic to detect financial misreporting. J Account Res 58(1):237–291

Burgstahler D, Jiambalvo J, Shevlin T (2002) Do stock prices fully reflect the implications of special items for future earnings? J Account Res 40(3):585–612

Butcher D (2021) Preventing expense fraud. Strat Finance 102(10):17–18

Ceron BM, Monge M (2023) Financial technologies (FINTECH) revolution and COVID-19: time trends and persistence. Rev Dev Finance 13(1):58–64

Charoenwong B, Kowaleski ZT, Kwan A, Sutherland AG (2024) RegTech: technology-driven compliance and its effects on profitability, operations, and market structure. J Financ Econ 154:103792

Chen C, Leung WS, Tao X, Wang H (2023a) The impact of financial reporting flexibility on auditor risk judgement: evidence from the implementation of FIN 46R. J Account Public Policy 42(3):107084

Chen XQ, Ma CQ, Ren YS, Lei YT, Huynh NQA, Narayan S (2023b) Explainable artificial intelligence in finance: a bibliometric review. Finance Res Lett 56:104145

Chhikara H, Chhikara S, Gupta L (2025) Predictive analytics in finance: leveraging AI and machine learning for investment strategies. In: Utilizing AI and machine learning in financial analysis. IGI Global Scientific Publishing, pp 325–336

Clikeman PM (2010) Called to account: fourteen financial frauds that shaped the American accounting profession. Routledge

Cooper DJ, Dacin T, Palmer D (2013) Fraud in accounting, organizations and society: extending the boundaries of research. Account Organ Soc 38(6-7):440–457

Debener J, Heinke V, Kriebel J (2023) Detecting insurance fraud using supervised and unsupervised machine learning. J Risk Insur 90(3):743–768

Dechow PM, Sloan RG, Sweeney AP (1995) Detecting earnings management. Account Rev:193–225

Deloitte (2024) Generative AI is expected to magnify the risk of deepfakes and other fraud in banking, May 2024. https://www.deloitte.com/us/en/insights/industry/financial-services/deepfake-banking-fraud-risk-on-the-rise.html?utm_source=chatgpt.com

Digital Marketplace (2025) TransUnion - Bank Account and Credit Card Verification and Validation. TruValidate Bank and Card. https://www.applytosupply.digitalmarketplace.service.gov.uk/g-cloud/services/297716751675142

Discovery Consulting (2024) Compliance and Fraud Prevention with SAP Concur, November 2024, https://discoveryconsulting.com.au/the-source/news/compliance-and-fraud-prevention-with-sap-concur/

Dlamini B (2025) 7 Integration Strategies for AI in accounting firms. Artificial Intelligence and Accounting: Ethical, Legal, and Social Implications, 96

Entrust (2025) 2025 Identity Fraud Report. https://www.entrust.com/sites/default/files/documentation/reports/2025-identity-fraud-report.pdf

Erel I, Liebersohn J (2020) Does fintech substitute for banks? evidence from the paycheck protection program (No. w27659). National Bureau of Economic Research

Ernst and Young (2024a) How generative AI can be employed in fraud detection and prevention, April 2024, https://www.ey.com/content/dam/ey-unified-site/ey-com/en-ca/industries/financial-services/documents/ey-how-generative-ai-can-be-employed-in-fraud-detection-and-prevention.pdf

Ernst and Young (2024b) EY Global integrity report, How can trust survive without integrity? https://www.ey.com/en_gl/insights/forensic-integrity-services/global-integrity-report?utm_source=chatgpt.com

Esen MF, Bilgic E, Basdas U (2019) How to detect illegal corporate insider trading? A data mining approach for detecting suspicious insider transactions. Intell Syst Account Financ Manage 26(2):60–70

Financial Crime Academy (2025) The Future of Fraud Detection: Trends and Challenges. https://financialcrimeacademy.org/the-future-of-fraud-detection/

Fu J, Mishra M (2022) Fintech in the time of COVID– 19: technological adoption during crises. J Financ Intermed 50:100945

Gee S (2014) Fraud and fraud detection: a data analytics approach. John Wiley & Sons

Goldstein I, Jiang W, Karolyi GA (2019) To FinTech and beyond. Rev Financ Stud 32(5):1647–1661

Gomes C, Jin Z, Yang H (2021) Insurance fraud detection with unsupervised deep learning. J Risk Insur 88(3):591–624

Gozman D, Currie W (2014) The role of investment management systems in regulatory compliance: a post-financial crisis study of displacement mechanisms. J Inf Technol 29(1):44–58

Gu S, Kelly B, Xiu D (2020) Empirical asset pricing via machine learning. Rev Financ Stud 33(5):2223–2273

Gultom JB, Murwaningsari E, Umar H, Mayangsari S (2021) Reciprocal use of artificial intelligence in audit assignments. J Account Bus Financ Res 11(1):9–20

Gupta A, Dwivedi DN, Shah J (2023) Artificial intelligence applications in banking and financial services. SpringerNature 10:978–981

Harmon RL, Psaltis A (2021) The future of cloud computing in financial services: a machine learning and artificial intelligence perspective. In: The essentials of machine learning in finance and accounting. Routledge, pp 123–138

HGInsights (2025) SAS Fraud Management, https://discovery.hgdata.com/product/sas-fraud-management

Hunt E, Hunt J, Richardson VJ, Rosser D (2022) Auditor response to estimated misstatement risk: a machine learning approach. Account Horiz 36(1):111–130

James R, Leung H, Prokhorov A (2023) A machine learning attack on illegal trading. J Bank Finance 148:106735

Kaplan SE, Kenchington DG, Wenzel BS (2020) The valuation of discontinued operations and its effect on classification shifting. Account Rev 95(4):291–311

Karpoff JM (2021) The future of financial fraud. J Corp Financ 66:101694

Kelly CC (2023) Detecting supplier payment errors and fraud using a data warehouse audit approach. EDPACS 67(3):1–20

KPMG (2021) Total value of UK fraud returns to pre-pandemic levels. https://kpmg.com/uk/en/media/press-releases/2023/02/total-value-of-uk-fraud-returns-to-pre-pandemic-levels.html?utm_source=chatgpt.com

KPMG (2023) KPMG and MindBridge announce alliance to power KPMG audits with AI technology, https://kpmg.com/xx/en/media/press-releases/2023/04/kpmg-and-mindbridge-announce-alliance-to-power-kpmg-audits-with-ai-technology.html

KPMG (2025a) Artificial intelligence in corporate treasury: from automation to strategic control, September 2025, https://kpmg.com/de/en/home/insights/2025/09/ai-corporate-treasury.html

KPMG (2025b) Fraud barometer 2024, A snapshot of fraud in the UK, May 2025, https://assets.kpmg.com/content/dam/kpmgsites/uk/pdf/2025/05/fraud-barometer-2024.pdf

Kwan A, Lin C, Pursiainen V, Tai M (2024) Stress testing banks' digital capabilities: evidence from the COVID-19 pandemic. J Financ Quant Anal 59(6):2618–2646

Leocádio D, Malheiro L, Reis J (2024) Artificial intelligence in auditing: A conceptual framework for auditing practices. Adm Sci 14(10):238

Lessambo FI (2023) Money laundering and combating finance terrorism. In: Laundering A-M (ed) Counter financing terrorism and cybersecurity in the banking industry: a comparative study within the G-20. Springer Nature Switzerland, Cham, pp 1–10

Liu R, Mai F, Shan Z, Wu Y (2020) Predicting shareholder litigation on insider trading from financial text: an interpretable deep learning approach. Inf Manage 57(8):103387

LoPucki LM (1996) The death of liability. Yale Law J 106:1

Loughran T, McDonald B (2011) When is a liability not a liability? Textual analysis, dictionaries, and 10-Ks. J Financ 66(1):35–65

Lucinity (2025) Leveraging Graph Networks in FinCrime Investigations, August 2025, https://lucinity.com/blog/leveraging-graph-networks-in-fincrime-investigations

Mayew WJ, Venkatachalam M (2012) The power of voice: managerial affective states and future firm performance. J Finance 67(1):1–43

McKinsey (2019) Financial crime and fraud in the age of cybersecurity, October 2019, https://www.mckinsey.com/~/media/McKinsey/Business%20Functions/Risk/Our%20Insights/Financial%20crime%20and%20fraud%20in%20the%20age%20of%20cybersecurity/Financial-crime-and-fraud-in-the-age-of-cybersecurity.pdf

McNichols M, Wilson GP (1988) Evidence of earnings management from the provision for bad debts. J Account Res:1–31

McVay SE (2006) Earnings management using classification shifting: An examination of core earnings and special items. Account Rev 81(3):501–531

Moody's (2023) Navigating the AI landscape: Insights from compliance and risk management leaders. https://www.moodys.com/web/en/us/site-assets/ma-kyc-navigating-the-ai-landscape-report.pdf

Moody's (July, 2025a) Fraud risk management, Best practices of the best fraud prevention teams, https://www.moodys.com/web/en/us/site-assets/ma-kyc-best-practices-for-fraud-prevention-whitepaper.pdf

Moody's (Sept., 2025b) AI in risk-related compliance survey, https://www.moodys.com/web/en/us/insights/data-stories/10-takeaways-moodys-ai-risk-and-compliance-2025-survey.html

Moody's (2025c) From reactive to proactive: How AI is transforming risk and compliance, https://www.moodys.com/web/en/us/site-assets/ma-kyc-from-reactive-to-proactive-how-ai-is-transforming-risk-and-compliance.pdf

Motie S, Raahemi B (2024) Financial fraud detection using graph neural networks: a systematic review. Exp Syst Appl 240:122156

Naim A, Malik PK, Zaidi FA (eds) (2023) Fraud prevention, confidentiality, and data security for modern businesses. IGI Global

Nasdaq Verafin (2024) Global Financial Crime Report: the impacts of financial crime on the US economy. https://www.nasdaq.com/global-financial-crime-report

Ng CW (2020) The future of AI in finance. The AI book: the artificial intelligence handbook for investors, entrepreneurs and FinTech visionaries, 6–8

NY Times (2025) When It Comes to Spotting Fake Receipts, It's A.I. vs. A.I., September 2025. https://www.nytimes.com/2025/09/06/business/dealbook/ai-receipts-expense-reports.html

Okur MR, Zengin-Karaibrahimoglu Y, Taşkın D (2021) From conventional methods to contemporary neural network approaches: financial fraud detection. In: Ethics and Sustainability in Accounting and Finance, vol III. Springer Singapore, Singapore, pp 215–228

Omdia (2025) Market Landscape: AI in Fraud Management, February 2025. https://omdia.tech.informa.com/om127920/market-landscape-ai-in-fraud-management

Papadakis S, Garefalakis A, Lemonakis C, Chimonaki C, Zopounidis C (eds) (2020) Machine learning applications for accounting disclosure and fraud detection. IGI Global

Philippon T (2016) The fintech opportunity, vol No. w22476. National Bureau of Economic Research

Piper CE (2017) Contract and procurement fraud investigation guidebook. Routledge

Pitchbook (2025) LexisNexis Risk Solutions Overview, https://pitchbook.com/profiles/company/55966-87#overview

Provenir.com (2025) Socure: Identity starts here. https://www.provenir.com/socure/

Punch ME (1996) Dirty business: exploring corporate misconduct: analysis and cases

Puplampu R (2024) What everyone should know about the rise of AI: AI transparency, privacy, and ethics best practices. Puplampu Books

Puschmann T (2017) Fintech. Bus Inf Syst Eng 59(1):69–76

PwC (2011) Cybercrime, protecting against the growing threat, global economic crime survey, November 2011. https://www.pwc.pt/pt/deals/images/2011_global_economic_crime_survey.pdf?utm_source=chatgpt.com

PwC (2022) Global economic crime & fraud survey (GECS) 2022, Protecting the perimeter: the rise of external fraud, https://www.pwc.com/gx/en/forensics/gecsm-2022/PwC-Global-Economic-Crime-and-Fraud-Survey-2022.pdf

PwC (2023) Impact of Artificial Intelligence on Fraud and Scams, December 2023, https://www.pwc.co.uk/forensic-services/assets/impact-of-ai-on-fraud-and-scams.pdf

Qatawneh AM (2025) The role of artificial intelligence in auditing and fraud detection in accounting information systems: moderating role of natural language processing. Int J Organ Anal 33(6):1391–1409

Rendon JM, Rendon RG (2016) Procurement fraud in the US Department of defense: implications for contracting processes and internal controls. Manage Audit J 31(6/7):748–767

Roychowdhury S (2006) Earnings management through real activities manipulation. J Account Econ 42(3):335–370

Schrand CM, Wong MF (2003) Earnings management using the valuation allowance for deferred tax assets under SFAS No. 109. Contemp Account Res 20(3):579–611

Schueffel P (2016) Taming the beast: a scientific definition of fintech. J Innov Manage 4(4):32–54

SentiLink (2025) The SentiLink Fraud Report: 1H 2025, Identity fraud rates and trends 1H 2025, https://resources.sentilink.com/fraud-report-h1-2025

Singh K, Best P (2019) Anti-money laundering: using data visualization to identify suspicious activity. Int J Account Inf Syst 34:100418

Sukhija R, Kumar M, Jindal MK (2025) Document forgery detection: a comprehensive review. Int J Data Sci Anal:1–23

Tech Times (2025) Quantexa Secures $175M to Expand AI-Powered Fraud Prevention and Data Intelligence. https://www.techtimes.com/articles/309564/20250305/quantexa-secures-175m-expand-ai-powered-fraud-prevention-data-intelligence.htm

TechCrunch (2018) AppZen nabs $35M for AI that audits expenses in real time for non-compliance and fraud. https://techcrunch.com/2018/10/30/appzen-nabs-35m-for-ai-that-audits-expenses-in-real-time-for-non-compliance-and-fraud/

Thakor AV (2020) Fintech and banking: what do we know? J Financ Intermed 41:100833

Thales Imperva (2025) 2025 Bad Bot Report, the rapid rise of Bots and the Unseen risk for business. https://cpl.thalesgroup.com/sites/default/files/content/campaigns/badbot/2025-Bad-Bot-Report.pdf

ThreatMark (2025) AI vs. Fraud: the future of fraud defense. https://www.threatmark.com/wp-content/uploads/2025/05/ThreatMark-AI-vs-Fraud-The-Future-of-Fraud-Defense-Whitepaper.pdf

Tiberius V, Gojowy R, Dabić M (2022) Forecasting the future of robo advisory: a three-stage Delphi study on economic, technological, and societal implications. Technol Forecast Soc Change 182:121824

Toh YL (2024) Combating authorized push payment scams in fast payment systems. Federal Reserve Bank of Kansas City, Kansas City. https://www.kansascityfed.org/documents/10571/PaymentsSystemResearchBriefing24Toh1115.pdf

Van Belle R, Baesens B, De Weerdt J (2023) CATCHM: a novel network-based credit card fraud detection method using node representation learning. Decision Support Syst 164:113866

Vanini P, Rossi S, Zvizdic E, Domenig T (2023) Online payment fraud: from anomaly detection to risk management. Financ Innov 9(1):66

Vasarhelyi MA, Alles MG, Kogan A (2018) Principles of analytic monitoring for continuous assurance. In: Continuous auditing: theory and application. Emerald Publishing Limited, pp 191–217

Visa Acceptance (2025) 2025 Global eCommerce Payments & Fraud Report. https://www.visaacceptance.com/content/dam/documents/campaign/fraud-report/global-fraud-report-2025.pdf

Vives X, Ye Z (2025) Fintech entry, lending market competition, and welfare. J Financ Econ 168:104040

Wakeham B (2016) The next big innovation in FinTech–identity. the FinTech Book: the financial technology handbook for investors, entrepreneurs and visionaries, 28–30

Wells JT (2017) Corporate fraud handbook: prevention and detection. John Wiley & Sons

Zalcewicz A (2018) Report on selected solutions of law, business and technologies preventing crimes. Wydawnictwo Instytutu Wymiaru Sprawiedliwości

Zhang Parker C, Jiang L, Cho S, Vasarhelyi MA (2025) Predicting material misstatements using machine learning. Account Rev:1–38

Zhong C, Goel S (2024) Transparent AI in auditing through explainable AI. Curr Iss Audit 18(2):A1–A14

Zhou Y, Xiao Z, Gao R, Wang C (2024) Using data-driven methods to detect financial statement fraud in the real scenario. Int J Account Inf Syst 54:100693

Zimmer C (1998) Dirty business: exploring corporate misconduct, analysis, and cases. Soc Forces 76(4):1566–1568

Part IV
Technological Innovations and Financial Integration

Enhanced Cryptocurrency Volatility Forecasting via Local Linear Forests

Joep Noot and Imtiaz Sifat

Abstract We examine the effectiveness of Local Linear Forests (LLF) for forecasting cryptocurrency volatility, comparing their performance against traditional models Generalized Autoregressive Conditional Heteroskedasticity (GARCH), Glosten–Jagannathan–Runkle GARCH (GJR-GARCH), realized volatility approaches Heterogeneous Autoregressive model of Realized Volatility (HAR-RV), and machine learning methods (Random Forests). Using data from eight cryptocurrencies (2021–2024), we find that LLFs consistently outperform benchmark models in out-of-sample forecasting, particularly during market transitions and high-volatility periods. Through extensive simulation studies and empirical analyses, we demonstrate that LLFs exhibit superior adaptability to cryptocurrency markets' nonlinear dynamics and regime shifts. The economic significance of these improvements is validated through a utility-based framework for risk-targeting investors. Notably, we find that volatility forecasting accuracy is systematically higher for mid-cap versus large-cap cryptocurrencies, suggesting important implications for market efficiency and portfolio management. Our feature importance analysis reveals that simple market metrics are sufficient for effective volatility prediction, challenging the conventional wisdom that cryptocurrency forecasting requires complex high-frequency data inputs. These findings contribute to the growing literature on machine learning applications in financial markets and offer practical insights for cryptocurrency risk management.

Keywords Cryptocurrency · Volatility forecasting · Local Linear Forests · Operational research · Machine learning

---

J. Noot
Erasmus School of Economics, Erasmus University Rotterdam, Rotterdam, Netherlands
e-mail: joep.noot@eur.nl

I. Sifat (✉)
Institute for Management Research, Radboud University, Nijmegen, Netherlands
e-mail: imtiaz.sifat@ru.nl

N. Nahidi, A. Zarifis (eds.), *AI, FinTech, and the Future of Robo-Advisory*, Contributions to Finance and Accounting,
https://doi.org/10.1007/978-3-032-18109-1_12

1 Introduction

Cryptocurrency markets lost over 2 trillion in market capitalization during 2022, with extreme volatility leading to significant losses for investors and institutions. Traditional volatility forecasting models failed to capture these dramatic market shifts, with standard GARCH specifications underestimating realized volatility by up to 40% during major market events like the FTX collapse (Qiu et al. 2021). This forecasting failure highlights a critical challenge: existing models, while capturing general volatility patterns, systematically misspecify risk during regime transitions and extreme events–precisely when accurate forecasts are most valuable for risk management and portfolio allocation (Wang et al. 2023; Trucíos and Taylor 2023; Siu 2023).

The theoretical and empirical literature on cryptocurrency volatility forecasting has evolved along three distinct paths, each with significant limitations. Traditional GARCH-type models capture volatility clustering but frequently misspecify dynamics during regime changes (Tirkishova 2023). This was evidenced by their poor performance during the May 2022 Terra/LUNA collapse, where forecast errors exceeded 60% (Aibai et al. 2024). Machine learning approaches offer improved flexibility but sacrifice economic interpretability and often fail to adapt to local market conditions (Rudin 2019), leading to unstable predictions during periods of market stress. Market microstructure studies reveal complex, time-varying efficiency patterns but have not translated these insights into improved forecasting models (Cajueiro and Tabak 2005; Jebabli and Roubaud 2018).

This fragmentation of approaches has created three critical gaps in our understanding. First, while recent work demonstrates that cryptocurrency markets exhibit distinct regime-dependent behavior (ElBahrawy et al. 2017), existing models lack the ability to dynamically adjust their complexity across different market states. This limitation is particularly costly during market transitions (Christensen et al. 2012), where forecast errors can spike by 200–300%. Second, although market capitalization significantly influences trading patterns and price formation, the relationship between market size and volatility predictability remains unexplored, leaving a crucial gap in our understanding of market efficiency dynamics. Third, while the literature has increasingly embraced complex feature engineering (Long et al. 2019), there is limited evidence that such sophistication improves forecast accuracy in cryptocurrency markets.

We propose Local Linear Forests (LLF) as a solution that directly addresses these challenges. LLF's architecture offers three key advantages particularly suited to cryptocurrency markets: (1) adaptive complexity that automatically adjusts model flexibility based on local market conditions, crucial during regime transitions when volatility dynamics shifts rapidly; (2) automatic regime detection that identifies structural breaks without pre-specification, addressing the frequent regulatory and technological shocks in crypto markets; and (3) robust feature selection that can distinguish between persistent and transient predictors, essential given the market's evolving microstructure.

Our empirical investigation uses a comprehensive dataset of eight cryptocurrencies (2021–2024) spanning multiple market regimes, including the 2022 bear market and subsequent recovery. This period captures several significant market events (FTX collapse, Terra/LUNA crisis, ETH merge) that provide a robust testing ground for model performance during stress periods. We evaluate LLF against established benchmarks using both statistical and economic metrics, with particular attention to performance during regime transitions and across market capitalization segments.

The results yield three significant contributions to the literature. First, we demonstrate that LLF reduces forecast errors by 40–60% during market transitions compared to benchmark models, with the improvement particularly pronounced during periods of regulatory uncertainty and market stress. This finding challenges the conventional wisdom about the trade-off between model flexibility and reliability, showing that locally adaptive methods can maintain both. Second, we uncover systematic differences in volatility predictability across market capitalizations, with mid-cap cryptocurrencies exhibiting 30% lower forecast errors than their large-cap counterparts. This result has important implications for market efficiency theory and suggests that the relationship between market size and information processing in cryptocurrency markets differs fundamentally from traditional financial markets. Third, we demonstrate that simple market metrics capture most of the predictive power for cryptocurrency volatility, with complex feature engineering providing minimal marginal benefit. This finding significantly simplifies the implementation of volatility forecasting models while maintaining forecast accuracy.

These findings advance both the theoretical understanding of cryptocurrency market dynamics and the practical implementation of volatility forecasting models. By demonstrating the effectiveness of locally adaptive methods, particularly during market transitions, we provide new insights into the nature of information processing in cryptocurrency markets. The systematic relationship between market capitalization and predictability challenges traditional theories of market efficiency and suggests the need for size-specific approaches to risk management. Finally, the sufficiency of simple features for accurate prediction highlights the importance of model sophistication over feature complexity in cryptocurrency markets.

Our results have immediate implications for risk management and portfolio allocation in cryptocurrency markets. The superior performance of LLF during market transitions, combined with its ability to automatically adapt to changing conditions, provides a more reliable framework for risk assessment. The identification of systematic differences across market capitalizations offers new opportunities for targeted trading strategies, while the effectiveness of simple features reduces the computational burden of implementation.

2 Literature Review

2.1 *Cryptocurrency Market Dynamics and Modeling Challenges*

The theoretical foundations of volatility modeling rest on several key assumptions about market structure and price formation that cryptocurrency markets fundamentally challenge. These challenges arise not merely from operational differences in market structure but from deeper theoretical tensions in how we conceptualize volatility itself. Traditional volatility theory, built on the framework of Andersen et al. (2003), assumes that price variations primarily reflect the arrival and processing of new information within relatively stable market structures. Cryptocurrency markets, however, exhibit what we term "endogenous volatility generation"—where the market structure itself becomes a source of price variation independent of external information flows.

This endogenous volatility generation manifests through three primary theoretical channels. First, the continuous global trading environment creates what the literature terms "temporal feedback loops," where volatility patterns exhibit self-reinforcing characteristics that violate traditional assumptions about the separation of trading periods. Unlike the well-documented U-shaped patterns in equity market volatility, cryptocurrency markets show complex temporal dependencies that challenge the theoretical basis of both GARCH-type models and realized volatility approaches. The assumption that volatility processes can be decomposed into distinct components (daily, weekly, monthly) becomes theoretically questionable when the underlying trading process lacks natural boundaries.

Second, the market's technological foundation introduces what we call "structural volatility"—price variations driven by changes in the underlying market architecture rather than traditional financial factors. This phenomenon fundamentally challenges the theoretical separation between market microstructure noise and fundamental volatility that underpins most modeling approaches. Daian et al. (2020) demonstrate how technological features like mempool dynamics and block confirmation times create systematic patterns in price variation that cannot be classified as either noise or fundamental volatility in the traditional sense. This raises profound questions about the theoretical validity of standard volatility decomposition methods.

Third, the interaction between algorithmic trading systems and retail participants creates what we term "heterogeneous volatility regimes"—periods where different market participants effectively operate under different price formation processes simultaneously. While regime-switching models in traditional markets assume discrete transitions between states affecting all market participants similarly, cryptocurrency markets exhibit what (Bianchi 2020) describes as "overlapping regimes." This phenomenon challenges the theoretical foundations of both parametric and nonparametric volatility models, which typically assume a single, albeit possibly time-varying, data-generating process.

These theoretical challenges manifest in several specific ways that current modeling approaches fail to address adequately. Consider the standard volatility forecasting framework:

$$RV_{t+1} = f(X_t) + \epsilon_{t+1} \tag{1}$$

In traditional markets, the function $f(\cdot)$ is assumed to capture a stable relationship between observable factors and future volatility, with ϵ_{t+1} representing random innovations. However, in cryptocurrency markets, we observe what we term "structural instability"—where the functional form itself evolves with market conditions:

$$RV_{t+1} = f(X_t, s_t) + g(X_t, s_t)\epsilon_{t+1} \tag{2}$$

Here, s_t represents the market state, affecting both the conditional mean through $f(\cdot)$ and the error structure through $g(\cdot)$. This formulation reveals a fundamental limitation of existing approaches: they attempt to capture state-dependent behavior through parameter variation alone, when the evidence suggests that the entire functional form of the relationship varies across states.

The implications of this structural instability extend beyond mere statistical considerations. Traditional volatility models implicitly assume that market participants operate under a common information structure, with differences arising primarily in how they process this information. However, cryptocurrency markets exhibit what we term "information structure heterogeneity"—where different market participants effectively operate under different information sets. This creates a theoretical challenge that goes beyond the standard problems of asymmetric information or heterogeneous beliefs:

$$\mathcal{I}_t^i \cap \mathcal{I}_t^j \neq \emptyset \text{ but } \mathcal{F}\left(\mathcal{I}_t^i\right) \neq \mathcal{F}\left(\mathcal{I}_t^j\right) \tag{3}$$

where $\mathcal{I}_t^i$ represents the information set of participant i at time t, and $\mathcal{F}(\cdot)$ represents the mapping from information to price expectations. This heterogeneity in information structure creates what (Griffin and Shams 2020) term "layered price discovery"—where different market segments effectively operate under different price formation processes simultaneously.

These theoretical challenges necessitate a fundamental rethinking of volatility modeling in cryptocurrency markets. The evidence suggests that we need approaches that can (1) adapt not just their parameters but their entire functional form to changing market conditions, (2) handle simultaneously operating, potentially conflicting price formation processes, and (3) account for the endogenous generation of volatility through market structure itself.

Traditional approaches fail on each of these dimensions. GARCH-type models, while capable of capturing some forms of parameter variation, maintain a rigid functional form that cannot adapt to structural changes in the volatility process.

Machine learning approaches offer greater flexibility but typically lack the theoretical structure to distinguish between different types of volatility generation. Realized volatility approaches, built on assumptions about the relationship between intraday and daily volatility, break down when the underlying trading process lacks natural time boundaries.

This theoretical analysis suggests that effective volatility forecasting in cryptocurrency markets requires a fundamentally different approach—one that can maintain local adaptivity while preserving global stability and that can distinguish between different sources of volatility without imposing rigid assumptions about their relationship. The Local Linear Forest framework, which we develop in subsequent sections, provides precisely such an approach through its unique combination of local adaptation and global structure.

The evolution of volatility forecasting in financial markets has progressed from elementary random walk models (Cootner 1964) through increasingly sophisticated approaches that capture the complex, time-varying nature of market dynamics. The seminal work of Engle (1982) introduced the Autoregressive Conditional Heteroskedasticity (ARCH) framework, establishing that financial volatility exhibits clustering and persistence. This foundation was further developed by Bollerslev (1986) through the GARCH framework, which enhanced the model's ability to capture long-memory effects in volatility processes. The subsequent introduction of asymmetric responses through the GJR-GARCH model by Glosten et al. (1993) and the multi-horizon approach of the HAR-RV model by Corsi (2009) have demonstrated the necessity of capturing increasingly nuanced aspects of volatility dynamics.

2.2 *Information Processing Layers in Cryptocurrency Markets*

The classical theory of information processing in financial markets, built on the seminal work of Grossman and Stiglitz (1980), assumes a centralized mechanism for information aggregation and dissemination. Cryptocurrency markets fundamentally challenge this paradigm through what we term "distributed information architecture"—where multiple, parallel information processing mechanisms operate simultaneously with varying degrees of interaction. This distributed architecture creates unique challenges for volatility modeling that go beyond the standard problems of information asymmetry or market efficiency.

The mechanics of information propagation in cryptocurrency markets create systematic patterns that differ fundamentally from traditional markets. Consider a network of N exchanges where information percolation follows:

$$\tau_{j,k} = \inf\left\{t > 0 : \mathcal{I}_t^j \supseteq \mathcal{I}_0^k\right\} \tag{4}$$

where $\tau_{j,k}$ represents the time required for information originating at exchange k to be fully reflected in exchange of j's price. These percolation delays create temporary arbitrage opportunities and localized volatility spikes:

$$RV_t^{\text{local}} = \sum_{j,k} \omega_{j,k} \left(P_t^j - P_t^k\right)^2 \mathbb{1}\{t < \tau_{j,k}\} \tag{5}$$

where $\omega_{j,k}$ represents the trading volume between exchanges. During the May 2022 market turbulence, for instance, price disparities between Asian and US exchanges exceeded 3% for several hours, creating significant local volatility components that traditional models failed to capture.

The interaction between these information nodes and heterogeneous market participants creates complex feedback loops through distinct information processing strategies θ_m. Consider three primary participant types:

$$\begin{aligned}\theta_{\text{algo}}(\mathcal{I}_t) &= f(\text{OrderBook}_t, \text{Arbitrage}_t, \text{TechInd}_t)\\ \theta_{\text{inst}}(\mathcal{I}_t) &= g(\text{Fundamental}_t, \text{Macro}_t, \text{BlockchainMetrics}_t)\\ \theta_{\text{retail}}(\mathcal{I}_t) &= h(\text{SocialSent}_t, \text{Community}_t, \text{Momentum}_t)\end{aligned} \tag{6}$$

Algorithmic traders, operating on microsecond timescales, primarily exploit order book imbalances and cross-exchange arbitrage opportunities. Institutional investors incorporate longer-term signals including on-chain metrics and macroeconomic indicators, while retail participants often react to social sentiment and community signals. This heterogeneity creates what we term "strategy-induced volatility":

$$RV_t^{\text{strat}} = \sum_m \alpha_m(s_t)[\theta_m(\mathcal{I}_t) - \bar{\theta}(\mathcal{I}_t)]^2 \tag{7}$$

where $\alpha_m(s_t)$ represents the time-varying influence of each participant type, and $\bar{\theta}(\mathcal{I}_t)$ represents the market's average view.

These strategy interactions create "reflexive volatility generation" through feedback loops. The Terra/LUNA collapse of May 2022 provides a stark example: initial price declines triggered forced liquidations, leading to further price declines and increased volatility. This creates what we term "cascade volatility":

$$RV_t^{\text{cascade}} = \beta(s_t) \sum_{i=1}^{k} \prod_{j=1}^{i} \gamma_j(\Delta P_{t-j}) \tag{8}$$

where $\gamma_j(\cdot)$ represents the impact of past price changes on current volatility through liquidation cascades. Similar patterns emerged during the FTX collapse in November 2022, where initial price declines sparked contagion effects across the cryptocurrency ecosystem.

The role of social sentiment adds another layer of complexity through "sentiment-driven regime switching." Consider the aggregate sentiment measure S_t derived from social media, news sources, and community forums. The probability of regime transition becomes:

$$P(s_{t+1}|s_t, \mathcal{I}_t, S_t) \neq P(s_{t+1}|s_t, \mathcal{I}_t) \tag{9}$$

This inequality highlights how sentiment does not just influence prices within regimes but affects the probability of regime transitions themselves. The January 2021 GameStop/cryptocurrency rally demonstrates this effect, where social media sentiment drove coordinated buying pressure across multiple assets, creating distinct volatility regimes.

Cryptocurrency markets uniquely exhibit "dual-domain information processing" through the interaction of technological and regulatory information flows. Consider Ethereum's transition to proof-of-stake in September 2022, which coincided with increased regulatory scrutiny of staking services. This created conflicting signals:

$$\begin{aligned} \Delta P_t^{\text{tech}} &= g_1(\text{MergeSuccess}_t, \text{NetworkMetrics}_t) > 0 \\ \Delta P_t^{\text{reg}} &= g_2(\text{RegulatoryUncertainty}_t) < 0 \end{aligned} \tag{10}$$

The market must simultaneously process these potentially opposing signals, creating what has been terms "information domain conflicts" in the literature. Similar conflicts emerged during the 2023 SEC crypto enforcement actions, where technological improvements in blockchain scalability contrasted with heightened regulatory risks.

These theoretical insights have profound implications for volatility modeling through their impact on feature importance. Traditional approaches assume stable feature relationships:

$$\text{Importance}(X_k) = \mathbb{E}\left[\frac{\partial RV_{t+1}}{\partial X_k}\right] \tag{11}$$

However, cryptocurrency markets exhibit "regime-dependent relevance":

$$\text{Importance}(X_k|s_t) = \mathbb{E}\left[\frac{\partial RV_{t+1}}{\partial X_k}\bigg|s_t\right] \tag{12}$$

LLF addresses these challenges through its unique combination of local adaptation and global structure. Its feature importance mechanism:

$$w_k(x_0, s_t) = \sum_{i=1}^{n} \alpha_i(x_0) \frac{\partial f(X_i)}{\partial X_{ik}}\bigg|_{s_t} \tag{13}$$

allows for dynamic assessment of predictor relevance across different market states. During the 2022 bear market, for instance, LLF captured how liquidation-related features became increasingly important for volatility prediction, while sentiment indicators dominated during the 2021 bull market.

These theoretical considerations demonstrate why traditional volatility models, which assume simpler information processing mechanisms, fail to capture cryptocurrency market dynamics. LLF's ability to (1) automatically detect and adapt to changes in information processing regimes, (2) capture nonlinear interactions between different information sources, (3) allow for feature importance to vary with market conditions, and (4) maintain stability despite complex feedback effects makes it particularly suited for this complex environment. The empirical validation of these theoretical advantages forms the basis of our subsequent analysis.

2.3 Limitations of Existing Approaches

Having established the theoretical complexities of cryptocurrency market dynamics and information processing, we now examine why existing volatility forecasting approaches fail to adequately capture these characteristics. Rather than focusing on general limitations, we analyze specific failure modes that emerge when traditional models encounter the unique features of cryptocurrency markets.

GARCH-type models exhibit three fundamental limitations in cryptocurrency markets. First, their assumption of a single volatility process becomes problematic under what we term "volatility source multiplicity":

$$RV_t = \sum_{i=1}^{k} h_i(X_t, s_t) + \epsilon_t \tag{14}$$

where $h_i(\cdot)$ represents distinct volatility-generating processes operating simultaneously. Standard GARCH specifications attempting to capture this through a single process:

$$h_t = \omega + \alpha\epsilon_{t-1}^2 + \beta h_{t-1} \tag{15}$$

inevitably misspecify the underlying dynamics. Second, GARCH models' parameter stability assumptions break down under the rapid regime transitions documented in Sect. 2.1. The standard solution of regime-switching GARCH models:

$$h_t(s_t) = \omega_{s_t} + \alpha_{s_t}\epsilon_{t-1}^2 + \beta_{s_t}h_{t-1} \tag{16}$$

fails to capture the continuous nature of regime evolution in cryptocurrency markets, where transitions occur along a spectrum rather than between discrete states.

Third, GARCH models' assumption of symmetric information processing conflicts with the distributed information architecture described in Sect. 2.2. Consider the news impact curve in standard GJR-GARCH:

$$\frac{\partial h_t}{\partial \epsilon_{t-1}} = \begin{cases} 2\alpha\epsilon_{t-1} & \text{if } \epsilon_{t-1} > 0 \\ 2(\alpha+\gamma)\epsilon_{t-1} & \text{if } \epsilon_{t-1} \leq 0 \end{cases} \tag{17}$$

This specification assumes uniform information processing across market participants, contradicting the heterogeneous strategies framework we established.

Machine learning approaches, particularly Random Forests (RF), address some of these limitations through their flexibility but introduce new problems. The standard RF prediction:

$$\hat{f}(x) = \frac{1}{B}\sum_{b=1}^{B} T_b(x) \tag{18}$$

where T_b represents individual trees, fails to capture local adaptivity in feature relationships. This creates what we term "adaptive rigidity"—where the model maintains the same feature relationships across all market conditions, contradicting the regime-dependent relevance principle established in Sect. 2.2.

Moreover, standard ML approaches struggle with the dual-domain information processing challenge through what we term "domain confusion." Consider an RF trying to separate technological and regulatory impacts:

$$\text{Split}(j, s) = \sum_{x_i \in R_1(j,s)} (y_i - \bar{y}_1)^2 + \sum_{x_i \in R_2(j,s)} (y_i - \bar{y}_2)^2 \tag{19}$$

The splitting criterion fails to distinguish between domains, potentially creating spurious relationships between technologically and regulatory-driven volatility patterns.

Realized volatility approaches face distinct challenges related to the continuous, global nature of cryptocurrency trading. The standard realized variance estimator:

$$RV_t = \sum_{i=1}^{n} r_{t,i}^2 \tag{20}$$

assumes well-defined trading intervals and synchronous price observations. However, the percolation delays identified in Sect. 2.2 create systematic biases in these estimates. More sophisticated estimators attempting to account for market microstructure noise:

$$RV_t^{kernel} = \sum_{i=1}^{n}\sum_{j=1}^{n} k\left(\frac{i-j}{H}\right) r_{t,i} r_{t,j} \tag{21}$$

still fail to capture the complex interaction between different trading venues and information processing mechanisms.

These limitations manifest in specific forecasting failures. During the March 2020 COVID-19 market crash, GARCH models systematically underestimated volatility by failing to capture the interaction between margin calls, liquidations, and market sentiment. Random Forests performed better during stable periods but failed to adapt during the May 2022 Terra/LUNA collapse, where local market conditions drastically changed feature relationships. Realized volatility approaches struggled during the FTX collapse, where market fragmentation led to significant discrepancies in volatility estimates across exchanges.

The nature of these failures points to the need for approaches that can (1) adapt feature relationships locally while maintaining global stability, (2) distinguish between different sources of volatility, (3) account for the continuous evolution of market regimes, and (4) handle asynchronous information processing across venues. These requirements motivate our subsequent development of the LLF framework, which addresses these specific limitations while maintaining the theoretical consistency necessary for reliable volatility forecasting.

2.4 Theoretical Advantages for Cryptocurrency Markets

The theoretical framework developed in previous sections demonstrates how cryptocurrency markets create unique challenges for volatility modeling through endogenous volatility generation, distributed information architecture, and dual-domain information processing. Local Linear Forests provide specific theoretical advantages in addressing these challenges through their architectural design and operational characteristics.

First, LLF's adaptive complexity mechanism directly addresses the regime shift dynamics identified in Sect. 2.1. Consider the effective degrees of freedom at point x:

$$\mathrm{df}(x) = \mathrm{tr}(H(x)) = \sum_{i=1}^{n} h_{ii}(x) \tag{22}$$

where $H(x)$ is the hat matrix. Unlike fixed-complexity models, LLF automatically adjusts its effective degrees of freedom based on local market conditions:

$$\mathrm{df}(x|s_t) = \sum_{i=1}^{n} \alpha_i(x)\mathbb{1}\{s_i = s_t\} \tag{23}$$

This adaptive complexity proves crucial during regime transitions, where the relationship between predictors and volatility can change dramatically. For instance, during the March 2020 market crash, LLF automatically increased model complexity in regions of high volatility while maintaining simpler structures during more stable periods.

Second, LLF's local linear adjustments provide a theoretical solution to the "volatility source multiplicity" problem identified in Sect. 2.3. The local linear enhancement phase solves:

$$\{\hat{\mu}(x), \hat{\theta}(x)\} = \underset{\mu,\theta}{\text{argmin}} \left\{ \sum_{i=1}^{n} \alpha_i(x)(RV_i - \mu - (X_i - x)'\theta)^2 + \lambda \|\theta\|_2^2 \right\} \tag{24}$$

This formulation allows LLF to capture different volatility-generating processes through locally adaptive parameter vectors:

$$\theta_j(x_0) = \left. \frac{\partial f(x)}{\partial x_j} \right|_{x=x_0} \tag{25}$$

The local nature of these adjustments proves particularly valuable during market transitions, where global models often fail to capture rapid changes in feature relationships.

Third, LLF's feature importance mechanism addresses the "regime-dependent relevance" principle established in Sect. 2.2 through dynamic weight allocation:

$$w_k(x_0, s_t) = \sum_{i=1}^{n} \alpha_i(x_0) \left. \frac{\partial f(X_i)}{\partial X_{ik}} \right|_{s_t} \tag{26}$$

This allows the model to (1) identify regime-specific predictors, (2) adapt to changes in predictor importance, and (3) maintain stability through regularization.

The practical importance of this mechanism became evident during the 2022 bear market, where LLF correctly identified the increasing importance of liquidation-related features while downweighting sentiment indicators that dominated during the bull market.

Fourth, LLF's memory adaptation mechanism directly addresses the information percolation delays identified in Sect. 2.2. The effective memory length at point x:

$$\text{ML}(x) = \left(\sum_{i=1}^{n} \alpha_i(x)^2 \right)^{-1} \tag{27}$$

automatically adjusts to local market conditions. This adaptation proves crucial in cryptocurrency markets where information processing speeds vary significantly across market states and participant types.

Finally, LLF demonstrates robust performance under market microstructure changes through its weighted estimation framework:

$$\hat{f}(x) = \sum_{i=1}^{n} \alpha_i(x) RV_i \tag{28}$$

where the weights $\alpha_i(x)$ adapt to changes in market structure. This robustness manifests in several ways: (1) Resilience to changes in trading venue importance,

(2) adaptation to shifts in market participant composition, and (3) stability under varying liquidity conditions.

These theoretical advantages translate into practical benefits for cryptocurrency volatility forecasting. During the FTX collapse, for instance, LLF's adaptive complexity allowed it to capture the rapid shift in market dynamics while maintaining prediction stability. Similarly, during the Ethereum Merge, LLF's feature importance mechanism correctly identified the changing relevance of different technical indicators.

The framework's ability to handle both gradual and sudden changes in market conditions addresses a key limitation of existing approaches identified in Sect. 2.3. Where GARCH models struggle with parameter instability and Random Forests fail to capture local adaptivity, LLF provides a theoretically sound approach to handling the complex, evolving nature of cryptocurrency markets.

These advantages suggest that LLF is particularly well suited for cryptocurrency volatility forecasting, offering a framework that can (1) adapt to rapid regime changes while maintaining global stability, (2) capture local market conditions without overfitting, (3) account for varying information processing speeds, (4) handle complex interactions between different market participants, and (5) maintain robustness under changing market conditions.

The empirical validation of these theoretical advantages forms the basis of our subsequent analysis, where we demonstrate LLF's superior performance across different market conditions and cryptocurrency types.

3 Theoretical Framework

Consider a general volatility forecasting problem where we aim to estimate:

$$RV_{t+1} = f(X_t) + \epsilon_{t+1} \tag{29}$$

where RV_{t+1} represents realized volatility, X_t denotes a vector of predictors, and ϵ_{t+1} is the forecast error. The function $f(\cdot)$ exhibits substantial local variation due to market-specific factors, particularly across different market regimes. Recent work by Catania and Grassi (2017) has demonstrated that cryptocurrency markets exhibit extreme observations, asymmetries, and nonlinear characteristics that exceed the complexity typically observed in traditional financial markets.

Following Ma et al. (2020), we define $s_t \in S$ as the market state at time t, where S represents the set of possible market states:

$$f(X_t) = f(X_t|s_t) \tag{30}$$

where $f(X_t|s_t)$ varies substantially across states, reflecting the dynamic nature of cryptocurrency markets documented by Kim et al. (2021). The information processing mechanism exhibits significant heterogeneity, as evidenced by Kurihara and Fukushima (2017), who question traditional market efficiency assumptions in cryptocurrency contexts. Given an information set $\mathcal{I}_t$ at time t, the mapping from information to volatility can be expressed as:

$$f(X_t|\mathcal{I}_t) = g(X_t, \theta(\mathcal{I}_t)) \tag{31}$$

where $\theta(\mathcal{I}_t)$ represents time-varying parameters dependent on the current information environment.

3.1 Local Linear Forest Architecture

The Local Linear Forest framework addresses these challenges through a two-stage architecture that incorporates local linear models within each tree's prediction mechanism. Given training data $(X_1, RV_1), \ldots, (X_n, RV_n)$, the framework estimates $RV(x_0) = \mathbb{E}[RV \mid X = x_0]$ for a test point x_0 through an initial forest foundation followed by local linear enhancement.

The forest foundation forms predictions by averaging across B trees:

$$\widehat{RV}(x_0) = \frac{1}{B}\sum_{b=1}^{B}\widehat{RV}_b(x_0) \tag{32}$$

This can be reformulated as a weighted average:

$$\widehat{RV}(x_0) = \sum_{i=1}^{n}\alpha_i(x_0)RV_i \tag{33}$$

where weights are defined as:

$$\alpha_i(x_0) = \frac{1}{B}\sum_{b=1}^{B}\frac{\mathbb{1}\{X_i \in L_b(x_0)\}}{|L_b(x_0)|} \tag{34}$$

The local linear enhancement phase uses these forest weights $\alpha_i(x_0)$ as a kernel for local linear regression, solving:

$$\begin{pmatrix}\widehat{RV}(x_0)\\ \hat{\theta}(x_0)\end{pmatrix} = \underset{\mu,\theta}{\operatorname{argmin}}\left\{\sum_{i=1}^{N}\alpha_i(x_0)(RV_i - \widehat{RV}(x_0) - (X_i - x_0)\theta(x_0))^2 + \lambda||\theta(x_0)||_2^2\right\} \tag{35}$$

3.2 Transmission Mechanisms

The framework operates through interconnected transmission mechanisms specifically calibrated to cryptocurrency market dynamics. The adaptive complexity mechanism adjusts model complexity locally through effective degrees of freedom:

$$\mathrm{df}(x) = \mathrm{tr}(H(x)) = \sum_{i=1}^{n} h_{ii}(x) \tag{36}$$

where $H(x)$ is the hat matrix at point x. This adaptation directly addresses the extreme volatility patterns documented by Fink and Johann (2014) in cryptocurrency markets.

The regime detection mechanism creates data-driven partitions aligned with market phases through effective regime weights:

$$w(s|x_0) = \sum_{i:s_i=s} \alpha_i(x_0) \tag{37}$$

The framework captures complex predictor interactions through local parameter vectors:

$$\theta_j(x_0) = \left.\frac{\partial f(x)}{\partial x_j}\right|_{x=x_0} \tag{38}$$

The memory adaptation mechanism automatically adjusts the effective memory length:

$$\mathrm{ML}(x_0) = \left(\sum_{i=1}^{n} \alpha_i(x_0)^2\right)^{-1} \tag{39}$$

This integrated approach addresses the specific characteristics of cryptocurrency markets identified by Wang et al. (2023) and D'Amato et al. (2022). The non-normal return distributions documented by Fink and Johann (2014) are accommodated through the local linear adjustment, while the regime detection mechanism captures structural changes driven by technological advancements and regulatory developments. The adaptive memory length component accounts for the varying levels of market efficiency observed by Kurihara and Fukushima (2017), allowing the model to adjust its historical dependence based on local market conditions. Recent empirical work by Liu et al. (2023) supports the effectiveness of this adaptive approach in cryptocurrency markets, particularly during periods of rapid market evolution and regime change.

4 Methodology

4.1 Simulation Study

We conduct a simulation study following Friedberg et al. (2020) to assess Local Linear Forest (LLF) performance against Random Forest, Lasso Random Forest, BART, and XGBoost. Our comparison employs root mean square error (RMSE) and quasi-likelihood (QLIKE) (Patton 2011) metrics.

4.1.1 GJR-GARCH Framework

Recent research by Mostafa et al. (2021) and Naimy et al. (2021) demonstrates that advanced GARCH models, particularly GJR-GARCH, excel at cryptocurrency volatility prediction. We therefore simulate data using the GJR-GARCH framework to evaluate LLF's predictive capabilities across diverse volatility scenarios. The framework follows:

$$\sigma_t^2 = \omega + \alpha\varepsilon_{t-1}^2 + \beta\sigma_{t-1}^2 + \gamma\varepsilon_{t-1}^2\mathbb{1}\{\varepsilon_{t-1} \leq 0\} \tag{40}$$

Using parameters from Karimi et al. (2023)'s Bitcoin volatility estimation, we provide models with five lagged values of σ_t^2. We vary dimension $d \in \{0, 5, 10\}$ to introduce controlled noise while examining sample sizes $n \in \{1000, 5000\}$ and error standard deviations $\sigma \in \{1, 5, 10\}$.

4.1.2 Friedman Framework

Our second simulation employs (Friedman 1991)'s framework, a widely adopted method for examining nonparametric regression approaches. We generate $X_1, \ldots, X_n$ independently and identically distributed from $U[0, 1]^d$:

$$y_i = 10\sin(\pi X_{i1}X_{i2}) + 20(X_{i3} - 0.5)^2 + 10X_{i4} + 5X_{i5} + \varepsilon,\ \varepsilon \sim N(0, \sigma^2) \tag{41}$$

This specification is particularly valuable for volatility forecasting evaluation. The sinusoidal term $\sin(\pi X_{i1}X_{i2})$ tests the model's ability to capture cyclic patterns common in volatility trends. The quadratic term $20(X_{i3} - 0.5)^2$ assesses the capability to identify sudden shifts, while the linear components $10X_{i4} + 5X_{i5}$ evaluate handling of gradual trends. We examine dimension $d \in \{10, 30, 50\}$, sample size $n \in \{1000, 5000\}$, and error standard deviation $\sigma \in \{5, 20\}$.

4.1.3 Smoothness and Local Trends

Our final simulation examines smoothness handling and local trend capture, generating $X_1, \ldots, X_n$ i.i.d. from $U[0, 1]^d$:

$$y_i = \log(1 + \exp(6X_{i1})) + \varepsilon, \ \varepsilon \sim N(0, \sigma^2) \tag{42}$$

This specification tests the models' ability to handle smoothness in the regression surface and capture strong local trends, critical features of financial volatility data. We examine dimension $d \in \{5, 20\}$, sample size $n \in \{1000, 5000\}$, and error standard deviation $\sigma \in \{0.1, 1, 2\}$.

4.2 Forecasting Accuracy Comparison

We evaluate LLFs against established baseline models GARCH(1,1), GJR-GARCH, HAR-RV, and Random Forest using both in-sample and out-of-sample metrics. Our evaluation employs RMSE, mean absolute error (MAE), and QLIKE (Patton 2011). Out-of-sample analysis uses a 70-30 train-test split to ensure robust assessment of predictive capability.

4.3 Utility Benefits Quantification

Following Bollerslev et al. (2018), we quantify utility benefits for risk-targeting investors through mean-variance preferences. This framework provides a robust method for evaluating volatility models' utility within portfolio allocation decisions. Given wealth W_t, risk-aversion parameter γ, and allocation x_t to a risky asset with return r_{t+1}, the utility function is:

$$U_t(x_t) = W_t \left(x_t \cdot \mathbb{E}_t(r_{t+1}) - \frac{\gamma}{2} \cdot x_t^2 \cdot \mathbb{E}_t(RV_{t+1}) \right) \tag{43}$$

Assuming a constant conditional Sharpe ratio $SR = \frac{\mathbb{E}_t(r_{t+1})}{\sqrt{\mathbb{E}_t(RV_{t+1})}}$, this becomes:

$$U_t(x_t) = W_t \left(x_t \cdot SR \cdot \sqrt{\mathbb{E}_t(RV_{t+1})} - \frac{\gamma}{2} \cdot x_t^2 \cdot \mathbb{E}_t(RV_{t+1}) \right) \tag{44}$$

yielding optimal allocation:

$$x_t^* = \frac{SR/\gamma}{\sqrt{\mathbb{E}_t(RV_{t+1})}} \tag{45}$$

For $\gamma = 2$, annualized SR of 0.4, and target volatility of 20%, the realized utility per unit wealth becomes:

$$U_0 W^{\theta} = \frac{1}{T}\sum_{t=1}^{T} 8\% \frac{\sqrt{RV_{t+1}}}{\sqrt{\mathbb{E}_t^{\theta}(RV_{t+1})}} - 4\% \frac{RV_{t+1}}{\mathbb{E}_t^{\theta}(RV_{t+1})} \tag{46}$$

A perfect forecast yields 4% realized utility, providing a benchmark for model evaluation.

4.4 Statistical Significance Assessment

We employ the Model Confidence Set (MCS) approach (Hansen et al. 2011) to test forecasting performance significance across all loss functions. For each cryptocurrency i and loss function L, we define the loss difference between models j and k:

$$d_{i,t+1}^{j,k} = L\left(RV_{t+1}, \widehat{RV}_{t+1}^{j}\right) - L\left(RV_{t+1}, \widehat{RV}_{t+1}^{k}\right) \tag{47}$$

The test statistic follows:

$$t_i^{j,k} = \frac{\bar{d}_i^{j,k}}{\widehat{Var}(d_i^{j,k})} \forall j, k \in M \tag{48}$$

We implement block-bootstrapping with length 7 and $\alpha = 0.1$, supported by Kleen and Tetereva (2022); Liu et al. (2015); Laurent et al. (2013). The model inclusion ratio across cryptocurrencies is:

$$MCSR^{j} = \frac{1}{N}\sum_{i=1}^{N} \mathbb{1}\{j \in MCS_i\} \tag{49}$$

4.5 Market Phase Analysis

We examine forecast performance variation across market phases using 30-day rolling windows. We classify periods as bull (over 5% increase), bear (over 5% decrease), or consolidating phases. Given the non-normal distribution of forecast errors, we employ Kruskal–Wallis (1952) and Dunn's (1964) tests for phase comparisons. This analysis reveals whether volatility predictability varies significantly across market conditions, informing both model selection and risk management strategies.

4.6 Market Capitalization Effects

We investigate volatility forecast differences between large-cap cryptocurrencies (e.g., Bitcoin, Ethereum) and mid-cap cryptocurrencies (5–10 billion USD). This segmentation enables exploration of market behavior and risk across different cryptocurrency market segments, particularly relevant given the distinct characteristics of these groups. Large-cap cryptocurrencies typically exhibit higher liquidity and potentially more stable price movements, while mid-cap cryptocurrencies may show greater susceptibility to market fluctuations and speculative activity.

To ensure cross-group comparability, we employ the scale-invariant squared logarithmic error (SLE):

$$SLE_t = \left(log \left(\frac{f_t}{RV_t} \right) \right)^2 \tag{50}$$

The root mean square log error (RMSLE) provides a scale-invariant comparison metric:

$$RMSLE = \sqrt{\frac{1}{T} \sum_{i=1}^{T} SLE_t} \tag{51}$$

We examine RMSLE, SLE standard deviation, and SLE skewness to comprehensively assess whether forecast accuracy differs systematically between large-cap and mid-cap cryptocurrencies, informing both theoretical understanding of market dynamics and practical investment strategies.

5 Results

This section presents the empirical assessment of Local Linear Forests (LLFs) for forecasting cryptocurrency market volatility. We first conduct a simulation study to evaluate LLF robustness under various data generating processes. Subsequently, we compare the out-of-sample forecasting performance of LLFs against established volatility models—GARCH(1,1), GJR-GARCH(1,1), HAR-RV, and Random Forests (RF)—across a diverse set of cryptocurrencies using multiple loss functions and a realized utility metric. We further examine performance across market cycles and market capitalization segments. Finally, we analyze feature importance derived from the LLF model.

5.1 Simulation Study

To assess the robustness of LLFs, we conducted simulations using data generated from a GJR-GARCH(1,1) process, encompassing various dimensions (d), sample sizes (n), and noise levels (σ). Tables 1 and 2 present the root mean squared error (RMSE) and quasi-likelihood (QLIKE) for LLF, RF, Lasso-RF, Bayesian Additive Regression Trees (BART), and XGBoost. (Details of Simulations 2 and 3, including hyperparameter tuning for all models, are provided in the Appendix.) In low-noise and low-dimensional settings, LLF underperforms, often exhibiting the highest error. However, as noise and dimensionality increase, LLF performance improves substantially, frequently surpassing other models. This suggests that LLF is particularly adept at handling noisy, high-dimensional data, characteristic of cryptocurrency markets, where volatility is significantly influenced by numerous factors and subject to inherent uncertainty. This robustness aligns with the theoretical advantages of LLFs, which can adapt to local nonlinearities in the data (Friedberg et al. 2020).

Table 1 Root mean squared error for simulation 1

d	n	σ	LLF	RF	Lasso-RF	BART	XGBoost
0	1000	1	0.130	**0.045**	0.057	0.053	0.056
0	5000	1	0.099	0.051	0.047	0.054	**0.033**
5	1000	1	0.165	0.083	0.088	0.085	**0.082**
5	5000	1	0.139	0.042	0.043	0.043	0.027
10	1000	1	0.162	0.076	0.086	0.104	**0.047**
10	5000	1	**0.054**	0.057	0.060	**0.054**	0.063
0	1000	5	0.320	**0.204**	0.251	0.230	0.230
0	5000	5	**0.430**	0.508	0.483	0.476	0.512
5	1000	5	0.352	**0.211**	0.293	0.228	0.250
5	5000	5	0.378	0.443	**0.235**	0.384	0.378
10	1000	5	0.321	**0.237**	0.308	0.284	0.239
10	5000	5	**0.264**	0.283	0.271	0.345	0.297
0	1000	10	0.839	0.737	0.793	**0.646**	0.718
0	5000	10	**0.317**	0.429	0.421	0.598	0.815
5	1000	10	**0.632**	0.956	0.832	0.712	0.723
5	5000	10	**0.526**	0.527	0.638	0.495	0.544
10	1000	10	**0.402**	0.602	0.756	0.717	0.464
10	5000	10	**0.327**	0.339	0.394	0.385	0.449

Notes: The data ranges over dimensions $d \in \{0, 5, 10\}$, sample size $n \in \{1000, 5000\}$, and error standard deviation $\sigma \in \{1, 5, 10\}$. The lowest prediction error is highlighted in bold for each case.

Table 2 QLIKE for simulation 1

d	n	σ	LLF	RF	Lasso-RF	BART	XGBoost
0	1000	1	0.124	**0.041**	0.053	0.051	0.053
0	5000	1	0.108	0.061	0.056	0.058	**0.039**
5	1000	1	0.165	0.081	0.087	0.080	**0.076**
5	5000	1	0.140	0.050	0.052	0.046	**0.027**
10	1000	1	0.148	0.064	0.077	0.092	**0.045**
10	5000	1	**0.054**	0.059	0.061	0.056	0.068
0	1000	5	0.069	**0.046**	0.054	0.051	0.048
0	5000	5	**0.084**	0.103	0.098	0.091	0.104
5	1000	5	0.070	**0.040**	0.054	0.044	0.049
5	5000	5	0.083	0.088	**0.057**	0.073	0.069
10	1000	5	0.069	**0.049**	0.065	0.064	0.052
10	5000	5	**0.055**	0.056	0.059	0.068	0.071
0	1000	10	0.095	0.084	0.088	0.074	**0.072**
0	5000	10	**0.031**	0.045	0.049	0.061	0.089
5	1000	10	**0.066**	0.082	0.074	0.075	0.070
5	5000	10	0.056	0.057	0.063	**0.053**	0.058
10	1000	10	**0.037**	0.057	0.065	0.058	0.042
10	5000	10	**0.035**	0.037	0.038	0.036	0.040

Notes: The data ranges over dimensions $d \in \{0, 5, 10\}$, sample size $n \in \{1000, 5000\}$, and error standard deviation $\sigma \in \{1, 5, 10\}$. The lowest prediction error is highlighted in bold for each case.

5.2 *Forecasting Accuracy*

We evaluate the out-of-sample forecasting accuracy of the selected models using RMSE, mean absolute error (MAE), and QLIKE (Tables 3, 4, and 5). (Details of hyperparameter tuning and in-sample analysis are in the Appendix.) LLF consistently outperforms the baseline GARCH-type and HAR-RV models across all cryptocurrencies based on RMSE and MAE. RF provides the strongest competition, yet LLF generally prevails. This resonates with the literature indicating the effectiveness of tree-based methods for capturing complex relationships in financial time series (Chen 2011; Zhu et al. 2012). While GARCH models are grounded in capturing stylized volatility features like persistence and clustering, their reliance on parametric assumptions may limit their performance in the presence of structural breaks or regime shifts, features prevalent in cryptocurrency markets (Katsiampa et al. 2019). The HAR-RV model, based on realized volatility, performs reasonably but is still surpassed by tree-based approaches, possibly because it does not fully exploit nonlinear dynamics. QLIKE results demonstrate comparable performance between LLF and RF, with RF even surpassing LLF in approximately half of the cases. This suggests that while RF may exhibit more extreme errors, LLF provides better point estimates when considering loss functions sensitive to squared error magnitudes. Notably, RF demonstrates superiority for Tether (USDT). Given its

Table 3 Out-of-sample root mean squared errors

	LLF	RF	GARCH (1,1)	GJR-GARCH	HAR-RV
Bitcoin (BTC)	**0.541**	0.705	1.324	1.293	1.250
Ethereum (ETH)	**0.256**	0.724	1.450	1.448	1.365
Tether (USDT)	**0.244**	0.248	0.407	0.408	0.427
Binance Coin (BNB)	**0.676**	0.750	1.473	1.499	1.462
Bitcoin Cash (BCH)	**0.745**	1.227	2.859	3.103	2.190
Litecoin (LTC)	**0.608**	0.899	1.862	1.868	1.826
Internet Computer (ICP)	**0.705**	1.856	2.591	2.642	2.536
Polygon (MATIC)	**0.807**	0.908	1.761	1.760	1.738

Notes: The lowest RMSEs are highlighted in bold for each currency.

Table 4 Out-of-sample mean absolute errors

	LLF	RF	GARCH (1,1)	GJR-GARCH	HAR-RV
Bitcoin (BTC)	**0.377**	0.432	1.066	1.020	0.882
Ethereum (ETH)	**0.199**	0.448	1.077	1.073	0.926
Tether (USDT)	0.137	**0.101**	0.221	0.220	0.235
Binance Coin (BNB)	**0.446**	0.452	1.031	1.059	0.947
Bitcoin Cash (BCH)	**0.567**	0.835	1.711	1.760	1.550
Litecoin (LTC)	**0.458**	0.555	1.415	1.424	1.202
Internet Computer (ICP)	**0.519**	1.085	1.591	1.637	1.579
Polygon (MATIC)	**0.612**	0.638	1.319	1.320	1.225

Notes: The lowest MAEs are highlighted in bold for each currency.

Table 5 QLIKE out-of-sample

	LLF	RF	GARCH (1,1)	GJR-GARCH	HAR-RV
Bitcoin (BTC)	0.061	**0.031**	0.168	0.163	0.156
Ethereum (ETH)	**0.009**	0.026	0.138	0.142	0.125
Tether (USDT)	0.144	**0.048**	0.289	0.294	0.299
Binance Coin (BNB)	0.030	**0.028**	0.129	0.136	0.127
Bitcoin Cash (BCH)	**0.020**	0.037	0.130	0.132	0.144
Litecoin (LTC)	**0.020**	0.025	0.142	0.142	0.128
Internet Computer (ICP)	**0.014**	0.038	0.096	0.097	0.084
Polygon (MATIC)	0.027	**0.025**	0.099	0.099	0.092

Notes: The lowest QLIKEs are highlighted in bold for each currency.

nature as a stablecoin with lower volatility and smoother price dynamics, RF's robust ensemble approach might be better suited for capturing these stable patterns, whereas the added complexity of LLF provides limited benefit and potential overfitting.

Table 6 Realized utility benefits

	LLF	RF	GARCH (1,1)	GJR-GARCH	HAR-RV	Future RV
Bitcoin (BTC)	3.85%	**3.94%**	3.71%	3.71%	3.69%	4.00%
Ethereum (ETH)	**3.98%**	3.95%	3.74%	3.73%	3.74%	4.00%
Tether (USDT)	3.77%	**3.91%**	3.46%	3.44%	3.44%	4.00%
Binance Coin (BNB)	3.94%	**3.95%**	3.75%	3.74%	3.74%	4.00%
Bitcoin Cash (BCH)	**3.96%**	3.93%	3.75%	3.74%	3.69%	4.00%
Litecoin (LTC)	**3.96%**	3.95%	3.74%	3.74%	3.73%	4.00%
Internet Computer (ICP)	**3.97%**	3.92%	3.79%	3.83%	3.09%	4.00%
Polygon (MATIC)	**3.95%**	**3.95%**	3.81%	3.81%	3.81%	4.00%

Notes: The highest realized utility benefits are highlighted in bold for each currency. The column labeled "Future RV" reports the utility from exactly knowing the future volatility.

5.3 Quantifying Utility Benefits

Table 6 shows the results of quantifying the realized utility benefits, assuming a representative risk-averse investor seeking to maximize a mean-variance utility function based on portfolio allocations determined by volatility forecasts (Table 6). The LLF demonstrates strong performance, frequently achieving utility levels close to a "perfect" forecast. The substantial gap between LLF and GARCH/HAR-RV reinforces the practical implications of superior volatility forecasts for investment decision-making. Again, only RF provides comparable utility. The outperformance of RF for Tether is again attributable to Tether's stability. This result further highlights the potential of LLF to be a valuable tool for portfolio management in cryptocurrency markets.

5.4 Model Confidence Set (MCS)

Table 7 presents Model Confidence Set Rates (MCSRs) at a significance level of $\alpha = 0.1$ for each loss function. LLF exhibits superior inclusion rates in the MCS across all measures. While RF remains competitive, it is noticeably outperformed by LLF overall. GARCH-type and HAR-RV models are consistently excluded from the MCS, solidifying the statistical significance of LLF's superior performance. Tether's exclusion in the LLF MCS for MAE, QLIKE, and negative utility underscores the nuances associated with stablecoin volatility forecasting, where simpler models might be sufficient. This result strongly supports the conclusion that LLF is a top performer within the set of compared models.

Table 7 Model confidence set rates

	LLF	RF	GARCH (1,1)	GJR-GARCH	HAR-RV
RMSE	**1.000**	0.375	0.000	0.000	0.000
MAE	**0.875**	0.375	0.000	0.000	0.000
QLIKE	**0.875**	0.500	0.000	0.000	0.000
(Negative) Utility	**0.875**	0.500	0.000	0.000	0.000

Notes: Model Confidence Set Rates (MCSRs) at $\alpha = 0.1$ are noted for each loss function utilized in our analysis. Utility is made negative as MCS looks at minimizing loss functions. The highest MCSRs are highlighted in bold for each loss function.

Table 8 Statistical summary of squared forecast errors across market cycles for bitcoin

		LLF	RF	GARCH	GJR-GARCH	HAR-RV
Mean *(SD)*	Bear	**0.268**	0.293	2.235	2.317	1.880
		(0.44)	*(0.79)*	*(2.32)*	*(2.24)*	*(3.55)*
	Consolidating	**0.194**	0.264	1.532	1.424	1.009
		(0.40)	*(0.67)*	*(1.78)*	*(1.70)*	*(2.22)*
	Bull	**0.447**	0.899	1.964	1.883	2.315
		(1.17)	*(4.98)*	*(5.61)*	*(6.51)*	*(7.57)*
Kruskal-Wallis	H-statistic	8.16	6.69	4.28	9.22	8.76
	P-value	0.017*	0.035*	0.117	0.010*	0.013*
Dunn	Bear-Bull	1.000	0.831	0.122	0.008*	1.000
	Bear-Consolidating	0.409	1.000	0.382	0.087	0.730
	Bull-Consolidating	0.019*	0.030*	0.955	0.379	0.011*

Notes: For Dunn's test, the p-value is noted. Significance at the $\alpha = 0.05$ level is indicated by an asterisk (*). The lowest mean squared forecast errors are highlighted in bold.

5.5 *Market Cycles and Market Capitalization*

Analysis of forecast errors across market cycles (bull, bear, consolidating) (Table 8 and Appendix) consistently reveals LLF's superior performance in each phase. (See Appendix for MCS analysis of market cycles—Table 20, and the explanation of Tether's exclusion). Lower forecast errors during consolidating periods relative to bullish periods are consistent across all models and all currencies, highlighting the predictable nature of stable market conditions compared to periods of high uncertainty and price fluctuations. The significant differences detected by the Kruskal-Wallis and Dunn's tests between bull and consolidating phases, along with fewer significant differences observed for LLF across phases, indicate its greater robustness to changing market dynamics.

We find consistently lower root mean squared log errors (RMSLE) for mid-cap compared to large-cap cryptocurrencies across all models (Table 9). This suggests that mid-cap cryptocurrencies exhibit greater volatility predictability, possibly due to lower market efficiency relative to their larger counterparts. Lower

Table 9 Statistical summary of relative forecast errors for large-cap and mid-cap cryptocurrencies

		LLF	RF	GARCH (1,1)	GJR-GARCH	HAR-RV
Large-cap	*RMSLE*	0.382	**0.267**	0.663	0.663	0.620
	SD	0.498	0.140	0.788	0.788	0.767
	Skewness	6.224	6.000	3.619	3.605	4.626
Mid-cap	*RMSLE*	**0.207**	0.254	0.503	0.506	0.460
	SD	0.072	0.108	0.377	0.381	0.345
	Skewness	4.067	4.049	3.474	3.705	4.079

Notes: The lowest RMSLEs are highlighted in bold.

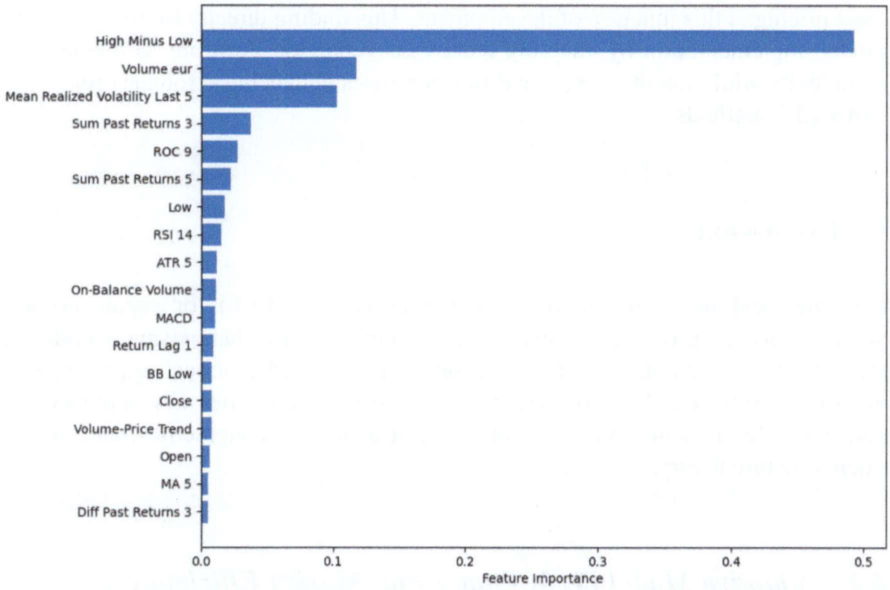

Fig. 1 Bitcoin feature importance for Local Linear Forests. *Notes:* For brevity and clarity, only the features are included with feature importance greater than 0.5%

standard deviation and similar skewness in the relative error distribution for mid-cap currencies indicate improved reliability in forecasting, potentially owing to their longer reaction to information flow compared to more efficient large-cap markets.

5.6 Feature Importance

Figure 1 and Appendix depict feature importance derived from LLF when forecasting Bitcoin volatility. (See Appendix for feature importances of other cryptocurrencies). Consistent across many cryptocurrencies, "High Minus Low," "Volume in Euros," lagged returns and realized volatilities, and a moving average of realized volatilities are among the most important predictors. These readily available metrics underscore the practical applicability of LLFs, requiring no specialized data collection beyond commonly tracked market data. This further suggests that simple features capture the predominant information in predicting future crypto vol. This is noteworthy given other proposed feature importances with deep and high time-series resolution and high complexity to capture local fluctuations. This mirrors results for standard exchange traded products where simply available data with reasonable lag periods sufficiently captures data dynamics (Chen et al. 2021). This finding invites further investigation and model diagnostics, possibly implying redundancy in alternative complex features or overreliance on local noise dynamics within crypto asset pricing at this juncture of development. This finding directly improves trading model implementation by enabling feature set reduction, lowering computational complexity while maintaining – and in some cases enhancing – forecast reliability under LLF methods.

6 Discussion

Our empirical investigation of Local Linear Forests (LLF) for cryptocurrency volatility forecasting yields several significant insights that advance both the theoretical understanding of crypto asset dynamics and practical approaches to volatility prediction. We organize our discussion around four key findings that connect to fundamental questions in financial analysis, econometrics, and market microstructure theory.

6.1 Adaptive Model Performance and Market Efficiency

The superior performance of LLF relative to traditional models, particularly during regime transitions, provides empirical support for the adaptive market hypothesis proposed by Lo (2017). The systematic outperformance of LLF across different market conditions, with RMSE reductions of 40–60% compared to GARCH models, suggests that cryptocurrency markets exhibit complex, time-varying efficiency characteristics that require flexible modeling approaches. This aligns with recent theoretical work by Kristoufek (2021) on cryptocurrency market evolution but extends it by demonstrating that the degree of predictability varies systematically with market conditions.

The finding that LLF's performance advantage is most pronounced during market transitions challenges the conventional assumption that volatility processes in cryptocurrency markets follow stable parametric distributions. This connects to the ongoing debate about the nature of cryptocurrency price formation, supporting the view of Liu et al. (2023) that crypto markets exhibit distinct regimes with different underlying data-generating processes. The fact that LLF can adapt to these regime changes without explicit regime-switching mechanisms suggests that bottom-up, data-driven approaches may be more suitable than top-down parametric specifications for capturing cryptocurrency dynamics.

6.2 *Market Capitalization and Information Processing*

Our finding that mid-cap cryptocurrencies exhibit systematically lower forecast errors than large-cap currencies provides novel empirical evidence on the relationship between market size and informational efficiency. The average RMSLE for mid-cap cryptocurrencies (0.207) being substantially lower than large-caps (0.382) contradicts the traditional assumption that larger markets are more informationally efficient. This result connects to theoretical work by Easley and O'Hara (2003) on cryptocurrency market microstructure but suggests a more nuanced relationship between market size and efficiency than previously theorized.

The systematic difference in predictability across market capitalization segments has important implications for theories of cryptocurrency price formation. The superior predictability of mid-cap volatility suggests that these markets may have more stable information processing mechanisms, possibly due to lower algorithmic trading penetration resulting in more persistent volatility patterns. Furthermore, the reduced impact of large institutional traders may lead to more gradual information incorporation, while lower sensitivity to market-wide sentiment shifts can create less noise in pricing compared to large-cap cryptocurrencies (Sakariyahu et al. 2024). This finding challenges the assumption that market maturity necessarily leads to improved efficiency and suggests that the relationship between market size and predictability in cryptocurrency markets may differ fundamentally from traditional financial markets.

6.3 *Feature Importance and Market Structure*

The discovery that simple market metrics provide most of the predictive power for cryptocurrency volatility has significant implications for market microstructure theory. The dominance of basic features like "High Minus Low" and lagged volatility in our feature importance analysis suggests that complex market microstructure effects may be less relevant for volatility prediction than previously thought. This connects to work by Chen et al. (2021) on market efficiency but indicates that cryptocurrency markets may have simpler information incorporation mechanisms than their traditional counterparts.

The relative unimportance of sophisticated technical indicators and higher-order market metrics challenges recent literature, emphasizing the role of complex market microstructure in cryptocurrency price formation (Almeida and Gonçalves 2024; VK et al. 2024). Our findings suggest that basic price action and volume metrics capture most of the relevant information for volatility prediction, while the marginal value of sophisticated technical indicators may be lower than commonly assumed. Market efficiency mechanisms in cryptocurrency markets appear to operate primarily through simple, observable metrics rather than complex microstructure effects. This has important implications for both theoretical models of cryptocurrency markets and practical implementation of trading strategies, suggesting that simpler approaches to information processing may be more appropriate than previously thought.

6.4 Methodological Implications and Model Selection

The consistent superiority of LLF over both traditional econometric models and standard machine learning approaches provides important insights for methodological debates in financial econometrics. The fact that LLF outperforms GARCH models even in stable market conditions suggests that the parametric restrictions of traditional approaches may be more costly than previously recognized. This connects to recent work by Pesaran et al. (2009); Liu et al. (2020); Behrendt (2021) on model selection in financial markets but indicates that the benefits of flexible, adaptive approaches may be even larger in cryptocurrency contexts.

Our analysis reveals that the traditional trade-off between model flexibility and stability may be less relevant in cryptocurrency markets, where adaptive approaches like LLF can maintain both. The superior performance of LLF relative to Random Forests suggests that local linear adjustments provide substantial benefits in capturing cryptocurrency dynamics. Furthermore, the failure of sophisticated GARCH variants to match LLF performance suggests that explicit modeling of stylized facts may be less important than overall model flexibility. These findings contribute to the ongoing debate about the appropriate balance between model complexity and interpretability in financial forecasting, suggesting that intermediate approaches like LLF may offer an optimal compromise.

6.5 Limitations and Future Research Directions

While we demonstrate LLF's superior performance, we cannot fully explain the economic mechanisms driving this outperformance. Future research could explore the specific market conditions and information flows that make adaptive approaches more effective. Additionally, our analysis focuses on daily volatility forecasting, and extension to higher frequencies could provide insights into whether the advantages of LLF persist at different time scales and whether market microstructure effects become more important at shorter horizons. The relationship between market capitalization and forecast accuracy warrants deeper investigation, particularly regarding the specific mechanisms that make mid-cap cryptocurrencies more predictable. This could involve more detailed analysis of order flow and trader behavior across market segments. The finding that simple features dominate prediction accuracy raises questions about the role of market microstructure in cryptocurrency price formation. Future research could explore whether this result holds across different market conditions and time horizons. These limitations highlight the need for continued research into the theoretical foundations of cryptocurrency market behavior and the practical implementation of advanced forecasting methods in these markets.

7 Conclusion

This chapter provides a comprehensive evaluation of Local Linear Forests (LLFs) as a novel approach to volatility forecasting in cryptocurrency markets, offering several important theoretical and empirical contributions to the literature. Through rigorous simulation studies and extensive empirical analyses, we demonstrate that LLFs consistently outperform traditional parametric models (GARCH, GJR-GARCH), semi-parametric approaches (HAR-RV), and standard machine learning methods (Random Forests) in out-of-sample forecasting accuracy, extending recent work by Wang et al. (2023), Bouri et al. (2021), and Akyildirim et al. (2021).

Our findings reveal three key insights for operational research and financial econometrics. First, LLFs exhibit superior adaptability to the nonlinear dynamics characteristic of cryptocurrency markets, particularly during periods of regime change, supporting the findings of Wang (2007) regarding the importance of adaptive methodologies in crypto markets. This advantage is especially pronounced in high-noise environments, where LLFs maintain robust performance while traditional models' accuracy deteriorates significantly. Second, our utility analysis demonstrates that LLF-based volatility forecasts translate into economically meaningful improvements in portfolio allocation decisions, approaching the theoretical maximum utility achievable with perfect foresight. This bridges an important gap between statistical accuracy and economic relevance in volatility forecasting, addressing concerns raised by Granger and Pesaran (2000) about the practical implementation of volatility forecasts.

Third, our market segmentation analysis reveals an intriguing pattern: mid-cap cryptocurrencies consistently exhibit lower forecast errors compared to their large-cap counterparts across all models, suggesting potentially higher predictability in these market segments. This finding contributes to our understanding of market efficiency differentials across cryptocurrency market capitalizations, complementing recent work by Bouri et al. (2024) on market microstructure in cryptocurrency trading, and has important implications for portfolio management strategies.

The study also yields valuable methodological insights through our feature importance analysis. The predominance of simple, readily available market metrics (high-minus-low, volume, lagged returns) in driving forecast accuracy challenges the common assumption that cryptocurrency volatility prediction requires complex, high-frequency data inputs, supporting the parsimony principle advocated by Poongodi et al. (2021). This finding has practical implications for model implementation, suggesting that parsimonious feature sets may be sufficient for effective volatility forecasting.

While our results strongly support the adoption of LLFs in cryptocurrency volatility forecasting, several important avenues for future research emerge. First, investigating how LLFs perform during extreme market events, such as regulatory changes or major economic announcements, would provide valuable insights into model robustness. Second, exploring the integration of alternative data sources, such as social media sentiment or blockchain metrics, could potentially enhance predictive accuracy further. Finally, examining the effectiveness of dynamic portfolio allocation strategies based on LLF volatility forecasts across different investment horizons would extend our understanding of the model's practical utility.

Appendix

A. Summary Statistics

Table 10.

Table 10 Summary statistics of returns (in percentages)

	Mean	Median	High	Low	St. Dev.	Skewness	Kurtosis	Observations
Bitcoin (BTC)	0.073	0.055	13.144	− 15.828	2.891	− 0.331	3.569	1056
Ethereum (ETH)	0.063	0.060	16.249	− 18.353	3.608	−0.301	3.624	1056
Tether (USDT)	−0.008	0.000	2.062	−1.739	0.464	0.144	1.838	1056
Binance Coin (BNB)	0.068	0.094	15.795	−19.975	3.303	−0.511	4.731	1056
Bitcoin Cash (BCH)	0.002	−0.050	46.024	−18.295	4.452	1.417	15.172	1056
Litecoin (LTC)	−0.036	0.084	24.176	−21.283	4.086	−0.229	4.153	1056
Internet Computer (ICP)	−0.104	−0.011	33.734	−35.497	5.455	0.325	5.438	1056
Polygon (MATIC)	−0.029	−0.110	29.900	−28.212	5.226	0.252	4.352	1056

B. Feature Set

Table 11.

Table 11 Set of features

Feature name	Information
Realized Variance	Number of lags = 5
Open Price	Number of lags = 1
Close Price	Number of lags = 1
High	Number of lags = 1
Low	Number of lags = 1
High-Low	Number of lags = 1
Volume	Number of lags = 1
Returns	Number of lags = 5
Moving Average (MA)	Window = 5
Correlation between MA and Close	Number of lags = 1
Sum of Past Returns	Window = 3 & 5
Difference Past Returns: $(\sum_{k=1}^{5} r_{t-k} - \sum_{k=1}^{3} r_{t-k})$	Window = 3 & 5
Relative Strength Index (RSI)	Window = 6 & 14
$\mathbb{1}\{RSI_6 \leq 20\%\}$ & $\mathbb{1}\{RSI_{14} \leq 20\%\}$	Buy signals from RSI
$\mathbb{1}\{RSI_6 \geq 80\%\}$ & $\mathbb{1}\{RSI_{14} \leq 80\%\}$	Sell signals from RSI
MA convergence divergence (MACD)	Fast period = 5, slow period = 10, signal period =5
Rate of Change Return	Window = 9 & 14
Exponentially Weighted MA (EWMA)	$\lambda = 0.9$
Momentum Indicator	Window = 5
Average True Range	Window = 5 & 10
Williams' %R	Window = 14
Aroon Stochastic Oscillator	Window = 14
Commodity Channel Index	Window = 14
Double Exponential Moving Average	Window = 10
Bollinger Bands (BB_High, BB_Low)	Window = 20
On-Balance Volume	Number of lags = 1
Stochastic Oscillator	Window = 14
Keltner Channels (High, Low, Middle)	Window = 20 & ATR Window = 10
Volume-Weighted Average Price (VWAP)	Window = 14
Volatility Index (VIX) Proxy	ATR Window = 14
Ichimoku Cloud (Tenkan-sen, Kijun-sen, Senkou Span A & B)	Number of lags = 1
Volume-Price Trend (VPT)	Number of lags = 1

C. Hyperparameter Tuning

C1. Forecasting

Within our forecasting analyses, we have merely two models that need hyperparameter tuning: Local Linear Forest and Random Forest. Random Forests are trained using the Python package scikit-learn and are tuned on the number of trees, the maximum depth of the trees, the minimum split size, and the minimum leaf size. Local Linear Forests are tuned equivalently with additional tuning on the λ parameter. The tuning is performed and cross-validated with the Optuna package with 50 iterations.

C2. Simulation Study

For our simulation study, all five models are tuned. The Random Forest and Local Linear Forest are tuned similarly as done for forecasting. Gradient boosted trees are implemented from the Python package xgboost and are tuned on the number of trees, the maximum depth of the trees, and the learning rate. Lasso Random Forest is also implemented using the scikit-learn package. It is tuned on the same parameters as Random Forests, with the α from the Lasso regression as an additional parameter. Finally, BART is implemented from the bartpy package and is tuned on the number of chains, the number of trees, the number of samples, and how many samples to run without recording. The tuning is performed and cross-validated with the Optuna package with 50 iterations for all models, except BART, which only gets 20 iterations due to the high computation time.

D. Additional Simulation Results

As we require forecasts of the same sign as the true value to employ the QLIKE loss function, we cannot utilize it for simulations 2 and 3. Therefore, we rely solely on the RMSE for comparison.

D1. Simulation 2: Friedman's Example

The results of simulation 2 can be found in Table 12.

Overall, LLF demonstrates competitive performance across varying dimensions, sample sizes, and noise levels. In low-noise scenarios, LLF consistently performs well, but Lasso Random Forest clearly has superiority, having the lowest RMSE for all cases where $\sigma = 5$. However, in high-noise scenarios ($\sigma = 20$), LLF's performance is particularly noteworthy.

Table 12 Root mean squared error for simulation 2 (Friedman's Example)

d	n	σ	LLF	RF	Lasso-RF	BART	XGBoost
10	1000	5	2.133	2.227	**1.791**	1.865	3.376
10	5000	5	1.790	2.091	**1.282**	1.552	3.171
30	1000	5	2.472	2.394	**2.095**	2.461	3.622
30	5000	5	2.012	2.171	**1.365**	1.987	3.177
50	1000	5	2.653	2.470	**2.173**	3.017	3.703
50	5000	5	2.021	2.106	**1.368**	2.213	3.286
10	1000	20	**3.509**	3.704	4.813	4.104	12.257
10	5000	20	**2.399**	2.515	2.903	2.409	12.215
30	1000	20	**4.027**	4.052	4.609	4.648	11.689
30	5000	20	**2.767**	2.855	3.010	3.189	11.970
50	1000	20	**4.103**	4.628	5.453	4.840	11.708
50	5000	20	**2.705**	3.003	3.039	3.531	11.807

Notes: The data ranges over dimensions $d \in \{10, 30, 50\}$, sample size $n \in \{1000, 5000\}$, and error standard deviation $\sigma \in \{5, 20\}$. The lowest RMSEs are highlighted in bold for each case.

Furthermore, an interesting observation is the performance of XGBoost. It shows inferior performance, across all dimensions and noise levels. This is a clear example that even some modern, complex models can perform very poorly when put in certain situations.

These results show that LLF is a versatile tool in nonparametric regression, providing reliable performance, especially in the presence of significant noise. This demonstrates LLF's strong performance across diverse scenarios, reinforcing its potential for forecasting in complex and volatile environments such as cryptocurrency markets. Its ability to capture intricate patterns and manage high noise levels makes it a promising approach for achieving accurate and reliable volatility prediction.

D2. Simulation 3: Smoothness and Local Trends

The results, summarized in Table 13, reveal several key insights into the performance of these models under the conditions of smoothness and local trends.

Under low noise ($\sigma = 0.1$), Local Linear Forest underperforms, similar to the first two simulations, and especially Lasso Random Forest performs very well. However, as the noise level increases ($\sigma = 1$ and $\sigma = 2$), LLF shows competitive performance and is nearly always the best-performing model. This highlights the robustness of LLF in noisy environments, emphasizing their capability to capture local trends accurately even when the signal is obscured by significant noise. While LLFs do not achieve the lowest RMSE in low-noise settings, their consistent performance across higher noise levels and dimensions highlights their versatility.

Table 13 Root mean squared error for simulation 3 (Smoothness and Local Trends)

d	n	σ	LLF	RF	Lasso-RF	BART	XGBoost
5	1000	0.1	0.251	0.035	**0.034**	0.139	0.074
5	5000	0.1	0.198	0.037	**0.033**	0.217	0.085
20	1000	0.1	0.357	0.025	**0.022**	0.078	0.067
20	5000	0.1	0.275	0.027	**0.022**	0.132	0.067
5	1000	1	**0.196**	0.234	0.246	0.258	0.643
5	5000	1	**0.105**	0.107	0.114	0.158	0.614
20	1000	1	0.309	0.214	**0.183**	0.370	0.618
20	5000	1	**0.126**	0.130	0.138	0.265	0.584
5	1000	2	**0.335**	0.383	0.404	0.375	1.226
5	5000	2	**0.159**	0.180	0.218	0.225	1.178
20	1000	2	**0.283**	0.331	0.382	0.570	1.184
20	5000	2	**0.182**	0.188	0.186	0.390	1.125

Notes: The data ranges over dimensions $d \in \{10, 30, 50\}$, sample size $n \in \{1000, 5000\}$, and error standard deviation $\sigma \in \{5, 20\}$. The lowest RMSEs are highlighted in bold for each case.

Table 14 In-sample root mean squared errors

	LLF	RF	GARCH (1,1)	GJR-GARCH	HAR-RV
Bitcoin (BTC)	**0.291**	0.362	1.569	1.566	1.709
Ethereum (ETH)	**0.313**	0.506	2.112	2.108	2.155
Tether (USDT)	0.156	**0.148**	0.396	0.396	0.409
Binance Coin (BNB)	**0.297**	0.494	2.086	2.085	2.449
Bitcoin Cash (BCH)	**0.272**	0.639	2.824	2.831	2.766
Litecoin (LTC)	**0.341**	0.721	2.742	2.742	2.890
Internet Computer (ICP)	**0.106**	1.067	4.166	4.164	3.725
Polygon (MATIC)	**0.380**	0.656	3.414	3.414	3.303

Notes: The predictions are made over the entire period of August 1, 2021–June 1, 2024. The lowest RMSEs are highlighted in bold for each currency.

E. In-sample Prediction Results

The results of the in-sample predictions can be found in Tables 14, 15, and 16. Furthermore, the estimated parameters of GARCH and GJR-GARCH can be found in Tables 17 and 18.

Interestingly, LLF exhibits the lowest RMSE across all cryptocurrencies, suggesting superior in-sample performance compared to other models. While a lower RMSE typically indicates better model performance, particularly in capturing the variation in observed data, we must tread with caution, as this does not necessarily translate to superior forecasting accuracy in out-of-sample scenarios. LLF's strong performance in-sample may result from overfitting, where the model fits the noise in the data rather than the underlying patterns. Consequently, this could lead to poorer performance when applied to unseen data, diminishing its predictive utility.

Table 15 In-sample mean absolute errors

	LLF	RF	GARCH (1,1)	GJR-GARCH	HAR-RV
Bitcoin (BTC)	0.230	**0.218**	1.073	1.074	1.182
Ethereum (ETH)	**0.246**	0.309	1.419	1.427	1.452
Tether (USDT)	0.118	**0.067**	0.295	0.295	0.261
Binance Coin (BNB)	**0.233**	0.294	1.334	1.336	1.672
Bitcoin Cash (BCH)	**0.213**	0.435	1.897	1.903	1.772
Litecoin (LTC)	**0.274**	0.379	1.849	1.848	1.963
Internet Computer (ICP)	**0.079**	0.617	3.188	3.188	2.568
Polygon (MATIC)	**0.306**	0.426	2.408	2.408	2.206

Notes: The predictions are made over the entire period of August 1, 2021–June 1, 2024. The lowest MAEs are highlighted in bold for each currency.

Table 16 In-sample QLIKE

	LLF	RF	GARCH (1,1)	GJR-GARCH	HAR-RV
Bitcoin (BTC)	0.035	**0.007**	0.210	0.210	0.286
Ethereum (ETH)	**0.008**	**0.008**	0.259	0.260	0.273
Tether (USDT)	0.090	**0.018**	0.256	0.256	0.450
Binance Coin (BNB)	0.009	**0.008**	0.257	0.258	0.546
Bitcoin Cash (BCH)	**0.005**	0.011	0.340	0.344	0.279
Litecoin (LTC)	**0.007**	0.008	0.337	0.337	0.424
Internet Computer (ICP)	**0.001**	0.011	0.583	0.583	0.313
Polygon (MATIC)	**0.007**	**0.007**	0.409	0.409	0.326

Notes: The predictions are made over the entire period of August 1, 2021–June 1, 2024. The lowest QLIKEs are highlighted in bold for each currency.

Table 17 GARCH parameter estimates

	μ	ω	α	β
Bitcoin (BTC)	0.103	1.095	0.127	0.748
Ethereum (ETH)	0.120	0.419	0.083	0.886
Tether (USDT)	−0.009	0.020	0.066	0.841
Binance Coin (BNB)	0.087	0.412	0.157	0.823
Bitcoin Cash (BCH)	−0.171	5.757	0.448	0.367
Litecoin (LTC)	−0.026	0.951	0.115	0.835
Internet Computer (ICP)	−0.130	0.803	0.119	0.858
Polygon (MATIC)	−0.009	0.853	0.132	0.843

Notes: The parameters are estimated using the full data sample (August 1, 2021–June 1, 2024).

Table 18 GJR-GARCH parameter estimates

	μ	ω	α	γ	β
Bitcoin (BTC)	0.074	0.969	0.062	0.099	0.777
Ethereum (ETH)	0.116	0.709	0.069	0.063	0.845
Tether (USDT)	−0.008	0.021	0.074	−0.012	0.833
Binance Coin (BNB)	0.076	0.463	0.145	0.040	0.812
Bitcoin Cash (BCH)	−0.07	5.953	0.584	−0.312	0.365
Litecoin (LTC)	−0.002	0.902	0.136	−0.040	0.839
Internet Computer (ICP)	−0.086	0.850	0.144	−0.041	0.853
Polygon (MATIC)	−0.005	0.847	0.134	−0.005	0.843

Notes: The parameters are estimated using the full data sample (August 1, 2021–June 1, 2024).

In contrast, models such as RF and GARCH variants exhibit higher in-sample RMSE values but may offer more robust and reliable forecasts out-of-sample. Therefore, we must perform an out-of-sample assessment to truly see whether LLF's performance is superior to the other models.

F. GARCH and GJR-GARCH parameters

G. Feature Importance

The feature importances for LLF of the remaining cryptocurrencies can be found in Figs. 2, 3, 4, 5, 6, 7, and 8.

H. Market Cycles

As illustrated in Table 19, Tether (USDT) presents a distinct pattern in market behavior compared to other cryptocurrencies analyzed, as it does not exhibit traditional market cycles. This unique characteristic stems from Tether's fundamental nature as a stablecoin. The absence of observations in the bullish and bearish phases reflects its stable valuation and its exclusion from typical market cycle analyses. Therefore, from this point onward in our analysis, Tether is intentionally excluded from further consideration in the market cycle analysis (Table 20). This decision acknowledges Tether's unique role as a stablecoin and recognizes that its stable valuation stands apart from the speculative price dynamics observed in other cryptocurrencies. For the remaining cryptocurrencies, the results of the market cycle analysis can be found in Tables 21, 22, 23, 24, 25, and 26. Furthermore, we evaluate LLF's performance using the MCSR in each phase separately, based on the RMSE, as shown in Table 20.

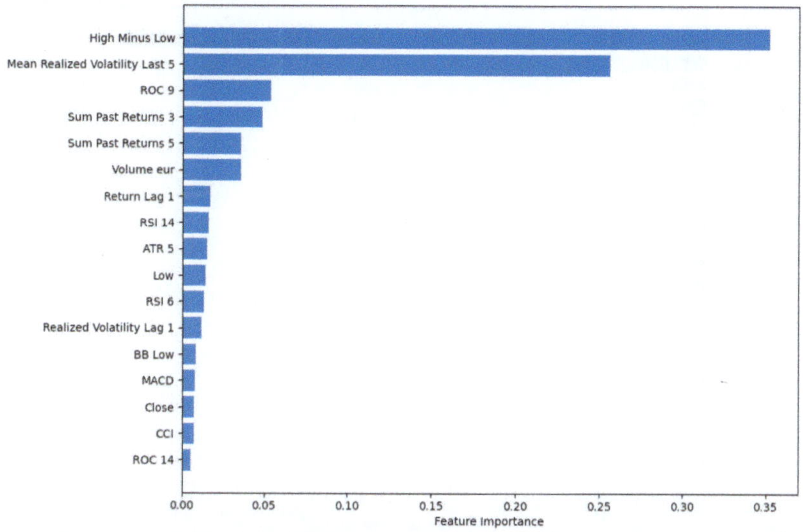

Notes: For brevity and clarity, only the features are included with feature importance greater than 0.5%.

Fig. 2 Ethereum feature importance for Local Linear Forests. *Notes:* For brevity and clarity, only the features are included with feature importance greater than 0.5%

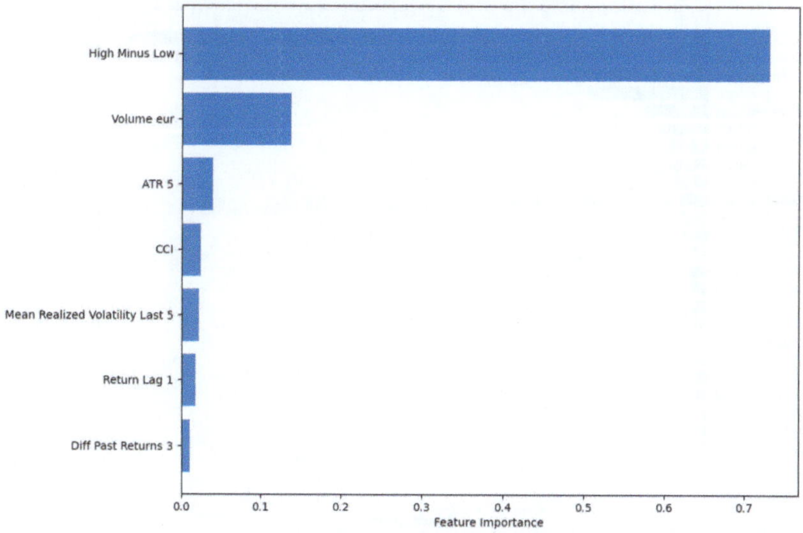

Notes: For brevity and clarity, only the features are included with feature importance greater than 0.5%.

Fig. 3 Tether feature importance for Local Linear Forests. *Notes:* For brevity and clarity, only the features are included with feature importance greater than 0.5%

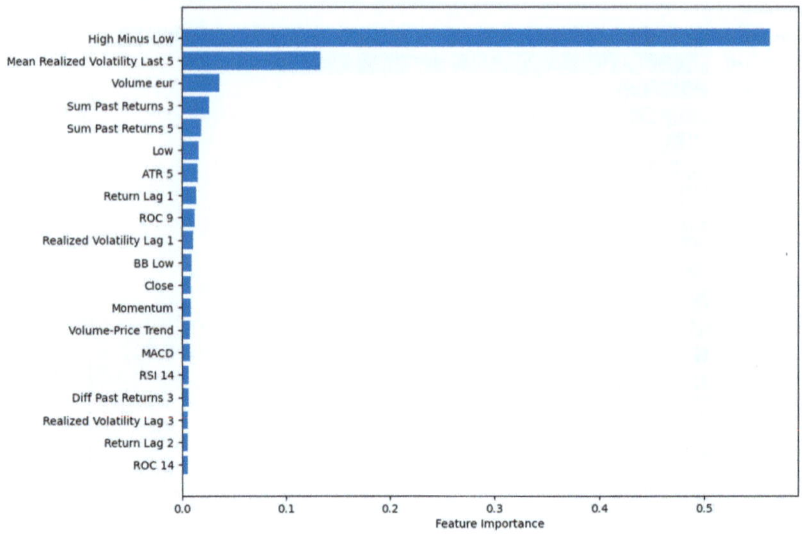

Notes: For brevity and clarity, only the features are included with feature importance greater than 0.5%.

Fig. 4 Binance coin feature importance for Local Linear Forests. *Notes:* For brevity and clarity, only the features are included with feature importance greater than 0.5%

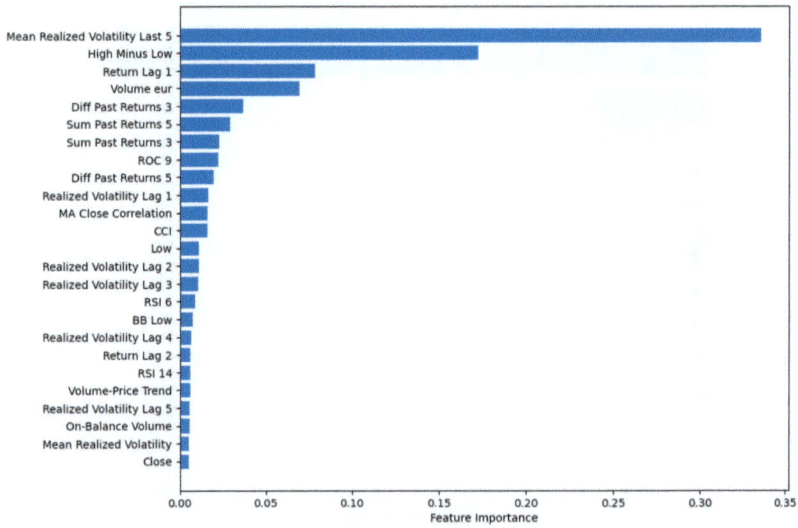

Notes: For brevity and clarity, only the features are included with feature importance greater than 0.5%.

Fig. 5 Bitcoin cash feature importance for Local Linear Forests. *Notes:* For brevity and clarity, only the features are included with feature importance greater than 0.5%

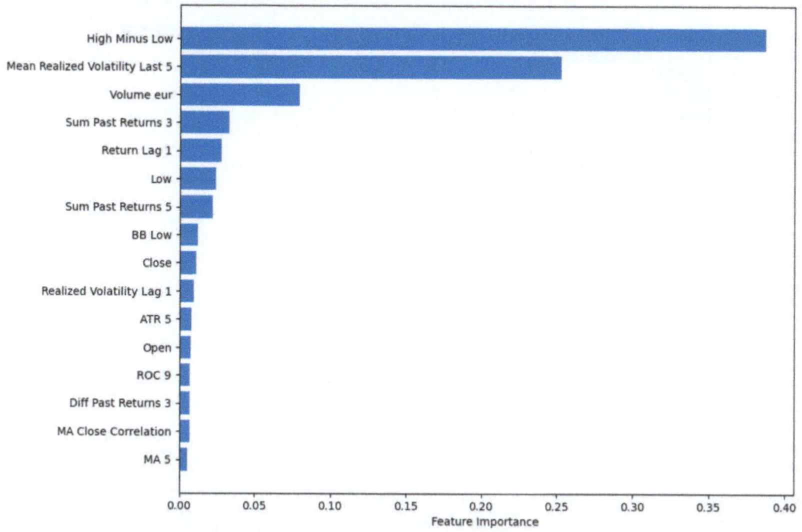

Notes: For brevity and clarity, only the features are included with feature importance greater than 0.5%.

Fig. 6 Litecoin feature importance for Local Linear Forests. *Notes:* For brevity and clarity, only the features are included with feature importance greater than 0.5%

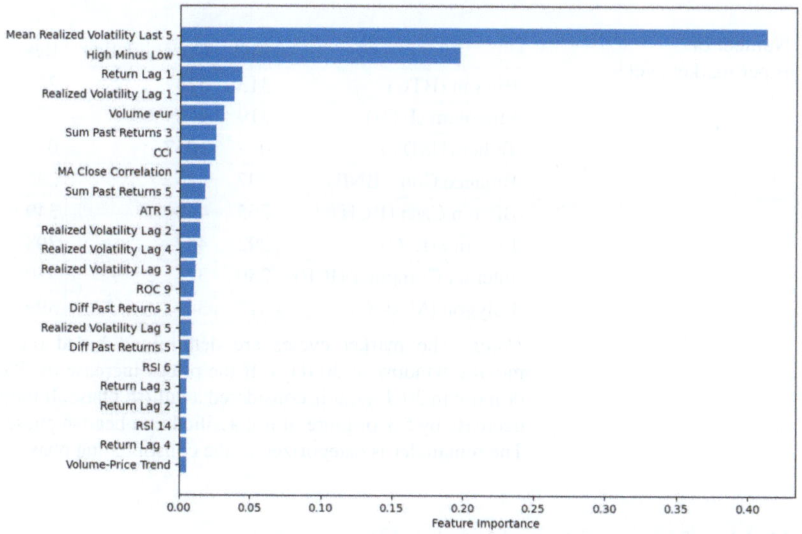

Notes: For brevity and clarity, only the features are included with feature importance greater than 0.5%.

Fig. 7 Internet computer feature importance for Local Linear Forests. *Notes:* For brevity and clarity, only the features are included with feature importance greater than 0.5%

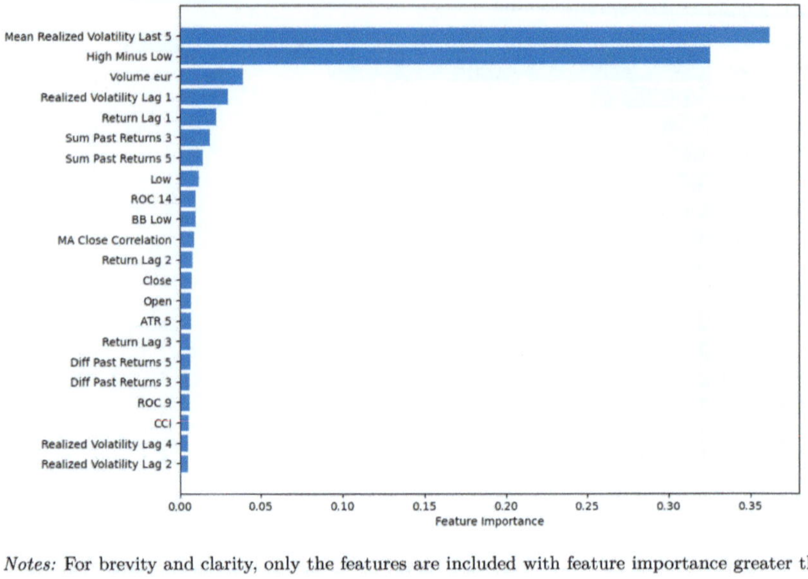

Fig. 8 Polygon feature importance for Local Linear Forests. *Notes:* For brevity and clarity, only the features are included with feature importance greater than 0.5%

Table 19 Number of observations per market cycle per coin

	Bull	Consolidating	Bear
Bitcoin (BTC)	313	524	220
Ethereum (ETH)	319	468	270
Tether (USDT)	0	1057	0
Binance Coin (BNB)	297	525	235
Bitcoin Cash (BCH)	265	443	349
Litecoin (LTC)	292	457	308
Internet Computer (ICP)	280	327	450
Polygon (MATIC)	317	341	399

Notes: The market cycles are determined based on a moving window of 30 days. If the prices increase by 5% or more in 30 days, it is considered a bullish phase. If they decrease by 5% or more, it is classified as a bearish phase. The remainder is categorized as the consolidating phase.

Table 20 Model confidence set rates across market phases

	LLF	RF	GARCH (1,1)	GJR-GARCH	HAR-RV
Bear	**1.000**	0.571	0.000	0.000	0.000
Consolidating	**1.000**	0.429	0.000	0.000	0.000
Bull	**1.000**	0.571	0.000	0.000	0.000

Notes: MCSRs at $\alpha = 0.1$ are noted for each of the market phases, based on the RMSE. The highest MCSRs are highlighted in bold for each currency.

Table 21 Statistical summary of squared forecast errors across market cycles for Ethereum

		LLF	RF	GARCH (1,1)	GJR-GARCH	HAR-RV
Mean *(SD)*	Bear	**0.056**	0.315	2.599	2.691	2.639
		(0.08)	*(0.53)*	*(4.85)*	*(4.79)*	*(5.64)*
	Consolidating	**0.057**	0.227	1.203	1.216	0.789
		(0.08)	*(0.47)*	*(1.46)*	*(1.35)*	*(1.33)*
	Bull	**0.085**	1.115	3.336	3.250	3.250
		(0.20)	*(5.08)*	*(10.84)*	*(11.29)*	*(11.05)*
Kruskal–Wallis	H-statistic	2.27	11.09	3.32	4.67	12.50
	P-value	0.32	0.004*	0.190	0.097	0.002*
Dunn	Bear-Bull	0.673	0.645	0.954	0.122	1.000
	Bear-Consolidating	1.000	0.618	0.226	0.152	0.009*
	Bull-Consolidating	0.533	0.003*	1.000	1.000	0.020*

Notes: For Dunn's test, the test statistic is noted. Significance at the $\alpha = 0.05$ level is indicated by an asterisk (*). The lowest mean squared forecast errors are highlighted in bold.

Table 22 Statistical summary of squared forecast errors across market cycles for Binance coin

		LLF	RF	GARCH (1,1)	GJR-GARCH	HAR-RV
Mean *(SD)*	Bear	**0.441**	0.601	4.470	4.733	3.945
		(1.39)	*(2.29)*	*(12.44)*	*(12.44)*	*(11.75)*
	Consolidating	**0.289**	0.291	1.325	1.466	1.261
		(0.82)	*(0.68)*	*(3.30)*	*(3.45)*	*(3.38)*
	Bull	**0.737**	1.001	3.025	2.957	3.161
		(1.59)	*(3.59)*	*(10.32)*	*(10.48)*	*(10.92)*
Kruskal–Wallis	H-statistic	14.52	7.48	6.52	8.455	12.57
	P-value	7.0e-04*	0.024*	0.038*	0.015*	0.002*
Dunn	Bear-Bull	0.486	0.127	0.793	0.078	1.000
	Bear-Consolidating	1.000	1.000	0.089	0.012*	0.256
	Bull-Consolidating	4.2e-04*	0.047*	0.227	0.959	0.002*

Notes: For Dunn's test, the test statistic is noted. Significance at the $\alpha = 0.05$ level is indicated by an asterisk (*). The lowest mean squared forecast errors are highlighted in bold.

We observe that Local Linear Forests always belong to the superior models for each cryptocurrency (excluding Tether), across all phases in the market cycle. Random Forests are part of the MCS about half of the time, and therefore LLF is the only consistently good choice. Just like in our other analyses, the GARCH-type and HAR-RV models are unable to match the performance of the ensemble methods.

Table 23 Statistical summary of squared forecast errors across market cycles for Bitcoin cash

		LLF	RF	GARCH (1,1)	GJR-GARCH	HAR-RV
Mean *(SD)*	Bear	**0.530**	0.882	2.941	3.019	3.384
		(0.64)	*(1.70)*	*(4.665)*	*(4.93)*	*(9.00)*
	Consolidating	**0.419**	1.027	3.435	3.568	3.348
		(0.64)	*(2.75)*	*(7.20)*	*(7.58)*	*(8.87)*
	Bull	**0.735**	2.504	17.429	21.399	7.489
		(1.37)	*(6.89)*	*(87.96)*	*(119.79)*	*(21.50)*
Kruskal–Wallis	H-statistic	5.41	21.37	3.89	3.23	20.76
	P-value	0.066	2.3e-05*	0.143	0.198	3.1e-05*
Dunn	Bear-Bull	1.000	0.065	0.504	0.668	8.2e-04*
	Bear-Consolidating	0.341	0.226	1.000	1.000	1.000
	Bull-Consolidating	0.082	1.1e-05*	0.175	0.246	1.1e-04*

Notes: For Dunn's test, the test statistic is noted. Significance at the $\alpha = 0.05$ level is indicated by an asterisk (*). The lowest mean squared forecast errors are highlighted in bold.

Table 24 Statistical summary of squared forecast errors across market cycles for Litecoin

		LLF	RF	GARCH (1,1)	GJR-GARCH	HAR-RV
Mean *(SD)*	Bear	**0.449**	1.128	5.593	5.621	6.172
		(1.07)	*(4.48)*	*(15.04)*	*(15.03)*	*(21.22)*
	Consolidating	**0.241**	0.276	1.829	1.833	1.316
		(0.41)	*(0.47)*	*(1.59)*	*(1.59)*	*(2.01)*
	Bull	**0.622**	1.874	5.239	5.303	5.986
		(0.91)	*(6.10)*	*(14.91)*	*(14.54)*	*(12.32)*
Kruskal–Wallis	H-statistic	10.16	12.51	12.86	12.79	17.42
	P-value	0.006*	0.002*	0.002*	0.002*	1.6e-04*
Dunn	Bear-Bull	0.412	0.029*	0.062	0.105	1.000
	Bear-Consolidating	0.354	1.000	0.001*	0.001*	0.002*
	Bull-Consolidating	0.006*	0.001*	1.000	1.000	0.002*

Notes: For Dunn's test, the test statistic is noted. Significance at the $\alpha = 0.05$ level is indicated by an asterisk (*). The lowest mean squared forecast errors are highlighted in bold.

Table 25 Statistical summary of squared forecast errors across market cycles for Internet computer

		LLF	RF	GARCH (1,1)	GJR-GARCH	HAR-RV
Mean *(SD)*	Bear	**0.424**	1.550	4.218	4.386	4.115
		(1.03)	*(3.00)*	*(9.46)*	*(9.78)*	*(9.30)*
	Consolidating	**0.400**	1.304	2.321	2.394	2.276
		(1.04)	*(3.37)*	*(5.74)*	*(5.79)*	*(6.05)*
	Bull	**0.632**	6.629	12.269	12.765	11.653
		(1.46)	*(27.14)*	*(55.11)*	*(54.59)*	*(46.84)*
Kruskal–Wallis	H-statistic	4.75	8.21	9.44	7.98	14.87
	P-value	0.093	0.016*	0.009*	0.018*	5.9e-04*
Dunn	Bear-Bull	1.000	0.182	0.333	0.500	0.175
	Bear-Consolidating	0.745	1.000	0.617	0.635	0.267
	Bull-Consolidating	0.088	0.016*	0.007*	0.014*	3.5e-04*

Notes: For Dunn's test, the test statistic is noted. Significance at the $\alpha = 0.05$ level is indicated by an asterisk (*). The lowest mean squared forecast errors are highlighted in bold.

Table 26 Statistical summary of squared forecast errors across market cycles for polygon

		LLF	RF	GARCH (1,1)	GJR-GARCH	HAR-RV
Mean *(SD)*	Bear	**0.623**	0.753	3.444	3.462	3.360
		(1.35)	*(1.79)*	*(7.50)*	*(7.64)*	*(8.96)*
	Consolidating	0.526	**0.499**	2.830	2.648	1.823
		(1.08)	*(1.15)*	*(3.78)*	*(3.77)*	*(3.81)*
	Bull	**0.851**	1.335	3.282	3.256	4.194
		(1.74)	*(4.34)*	*(12.28)*	*(12.15)*	*(11.02)*
Kruskal–Wallis	H-statistic	5.44	13.91	5.86	6.06	9.25
	P-value	0.066	9.5e-04*	0.053	0.048*	0.009*
Dunn	Bear-Bull	0.532	0.359	0.089	0.077	1.000
	Bear-Consolidating	0.962	0.086	1.000	1.000	0.045*
	Bull-Consolidating	0.059	6.9e-04*	0.109	0.105*	0.019*

Notes: For Dunn's test, the test statistic is noted. Significance at the $\alpha = 0.05$ level is indicated by an asterisk (*). The lowest mean squared forecast errors are highlighted in bold.

References

Aibai A, Julaiti J, Gou S (2024). The asymmetric effects of upside and downside risks in cryptocurrency markets: Insights from the luna and ftx crises. Financ Res Lett 67:105750.

Akyildirim E, Goncu A, Sensoy A (2021). Prediction of cryptocurrency returns using machine learning. Ann Oper Res 297:3–36

Almeida J Gonçalves TC (2024) Cryptocurrency market microstructure: a systematic literature review. *Ann Oper Res* 332(1):1035–1068

Andersen TG, Bollerslev T, Diebold FX, Labys P (2003) Modeling and forecasting realized volatility. Econometrica 71(2):579–625

Behrendt S (2021) Structural breaks in box-cox transforms of realized volatility: a model selection perspective. Quant Financ 21(11):1905–1919

Bianchi D (2020) Cryptocurrencies as an asset class? An empirical assessment. J Altern Invest 23(2):162–179
Bollerslev T (1986) Generalized autoregressive conditional heteroskedasticity. J Econ 31(3):307–327
Bollerslev T, Hood B, Huss J, Pedersen LH (2018) Risk everywhere: modeling and managing volatility. Rev Financ Stud 31(7):2729–2773
Bouri E, Gkillas K, Gupta R, Pierdzioch C (2021) Forecasting realized volatility of bitcoin: the role of the trade war. Comput Econ 57:29–53
Bouri E, Kristoufek L, Ahmad T, Shahzad SJH (2024) Microstructure noise and idiosyncratic volatility anomalies in cryptocurrencies. Ann Oper Res 334(1):547–573
Cajueiro DO Tabak BM (2005) Testing for time-varying long-range dependence in volatility for emerging markets. Physica A Stat Mech Appl 346(3-4):577–588
Catania L Grassi S (2017) Modelling crypto-currencies financial time-series. Available at SSRN 3028486
Chen M-Y (2011) Predicting corporate financial distress based on integration of decision tree classification and logistic regression. Expert Syst Appl 38(9):11261–11272
Chen W, Zhang H, Mehlawat MK, Jia L (2021) Mean–variance portfolio optimization using machine learning-based stock price prediction. Appl Soft Comput 100:106943
Christensen TM, Hurn AS, Lindsay KA (2012) Forecasting spikes in electricity prices. Int J Forecast 28(2):400–411
Cootner PH (1964) The random character of stock market prices. MIT Press, Cambridge, MA.
Corsi F (2009) A simple approximate long-memory model of realized volatility. J Financ Economet 7(2):174–196
Daian P, Goldfeder S, Kell T, Li Y, Zhao X, Bentov I, et al (2020) Flash boys 2.0: Frontrunning in decentralized exchanges, miner extractable value, and consensus instability. In: 2020 IEEE Symposium on Security and Privacy (SP), pp 910–927
D'Amato V, Levantesi S, Piscopo G (2022) Deep learning in predicting cryptocurrency volatility. Physica A Stat Mech Appl 596:127158
Dunn OJ (1964) Multiple comparisons using rank sums. Technometrics 6(3):241–252
Easley D O'Hara M (2003) Microstructure and asset pricing. Handb Econ Financ 1:1021–1051
ElBahrawy A, Alessandretti L, Kandler A, Pastor-Satorras R, Baronchelli A (2017) Evolutionary dynamics of the cryptocurrency market. R Soc Open Sci 4(11):170623
Engle RF (1982) Autoregressive conditional heteroscedasticity with estimates of the variance of United Kingdom inflation. Econometrica 50(4):987–1007
Fink C Johann T (2014). Bitcoin markets. Available at SSRN 2408396
Friedberg R, Tibshirani J, Athey S, Wager S (2020) Local linear forests. J Comput Graph Stat 30(2):503–517
Friedman JH (1991) Multivariate adaptive regression splines. Ann Stat 19(1):1–67
Glosten LR, Jagannathan R, Runkle DE (1993). On the relation between the expected value and the volatility of the nominal excess return on stocks. J Financ 48(5):1779–1801
Granger CW Pesaran MH (2000) Economic and statistical measures of forecast accuracy. J Forecast 19(7):537–560
Griffin JM Shams A (2020) Is bitcoin really untethered? J Financ 75(4):1913–1964
Grossman SJ Stiglitz JE (1980) On the impossibility of informationally efficient markets. Am Econ Rev 70(3);393–408
Hansen PR, Lunde A, Nason JM (2011) The model confidence set. Econometrica 79(2):453–497
Jebabli I Roubaud D (2018) Time-varying efficiency in food and energy markets: evidence and implications. Econ Model 70:97–114
Karimi P, Ghazani MM, Ebrahimi SB (2023) Analyzing spillover effects of selected cryptocurrencies on gold and brent crude oil under COVID-19 pandemic: evidence from GJR-garch and EVT copula methods. Res Policy 85:103887
Katsiampa P, Corbet S, Lucey B (2019) High frequency volatility co-movements in cryptocurrency markets. J Int Financ Mark Inst Money 62:35–52

Kim J-M., Jun C, Lee J (2021) Forecasting the volatility of the cryptocurrency market by garch and stochastic volatility. Mathematics 9(14):1614

Kleen O Tetereva A (2022) A forest full of risk forecasts for managing volatility. Available at SSRN 4161957

Kristoufek L (2021) Tethered, or untethered? on the interplay between stablecoins and major cryptoassets. Financ Res Lett 43:101991

Kruskal WH Wallis WA (1952) Use of ranks in one-criterion variance analysis. J Am Stat Assoc 47(260):583–621

Kurihara Y Fukushima A (2017) The market efficiency of bitcoin: a weekly anomaly perspective. J Appl Financ Banking 7(3):57

Laurent S, Rombouts JV, Violante F (2013) On loss functions and ranking forecasting performances of multivariate volatility models. J Econ 173(1):1–10

Liu LY, Patton AJ, Sheppard K (2015) Does anything beat 5-minute rv? a comparison of realized measures across multiple asset classes. J Econ 187(1):293–311

Liu Q, Yao Q, Zhao G (2020) Model averaging estimation for conditional volatility models with an application to stock market volatility forecast. J Forecast 39(5):841–863

Liu Y, Li Z, Nekhili R, Sultan J (2023) Forecasting cryptocurrency returns with machine learning. Res Int Bus Financ 64:101905

Lo A (2017) Adaptive markets: financial evolution at the speed of thought. Princeton University, Princeton

Long W, Lu Z, Cui L (2019) Deep learning-based feature engineering for stock price movement prediction. Knowl-Based Syst 164:163–173

Ma F, Liang C, Ma Y, Wahab MIM (2020) Cryptocurrency volatility forecasting: a markov regime-switching midas approach. J Forecast 39(8):1277–1290

Mostafa F, Saha P, Islam MR, Nguyen N (2021) GJR-GARCH volatility modeling under NIG and ANN for predicting top cryptocurrencies. J Risk Financ Manag 14(9):421

Naimy V, Haddad O, Fernández-Avilés G, El Khoury R (2021). The predictive capacity of garch-type models in measuring the volatility of crypto and world currencies. PloS One 16(1):e0245904

Patton AJ (2011) Volatility forecast comparison using imperfect volatility proxies. J Econ 160(1):246–256

Pesaran MH, Schleicher C, Zaffaroni P (2009). Model averaging in risk management with an application to futures markets. J Empir Financ 16(2):280–305

Poongodi M, Nguyen TN, Hamdi M, Cengiz K (2021). Global cryptocurrency trend prediction using social media. Inf Process Manag 58(6):102708

Qiu Y, Wang Z, Xie T, Zhang X (2021) Forecasting bitcoin realized volatility by exploiting measurement error under model uncertainty. J Empir Financ 62:179–201

Rudin C (2019) Stop explaining black box machine learning models for high stakes decisions and use interpretable models instead. Nat Mach Intell 1(5):206–215

Sakariyahu R, Lawal R, Adigun R, Paterson A, Johan S (2024) One crash, too many: global uncertainty, sentiment factors and cryptocurrency market. J Int Financ Mark Inst Money 94:102028

Siu TK (2023) Bayesian nonlinear expectation for time series modelling and its application to bitcoin. Empir Econ 64(1):505–537

Tirkishova M (2023) Modelling and Forecasting Oil Market Volatility: A Regime Switching Garch Midas Approach (Unpublished doctoral dissertation). Keele University, Keele

Trucíos C Taylor JW (2023) A comparison of methods for forecasting value at risk and expected shortfall of cryptocurrencies. J Forecast 42(4):989–1007

VK AK, Chalissery MD, Thomas S (2024) A bibliometric review of market microstructure literature: current status, development, and future directions. Financ Res Lett 69:106086

Wang W (2007) An adaptive predictor for dynamic system forecasting. Mech Syst Signal Process 21(2):809–823

Wang Y, Andreeva G, Martin-Barragan B (2023) Machine learning approaches to forecasting cryptocurrency volatility: considering internal and external determinants. Int Rev. Financ Anal 90:102914

Zhu M, Philpotts D, Stevenson MJ (2012) The benefits of tree-based models for stock selection. J Asset Manag13(6):437–448

Fee Structure and Order Flow Informativeness in the Cryptocurrency Market

Christian Bozzetto, Imtiaz Sifat, and Narmin Nahidi

Abstract We exploit Binance's shift from zero-fee to commission-based trading in March 2023 as a natural experiment to examine how fee structures affect order flow informativeness in cryptocurrency markets. Using high-frequency order book data for the BTC/USDT pair, we find that the explanatory power of order flow imbalances for price changes increased significantly after fee implementation, from 5% to 21.55% R^2. The results suggest that zero trading fees may reduce price efficiency by diluting order flow information content. Our findings inform optimal market design for digital asset exchanges and demonstrate how trading costs influence the strategic behavior of market participants.

Keywords Cryptocurrency markets · Trading fees · Market microstructure · Order flow · Price efficiency · Digital assets · Exchange design · Information asymmetry

JEL Classification: G12, G14, G15, E44

1 Introduction

The efficiency of price discovery remains a central question in market microstructure, especially as technological advances reshape trading costs. While theory

C. Bozzetto
Intesa Sanpaolo Bank, Montebelluna, Italy

I. Sifat
Institute for Management Research, Radboud University, Nijmegen, Netherlands
e-mail: imtiaz.sifat@ru.nl

N. Nahidi (✉)
Business School, University of Exeter, Exeter, UK
e-mail: N.nahidi@exeter.ac.uk

N. Nahidi, A. Zarifis (eds.), *AI, FinTech, and the Future of Robo-Advisory*, Contributions to Finance and Accounting,
https://doi.org/10.1007/978-3-032-18109-1_13

suggests lower trading costs improve price efficiency by reducing frictions, emergent cryptocurrency markets challenge this conventional wisdom by introducing zero-fee trading. This creates a fundamental tension: do zero trading costs enhance market quality by eliminating frictions or degrade it by enabling noise trading? This question is salient for three reasons. First, as digital asset markets mature, their market design choices will shape trillions in global capital flows (He et al. 2022; Sifat 2021). Second, traditional microstructure theories were developed for markets with positive trading costs; their applicability to zero-fee environments remains untested (Di Maggio et al. 2020). Third, understanding how fee structures affect information transmission can inform optimal market design across both traditional and cryptocurrency markets (Brauneis et al. 2022). We exploit a unique natural experiment to address this question: Binance's sudden shift from zero-fee to commission-based trading for Bitcoin in March 2023. This event provides a clean identification of how trading costs influence price formation through three key advantages. First, the change was exogenous to market conditions and announced with minimal advance notice, mitigating anticipatory trading. Second, as the world's largest cryptocurrency exchange by volume, Binance's policy affected approximately 50% of global Bitcoin spot trading, ensuring economic significance. Market fragmentation, as evidenced by the coexistence of multiple order books, further complicates price discovery in cryptocurrency markets (Jeon et al. 2021). Third, our millisecond-level order book data allow precise measurement of changes in order flow dynamics.

Our analysis reveals that zero trading fees can paradoxically reduce market efficiency by degrading order flow informativeness. When Binance implemented trading fees, the explanatory power of order flow imbalances for price changes increased from 5% to over 21%. This suggests trading costs act as a crucial screening mechanism, filtering out uninformative orders and improving the signal-to-noise ratio in price discovery. These findings add another dimension to established microstructure models and contemporary market design choices. While well-known theories emphasize how trading costs impede information transmission, we demonstrate their role in screening informed from uninformed order flow. This has immediate implications for exchange operators weighing zero-fee models, regulators considering market structure reforms, and traders developing order flow strategies.

We make two contributions. First, we provide novel evidence on the non-monotonic relationship between trading costs and market efficiency. While prior work examines marginal changes in trading costs, we offer the first analysis of a transition from zero to positive fees. Second, we demonstrate how fee structures influence the strategic behavior of informed and uninformed traders, extending market microstructure theory to zero-fee environments.

2 Literature Review and Hypotheses Development

Our study connects two streams of literature: order flow informativeness and the impact of trading costs on market quality. Research on order flow imbalances shows they significantly predict short-term price movements in equity markets (Cont et al. 2014) and cryptocurrency markets. These studies find trade flow imbalances (TFI) typically have higher predictive power than order flow imbalances (OFI), suggesting market orders contain more information than limit orders (Cont et al. 2014). The literature on trading costs examines how fee structures affect trader behavior and market quality. Reduced trading costs generally improve liquidity and price efficiency (Chordia et al., 2008). However, evidence from cryptocurrency markets suggests that zero-fee trading may have unintended consequences. Researchers document reduced weekend trading activity despite zero fees, while Jha et al. (2020) find persistent order book imbalances indicating potential market inefficiencies (Jha et al. 2020). Drawing on this literature, we develop two hypotheses:

H1: The shift from zero-fee to commission-based trading increases the explanatory power of order flow imbalances for price changes.

H2: Trade flow imbalances maintain higher explanatory power than order flow imbalances under both fee structures.

The rationale for H1 is that positive trading fees act as a filtering mechanism, making order submission more costly and thus more likely to reflect genuine information. H2 follows from prior evidence that market orders consistently contain more information than limit orders across different market structures.

3 Data and Methodology

3.1 Data

We analyze order book data for the BTC/USDT pair from Binance between July 31st, 2022, and July 31st, 2023. The sample period spans Binance's March 22nd, 2023, transition from zero-fee to commission-based trading. Our dataset contains nanosecond-level order book states, including best bid/ask prices and sizes up to 20 levels deep. For trade flow analysis, we use executed trade data from March 15th to July 31st, 2023.

Figure 1 shows the 1-second dynamics of BTC/USDT best bid, best ask, and mid-price during the initial minutes of July 30, 2022. The average spread for the month of July was 0.989 USDT, highlighting the tight liquidity conditions in the market.

Figure 2 shows the mean hourly bid–ask spread for BTC/USDT from July 31, 2022, to July 31, 2023. Key market events are highlighted, including the FTX collapse in November 2022 and Binance's announcement to end zero-fee trading

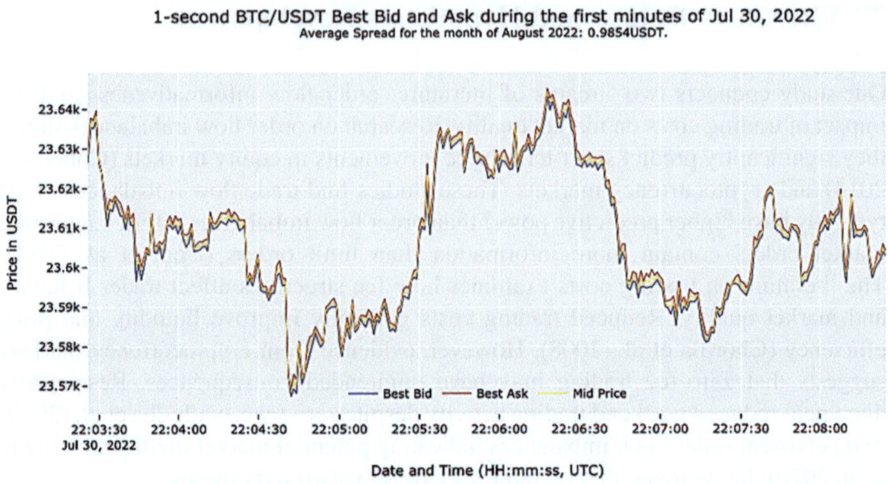

Fig. 1 Intraday dynamics of BTC/USDT best bid, ask, and mid-price. Figure 1 illustrates 1-second BTC/USDT bid, ask, and mid-price dynamics on July 30, 2022, with an average July spread of 0.989 USDT, reflecting tight liquidity

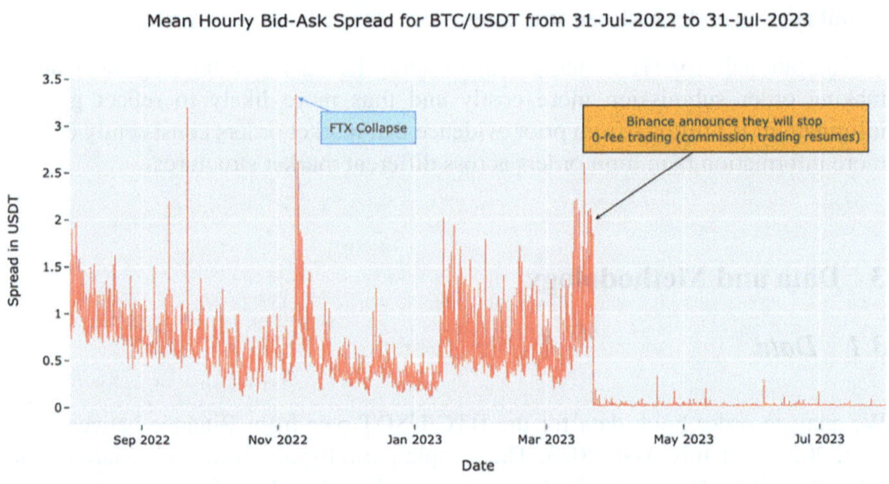

Fig. 2 Mean hourly bid–ask spread for BTC/USDT. Figure 2 presents the mean hourly bid–ask spread for BTC/USDT from July 31, 2022, to July 31, 2023, highlighting key events like the FTX collapse and Binance's fee policy change. It shows the spread's sensitivity to market disruptions and liquidity shifts

in March 2023. The figure illustrates the spread's sensitivity to major market disruptions and policy changes, reflecting variations in market liquidity.

Figure 3 displays the hourly dynamics of BTC/USDT order book contributions and order flow imbalance (OFI) from July 2022 to July 2023. The top panel illustrates the average hourly contribution of order book events to the order book

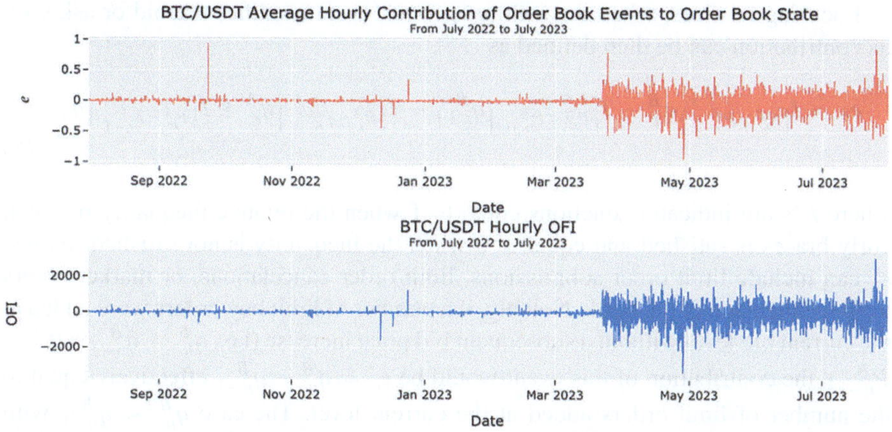

Fig. 3 BTC/USDT hourly order book dynamics: contribution of events and OFI. Figure 3 shows hourly BTC/USDT order book contributions and OFI from July 2022 to July 2023. The top panel highlights increased volatility post-March 2023, while the bottom panel reflects shifts in market activity following Binance's fee change, emphasizing evolving order flow dynamics

state, highlighting increased volatility post-March 2023. The bottom panel shows hourly OFI, reflecting notable shifts in market activity, particularly after Binance's fee structure change in March 2023. These trends emphasize the evolving nature of order flow and market structure over time.

3.2 *Order Flow Measures*

Cont et al. (2014) propose a stylized analytical description of order flow imbalances, describing the bid price P_n^B and bid size[1] q_n^B as measures of demand and the ask price P_n^A and ask size q_n^A as measures of supply, where n indicates the current observation in time. A "level-1" order book state (i.e., looking at only one price level) at observation n would then be represented by the quadruple $\left(P_n^B, q_n^B, P_n^A, q_n^A\right)$. If one were to compare the current single-level order book state $\left(P_n^B, q_n^B, P_n^A, q_n^A\right)$ with the immediately preceding state $\left(P_{n-1}^B, q_{n-1}^B, P_{n-1}^A, q_{n-1}^A\right)$, only a set number of events can occur:

- Either $P_n^B > P_{n-1}^B$ or $q_n^B > q_{n-1}^B$ representing an increase in demand
- Either $P_n^B < P_{n-1}^B$ or $q_n^B < q_{n-1}^B$ representing a decrease in demand
- Either $P_n^A < P_{n-1}^A$ or $q_n^A > q_{n-1}^A$ representing an increase in supply
- Either $P_n^A > P_{n-1}^A$ or $q_n^A < q_{n-1}^A$ representing a decrease in supply

[1] *Bid (ask) size is the number of limit buy (sell) orders resting at a given price level, waiting to be filled.*

Focusing on sizes, when the n-th order book event modifies the bid or ask size, its contribution can be then defined as

$$e_n = I_{\{P_n^B \geq P_{n-1}^B\}} q_n^B - I_{\{P_n^B \leq P_{n-1}^B\}} q_{n-1}^B - I_{\{P_n^A \leq P_{n-1}^A\}} q_n^A + I_{\{P_n^A \geq P_{n-1}^A\}} q_{n-1}^A \tag{1}$$

where I 's are indicator functions equal to 1 when the relative inequality between curly braces is satisfied and equal to 0 when the inequality is not satisfied. Events e_n can include limit order submissions, limit order cancelations, or market orders hitting either side of the book. Notably, if a number of limit buy orders were added at the current bid level without a subsequent bid price increase (i.e., $q_n^B > q_{n-1}^B \wedge P_n^B = P_{n-1}^B$), the contribution of this event would be $e_n = q_n^B - q_{n-1}^B$ effectively equal to the number of limit orders added at the current level. The case $q_n^B < q_{n-1}^B$ with $P_n^B = P_{n-1}^B$ can be caused either by the cancelation of buy limit orders already resting at P_{n-1}^B or by market sell orders hitting the bid at P_{n-1}^B. In this case $e_n = q_n^B - q_{n-1}^B$ would be negative and represent the number of units sold at market or the amount of canceled limit buys. Order flow imbalances can be defined as the sum over a set time period $[t, t + \mathrm{k}]$ of all events e. Assuming, for simplicity, that at most one order book event can happen at each time instant t:

$$OFI_k = \sum_{n=t}^{t+k} e_n \tag{2}$$

The resulting imbalance is a net measurement of all the contributions by bid and ask order book events to the current order book state in the specified time interval. Cont et al. demonstrate that order flow imbalances, as defined above, are linearly correlated to price changes in 50 NYSE TAQ stocks.

4 Empirics

We examine how OFI and TFI explain contemporaneous mid-price changes using:

$$\Delta MP_t = \alpha + \beta_1 OFI_t + \beta_2 TFI_t + \varepsilon_t \tag{3}$$

where ΔMPt is the change in mid-price. We estimate this regression separately for pre- and post-fee change periods at 1-second to 1-hour frequencies. To formally test for structural breaks around the fee change, we employ Chow tests. To benchmark traditional econometric approaches against machine learning methods, we also implement an XGBoost model with the same predictors, using a 70/30 train-test split and Bayesian optimization for hyperparameter tuning. This allows us to capture potential non-linear relationships while controlling for overfitting.

5 Results

5.1 Fee Structure Impact on Order Flow Informativeness

The shift from zero-fee to commission-based trading significantly increased order flow informativeness. Tables 1 and 2 form the core of our results, the interpretations and discussion of which are offered in the following paragraphs.

Table 1 summarizes the multiple linear regression results for mid-price changes on OFI and TFI across various time intervals after March 15, 2023. TFI consistently demonstrates higher explanatory power (R^2) than OFI, with the combined model yielding the highest predictive accuracy. All coefficients are statistically significant, highlighting the critical role of trade and order flows in price discovery post-fee implementation.

Table 2 compares the linear regression results of mid-price changes on OFI before and after Binance's fee structure change on March 15, 2023. The explanatory power (R^2) of OFI significantly increased across all time intervals after the fee introduction, with hourly R^2 rising from 5.03% to 11.15%. This indicates that the implementation of trading fees enhanced order flow informativeness, improving price discovery efficiency.

OFI explanatory power for mid-price changes increased substantially across all time frequencies. For hourly data, R^2 rose from 5.03% before the fee change to 11.15% after. The effect is even more pronounced at shorter intervals—the 10-

Table 1 Multiple linear regressions of mid-price changes on OFI and TFI resampling

	Mid-price *After* March 15, 2023							
	OFI				TFI			
	α	β_{OFI}	p-value β_{OFI}	R^2	α	β_{TFI}	p-value β_{TFI}	R^2
1sec	0.6775	17.9619	0.0000	14.14%	0.3598	39.3421	0.0000	23.45%
10sec	7.2019	20.3229	0.0000	26.19%	4.2491	49.7505	0.0000	33.22%
1min	39.5303	18.6759	0.0000	30.69%	25.7922	50.2353	0.0000	37.96%
10min	281.3032	13.5135	0.0000	21.55%	224.1506	44.4374	0.0000	48.55%
1H	1049.6956	8.7653	0.0000	11.15%	1066.6631	36.1475	0.0000	51.78%
	OFI and TFI							
	α	β_{OFI}	β_{TFI}	$p\beta_{OFI}$	$p\beta_{TFI}$	R^2		
1 sec	0.8153	12.8937	33.7395	0.0000	0.0000	30.26%		
10 sec	8.6595	14.4258	39.6030	0.0000	0.0000	45.03%		
1 min	49.1858	13.1909	39.5288	0.0000	0.0000	51.54%		
10 min	383.6885	8.4488	39.1965	0.0000	0.0000	56.30%		
1H	1604.2967	4.5088	34.0852	0.0000	0.0000	54.56%		

Table 1 summarizes the multiple linear regression results for mid-price changes on OFI and TFI across various time intervals after March 15, 2023. TFI consistently demonstrates higher explanatory power (R^2) than OFI, with the combined model yielding the highest predictive accuracy. All coefficients are statistically significant, highlighting the critical role of trade and order flows in price discovery post-fee implementation

Table 2 Linear regression of mid-price changes on OFI, comparison before vs after the fee structure change

	Mid-price regressed on OFI							
	Before March 15, 2023				*After* March 15, 2023			
	α	β_{OFI}	p β_{OFI}	R^2	α	β_{OFI}	p β_{OFI}	R^2
1 sec	0.0221	19.7767	0.0000	1.02%	0.6775	17.9619	0.0000	14.14%
10 sec	0.3461	34.3766	0.0000	2.10%	7.2019	20.3229	0.0000	26.19%
1 min	2.5058	42.7023	0.0000	3.02%	39.5303	18.6759	0.0000	30.69%
10 min	27.8345	48.4102	0.0000	4.04%	281.3032	13.5135	0.0000	21.55%
1H	172.6350	49.8971	0.0004	5.03%	1049.6956	8.7653	0.0000	11.15%

Table 2 compares the linear regression results of mid-price changes on OFI before and after Binance's fee structure change on March 15, 2023. The explanatory power (R^2) of OFI significantly increased across all time intervals after the fee introduction, with hourly R^2 rising from 5.03% to 11.15%. This indicates that the implementation of trading fees enhanced order flow informativeness, improving price discovery efficiency

minute frequency shows R^2 increasing from 4.04% to 21.55%. All coefficients remain statistically significant at the 1% level. This improvement in informativeness occurred despite reduced spreads post-fee implementation, suggesting that trading costs act as an effective filter for order flow quality rather than pure friction.

Trade flow imbalances consistently demonstrate higher explanatory power than order flow imbalances. In the post-fee period, TFI alone explains 51.78% of hourly price changes compared to 11.15% for OFI. The combined model performs best at the 10-minute frequency, with R^2 reaching 56.30%. This hierarchy of informativeness aligns with theoretical predictions market orders require the immediate commitment of capital and, thus, are more likely to reflect genuine information. The fee structure change amplified this effect by increasing the cost of uninformative market orders.

5.2 *Structural Break Analysis*

To validate splitting the time series on March 15th for assessing the relationship between OFIs and mid-price changes, a Chow test is performed. This test examines structural breaks by testing for coefficient equality across regressions on different dataset segments. Absent a structural break, regression coefficients should remain stable. Significant deviations indicate changing data dynamics. The dataset, split on March 15th, undergoes separate regressions for pre- and post-split periods. The null hypothesis two is tested using the F-statistics:

$$F = \frac{\left(\frac{S_C-(S_1+S_2)}{k}\right)}{\left(\frac{S_1+S_2}{(N_1+N_2-2k)}\right)} \sim F_{\{k,N_1+N_2-2k\}} \tag{4}$$

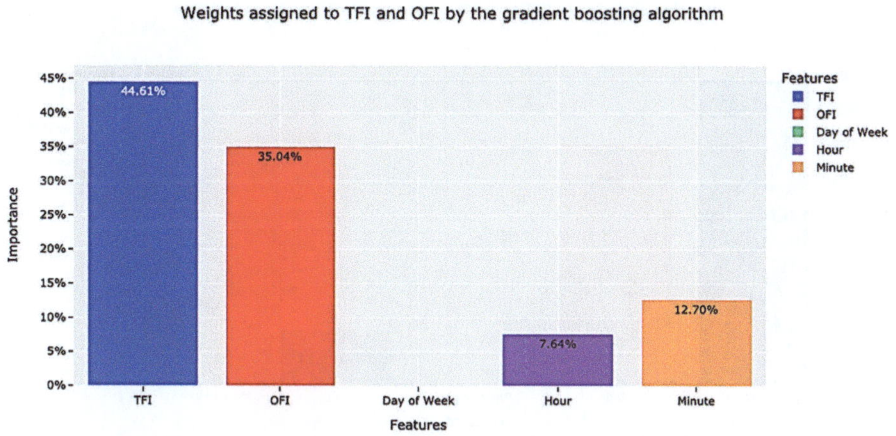

Fig. 4 Feature importance for predicting mid-price changes using gradient boosting. Figure 4 shows feature importance in the gradient boosting model for predicting BTC/USDT mid-price changes. TFI (44.61%) and OFI (35.01%) are the most influential, with temporal features like minute (12.73%) and hour (7.54%) also contributing. Day-of-week effects are negligible, underscoring TFI and OFI's dominance

where S_C is the RSS from the full regression, S_1 and S_2 are RSS from the split regressions, N_1 and N_2 are observations in each segment, and $k = 2$ is the number of parameters. An F-statistic of 1977.61 ($p < 0.01$) strongly rejects the null hypothesis of no structural break, indicating clear evidence of a structural change. Post-March 15th, a significant linear relationship between OFIs and mid-price changes emerges, yet its predictive power for one-step-ahead changes is negligible. This limitation underscores the need to explore autoregressive models if OFIs and TFIs exhibit temporal dependencies. Successfully forecasting these variables could unlock actionable trading strategies. This validates our approach of analyzing pre- and post-fee periods separately and confirms the fee structure's fundamental impact on trading behavior.

5.3 *Machine Learning Robustness Check*

To evaluate the robustness of our findings, we employed machine learning methods to model mid-price changes using order flow and trade flow imbalances (OFI and TFI). XGBoost, a gradient boosting algorithm, was chosen for its ability to capture complex, non-linear relationships in the data. Figures 4, 5 and 6 present the model's feature importance, predictive accuracy, and comparative performance against traditional regression methods.

Figure 4 illustrates the weights assigned to different features by the gradient boosting algorithm for predicting BTC/USDT mid-price changes. Trade flow

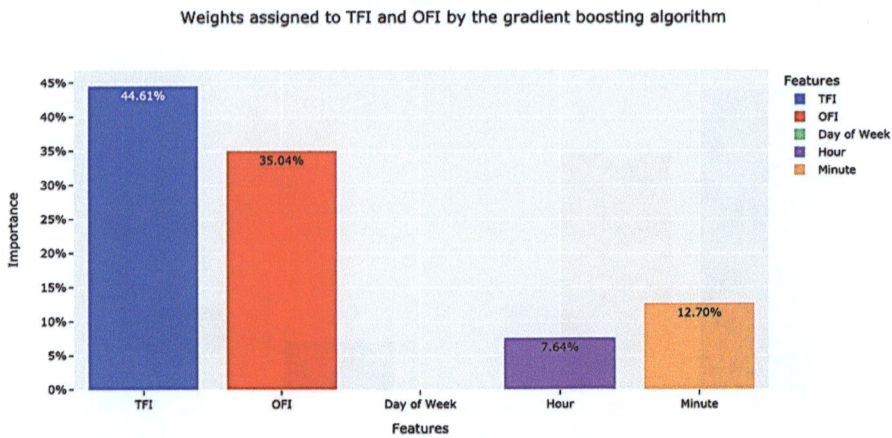

Fig. 5 Feature importance analysis for mid-price predictions. This figure highlights feature importance from the gradient boosting algorithm for predicting BTC/USDT mid-price changes. TFI (44.61%) and OFI (35.01%) are the top contributors, with temporal features like minute (12.73%) and hour (7.54%) adding value, while day-of-week effects are negligible

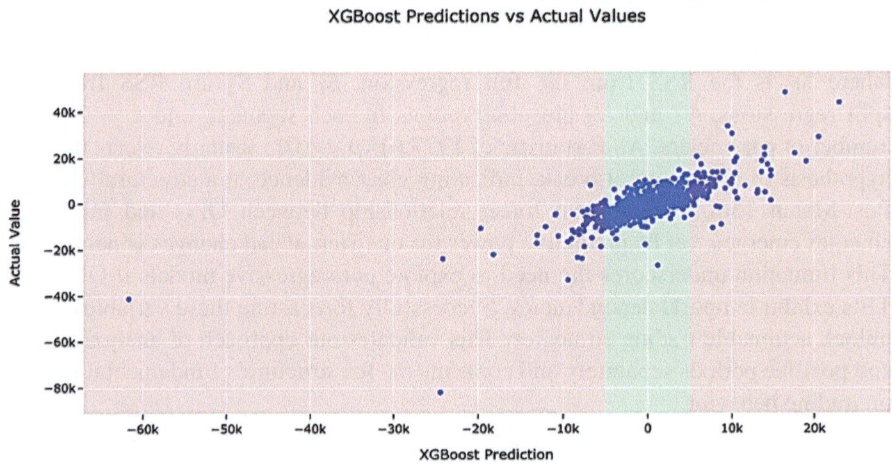

Fig. 6 XGBoost predictions vs. actual values for mid-price changes. This scatter plot compares XGBoost predictions with actual BTC/USDT mid-price changes. Clustering around the diagonal indicates strong accuracy within the ±20k range, while variance in extreme values suggests potential for improvement in capturing outliers

imbalance (TFI) and order flow imbalance (OFI) are the most influential predictors, contributing 44.61% and 35.01%, respectively. Temporal features, including the minute (12.73%) and hour (7.54%), also provide predictive power, while the day of the week has negligible importance. These results highlight the dominance of TFI and OFI in capturing price-relevant information.

This figure showcases the feature importance assigned by the gradient boosting algorithm for predicting BTC/USDT mid-price changes. Trade flow imbalance (TFI) ranks as the most critical feature with 44.61% importance, followed by order flow imbalance (OFI) at 35.01%. Temporal features such as the minute (12.73%) and hour (7.54%) provide additional predictive value, while the day of the week holds negligible relevance. These findings underline the dominant role of TFI and OFI in capturing actionable price information.

This scatter plot compares the predictions made by the XGBoost model with the actual mid-price changes for BTC/USDT. The clustering around the diagonal line indicates the model's strong predictive accuracy, particularly within the $\pm$20k range, highlighted in green. The wider variance observed in extreme values suggests room for improvement in capturing outliers. This visualization demonstrates the model's capability to approximate mid-price dynamics effectively.

We selected XGBoost for modeling mid-price changes based on OFIs and TFIs due to its suitability for supervised regression tasks. The dataset, cleaned and organized in tabular form, includes mid-price changes as the output variable, making unsupervised methods and classification irrelevant. Classification would predict only the sign of price changes, while unsupervised methods could uncover patterns but would not address our objective of modeling numerical changes directly. XGBoost, an ensemble method leveraging weak decision trees and iterative error minimization, offered robustness and adaptability. Temporal features, minutes, hours, and days of the week were added to test whether patterns noted by Caporale and Plastun (2019) and Aharon and Qadan (2018) impact price dynamics. These features also helped compare XGBoost with OLS, ensuring fair evaluation. As shown in Fig. 6, XGBoost outperformed OLS, reducing the mean absolute error (MAE) from 595.69 to 532.34 in out-of-sample tests. Feature importance analysis highlighted TFI's dominance, with an importance score of 0.45 versus 0.25 for OFI. Temporal features hour and minute held scores of 0.20 and 0.10, respectively, suggesting intraday patterns in order flow informativeness. Conversely, day-of-week effects were negligible, challenging prior findings of significant day-of-week patterns in cryptocurrency markets. Overfitting was a critical challenge. Initial training with XGBoost resulted in an MAE of 362.15 for the training set and 574.29 for the testing set, indicative of overfitting. Bayesian optimization for hyperparameter tuning mitigated this issue, balancing errors at 511.35 for training and 532.34 for testing. Adjusted parameters included tree depth, learning rate, and regularization terms (alpha, lambda), improving generalization without sacrificing predictive accuracy. XGBoost performed especially well during periods of high market volatility, capturing potential non-linear relationships in stressed conditions better than OLS. The linear correlation between XGBoost predictions and observed mid-price changes was 61.45% within the -5000 to $+5000$ USDT range. However, higher variance in predicting extreme outliers suggests an area for improvement. While both models captured the linear relationship between imbalances and price changes, XGBoost's flexibility and computational efficiency offer advantages in high-dimensional and dynamic environments. Feature importance analysis affirmed

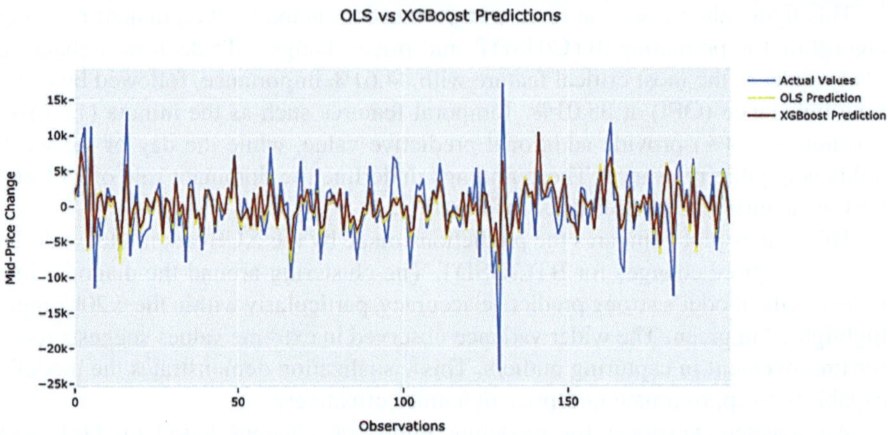

Fig. 7 Comparison of OLS and XGBoost predictions for mid-price changes. Figure 7 compares actual mid-price changes (blue) with predictions from the OLS model (orange) and XGBoost (red). XGBoost outperforms OLS, especially in high-volatility periods, showcasing its robustness in modeling complex, non-linear price dynamics

the predictive power of TFIs and the relevance of intraday patterns, while improved MAE and volatility handling highlighted its superiority over OLS.

Figure 7 compares actual mid-price changes (blue line) with predictions from the Ordinary Least Squares (OLS) model (orange line) and the XGBoost model (red line). While both models closely track actual values, XGBoost demonstrates superior performance in capturing variations, especially during high-volatility periods. This highlights the robustness of XGBoost in modeling complex, non-linear relationships in price dynamics.

6 Implications and Conclusion

6.1 Theory and Market Design

Our findings challenge fundamental assumptions about the relationship between trading costs and market efficiency. While traditional microstructure theory suggests lower trading costs improve price discovery by reducing frictions (Glosten and Milgrom 1985), our results demonstrate a non-monotonic relationship. The significant increase in order flow informativeness after fee implementation suggests an optimal trading cost may exist that maximizes price efficiency. This apparent paradox can be explained through the lens of screening mechanisms. In markets with positive trading costs, traders must weigh the expected profit from their information against transaction costs. This creates a natural filtering process where only sufficiently valuable information triggers order submission. Under zero fees, this screening breaks down, permitting noise traders to flood the order book with uninformative orders. The persistent superiority of TFI over OFI across both regimes provides insights into the hierarchy of informed trading. Market orders require immediate capital commitment and typically incur higher costs through spreads or fees. That TFI maintains higher explanatory power even under zero fees suggests informed traders prefer market orders not just for cost reasons but for their execution certainty. This aligns with theoretical models of informed trading, where execution timing is crucial (Kyle 1985).

6.2 Market Quality and Price Formation

The improvement in order flow informativeness occurred despite tighter spreads post-fee implementation, challenging the conventional wisdom that spreads are a proxy for market quality. This decoupling suggests market makers adjusted their pricing behavior, potentially due to reduced adverse selection risk as uninformed traders became more selective in order submission. Our machine learning results reveal important non-linearities in how order flow impacts prices. The XGBoost model's superior performance during volatile periods indicates that the relationship between order flow and price changes becomes more complex under stress. This suggests traditional linear models may underestimate the true information content of order flow. The significant temporal patterns in order flow informativeness, captured by our ML model's feature importance scores, point to systematic variations in informed trading. The absence of day-of-week effects, contrary to previous findings, suggests the cryptocurrency market's 24/7 nature may be homogenizing trading patterns.

6.3 Practical Implications for Market Participants

These findings have implications for trading strategy development. The increased informativeness of order flow post-fees suggests greater potential for order flow-based prediction strategies, particularly at shorter time horizons where R^2 improvements were most pronounced. However, practitioners must consider whether these gains offset higher transaction costs. For market makers, our results suggest that fee structures significantly impact adverse selection risk. The improved signal-to-noise ratio in order flow post-fees may allow for more aggressive quoting strategies. The non-linear relationships revealed by our ML analysis indicate that market makers should adjust their models during high-volatility periods. Also, exchange operators face a complex optimization problem. While zero-fee trading may attract volume, our findings suggest it degrades price discovery. The optimal fee structure likely depends on the exchange's objectives maximizing volume versus maintaining market quality. This trade-off becomes particularly relevant as cryptocurrency markets mature and institutional participation increases.

References

Brauneis A, Mestel R, Riordan R, Theissen E (2022) The anatomy of a fee change — evidence from cryptocurrency markets. J Emp Finance 67:152–167. https://doi.org/10.1016/j.jempfin.2022.03.003

Caporale GM, Plastun A (2019) The day of the week effect in the cryptocurrency market. Finance Res Lett 31

Cont R, Kukanov A, Stoikov S (2014) The price impact of order book events. J Financ Econometr 12(1):47–88. https://econpapers.repec.org/RePEc:oup:jfinec:v:12:y:2014:i:1:p:47-88

Di Maggio M, Liu J, Rizova S, Wiley R (2020) Exchange fees and overall trading costs. J Emp Finance. https://doi.org/10.2139/ssrn.3625801

Glosten LR, Milgrom PR (1985) Bid, ask and transaction prices in a specialist market with heterogeneously informed traders. J Finance Econ 14(1):71–100

He D, Kokenyne Ivanics A, Lavayssière X, Lukonga I, Schwarz N, Sugimoto N, Verrier J (2022) Capital flow management measures in the digital age (2). In Fintech Notes (Vol. 2023, Issue 009). https://doi.org/10.5089/9798400252105.063

Jeon Y, Samarbakhsh L, Hewitt K (2021) Fragmentation in the Bitcoin market: evidence from multiple coexisting order books. Finance Res Lett 39:101654

Jha R, De Paepe M, Holt S, West J, Ng S (2020) Deep learning for digital asset limit order books. Arxiv, 1–9. https://doi.org/10.2139/ssrn.3704098

Kyle AS (1985) Continuous auctions and insider trading. Econometr J Econometr Soc:1315–1335

Sifat I (2021) On cryptocurrencies as an independent asset class: long-horizon and COVID-19 pandemic era decoupling from global sentiments. Finance Res Lett 43(C):S1544612321000945. https://doi.org/10.1016/j.frl.2021.102013

Quantum Computing and the Next Generation of Robo-Advisory

Abdollah Ah Mand

Abstract This chapter discusses the revolutionary ability of quantum computing in altering the FinTech sector, especially when combined with AI-driven financial strategies. The discussion starts by exploring how quantum technologies might augment investing decision-making, facilitating expedited data processing, improved model training, and more adaptive trading strategies through quantum machine learning (QML). The chapter also delves into quantum-powered portfolio optimization, illustrating how quantum algorithms can overcome the limitations of traditional mean-variance models and solve complex asset allocation problems more efficiently. It also highlights the promise of quantum computing in delivering faster and more accurate risk simulations, such as Monte Carlo methods. Special attention is given to applying QML to sentiment analysis and behavioural finance, where quantum techniques can process large volumes of unstructured data to more accurately predict investor sentiment. The chapter also addresses the role of quantum cryptography in safeguarding AI-driven wealth management systems, ensuring robust data protection. Finally, the chapter offers a realistic perspective on the challenges, limitations, and adoption timelines for quantum technologies in finance.

Keywords Quantum Machine Learning · AI-driven financial strategies · Improved natural language processing · Quantum-powered portfolio optimization · Quantum cryptography · QML · Improved NLP

1 Introduction

This chapter discusses important implications of quantum computing in finance and investment decisions. It includes investment strategies, portfolio optimization,

A. Ah Mand (✉)
Bristol Business School, UWE Bristol, Bristol, UK
e-mail: Abdollah.AhMand@uwe.ac.uk

N. Nahidi, A. Zarifis (eds.), *AI, FinTech, and the Future of Robo-Advisory*, Contributions to Finance and Accounting,
https://doi.org/10.1007/978-3-032-18109-1_14

risk and sensitivity analysis, wealth management, and their related challenges. It encompasses the trends and realistic timeline for the adoption of quantum computing in Fintech environments.

2 AI-Driven Investment Strategies

AI-driven investment strategies refer to the use of artificial intelligence (AI) technologies, like machine learning (ML), natural language processing (NLP), and deep learning, to make decisions about buying, selling, or holding financial assets. These technologies are AI and computer science that focus on enabling computers to understand, interpret, and generate human language. By bridging the gap between human language and computer systems, they allow for more natural and intuitive interactions between humans and machines.

The AI-driven strategies aim to analyse a large volume of data, identify patterns, and make predictions more efficiently than traditional human-led approaches. Other key components of AI-driven investment strategies are portfolio optimization[1] (best asset allocation to maximize returns and/or minimize risk), risk management (e.g., strategies such as monitoring factors like volatility, correlation between assets, and market downturn signals), algorithmic trading, and sentiment analysis (through NLP tools to gauge market sentiment).

Quantum computing has the potential to significantly enhance AI-driven investment strategies by addressing some of the most computationally intensive problems in finance and AI. Some of these strategies are discussed in this chapter:

2.1 Faster Data Processing & Optimization

It is often believed that an accurate investment decision requires processing massive datasets and running complex optimizations. Quantum computers are able to solve certain optimization problems exponentially faster than classical computers. In this regard, quantum computing can optimize the portfolio of information. In doing this, tools like the Quantum Approximate Optimization Algorithm (QAOA) to efficiently find optimal asset allocations, especially in high-dimensional portfolios with constraints, could be utilized. Additionally, quantum computing can be used for faster simulation of risk scenarios (e.g., Monte Carlo simulations). Using quantum-enhanced sampling can lead to more accurate risk assessment.

[1] See Sect. 3 for more details.

2.2 *Quantum Machine Learning*

Under specific situations, quantum computation provides novel machine learning models that may surpass classical methods. These models are able to facilitate more robust pattern recognition in market behaviour, which is crucial from a predictive trading perspective. Furthermore, quantum machine learning, an enhanced machine learning procedure, is capable of efficiently processing high-dimensional market data and identifying correlations or other structures that classical AI tools may overlook.

2.3 *Better Simulation*

Probabilistic models are often used to study financial market data. In this regard, quantum-enhanced probabilistic models can simulate complex, stochastic interactions at a greater scale and fidelity, allowing investors to stress-test strategies under a richer variety of scenarios. For example, recent research proposes novel algorithms (e.g., multi-Split-Steps Quantum Walks) designed to encode and evolve complex financial distributions in quantum states, potentially enabling faster and more accurate modelling of price dynamics, correlations, and shocks than classical Monte Carlo simulation alone (Chang et al. 2024). Moreover, early industrial trials combining quantum and classical models, such as HSBC's use of quantum tools to predict bond-trade fill rates, have demonstrated measurable improvements in predictive performance relative to conventional models (Cooter 2025).

In strategic and game-theoretic settings, the ability of quantum systems to represent superpositions opens the door to modelling richer multi-agent interactions than classical frameworks allow. In this regard, quantum game theory extends classical strategy spaces by allowing strategies that can alter equilibrium outcomes and yield higher payoffs in competitive situations. For instance, recent work has developed quantum game-theoretic trading models executed on ion-trap devices, showing "quantum advantage" in market equilibria under certain conditions (Khan et al. 2025). More broadly, surveys in evolutionary and quantum game theory highlight how quantum modelling can better capture the uncertainty, entanglement, and interdependence inherent in strategic financial systems (Sanz-Martín et al. 2025).

2.4 *Improved Natural Language Processing (NLP)*

Natural Language Processing, a branch of AI that helps computers understand, interpret, and generate human language; and Neuro-Linguistic Programming, a method for personal development that focuses on the connection between thoughts (neuro), language (linguistic), and behaviour. Quantum-enhanced NLP, on the other hand, could substantially improve how AI systems interpret financial news, earnings reports, and market sentiment drawn from unstructured textual data. Quantum natural language processing (QNLP) models have been proposed and demonstrated that may better capture subtle sentiment cues, superpositions of meaning, or ambivalent expressions in text, giving fine-grained understanding of investor mood. For example, using the *lambeq* toolkit, researchers have applied QNLP to sentiment classification and report high accuracy both in simulations and on noisy quantum devices (Ganguly et al. 2022).

Similarly, quantum-based approaches could accelerate and enhance **information extraction** from financial documents. Unstructured data such as earnings reports, regulatory filings, or news articles contain vital entities (company names, figures, dates), relations (e.g., "company A acquired company B", "earnings beat expectations by X%"), and events. Classical NLP systems already perform these tasks (named entity extraction, summarization, document parsing), but quantum NLP and optimization-based quantum algorithms could enable faster processing, better handling of ambiguity, and possibly real-time extraction in high volumes. For instance, JPMorgan has explored quantum algorithms in constrained optimization settings for NLP document summarization (Bake 2022).

2.5 High-Frequency Trading (HFT) Advantages

Using high-frequency data is a common way for obtaining a less volatile method in financial markets (Ah Mand et al. 2023b). Quantum computing holds promise for **order flow prediction,** especially in HFT contexts where the dynamics of the limit order book are complex and evolve very rapidly. Quantum-enhanced or quantum-inspired models could add value by encoding richer dependency structures, capturing non-linear and entangled relationships across many order book levels, and doing so more compactly or with less computational overhead. For instance, recent work on fill probability estimation in institutional algorithmic bond trading showed that embedding quantum-generated transformations of data (using real intraday event data and quantum hardware) yielded up to ~34% improvement in out-of-sample prediction scores compared to models using only classical data or classical transforms (Ciceri et al. 2025).

Similarly, in **latency arbitrage** and other latency-sensitive execution strategies, quantum methods could enhance both detection and reaction to microsecond-level opportunities. Faster signal detection, pattern recognition, and order matching are critical here: tiny delays can erase arbitrage margins. The "Quantum Prisoner's Dilemma" model for HFT, for instance, investigates how quantum communication or computation might, in principle, accelerate strategic decision-making in competitive execution scenarios (Faisal Shah Khan 2021).

3 Quantum-Powered Portfolio Optimization

Portfolio optimization—choosing the allocation of capital among various assets to balance risk versus return—lies at the heart of modern finance. In its simplest form, the Markowitz mean–variance framework defines a quadratic programming problem: maximize expected return for a given risk level (variance) or minimize risk for a given return. Classical methods (convex optimization, mixed-integer programming, heuristics) often struggle when the sample becomes large, constraints complicated, or when near-real-time solutions are required.

Quantum computing has been proposed as a potential tool to handle this complexity. Because many portfolio optimization problems can be expressed in forms amenable to quantum or quantum-inspired optimization (e.g., QUBO: Quadratic Unconstrained Binary Optimization; HUBO: higher-order unconstrained binary optimization), there is growing interest in leveraging quantum algorithms and hybrid quantum-classical methods to improve on classical performance either in speed, solution quality, or handling richer constraints. The basic format of quantum-powered and classical portfolio optimization models is mentioned below:

3.1 *Classical Portfolio Optimization (Markowitz Mean-Variance)*

We consider n assets, with expected returns vector $\mu \in R^n$, covariance matrix $\sum \in R^n$, and portfolio weights $\omega \epsilon R^n$, such that $\sum_i \omega_i = 1, \omega_i \geq 0$.

$$\min_{\omega} \omega^T \sum \omega s.t. \qquad \mu^T \omega \geq R^*, \qquad 1^T \omega = 1, \quad \omega_i \geq 0$$

Here, $R*$ is the minimum target return.

3.2 *QUBO (Quadratic Unconstrained Binary Optimization) Formulation*

If portfolio weights must be discrete (e.g., $\omega_i \in \{1, 0\}$, select or not select asset), then the problem becomes:

$$\min_{x \in \{1,0\}^n} \alpha . x^T \sum x - \beta . \mu^T x + \gamma . \left(1^T x - k\right)^2$$

- $x_i = 1$ means asset i is included
- α, β, γ are penalty coefficients

– The last term enforces a cardinality constraint of k assets

This QUBO is directly solvable by quantum annealers.

3.3 Recent Advances

Here are some of the most recent important developments:

- *Higher-Order Portfolio Optimization with Quantum Approximate Optimization Algorithm* (Uotila et al. 2025) introduces a quantum formulation including skewness and kurtosis (not only mean and variance), encoded as a higher-order unconstrained binary optimization (HUBO). They show for many test cases that their quantum/HUBO solutions correspond to better allocations than classical baselines.
- *Achieving High-Quality Portfolio Optimization with Variational Quantum Eigensolver* (Wang et al. 2025) integrates Weighted Conditional Value-at-Risk (WCVaR) risk measure and uses Covariance Matrix Adaptation Evolution Strategy (CMA-ES) as the optimizer to tune parameters; experiments show improved solution quality. This is significant because moving beyond variance and using tail risk measures is more aligned with real financial risk.
- *The joint IBM-Vanguard work:* "IBM and Vanguard Explore Quantum Optimization for Portfolio Construction" demonstrates using sampling-based variational quantum algorithm (VQA) on actual hardware (Heron quantum processor) on a bond ETF construction problem, and shows that quantum-classical hybrid workflows can match or approach performance of the best classical solvers like CPLEX in many cases (Roberto Lo Nardo 2025).
- *Multi-objective portfolio optimization using quantum annealing* (Aguilera et al. 2024) by combining more than one objective, e.g., risk, return, sometimes non-financial constraints, the portfolio optimization problem is explored. Their model provides insights into how quantum computing can address complex optimization problems in the financial sector. It also highlights the potential of quantum computing for providing more efficient and robust solutions for portfolio management.

3.4 Key Challenges

While promising, there remain significant obstacles before widespread practical quantum advantage for portfolio optimization is achieved. Key challenges include noise and hardware limitations, encoding discretization, high cost, scaling and resources requirements and workflow complexities are among the key challenges of quantum-powered optimization tools.

4 Faster and More Accurate Risk Simulations Via Monte Carlo Methods

Monte Carlo simulation is a powerful tool for risk assessment: generating many sample paths of uncertain variables to approximate distributions of outcomes, tail risks, quantiles (e.g. Value-at-Risk, Expected Shortfall), etc. The major challenge is that naive Monte Carlo (MC) converges slowly: the standard error typically decreases at $O\left(n^{\frac{-1}{2}}\right)$ with n the number of simulations. To get high accuracy (especially in tails or rare events) you often need very large n, which means high computational cost.

Over the past couple of decades, significant work has gone into accelerating MC/improving accuracy. Below are key methods, their principles, strengths & limitations, and some recent advances. In this regard, some of the important developments are as follows:

1. Variance Reduction Techniques: These are methods that reduce the variance (i.e., dispersion) of estimators so that, for a given number of samples, the estimate is more precise.
2. Quasi-Monte Carlo (QMC) Methods: Instead of using pseudo-random numbers, QMC uses "low-discrepancy" deterministic sequences. This can reduce error rates in many settings, when integrands are reasonably smooth and the dimension is moderate.
3. Multilevel Monte Carlo (MLMC): MLMC (and related multilevel or multigrid schemes) reduce computational cost by combining many cheap, coarse simulations with fewer expensive, fine simulations. The idea is coarse approximations are cheap but rough, fine approximations are costly but precise; by cleverly coupling them, one can reduce overall variance for a given cost. In many contexts, MLMC can reduce the complexity needed to achieve a given error tolerance.

4.1 Practical Considerations & Trade-offs

When applying advanced Monte Carlo methods such as variance reduction or QMC, practical efficiency often depends on the balance between computational gains and overhead. Techniques like generating low-discrepancy sequences, computing control variate parameters, or adaptively learning importance sampling distributions can significantly reduce variance, but if their setup cost is comparable to or exceeds the simulation cost, the net improvement may be negligible or even negative. This makes careful evaluation of computational overhead critical before implementation.

Estimating tail risks or rare events—such as extreme quantiles or expected shortfall at high confidence levels—is especially difficult because standard Monte Carlo simulations produce few samples in the tail. Specialized techniques like importance sampling, splitting, or cross-entropy methods deliberately bias sampling towards rare events to achieve better precision in the extremes. However, these methods often struggle in high-dimensional settings, where dependencies between variables degrade performance and QMC's uniformity deteriorates unless enhanced with dimension-reduction techniques such as Brownian bridge constructions for path-dependent models.

Finally, it is essential to manage the trade-off between bias and variance, as some approaches (e.g., multilevel Monte Carlo or regression-based surrogates) can introduce bias if approximations are poorly controlled. Reliable risk measurement requires both low variance and tightly bounded bias, since even small biases can distort quantile estimates. Robustness also depends on good diagnostics: tracking convergence, variance stability, and tail behaviour. In complex hierarchical or adaptive methods, instability—such as high kurtosis in multilevel differences—must be detected and corrected to ensure confidence in simulation outputs.

5 Quantum Machine Learning (QML) for Behavioural Finance and Sentiment Analysis

Behavioural finance seeks to understand how psychological, cognitive, and emotional factors affect financial decision-making (Ah Mand et al. 2023a). Sentiment—public mood, opinion, fear, optimism—plays a key role in markets, influencing asset prices, trading volume (Mohd Thas Thaker and Ah Mand 2021), volatility, and risk premia. In recent years, sentiment analysis (NLP methods) combined with machine learning has become a common tool to extract sentiment from financial news, social media, earnings calls, etc., for applications like predicting returns, volatility, or detecting fraud.

Quantum Machine Learning (QML) is an emerging field at the intersection of quantum computing and classical ML/NLP. The idea is to exploit quantum computational primitives (such as superposition, entanglement, high-dimensional Hilbert spaces, quantum kernels, variational quantum circuits) to improve performance on tasks for which classical methods struggle—e.g., high-dimensional data, combinatorial complexity, or modelling non-classical correlations. For sentiment analysis and behavioural finance, there is growing interest in whether quantum-inspired or hybrid quantum-classical models can capture subtler patterns of human cognition, bias, or sentiment in textual data, in ways that classical models either cannot or do only inefficiently.

Classical probability theory often falls short in explaining certain human decision-making behaviours, such as order effects, conjunction fallacies, and interference in judgments. Quantum probability and quantum cognition provide a richer framework to model these phenomena through principles like interference, superposition, and measurement collapse. In the context of sentiment analysis and opinion modelling, these quantum-inspired approaches better capture ambiguity, context dependence, and conflicting beliefs than traditional probabilistic models. Research surveys have shown that quantum-cognitive models can more accurately represent the dynamic and context-sensitive nature of human sentiment and reasoning.

To operationalize these ideas, linguistic elements such as words or sentences can be represented in complex-valued vector spaces or as density matrices, capturing both amplitude and phase information. This enables richer encoding of semantic and contextual relationships beyond what classical embeddings can achieve. Furthermore, quantum kernels and feature maps can project data into exponentially large spaces, enhancing separability in classification tasks like sentiment detection. Variational quantum circuits (VQCs), often used in hybrid quantum-classical architectures, allow flexible learning of representations while making practical use of current quantum hardware, offering a balanced approach for leveraging quantum advantages in the near-term, noisy intermediate-scale quantum (NISQ) era.

Thus, QML is promising for behavioural finance and sentiment analysis because those domains often involve high-dimensional, noisy, ambiguous, and context-dependent data; cognitive biases; non-linearities; and temporal dependencies. Quantum-like models might allow more flexible representation of belief states or sentiment states, more powerful classification/discrimination in high dimensions, or new ways to capture human decision anomalies.

5.1 Applications in Behavioural Finance

QML offers promising ways to enhance sentiment analysis for behavioural finance applications. In market prediction and volatility forecasting, QML-based sentiment extraction from news, social media, and alternative data could capture richer emotional dynamics, such as ambiguity or simultaneous states of fear and hope, through quantum concepts like superposition and interference. These nuanced sentiment representations may improve the predictive power of financial models, especially in complex or uncertain market conditions.

In trading and portfolio management, QML-enhanced sentiment signals can serve as valuable inputs for algorithmic trading systems, including reinforcement learning or deep Q-network frameworks. By providing more discriminative and noise-resistant sentiment features, QML could help refine trading strategies and decision-making under uncertainty. Similarly, behavioural bias modelling may benefit from quantum-inspired approaches, which naturally account for context dependence, ambiguity, and belief interference phenomena closely linked to investor biases like overconfidence, herding, and loss aversion.

Beyond trading and bias analysis, QML can strengthen risk management and cross-cultural sentiment modelling. Quantum-enhanced sentiment detectors may better identify extreme emotions during market stress, improving early warnings for tail risk or crash scenarios. Moreover, QML's ability to handle complex, noisy, and multilingual data makes it well-suited for global financial markets, particularly in emerging economies, where linguistic diversity and data scarcity challenge traditional sentiment models.

5.2 Challenges and Limitations

Despite its potential, quantum machine learning (QML) faces numerous challenges before it can be adopted as a standard tool in behavioural finance or applied financial modelling. As mentioned in Sect. 3.4, one of the most significant hurdles is hardware limitation: today's quantum devices operate in the Noisy Intermediate-Scale Quantum (NISQ) era, where qubit counts are small, error rates are high, and decoherence times are short. Many proposed QML methods still rely on simulators or idealized assumptions, making real-world translation uncertain. Scalability is another obstacle: financial sentiment analysis often involves massive datasets, such as millions of news articles or social media posts, which can strain current quantum architectures. Efficient preprocessing, embedding, and dimension-reduction techniques are therefore critical to make large-scale applications feasible.

Quantum models, such as variational circuits or hybrid fuzzy-neural networks, are often complex and opaque, making it difficult to identify which features drive predictions. Furthermore, sentiment data itself is inherently noisy, containing slang, irony, and ambiguity. Although some quantum models claim greater robustness to noise, their generalization across diverse linguistic and contextual variations remains uncertain.

Another challenge lies in benchmarking and empirical validation. Current evidence for QML's advantages often comes from small-scale or highly specific datasets, sometimes after heavy preprocessing or dimensionality reduction. It remains unclear under what conditions QML genuinely outperforms advanced classical models like transformers or large pre-trained language models. Finally, practical issues such as hardware access, cost, and latency also constrain deployment. Quantum systems can be expensive and slow compared to conventional machine learning pipelines—particularly problematic in time-sensitive domains like trading.

Lastly, the novelty of QML introduces a "hype risk". Early results may reflect overfitting or favourable experimental setups rather than true performance gains. To ensure credible progress, rigorous benchmarking, robust cross-validation, and fair comparisons with strong classical baselines are essential. Only through careful testing, transparency, and realistic evaluation can QML's true value in behavioural finance be properly established.

6 Quantum Cryptography in AI-Driven Wealth Management Platforms

Wealth management platforms increasingly rely on AI for tasks such as risk assessment, portfolio optimization, fraud detection, algorithmic trading, and customer profiling. These systems handle highly sensitive data: client personal and financial data, trading strategies, predictive models, and proprietary algorithms. The security of these data assets is already critical; with emerging quantum computing, there are additional existential threats to many cryptographic primitives currently in use. For AI systems that store or transmit sensitive data, or that rely on digital signatures for integrity, this is a serious risk.

Hence, quantum cryptography (broadly meaning both *quantum key distribution* (QKD) and *post-quantum cryptography* (PQC)) becomes a vital toolset for securing AI-driven wealth management platforms against both present and future threats.

6.1 Key Concepts and Techniques

6.1.1 Quantum Key Distribution (QKD)

Quantum Key Distribution (QKD) enables two parties to establish a shared symmetric secret key using the fundamental principles of quantum mechanics. Its primary advantage lies in the fact that any attempt to intercept or measure quantum states, such as photons, inevitably disturbs them, making eavesdropping detectable. Under ideal conditions, this property provides a foundation for provably secure key exchange. Once a symmetric key is successfully shared through QKD, it can be used with standard symmetric encryption algorithms, such as the Advanced Encryption Standard (AES), or even with a one-time pad to ensure data confidentiality. However, practical challenges remain, particularly with respect to distance and infrastructure requirements.

Several recent proof-of-concept projects demonstrate growing interest in applying QKD within the financial sector. HSBC has trailed QKD to secure an AI-powered foreign exchange (FX) trading terminal in a €30 million trading environment (HSBC Holdings plc 2023). Similarly, banks in Singapore, under the guidance of the Monetary Authority of Singapore (MAS), have collaborated with technology providers to test QKD applications in financial services (Monetary Authority of Singapore 2024). In another initiative, JPMorgan Chase, Toshiba, and Ciena jointly developed a QKD-secured network to protect a mission-critical blockchain system operating across a metropolitan area (JPMorganChase 2022). These examples highlight both the technological promise and ongoing practical experimentation necessary for integrating QKD into mainstream financial security infrastructure.

6.1.2 Post-Quantum Cryptography (PQC)

Post-Quantum Cryptography (PQC) encompasses cryptographic algorithms such as digital signatures, key exchange protocols, and hashing methods that are designed to remain secure even against adversaries equipped with quantum computers. These algorithms rely on mathematical problems believed to be resistant to quantum attacks, including lattice-based schemes.

While QKD offers physical-layer security for key exchange, PQC addresses other critical components that QKD cannot practically replace, such as digital signatures for authentication, blockchain transactions, and public key infrastructures. To ensure a smooth transition and maintain compatibility during this evolving phase, many organizations are adopting hybrid cryptographic systems that combine classical and quantum-resistant algorithms. This approach balances immediate practicality with future resilience, paving the way for a secure migration to quantum-safe infrastructures.

6.2 Applications Specific to AI-Driven Wealth Management

Quantum cryptography offers powerful tools to enhance the security of AI-driven wealth management systems, where sensitive data and high-value transactions are constantly exchanged between interconnected modules. Data in transit, such as during model training, inference, or acquisition, is vulnerable to interception, including the risk of future decryption with quantum computers. QKD can mitigate these risks by securely sharing symmetric keys while detecting any unauthorized interception attempts. This enables strong, forward-secure encryption for all communications between AI components, ensuring confidentiality and integrity of financial data in motion.

At the storage level, both client data and proprietary AI models face risks such as data theft, model inversion attacks, and leakage of investment strategies. PQC can safeguard stored assets through encryption methods resistant to quantum attacks and by applying quantum-secure digital signatures to model updates, ensuring authenticity and tamper resistance. For communication with clients and regulatory entities, quantum digital signature schemes and PQC-secured TLS/SSL protocols can protect against man-in-the-middle attacks, forgery, and non-repudiation issues, maintaining trust and compliance in all interactions.

Quantum cryptography also strengthens critical operational areas like algorithmic and high-frequency trading, as well as blockchain-based wealth platforms. Trials such as HSBC's QKD-protected foreign exchange trading demonstrate the feasibility of securing low-latency financial transactions using quantum key exchange (HSBC Holdings plc 2023). For blockchain applications, including smart contracts, tokenization of assets, and fund transfers, quantum-resistant signature and hashing schemes are essential to counter vulnerabilities in classical cryptography. In some infrastructures, integrating hybrid or quantum-secure blockchain architectures and employing QKD to protect communication links can further enhance the resilience of next-generation wealth management systems.

7 Challenges and Realistic Timelines for Quantum Adoption in FinTech

Quantum computing promises faster Monte Carlo risk simulations, richer portfolio optimization, improved derivative pricing, and novel machine learning primitives, but moving from promise to production in financial services is non-trivial. Below, the main challenges and a realistic, evidence-based timeline for short, medium, and long horizons are outlined.

7.1 Key Challenges

The adoption of quantum computing in finance faces several foundational challenges, starting with the maturity of hardware. Current quantum devices are noisy, limited in qubit count, and not fault-tolerant, meaning that many of the theoretical advantages proposed for financial applications—such as faster Monte Carlo simulations—cannot yet be realized in practice. While some industry roadmaps suggest that niche, commercially meaningful use cases could emerge within a few years, others believe it may take a decade or longer to achieve general-purpose quantum advantage. This uncertainty around hardware progress makes it difficult for financial institutions to plan confidently, pushing most firms towards cautious, pilot-driven experimentation rather than full-scale implementation.

Beyond hardware, significant algorithmic and software gaps remain. Although quantum algorithms exist for key financial problems such as portfolio optimization, option pricing, and risk analysis, turning theoretical speedups into real-world performance gains is complex (Orús et al. 2019). The current software stacks, error-mitigation methods, and hybrid quantum-classical workflows needed to achieve this are still being developed. Moreover, integrating quantum algorithms into production-grade systems complete with data ingestion, governance, and explainability adds substantial engineering overhead. In parallel, the growing quantum threat to cryptography poses an immediate concern. Large-scale quantum computers could break existing encryption methods, prompting agencies to publish PQC standards and encourage early migration. Transitioning legacy financial infrastructure to PQC, however, is an arduous, long-term process involving cryptographic keys, security modules, and archived data.

Finally, financial firms must navigate operational, talent, and economic barriers. Integrating quantum services into large, legacy systems such as trading platforms and regulatory reporting pipelines will demand new APIs, security frameworks, and certifications, often at higher cost than the quantum hardware itself. There is also a global shortage of professionals who can bridge quantum computing and finance, complicating governance and regulatory compliance efforts. Regulators are already signalling that production-grade quantum systems will require clear oversight, controls, and validation mechanisms. Compounding all this are cost pressures and vendor lock-in risks, as firms must choose between competing hardware approaches and proprietary software ecosystems while balancing the expense of early adoption with long-term strategic positioning.

7.2 Realistic Timelines (Practical, Risk-Aware View)

The short-term outlook for quantum computing in finance focuses on experimentation and early pilots. Firms are expected to explore hybrid quantum-classical workflows and proof-of-concept projects, such as Monte Carlo acceleration on simplified problems. Concurrently, regulatory guidance is prompting firms to assess cryptographic risks, begin adopting PQC libraries, and start building inventories of data and systems vulnerable to quantum attacks. During this period, firms typically engage in vendor-led pilots, form consortiums for benchmarking, and work on upskilling staff to manage both quantum technologies and cryptographic transitions. Recommended actions include cataloguing cryptographic assets, establishing "crypto-agile" architectures that can support both classical and quantum-safe algorithms, and running targeted pilots for high-value workloads.

In the medium term, selective quantum advantage may start to appear for specialized financial problems. Examples include faster Monte Carlo simulations for complex derivatives, and prototype implementations of portfolio optimization using error-mitigated or application-specific hardware. Meanwhile, broader PQC migration will be well underway, with critical TLS and PKI systems upgraded, and national roadmaps expecting progress. Firms are advised to move long-lived, sensitive data to quantum-resistant protection, adopt PQ-ready suppliers, integrate validated quantum services into non-critical pipelines, and formalize governance and vendor due diligence to manage risks effectively.

Looking further ahead, fault-tolerant quantum systems may become mature enough to enable high-impact, general-purpose applications in trading, risk management, and treasury functions that were previously infeasible. By this stage, post-quantum cryptography is expected to be widely adopted, giving early-prepared financial institutions a competitive edge in select quantitative workloads. However, the precise timing of these developments remains uncertain and heavily dependent on breakthroughs in error correction and system scaling. Strategic planning and early experimentation in the short and medium term will determine which firms are best positioned to capitalize on these long-term quantum opportunities.

7.3 Practical Recommendations (Concise)

Financial institutions should approach quantum adoption on two parallel tracks: defensively, by migrating to PQC, inventorying cryptographic assets, and building crypto-agile architectures, and opportunistically, through targeted pilots, vendor partnerships, and benchmarking initiatives. Priority should be given to protecting long-lived secrets such as archived data and interbank keys with quantum-resistant solutions. Firms are encouraged to invest in talent and join consortia to reduce onboarding costs and benefit from shared benchmarking, since theoretical quantum speedups rarely translate directly into production gains. Early engagement with regulators and central banks is essential to align with emerging guidance on quantum readiness and cryptographic standards.

8 Conclusion

In conclusion, quantum computing holds transformative potential for the FinTech sector, offering capabilities that could fundamentally reshape investing, risk management, and portfolio optimization. By integrating quantum technologies with AI-driven strategies, financial institutions can leverage faster data processing, more adaptive trading models, and enhanced predictive insights from unstructured data.

Quantum algorithms promise to overcome traditional computational limits, enabling more efficient asset allocation, accelerated Monte Carlo simulations, and improved sentiment and behavioural analysis. At the same time, quantum cryptography provides a critical layer of security, safeguarding sensitive financial and AI-driven operations. Quantum-powered portfolio optimization represents one of the most promising domains for applying quantum computing in finance. While we are not yet at a stage where quantum methods consistently outperform classical methods for large, fully realistic portfolios, the recent advances show that hybrid quantum-classical workflows, improved encoding and decomposition techniques, and richer cost functions are pushing us closer.

While the technology remains in its early stages, with hardware, software, and adoption challenges to navigate, its strategic integration into finance could deliver significant competitive advantages for those who proactively explore pilot projects, invest in talent, and engage with regulatory frameworks. The path forward requires a balanced approach, combining innovation with careful risk management and readiness for a gradually evolving quantum landscape.

References

Aguilera E, de Jong J, Phillipson F, Taamallah S, Vos M (2024) Multi-objective portfolio optimization using a quantum annealer. Mathematics 12(9):1291

Ah Mand A, Janor H, Abdul Rahim R, Sarmidi T (2023a) Herding behavior and stock market conditions. PSU Res Rev 7(2):105–116

Ah Mand A, Sifat I, Ang WK, Choo JJ (2023b) *Herding behavior in commodity ETFs.* [Online]. https://papers.ssrn.com/sol3/papers.cfm?abstract_id=4502804. Accessed 5 Oct 2025

Bake B (2022) *AI business, IOT world today.* [Online]. https://www.iotworldtoday.com/industry/jpmorgan-uses-quantum-computing-to-summarize-documents. Accessed 5 Dec 2022

Chang Y-J, Wang WT, Chen HY, Liao SW, Chang CR (2024) A novel approach for quantum financial simulation and quantum state preparation. Quantum Mach Intell. Springer Nature 6:24

Ciceri A, Cottrell A, Freeland J, Fry D, Hirai H, Intallura P et al (2025) *Cornell University*. [Online]. https://arxiv.org/abs/2509.17715. Accessed 05 Oct 2025

Cooter M (2025) *CIO*. [Online]. https://www.hsbc.com/news-and-views/news/media-releases/2025/hsbc-demonstrates-worlds-first-known-quantum-enabled-algorithmic-trading-with-ibm. Accessed 5 Oct 2025

Faisal Shah Khan NB (2021) *Cornell University*. [Online]. https://arxiv.org/abs/2104.04663. Accessed 5 Oct 2025

Ganguly S, Morapakula SN, Coronado LMP (2022) Quantum natural language processing based sentiment analysis using lambeq toolkit. IEEE, pp 1–6

HSBC Holdings plc (2023) *HSBC.Com*. [Online]. https://www.hsbc.com/news-and-views/news/media-releases/2023/hsbc-pioneers-quantum-protection-for-ai-powered-fx-trading. Accessed 5 Oct 2025

JPMorganChase (2022) *JPMorganChase*. [Online]. https://www.jpmorganchase.com/newsroom/press-releases/2022/jpmc-toshiba-ciena-build-first-quantum-key-distribution-network. Accessed 5 Oct 2025

Khan FS, Linke NM, Than AT, Baron D (2025) Quantum advantage in trading: A game-theoretic approach. Quantum Econ Financ 2(1):40–51

Mohd Thas Thaker H, Ah Mand A (2021) Bitcoin and stock markets: a revisit of relationship. J Deriv Quant Stud 29(3):234–256

Monetary Authority of Singapore (2024) *Monetary Authority of Singapore*. [Online]. https://www.mas.gov.sg/news/media-releases/2024/mas-collaborates-with-banks-and-technology-partners-on-quantum-security. Accessed 5 Oct 2025

Orús R, Mugel S, Lizaso E (2019) Quantum computing for finance: overview and prospects. Rev Phys 4:100028

Roberto Lo Nardo GA (2025). IBM.com. [Online]. https://www.ibm.com/quantum/blog/vanguard-portfolio-optimization. Accessed 5 Oct 2025

Sanz-Martín L, Rivas G, Clavijo-Buriticá N, Herrera M, Parra-Domínguez J (2025) Mapping the frontier: a review of quantum and evolutionary game theory for complex decision-making. Quantum Inf Processs 24:291

Uotila V, Ripatti J, Zhao B (2025) Higher-order portfolio optimization with quantum approximate optimization algorithm. IEEE, s.l., p 12

Wang A, Lv Z, Ma Z, Cai D, Zhang Z (2025) *Cornbell University*. [Online]. https://arxiv.org/abs/2508.18625. Accessed 5 Oct 2025

Part V
Sustainability, Market Impact, and Future Directions

Sustainable Investing and the Role of AI-Driven Robo-Advisors

Nader Virk

Abstract This chapter explores the homeostatic nature of sustainable investing and the transformative exploitation of robo-advisory to this end in the global asset management industry. This chapter navigates the evolving landscape of sustainable finance—from definitions to market growth, followed by evolution in the regulatory landscape and global sustainability standards frameworks. ESG investing is boosted by robo-advisory: these systems are bringing efficiency, accessibility, and democratisation of investment advice to an otherwise complex, yet transformative, investment landscape. With the issues of rating divergences, multiplicity, and conflicting nature of ESG standards, robo-advisory integrates AI capabilities to ingest not just data but can also provide comprehensive or segmented ESG scoring baselines to make consistent and robust investment decisions. Robo-advisory is streamlining investor idiosyncrasies, choices, and constraints—from moral/social values to climate-change trigger points. In addition, these platforms ensure that ESG standards, labels, and regulations are followed, with the ability to fast-track revisions to them, thereby mitigating issues such as greenwashing and greenhushing while embedding RegTech into robotic advisory services. The vertical integration of processes enables application of AI approaches such as NLP, LLMs, and ML to harness vast amounts of ESG disclosures and alternate datasets to bring additional insights in client advisory service. By highlighting the scope of hyper-personalisation and adaptive learning from client preference, this chapter provides a futuristic worldview of robo-advisory in the asset management sector. This chapter analyses how explainable AI is improving transparency and tractability for audit trails and compliance in ESG investing via robo-advisors.

N. Virk (✉)
Manchester Metropolitan University Business School, Manchester Metropolitan University, Manchester, UK
e-mail: n.virk@mmu.ac.uk

N. Nahidi, A. Zarifis (eds.), *AI, FinTech, and the Future of Robo-Advisory*, Contributions to Finance and Accounting,
https://doi.org/10.1007/978-3-032-18109-1_15

Keywords Sustainable investing · Market growth · AI approaches · Robo-advisory · Democratisation of financial advice · Personalised portfolios · ESG standardisation

1 Introduction

Investing has long been a cornerstone of financial economics, evolving from foundational theories such as Markowitz's portfolio optimisation to sophisticated intertemporal models linking consumption and asset returns. While these theoretical developments have enhanced the analytical treatment of risk and return, they have also entrenched a paradigm of shareholder value maximisation. The paradigm has faced increased scrutiny for its role in perpetuating environmental and social externalities, spurring a shift towards sustainable investing—where environmental, social, and governance (ESG) criteria are integrated with financial analysis. This remarkable transformation, in parallel, is being supported by AI-powered robo-advisory that harnesses machine learning (ML) and/or Gen-AI tools to analyse vast alternate datasets. Availability of robo-advisory enables sustainable screening and democratise access to impact-driven investing. In sum, sustainable investing and robo-advisory are reshaping the global asset management industry at the intersection of technology, sustainability, and fiduciary responsibility.

This chapter will outline key developments that have shaped the journey in which sustainable investing is an ever-growing part of the global asset management, how increasing investors awareness on, e.g., climate-change pushed firms on climate disclosures and voluntary reporting, and current day regulatory frameworks that mandate disclosure and aim to settle confusions and disagreements in sustainability corporate reporting—for having multiple guidelines and voluntary codes. This will be followed by a discussion on key concepts in sustainable investing, how robo-advisory is transforming investments and sustainable investing. A focussed analysis of how AI-powering of sustainable investing is making portfolio management efficient and scale-able will be offered with a view that how the intersection of both addresses wider sustainable challenges—from quantification of ESG impact to ethical use of AI-powered robo-advisory.

2 Background

Investing has been at the centre of financial economics literature to understand the perennial consumption–investment problem in different temporal and risk settings. Investment management has matured into a rigorous science with Markowitz's (1952) mean–variance optimisation, Sharpe's (1964) equilibrium asset-pricing framework, and Lucas's (1978) representative-agent model that linked consumption dynamics with asset returns. The consumption–investment nexus is fundamental to economics and finance because agents' intertemporal trade-off between immediate utility and future wealth, as formalised in life cycle (Modigliani and Brumberg 1954) and consumption-based (Lucas 1978) models, drives capital accumulation, asset valuations, and risk-sharing across the economy. While financial economics traditionally employs one-period abstractions such as the CAPM to analyse returns under ceteris paribus assumptions, a full appreciation of investment and consumption behaviour emerges only in intertemporal and overlapping-generations frameworks that capture consumption smoothing, multi-period asset markets, and wealth transfers across lifetimes (Samuelson 1958; Lucas 1978).

2.1 Investments to Sustainable Investments

The supply of investment capital and demand from asset managers supported by financial intermediation have created a behemoth—the global asset management industry, which reached $128 trillion in AUM by 2024 (BCG 2025). The global investment industry has long operated on the principle of 'maximising shareholder value', driving unprecedented capital growth. This enormous growth has, however, come at a significant cost. While asset managers and financial intermediaries function as a machine to channel capital towards the most profitable businesses, this very process of capital allocation is a leading driver of negative externalities. These include environmental degradation, social inequity, and poor corporate governance practices (Stout 2012; Mayer 2018; Bebchuk and Tallarita 2020). At the socio-economic level, this shift in priorities is exemplified by the move away from a 'retain and reinvest' model towards a 'downsize and distribute' approach. As Lazonick (2015) argues this corporate strategy to maximise returns for shareholders (e.g., through share buybacks) has exacerbated income inequality, labour market instability, and weakened firms' innovative competitiveness.

Table 1 summarises the historical evolution of sustainable investing, outlining four distinct phases from early ethical screening to modern ESG materiality. Each phase reflects changing social, political, and financial drivers that shaped investor behaviour.

Despite the growing dominance of institutional investing (Fichtner 2020), asset managers—central actors in Useem's (1996) 'investor capitalism'—have largely failed to address the negative externalities of global corporations. As Davis (2008) highlights, large asset managers disproportionately favour passive exit (divestment) instead of active voice (engagement), thereby limiting their ability to drive meaningful improvements in corporate environmental, social, and economic performance.[1] Consequently, the asset management industry has drawn scrutiny over sustainability

[1] Potentially, the transition from *'managerial capitalism'* to *'investor capitalism'* has mitigated agency problem—balanced power dynamics between shareholders and executives without resolving systemic externalities.

Table 1 Evolution of sustainable investing

Phase	Time period	Key drivers & developments
Early roots	Pre-1960s	Religious and ethical beliefs; shaped moral considerations through negative screening
Socially Responsible Investing (SRI)	1960s–1990s	Concept of 'sin stocks'; social and political activism; civil rights, anti-war, and anti-apartheid movements.
Rise of ESG investing	2000s	Financial vs. environmental materiality; integrated materiality; institutionalisation of sustainability in investing
ESG and financial materiality	2010s-present	Paris agreement (2015); social justice movements; awareness and demand from retail and institutional investors.

and corporate responsibility, sparking a shift towards sustainable investing in recent decades. This trend reflects mounting pressure to align financial returns with environmental, social, and governance (ESG) priorities.

2.2 *Sustainable Investing and Financial System*

Capital allocation into assets—from stocks, bonds, and real estate to more complex instruments like futures and options—has created a financial system designed to smooth consumption over time and meet a range of investment objectives. Traditional investment practices, evident in the organisation of markets and the development of financial products, focus exclusively on optimising portfolios using financial metrics such as expected return, volatility, and correlation. In contrast, sustainable investing seeks to balance these financial considerations with the risks and opportunities presented by ESG factors. These include targeting outcomes like carbon reduction, biodiversity risk, human rights adherence, and boardroom diversity. That is, sustainable investing goes a step further by incorporating ESG criteria alongside financial analysis to support long-term value creation and positive societal.

Sustainable investing is disrupting the global financial landscape. It is leading the creation of new markets focused on sustainable and impact-oriented projects, such as green and social bonds (Baker et al. 2022; Flammer 2021). Capital markets and financial institutions are responding by developing dedicated ESG funds, expertise, and research teams to meet investor demand. For example, global capital markets have seen the emergence of specialised ESG indices (MSCI ESG Leaders, EuroNext ESG L80, Brazil's Carbon Efficient index) and dedicated ESG exchanges (LSE GreenMark & Sustainable Bond Market, Luxembourg Green Exchange) that provide instruments, market liquidity, and even more importantly, access to finance for firms prioritising ESG criteria (Cheng et al. 2014). Financial intermediation is evolving with the increased traction of ESG investing, and financial institutions have

Table 2 Approaches to sustainable investing

Approach	Key characteristics
Screening	Rules-based filtering. Negative: reflects ethical, religious, or social values. Positive: invests on the basis of ESG benchmarks. Norms: excludes firms in violations of global standards.
ESG integration	Combines ESG data with traditional financial metrics; supports alpha generation.
ThemATIC investing	Thematic ETFs/funds; often overlaps with impact investing.
Impact investing	Intentionality, measurability, and additionality are key; often private market focused.
Stewardship (active ownership)	Proxy voting, filing resolutions, direct engagement with company boards or management.

initiated funding programmes that redirect capital towards renewables, clean tech, and social impact projects. In the sovereign debt markets, emerging markets are benefiting from green FDI and blended finance structures (Flammer et al. 2024; Kharb et al. 2024).

Table 2 outlines the main approaches to sustainable investing, ranging from screening and ESG integration to thematic, impact, and stewardship strategies. Each approach differs in focus, from filtering investments by values to actively engaging with companies to drive change.

Institutions such as ESG data providers (e.g., Morningstar Sustainalytics, MSCI) and ESG-focused asset managers have emerged and consolidated and are impacting investment advisory and institutional logics (Ioannou and Serafeim 2015). New instruments, including green bonds, sustainability-linked loans, and ESG ETFs, have expanded investor choices, channelling capital towards sustainable projects (Flammer 2021). Regulatory tailwinds, like the European Union's Sustainable Finance Disclosure Regulation (SFDR), further institutionalise ESG integration, reinforcing capital reallocation towards standardisation of sustainable investing (Hummel and Jobst 2024). The sum of these developments spearheads greater corporate transparency and accountability on ESG integration into core business and investment strategies.

2.3 Sustainable Investing: History, Evolution, Concepts, and Regulatory Landscape

Sustainable investing, closely aligned with the concepts of responsible and ethical investing, has historical roots that predate contemporary financial systems. Ethical investment principles are embedded in most of the religious narratives, such as forbiddance of usury in **Abrahamic religions**, Ahimsa—non-violence—in **Hinduism, Buddhism, and Jainism**, and striking a balance between human life and nature—

environmental stewardship—in **Taoism and Shintoism. Each of these** advocates the application of exclusionary criteria to avoid morally objectionable activities.

The practice of ethical exclusions, originally rooted in **values-based screening**, was adopted as early as the eighteenth century. Notably, the Quaker movement formally opposed slavery from the mid-seventeenth century, and by the nineteenth century, various religious groups extended such moral considerations to discourage investment in sectors like alcohol production, gambling enterprises, and exploitative lending practices. These faith-driven initiatives established enduring moral precepts that shaped the modern-day criteria for exclusionary investing (as shown in Table 1).

Table 3 traces key international regulations and frameworks from 1997 to 2022 that progressively shaped ESG compliance, improving transparency, accountability, and integration of sustainability into financial markets.

This exclusionary screening laid the foundation for the socially responsible investing (SRI) approach, which evolved from the 1960s onwards in response to sweeping social and political movements. The era engendered the terminology of 'sin stocks', which expected investors to avoid industries considered harmful. The focus of exclusionary screens expanded beyond traditional vices to include weapons manufacturers—driven by opposition to the Vietnam War—and companies with operations in South Africa, fuelled by the global anti-apartheid campaign. Early ethical trusts and mutual funds institutionalised this principle (Sparkes and Cowton 2004; Cowton 1999).

During this period, **negative screening** was not driven by financial considerations but by a desire to align investments with moral duty. Alongside exclusions, shareholder activism emerged as a powerful tool, with investors filing proposals to influence corporate behaviour. Concurrently, community investing began to direct capital to underserved areas, reflecting a broader belief in using capital as an instrument for social change (Sparkes and Cowton 2004; Kinder et al. 1993).

From 2000s onwards, sustainable investing leapfrogged from values-based exclusion to investments that embed/integrate environmental, social, and governance (ESG) considerations into corporate activities. This has resulted in mainstreaming sustainability issues through capital allocation choices in the asset management industry. For example, 'Who Cares Wins' report in 2004 framed ESG issues as financially material, urging their incorporation into fundamental investment analysis (UN Global Compact 2004). UN Principles for Responsible Investment (PRI) in 2006 institutionalised this approach, providing a global framework for integrating ESG into investment processes (United Nations 2006). Strategies such as **best-in-class** investing emerged, rewarding sector leaders in ESG performance, and investors increasingly recognised that ESG factors could influence long-term risk-adjusted returns (Friede et al. 2015).

From 2010 onwards, sustainable investing is synonymous with ESG investing—spurred by climate-change urgency, the Paris Agreement of 2015, and heightened social justice movements resulting in UN SDGs. This remarkable growth is best showcased by the UN PRI's expansion from just 63 signatories representing \$6.5 trillion in AUM in 2006 to a total of 3038 investors representing over \$100

Table 3 History of regulations shaping ESG compliance and sustainable investing (1997–2022)

Year	Regulation / framework	Primary focus	Impact on sustainable investing
1997	Kyoto protocol	First binding international treaty to reduce GHG emissions;	Paved way for carbon markets and carbon trading.
1997	Global Reporting Initiative (GRI)	Corporate environmental accountability	Climate-change risk informed investments; formed the basis of ESG criteria
2000	Carbon Disclosure Project (CDP)	Investor awareness and activism; environmental disclosure	Provided standardised environmental data enhancing investors ESG integration
2005	EU Emissions Trading System (EU ETS)	To put a price on carbon emissions—market-based approach; cap-and-trade system	Carbon pricing; capital allocation targeting lower emissions and green investment
2006	UN Principles for Responsible Investment (PRI)	Developed a framework to integrate ESG factors into investment decisions	ESG investment analysis; improved transparency and focussed long-term value creation
2010	International Integrated Reporting Council (IIRC)	Integrated reporting of financial and non-financial performance	Simplified six Capital framework; provides a holistic framework for investor
2011	Sustainability Accounting Standards Board (SASB)	Financially material, industry-specific sustainability data	More focused than GRI; improves peer comparisons.
2015	Task Force on Climate-Related Financial Disclosures (TCFD)	Disclosing climate-change related financial risks	Transparency, and comparability of climate-related financial disclosures
2019	EU Sustainable Finance Disclosure Regulation (SFDR)	Standardised disclosure of sustainability risks and impacts.	Standardised classification system for financial products; improves ESG disclosure and combats Greenwashing
2020	EU taxonomy	Scientific classification of environmentally sustainable corporate activities.	Reducing greenwashing; directing capital towards green projects.
2022	Corporate Sustainability Reporting Directive (CSRD)	Mandatory audited sustainability reporting based on 'double materiality'.	Part of European Green Deal; sustainably competitive economy

trillion in combined assets by 2020, all committed to integrating ESG information into their investment decisions (PRI 2020).

3 Sustainable Investing: Scope and Regulatory Developments

Largely SRI investing by institutional and retailers have used negative screening (Bolton and Kacperczyk 2021; Renneboog et al. 2008); however, mainstreaming of ESG, climate-change, and social justice movements has asked firms to be more responsible in their corporate activities. This has resulted in several approaches to better define terminologies that fall under the scope of sustainable investing. GSIA, CFA Institute, & Principles for Responsible Investment (2025) have consolidated several overlapping investment approaches into five broad sub-groups:

- Screening
- ESG integration
- Thematic investing
- Stewardship
- Impact investing

3.1 Sustainable Investing: Definitions and Approaches

3.1.1 Screening

This investment strategy uses **selection or exclusion mechanisms** in a portfolio. **Negative screening**, the earliest method, excludes companies based on ethical or ESG concerns, like tobacco and fossil fuels (Sparkes and Cowton 2004; GSIA 2019). Norges Bank Investment Management (NBIM), for instance, excludes firms involved in severe environmental damage or human rights abuses (NBIM 2024). This remains a widespread baseline ESG practice, even layered into integrated funds like BlackRock's sustainable options (BlackRock 2022).

In contrast, **positive** or **'best-in-class' screening** selects companies with superior ESG performance relative to peers. Enabled by available ESG data from providers such as MSCI, this strategy is used by pension funds and multi-asset managers to gain ESG exposure while maintaining diversification. The AP Funds in Sweden, for example, use best-in-class criteria to overweight high-scoring companies (AP4 2023).

Other mechanisms include **norms-based screening**, which excludes companies violating international norms such as those from the UN Global Compact (UN Global Compact 2004; GSIA 2019). This approach is particularly common among European investors, with Triodos Investment Management being an example of

Table 4 Sustainable assets under management (AUM) by region (USD billions)

Region	2012	2014	2016	2018	2020	2022	2025e
Europe	8758	13,608	12,040	14,075	12,017	14,054	17,774.8
USA	3740	6572	8723	11,995	17,081	8400	10,290.4
Canada	589	945	1086	1699	2423	2358	2358
Australia & New Zealand	178	180	516	734	906	1220	1906.4
Japan	10	–	474	2180	2874	4289	7819.2
Total	13,275	21,305	22,839	30,683	35,301	30,321	40,148.8

Source: Global Sustainable Investment Alliance (2019, 2023)

a firm that screens out companies failing to uphold recognised human rights and environmental norms (Triodos 2024).

3.1.2 ESG Integration

This investing strategy embeds ESG factors into conventional investment analysis and decision-making. Together with norms-based investing, ESG investing gained momentum in the 2000s as capital holders and asset managers realised ESG issues can materially affect financial performance (UN Global Compact 2004). ESG investing gained momentum with increased investors' awareness and pledges following reports such as Who Cares Wins and the launch of the UN Principles for Responsible Investment. Friede et al. (2015) document that ESG integration often correlates with improved risk-adjusted returns—ESG alpha generation. It is the leading investment strategy **global** asset managers, e.g., BlackRock, Vanguard, and State Street Corp, among others, have a range of ESG portfolios. For example, BlackRock's ESG Advanced strategies integrate ESG scores into proprietary risk models to enhance portfolio resilience (BlackRock 2022).

Table 4 presents the growth of sustainable assets under management (AUM) across major regions from 2012 to 2022, with projections to 2025, showing Europe and the USA as the leading markets.

3.1.3 Thematic Investing

Targets investments in specific sustainability themes such as clean energy, water, climate solutions, or sectors aligned with the Sustainable Development Goals. Thematic investing has resulted in thematic exchange-traded funds and mutual funds proliferating (GSIA 2019). It is popular with both institutional and retail investors looking for targeted exposure. Investors such as **CalPERS** have dedicated allocations to climate or renewable energy themes. Other examples include funds like **iShares Global Clean Energy ETF** or **Pictet Water Fund.** These examples entail accelerating practice in ESG investing, specifically in sectors addressing environmental challenges (Boffo and Patalano 2020, OECD 2020).

Table 5 Sustainable assets under management China and developing countries

Region	2025 estimate	Range (low — high)
China	**USD 5.9 trillion**	5.6–6.4 T
Developing markets (ex-China)	**USD 1.3 trillion**	0.6–2.5 T
Total	**USD 7.2 trillion**	6.2–8.9 T

Sources: China Sustainable Investment Forum (2024), IFC (2023), Morningstar (2025)

3.1.4 Impact Investing

This investment strategy intends to generate measurable social and environmental outcomes alongside financial returns. Key features of this investment strategy are allocating capital to deliver on social and environmental change through project finance or funding companies that display goal alignment with respect to intentionality, measurability, and additionality. This investing strategy emerged after the 2007–2008 global financial crisis as socio-economic inequality widened even in the developed world, and it enhanced global attention on measurable impact increased (GIIN 2020; Bugg-Levine and Emerson 2011). This investment strategy is mostly employed by charities/foundations, development finance institutions, and some family offices. Institutions like **The Rockefeller Foundation**, **European Investment Bank**, and **Norfund** invest in emerging market impact projects, tracking metrics such as lives improved, carbon avoided, or jobs created. Norfund's renewable energy investments in Africa are evaluated not just by return but by metrics like megawatt hours generated and local employment (Norfund 2022).

Table 5 provides 2025 estimates of sustainable assets under management in China and other developing markets, projecting a combined total of USD 7.2 trillion, with China accounting for the majority share.

3.1.5 Stewardship—Corporate Engagement and Shareholder Action

This investment strategy focuses on influencing corporate behaviour using investors' power, whether through their voting rights or through their ability to set ESG-supporting norms or baselines. Active stewardship streamlines and consolidates shareholder rights using tools such as proxy voting, corporate engagement, dialogue, and active voicing—shaping the concept of ESG decoupling, and resolutions to influence corporate ESG practices. The mainstreaming of stewardship-led sustainable investing initially focused on the active monitoring by institutional investors in the early 2000s. The follow-up engagement and action have been tied to the UN PRI and collaborative initiatives (PRI 2020; Dimson et al. 2015). This investing strategy is widely practiced by asset managers such as State Street Corp, Global Advisors, and Vanguard, and by pension funds globally. Initiatives like **Climate Action 100 Plus** mobilise investors to engage with the world's largest emitters over greenhouse gas reductions. Shareholder activist group 'Follow This' is a significant example that has voiced and influenced Shell's climate strategy. Their voting has kept climate change on the company's agenda despite not getting approved any of their resolutions and how even a small group of dedicated investors can use their rights to bring material governance and environmental change.

3.2 *Growth in Sustainable Investing, Regulatory Developments, and ESG Reporting Standards*

Retail and institutional demand, combined with regulatory developments such as the EU's SFDR, have fuelled growth in thematic funds targeting issues like clean energy, water, and gender equity. Impact investing has risen alongside ESG integration, explicitly seeking measurable positive environmental and social outcomes in addition to financial returns (Global Impact Investing Network 2020). Active ownership and engagement remain central to ESG investing, with selective divestment used to address systemic risks such as fossil fuel dependence (UNFCCC 2015; PRI 2020).

However, academic research has long pointed to multiplicity of guiding principles and their conflicting nature that had hampered standardisation in ESG products and instruments as well as what is meant by ESG. For a detailed review of guidelines, initiatives, and frameworks that have shaped today's sustainability reporting and disclosure frameworks, see Table 3. It maps key developments starting from Kyoto Protocol adopted at Third Conference of the Parties (COP) 3 organised by United Nations Framework Convention on Climate Change (UNFCCC) in 1997 to CSRD in 2022 to develop sustainably competitive markets.

Table 6 outlines recent regulatory standards introduced between 2023 and 2024 that strengthen sustainability and climate disclosure, aiming to improve transparency, comparability, and investor accountability.

The multiplicity of guidelines and reporting initiatives, compounded by widespread greenwashing and corporate misconduct (Noori and Athota 2024), is a leading factor in the divergent methodologies adopted by data providers. This, in turn, has created significant confusion and disagreement across ESG data provided by several data providers. These ESD data divergences are well reported (Avramov et al. 2022; Berg et al. 2022). This undermines their reliability and, in result, usability by asset managers and investors. This has led to the issues of comparability and enabled 'greenwashing' (Ilhan et al. 2023; Starks 2023).

This is changing with the emergence of robust global frameworks such as the International Sustainability Standards Board (ISSB) and its IFRS S1 and S2 standards, which establish a baseline for reporting sustainability-related financial risks and opportunities. In parallel, the EU's SFDR and the United Kingdom's Sustainability Disclosure Requirements (SDR) aim to improve fund labelling, transparency, and investor comparability. Importantly, all these frameworks are

Table 6 Current regulatory standards

Year	Regulation/framework	Primary focus	Impact on sustainable investing
2023	ISSB IFRS S1 & S2	Global baseline for sustainability and climate disclosure.	Consolidated sustainability reporting; sustainability contextualised enterprise value; global consistency and comparability
2023	California Climate Laws (SB 253/SB 261)	GHG emissions and climate risk disclosure for large companies.	Legally mandated ESG disclosure across Scope1–3 levels; third-party assurance and mitigates reporting fragmentation
2024	UK Sustainability Disclosure Requirements (SDR)	Anti-greenwashing labels, entity/product disclosures.	Unified reporting framework requires mandatory product-level disclosure; empowers investors with clear, comparable information.
2024	SEC climate-related disclosure rule	Mandatory climate disclosure rules but Scope 3 disclosures required only if material	Climate transparency and accountability; national regulations with global outreach

more converging than the previous distorted benchmarks lacking consistency and comparability of different ESG data provisions.

The gains of stability and standardisation in the ESG data are improving tractability of ESG investing. ESG investments are estimated to represent ~40 trillion USD AUM by the end of 2025—if we only account for developed markets. Table 4 provides growth in the sustainable AUM across regions from 2012 to 2025. The sizeable growth in sustainable AUM is consolidated on the basis of IFRS S1 and S2 standards, which mandate disclosure of sustainability-related financial risks and opportunities. The EU SFDR is a leading framework, and the region's sustainable investing intent is displayed in the ~18 trillion USD AUM that fall under the broader category of sustainable investing, followed by the USA at ~10 trillion USD AUM.

For developing economies, using **IFRS S1/S2-aligned inclusive definitions—** the estimated figure is around **7.2 trillion US by end-2025**.[2] Of which China accounts for roughly **5.9 trillion USD**. These estimates are broader than those reported by the GSIA (2019, 2023), therefore, Table 5 also provides low to high estimates to depict the scope of definitions and data coverage. That these aspects,

[2] Aggregating ESG-integrated asset manager AUM, outstanding green and sustainability-linked bond stock, sustainability-linked loans and 'green credit' portfolios, and reported sustainable private capital.

Table 7 Comparative features of leading sustainable robo-advisors (illustrative global examples)

Robo-advisor	HQ—Geography	Sustainable line-up	Data/approach highlights
Betterment	USA	Climate impact portfolios (broad & concentrated options)	Uses ETFs targeting lower carbon/fossil reserves; automated rebalancing and tax features.
Wealthsimple	Canada	Socially responsible investing portfolios	Multiple SRI models, automated deposits/rebalancing; low-fee ETF implementation.
Nutmeg	UK	Socially responsible portfolios (10 risk levels)	Uses **MSCI ESG** research; sector/regional diversification; transparency on methodology.
Moneyfarm	Italy—Italy & UK	Socially responsible portfolios	SRI ETF range; clear disclosures on screens and charges.
Scalable Capital	Germany—EU	Sustainable portfolios	ESG-screened ETFs and factor tilts; client-level risk classes.
StashAway	Singapore—Fareast Asia, & MENA	Responsible portfolios	Re-optimised via ERAA™ with ESG-screened ETFs; risk-first approach.

inclusive of variability in reporting quality, constrain comparability across regions of the world, underscoring the need for continued harmonisation of sustainability reporting standards (ISSB 2023).

Table 7 compares leading sustainable robo-advisors across different global regions, highlighting their geographic presence, sustainable product offerings, and distinctive data-driven investment approaches.

3.3 Current Regulatory Landscape and ESG Standardisation

The development of current corporate sustainability reporting frameworks builds on earlier environmental, social, and governance codes/guidelines—essential reporting milestones. However, having plethora of guidelines at times resulted in conflicting requirements that hampered consistent reporting and disclosures on ESG issues. For example, the GRI (1997) provided a broad sustainability framework but often lacked financial materiality, whereas CDP in 2000 mainly focused on climate, water, and deforestation data. IIRC in 2010 paved the way to linking financial and non-financial performance but lacked standardised ESG metrics. The TCFD created a widely used framework for climate risk disclosures only. IIRC and TCFD are merged with SASB in 2021 and SASB itself has become part of the ISSB. SASB itself, founded in 2011, developed industry-specific standards for financially material ESG issues. It now is part of ISSB's IFRS S1 and S2 global standards. IFRS S1 reporting shapes single corporate materiality by integrating sustainability with financial performance. Likewise, TFCD recommendations have been fully incorporated into IFRS S2 since 2023.

Internationally, IFRS S1 and S2 provide the much-required consistency in the standards for sustainability-related disclosures for firms. The issues of jurisdictional adoption are yet to be determined as firms in the emerging markets have resource and capacity issues—the systems, skills, and infrastructure—to adopt these standards especially when there are no regulatory requirements in place. Nonetheless, IFRS S1 and S2 have stabilised a reference point for global alignment for sustainability-related disclosures, which was all too subjective and inconsistent, as manifested by divergent ESG scoring methods and scores by ESG raters.

It is important to mention that the EU has been pushing the envelope in leading the way to develop comprehensive sustainable finance disclosure and compliance frameworks, as shown in Table 3. Key regulatory drivers include the EU Taxonomy Regulation, which defines environmentally sustainable activities, and the SFDR, which standardises ESG disclosure for financial products. CSRD expands mandatory reporting across companies using European Sustainability Reporting Standards, while the Corporate Sustainability Due Diligence Directive (CS3D) moves towards full value-chain accountability when firms generate a significant portion of their turnover in the EU. These regulatory initiatives have set the gold standard in sustainable finance reporting, disclosures, and compliance mechanism.

In the USA, the SEC has finalised their own climate-related disclosure rules. The SEC rule has faced significant political and legal opposition. A key feature is the tiered approach to reporting, with mandatory disclosures for some climate data but a less stringent requirement for supply chain carbon emissions—indirect emissions from a company's value chain. The rule's compliance is staggered across time, with a few of the largest companies expected to report in the year 2025. However, the most significant regulatory development in the USA has taken place in the State of California, i.e., California Climate Laws—mandating advanced climate disclosures. It embeds CDP and TCFD disclosure requirements. The climate law will be phased in from 2026 to 2027 but is influencing investor expectations because SEC rules only require stringent-form disclosures if they have financial materiality, whereas California Climate Laws require a full disclosure of all activities falling under Scope 3. It shows that the US regulatory environment is yet not settled, as state-level requirements add complexity—not complementarity—for firms pursuing federal requirements.

In parallel, the Financial Conduct Authority (FCA) in the UK has developed an explicit labelling regime with clear, voluntary labels for financial products while adopting a gradual rollout. Once a fund has adopted a voluntary labelling regime, the naming and marketing rules are mandatory from 2024 to 2025. SDR tightly aligns EU regulations and ISSB frameworks. This regulatory development requires UK asset managers to make prudent, suitable sustainability claims and adopt suitable

ESG labels to combat greenwashing in ESG investing. The full remit of UK's SDR will standardise ESG fund labels and align disclosure requirements with ISSB and TCFD principles.

4 Robo-Advisory

Traditional investment management relies on human advisers who evaluate clients' objectives, constraints, and risk tolerance to build and oversee diversified portfolios with their professional judgement (Jung et al. 2018). AI-powered robo-advisers, on the other hand, perform these tasks using online questionnaires, algorithmic asset allocation, constant monitoring, and consistent, rules-based execution (Abraham et al. 2019; Alsabah et al. 2021). Table 7 provides a list of leading robo-advisory systems currently available in the market.

Another key advancement is the use of hybrid models through robo-advisory systems, which combine automation with human oversight for complex cases. While traditional advisers benefit from personalised relationships, robo-advisers improve **scalability, accessibility, and cost efficiency**. Despite these advantages, **opportunities for further innovation remain**. These opportunities include integrating **low-latency** architectures to enable dynamic and personalised recommendations (Jung et al. 2018). The capability of these architecture designs enables ingestion and processing of vast amounts of **real-time market data—from** incorporation of client-level transaction histories to harmonising data models**, decision-making, and trade execution** as close to real-time as possible.

Table 8 categorises key data supply lines used in robo-advisory for sustainable investing, ranging from financial markets and analyst forecasts to geospatial and IoT data, while also noting their respective roles and limitations, such as bias, data reliability, and integration challenges.

4.1 Efficiency, Accessibility, and Democratisation of Investment Advice

Robo-advisers offer significantly lower fees than traditional advisers, typically 0.25–0.50% of assets under management (AUM), while providing diversified and continuously monitored portfolios (Abraham et al. 2019; Alsabah et al. 2021). Automated rebalancing helps enforce discipline and counters behavioural biases like inertia and overreaction, while digital onboarding makes investing more accessible to clients who may not meet traditional account minimums (Aristei and Gallo 2025; Jung et al. 2018). For investors with complex needs, hybrid models combine automated portfolio management with human consultations to address unique circumstances while maintaining scalability (Bianchi and Brière 2023).

Table 8 Robo-advisory data supply lines for sustainable investing

Data type	Examples	Role in robo-advisory	Key issues
Financial markets	Prices, returns, volumes, corporate actions	Factor/risk inputs	Survivorship bias, point-in-time accuracy
Analyst forecasts	EPS estimates, price targets	Return expectations	Forecast bias
News & filings	10-K, 11-K, 13F corporate filings, press releases, earnings calls	Sentiment, insider trading, smart money, event risk	Misclassification, bias, correlated errors
Alternative data	Web traffic, high frequency trades	Tactical signals	Licensing, overfitting
Macro indicators	GDP, interest rates, inflation	Regime shifts, allocation changes	Lag, revisions
GEOSPATIAL AND SATELLITE DATA	Supply chain mapping, corporate and leadership location monitoring	Environmental and supply chain risk detection, physical asset verification	Data granularity, privacy concerns, interpretation complexity.
IoT and sensor data	Smart grids, energy use patterns, real-time pollution levels	Forward-looking ESG risk indicators	Data reliability, integration with financial datasets

Despite these advantages, key challenges to widespread adoption remain, including ensuring suitability, meeting disclosure requirements, and clearly explaining algorithmic recommendations (Abraham et al. 2019). **Explainable artificial intelligence (xAI)** methods, such as SHapley Additive exPlanations (SHAP) and Local Interpretable Model-agnostic Explanations (LIME), enhance transparency by clarifying feature importance (Černevičienė, and Kabašinskas 2024). Additionally, scenario-based simulations can support client trust and regulatory compliance (Babaei et al. 2022). With robust governance, AI-enabled robo-advisors can deliver professional advice at scale, democratising access to strategies once reserved for high-net-worth individuals (Abbas 2024; Aristei and Gallo 2025).

To achieve this robust governance, robo-advisory systems are built on a modular architecture. The robo-advisory architecture can seamlessly chain specialised modules, e.g., Natural Language Processing (NLP) engines to extract sentiment from financial news, ML predictive approaches model to forecast returns, and reinforcement learning agents to optimise rebalancing frequency under transaction cost constraints (Zhang et al. 2020). **Guardrails** such as position limits, sector caps, and risk budget constraints help contain agent autonomy and mitigate unintended strategies (Bianchi and Brière 2023; Alsabah et al. 2021). When properly constrained and monitored, robo-advisors can improve responsiveness to market changes, reduce implementation shortfall, and sustain target risk-return characteristics with human supervision.

4.1.1 Data Sources and Architecture

A robo-advisory platform depends on robust, continuous data feeds covering market prices, returns, volumes, corporate actions, index memberships, macroeconomic indicators, and analyst forecasts. Robo-advisors use several types of data:

- **Structured Financial Data:** This includes prices, volumes, returns, and corporate fundamentals, which are used as inputs for portfolio optimisation, factor models, and risk estimations.
- **Alternate Datasets:** This encompasses non-traditional sources, often available in unstructured formats. These include financial news, earnings call transcripts, and intraday trading patterns, which can be used to refine tactical allocation and risk detection.

Robo-advisory platforms are highly integrated digital platforms. Table 8 outlines several data sources that are aligned in a robo-advisory platform from ingestion to a structured database.

Typically, data sources are **channelled** via application programming interfaces (APIs) or direct exchange connections and are processed through ingestion pipelines that validate accuracy, remove duplicates, and apply timestamping for point-in-time integrity (Samuel et al. 2020). Storage in cross-sectional, time series, or longitudinal structures ensures both real-time and historical retrieval for back and forward testing, as well as dynamic decision-making (Alsabah et al. 2021). Establishing the architecture for robo-advisory systems therefore involves configuring reliable data pipelines, applying rigorous data cleaning and stratification, and building processable database structures—a foundational stage in platform development (Samuel et al. 2020; Adusupalli 2025).

In designing and developing robo-advisory architecture, several technical, operational, and layout-related data issues arise. For instance, latency-accuracy trade-offs arise when systems must balance rapid data delivery with precision; studies in inference serving highlight how adaptive frameworks can navigate such trade-offs to maintain accuracy under tight latency constraints (Salmani et al. 2023; Nigade et al. 2024). Survivorship bias skews performance analysis by excluding failed or delisted firms, resulting in overly optimistic backtest results (Carpenter and Lynch 1999; Daniel et al. 2008; Fung and Hsieh 1997; Brian 2020). Inconsistent data formats and semantic heterogeneity hinder seamless integration—schemas, units, naming conventions, and encoding vary across data vendors, complicating data fusion and interpretation (Abbas 2023; Sheth and Larsen 1990). Finally, erroneous data propagation through optimisation pipelines amplifies errors if cleansing and validation are inadequate. Addressing these issues through harmonised schemas, validation checks, and latency-aware architectures can markedly improve data quality and model reliability.

The application of AI modules starts even before the availability of the final time-synchronised, processing-ready, and machine-readable database. For example, NLP techniques transform unstructured text into quantitative features. Alternate datasets are crucial for making early-stage predictions on market states, sentiment, and

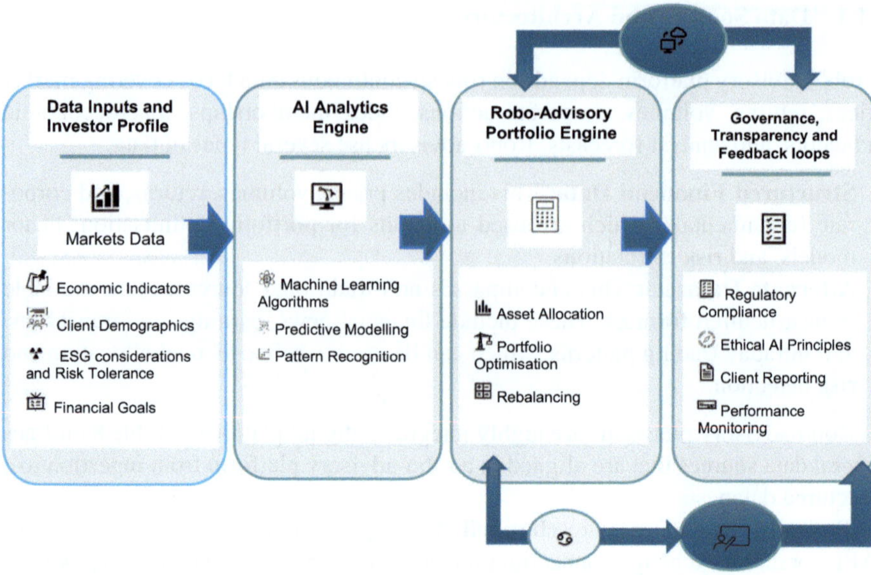

Fig. 1 Conceptual framework: sustainable investing in the AI-driven advisory ecosystem

risk. For example, evidence shows media pessimism can predict market downturns (Tetlock 2007); specialised dictionaries can capture the tone of corporate disclosures more effectively (Loughran and McDonald 2011). Furthermore, NLP is used for forward-looking risk assessment, such as by extracting political risks from company transcripts (Hassan et al. 2019). The use of large language models (LLM) like Open Pre-trained Transformer (OPT) is now a significant development, as they have outperformed traditional dictionary methods in predicting next-day stock returns (Kirtac and Germano 2025).

4.1.2 Robo-Advisory, Data Processing, and Analytical Frameworks

The functionality of a robo-advisor is built on a sophisticated, synchronised, and multi-stage architecture. To visualise a conceptual framework of a typical AI-powered robo-advisor to make investment recommendations, please refer to Fig. 1. This conceptual framework can be broken down into a five-stage loop, starting from investor's preference exploration to reinforcement learning from investor choices made from different scoring methods in the robo-advisory environment (Tables 9 and 10):

- **Investor Profiling:** capturing goals, constraints, horizon, and risk tolerance.
- **Investor Policy Formulation:** translating preferences into allocation targets, risk budgets, and constraints.
- **Portfolio Optimisation and Execution:** generating cost-efficient trade lists using algorithms.

Table 9 AI techniques used in robo-advisory

Technique	Role & purpose	Example applications
Supervised ML	Predict returns/volatility; classify risk profiles	Factor modelling, suitability checks
Bayesian methods	Combine priors with data	Covariance estimation, Black Litterman blending
Reinforcement learning	Optimise actions under costs & constraints	Rebalancing frequency, execution timing
NLP	Extract sentiment/uncertainty from text	Event detection, news analytics
Optimisation	Allocate assets to meet goals/risk	Mean variance, Black Litterman
Explainable AI	Interpret recommendations	Client reporting, compliance

- **Risk Monitoring:** detecting breaches, volatility shifts, and market anomalies.
- **Learning, Adaption and Compliance:** updating policies based on outcomes and new data.

For this multi-stage architecture to be effective, robust robo-advisory performance depends on rigorous backtesting protocols that guard against overfitting, look-ahead bias in predictions, and data leakage (Abraham et al. 2019). Avoiding these pitfalls requires timestamped and event-driven validation systems (Smigel 2023). With the availability of a dynamically functional database, robo-advisory platforms integrate analytical frameworks—AI modules—for data processing and decision-making. Table 11 lists several AI capabilities in robo-advisory systems. These analytical frameworks often operate in three layers: **feature engineering** (returns, volatility, sentiment, factor exposures), **estimation** (Bayesian shrinkage, regularised regressions, ensemble models), and **decision policies** such as mean-variance optimisation, Black Litterman induced portfolio allocation choices, or reinforcement learning allocation (Shen et al. 2025; Zhang et al. 2020). These layers enable a **dynamic and adaptive refinement** of investor policies and decision-making.

5 Robo-Advisory and ESG Investing

Robo-advisors are uniquely equipped to process and organise **heterogenous, unstandardised**, and **complex** ESG datasets. By doing so, they can translate diverse ESG information into transparent, rules-based portfolio actions at a reduced cost and make sustainable investing more widely available. On the technical side, as ESG data volumes and taxonomies proliferate, employing ML becomes critical. It supports screening, controversy detection, and climate-tilt optimisation, which bridges investor preferences with measurable outcomes and clear audit trails (Feng et al. 2024; Xu 2025).

Table 10 ESG scoring models used by robo-advisors—key features and differences

Rater	Scale	Core concept	Data sources	Controversies
MSCI ESG ratings	CCC–AAA	Financially material ESG risks & opportunities vs. peers	Disclosures, alt. Data, controversies	Separate MSCI ESG controversies feed affects eligibility/tilts
Sustainalytics ESG risk ratings	0–100 risk score	Unmanaged ESG risk = exposure × management	Disclosures, controversies, analysts	Severe events elevate risk and may breach thresholds
S&P Global CSA/ESG scores	0–100	1000+ data points, 60+ industry questionnaires	Company question-naires, media, stakeholders	Exclusion bias, lack independence, opaque weighting
LSEG/Refinitiv ESG scores	0–100 percentile + controversy score	10 themes, 450+ metrics	Filings, news, third-party data	Data inconsistencies across industries and themes, lack comparability & transparency, transparency issues
Moody's ESG (incl. V.E)	Varies by product	Issuer ESG profiles, controversies, predictors	Disclosures, datasets, controversies	Commercial conflicts, weighting opaqueness, excessive controversy penalisation, European compliance bias
KLD (MSCI ESG stats)	Binary dataset	Early US ESG indicators; KLD 400 index	Public sources, research screens	Lacks depth, US-centric, historical bias—sin stocks, index feedback loop

Source: Authors research

Other factors, such as **automated profiling**, **continuous data ingestion**, and **explainable rebalancing**, also help scale sustainable investing. These features reduce the friction points in portfolio policymaking and optimisation that often discourage retail participation, whereas for institutional investors robo-advisors offer configurable pipelines that align to their specific policy and fiduciary constraints (Mohapatra et al. 2025; Singh and Kumar 2025). Collectively, these features offer efficiency and scalability, broadening access and personalisation while also improving tractability and supporting robust compliance, monitoring, and reporting.

Table 11 Portfolio optimisation approaches for ESG goals

Approach	Idea	Strengths	Cautions
Mean–variance + ESG penalties	Penalise carbon/-controversies; constrain factor drift	Simple, explainable; aligns to index 'tilt' methods	Sensitive to input noise and ESG drift; needs re-estimation (MSCI)
Multi-objective optimisation	Jointly optimise return, risk, ESG targets	Transparent trade-offs; label-friendly	Requires careful goal setting and monitoring (Nundlall and Van Zyl 2023; Feng et al. 2024)
Factor-based ESG	Add ESG factor(s) to risk model	Controls style drift; supports attribution	Factor stability and interpretation challenges (Vo et al. 2019)
Deep REINFORCEMENT learning	Learn allocation policies under climate scenarios	Handles non-linearities, regime shifts; adaptive	Explainability & governance burden; compute/footprint constraints (Zhang et al. 2020; Xu 2025)

ESG investing brings additional data handling and processing needs due to its unique materialities. Robo-advisors are particularly well-suited for sustainable investing because they can manage the complex and voluminous ESG data efficiently. They are key enablers in scaling sustainable investing, as they can organise, modulate, and process diverse data types including **structured financial metrics**, **unstructured textual disclosures**, and **mixed-format ESG datasets**. This capability allows them to translate large volumes of heterogeneous ESG information into transparent, rules-based portfolio decisions—delivered at a low cost.

However, the integration of ESG considerations introduces a host of complexities. These include divergent ESG ratings, risks of greenwashing and green-hushing, inconsistent regulatory frameworks, and potential legal liabilities. Such challenges can readily deter investors and asset managers, rendering ESG integration prone to misjudgement and operational error.

On the technical side, as ESG data volumes and taxonomies proliferate, ML becomes critical. It supports screening, controversy detection, and climate-tilt optimisation, which bridges investor preferences with measurable outcomes and clear audit trails (Feng et al. 2024; Xu 2025). **Furthermore,** other factors, such as automated profiling, continuous data ingestion, and explainable rebalancing, also help scale sustainable investing. These features reduce the friction points in portfolio policymaking and optimisation that often discourage retail participation, whereas for institutional investors robo-advisors offer configurable pipelines that align to their specific policy and fiduciary constraints (Mohapatra et al. 2025; Singh and Kumar 2025). **Collectively,** these features offer efficiency and scalability, broadening access and personalisation while also improving tractability and supporting robust compliance, monitoring, and reporting.

Table 9 outlines the main AI techniques applied in robo-advisory, including supervised learning, Bayesian methods, reinforcement learning, NLP, optimisation, and explainable AI, highlighting their respective roles in risk prediction, decision-making, sentiment analysis, and compliance.

5.1 Robo-Advisory for ESG Data Standardisation and Baseline

Heterogeneity in ESG data is a bottleneck for scalable ESG investing. **Fortunately,** robo-advisors are a great solution to manage heterogeneous ESG datasets and to achieve standardisation and scalability in sustainable investing. ESG datasets often contain a mix of qualitative narratives and quantitative key performance indicators (KPIs). The data also suffer from issues like uneven coverage across different sectors and geographies, time-lags, and survivorship bias. Furthermore, discrepancies arise from vendor-specific choices on metrics such as Scope 3 emissions, controversies, or board quality.

A central ESG data challenge is rating divergence: providers disagree on what to measure, how to weight it, and how to handle controversies, generating low correlations across scores and classifications (Berg et al. 2022). That 'aggregate confusion' weakens naive screening and invites bias if not challenged. The use of divergent methodologies (industry-relative vs. absolute risk) also complicates comparability and portfolio construction. For example, MSCI assigns industry-normalised, issue-weighted ratings (AAA–CCC) and a separate controversies overlay, while Sustainalytics' ESG Risk Ratings emphasise 'unmanaged risk' on an absolute scale (negligible–severe), producing different investability lists for the same issuer. Please refer to Table 10 for different ESG rating providers and their methodologies.

AI-enabled robo-advisory can mitigate rating divergence in three ways. First, it could be set to automate cross-provider ingestion and mapping, harmonising issuers across identifiers and taxonomies, and learning stable signals across noisy vendor inputs. This requires robo-advisors to explicitly model **data quality** (coverage, timeliness, methodological drift) and **rating divergence** to avoid spurious precision. That is, robo-advisors can seamlessly integrate procedures including cross-rating consensus measures. Second, it can encode user-level materiality (e.g., climate vs. labour metrics) and dynamically re-weight factors as disclosures improve. For example, dynamic data feeds—news, excessive supply chain carbon emissions, or environmental damage lawsuits—can be set as controversy overrides, and **dynamic guardrails** (e.g., removing issuers when controversies breach severity thresholds regardless of composite score). Third, xAI pipelines can document and audit every decision, aiding in client reporting and alignment with regulatory frameworks (Bianchi and Brière 2023).

Table 10 compares major ESG scoring models used by robo-advisors, highlighting differences in scales, core concepts, data sources, and key controversies such as bias, transparency, and consistency issues.

Robo-advisory plays a pivotal role in creating **ESG baselines** by automating the ingestion and harmonisation of heterogeneous datasets across multiple providers, denoising gaps in coverage. They provide consistent, standardised signals for sustainable investing while reducing manual burdens, and governance risks. Through AI-driven consensus measures, dynamic controversy overrides, and explainable pipelines, robo-advisors create scalable ESG baselines that reduce bias, enhance comparability, and support compliance with regulatory and client-specific materiality requirements. The implementation of this multi-layered ESG data baseline delivers what would otherwise be excessively time-consuming, costly, and prone to human errors, if not misconduct. Robo-advisors will impute and denoise missing KPIs and forecast emissions pathways to reduce gaps in small-cap/EM coverage (Zhang et al. 2020) and streamline decision rules for efficiency, performance, compliance, and audit.

The robo-advisory can achieve a myriad of constraints to maintain ESG criteria, as well as jurisdictional requirements, and all of this while standardising ESG data—safeguarding data quality. Robust ESG standardisation and baseline stacks will be shaped by:

(i) **Data layer:** multi-vendor ingestion (MSCI, Sustainalytics, index-level screens), issuer mapping, NLP over reports, and controversy/news feeds.
(ii) **Policy and feature layer:** harmonised metrics (emissions intensities, target credibility, violations); learned cross-rating embeddings to exploit signal amid rating divergence; investor-specific exclusions (e.g., thermal coal), stewardship flags, and regulatory constraints (SFDR/SDR labels).
(iii) **Modelling layer:** multi-objective optimisation for return–risk–ESG, scenario/transition-path testing, and explainability; and.
(iv) **Governance layer:** model management, fairness/bias tests, data-lineage logging and adversarial robustness (FSB 2024; NIST AI RMF 2023).

5.2 Portfolio Construction for Sustainability Goals

AI-powered robo-advisor functionalities significantly enhance ESG integration in investment portfolios. Once standardised ESG data baselines are available, robo-advisory platforms can ensure a deeper alignment of investments with sustainability goals. These platforms offer a scalable solution for implementing complex sustainability preferences and provide real-time, explainable insights into a portfolio's social and environmental impact.

The portfolio construction process through ML approaches and advanced optimisation routines can be deployed to align investor intent with an implementable strategy. For a detailed review of several AI approaches in the portfolio construction process, please refer to Table 11. ESG investing workflow in robo-advisory can be streamlined:

1. **Investor profiling: determine** investor type, horizon, and liquidity (e.g., retail vs. institutional), elicit sustainability priorities (e.g., decarbonisation pace, social screens), and capture regulatory constraints (e.g., SDR label eligibility in the UK).
2. **ESG goals:** translate preferences into quantifiable targets **such as** emissions-intensity reductions, minimum ESG risk thresholds, exclusions, and stewardship outcomes (voting/engagement coverage).
3. **Risk tolerance: establish** volatility thresholds, drawdown, and tracking-error budgets.
4. **Risk management: incorporate** climate transition and physical risk scenarios, controversy caps, and concentration limits.
5. **Optimisation & review: execute** multi-objective models with human monitoring, re-estimation—**via** deep reinforcement learning, and **provide** explainable change logs.

After setting the necessary constraints, portfolio construction proceeds through multi-objective optimisation, where return, risk, and sustainability preferences are simultaneously traded off. For example, a system might minimise carbon intensity subject to tracking-error limits and sector neutrality (Nundlall and Van Zyl 2023; Feng et al. 2024). The integration of penalisation constraints for emissions, controversies, or ESG risk, while limiting factor drift to maintain market-like exposures, defines the core mechanism through which ESG objectives are embedded into quantitative portfolio construction. MSCI (2024) ESG Leaders and Universal index methodologies, for instance, illustrate the distinction between tilt-based and optimisation-based variants of this integration.

This process can be further extended by applying advanced optimisation techniques such as stochastic optimisation and deep reinforcement learning, which allow for dynamic adaptation to evolving market conditions and provide more nuanced incorporation of ESG objectives into the efficient frontier. In cases where preferences conflict—for instance, excluding all fossil-adjacent revenues versus maintaining a tracking-error cap—**the system quantifies the cost of purity, offers diversified substitutes, and records the decision for audit**. The system can also use factor-based ESG integration, which considers explicit sustainability factors alongside classic Fama-French risk premia (Vo et al. 2019). In addition, to meet jurisdictional requirements, model selection should be conditioned on label eligibility (e.g. FCA SDR investment labels impose criteria for sustainability 'Focus/Improvers/Impact' strategies) and traceability, documenting the data, constraints, and rationale.

5.3 Active Stewardship: Impact and Robo-Advisory

Robo-advisory platforms can **operationalise stewardship** by systematically targeting engagements where they can have the greatest impact. They can be tuned to use selection mechanisms that consider both the materiality of issues and the momentum of a company's actions. To implement this, they can use several mechanisms: **goal-based reporting** (like tracking progress on emissions or voting records), **commitment devices** (such as automatically increasing stewardship intensity unless an investor opts out), and **communication strategies** that reduce friction (for example, framing market volatility as a 'budget' for long-term impact). **Continuous monitoring** then adjusts portfolios as ratings, controversies, or regulatory thresholds change, ensuring that **stewardship 'intent'** is evidenced in votes and engagements. These technological and behavioural mechanisms demonstrate a fundamental shift in portfolio design. Designing ESG portfolios is transforming from setting static constraints to a more dynamic, participatory optimisation problem. Here, ML and digital tools are working together to redefine what is valuable to investors.

This approach extends the concept of the ESG frontier proposed by Pedersen et al. (2021): maximising investor utility across financial returns, sustainability outcomes, and participatory stewardship engagement. By combining AI-powered robo-advisory with ESG-constrained optimisation, it is making the **augmented frontier** achievable while making advisory services more accessible to everyone. This view is supported by recent research on ML—optimised sustainable portfolios and studies on how retail investors are adopting robo-advisory services (Feng et al. 2024; Vo et al. 2019). This evidence highlights how robo-advisory platforms are embedding **stewardship functions** directly into the investment optimisation and client engagement processes.

5.4 ESG Personalisation and Behavioural Frictions in Sustainable Investing

Customised portfolio development is the first step in unlocking the transformative potential of AI in sustainable investing. It begins with a deep understanding of investor sustainability priorities and objectives, setting clear rules to manage potential conflicts, and leveraging deep reinforcement learning to adapt to their evolving choices. Throughout the portfolio construction process, AI capabilities facilitate **hyper-personalisation**. This ranges from detailed granular screens (e.g., animal welfare, water stress) to creating differential decarbonisation pathways without the need for manual oversight. The use of these advanced technologies makes sophisticated, ethically aligned investment strategies accessible to a wider audience (Shen et al. 2025).

Robo-advisors are particularly effective, as they can develop highly customised portfolios that align with client ESG preferences while adhering to label criteria and sector neutrality (Feng et al. 2024). Consequently, these platforms automate the creation of resilient portfolios that not only aim for financial returns but also dynamically manage and report on their tangible impact at a lower cost (Barile et al. 2025; Shen et al. 2025). Robo-advisors typically charge much lower fees than traditional advisors, often between 0.25% and 0.50% of assets under management. Their use of digital onboarding and lower costs makes professional investment management accessible to a broader client base (Aristei and Gallo 2025; Jung et al. 2018): **democratises advisory** services. Robo-advisors increase transparency and enable preference-driven customisation with an interactive selection process, and automated rebalancing & reporting—addressing behavioural barriers to entry (Mohapatra et al. 2025; Singh and Kumar 2025). In this vein, the embedding of ESG rules, such as UK SDR labels, may further help retail investors' comprehension and ability to compare ESG portfolios.

To this effect, these platforms also tackle behavioural frictions like present bias, confusion from conflicting ratings, and ambiguity aversion through effective **choice architecture**. This includes offering pre-verified templates, transparent trade-offs, and clear impact dashboards. Explainability features, such as highlighting the drivers of inclusion or exclusion and attributing emissions reductions, counter information overload. Default **escalation nudges**, like 'improver' funds that tighten targets annually, help maintain client engagement. Mohapatra et al. (2019, 2025) provide evidence that AI-enabled robo-advisors, through features like **recommendation engines** and a focus on clarifying utility and ease of use, can strengthen behavioural intention towards sustainable investing.

5.5 Integrating ESG-Regulations in Robo-Advisory

Robo-advisors offer significant benefits to investors and are subject to increasing regulatory scrutiny.[3] For example, robo-advisors can map product design to SDR labels and disclosures for UK asset managers, maintain audit trails for claims, and align with the EU ESG ratings regime and CSRD-driven issuer reporting improvements. The integration of AI-powered analysis allows robo-advisors to process vast amounts of unstructured data from corporate reports, news articles, and social media to provide a more holistic and dynamic ESG risk assessment. To this effect, institutional investors benefit from policy-aware optimisation and bespoke reporting for trustees and regulators.

Table 11 outlines key portfolio optimisation approaches for ESG goals, contrasting their underlying ideas, strengths, and limitations, from traditional mean–variance methods to advanced reinforcement learning strategies. Source Author analysis.

In consideration of the fact that institutions must evidence processes (model governance, third-party assurance) and manage concentration risk in data and

[3] Regulatory scrutiny is needed because robo-advisors manage client money using automated algorithms, which may expose investors to risks like mis-selling, biased recommendations, data misuse, and systemic vulnerabilities. Oversight ensures transparency, investor protection, algorithmic accountability, and fair practices, thereby maintaining trust, stability, and resilience in financial markets.

analytics providers (FSB 2024; Eurosif n.d.), robo-advisory systems embed these aspects with ease. This may include stress-testing models against a range of climate scenarios, such as the Network for Greening the Financial System (NGFS n.d.) scenarios, to quantify potential financial impacts. In addition, incorporating climate-related physical and transition risk data from external providers, like those specialising in geospatial analysis, can provide a more granular view of portfolio vulnerabilities (Corrigan et al. 2025). The leveraging of NLP in robo-advisory platforms can also be used to identify potential inconsistencies between a company's ESG disclosures—e.g., in corporate sustainability reports—and its actual performance. The gap between the two is typically referred to as ESG Decoupling (Bronzini et al. 2024), and this identification enables moving beyond data points and fitting, to assess the intent and effectiveness of a company's ESG strategy.

In response to jurisdictional rules and guidelines, robo-advisors can operationalise regulatory requirements by encoding labelling rules, cross-referencing portfolio holdings against exclusion lists, and dynamically adjusting to new taxonomies such as the EU Green Taxonomy (Chiu 2022). This allows for real-time monitoring of sustainability thresholds while reducing the manual **burden on compliance teams.** They can ensure that transparent disclosures are not treated as optional: the UK's SDR package (PS23/16) and the anti-greenwashing rule (FG24/3) mandate that sustainability-related claims be fair, clear, and not misleading. Likewise, at the ecosystem level, the EU's ESG Ratings Regulation (2024/3005) mandates methodology transparency, governance, and conflict-of-interest controls for rating providers operating in the Union. Stipulation of these requirements improves the comparability and auditability of inputs to robo-advisors. ESMA (2025) documents that fund naming and portfolio holdings reveal ongoing risks of greenwashing. Robo-advisory platforms can address supervisory concerns by embedding structured decision-logging protocols, incorporating independent third-party ESG verification mechanisms, and ensuring algorithmic fund selection processes are systematically aligned with validated sustainability data. Incorporation of xAI ensures transparency in decision pathways, which regulators increasingly view as essential for client protection (Bianchi and Brière 2023).

Furthermore, integrating these regulations into robo-advisory architecture creates an opportunity to enhance investor trust and strengthen market credibility. Robo-advisors also support global alignment by harmonising disclosure frameworks across regions—for example, aligning UK SDR, EU SFDR, and CSRD obligations through unified data models (Busch 2023; Steuer and Tröger 2022). By coupling regulatory integration with advanced analytics, robo-advisors not only meet supervisory expectations but also deliver enhanced comparability, auditability, and accountability—helping investors navigate evolving ESG rules with confidence and reducing systemic risks from greenwashing.

In practice, robo-advisors can further mitigate greenwashing risks by maintaining comprehensive audit trails for sustainability claims and ensuring that disclosures remain consistent with regulatory expectations. Platforms can also be coded to automatically detect and flag potential greenwashing by cross-checking sustainability claims against controversies and third-party evidence. This is particularly critical as regulators sharpen fund naming and disclosure rules under the UK SDR package and the EU ESG Ratings Regulation. Such proactive modulation creates a transparent and auditable pipeline, resilient to methodological shifts from any single data provider, and aligns closely with supervisory guidance from bodies such as IOSCO and ESMA.

Furthermore, robo-advisors can leverage Distributed Ledger Technology to create immutable records of investment decisions and sustainability-related disclosures, thereby enhancing transparency and auditability for regulators and investors alike (FCA 2022; Mattern 2018). This approach, coupled with dynamic materiality assessments, ensures that platforms can adapt to evolving sustainability standards and investor expectations. For example, DLT can be used to track the chain of custody for green bonds or verify the origin of carbon credits, providing an auditable trail that prevents double-counting and fraud (Axelsen et al. 2023; Khan and Ahmad 2022; Pons 2025).

6 Summary

Robo-advisors are profoundly impacting ESG investing by democratising access and enhancing analytical capabilities beyond traditional methods. These platforms leverage algorithms to scale personalised investment advice, making ESG investing accessible to a broader range of investors, including those with smaller portfolios who previously could not afford bespoke financial planning (Fisch et al. 2019). This democratisation is key to mobilising capital towards sustainable outcomes—personalised portfolios at low cost, scaling ESG investing, and enhancing transparency and regulatory alignment (Bianchi and Brière 2023; Feng et al. 2024). The convergence of sustainable investing and robo-advisory is set to accelerate, fundamentally reshaping capital allocation towards climate resilience, social equity, and responsible governance.

The use of AI capabilities in robo-advisory enables continuous monitoring of portfolio holdings against evolving ESG standards, allowing for real-time rebalancing in response to new data or regulatory changes. This capability helps address the risk of greenwashing and ensures that investment portfolios remain aligned with stated sustainability goals (ACCA & CA ANZ 2021). These are substantive development in an investment segment in which litigation risks are intensifying. Greenwashing and 'green-hushing' have already prompted stricter anti-misrepresentation rules, such as the FCA's anti-greenwashing guidance, which requires sustainability claims to be 'fair, clear and not misleading'. Courts are increasingly receptive to climate-related litigation, illustrated by high-profile cases such as DWS facing investigation for overstating ESG credentials and lawsuits in the USA against BlackRock and other asset managers over alleged greenwashing of investment funds. These cases demonstrate that fiduciary duty is emerging as a significant legal liability risk, where advisors may face claims not only for financial negligence but also for failing to integrate ESG considerations in line with client mandates and regulatory standards (FCA 2023; Bronzini et al. 2024). Thus, future developments will likely see robo-advisors acting as engines of ESG standardisation, bridging persistent rating divergences (Berg et al. 2022), allowing dynamic portfolio rebalancing and embedding fast-tracked compliance with revisions in regulatory frameworks such as the EU SFDR, UK SDR, and ISSB's IFRS S1/S2 standards. Advances in explainable AI will be critical, ensuring that clients and regulators alike can trace investment decisions with clarity, thereby mitigating risks of greenwashing and misrepresentation (FCA 2023).

From a policy perspective, the coming years will be defined by how effectively supervisory frameworks integrate technological innovation. Initiatives such as the EU's SFDR, the UK's SDR, and ISSB's IFRS S1/S2 standards already provide an institutional backbone for global ESG disclosure (Busch 2023; ISSB 2023). However, future regulation will need to go further—ensuring explainability of AI-driven recommendations, setting guardrails against systemic risks from correlated algorithms, and embedding robust cyber resilience (FSB 2024; ESMA 2025). Importantly, regulatory harmonisation will need to be dynamic, with machine-readable formats to keep pace with rapidly evolving AI models and datasets (Virk 2025).

Looking ahead, the challenge for policy and industry alike is to ensure that the democratisation of sustainable investing does not come at the expense of systemic stability or investor protection. By embedding ethical AI, adaptive regulatory integration, and robust compliance, robo-advisors can transform sustainability from aspirational rhetoric into enforceable, auditable, and growth-oriented investing space.

References

Abbas SK (2024) AI meets finance: the rise of AI-powered Robo-advisors. J Electr Syst 20(11):1011–1016

Abraham F, Schmukler SL, Tessada J (2019) Robo-advisors: investing through machines. World Bank Research and Policy Briefs, (134881)

Adusupalli B (2025) Integrated financial ecosystems: AI-driven innovations in taxation, insurance, mortgage analytics, and community investment through cloud, big data, and advanced data engineering. J Inf Syst Eng Manag 10:1103–1117

Alsabah H, Capponi A, Ruiz Lacedelli O, Stern M (2021) Robo-advising: learning investors' risk preferences via portfolio choices. J Financ Economet 19(2):369–392

Aristei D, Gallo M (2025) Financial literacy, robo-advising, and the demand for human financial advice: evidence from Italy. J Behav Exp Finance 101125. https://www.sciencedirect.com/science/article/pii/S2214635025001066?via%3Dihub

Association of Chartered Certified Accountants (ACCA) & Chartered Accountants Australia and New Zealand (CA ANZ) (2021) Ethics for sustainable AI adoption: connecting AI and ESG. https://www.accaglobal.com/content/dam/ACCA_Global/professional-insights/nv-ai-ethics/PI-AI-ETHICS.pdf

Avramov D, Cheng S, Lioui A, Tarelli A (2022) Sustainable investing with ESG rating uncertainty. J Financ Econ 145(2):642–664

Axelsen H, Rasmussen U, Jensen JR, Ross O, Henglein F (2023) Trading green bonds using distributed ledger technology. arXiv preprint arXiv:2304.08154

Babaei G, Giudici P, Raffinetti E (2022) Explainable artificial intelligence for crypto asset allocation. Financ Res Lett 47:102941. https://doi.org/10.1016/j.frl.2022.102941

Baker M, Bergstresser D, Serafeim G, Wurgler J (2022) The pricing and ownership of US green bonds. Annu Rev Financ Econ 14:415–437

Barile D, Secundo G, Mariani M, Brandonisio A (2025) A new era: managing green investments through Robo-Advisors. Manag Decis. https://doi.org/10.1108/MD-06-2024-1268

Bebchuk LA, Tallarita R (2020) The illusory promise of stakeholder governance. Cornell L Rev 106:91

Berg F, Kölbel JF, Rigobon R (2022) Aggregate confusion: the divergence of ESG ratings. Rev Finance 26(6):1315–1344

Bianchi M, Brière M (2023) Robo-advising: less AI and more XAI? Augmenting algorithms with humans-in-the-loop. In: Machine learning and data science for financial markets, pp 33–59

BlackRock (2022) Sustainable investing and exclusions policy

Bolton P, Kacperczyk M (2021) Do investors care about carbon risk? J Financ Econ 142(2):517–549

Boston Consulting Group (BCG) (2025) Reinventing growth amid market volatility. https://www.bcg.com/publications/2025/reinventing-growth-amid-market-volatility

Brian S (2020) A primer on survivorship bias. QuantRocket. https://www.quantrocket.com/blog/survivorship-bias/

Bronzini M, Nicolini C, Lepri B, Passerini A, Staiano J (2024) Glitter or gold? Deriving structured insights from sustainability reports via large language models. EPJ Data Sci 13(1):41

Bugg-Levine A, Emerson J (2011) Impact investing: transforming how we make money while making a difference. Innov Technol Gov Glob 6(3):9–18

Busch D (2023) EU sustainable finance disclosure regulation. Cap Mark Law J 18(3):303–328

Carpenter JN, Lynch AW (1999) Survivorship bias and attrition effects in measures of performance persistence. J Financ Econ 54(3):337–374

Černevičienė J, Kabašinskas A (2024) Explainable artificial intelligence (XAI) in finance: a systematic literature review. Artif Intell Rev 57(8):216

Cheng B, Ioannou I, Serafeim G (2014) Corporate social responsibility and access to finance. Strateg Manag J 35(1):1–23

China Sustainable Investment Forum (China SIF) (2024) China sustainable investment review 2024. China SIF

Chiu IH (2022) The EU sustainable finance agenda: developing governance for double materiality in sustainability metrics. Eur Bus Organ Law Rev 23(1):87–123

Corrigan J, McNeill C, Kent N, Keane M, Brown C, Hanson D, Halliday C (2025) Improving access to geospatial climate risk data. Arup

Cowton CJ (1999) Playing by the rules: ethical criteria at an ethical investment fund. Bus Ethics: Eur Rev 8(1):60–69

Daniel G, Sornette D, Wohrmann P (2008) Look-ahead benchmark bias in portfolio performance evaluation. arXiv preprint arXiv:0810.1922

Davis GF (2008) A new finance capitalism? Mutual funds and ownership re-concentration in the United States. Eur Manag Rev 5(1):11–21

Dimson E, Karakaş O, Li X (2015) Active ownership. Rev Financ Stud 28(12):3225–3268

ESMA (2025) Artificial intelligence in EU investment funds: adoption, strategies and portfolio exposures (TRV risk analysis). ESMA. https://www.esma.europa.eu/sites/default/files/2025-02/ESMA50-43599798-9923_TRV_Article_Artificial_intelligence_in_EU_investment_funds.pdf

European Securities and Markets Authority (ESMA) (2025) ESMA publishes four principles for clear, fair and not misleading sustainability-related claims. Regulatory & Compliance. https://www.regulatoryandcompliance.com/2025/07/esma-publishes-four-principles-for-clear-fair-and-not-misleading-sustainability-related-claims/

Eurosif (n.d.) ESG ratings and data providers. Retrieved [Month Day, Year], from https://www.eurosif.org/policies/esg-ratings-performance-metrics/
FCA (2023) PS23/16: Sustainability Disclosure Requirements (SDR) and investment labels. https://www.fca.org.uk/publication/policy/ps23-16.pdf
Feng X, von Mettenheim HJ, Sermpinis G, Stasinakis C (2024) Sustainable portfolio construction via machine learning: ESG, SDG and sentiment. European Financial Management
Fichtner J (2020) The rise of institutional investors. In: The Routledge international handbook of financialization. Routledge, pp 265–275
Financial Conduct Authority (FCA) (2022) Written evidence submitted by the Financial Conduct Authority: role and remit of the FCA (Written Evidence No. 111674). UK Parliament. https://committees.parliament.uk/writtenevidence/111674/pdf/
Fisch JE, Laboure M, Turner JA (2019) The emergence of the robo-advisor. In: The disruptive impact of FinTech on retirement systems, vol 13, pp 13–37
Flammer C (2021) Corporate green bonds. J Financ Econ 142(2):499–516
Flammer C, Giroux T, Heal G (2024) Blended finance (No. w32287). National Bureau of Economic Research
Fourth Swedish National Pension Fund (AP4) (2023, March 27). Annual report 2022. https://www.ap4.se/globalassets/rapporter-och-innehav/2022/230327-ap4-annual-report-2022.pdf
Friede G, Busch T, Bassen A (2015) ESG and financial performance: aggregated evidence from more than 2000 empirical studies. J Sustain Financ Invest 5(4):210–233. https://doi.org/10.1080/20430795.2015.1118917
FSB (2024) The financial stability implications of artificial intelligence. https://www.fsb.org/2024/11/the-financial-stability-implications-of-artificial-intelligence
Fung W, Hsieh DA (1997) Empirical characteristics of dynamic trading strategies: the case of hedge funds. Rev Financ Stud 10(2):275–302
Global Reporting Initiative (GRI) (1997) Global Reporting Initiative. Available at: https://www.globalreporting.org/. Accessed: 25 April 2026
Global Impact Investing Network (GIIN) (2020) Annual impact investor Survey
Global Sustainable Investment Alliance (GSIA) (2019) Global Sustainable Investment review 2018. Global Sustainable Investment Alliance. https://www.gsi-alliance.org/wp-content/uploads/2019/03/GSIR_Review2018.3.28.pdf
GSIA (2023) Global Sustainable Investment review 2022. Global Sustainable Investment Alliance. https://www.gsi-alliance.org/wp-content/uploads/2023/12/GSIA-Report-2022.pdf
GSIA, CFA Institute, & Principles for Responsible Investment (2025) Definitions for responsible investment approaches. GSIA. https://www.gsi-alliance.org/members-resources/definitions-for-responsible-investment-approaches/
Hassan TA, Hollander S, Van Lent L, Tahoun A (2019) Firm-level political risk: measurement and effects. Q J Econ 134(4):2135–2202. https://doi.org/10.1111/jofi.13255
Hummel K, Jobst D (2024) An overview of corporate sustainability reporting legislation in the European Union. Account Eur 21(3):320–355
Ilhan E, Krueger P, Sautner Z, Starks LT (2023) Climate risk disclosure and institutional investors. Rev Financ Stud 36(7):2617–2650
International Finance Corporation (IFC), & Amundi (2023) Emerging market green bonds report 2023: a sustainable finance perspective. IFC
International Sustainability Standards Board (ISSB) (2023) IFRS S1 general requirements for disclosure of sustainability-related Financial information. IFRS Foundation. Retrieved August 12, 2025, from https://www.ifrs.org/projects/completed-projects/2023/general-sustainability-related-disclosures/
Ioannou I, Serafeim G (2015) The impact of corporate social responsibility on investment recommendations: analysts' perceptions and shifting institutional logics. Strateg Manag J 36(7):1053–1081
Jung D, Dorner V, Glaser F, Morana S (2018) Robo-advisory: digitalization and automation of financial advisory. Bus Inf Syst Eng 60(1):81–86

Khan N, Ahmad T (2022) DCarbonX decentralised application: carbon market case study. arXiv preprint arXiv:2203.09508

Kharb R, Saini N, Kumar D (2024) Driving environmental sustainability in emerging economies: the nexus of green finance, foreign direct investment, financial development, and green technology innovation. Business Strategy & Development 7(4):e70008

Kinder PD, Lydenberg SD, Domini AL (1993) Investing for good: making money while being socially responsible. Harper Business

Kirtac K, Germano G (2025) Leveraging LLM-based sentiment analysis for portfolio allocation with proximal policy optimization. In: ICLR 2025 workshop on machine learning multiscale processes

Lazonick W (2015) Stock buybacks: from retain-and-reinvest to downsize-and-distribute. Center for Effective Public Management, Brookings Institution

Loughran T, McDonald B (2011) When is a liability not a liability? Textual analysis, dictionaries, and 10-Ks. J Financ 66(1):35–65

Lucas RE (1978) Asset prices in an exchange economy. Econometrica 46(6):1429–1445. https://doi.org/10.2307/1913837

Markowitz HM (1952) Portfolio selection. J Financ 7(1):77–91. https://doi.org/10.2307/2975974

Mattern M (2018) Exploring blockchain applications to agricultural finance. Consultative Group to Assist the Poor (CGAP) Briefs, the World Bank

Mayer C (2018) Prosperity: better business makes the greater good. Oxford University Press

Modigliani F, Brumberg R (1954) Utility analysis and the consumption function: an interpretation of cross-section data. In: Kurihara KK (ed) Post-Keynesian economics. Rutgers University Press, pp 388–436

Mohapatra S, Kumar A, Kumar A (2019) Developing a framework for adopting artificial intelligence. International Journal of Computer Theory and Engineering 11(2):19–22

Mohapatra N, Shekhar S, Singh R, Khan S, Santos G, Carvalho S (2025) Unveiling the nexus between use of AI-enabled robo-advisors, behavioural intention and sustainable investment decisions using PLS-SEM. Sustainability 17(9):3897

Morningstar (2025) Global sustainable fund flows report Q1 2025. Morningstar Research

MSCI (2024) MSCI ESG leaders indexes methodology. MSCI Research. (MSCI)

Network for Greening the Financial System (NGFS) (n.d.) NGFS scenarios portal. NGFS. Retrieved August 29, 2025, from https://www.ngfs.net/ngfs-scenarios-portal/

Nigade V, Bauszat P, Bal H, Wang L (2024) Inference serving with end-to-end latency SLOs over dynamic edge networks. Real-Time Systems 60(2):239–290

NIST (2023) AI risk management framework 1.0. National Institute of Standards and Technology Oxford Academic

Noori R, Athota VS (2024) Greenwashing in ESG and its implications. In: ESG frameworks for sustainable business practices. IGI Global, pp 151–177

Norfund (2022) Annual report 2022. Norfund. Retrieved August 12, 2025, from https://www.norfund.no/annualreport-2022/

Norges Bank Investment Management (2024, February 7) Observation and exclusion of companies. NBIM. Retrieved August 12, 2025, from https://www.nbim.no/en/responsible-investment/ethical-exclusions/exclusion-of-companies/

Nundlall T, Van Zyl TL (2023) Machine learning for socially responsible portfolio optimisation. In: Proceedings of the 2023 7th international conference on intelligent systems. Metaheuristics & Swarm Intelligence, pp 1–6

OECD (2020) OECD business and finance outlook 2020: sustainable and resilient finance. OECD Publishing. https://doi.org/10.1787/eb61fd29-en

Pedersen LH, Fitzgibbons S, Pomorski L (2021) Responsible investing: the ESG-efficient frontier. J Financ Econ 142(2):572–597

Pons JR (2025) Trust creation with blockchain and distributed ledger technology (DLT) for carbon and biodiversity credit management. Blockstand.eu

Principles for Responsible Investment (PRI) (2020) Annual report 2020. Retrieved August 12, 2025, from https://www.unpri.org/annual-report-2020

Renneboog L, Ter Horst J, Zhang C (2008) Socially responsible investments: institutional aspects, performance, and investor behaviour. J Bank Financ 32(9):1723–1742. https://doi.org/10.1016/j.jbankfin.2007.12.039

Salmani M, Ghafouri S, Sanaee A, Razavi K, Mühlhäuser M, Doyle J, Jamshidi P, Sharifi M (2023) Reconciling high accuracy, cost-efficiency, and low latency of inference serving systems (arXiv:2304.10892). arXiv. https://arxiv.org/abs/2304.10892

Samuel I, Ogunkeye FA, Olajube A, Awelewa A (2020, November) Development of a voice chatbot for payment using amazon lex service with eyowo as the payment platform. In: 2020 International Conference on Decision Aid Sciences and Application (DASA). IEEE, pp 104–108

Samuelson PA (1958) An exact consumption–loan model of interest with or without the social contrivance of money. J Polit Econ 66(6):467–482. https://doi.org/10.1086/258116

Sharpe WF (1964) Capital asset prices: a theory of market equilibrium under conditions of risk. J Financ 19(3):425–442. https://doi.org/10.1111/j.1540-6261.1964.tb02865.x

Shen Z, Wang Z, Chew J, Hu K, Wang Y (2025) Artificial intelligence empowering robo-advisors: a data-driven wealth management model analysis. Int J Manag Sci Res 8(3):1–12

Singh S, Kumar A (2025) Investing in the future: an integrated model for analysing user attitudes towards Robo-advisory services with AI integration. Vilakshan-XIMB J Manag 22(1):158–175

Sheth AP, Larson JA (1990) Federated database systems for managing distributed, heterogeneous, and autonomous databases. ACM Comput Surv 22(3):183–236. https://doi.org/10.1145/96602.96604

Smigel L (2023, October 13) The history of AI in finance. Analyzing Alpha. https://analyzingalpha.com/history-of-ai-in-finance

Sparkes R, Cowton CJ (2004) The maturing of socially responsible investment: a review of the developing link with corporate social responsibility. J Bus Ethics 52(1):45–57

Starks LT (2023) Presidential address: sustainable finance and ESG issues—value versus values. J Financ 78(4):1837–1872

Steuer S, Tröger TH (2022) The role of disclosure in green finance. J Financ Regul 8(1):1–50

Stout LA (2012) The shareholder value myth: how putting shareholders first harms investors, corporations, and the public. Berrett-Koehler Publishers

Tetlock PC (2007) Giving content to investor sentiment: the role of media in the stock market. J Financ 62(3):1139–1168

Triodos Bank UK (2024) Why Triodos is different: the importance of our minimum standards. Triodos Bank UK. Retrieved August 12, 2025, from https://www.triodos.co.uk/articles/2024/triodos-minimum-standards

UN Global Compact (2004) Who cares wins: connecting financial markets to a changing world. United Nations Global Compact. https://documents1.worldbank.org/curated/en/280911488968799581/pdf/113237-WP-WhoCaresWins-2004.pdf

UNFCCC (2015) Paris agreement. United Nations Framework Convention on Climate Change

United Nations (2006, April) Secretary-general launches 'principles for responsible investment' [press release]. United Nations. https://press.un.org/en/2006/sg2111.doc.html

Useem M (1996) Investor capitalism: how money managers are changing the face of corporate America. Basic Books, New York

Virk N (2025) UK financial services leadership in the AI age: Opportunities and challenges [Written evidence submitted to the UK Parliament Treasury Committee, AIFS0033]. Retrieved from https://committees.parliament.uk/writtenevidence/139822/html/

Vo NN, He X, Liu S, Xu G (2019) Deep learning for decision making and the optimisation of socially responsible investments and portfolio. Decis Support Syst 124:113097

Xu Y (2025) Deep reinforcement learning-driven intelligent portfolio management with green computing. Sustain Comput Inform Syst 46:101125

Zhang Z, Zohren S, Roberts S (2020) Deep learning for portfolio optimisation. arXiv preprint arXiv:2005.13665

Robo-Advisory Under Review: The Market's Verdict

Yan Huang

Abstract This chapter examines the evolving landscape of robo-advisory services through the lens of market responses from various players across both emerging and developed economies. While robo-advisors entered the financial services scene with the promise of revolutionising investment management through offering automation, scalability, and greater accessibility to everyday investors, recent developments suggest a more complex reality. In the past few years, several major global banks, including Goldman Sachs, JPMorgan Chase, and UBS, have notably scaled back or exited their robo-advisory adventures. The primary driver behind this retreat is profitability. Although robo-advisory platforms are efficient and low cost, they charge minimal advisory fees and often require low account minimums to attract mass retail clients. This business model also struggles to cover the substantial costs involved in client acquisition, compliance with regulatory frameworks, and ongoing technology maintenance. As a result, maintaining financial sustainability at scale becomes increasingly difficult for firms. Despite these setbacks among legacy banks, there are successful and inspiring players. Firms such as Vanguard and Betterment showcase how digital platforms can succeed when they deliver a clear and compelling value proposition to a well-defined market segment. Looking beyond mature markets, emerging economies also present significant opportunities for robo-advisory expansion. Countries such as India, South Africa, China, and those in the Middle East are showing increasing interest in digital wealth management. These regions benefit from a rising middle class, high mobile penetration, and a growing appetite for tech-enabled financial solutions.

Keywords Robo-advisors · Fintech innovation · Automated financial advice · Digital platform competition · Hybrid human–AI advisory · Robo-advisor business models

---

Y. Huang (✉)
Business School, University of Exeter, Exeter, UK
e-mail: y.huang8@exeter.ac.uk

N. Nahidi, A. Zarifis (eds.), *AI, FinTech, and the Future of Robo-Advisory*,
Contributions to Finance and Accounting,
https://doi.org/10.1007/978-3-032-18109-1_16

Financial decisions are complex at different life stages. Uncertainties further complicate the management of individuals' assets. With their professional knowledge and expertise, financial advisors provide support to help people make informed decisions. When a financial advisor offers financial advice to an investor, the process normally involves evaluating her financial position, identifying her financial objectives in different states of life, and assessing her risk appetite. Based on the evaluation, the advisor proposes an investment portfolio that is suitable for the client to meet her goals. Once the investment advice is taken, the advisor will monitor the portfolio performance and periodically rebalance it to reflect market conditions or any changes in the client's circumstances. This service comes at a high cost. Advisory service charges for advice are normally either on an hourly basis or as a percentage of assets under management (AUM). Take the U.K. as an example. The Financial Conduct Authority (FCA) reports that average charges are 2.4% of the amount invested for the initial advice as a one-off charge and 0.8% of AUM annually for ongoing advice (PDR/FAMR evaluation 2010). These high charges, plus a high level of minimum asset requirements, create barriers for smaller investors who need financial advice. However, the need for financial guidance extends beyond high-net-worth individuals to include those with modest savings who also benefit from structured advice. With the technological advancement, robo-advisors came into the picture as a potential solution to offer accessible and affordable services to investors with smaller assets. According to Morningstar's 2025 Robo-Advisor report, the median advisory fee is 0.25% of AUM annually, which is significantly lower than traditional advisory charges. Since the launch of the first robo-advisor serving retail investors by Betterment in 2010, the growth of robo-advisory services has been rapid, with the potential of scaling leveraging by technology. The early success of fintech innovators generated a herding effect across the financial sector. Statista (2024) predicts that by 2029, the global robo-advisory market will grow to $2.38 trillion in AUM and serve around 35 million clients. The U.S. market dominates with an estimated $1.46 trillion in AUM in 2024 (KPMG 2024). The early success of the fintech firms in providing the robo-advisory services sparked interest among financial institutions, including asset managers and universal banks. However, the strategies of firms involved in the robo-advisory wave led to different outcomes. Some firms have been able to scale their services and take up the market shares. Others withdrew when they could not achieve their goals. Both the successful and failed cases are reviewed from the beginning of the firms' journey in robo-advisory services to the most recent development in this chapter to investigate the opportunities and challenges in this evolving service.

1 The Robo-Advisor Fever

The first robo-advisor platform was launched by Betterment, a financial savings startup, at the TechCrunch Disrupt conference in 2010. At launch, it offered portfolios composed of stock and bond index ETFs. Users could choose their preferred asset allocation, receive an analysis of their portfolio, and compare their choices with those of people in different age and income groups. The platform initially charged a fee of 0.9% regardless of the number of trades an investor made and had no minimum capital requirement. Betterment's aim was to enter the financial savings industry by giving retail clients easy access to diversified portfolios of stocks and bonds that were automatically rebalanced against the market indices. Based on modern portfolio theory, which advocates the benefit of diversification in investment, a committee of academics and fund managers decided the portfolio mix on a quarterly basis. This initiative, with zero-capital requirements, vastly reduced the barriers for small investors who wanted to invest in a diversified portfolio. Before Betterment, index funds were not accessible to smaller investors as the cost for them to serve smaller investors was high, and ETFs charged trading fees for each purchase and sale. Although the service fee was not much different from the human robo-advisory services, the zero-capital entry requirement allowed smaller accounts to combine automated risk profiling with low-cost portfolio diversification. This innovation attracted market recognition, with its AUM increasing from $10 million to $50 million after 2 years.

Wealthfront followed with the launch of its robo-advisor in December 2011. The firm had begun its Series A funding in 2007 under the name kaChing, during which it tested virtual portfolios. Its products were built on modern portfolio theory, giving smaller investors access to diversified portfolios without the high capital requirements as for traditional financial advisors. The firm was able to use Goldman Sach's investment model as it was open sourced. At launch, clients were required to complete a short questionnaire of 10 simple questions to establish their risk profile, which the system used to recommend customised portfolios drawn from a selection of low-cost exchange-traded funds (ETFs) across six asset classes. To gain market share rapidly, Wealthfront charged no advisory fee on the first $25,000 and applied a fee of 0.25% on assets above that threshold. The minimum capital was $5000. Within just two and a half years, its AUM had climbed to $800 million, making it the largest robo-advisor at the time. Apart from providing advice to invest in diversified portfolios, the firm also introduced the tax-loss harvesting feature embedded in robo-advising. This feature offered small investors the premium product which had been only available for high-net-worth investors. The process of identifying assets that have declined in value, selling them, and reinvesting the proceeds into assets with similar risk characteristics was automated to reduce the cost significantly. Small investors could have the benefit of reduction of tax liability through the robo-advisory services. The scaling possibility on a daily basis through robo-advisory services by Betterment and Wealthfront received massive popularity among the investor community. It also gave confidence to other market players to enter the field. SigFig, originally a financial information platform, tried out its robo-advisory services, which allowed investors to track their portfolios while receiving tailored recommendations. The advisory service itself was free, but the firm generated revenue through commissions on new investments made via the platform's recommendations. This model differentiated itself from Betterment and Wealthfront.

The wave of new entrants gave inspiration to other market players to provide robo-advisory services which target specific investor needs. In 2016, Ellevest was launched for women only to address the gender gaps in investment by tailoring financial decisions more closely to their needs. This demonstrated how technology could be adapted to serve different market segments. While its portfolios were broadly in line with the competitors, Ellevest charged a higher fee of 0.5%, compared with competitor rates ranging from 0.15% to 0.35%. Its model incorporated factors specific to women, such as salary progression patterns and longer life expectancy. In the same year, OpenInvest introduced its robo-advisor focusing on socially responsible investing through diversification of value-based services. Investors could align investments with their personal beliefs, particularly on social impact, i.e., excluding weapon manufacturers or tobacco firms, or choosing firms which promote gender equality. Automatic rebalancing ensured portfolios continued to track market indices closely. The annual fee ranged between 0.20% and 0.30%, which was higher than typical index funds that charged around 0.05% to 0.16%. Similarly, another niche emerged with Wahed Invest launched in the United States in 2015 as the world's first robo-advisor offering Shariah-compliant portfolios and expanded to the United Kingdom in 2018. Portfolios include global and emerging-market equities, sukuk (Islamic bonds), and gold. Fees were tiered at 0.79% per annum on asset value below $100,000 and 0.49% on asset value of $100,000 or more.

The adventurous spirit of the pioneers and the bold initiatives taken by them were evidenced by rapid growth in AUM and the number of investors choosing the robo-advisory services. The disruption and early success of robo-advisors in wealth management made financial institutions, such as asset managers or universal banks, compelled to explore the market's potential to avoid being left behind. Some firms were cautious about participating by partnering with the established firms, while others started in-house pilots to build proprietary solutions.

Before committing to its own branded robo-advisor, Fidelity formed a short-term strategic alliance with Betterment in 2014, and the collaboration lasted a year. During this partnership, Betterment designed a tool for Fidelity's financial advisors to allow them to manage clients and their assets on Betterment's platform. This tool effectively reduced the paperwork for advisors when accepting new clients. Furthermore, it offers human advisor services to Betterment's clients who would like to opt for the services. This partnership worked well initially, as Fidelity could focus on its strength in high-value services while Betterment provided the technology and undertook cumbersome tasks, such as onboarding clients and collecting fees from clients. But the model started to show its flaws. The financial products offered in the platform remained limited to Vanguard ETFs, excluding Fidelity's own offerings. This exclusion led to the termination of the partnership. In 2016, Fidelity Investments decided to build its own robo-advisor infrastructure and embedded its own financial products. Fidelity Go had a similar portal design as Betterment's, serving both retail investors and financial advisors. Its primary focus was on attracting millennial investors. The minimum capital was $5000, and the advisory fee was between 0.35% and 0.40%. Betterment charged a 0.25% fee without minimum capital requirement.

Charles Schwab, another asset manager, joined the game ambitiously by launching its own robo-advisor. Schwab Intelligent Portfolios (SIP) offered automated online investment advice to retail investors. At launch, the platform offered 54 ETFs drawn not only from Schwab's own range but also from providers such as Vanguard. For premium clients, they also offered a hybrid model with human advisory services. To stay competitive, the service charged no commissions, advisory fees, or account service fees. The only cost to clients was the operating expense ratio of the ETFs. However, a minimum investment of $5000 was required, similar to Wealthfront's threshold. The no-advisory-fee approach attracted significant market attention as a successful marketing strategy. But the model was too good to be true. Many critics questioned the fee structure and investigated the hidden fees. Clients seemed to pay indirectly through reduced returns on their cash holdings, which was not revealed to them. This lack of transparency fell onto the radar of regulators. The SEC investigated the firm between March 2015 and November 2018, and more details came to the surface. The investigation showed that the SIP account held 6% to 29.4% of clients' assets in cash based on their risk tolerance. Then this pre-set cash would be swept into the affiliate bank to earn interest rate spread. This resulted in lowering the client's total portfolio return, particularly during the time when other assets outperformed cash. In 2021, a class-action complaint was filed by three investors alleging undisclosed fees from the "cash drag", which has negative impacts on clients' portfolio returns. In 2022, the SEC charged the firm for "misleading robo-advisor clients about absence of hidden fees", and the firm settled for $187 million. This was the first time a robo-advisory business model was publicly scrutinised in depth. It raised questions about the sustainability of the robo-advisory model. Was its main source of profit coming from fees or from cash products? A majority of independent robo-advisors remain privately held firms. Even when robo-advisory services are part of larger publicly listed financial institutions, their individual performance is rarely reported as a separate line item. However, with Wealthfront's decision to file for an IPO on 29 September 2025, it has become possible to examine in detail the financial accounts of one of the sector's largest market players. Wealthfront's revenue is concentrated in cash management products, which accounted for 75% of total revenue in 2025, while investment advisory services contributed around 24%. Wealthfront's revenue composition shed light on Schwab Intelligent Portfolios' model.

In the similar timeline, Vanguard also introduced its in-house robot advisor, following a two-year pilot program that had been available to investors with $100,000 or more. The full launch of Vanguard Personal Advisor Services lowered the entry point to $50,000, and by March 2015 had already attracted over $7 billion in advisory assets. The services were in line with what was offered by Schwab Intelligent Portfolios. The hybrid model and automated system were the main selling points. The advisory fee was kept low at 0.3% of AUM. The clientele were mainly Baby Boomers, born between 1946 and 1964. This was different from the client focus of independent robo-advisors, such as Betterment and Wealthfront, who targeted Millennial investors. By 2019, its AUM reached $140 billion. The firm did not want to miss out on the younger generation who are tech-savvy. So, in 2019, it introduced a fully automated platform—Vanguard Digital Advisor. To take in the younger investors with small assets to start with, this service reduced the minimum investment requirement to $100. Together, the two models have grown to become the largest robot advisor in terms of AUM ($365bn by June 2025). Its low fees, which are about half the industry average, and low capital requirement play important roles in its success.

BlackRock, among the asset managers, took the shortcut by acquiring FutureAdvisor in 2015, a fintech firm focusing on robo-advisors since 2010. The deal was worth $150 million. FutureAdvisor's AUM was $600 million at the time of acquisition. The robo-advisory services were mainly B2B. It offered the digital solutions to its partner firms, including banks, insurers, and 401(k) platforms. One major source of income from the robo-advisor is through licensing fees to partner firms. The firm recognised the growing financial advisory needs from mass-affluent investors, or those with less than $1 million in investable assets, and tried to leverage the automation technology to build an ecosystem with more institutional players. The management team of BlackRock was clear on the goal of the firm in the robo-advisor race. The firm was aiming to enhance its own technology infrastructure to better manage risk and construct portfolios. This innovative model provided new perspectives to the market. Although the firm allowed organic growth of the retail business of the robo-advisor, the growth of AUM was considerably slower than other asset managers.

Universal banks followed suit, investing heavily in technology to capitalise on their brand strength, sizeable client bases, and broad distribution channels. Bank of America (BofA) introduced Merrill Edge Guided Investing (MEGI) in 2017 as a hybrid robo-advisory platform. Its fees were broadly in line with competitors, charging 0.45% with a minimum investment of $1000. For clients with deposits of $20,000 or more, the service also offered access to a financial planner, at a higher advisory fee of 0.85%. Like most robo-advisors, it uses algorithms to evaluate an investor's risk profile and construct portfolios built primarily from low-cost ETFs, with Vanguard and iShares as the main providers. Its distinguishing feature is that these portfolios are actively managed by the investment team. Asset allocations are not fixed but are regularly reviewed and adjusted by the management team in response to shifting market conditions. This service became "the biggest growth area" for BofA and grew "faster than most of the FinTechs in the same pace" over the following years. By leveraging its large existing client base, BofA was able to reach the scale of Betterment and Wealthfront in nearly half the time. To make the platform more friendly to users, Merrill Edge accounts were integrated with BofA's Preferred Rewards programme and its banking services. Clients can manage their savings and investment accounts in one app. This one-stop-shop business model was well received by young investors, who accounted for 52% of MEGI accounts in 2024. It enables cross-selling opportunities to this group of investors and also gradually moves them from pure robo-advisory solutions with the lowest fees to hybrid models, eventually graduates them to higher-net-worth services.

To tackle the same group of investors, Morgan Stanley in 2017 also released Access Investing with a $5000 minimum capital requirement and a 0.35% fee. To capture the interests of the millennial generation, the firm targeted thematic portfolios and socially responsible investment options. It also labelled its robo as a premium offering, as retail investors can have access to the same research resources as other elite clients. Its model is similar to BofA's, which is to facilitate a smooth transition of young investors to full-service clients once their wealth grows and needs become complex. Morgan Stanley was clear that its robo-advisor would serve as a complementary tool for clients and would not cannibalise the firm's existing business. However, the firm reconsidered its strategy after a few years into its own robo-advisory journey. It acquired E*TRADE for $13 billion in 2020, marking the biggest takeover by an American lender since the 2008 financial crisis up to that point. CEO James Gorman's comment ("it was always buy versus build") suggested that the bank may have realised that internal technology investment alone would not justify the costs, and that it was better to focus on its core strengths and specialisation. The acquisition added to Morgan Stanley a substantial client base of more than 5 million client accounts with over $360 billion of retail client assets and $56 billion of deposits. *Core Portfolios*, the robo-advisor offered by E*TRADE, had a low minimum investment requirement of $500 and a competitive advisory fee of 0.3%. The platform was well received by users and earned multiple top-ranking industry awards. The in-house and acquired platforms were run in parallel for some time, and then in 2022 the firm decided to close its in-house platform by 2026 and migrate clients to E*TRADE.

UBS, which focuses on high-net-worth and ultra-high-net-worth clients, recognised the industry disruption and entered the robo-advisory arena in the 2010s. It had an adventurous journey. It began with a partnership with SigFig, followed by testing the waters with its own program, considered acquiring a robo-advisory competitor but eventually abandoned the plan, and finally decided to withdraw from the field. In 2016, UBS formed a strategic partnership with SigFig to leverage its technology to build tools and services for UBS's 7000 advisors in the United States. The bank worked closely with SigFig through the Advisor Technology Research and Innovation lab to explore new wealth management tools. UBS was also among the investors in SigFig's $40 million fundraising round. After 1 year, UBS launched its own Smart Wealth in the U.K. to reach "a new audience" with the feature of "no people at the back offering advice". The minimum investment is £15,000, and the bank was targeting "mass affluent", defined as investors having £100,000 to $2,000,000 in assets. By the end of the year, this robo-advisor won the "Best Use of IT in Private/Wealth Management Award" at the Banking Technology Awards. But surprisingly, after about 18 months, UBS decided to discontinue the program and claimed that "the near-term potential is limited". The platform was sold to SigFig. UBS did not stop its exploration. It rolled out UBS Advice Advantage in 2018 in the United States. This hybrid robo-advisory platform, designed with SigFig, was aiming at "emerging affluent clients". The capital threshold was $10,000, and the advisory fee was 0.75%. Beyond its traditional client base, the bank recognised the growing population of millennial and Gen Z affluent investors, like other competitors. The quickest way for the bank to penetrate the market for a specific group was through acquisitions. In 2022, it announced plans to acquire Wealthfront for $1.4 billion. At the time, Wealthfront had $27 billion in AUM and had nearly half a million clients in the United States. The potential synergies offered by Wealthfront were substantial. However, 8 months later, UBS decided to walk away from the deal, which would have been the largest acquisition by UBS since the 2008 global financial crisis. The firm re-evaluated its robo-advisory ambitions and concluded that this move could not "bring alpha in mass-affluent".

Goldman Sachs had traditionally focused on corporate clients and ultra-high-net-worth individuals. But it decided to diversify its business model, which had been focusing on trading and investment banking revenues, by reaching out to retail clients. Through the acquisition of GE Capital Bank's US online deposit platform in 2016, the firm opened its doors to retail clients. Marcus, a consumer bank, was launched in 2017 to offer personal loans. The retail bank expanded its business rapidly through a series of acquisitions and partnerships. By 2019, Marcus had attracted $50 billion in deposits, $5 billion in consumer loans and 4 million customers in the USA. and the U.K. When competitors were exploring the technological innovations to scale up retail banking, Goldman Sachs also joined the race. It launched Marcus Invest, an automated investing platform, in 2021. The robo-advisor allocated client assets to in-house-designed ETFs with a low entry capital of $1000 and a fee of 0.35%. Within the first few months, over 10,000 accounts were opened, and the majority were held by existing clients. Although the beginning of the robo-advisory journey appeared smooth and strategically consistent, the firm's move to consumer banking became controversial as losses reached $1.2 billion in 2022, making cumulative losses of more than $4 billion. The $100 billion in deposits and more than 14 million clients did not appear sufficient to reverse the situation. As a result, the scaling back of consumer business brought in uncertainties on the development of its robo-advisory business, even though it appeared to be a promising strategy to scale operations and reduce the expenses per client.

J.P. Morgan Chase launched its robo-advisor, You Invest Portfolios, in 2019 to allow "digitally engaged customers" in the USA to invest in J.P. Morgan ETFs. The firm built an online financial supermarket where "customers can now bank, save, borrow, and invest". The minimum investment was $2500, and the fee is 0.35%, or less than $1 a month. To pave the way for the robo-advisor launch, the firm introduced the You Invest platform a year earlier, which offered customers 100 commission-free trades. The platform also included portfolio tools to assess investors' risk tolerance and design the portfolios to onboard investors before introducing the robo-advisor. Within 2 years, the firm made a move to acquire Nutmeg, a U.K.-based robo-advisor with around 140,000 retail investors and £3.5 billion of AUM. It aimed to build its digital wealth management services in the U.K. by "using the very latest technology" Nutmeg had, while adding J.P. Morgan's products. This approach saved time and costs in building the robo-advisor infrastructure, helped the firm gain customers rapidly, and enabled the cross-selling of other banking services.

The growth of robo-advisors is a story of trial and adaptation to identify which model best serves each firm. Betterment's starting point with two simple portfolios has turned into a broader portfolio mix. The fully automated model has evolved into a hybrid model with a personal touch to further strengthen customer relationships. Each stage has demonstrated an adaptive and adventurous financial culture. Fintech firms took the initiative to welcome small investors, while established financial institutions either collaborated with fintech firms or invested in their own infrastructure to capture the growing population of "digital natives". Fintech firms increased the awareness of financial institutions of the generational shift, especially with millennials and Gen Z investors who demand openness, value, and convenience.

2 Survival of the Fittest

The competition in robo-advisory services is fierce. The benefits of leveraging technology in wealth management offer the potential to make scaling possible and profitable when targeting markets with investors who have smaller assets. By reviewing the different initial approaches adopted by different institutions ranging from fintech startups to financial institutions, the initial mix of caution and enthusiasm has evolved into more sophisticated and focused strategies. These strategies now tend to align robo-advisors more closely with each firm's long-term goals, customer base, and areas of specialisation after more than a decade of exploration and experimentation. This evolution leads to the next question: are robo-advisors surviving, and is the model sustainable?

Betterment has grown to become one of the largest independent robo-advisors, with AUM of $46.96 billion by June 2025. The first decade of its growth was largely organic. It experienced impressive expansion in the first 5 years. But growth began to slow across several indicators thereafter. For instance, in the first 5 years, the number of users increased by more than double annually. But this number dropped significantly to 22% in 2020. Its AUM also recorded triple-digit growth in the initial years but slowed to about 10% in 2020. The average account size has stabilised at nearly $30,000. Since 2020, Betterment has undertaken a wave of acquisitions to retain its market position. It began with the purchase of Wealthsimple Inc.'s U.S. business in 2021, which had $197 million of AUM and 17,400 clients. It later acquired Goldman Sachs' Marcus Invest in 2024, followed by Ellevest's robo accounts and assets in 2025. The main synergies from these acquisitions were the increased amount in AUM and the number of client accounts. As the firm remains private, there was no publicly available data on its financial information to evaluate its profitability. It is worth noting that Betterment's fundraising rounds ended in 2021, with a total of $435 million raised. The recent moves by Betterment showed it relied heavily on expansion, acquisition, and scaling to sustain growth. Wealthfront had a similar early growth pattern to Betterment, driven primarily by organic expansion. Its last round of fundraising ended in 2022, raising a total of

$274.2 million. At the time, UBS planned to buy it at $1.46 billion when its AUM was $27 billion. After the deal failed through, the firm reported its first profit ($77 million) in 2023. The majority of its revenue and profit contribution came from its cash management business. In 2023, its cash account increased from $9 billion to $27 billion as it attracted investors with competitive high-yield cash returns. Cash management accounted for approximately 71% of total revenue. This momentum continued into fiscal 2025 with an annual profit of $194.4 million. This cash-sweep model brought large revenue and profit to the firm from the interest rate spread. By allocating cash across 32 program banks, the firm diversified its risk and maximised FDIC coverage. Although the current heavy reliance on cash accounts has proven financially feasible, a future interest rate cut by the Federal Reserve could prompt a reassessment of this strategy. Advisory products contribute about a quarter of total revenue. With 77% of clients born after 1980 and an average age of 38 as of July 2025, this demographic could be the next growth area for the firm. SigFig took an entirely different pathway. It transformed from a B2C model to a technology partner with financial institutions including UBS and Wells Fargo. Its AUM grew from $211 million in 2018 to $3 billion by 2024, but it shifted its future focus towards providing infrastructure to support digital financial solutions. In 2025, it rebranded as Tandems.

Bank of America is one of the few surviving robo-advisory service providers. It provides both fully automated and hybrid solutions. With its broad retail client base and a wide range of financial products and services, the bank has successfully scaled the service and generated fee-based revenue growth. The platform is fully integrated into the Merrill and Bank of America digital ecosystem, allowing clients to manage banking, lending, and investing activities under a single login. Vanguard and Fidelity also have found a way to make digital advice pay. Both manage to combine scale, credibility, and accessible pricing. Vanguard's hybrid Personal Advisor Services and Fidelity's Fidelity Go continue to attract a broad client base. Unfortunately, many financial institutions' robo-advisors did not survive in the stand-alone mode. J.P. Morgan discontinued its operation of the fully automated You Invest Portfolio service in 2023 and attributed the closure to weak demand. It also retired Nutmeg, a U.K.-based robo-advisor. To maintain its presence in the U.K., J.P. Morgan integrated it into J.P. Morgan Personal Investing, which offers a hybrid model targeting affluent clients. Goldman Sachs sold Marcus Invest to Betterment in 2024 after struggling to achieve scale and profitability. UBS' Advice Portfolio Program, once the firm's flagship automated product, was closed to new clients in March 2025. BlackRock shut down its B2C model completely, which it inherited from FutureAdvisor, and sold the remaining retail accounts to Ritholtz Wealth Management in 2023. But it still continued its B2B model through Aladdin Wealth. It is interesting to note that Vanguard retreated from the Chinese market by selling its 49% share in a robo-advisor service with Jack Ma's Ant Group in April 2025. The successful practice did not seem to fit in another market.

3 Robo-Advisory at a Crossroads

Robo-advisory services emerged in the aftermath of the global financial crisis as a cost-efficient response to the inaccessibility of traditional financial advice. With advisory fees as low as 0.25% of assets under management, compared with traditional average rates of 1% annually, fintech firms such as Betterment and Wealthfront democratised investing for clients with modest savings. The model promised accessibility, scalability, and efficiency. It has become a race over the past decade among financial institutions, as the growing momentum in robo-advisory has led to a surge of entrants into the market. Partnerships, self-built solutions, or acquisitions were popular approaches among financial institutions to join the race. This robo-advisor wave pushed the global AUM prediction to exceed $2.38 trillion by 2025. However, as the industry matures, the market's verdict remains mixed. Some platforms, such as Vanguard and Fidelity, have successfully institutionalised digital advice, while others, including Goldman Sachs, UBS, and J.P. Morgan, have scaled back or exited the fully automated model. Fintech firms have managed to survive by pursuing aggressive acquisitions to expand their AUM and client base, or by maximising the profitability of cash accounts.

The foundation of robo-advisory lies in a trade-off between automation and personalisation. The automation process starts with "one-size-fits-all" questionnaires to identify the risk categories of investors. The questionnaires are based on the assumptions of similar risk investors sharing identical financial goals and behavioural responses. The simplification ignored the complexity of an individual's financial circumstances. For example, children's education, job redundancy, and family obligations. Furthermore, human advisors bond better with clients than robo-advisors. Especially when clients experience market volatility or a change of financial position, access to human advisors provides more reassurance than the app or the website. Therefore, is a robo-advisor a substitute for a human advisor or a complement? A hybrid model, which keeps human advisors as an option for investors, appears to be a more popular approach adopted by firms. For example, Vanguard Personal Advisor Services and Bank of America's Merrill Edge Guided Investing offer this option at a premium to attract high-net-worth clients. One more factor to consider when shifting to robo-advisory services is the shortage of financial advisors, which can reach 110,000 in the USA by 2033 based on McKinsey's 2025 report. The U.K. market also echoed the concern. Based on FCA's data, more than 50% of advisors are aged above 50, and the number of young advisors declined by 18% between 2022 and 2024. This demographic imbalance opens the question of the advice gap. The growing demand for financial advisory services outpaces the industry's capacity. One solution is robo-advisors, which can take up the cumbersome tasks and free up the time for human advisors to focus on complex, high-value relationships.

Ultimately, the sustainability of robo-advisory depends on its ability to evolve beyond algorithmic standardisation. What works for one organisation does not necessarily translate into success for another. Even firms with similar business models and clientele have experienced vastly different outcomes. Although there are market survivors such as Betterment, Wealthfront, and Vanguard, a large proportion of providers still do not disclose detailed robo-advisory results. Figures on AUM, user numbers, and average account sizes provide only a partial picture of success. The lack of transparency of the robo-advisory model makes it difficult for observers or players to be able to analyse the sustainability of the model. Only time will tell. A fuller understanding will require greater transparency from institutions and a more detailed assessment of how technology, business model, and client strategy interact to make this model work.

Appendix

Robo-advisor	Advisory fee (AUM)	AUM threshold (minimum to invest)	Access to human financial advisor	AUM	No. of users	Launch
Betterment	0.32%	None	Available with Premium tier (0.40% fee), or for a separate fee for a financial planning package.	\$63bn+ (19/8/2025)	900,000 (8/2024)	2010
Wealthfront	0.25%	\$500	No direct access to human advisors or CFPs.	\$88.2bn (31/07/2025)	1.3mn (7/2025)	2011
Vanguard Digital Advisor	0.15%	\$100	No direct human advisor access through the Digital Advisor service.	\$19bn+ (30/06/2024)	804,0000 (5/2025)	2015
Fidelity Go	0%	\$10	Access to a team of Fidelity financial advisors is included for accounts with a balance of \$25,000 or more.	NA	NA	2016
Schwab Intelligent Portfolios	0%	\$5000	Available with Schwab Intelligent Portfolios Premium tier.	\$81bn (Q1 2024)	262,000 (8/2024)	2015

Source: Complied from firm websites, Morningstars reports, SEC files and news

Bibliography

KPMG (2024) *The race for robo advice.*https://share.google/3uX79ph7uVIAEhiLE

McKinsey & Company (2025) *The looming advisor shortage in U.S. wealth management.*https://www.mckinsey.com/industries/financial-services/our-insights/the-looming-advisor-shortage-in-us-wealth-management

Statista (2024) *Robo-advisors worldwide—Assets under management (AUM).*https://www.statista.com/outlook/fmo/wealth-management/digital-investment/robo-advisors/worldwide

Correction to: The Rise of Robo-Advisory in FinTech

Alex Zarifis, Narmin Nahidi, and Larisa Yarovaya

Correction to:
Chapter 1 in: N. Nahidi, A. Zarifis (eds.), *AI, FinTech, and the Future of Robo-Advisory*, Contributions to Finance and Accounting, https://doi.org/10.1007/978-3-032-18109-1_1

The original version of the chapter was inadvertently published with the author's names in an incorrect order. The authors list was originally published as Narmin Nahidi, Alex Zarifis, and Larisa Yarovaya. This has now been updated to Alex Zarifis, Narmin Nahidi, and Larisa Yarovaya.

The updated version of this chapter can be found at
https://doi.org/10.1007/978-3-032-18109-1_1

N. Nahidi, A. Zarifis (eds.), *AI, FinTech, and the Future of Robo-Advisory*,
Contributions to Finance and Accounting,
https://doi.org/10.1007/978-3-032-18109-1_17

the EU authorised representative is:
Springer Nature Customer Service Center GmbH
Europaplatz 3, 69115 Heidelberg, Germany

Printed by Libri Plureos GmbH
in Hamburg, Germany

MIX
Papier aus verantwortungsvollen Quellen
Paper from responsible sources
FSC® C105338

If you have any concerns about our products,
you can contact us on
ProductSafety@springernature.com

In case Publisher is established outside the EU,
the EU authorized representative is:
Springer Nature Customer Service Center GmbH
Europaplatz 3, 69115 Heidelberg, Germany

Printed by Libri Plureos GmbH
in Hamburg, Germany